The L

# of Political Victory . . . and Defeat

THE BLOOD, SWEAT, AND TEARS OF POLITICAL VICTORY... AND DEFEAT

R. R. Bob Greive

University Press of America, Inc.
Lanham • New York • London

Copyright © 1996 by
R. R. Bob Greive
University Press of America,® Inc.
4720 Boston Way
Lanham, Maryland 20706

3 Henrietta Street
London, WC2E 8LU England

All rights reserved
Printed in the United States of America
British Cataloging in Publication Information Available

Library of Congress Cataloging-in-Publication Data

Greive, R. R. Bob
The blood, sweat, and tears of political victory--and defeat// R. R. Bob
Greive
p.   cm.
1. Politics, Practical--United States.   2. Campaign management--
United States.   3. Electioneering--United States.   I. Title.
JK1726.G74   1996   324'.0973--dc20   96-8060 CIP

ISBN 0-7618-0361-0 (pbk: alk. ppr.)

⊖™The paper used in this publication meets the minimum
requirements of American National Standard for information
Sciences—Permanence of Paper for Printed Library Materials,
ANSI Z39.48—1984

Until you've been in politics, you've never really been alive. It's rough and sometimes it's dirty and it's always hard work and tedious details. But, it's the only sport for grownups-all other games are for kids.
　　—Heinlein[*]

---

[*]Plaque on the desk of Senator Edward Kennedy, Democrat, Massachusetts.

Thank You

Many people helped as I wrote this book, but I reserve special thanks for four:

Dr. George Blair, former dean of Claremont Graduate School: One of a kind, who is remembered for his warmth and character, and for his encouragement and inspiration. He kept my dream of this book alive, just as he did the dreams of hundreds of his students.

Betty Oliver, administrative assistant: Whose efforts don't show directly in these pages, but who contributed in numerous ways to everything I have done during their writing. Without her valuable support, I could not have written this book.

Dr. Toni Reineke: Friend, colleague, critic, and word processor par excellence, who demonstrated creative genius in knowing when to cut as she edited.

Barbara Cough Shea: A quiet voice of reason when judging an activity that is filled with gimmickry and exaggeration. Her sense of quality and style and incredible patience left a mark on both me and the manuscript.

Contents

Part 4   Advertising

Part 5   Anatomy of a Smear

Part 6   News as a Political Tool

Part 7   Political Strategy

Part 8   Reporting, Regulation, and Taxation of Campaign Funds

Part 9   Making the Decision

Chapter Notes   593

In a Nutshell:

Preface

There are some things this book will not do or be. First, it will not present the reader with an oversimplified panacea or recipe I allege to be the correct way to conduct a political campaign. Instead, this book is designed to be a compendium or sourcebook of the ideas on getting elected that I've gathered throughout a political lifetime from every source that I could put my hands on. The examples are taken from several sides of the political fence; from successful and unsuccessful candidates, both friend and opponent; from political consultants, advisors, and media strategists; from the media; from election campaigns in other countries; and from my extensive personal campaign files. While traveling I have collected every book, pamphlet, and article available on the topic. The best ideas are presented here.

Many of the nuggets are deliberately chosen from past history, so as to avoid problems with contemporary political figures. While these stories have been around a while, they to my knowledge had not been gathered into a single source. I have chosen to present so many because the anecdotes make for good, easy reading and because the more ideas candidates have to draw on the more likely they will hit on those that suit their own chemistry.

As I have said, many of the illustrations have been drawn from losing as well as winning campaigns. The candidate might ask, "Why should I look at techniques used in losing campaigns?" It's wise to look around. Most issues, ideas, and techniques are not really new. Even professional political consultants, who are highly familiar with current strategies and are paid because of their ability to shape, create, and merchandise political images, do not win all their campaigns. A survey of their success/loss ratio showed that in a typical year the loss record of the nation's leading consultants (each of whom handled more than one campaign) was "4-3, 3-3 and 5-4."[1]

Candidates and their planners therefore should make a real effort to carefully discuss an idea, issue, or technique, and if possible test public reaction before accepting or summarily rejecting it. A given technique should be rejected only if it was obviously the reason for campaign failure.

The book is organized into several sections. Part one is an overview of the simpler aspects of campaign basics. Parts two through eight cover those more complex topics that warrant an entire section of their own (raising money, polling, advertising, the smear campaign, using news as a political tool, political strategy, and public disclosure requirements). Finally, Part 9 is an overview of the factors and issues the prospective candidate must grapple with even before making the decision to run.

Throughout the book, I have where possible condensed the ideas into nutshell form. These might simply serve as memory refreshers or they might be copied to use in planning. For ease of access and so as not to interrupt the thread of text, I often have placed them at the ends of the relevant chapters.

I believe this book will prove useful to the beginner as well as to the old pro. But if the reader wants a simple handbook approach ("Don't muddle me with facts; just tell me what to do"), there are several reasonably good books available (some listed at the end of the chapter notes, under Additional Reading). If, however, the reader wants a fairly comprehensive sourcebook of entertainingly presented ideas, read on!

Part 1

Merchandising the Common Touch

Chapter 1

Introduction to Reality

> The best way to make your dreams come true is to wake up.
> —J. M. Power, in *Sign* magazine[1]

Some call it a war—which it is not. Some call it a horse race—which it is not. Some call it a game—which it is not. Whatever a campaign for political office is called, there is a need for realism. The candidate who ignores reality conducts the campaign in a fantasy world in which only winners live—at least until the votes are counted.

When applied to a political campaign, reality has many faces. Realism in any context requires judgment. Thus, candidates and their friends will find that there is a lot of room to differ on what is and is not realistic. What is realistic ranges from candidates who are shoo-ins to those who may have to claim they are certain of victory simply to keep the spirits of their campaign staffs and volunteers alive. In his day-after-the-election speech in New York, candidate for president Barry Goldwater described reality this way: "What can you say in a city you lost by 1,387,021 votes? It's nice to be among friends, even if they are not yours."[2]

A candidate and his or her staff can be realistic and still have differences, but the realistic candidate needs to expect and consider alternative suggestions in perspective. Campaign reality can be likened to the story of the wise men in a parable taken from the Muslim Koran that speaks of a ruler who called before him three advisors and said to them, "Wise and holy men, before you is an elephant, and since each of you has been blind from birth, I pray you to approach this creature and describe it to me."

The first holy man, on being led to the elephant and feeling of its side, said, "Sire, most magnificent ruler, this creature is a large, somewhat furry wall." The second was led to the elephant. He felt of his leg and said, "Sire, the most magnificent king, this creature is like a column that supports the temple wherein we worship." When the third was led to the elephant, he felt of its trunk and exclaimed, "Great Sire, it is clear that this creature is like a snake and may in fact be a snake."[3]

Realism requires both big-picture perspective and bottom-line understanding. I suggest the candidate answer three preliminary questions before plunging into campaign planning. First, the candidate should ask, "How badly do I want to win?" The value of motivation was best articulated by Ray Croc, founder of the MacDonald's hamburger chain:

Nothing in the world can take the place of persistence. Talent will not; nothing is more common than unsuccessful men with talent. Genius will not; unrewarded genius is almost a proverb. Education will not; the world is full of educated derelicts. Persistence and determination alone are omnipotent.[4]

Assuming that the candidate *really* wants to be elected, the second question is "What do I need to do to win?" In short, the pragmatic candidate must be able to project confidence, persuade financial contributors, inspire volunteers, bargain with special interests, and finally—most importantly—convince the voters that he or she can do something that the opponent can not or will not do. And if they both promise the same thing, the candidate must persuade the voter he or she can do it better.

The third question is "What about the possibility of defeat?" "Defeat" is a dirty word in campaigning, but I bring it up early in the book because it's an aspect of reality the candidate must face early on. Let me explain. The typical candidate filing for office is an optimist. Then the staff and volunteers join the candidate in creating a wild, heady environment that feeds on rumors and publicity that then reinforces the predictions of victory. In this environment, it's easy to forget reality—that somebody has to lose.

In reality the candidate and insiders must keep from wallowing in over-confidence. Conversely, they cannot drown in despair, which turns off campaign contributions and dries up volunteer support. I bring up the possibility of defeat partly to invoke the same emotion used by a mother when she threatens to spank a child—an emotion we all recognize: fear. In the candidate's case the possibility of defeat may not help his or her ego, but it is sure to motivate.

Chapter 2

The Perils of the Top Brass

> A political campaign is like an insane asylum run by the inmates.[1]
>
> Should amateurs do the navigation or should there be a
> professional pilot . . . called in to share the blame?
> —Anonymous

The Steering Committee

Candidates often seek relief from the secret panic they feel when faced with the details of advertising, attacks, contributions, etc., so they turn campaign decisions over to a committee. This group can relieve the candidates who are afraid to depend on their own expertise when setting strategy; studying issues, voting records, or sources; or making the search for political allies.

Formal steering committees usually include the candidate's campaign managers, finance chairs, and other politically savvy individuals who enjoy being on the inside. A journalist, for instance, might serve anonymously (as exposure might embarrass their publishers and evoke the antagonism of rivals).

In the opinion of Peter O'Donnell, one-time Republican chair for Texas, such a committee is the key to an effective campaign. "Planning a campaign is like playing three-dimensional chess; no one can see all the plays."[2]

Sometimes this steering committee will generate "position papers" addressing the key issues of the campaign. Or it might direct the campaign managers. Usually it is consulted as strategic sounding board before any major public positions are taken on controversial matters.

Speaking of the first Tower for U.S. Senate Campaign, O'Donnell stated: "Our group met from time to time in 1965 and 1966. . . . During the last four months of the campaign we thought that [the Sunday] that we spent planning and taking stock of our thoughts made the other six days of the week much more productive."[3]

However, candidates must be leery of a campaign in which too many fancy themselves policymakers. A group too hastily thrown together may not be able to work as a team when planning campaign strategy and timing.

The Management Team

Most campaigns are run by the candidate's campaign managers and a few advisors. Occasionally, they have one or two paid staff people. A skilled management team should be recruited months before the election so candidates can activate those on whom they will rely as soon as they are available. See the "Organizing" nutshell (over) for some ideas on getting started.

Choosing a competent campaign manager is the most important early task. The team should also a include a treasurer and a secretary. See the nutshell, "Choosing the Manager."

In a small campaign the functions of manager, secretary, and scheduler are combined. Whoever performs this function should sit in when strategy is decided, because he or she will have to set priorities when timing coffee hours, doorbelling, receptions, and a place in the candidate's schedule for visits with key political and news people. An overview of the aspects of the campaign the manager will need to oversee is shown in the Manager's Checklist nutshell at the end of this chapter.

Choosing the Manager

Note: Titles vary but every campaign needs a whipcracker. All too often campaigns are run by volunteers who don't get paid and can't be fired or disciplined. They often agree to do a specific task then lose interest and fail to follow through, perhaps even failing to notify the campaign staff. Therefore, a dynamo must calendar all of the tasks that must be accomplished during the entire run of the campaign. This person must be in a position, diplomatically or not, to motivate volunteers in advance. They must track the duties given to each volunteer (dates, times, places), calendar the data, and constantly remind all others what must be done.

Usually this person is the manager. They must keep in constant contact with the candidate. Their highest priority will be fundraising phone calls. He/she also needs to prepare weekly (daily, when nearing election day) status reports prior to each campaign meeting.

Commitment/Abilities
Is he/she a supporter?
Will there be compensation? (must come out of budget in advance)
What makes candidate think he/she can handle details?
Able to recruit others?
Able to orchestrate myriad people and tasks?
Will he/she be competent enough to speak for candidate?

★ ★ ★ ★ ★ **In A Nutshell** ★ ★ ★ ★ ★

★ ★ ★ ★ ★ ★ ★ ★ ★ ★ ★ ★ ★

Organizing

Note: No one volunteers unless asked. Expect staff and volunteers to turn over in the campaign.

	Target Date	Date Compl.
Ask potential supporters to participate in campaign committee; most candidates act as chair.		
Tie down committee meeting dates.		
Designate secretary to take notes at meetings.		
Appoint treasurer, open a bank account, study public-disclosure requirements.		
Consider hiring political consultant; clearly define extent of authority.		
Committee agenda (repeat often throughout campaign.): potential opposition; campaign strategy; issues; community attitudes; name recognition; potential sources of support		
Set a tentative date and event to announce candidacy.		
Collect information		
Study voting patterns in recent elections.		
Check costs for printing, mailing, advertising.		
Assemble materials		
Make preliminary budget.		
Begin fundraising.		
Draft candidate fact sheet.		
Draft and print signup cards for pledges, endorsements, and/or volunteers.		
List potential supporters, contributors, volunteers.		

★ ★ ★ ★ ★   In A Nutshell   ★ ★ ★ ★ ★

If a formal committee structure is used, the candidates appoint individual chairs who are responsible for such duties as finance, doorbelling, coffee hours, signs, office help, etc.

The number of committees and what they do depend on the finances, size, and complexity of the campaign. The chairs of these committees should be able to recruit and lead other volunteers in performing their tasks, and they should be given the authority to make decisions related to their tasks. Check the "Planning" nutshell for ideas.

★ ★ ★ ★ ★ ★ ★ ★ ★ ★ ★ ★ ★ ★

Planning

Note: *I repeat,* no one volunteers unless asked. Expect staff and volunteers to turn over in the campaign.

	Target Date	Date Compl.
Establish planning group (and make sure each planner also has campaign function).		
Set firm schedule for meetings.		
Decide on strategy:		
–Date to declare candidacy		
–How to handle opposition		
–Specific issues		
–Priorities, define specific positions		
–Ways to handle attacks		
–General fund-raising plan		
–General spending plan		
–How to make announcement (early or late, news conference or reception, etc.)		
Discuss an advertising and publicity plan:		
–Where (newspaper, radio, TV)		
–What types of ads (display, voice, signs)		
–When to release		
Decide on strategy for getting endorsements.		
Decide on phone bank strategy (e.g., to urge support).		
Decide on general strategy for get-out-vote drive.		
Plan schedule of appearances and debates.		

★ ★ ★ ★ ★ **In A Nutshell** ★ ★ ★ ★ ★

The candidates and advisors might decide on day-to-day operations, or they might manage a marketing strategy similar to that finally adopted by President Nixon in his second successful presidential campaign, when he created an in-house advertising staff called The November Group, headed by Peter Daily. They worked full-time, planning advertising strategy, which they then executed for not only the official Republican Nixon campaign effort, but also for that of the Democrats for Nixon and Agnew, headed by a former Democrat, one-time Texas Governor John Connolly. This in-house advertising agency was later revived to handle both Ford and Reagan's Presidential campaign advertising.[4]

Unfortunately, some campaign managers and advisors may be more concerned about their own success instead of worrying about the overall performance of the campaign team. For example, in theory, personnel should be transferred to the activities in which they can produce maximum results. In Ohio, Carl P. Rubin, who managed the successful Taft for Congressman at Large campaign in 1968, employed a computer to keep tabs on volunteers with special skills. If a typist was needed, the computer would come up with that person. However, he found that transferring volunteers from one function of the campaign to another one is not easy. The local campaign leaders who recruited the skilled volunteers did not want to release their best workers, so, instead of filling out and sending information cards into headquarters, they hoarded these recruits.[5]

Changing/Adding Personnel

The campaign structure should be such that there are open places in the management to be filled by newly found dynamos. This encourages other volunteers to graduate from the ranks of casual workers into the dynamo class. Candidates should also make these battlefield commissions the subject of public presentations.

However, the candidate should be careful when giving out mid-campaign honors, since a campaign is a short-run, high-pressure experience in which even minor events can cause dissension. In the first Howard Baker for United States Senate from Tennessee campaign, two or three of Senator Baker's staff felt it necessary to have personal mailboxes. Finally, it became a status symbol, and all in the headquarters had boxes with their names.[6]

A candidate should be even more careful about drastic shakeups in campaign management, or about putting out publicity releases announcing that someone has been named coordinator, assistant coordinator, or division chief. If the candidate creates new titles, their holders are going to want to make changes in the direction or structure of the campaign. This attitude is not new or unique. Because there are no hard-and-fast rules, everything depends on tradeoffs. If the campaign is in trouble and there is need for new direction, certainly such a change can be justified. If this is not the case, there should be great reluctance to ruffle egos. The present leaders should be consulted before new leaders are added. Even then such a move is not calculated to please those who are already recognized as campaign leaders. Jealousies and insubordination will follow conflicts in egos.

This has happened to important campaigns. For example, Stephen Shadegg reported, "The kindest thing which can be said about the 1964 Nixon for President campaign is that it lacked direction." It is difficult to say who really managed that Nixon campaign. Len Hall had the official responsibility. Bob Finch had some limited authority. Arthur Flemming and Attorney General Rogers are credited by insiders with Nixon's endorsement of welfare state proposals.[7] When Nixon met with Rockefeller in New York to discuss the Republican platform, his manager, Len Hall, was furious. He didn't even know the meeting was scheduled.

Someone must be appointed to settle squabbles. In some campaigns the responsibility is given to the manager. In the (Spiro) Agnew for Governor of Maryland Campaign, Robert Goodman said they left this task to the campaign manager, who was a decisive persuader of people, a solver of problems . . . a man who knew how to protect the candidate from his friends and project him to the public.[8]

If there is no such person, the candidate must appoint someone to hear complaints and effect compromises. In most cases, no one will be satisfied unless the decision is made by the candidate, but this has emotional ramifications. Disgruntled campaigners may seek revenge by selling out to the enemy, squealing to the press, or doing dirt in other ways.[9]

The Hired Gun

With the demise of the old political machines and the rise of political volunteers, consultants have become important factors in major campaigns and, contrary to what some would have us believe, hiring consultants is not un-American. Major candidates have always depended on outside help. President Franklin Pierce won the Presidency in 1852 due in part to the writing of one of America's early great novelists, Nathaniel Hawthorne. And in the Presidential campaign of 1874, Abraham Lincoln had much of his campaign rhetoric written by a famous novelist of that day, William Dean Howells.[10]

Looking at the forerunners who formed the techniques of today's political consultants, I am particularly fascinated by the strategy of a 19th century politician who was neither a traditional big city boss, nor a mayor, governor, or president. He was a legislator but he sponsored little legislation. The thing that fascinated the historians was expressed by one-time Secretary of State John Hay: "He was a born general in politics, who ruled not among crowds or elegance, but from a desk in his private office." One hundred years later he has become a legend, a symbol of his party's alliance with big business. On the field of political battle he was the driving genius who elected McKinley president.

This man, U.S. Senator Mark Hanna, understood the importance of money in influencing mass psychology. He was a political technician who recognized that the electorate was more than a single unidentifiable mass. It saw the electorate as having geographical, sexual, racial, income, religious, political, and age differences that could be targeted and channeled money and resources in a way best calculated to produce votes. In 1889, he was responsible for distributing more than 100 million pieces of campaign literature that encompassed 272 different messages to groups with diverse languages, economic interests, and ethnic origins.[11]

Hanna's political descendants—today's consultants—are practical, often ruthless, men and women. They are not employed because they are loved. They know the political terrain and are constantly watching, prepared to magnify small tactical errors to their advantage. They excel in interpreting polling information and raising money.

Consultants have first-hand contacts with pollsters who understand mass psychology. They know the market, the costs of the various media, and how to set political tone. When television is involved, they know how to use experts in design, lighting, and sound effects who can pick the appropriate production personnel, artists, and writers.

One satisfied customer gave testimonial to the fact that consultants excel in the technical functions needed to make a persuasive piece of campaign advertising. When sparring with newsmen following a tough, come-from-behind victory in November of 1977, New Jersey's Governor Byrne said, "Do I look enough like the Garth spots?" What he meant was how did he compare with the advertised image given him by the best-known of the political hired guns, David Garth, who was credited with erasing Byrne's weak and ineffective image and substituting the image of a forceful governor "who had the courage to make the tough decisions."[12]

In spite of their obvious expertise, the local opposition—and often the local media—intimate that the hired gun has reduced the candidate's image to that of a puppet, and that there is something un-American and unsporting about candidates who place their fate in the hands of a consultant. But candidates and their advisors should ignore this criticism and concentrate on the primary purpose of the political campaigns—to win.

Let's draw an analogy to the American Revolution. In school, students are taught that local militiamen were superior fighters to be admired for their hit-and-run tactics, deadly aim, and Indian-style fighting. Though the myth of the "citizen soldier" has persisted, they were not entirely responsible for the victory. The military force that won the war was composed of a few crack American regiments that held the rest of the army together, plus the French who supplied weapons and strategy from the time the colonists declared their independence in 1776. The army that forced Cornwallis's surrender at Yorktown and virtually ended the war was two-thirds French professional soldiers.[13]

So candidates should hire professional consultants and when they do should expect criticism, refusing needed outside help only after they have carefully considered the tradeoffs and concluded that the criticism will lose more votes than the help will gain.

Most candidates do not hire outside political consultants to oversee the entire campaign because they can't afford it. But they might be able to hire a consultant for a limited purpose, perhaps for their experience and understanding of strategy or advertising, or sometimes to raise money or recruit public relations men, pollsters, or research specialists. Or a hired gun also might lay out general campaign themes and overall strategies.

★ ★ ★ ★ ★ ★ ★ ★ ★ ★ ★ ★ ★ ★ ★

Tracking the Campaign: The Manager's Checklist

Note: Most of the following items appear in other nutshells in relation to the given event or task. They appear here again so they can be *calendared and tracked* by the whipcracker.

Ongoing planning

Constantly evaluate effectiveness of publicity campaign as well as issues and personalities that are impacting the campaign.

Identify responsibilities for each.

Set a firm schedule for meetings.

Discuss advertising and publicity plan: where (newspaper, radio, TV), what types of ads (display, voice, signs), when to release.

People coordinating

Appoint a chair.

Conduct first-round recruitment.

Set up master assignment list.

Pick up volunteer sign-up sheets from special events; contact volunteers offering to work or contribute.

Coordinate plans with event personnel and campaign staff (candidate, event chair, master of ceremonies, campaign manager, and program, finance, and hospitality committees).

Candidate appearances, special events

Schedule date and event to announce candidacy.

Schedule events, from coffees to fundraising dinners, etc.

Get written briefings to candidate for each appearance

★ ★ ★ ★ ★ **In A Nutshell** ★ ★ ★ ★ ★

★ ★ ★ ★ ★ ★ ★ ★ ★ ★ ★ ★ ★

Tracking the Campaign: The Manager's Checklist (cont.)

Assemble list of prospects to invite
(include name, spouse's name, home
address, phone).

Establish date invitations must be ready.

Design and prepare invitations.

Schedule entertainers, guest speakers; keep
in touch.

Deliver campaign literature at least day
before event.

Day after, pick up surplus materials.

Additional fundraising

Maintain calendar of fundraising
activities/events

Send "Dear Friends" fund-raising letters
with contribution-return envelopes.

Send 2nd "Dear Friends" bulk mailing

Publicity: Broadcast media

As needed, issue news releases, or if the
candidate packs enough clout, hold
news conferences.

Schedule TV ads. Remember that TV and
radio time must be purchased early,
requiring early money and early
decisions on type, length, issues to be
covered, etc.

Recheck radio and TV spots; make
changes if necessary, adding
endorsements where appropriate.

–Schedule newspaper ads:

–Schedule date(s) ad appears.

–Date layout must be prepared.

–Proofreading deadlines.

–Camera-ready copy deadline.

–Write work order, deliver with layout
and copy.

Publicity: Direct mail

Coordinate "Dear Friend" card mailings.

Do direct publicity mailing, sending a
major campaign piece to all good
voters.

–Check on postal requirements.

–Purchase appropriate mailing permits
from post office.

–Obtain precinct/district mailing list if
available or label sets.

–Choose between mailing agent or
volunteers.

Design pieces (consult with mailing
agent/post office).

Print.

Deliver to mailing agent or volunteers for
folding, labeling, and sorting.

Fill out appropriate postal forms.

Deliver to the post office.

Publicity: Signs, miscellaneous

Recruit volunteers to distribute yard signs.

Distribute posters and bumper strips to
businesses or homeowners 30-45 days
before election.

Post second wave of signs.

Replace signs during last 10 days of
campaign.

Hold additional news-making events (e.g.,
use foot soldiers for last-minute
pamphlet blitz).

★ ★ ★ ★ ★   **In A Nutshell**   ★ ★ ★ ★ ★

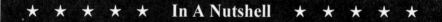

Tracking the Campaign: The Manager's Checklist (cont.)

Polling, phone banks

Select phone sites.

Designate a supervisor to be available to callers.

Make up a schedule for callers.

3 to 5 weeks before election day, schedule people for last- minute phone bank effort.

Miscellaneous

Expand the candidate's holiday greeting card list.

On appropriate occasions (anniversar-ies, special achievements, con-dolences, etc.), write notes to constituents.

Send thank-you notes as needed.

Prompt candidate and volunteers to write thank-you letters.

Recordkeeping

Keep financial files up to date.

Set up card files, file.

Clip newspapers, maintain a scrapbook, etc.

Post-election

Have volunteers promptly remove signs.

Get deposit(s) refunded from city/ county agency and/or businesses.

★ ★ ★ ★ ★ **In A Nutshell** ★ ★ ★ ★ ★

Chapter 3

Smilin', Recognizin', and Charmin'

> He gives you a smile,
> He's so full of charm,
> He walks down the aisle,
> He touches your arm,
> He'll hold your hand,
> Words gush from his throat, he looks
> in your eyes-he's after your vote.
> —Dorothy Dalton, *Modern Maturity*[1]
>
> Most politicians are vaccinated with a long-playing needle.
> —Congressman Henry J. Hyde[2]
>
> My name is Jimmy Carter and I am running for President. It's
> been a long time since I said those words for the first time . . . and
> now I stand here to accept your nomination."[3]

Political Barnstorming

When President Jimmy Carter used the above lines he was acknowledging that in truth he had succeeded in creating a ripple effect in his grassroots campaign, when the local precinct committeeman, barber, or department store clerk told his or her friends and neighbors of their encounter.

When a politician attempts to stretch his or her political personality, it is by what is dubbed "barnstorming." This term, William Safire said, was "derived from the old custom of using a barn for performances by itinerant players," and was applied to candidates because politicking was something of a rural amusement.[4]

Although it includes a number of different types of political contacts, when we think of barnstorming most of us picture a speech by William Jennings Bryan or a Lincoln-Douglas debate as typifying the campaigns of the past. Such showbiz speaking engagements occasionally work, but usually only for the more visible public offices such as mayor, governor or U.S. Senator, whom the public sees as political stars or at least feature players.

In most small campaigns the schedulers do what they can to keep the candidates abreast of local politics by talking in advance to those who know and understand local issues. But the amount of preparation and the size of the advance team escalates with the importance of the campaign. Major candidates have writers and researchers to prepare new ideas. They try to have something fresh and vital to say nearly every time they speak in public, which they drop into their standard speech as they cover a vast constituency. To such political stars the live audience is little more than a prop. They measure success by the space their visits command in the local paper, on the radio or the six o'clock TV news.

Before announcing their campaign, political candidates should do more than hope for invitations to speak. In even the most obscure races, there should be people charged with seeking opportunities for public exposure. They might write or call labor unions and business groups. A few church, fraternal, and service groups will permit speakers to discuss topical issues.

Once candidates have filed, most of these groups don't invite candidates because they want to steer clear of partisan involvement. This leaves the candidates making a circuit of sometimes poorly attended meetings-League of Women Voters, labor unions, business groups, B'Nai B'Rith-where a few activist groups interested in public affairs actively seek out and invite candidates to speak.

Thus, lesser candidates often find their appearances are sandwiched together at events that don't attract either electronic media or press comment. Still, most political bit players need to appear before perhaps five to fifty small groups during the course of their campaign. For some it is because they need the exposure, while others fear that failure to attend will be observed and reported by the press, or that the sponsors of the event will note their failure to show up.

What to Say

Candidates should understand that campaign speeches require what is referred to in business literature as a "standard presentation." Candidates would do well to follow the example of firms in the world of commerce where sales managers insist that new salesmen learn speeches thoroughly and then practice until they can deliver them with ease.[5]

Standard presentations are often difficult for newcomers. They fret that they are repeating themselves or that their messages will become stale. However, most campaign speeches are not carried on radio or television, or fully reported in the press. So it is rare that a voter will hear candidates more than once.

And what if they do? Hundreds of those who attended the Democratic National Convention came roaring to their feet at the close of William Jennings Bryan's stirring "cross of gold" speech. History records that they were not troubled by the fact that he was thoroughly familiar with the speech, because he had delivered it up to 100 times as he traveled throughout the central farming states![6]

Most audiences expect candidates to take the tack that their opponents are unfit or unqualified. But if they do, it is wise to go into details. If possible, he or she should cite specific examples from the records and then show why their opponents should not have acted as they did. Beyond this, most audiences will not be impressed with detail unless candidates are addressing groups with special interests.

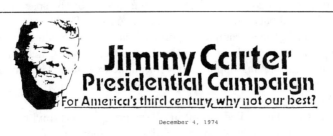

Jimmy Carter Presidential Campaign

For America's third century, why not our best?

December 4, 1974

My dear Friend,

Before the official announcement is made on December 12, I would like you to know that I intend to seek the Democratic nomination and election as President of the United States in 1976.

You may have anticipated this news. Some national political forecasters repeatedly predict that a governor will win the nomination, and my name has often been mentioned as a strong possibility.

I would not enter this formidable race if I did not believe that I can win; but neither would I run for President without a deep conviction that I can make an essential contribution to the United States government and the people it serves.

In my four years as Governor and in travels throughout the country, I have listened to may people who are frustrated and dissatisfied with government. They feel alienated from the decision-making process. They are troubled by the dishonesty of public officials. They deplore the absence of effective business management in government. They are bewildered by shortages and runaway inflation. With good reason, they have lost faith in federal programs that waste their taxes while the needs of the people go unmet.

I believe that the problems which plague our people can be solved with bold, competent, honest leadership.

With the support of many dedicated Georgians, we have proved in our state that government can be responsive, practical and fair.

We brought closed meetings out into the open. We adopted efficient, dollar-saving methods of organization, budgeting and planning. We reduced bureaucratic red tape and increased services. We proved that government can be sensitive to the needs of the individual.

I think that you will agree that those principles of reform are needed at the national level. With help from you and thousands of other concerned Americans, I intend to take them to Washington.

Some people might say that we face an impossible task. They have overlooked several important facts.

P.O. Box 7667 Atlanta, Georgia 30309 404/897-7100

I will deeply appreciate your participating in this campaign -- your comments, suggestions, contributions or pledge. May I hear from you soon? Thank you.

Sincerely,

Jimmy Carter
Jimmy Carter

Fig. 1-1. Democratic presidential campaign announcement letter, Jimmy Carter Campaign Committee, Atlanta, Georgia, 1974.

As much as a candidate running ahead might want to avoid controversial issues, most reject this sterile "don't rock the boat" approach because they instinctively feel they should make some references to issues, if only to let the voters know that they are not political lightweights. Also, they do not want to fall into the rut described by U.S. Senator William Gibbs McAdoo, when referring to President Warren Harding's speeches: "They . . . leave the impression of an army of pompous phrases moving over the landscape in search of an idea. Sometimes these meandering words would capture a struggling thought, and bear it triumphantly to a prison of servitude and overwork."[7]

How does a first-time candidate for mayor of a small town learn the issues? Normally, someone with first-hand information from the candidate's party is willing to help. Some candidates prefer learning from books, or may interview political science or economics professors at nearby colleges or universities. Better still is to stay abreast of current events.

Grooming

It is important that the candidate appear well groomed and clean when meeting the public. The candidate should remember, however, that he or she is running for public office and not going out for the lead in a musical. A male candidate should wear conservative suits, shirts, and ties for most occasions. In less formal circumstances, slacks and a nice sweater or sports jacket will do.

Like it or not, female candidates still have to worry more about personal appearance than do men. Choose simple, tailored suits and shirtdresses, and keep jewelry to a minimum. Don't try to become a femme fatale. Sex appeal is okay in moderate amounts for male candidates, but not for females. If she has a Liz Taylor face, use it, but don't emphasize it. The woman candidate should also keep their hair style and makeup simple. Usually they can't afford the time to powder their noses or fix their hair.

Fig. 1-2. Ben Wicks, *The Vancouver Province*, February 12, 1980.

One woman candidate got bored with her looks part way through her campaign. She came into headquarters with a Dolly Parton blonde wig covering her short, dark hair. The staff finally convinced her that nobody would recognize her as a curly blonde-this was a good ploy; candidates hate not being recognized-and that, even if they did, she would be in for a hard time, especially from snide columnists. A wig might be considered for emergencies, but it should be as close to the candidate's own hair style and color as possible.

Speaking Style

There is no agreement as to what is the best speaking style, except to say that candidates are also in showbiz. Successful candidates use different formats to avoid boring their audience. They lace their presentations with simple humor, stories, and homey illustrations.

Harry Truman, remembered for his whistle-stop campaigning, delighted audiences by giving his opposition in the 80th Congress "hell." However, that was not the only reason Harry's whistle-stop campaign succeeded. His stops followed a carefully orchestrated ritual. When his train pulled into a station he was met by a local band that played "Hail to the Chief" and the "Missouri Waltz." Truman then appeared on the train's back platform accompanied by some local politicians, who presented him with an item of local produce or manufacture, after which he was introduced to the assembled people as the President of the United States.

Truman always mentioned a carefully selected event of local interest or history. In Charlesburg, Virginia, he said that he had been a student of the war between the states and remembered that "Stonewall Jackson was born here." He told the farmers of Dexter, Iowa, "I can plow a straight furrow. . . . A prejudiced witness, my mother, said so." In Hammond, Indiana, he said that the Allied armies all over the world were grateful for the high quality of work turned out there.[8]

Of course, Truman was President. Obviously, the ritual will be different for a lesser candidate, who might invite opponents to debate. Even if the opponent doesn't show, the candidate can turn this to advantage by addressing embarrassing questions to an empty chair.

On occasion, candidates may be able to give theatrical performances. "Big Jim" Folsom, a man 6'8" with size 16 shoes, ran for governor when Alabama was still ruled by Southern courthouse politics. Though he finished a distant second when he ran against the established politicians in 1942, in 1946 he added a hillbilly band, the "Strawberry Pickers," and ran again as a reform candidate. He flourished a cornhusker mop and vowed that he would "scrub out that capitol up there in Montgomery." His message appealed to the crowds that were sprinkled with disgruntled silent youths wearing remnants of their wartime uniforms. They responded warmly when he said, "I ain't got no campaign manager. Y'all the only campaign managers I got. I don't want no others."[9]

Person to Person Rather than the Speech Circuit?

Not all politicians are charismatic. They may not only bore audiences, but stump speeches may not fit their personality. There may be other reasons peculiar to the candidate. Some are shy and want to avoid speeches. They should substitute events that do not require speeches. Their task then becomes one of finding and appearing at events which in themselves attract a crowd.

Candidates for state-wide office, or even Congress, may be able to profit from shaking thousands of hands, as future cabinet member Margaret Heckler did when she was a running for Congress. As she puts it, "Throughout my campaigns, I had a quota of shaking 1,000 hands before noon. In my district, this is not very hard to do, because we have many factories. I simply go through them from 5:00 in the morning to 12:00 noon, and then went on to my other campaign responsibilities. It was these 1,000 hands before noon that made a difference."[10]

This format may not work for a local candidate who is playing to a limited constituency. In their case, handshaking tours may be lost on workers of a giant industrial plant. Part of its workers may live and vote in neighboring counties. On the other hand, in a smaller, remote factory town, this technique may be a winner because the employees live and vote where the plant is located.

One handshaker has become a legend in the bluegrass country of Kentucky. For over fifty years Democrat Happy Chandler held forth as one of the nation's most durable politicians. In all, this master of the political handshake was the winner in twelve of his thirteen races. He was state senator at 30, governor at 36, then later United States Senator and Commissioner of Baseball. A generation later he was again elected governor of Kentucky.

Incidentally, handshaking can be a physical ordeal. Candidates frequently get sore hands, and President Lyndon Johnson occasionally got fungus infections during a campaign. Old political pros advise never wear rings and always jam the hand between the other person's thumb and forefinger, because, as former Bergen County, New Jersey, Sheriff Joe Job, put it, "I didn't know that a guy squeezed so hard; he put me out of commission for three days."[11]

In a memo to his Republican colleagues, U.S. Senator Rudy Boschwitz of Minnesota advised:

> Give very few speeches. Campaign wholesale at gates to state fairs, or get to sporting events, plant gates, walk the bleachers." Speaking of his reelection campaign, he explained, "From July 1 on, I gave few speeches except to high schools, who would assemble 500-800 kids, and I would be in and out in an hour (no reception, cocktails, etc.).[12]

Boschwitz continued:

Parades are great. Take your spouse. Walk behind your car, don't ride. Rush over and shake some hands at the curb (with spouse). Stop every 100 yards and conspicuously wipe the sweat off your brow. Caution, parades often have 200 units. If you arrive on time and are unit 180, there's a long wait. But if you're unit 5 in one and 180 in another, you can knock off two parades in a morning 25 miles apart!!![13]

On occasion, the person-to-person strategy has worked minor miracles. In 1976, Salem auto dealer and conservative legislative leader Victor Atiyeh logged over 40,000 miles as he crisscrossed the state in an old fashioned, person-to-person political effort. He beat the incumbent and early favorite-an acknowledged master of television-Governor Robert Straub.[14]

One might expect a man whose grandfather was President and his father Mr. Republican of the U.S. Senate to be at home on the public platform. But this was not true of former Congressman, later U.S. Senator, Robert Taft of Ohio. When he ran for office, as an alternative to campaign speeches, his schedulers assigned local chairmen specific times Taft would be in their neighborhoods. They planned activities to fill that time, such as parties and teas, visiting bowling alleys, restaurants, and nursing homes. Commenting on the success of this technique, Carl Rubin, who managed Taft's successful campaign for congressman at large, said: "We could not convince people that Bob Taft is a warm friendly person until he tried going around meeting people.[15]

As with any other facet of the campaign, there are limitations. For example, before schedulers reserve large quantities of time for candidates to go out and "press the flesh," they should make an analysis of both the place and the constituency.

The schedulers should check before handshaking tours are held in shopping malls or at plant gates. Such tours may require police permits or a city license. And if candidates use private property, such as shopping malls or entrances to plants, they may have to get permission from the management-and should in any case ask as a matter of courtesy. When quantities of campaign literature are distributed, candidates should make arrangements to clean up the debris. When Assemblyman Antonio G. Oliverieri of New York shook hands with subway travelers, his paraphernalia included a large barrel so voters could throw away his literature after they had read it.

Gimmicks: Enhancers of the Person to Person Strategy

Some politicians combine personal contact with gimmicks to get attention and publicity. Illinois Governor James Thompson liked to "trap" women under beauty salon hair dryers-"They say they are embarrassed, but they love it." He even visited a Chicago sauna to meet "the guys wrapped in sheets."

Some of the best gimmicks emphasize some unique characteristic of the candidate or the candidate's name. Congressman J. J. (Jake) Pickle liked to toss out green plastic "pickle whistles" to his supporters. "I realize it's kind of silly, me bein' a Congressman and goin' down the street throwin' out plastic pickles. But then, I'm lucky my last name isn't melon," he said.[16]

Minnesota U.S. Senator Rudy Boschwitz-a favorite innovator-worked the Minnesota State Fair, which he described as "BIG DOINGS." He held forth at Rudy's Super Duper Milkhouse, where he sold upwards of 200,000 glasses of milk. Reminiscing about his 1984 experience, he said, "At a quarter a glass, I either dispensed or stood out front 8-10 hours a day for 10 straight days. A million people must have seen me!"[17]

Turning again to U.S. Senator Rudy Boschwitz's advice, he commented: "County fairs-we have 87 of them!! I got to half of them. . . . I pulled more cows, ate very little of the food, had volunteers with me, and my favorite was calling a couple of games at the bingo tent. I went through grandstands and shook hands at tractor pulls and demolition derbies. Most Minnesotans recognize me, but a volunteer should carry a sign saying, 'Meet U.S. Senator Rudy Boschwitz,' because people savoring the delicacies of a corn dog may otherwise not notice you."[18]

Some observers find it unusual that, when campaigning, some politicians go into a back-slapping, baby-kissing, hand-shaking ritual. But person-to-person, eyeball-to-eyeball, hand-to-hand contact has been a part of political campaigning since there have been elections. Even in this age, when political images are marketed like soap, cars, and toilet paper, candidates continue to shake scores of hands in union halls, Democratic or Republican clubs, bars, and church basements.

Why do candidates go out of their way to stretch their presence as though it was a precious commodity? Because they continue to believe that no matter how powerful television has become, personal contact-and only personal contact-remains magic.

For some additional ideas on planning voter contact, see the "Person to Person" nutshell on the next page.

★ ★ ★ ★ ★ ★ ★ ★ ★ ★ ★ ★ ★

Person to Person:

Planning Voter Contact Strategy

On the stump

Barnstorm; plan joint appearances.
Don't overlook study and practice with staff (press will be judgmental).
Look for opportunities (mostly oral) to carry message.
Stick to your own style.
For most offices, don't limit appeal to a single issue.
Decide who can speak for candidate.

Preparing the stock speech

State motive(s) for running, what the candidate would like to accomplish.
Emphasize why voters should choose candidate.
Underscore the biggest issue(s) facing voter in this campaign

Convincing contributors or power brokers that candidate is a winner:
Remember that people making the decision to contribute or throw their support to a candidate are conscious of their own egos and reputations and will want to know:
–That campaign is strong.
–That candidate will work hard to make the campaign fly.
–How recruiting is going.
–What the polls say are the candidate's chances.

Doorbelling:

Will candidate go alone or with help? Check voting history of doorbelling area for predisposition of voters.
Make up or buy walking lists.
Variations: Mass canvassing, individually recruited doorbellers.
Choose strategies for: Sparsely settled areas, apartments or condos.
Campaign in rain (they'll be home and/or feel sorry for doorbeller).
Miscellaneous factors: Dogs, timing, what to say.
Not-at-homes: leave a message, mail a follow-up letter.

Keep records (notebook for ideas/ problems picked up on the go):
–Ideas from opponents, other offices.
–Complaints/suggestions by voters.
–Comments that need followup.

Other one-on-one contacts: (Check ordinances for legal requirements before doing these)
Visiting retail shops in neighborhoods.
Making street corner speeches.
Shaking hands at factory gate (have printed material or some gimmick to make them remember the name).
Telephoning (see also telephone bank nutshell)
–Candidate calls personally.
–Supporters make calls.
–Candidate's recorded message.

★ ★ ★ ★ ★   **In A Nutshell**   ★ ★ ★ ★ ★

Chapter 4

Merchandising the Common Touch—Machine Style

> Organize the whole state so that every Whig can be brought to the polls . . . divide (the) country into small districts . . . make a perfect list of all the voters and . . . ascertain with certainty for whom they will vote . . . keep a CONSTANT WATCH ON DOUBTFUL VOTERS . . . and on election day see that every Whig is brought to the polls.
> —A. Lincoln[1]

The modern campaigner can learn a great deal from the political machines of old. Whatever else the machine was, it excelled at "merchandising the common touch." By that I mean that they made individuals feel that they and their votes were important.

When machines flourished, tax rates were high. Most were corrupt. In some machines no one in the organization dared to speak out against the Boss, such as Tweed and his associates of Tammany Hall fame, who had incomes many times that of their official salaries. I make no attempt to justify the morality of those who were corrupt and in some cases provided mediocre—or more often rotten—government.

I'm interested in the old-fashioned political machine because they knew how to win elections.

Today, political parties, unions, and a host of nonpartisans and pressure groups conduct registration and get-out-the-vote drives. However, even today's multi-media campaigns do not get most eligible voters to the polls. Simply stated, today's campaigns have not given the voters the "feeling of importance" described by Dale Carnegie.[2]

In fact, most political campaigns are designed to ignore nonvoters, the people described by Michael Barone in the *New York Times Magazine* as "the overwhelming majority of [those] who believe their vote will never make any difference."[3]

In the twentieth century, turnout fell from a peak of 63.1 percent of the voting population of 1960 to 55.4 percent in 1972 and to approximately 50 percent in 1980. A Washington-based committee studying the American electorate, attempting to probe the reasons, found that fifty percent of those in the study who did not vote gave as their reason, "I just don't bother with politics."

The problem of registering voters and getting them to the polls has existed since at least 1824. In that campaign there were only 355,000 votes cast for the President of the United States, which was far from the majority of those eligible.

This happened because candidates for president were sectional and the opponents didn't bother to challenge each other in their home states.

The states of Tennessee and Pennsylvania strongly supported the candidacy of Andrew Jackson. The John Quincy Adams forces were in complete command in Massachusetts. In Virginia, the third candidate, W. H. Crawford, had the electoral vote sewn up. When the returns were in, Jackson had the most popular and electoral votes, but no candidate had a majority. The choice was made not by the electorate, but, as   the Constitution required, by the U.S. House of Representatives. They chose a "minority president," John Quincy Adams.[4]

This shocked the Jackson forces, who started organizing in all states. After they worked for four years, they registered and turned out the vote in the next presidential election. In 1828, Andrew Jackson rode to a landslide victory in an election in which not just 335,000 but 1,155,000 voted.[5]

Typical of those who used the power of an organized machine was the Democratic County Chairman of Cook County, Illinois, Richard J. Daley, whom I'll call exhibit one. In 1953, he decided he wanted the position of mayor. To get it, he had to beat an incumbent Chicago mayor, Martin Kennell, who had been the organization's choice four years before and who had name familiarity and newspaper support. On his side, party Chairman Daley had the loyalty of the regular party organization.

Daley budgeted his time and money on the eleven city wards that were the most constant in their support of the Democratic organization. He defeated the incumbent by 100,000 votes, picking up 99,000 of that plurality from these eleven wards.

This set a pattern. These wards later gave Daley a plurality of 134,000. In 1972 they gave Hubert Humphrey a 183,000 margin over then Vice-President Nixon. In 1968 they provided President Kennedy with a 168,000 margin and made it possible for him to carry the state of Illinois.[6]

A second successful political machine was run by the portly, ruddy-faced man who ruled Jersey City and Hudson County, New Jersey, with a heavy hand from 1917 until he voluntarily retired from office in 1948. He was a man who fit the movie image of a big-city political boss. Though "I am the Boss" Frank Hague is among the most controversial of politicians, no one has ever denied that he knew how to run an effective vote-getting organization.[7]

Boss Hague made sure his troops didn't lose the common touch. In his era, most Jersey City voters lived in walk-up apartments. Hague knew the constituent who lived at the top of a long flight of stairs was going to be flattered when someone walked up to ask for his or her vote. So several weeks before each election, Boss Hague insisted his block workers, most of whom were his city employees, go to a gym and train so that they would be in shape to climb stairs.

And he insisted they campaign in the rain, because it impressed the voter that they thought enough of his or her vote to get out and really work for it.[8]

They left nothing to chance. Prior to the opening of the polls were weeks of careful preparation, and just two days before the vote, all district leaders attended a rally where they heard a stoney-faced Frank Hague say with meaning, "364 days you want favors from me. Now, one day of the year, I come to you and I expect you to do your duty."

Fig. 1-3. Morton Keller, *The Art and Politics of Thomas Nast* (London: Oxford University Press, 1968), pp. 127, 131.

On election day the machine's poll-watchers got an official list of eligible voters, and they checked off organization supporters as they came in to vote. Party headquarters was converted to a war room. Its walls were covered with huge precinct maps, which were duplicates of those at the various district headquarters. Every voter's name was coded on these maps so the organization could see if they were: "Friendly, Okay," "Republican, No Good," "Republican, but Friendly," and "Receives Favors, Proved Ingrate."9   Here Hague operated like a Prussian general. As his runners periodically reported, a nervous Boss paced the floor, barked orders, or paused to talk to his aides and go over statistics. Occasionally, he inspected the charts, measuring what percentage of the vote should be in, say, by 1:00 p.m., 3:00 p.m. or 5:00 p.m.

If the totals in any precincts were falling behind their expected vote quotas, Hague would make phone calls to the ward lieutenants or precinct captains demanding to know what was wrong. Usually, he got an explanation: Maybe a building in the precinct had been torn down, but the voters' registrations had not been transferred. If there was no reason, then a furious Hague would dispatch reserves to supplement local workers who he assumed just weren't around hustling the voters to the polls.

During his heyday, Hague boasted 92 percent registration in Jersey City and Hudson County, and 85 percent turnout among those registered.10   This permitted him to dominate the politics of Jersey City and Hudson County, electing five governors in a row, and making him responsible for the election of most of New Jersey's U.S. Senators.

In the 1930s and 1940s, a third incredible Republican-run Philadelphia machine successfully swam against the popular Democratic New Deal tide of that era. The reason it succeeded was its 2,074 ward heelers. They were ready 365 days a year when individuals needed help.

The important cogs in that machine were ward committeemen who were duly elected to a two-year term in their regular party primary elections. Once elected, they were given a paying job at city hall. But whatever their paying job was, that was only the beginning of their public service. They ran award clubs, conducted outings and excursions, headed church fund drives, collected money for charity, and in times of need, produced food for the poor.11

To get the day-to-day story, let's follow the activities of one of those Republican ward committeemen, Joe Haggerty. On a typical day he got home from his (paid) job at City Hall rather early in the afternoon. He found telephone calls waiting for him and often somebody waiting on his stoop. He would spend the rest of the day, and often half the night, fixing things for people—getting this one excused from jury service, getting that one's hearing in magistrate's court postponed, obtaining bail bondsmen for a constituent's son—and was always available when there were complaints about garbage pickups, police, or fire protection.12

The modern political machine style is slightly different—a mixture of machine, activism, and volunteerism.

Today Orval Faubus is remembered because of his advocacy of white supremacy. However, when he ruled as Arkansas' governor, his political power depended on more than rhetoric. He shrewdly used his position to befriend 20,000 state employees. As governor he appointed 125 state boards or commissions that spent a quarter of a billion dollars a year and controlled the wages, hours, and working conditions of an additional 20,000 people. Faubus was a strong friend of education, which, of course, endeared him to as many as 15,000 teachers.13

In their heyday, the party bosses imposed vote quotas on each division or ward and set goals or quotas for their workers.14   The local committeeman knew exactly what to expect from each precinct.

As one-time president of the Philadelphia Republican city committee William Devlin explained: "Human beings will do only what you ask them to do. If I ask a party worker to get 106 votes out of his division, then he knows that is what he has to get out, and he will work on it. If I left him alone . . . we may need 98 votes from him, but because he got 90, he may think he did a good job winning his division by 20 votes."[15]

How did the major national and state office holders benefit from the local ward captain efforts? And how did the local candidate profit from having popular leaders at the head of the national, state, and local tickets, as they fought voters' tendency to drop off as the voting moved from national and state office down the ballot to the local candidates? In 1899, the Indiana bosses solved this problem by creating a straight-party ticket. All participants in the machine benefited from the huge party majority in precincts loyal to the party. This then permitted the voter to mark a ballot once and support all the party's candidates. This was adopted in most states after it was promoted ardently by party professionals, and it remains intact in most jurisdictions to this day.[16]

To understand how modern techniques differ from those used by the old-fashioned political machine, let's look at the machine's registration and getting-out-the-vote efforts. When anyone moved into a loyal precinct, he or she was visited long before the election. At that time the worker would inquire as to their party preference, how many there were in the household, etc.[17] If they were friendly to his party, unregistered, and the worker believed they would potentially support the ticket, they would be asked to fill out cards.

These cards were dropped off at district headquarters, where under ordinary circumstances they were picked up by a deputy registrar who was a party wheelhorse. The wheelhorse then called on the new residents and performed a little registration ceremony. At the same time, he made a sales pitch designed to impress the residents with the organization's power and interest in their well-being, finally telling them that in the future they could expect regular calls from the local party worker to find out if they needed help.

Before an election it was the precinct captains' duty to find out who would be unable to get to the polls and then assist them. If they were home sick, in the service, or going out of town on election day, the captain made sure they voted absentee, and loyal party workers visited all nursing homes, hospitals, jails, and even insane asylums to register residents of those institutions and help them vote.

The machine did more than concentrate on the high-performance precincts; they gingerly approached areas with a historical preference for the opposition. They recognized that it would only encourage opposition participation if they were to campaign vigorously, so they ignored most voters. However, like bookkeepers, they kept track of those leaning in their direction and those who had received past favors, and made sure these individuals got to the polls.

On occasion this getting-out-the-vote ritual epitomized corruption, as it did in Kansas City in 1944. In that election there were 41,805 votes cast on behalf of the 38,401 who lived there—and that counts children and babies.[18] Or if a landlord was having some painting done the committeeman might make a regular call and ask, "Why didn't you tell me you needed painters? I know some good men." If the landlord was apologetic and promised to consult the committeemen next time, the situation was usually smoothed over. If, on the other hand, the landlord insisted on hiring his own painters, he might get a surprise visit from health, fire, and plumbing inspectors, who would find all sorts of expensive necessary corrections.

But most fair historians contend that it was the system and attention to organizational detail rather than the corruption that really accounted for the machines' continued success. To their credit it was the machines that first recognized the importance of servicing the poor and minorities.

What has happened to the old-fashioned political machine? Why doesn't the machine flourish today? The answer is simply that times have changed, and the public will no longer support the corruption and the heavy-handed methods used to build and hold voter loyalty.

Chapter 5

Changing the Guard: Goodbye Machine, Hello Volunteer

> This civil service law is the biggest fraud of the age. It is the curse of the nation. How are you goin' to interest our young men in their country if you have no offices to give them when they work for their party? . . . These men were full of patriotism but when we tell them that we can't place them, do you think their patriotism is goin' to last? Not much. . . . I know more than one young man in past years who worked for the ticket and was just overflowin' with patriotism, but when he was knocked out by the civil service humbug, he got to hate his country and became an Anarchist.
> —George Washington Plunkett[1]

With the dawn of a new century came career service. In spite of the straight party ballot, determined efforts of the machine politician, and even the fact that the machines won elections, the machines simply lost their army. As civil service, the merit system, and government unions emerged, one by one the old-fashioned political machines disintegrated.

But political victory does not simply happen. Someone still finances the campaign, motivates the doorbelling, puts on coffee hours, and gets out the mail. In theory this burden is on the political party. But in an every-man-for-himself elective atmosphere, candidates must depend on personal political organizations composed of recruited volunteers. (See Figure 1-4 for some volunteer-recruitment advertising ideas.)

What Makes the Volunteer Respond?

Because much of what the candidate must ask volunteers to do is menial work, some candidates are reluctant to ask because they know they will not be able to reciprocate. No doubt some workers do expect return favors, but a public survey conducted by the Republican National Committee found that this need not necessarily be so:

- 90 percent of those asked said they had never worked for a candidate of either party.
- 89 percent had not been contacted in a get-out-the-vote drive.
- 76 percent had not been personally asked to support a candidate.
- 88 percent had not been asked for a financial contribution.
- 50 percent of those surveyed indicated that if they had been asked by the party or candidate they supported they would have become involved.2

It is obvious that a political campaign is no place for candidates who are shy and reluctant to ask people to work for them. On the contrary, they should ask and

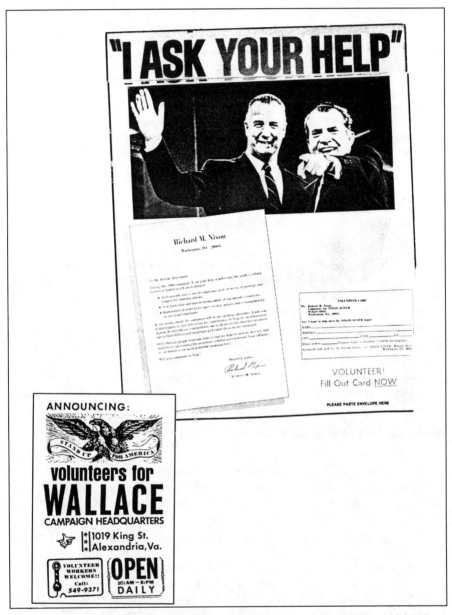

Fig. 1-4. Gary Yanker, *Prop Art* (New York: Darien House, Inc., 1972), pp. 136-137.

be willing to play the percentages, which means accepting numerous turndowns for every success.

What makes the volunteer respond? After friendship, there is self-interest. Orval Faubus's befriending of 20,000 state employees, mentioned earlier, is a case in point. Some enjoy the opportunity to bask in the reflected glow of the candidate's star quality. Some volunteer because they enjoy the excitement of being on the inside (of the campaign), and occasionally they volunteer because of the chance to meet and fraternize, or simply because it's fun.

Once candidates forget pride and recruit directly among friends and others with whom they come in contact, they often find there are many with strong interest they didn't even know about—those active in unions or in other organizations with political agendas.

What do candidates say to motivate people to volunteer? In his book *Winning Elections*, Chicago reform leader Dick Simpson says the volunteer responds to such phrases as, "Let me just put it to you, will you help?" "Will you take some personal responsibility to help us here? I've got some cards that I'd like to pass out. . . ." "If you are willing to work in our headquarters between now and election day, it can be a tremendous experience." "Please join with us. If you can't give money, give time. If you can, do both. If you can't do either, vote for us."[3]

Who and How to Recruit

Ordinarily, if the candidate is a known and respected liberal or conservative activist, he or she will find help within party ranks. After that, the best prospects are those who share a common interest, such as government employees or teachers. Help may be available from single-issue groups who support candidates willing to take public stands that are consistent with the candidate's convictions. These may include, but are not limited to, controversial groups such as pro-life or pro-choice, gay rights, and women's rights advocates.

Wise candidates also try to engage those who do church work or help the Red Cross, United Way, and/or other civic groups. Here recruiters should be aware that civic-minded citizens have mental pictures of themselves that make them respond to candidates who appear to be amateurs because they then feel they are performing a civic duty.

A related strategy is for the candidate to be—or appear to be—a "reform" candidate. Chicago reform leader Dick Simpson describes one technique to accomplish this. "Two or three months before candidate petitions must be filed, the leaders of a community group or independent organization invite 60 to 70 people to a meeting; and about 50 may actually appear."[4] With appropriate fanfare this reform group announces that they are tired of the incumbent, and they set about selecting an opponent. This group then nominates a selection committee. If the right people have been involved from the beginning, they become the dynamos that carry the campaign. When appointing the selection committee, Simpson warns that they take care not to appoint potential candidates or members of their families, so that it cannot be charged that the committee was "rigged from the beginning," as it is important that volunteers not feel they are pawns of special interest (e.g., Figure 1-5).

Fig. 1-5. Arnold Fochs, *Advertising That Won Elections* (Duluth, MN: A. J. Publishing, 1974), p. 123; Bob Strong, "Graphics That Grab You," *Campaign Insight*, July 1973.

If those with upper income adopt a candidate, they will phone their circle of acquaintances, hold meetings at their homes, organize committees to send out mailings, conduct phone campaigns, or even stage fashion shows and dances to raise money.

The Young and the Senior

In addition to traditional sources of volunteers, there are the young. No doubt some serious young people feel that the world they are inheriting has been badly botched by their elders. However, given new challenges, they miraculously find they are disenchanted with politicians, not politics.

Some examples: In 1969-1970, Congressman Meskill followed the local press and high school papers, and then sent congratulatory letters to every young person graduating from high school, winning a scholastic or sports award, getting elected to school office, etc.[5]

A former Republican youth coordinator, Robert F. Bonitati, tells how teenagers were deployed in Howard Baker's first campaign for U.S. Senator: "We established an organization called 'Young Tennesseans for Baker.' We had a high school division and a college division and enlisted between 5,000 and 7,500 high school and college students, who formed over 200 clubs throughout the state. These students could not vote, but . . . they had their own program because we believed in giving them responsibility."[6]

If they're on the candidate's team, young people will do nearly any chore. Typically, these youngsters react as they do when cheering at football games; the whole town will know the campaign is going on. However, they can have a drawback. They sometimes behave like savages when reacting to the opposition, especially if they hear a slur against their idol.[7] And young people are often less persuasive at the door, so some campaigns do not use teenagers in the initial stages, but save them for mass doorbelling when the campaign hits its final stages.

Candidates should not forget seniors. This group is best described by a sign at a retirement village in Palm Springs, California: "Drive carefully. Grandparents are at play."[8]

Fig. 1-6. Gary Yanker, *Prop Art* (New York: Darien House, 1972), p. 115.

A political campaign gives them opportunity to be active where their efforts are appreciated. No one is critical if they are a little slower, and all appreciate the fact that they are steady workers. Besides, you get the benefit of their enormous and diverse experience with the world.

Show Horses

In addition to ordinary volunteers, some campaigns recruit prestigious supporters to give the campaign a touch of class. For example, highly-honored, retired Fleet Admiral Chester Nimitz, of World War II fame, was persuaded to act as general chairman of the campaign conducted on behalf of private-school forces opposing a controversial California initiative that would strip them of their property tax exemption.

Sometimes these figureheads permit their names to appear on letterheads and ads, like golf enthusiast, Bob Hope, who lent his support to a statewide California initiative to limit tax burdens on golf courses.[9]

Taking Advantage of Volunteer Skills

Getting Organized. Today campaigns are usually run by a small group of dynamos who need little encouragement to give their all to make the campaign succeed. Beyond that it is all uphill. Few political patronage jobs are at stake, so no one has any power to order volunteers to do anything. Volunteers have different degrees of commitment. The result is that candidates and others charged with the responsibility of campaigns spend many hours trying to involve helpers, hoping that they will become interested enough to work a few hours.

There is no one way to run a political campaign. There are many good ones. On the following pages I describe the workings of a conventional campaign.

The first day sets the tone. The Democratic National Committee advises its followers to give volunteers specific instructions and neatly assigned tasks, and that there be definite lines of authority. Wise managers should take advantage of momentum when the volunteer first comes aboard. They have a supply of tasks waiting on the runway, ready to take off as volunteer help becomes available. These tasks vary with the type of campaign. In a big campaign, they can be quite specific; in smaller campaigns one volunteer may have to do several tasks. Tasks volunteers might do are summarized in the nutshell opposite.

Carefully preparing for the volunteer will overcome the common complaint that "I offered to help, but no one got in touch with me" or "I came down to headquarters, but everything was totally disorganized so I left." For those who do agree to work at headquarters, it is important that even drop-in volunteers be encouraged to use a sign-in sheet and mark their next work time on a large calendar. This is more than a formality because if they think someone is depending on them it is easier to persuade them to come back.

Putting Volunteers To Work

Again, I repeat: No one volunteers; they expect to be asked.

Headquarters tasks
Answer phones, make calls
Make photocopies
Distribute materials
Keep calendars updated
Maintain bulletin board
Type/word process

Recordkeeping
Keep files up to date
Set up card files, file
Check candidate's petitions
Check opponent's petitions

Public relations
Take pictures
Clip newspapers, maintain a scrapbook

Financial/Budget
List contributors and potential supporters
Establish a fundraising budget
Keep track of budget
File public disclosure reports
Set up calendar of fundraising events, activities

Events
Organize events, e.g., host coffee hours, line up other hosts
Address invitations
Write/type thank-you letters

In general
Make up voting lists, precinct maps
Paint or buy signs
Scout for and get permission for yard sign sites
Drive car, run errands
Doorbell
Distribute literature
Telephone voters (alone or in telephone bank)
Collect intelligence re resources
Gather info on filing, mailing, advertising, printing, other costs
Do research on issues, voting patterns
Staff phone bank polls
Operate loudspeaker trucks, bullhorns
Drive voters to the polls
Organize election day get-out-the vote drive
Recruit more volunteers

★ ★ ★ ★ ★   **In A Nutshell**   ★ ★ ★ ★ ★

Identifying Special Skills. A common complaint is "Why didn't they use my skills instead of paying a fantastic price for something I could have done for nothing?" Efficiency, tact, and diplomacy require that the candidate, manager, or staff person try to find out what the volunteer can and will do before assigning tasks. For example, the activity in headquarters will not suit all recruits. A woman with three children may not be free to leave home, but may be willing to address envelopes, doorbell her neighborhood, or make telephone calls.

In a major campaign, recruiters should look for volunteers with highly specialized skills or expertise that must otherwise be paid for. How can this information be obtained? One way is to encourage, but never require, the volunteer to fill out a checklist, one that includes information detailing the service(s) the particular individual can perform (see, for example the Leadership Inventory shown in Figure 1-7, opposite). The procedure should be in place to forward the name and address of the person volunteering to the proper chairperson, so the resulting information should be kept on cards, on computer or, better still, both.

Who knows? Someone might surface as a copywriter, a money-raiser, or with experience in handling publicity. He or she might be used to contact the media to get maximum mileage from the candidates' appearances, or to schedule news conferences and visits to local editors and radio or television newscasters.

Staying on Task. The candidate may quickly learn what was apparent to those who led the Colonial army of the American Revolution in 1776: The volunteer can be a questionable asset. Like the militiamen in the Continental Army, whose terms of enlistment were vague or limited to sixty days active duty, these volunteers can be hard to manage.

It is common for volunteers to complete only part of their tasks or to change their minds about working when they are given a specific job. Knowing this, managers should set up timetables and call those who accept responsibility, asking them for the work when it is due. If the work is not done and there is no satisfactory explanation, the manager should immediately give the task to someone else.

In spite of the fact that enthusiasm usually rises as the campaign progresses and reaches its peak just before the election, I disagree with a strategy that leaves essential chores to the last minute. There is no reason to procrastinate when recruiting volunteers who do the doorbelling, get out the mail, make telephone calls, etc. The candidate should start early but still be prepared to take advantage of the increase in the number and activity of those who respond within the last three weeks to ten days before the election.

Solving Problems with Volunteers. Later it may become apparent that some volunteers may not have the skills they claimed they had. Or they may have ideas about how the campaign should be run that do not mesh with those of the campaign strategist. Still, when volunteers make suggestions, it is important that they be carefully considered, and it is essential that they know the candidate is grateful even if the suggestion is rejected.

Also the campaign may not find it efficient to allow volunteers a free hand in selecting their campaign jobs because this will leave tasks to which no one is assigned. It is not possible to please everyone.

LEADERSHIP INVENTORY

MORE WAYS TO WIN

Name_____ Phone _____
               (Please Print)

Address _____
                 (Street No.)   (City)

Birth Date_____ Married or Single_____

Occupation _____

Education: High School ( ) College ( ) Years ( ) Degree ( )

Your County_____ Town_____ Ward_____ Precinct_____

Have you been active in Republican Politics?____ If so, how long?_____

Do you hold Party position now?_____ If so, what? _____

What other work have you done for the Party?_____

_____

How many hours a week do you estimate you can devote to the Party? _____

Have you been active in Civic Clubs ( ) Athletics ( ) Veterans Organizations ( ) Lodges ( ) Professional Clubs ( ) Others ( ) _____

Have you even held elective position in an organization? _____ If so, what?

_____

Could you say in a few words what you think is the most important job for
the Party to undertake at this time?_____

_____

Fig. 1-7. Leadership inventory, *More Ways to Win* (Republican National
Committee in cooperation with Nebraska Republican State Central Committee,
1966).

HANDY CHECK LIST

In past campaigns I have been active as:

In the coming campaign I would like to be considered to work as:

In past campaigns I have been active as:	In the coming campaign I would like to be considered to work as:
( ) Campaign manager	( ) Campaign manager
( ) Precinct worker	( ) Precinct worker
( ) Party official	( ) Party official
( ) Candidate	( ) Candidate
( ) Receptionist at headquarters	( ) Receptionist at headquarters
( ) Telephoner	( ) Telephoner
( ) Door-to-door worker	( ) Door-to-door worker
( ) Baby sitter	( ) Baby sitter
( ) Speaker	( ) Speaker
( ) Office manager	( ) Office manager
( ) Advertising copywriter	( ) Advertising copywriter
( ) Speech writer	( ) Speech writer
( ) Money raiser	( ) Money raiser
( ) Election day worker	( ) Election day worker
( ) Election day transportation aide	( ) Election day transportation aide
( ) Precinct official	( ) Precinct official
( ) Typist	( ) Typist
( ) Filing clerk	( ) Filing clerk
( ) Envelope addresser	( ) Envelope addresser
( ) Other - describe	( ) Other - describe

Names of 2 friends I would recommend as new Republican workers:

(Name)	(Address)	(Phone)
(Name)	(Address)	(Phone)

Fig. 1-7. Continued.

Creating and Maintaining Morale and Esprit de Corps

Once the campaign has established a minimum number of volunteers, this figure must be increased by at least 50 percent and sometimes by 200 percent. Holding volunteers' interest will depend upon the candidate's need and the prospects of victory. If possible, candidates should make their supporters believe the contest is so close that their volunteer efforts will make the difference. Yet much as they love to see it, candidates must be wary of a good standing in the polls and a large primary vote because it can backfire when workers become over-confident and stop campaigning.

The volunteers themselves can be used to increase recruits; the key to this is maintaining the zeal of those already on board. All must see the campaign as an adventure or an idealistic opportunity to promote something. To do this, it is important that the campaign have a sense of belonging and loyalty.

To accomplish this, some campaigns publish a periodic "insiders" newsletter designed to let everyone know of new endorsements, the results of current confidential polls, decision strategy, or even the dirty tricks the opposition is employing. Publishing a newsletter depends on the financial situation of the campaign, available help, and the number of workers involved. In some campaigns such a project may be rejected because inside information might fall in the hands of the opposition.

Another aspect of volunteer constancy is the candidate's visibility. When there is work to be done, the candidate should help. If this is not feasible, he or she should at least visit while a work party is in progress and thank the volunteers for their valuable service. Alternatively, the candidate might send a mid-campaign letter.

There are other ways a campaign can recognize volunteer excellence. The first Howard Baker for United States Senate (Tennessee) campaign simply compiled a list of names entitled, "Baker Campaign Key Workers," which they posted in a prominent place at headquarters.[10]

A candidate who used this form of recognition to its fullest was a man who had only a high school education, who inherited no wealth, had no profession, and no business or family connections. He wasn't handsome, and those who knew him say he wasn't brilliant. Yet he rose to become a Coca-Cola executive, Chairman of the Democratic Party, and Postmaster of the United States. James A. Farley did not minimize the political importance of image and the mass media, but, pointing out its limitations, he commented, "The media cannot gather signatures for nominating petitions, buttonhole a voter, or help them to the polls." In his heyday Farley remembered names, shook hands, and kept in contact with about 150,000 party workers. After forty years in politics he left a legacy in the form of letters sent during and after campaigns praising political workers for their efforts. Even today there are thousands of them signed "Jim" in green ink that have been passed down to children and grandchildren as treasured family heirlooms.[11]

Time—A Psychological Factor

Time has a psychological effect upon contributions—not only monetary contributions but also the time volunteers contribute to a campaign. For the vast majority who volunteer their time and money to a political campaign, the sense of the contest and the pleasure of participation are the only rewards. It is no surprise then that volunteers are enthusiastic at the beginning of a campaign, but toward the middle their interest drags and only reaches greater heights just prior to election.

This mid-campaign droop is aggravated by the fact that volunteers usually do not see the candidate, who is away from headquarters contacting voters. The wise strategist times a mid-campaign letter from the candidate to lift the volunteers' spirits. In this letter the candidate should thank the volunteers, praise their individual efforts, and discuss the final push to come. The letter should also extend a personal invitation to join the victory party on election night.

No matter how well plans are made, the campaign staff will not be ready to meet unforeseen emergencies that come during the campaign's final windup. This is when maximum volunteer help is needed to put up signs, complete mailing, get out the vote, etc.

During the 1966 campaign for governor of Maryland, Republican nominee Spiro Agnew realized the importance of last-minute volunteer support. He was supported by a group of affluent dedicated volunteers who viewed the campaign as a crusade against an opponent whom they considered a racist. While the volunteer feeling was running high, Agnew's staff persuaded many of the key workers to arrange their vacation schedules so they would be available in the campaign's closing days when their support would be crucial.[12]

The primary key to campaign morale is, of course, how the candidate is faring. If the candidate looks reasonably good in the polls or the primary election, it is easier to attract and retain volunteers. For candidates who are behind, keeping up this front is more difficult, especially in today's poll-oriented campaigns, where poll results can't be hidden from volunteers. Still, maintaining the facade is usually not difficult. Volunteers want to believe the candidate and his or her managers have some magic insight. They are inclined to take at face value predictions of success or pronouncements by the candidate or their managers that the election is too close to call. For example, at the time of his nomination, when his campaign seemed hopeless, Harry Truman said, "Vice President Barkley and I are going to win and make the Republicans like it." Just before his defeat, Democratic Presidential nominee Fritz Mondale said to his supporters, "Don't despair. Don't give up. . . . The Republicans are in for a big surprise."[13]

November 1972 polls showed U.S. Senator George McGovern's ill-fated presidential efforts going down to defeat by a margin greater than any presidential candidate since 1924. Yet two McGovern supporters authored a serious little book titled, "How McGovern was Elected President and Why the Polls Were Wrong."[14]

Come to think of it, how often have we heard any politician admit that he or she is going to lose an election? Yet we know some are going to lose. Does that mean, as Pierre de Beaumarchais, 18th Century French playwright, author of "The Marriage of Figaro," and an active supporter of the American Revolution, once said, "to be a politician . . . is to pretend knowledge of what you are totally ignorant, decline to listen to what you hear, attempt what is beyond capacity, hide what ought to be exposed, appear profound when you are dull-witted. . . ?"[15]

Of course, if necessary! Though some believe they are right when they claim victory, others believe good campaign staff morale demands that they predict victory, no matter how slim their chances.

Chapter 6

Doorbelling

Confucius say, "He who cover chair instead of territory is on bottom all time."

Person-to-person canvassing can be used in many different ways to solicit votes. A primary objective is of course to increase the candidate's name familiarity. Another objective of doorbelling is to register voters and then get them to the polls in areas populated by those who overwhelmingly support a particular party. In Texas, well over one third of the vote potential is Hispanic or black, who traditionally strongly support Democratic candidates. However, a high percentage of this potential is not registered, and those who are registered don't turn out. In such cases, it benefits Democratic candidates to combine in a statewide effort to get minorities registered and to the polls.

Getting Organized

Voters who live in sparsely settled areas make especially good targets because they rarely see a doorbeller. Attention to the rural voter launched the career of a notable Wisconsin politician when, as a brash young lawyer, Joseph McCarthy decided to run against an incumbent district court judge. Six months before the election, he started visiting the farms that dotted the countryside. As he went about this task, he joked with farmers' wives, praised their cooking, and patted the heads of their children. He made notes of the first names of family members, watch dogs, and ailing cows.

The very next day, he sent follow-up letters mentioning his visits in some detail. On the eve of the election, every farm and village housewife received a postcard bearing a picture of a freckle-faced boy wearing a baseball mitt with a handwritten message mentioning a name or incident or something else designed to make it personal. Another message urged the wife to shanghai her husband and get to the polls early.

How did he do it? After each visit, he returned to his car, plugged a recording device into the generator of his car and, while his memory was still fresh, dictated a letter. Each night he turned his recordings over to a stenographer who typed letters to be mailed the next day. Actually, these letters were not all originals. McCarthy did what every candidate who uses this technique does. He used a form letter to which he added a few personal touches.

The followup letters flattered the farm wife, the restaurant proprietors of places he stopped for lunch, the motorists he pulled out of the mud, and the village retirees he passed some time with. By mentioning some inconsequential but personal thing about his visit, it conveyed the impression that their meeting was the high point of the candidate's campaign day.

McCarthy rolled up a huge majority among these rural folks and the strategy worked; he beat the incumbent. After that victory, Joseph McCarthy went on to become U.S. Senator. It's hard to reconcile this picture with the notorious McCarthy who ran the infamous Communist hearings in the 1950s, but they are one and the same.[1]

Preparation

Generally speaking, incumbents with political followings and an ongoing organization might time the mailing and the doorbelling effort about six to eight weeks before the election. Challengers should start recruiting doorbellers *before* they file.

The first task is to select the areas to be doorbelled. The logical way to start making doorbell assignments is to identify the precincts on a map. At the outset, it is important that those coordinating this effort get a recent, detailed, large-scale map to use when making volunteer assignments and for marking the areas covered. Typically precinct maps show only boundaries, but not street number information.

Details of the specific households to be targeted are refined using a walking list, a list in which the names of the registered voters are arranged not only geographically, but in sequence by address (see Figure 1-8, next page, for a sample). Some identify residences by voting history and party affiliation. With such a tool, addresses can be skipped where no one is registered, and in a primary where registration is by party, they may want to skip those registered with the opposition.

In many jurisdictions, candidates can buy such a computerized precinct walking list. This resource also permits the doorbeller to heed Dale Carnegie's advice that "A person's name is the sweetest sound on earth."[2] With such a list, doorbellers can further "merchandise the common touch," greeting voters by name at the door.

Where do candidates or doorbell managers get such walking lists? The answer varies with the jurisdiction. Candidates might try the registrar of voting records or their political party headquarters. In some areas, private computer firms sell walking lists.

If these efforts fail, I would advise the candidate to see the local telephone company. They won't have anything that shows party affiliation, but they will have for purchase a reverse directory, which lists subscribers in geographic

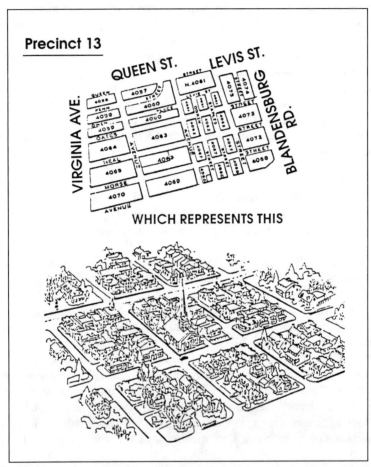

Fig. 1-8. *More Ways to Win* (North Platte, Nebraska: Nebraska Republican State Central Committee, 1966).

sequence. The list is then compared with a computer printout of registered voters, for example, which are crossed off the block lists, leaving a list of unregistered voters who can be solicited door to door.

Treating the Doorbeller with Tender Loving Care

The second task is to recruit volunteers, an ongoing task. The techniques used to recruit doorbellers are the same as for other volunteers, detailed in the previous chapter.

Doorbelling promotes the candidate and flatters the voter but doesn't do much for the canvassers' egos. Unless they have considerable motivation, they will not put up with the aches and pains that accompany climbing stairs and the embarrassment that goes with the occasional rejection by an opposition supporter. To supply this motivation, candidates in a small campaign—and managers and/or the doorbell chair in large ones—should maintain close daily communication with the doorbellers, striving to make them feel the responsibility and satisfaction of being part of an organized effort. Nevertheless, the attrition rate is high, and constant recruiting is necessary because, no matter how well they are treated, most volunteers do not expect or want to ring doorbells.

Although it pays to doorbell in the rain, to be realistic, there are going to be few doorbellers dedicated enough to brave the elements. This means the candidate or doorbell chairman must find imaginative ways to keep the crew working in bad weather. One way is to skip the apartments in dry weather, then have a driver pick up and deliver doorbellers there when it rains.

Speeding Up the Process

When the effort required to cover constituencies at the door is massive, the campaign may not have the option of covering the entire territory and must choose which voters to doorbell. A precinct can be measured on a scale of past party performance. One strategy is to target the precincts that made the greatest vote contribution first, on the theory that if the voter goes to the polls the candidate has a good to excellent chance of getting his or her vote. Then work from there to those precincts that contributed the fewest votes.

Another strategy is to avoid precincts where either party is strong and concentrate on those where the contest is close, or perhaps where there are a substantial number of ticket splitters. Former Michigan Governor George Romney's phenomenal success was due in large part to his popularity with these ticket-splitters. When pursuing them, Romney used a complicated computer formula to determine the likelihood that they would split their tickets. For example, Burton Township was shown as 7.93 percent of the state population; 41.4 percent Romney. His campaign provided for a door-to-door canvass in the eight precincts where his computer program showed these voters were concentrated, with a neighborhood rally in at least one of them.[3]

Whatever technique is used, most campaigns avoid areas that strategist Edward Schwartzman warns of where "the opponent is so strong you run the risk of reinforcing his (or her) vote rather than increasing your own."[4]

Making Assignments

When making assignments, the dispatcher can't assume two precincts with the same number of voters will take the same amount of effort. It's easier, for example, for a doorbeller to cover all the apartments in one building than to cover the same number of private homes. The difference is even more exaggerated in a widely separated rural area. So it is helpful if doorbell chairs know the physical area included in the assignments since, even with good maps, speed of doorbell operations depends on population concentration.

Apartments and condos deserve special attention when calculating the number of dwellings an individual or crew of doorbellers is to cover. There may be as few as twenty or as many as several hundred voters in high-rise living units.

Nothing can be done about topography, except that, when laying out doorbell areas, managers should recognize that it takes more dedication and time to contact voters who live in a hilly territory or in sparsely settled areas. It is wise, if candidates want to prevent these areas from getting lost in the last-minute rush, to arrange doorbelling efforts to concentrate on the hilly and more sparsely populated areas early, leaving the flat and more densely populated areas to a time when the campaign reaches a climax and when volunteers are increasing as election day approaches.

Volunteers working singly in their own neighborhoods are typically assigned between 20 to 60 residences. The numbers assigned to those working in teams can be greater.

Literature Related to Doorbelling

Once the area and households to be doorbelled have been selected, and sufficient volunteers have been signed up, it is important, particularly for first-time candidates, to direct a barrage of direct mail advertising, publicity, signs, etc., toward precincts about to be doorbelled.

At this point, packets should also be ready to hand out to the doorbellers containing candidate literature, "missed you" cards, maps where needed, an instruction sheet (including a sample "what to say" speech), volunteer sign-up cards, request-for-more-info forms, and information on local registration sites. Ideally, a staffer or the candidate delivers the campaign kits personally to those doorbellers working individually in their own neighborhoods, but if necessary the packets can be mailed. Either way, a staffer should check back in a few days to make sure the house-to-house calls were made and ask if the workers would be willing to work another block.

Doorbelling Strategies

The most popular way to doorbell is to give volunteers small, compact areas to cover on their own. This way the doorbelling can be done at the canvasser's own speed and leisure. Unsupervised individual effort, however, can and usually does fall victim to inertia or apprehension and can encourage deception.

To overcome these problems, the innovative campaigner supplies a form on which the doorbeller is asked to list the name and address of each family called on, with a space and special box to note the voters who will support the candidate. This encourages the volunteer to make the calls, and gives the campaign a list of probable supporters.

A more effective strategy is mass doorbelling. Master strategist Matt Reese commented, "The tube is impersonal, it doesn't make you part of anything. An organization makes you part and gives you satisfaction."[5] Even the experienced enjoy the esprit de corps of campaigning together as well as the fun of having coffee and swapping stories when they finish. Most candidates prefer mass doorbelling because it is easier to maintain a regular schedule. It is also more efficient and they can be sure the territory is covered.

Early in the campaign, while the registration lists are still open, candidates or their parties can arrange to have a volunteer designated as a deputy registrar to accompany crews, so nonvoters can be registered on the spot.

Generally, mass doorbelling efforts start with the volunteers rendezvousing at a predetermined location. After a quick pep talk, volunteers are paired, given their territory and materials, and sent out. They quit when they run out of literature or territory.

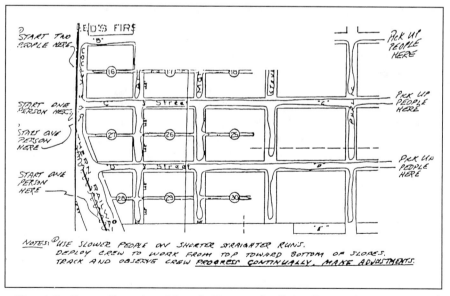

Fig. 1-9. From *Campaign Manual*, Democratic State Senate Caucus State of Washington, 1968.

To take advantage of any extra volunteer time, doorbelling crews can use the "partially mechanized variation." The volunteers are divided into crews, then transported and dispatched by car. The driver spends full time picking up and dropping off six to eight people (see Figure 1-9).

In suburban residential neighborhoods where homes are in rows, a two-person crew is dropped off. Then the second crew of two people is placed at the next street, and then two more are placed, etc. The driver constantly checks the progress of the crews, then picks them up and delivers them to the next street. When nearing time to quit, the last few streets are covered by placing those who have completed their assignments at opposite ends of the uncovered streets, and letting them meet in the middle. In suburban or residential areas, this technique can double the number of calls a crew can make in a given time period.

Like any other technique, massive doorbelling has its drawbacks. Coordinating can be difficult. It is hard to incorporate willing volunteers who will agree to meet at specified times, and a whole crew can be held up if one person is late.

Some doorbell managers believe that it will impress the voter more if two people rather than one call at the door. Though I have no doubt it is effective, usually candidates can't justify the time of two volunteers. It is advisable, however, for safety and reassurance, to have doorbellers work in pairs. They take opposite sides of the same street or, in apartments, different doors.

If by chance the campaign has a doorbeller surplus, it is my view that they should be saved for a few days or weeks so the doorbeller crew can call on voters a second time.

The Candidate Should Be Involved

As a rule of thumb, canvassing succeeds in direct proportion to how much the voters' egos are flattered. It is most effective when they are doorbelled by someone they consider important. And take it from one with 40 years of experience in the political trenches, voters consider the candidates or their families important. If they are to be effective, the candidate personally should contact as many voters as possible. (So doorbelling should start early, possibly even four months prior to the election.)

With this in mind, one of the most effective ways to add enthusiasm and to get recruits is to publicize in advance that the candidate is participating in the doorbelling effort. One-time Seattle Mayor Wes Uhlman often participated personally in his doorbelling efforts, as did U.S. Senators from Washington State Dan Evans and Slade Gorton.

However, as illustrated by the following story, it is often difficult to get candidates to doorbell. An incumbent councilman of my acquaintance represented a district of 150,000. He was at ease around the campaign headquarters, raising money, discussing strategy, giving orders, but had refused to doorbell. As the campaign progressed, it became apparent that it was in deep trouble. After analysis, it was agreed that the only way he could win was to go out and to do the thing he hated most—meet the public.

He and his campaign staff invited almost a hundred supporters for a Sunday kickoff breakfast. It was understood that the candidate would lead a massive doorbell effort. The breakfast went well. There were appropriate pep talks, and the workers left in teams of two or three to a car to their appointed precincts. Except the incumbent. He went by himself.

As they proceeded to the areas to be doorbelled, little by little the incumbent's car slowed down. He waved and smiled as he let all the cars carrying the doorbellers pass. His campaign manager, who was bringing up the rear, got suspicious and decided to follow him. When the other supporters were out of sight, the manager also passed, but he kept an eye on the candidate's car in his rear-view mirror. When the candidate's car stopped, a furious campaign manager turned his car around and went back. A violent argument ensued. The candidate refused to doorbell. The campaign lost its manager and, not incidentally, the election.

Other Innovations

In his 1974 campaign for prosecuting attorney of St. Louis, Missouri, Gene McNary used volunteer squads, which included businessmen, housewives, and high school seniors. They would meet late every afternoon to be dispatched by a decorated van loaded with literature and equipped with a tank of helium to blow up balloons.

When they arrived at a precinct, the volunteers canvassed residents, inviting them to come out and meet McNary, who stood at the corner ready to talk. Meanwhile, other workers handed out bumper stickers, brochures, and balloons.[6]

The National Association of Manufacturers candidate's manual suggests an alternative that eliminates ringing the doorbell or knocking on the door. A volunteer hangs a card printed on a piece of light cardboard, which says, "I didn't want to disturb you, but I hope you will read this before you vote."[7] The theory is that the householder will think more kindly of the candidate because they were not disturbed. In my opinion this technique lacks the most important ingredient of a door-to-door effort, personal contact, and should be reserved for campaigns in which opponents have doorbelled heavily and the candidate wants to catch up.

In some campaigns, doorbellers carry two types of campaign pieces. One is the standard campaign literature and the other is an alternate brochure targeted at those not at home, giving the illusion that the candidate actually called. The message can be handwritten in advance by the candidate, or even printed on the brochure, but in a different color ink.

There is another even more effective variation. When householders are not at home, workers not only leave literature with a message, but send a note to the householders. To do this, the doorbeller keeps a list of the addresses where no one answers. After the workers finish for the evening, they consult a walking list or, if one is not available, a reverse telephone directory and identify the householders by name. Then a personal letter is sent back to the not-at-homes. Some candidates even pretend they called.

True, this flatters the "not at homes," but it is fraught with danger. No candidate should take this chance unless he or she was with the doorbell crew when the calls were made, because if the opposition can prove the candidates were somewhere else they can and will make an issue of it.

What to Say? What to Do?

Once signed up, the volunteer is sure to say, "I've got my literature and I've got my street assignment. What do I do when somebody answers the door?"

There isn't a uniformly accepted answer to this question. Most experienced doorbellers, after knocking or ringing, take a step back so as not to be right on top of the person who answers. Then they go into their memorized talk. Some recommend an "opening icebreaker," such as this suggested by the Republican National Committee: "Our children play together, but I don't believe we've ever met. I'm a neighborhood worker for the Republican party. . . ."

To bring up the subject of registration by that same Republican worker, in an affluent neighborhood with a good turn-out record, just a straightforward, "I'm a Republican representative in this neighborhood," may do the trick. In a heavily Democratic neighborhood, the openers might go like this: "We're all strongly affected by our government, but in this district only 40 percent of our voters went to the polls last election. This time we have got to get everybody out. Are you folks registered?" (Or ". . . planning to vote?") Or maybe, "You are probably as concerned as I am about [mention a current issue]. The [Democratic, Republican] party has splendid candidates, who I know will uphold the best interests of this community. Could I talk with you a few minutes about this?"

The Manufacturers Association guide emphasizes repeating the candidate's name over and over again like this, "I am a personal friend of John Candidate. John Candidate is running for Congress. May I offer you some material that will give you information regarding John Candidate's background and qualifications. Thank you for your time and I hope you will vote for John Candidate for Congress. Thank you for a good afternoon."[8]

If for some reason volunteers don't like these formats, I encourage them to work out one of their own. For example: "Good evening. I am calling to remind you to be sure to vote next Tuesday. When you do, I hope you'll vote for John Candidate. Here's some literature that I know you'll find interesting. Speaking for myself, I can say [he or she] is an outstanding [citizen, educator, or some other complimentary thing]." Or "I know him personally, and I can guarantee that he will do a good job representing us in the state legislature."

Occasionally, doorbellers want to know what to wear when doorbelling. This reminds me of the most unforgettable doorbeller I ever met, Patrick Jerome Murphy. I still remember his first phone call. He sounded as if he had been drinking, which he probably was. I was about to hang up when he used the magic words, "Let me help you canvass for votes." Late the next morning, I looked up the caller, who lived on Skid Row in Seattle, which at the time was included in my district.

On arriving at his one-room living quarters, I met a tall, thin, sharp-nosed man of 70-plus years with white hair and a missing front tooth. His clothes were shabby but clean. As we talked, he explained that he was a retired merchant seaman, living alone on a very small pension. Although I had reservations, I decided to let him help—first as part of a doorbell crew and later on his own during daytime hours.

When he "canvassed," as he called it, the voter saw a wrinkled old man who (they probably suspected) drank more than he should carrying a shopping bag full of my literature. I kept wondering if Murph's appearance would turn off my constituents, most of whom lived in suburban single-family residential areas. Sensing my apprehension, he assured me that he was a "Boston professional," which I later came to realize meant that he was a "gentleman of the old school." And in spite of his disheveled appearance, he charmed the women of the house with generous quantities of blarney, always closing with "God loves you."

Things went very well until Halloween night, when I got a phone call from the local police who were responding to a complaint from a woman who said she had been "scared by a 75-year-old trick-or-treater." They wanted to know if he was legitimate.

After the election, I made a statistical comparison of the areas he covered with those covered by others. The results convinced me blarney far outweighed his appearance. I've concluded that clothes are helpful but not everything. Nevertheless, I would advise volunteers to dress for comfort in simple conservative attire.

Most volunteers fret about interrupting voter mealtimes. Individual doorbellers working their own neighborhood can usually wait until after mealtime to do their canvassing. However, when conducting a mass doorbelling effort, time is usually too precious and mealtimes too varied to be considered. As for quitting time, it should be before 9:00 p.m.

The volunteer who has never doorbelled also asks, "What about dogs?" The answer should be that, if the worker is afraid, stay away from houses with dogs.

The volunteer should also be reminded that, by federal law, even though householders buy them, mailboxes are government property, and putting anything in them is illegal unless it carries appropriate postage. So doorbellers should not put brochures in mailboxes when no one is home. Nor should they leave brochures on the floor where they will be walked on and kicked aside. Instead they should try to place them in a prominent place—say the handle of a door, or inside the screen door. It is common to write "Sorry you weren't at home" on the campaign brochure or to attach a preprinted note that asks householders to call or write if they have questions or an interest in helping.

Doorbell volunteers also should be instructed not to get into issues. The volunteer gives the householders a simple message and requests that they read a folder describing the candidate, because, as suggested by the National Association of Manufacturers, their function is to promote the candidate's *name*.[9] A few candidates have the doorbeller carry a special reference sheet designed for the voter who wants to know more about the candidate's positions on major issues. Or volunteers are instructed to take the voters' name, address, and a brief note of their concerns and forward it to the campaign manager, who will arrange to answer. More cautious candidates instruct the doorbeller to ask the voter to write a letter or fill out cards, which are submitted to specially designated staffers.

When doorbelling is completed for the day, the volunteers should be encouraged to return to a central meeting place for coffee and a sweet. There they can mingle and swap experiences and funny stories. They should be met and thanked by the candidate, who should ask them to sign up for another stint. A nice touch would be for the candidate to write personal thank yous to the doorbellers.

One-time Washington State Senator Pete Francis made up an instruction sheet that he gave to his doorbellers, entitled "The Do's and Don'ts of Doorbelling" (see nutshell). I recommend candidates and managers examine it and adapt it to their needs.

Instructions to Doorbellers

Work weekdays, 6:00 p.m. to 9:00 p.m. (Do not go beyond 9:30 p.m.)

Never ring a doorbell if the house is dark.

Always carry a pencil and paper.

After knocking on the door, take a step back so as not to be right on top of the person who answers the door.

The greeting should be familiar and short. *Example*: "Hello, my name is _____, and I'm here on behalf of your State Senator, Pete Francis."

Then offer the brochure and ask that they read it. Place it in the person's hand with the name "State Senator Pete Francis" in a position so it can be read. In most cases, no more conversation will be necessary or appropriate.

DON'T ARGUE. You probably do not know exactly how Pete thinks on each issue. Merely respond to questions about Pete's position on issues by inviting them to come to his home on Friday evening, after 8:30, when there is always open house.

If they indicate support for Pete, ask them if they would be willing to have a Pete Francis sign in their yard, or an easily removable, non-messy bumper strip on their cars.

If people exhibit further interest, inquire if they would like to become more active in the political process. We of course especially need people who are willing to hold coffee hours. Of course, there is doorbelling, work on mailings, and other work. BE CERTAIN TO WRITE DOWN WHATEVER THEY WANT and turn it in.

If you get no response, leave the material in a permanent place (handle of door, between screen and storm door, or inside door) never in a mailbox or on the floor, if possible.

HAVE FUN! All funny stories are gone over after each session at headquarters.

Fig. 1-10. Courtesy former Washington State Senator Pete Francis.

Chapter 7

Person to Person: The Power of the Telephone

> Skinner's Laws: Anyone who owns a telephone is at the mercy of any damn fool who knows how to dial.
> —Jean Skinner Ostlund[1]
>
> Two of the cruelest, most primitive punishments . . . the empty mail-box and the silent telephone.
> —Hedda Hopper[2]
>
> The telephone is the greatest nuisance among conveniences, the greatest convenience among nuisances.[3]

The telephone is an essential tool for the modern campaigner. Beyond the ordinary uses, it can be used to solicit monetary and voter support, to increase registration among supportive constituencies, and to help supports get to the polls on "judgment day." The telephone can also be used as a substitute for doorbelling and to recruit campaign volunteers. Indeed, the use of "boiler room" phone banks to recruit volunteers was one of the political sensations of the 1950s and early 1960s. (See the section on polling for a very different kind of telephone use.)

Among the most striking and earliest examples of effective telephone use to win voter support comes out of San Francisco in 1944. At this time the city by the bay ran its own municipal railroad, which competed with the privately owned Market Street Railroad. The city fathers wanted to merge the two systems so transit passengers could have universal transfer privileges. Five times, the merger was submitted to the voters, and each time they voted it down. Undeterred Mayor Roger B. Lapham decided to submit it again, but this time he threw an innovative twist into selling it. Each morning during that campaign he opened the phone book at random and called up a dozen people whom he startled by saying, "This is Roger Lapham. Will you help me straighten out the transportation tangle?"[4] Word soon spread. The media publicized the calls and the replies. The voters were impressed. The merger went through.

In 1952, cynical political pros scoffed at a bunch of crewcut cheerleader types who were forming Young Industry for Eisenhower. This group's first project was sending a task force out to Boise, Idaho, where presidential candidate Eisenhower was scheduled to speak. There they organized a chain of telephone calls covering every name in the phone book. In a town that at the time had a population of 34,000, they drew a crowd of 19,000 for Ike. The scoffing stopped.

When the local Democratic party organization turned against him in 1967, the renominated Mayor James H. J. Tate of Philadelphia was imperiled. He called in "hired political gun" Matt Reese, who used a battery of telephone operators to make 18,000 calls a day. They recruited 10,054 people to act as precinct captains, enabling Tate to win the primary, then the general election—by nearly two to one.

No doubt, professional telephone recruiting is expensive. (More about expenses at the end of this chapter.) But the high cost must be measured against the cost-effectiveness of other methods. For example, in 1970, Indiana Democrat and former U.S. Senator Vance Hartke spent a huge sum recruiting an instant organization in Marion County (Indianapolis). However, he considered it money well spent because it was responsible for holding the expected Hartke loss of 25,000 to 30,000 in this Republican bastion to fewer than 12,000, which accounted for his winning margin.[5] It's hard to imagine another method that could reliably produce this large an effect in so short a time. Even if the phone calls do not succeed in enlisting a recruit they are still useful because the operators are getting the candidate's name and message to the voters.

Former Congressman Bradford Morse of Massachusetts once commented, "You can spend thousands of dollars preparing a personal telephone campaign, and it will be worth every minute. Nine of ten calls will result in votes, whereas in a printed broadside canvass, if you get one vote out of 100, you will be doing well."[6]

Getting Out the Vote: Using the Telephone to Maximum Advantage

Much has changed since these early days of telephoning. Contemporary political campaigns apply the phone's power to a range of strategic uses. Campaign managers use telephones for daily conferences with the candidate's key campaign strategists and chairmen. Telephones are equally important for communications between candidates and supporters, candidates and contributors, or between the candidate and his or her opponents. Candidates can use the telephone to send personal messages to voters and it may be the only feasible method of person-to-person campaigning in widely scattered rural areas or in city apartment dwellings where doorbellers are not permitted.

Electronic Mass Merchandising. Modern campaigns tape messages and transmit them to voters using computerized telephone equipment so sophisticated it does everything, including dialing the phone number. Most recorded statements have a major disadvantage in that most people instantly recognize them as canned political speeches (they don't mention voters' names or answer questions). However, follow-up polls show that recorded statements do impress a minority of approximately 40 percent who feel the candidate has talked to them personally.[7] Forty percent is a substantial proportion and computerized phoning is far less expensive than paid professional phoning. Moreover these two techniques can be efficiently combined.

Murray Roman heads Campaign Communications, Inc., of New York, an organization that uses the phone to transmit candidates' personally recorded statements introduced by a live operator. This technique increases the percentage who think they have received a *personal* message right off the top and this alone can give a powerful boost to name familiarity and image. The operator then follows up the candidate's statement by asking if the listener will give one or two hours of their valuable time to contact ten or fifteen neighbors.

Other telephone specialists vary this routine, aiming at minorities who share an identifiable ethnic background or language. Consultant Stephen Shadegg notes that prominent leaders such as Jewish leader Theodore Bikel and Herman Badillo of the Puerto Rican community used this technique to send a tailored message from a person whom targeted voters both recognized and respected as one of their own.[8]

When targeting a racial or ethnic minority that is not proficient in English, it helps enormously if operators share the language and cultural background. This technique too has its costs, as some voters may be insulted if a foreign tongue is used. Therefore, it requires perceptive operators who are able to sense language problems and know when it is wise to speak in the prospect's native language.

Using the Telephone to Build an Organization. Once a phone list is established, calls are made on an organized basis by staff or campaign workers designed to recruit volunteers (see next section), and party workers use it early in the campaign to prospect for those desiring absentee ballots. The telephone can also be used to call a selected list on election day to see if all have voted and, if not, if they need rides or babysitters, which the organization will provide.

Where do campaigners get prospect lists? In a jurisdiction where the voters must declare party, the party faithful are the first priority. In a primary, or where the candidate is running in a jurisdiction where voters are not registered by party preference, the organization can (and should) start weeks—even months—in advance by taking a preliminary survey of all telephone subscribers.

The conventional approach has solicitors using a "soft sell" when taking the survey, opening the conversation with something like: "Good afternoon, Mrs. Subscriber (use name). This is Dorothy Solicitor (give name). We are taking a political survey in your neighborhood. May I ask if you are registered to vote?" The caller then asks the listener if he or she will answer a few questions. If the answer is yes, the caller asks, "Do you consider yourself a Republican, Democrat, or Independent voter? (After the primaries, the operator substitutes the words "undecided" for "independent.")

Following his initial election, and prior to his reelection bid, the first Republican Governor of the State of Arkansas, Winthrop Rockefeller, used this process of generating prospect lists to eliminate the handicap presented by the absence of a Republican party organization in the state. At first, working with an existing nucleus, he decided to canvass Arkansas' thirty most heavily populated areas. However, it soon became obvious that recruiting a door-to-door army big enough to do the job was more than his small organization could handle so he hired professionals who kept nine phones busy for three months.

As each telephone subscriber was surveyed, they were asked their registration status and political preference, willingness to volunteer, and other background factors. The information was computerized, and the results were used to register favorable voters, target the undecided, recruit doorbellers, and get favorable voters to the polls on election day. This effort was responsible for reaching 90 percent of the homes in Pulaski County (Little Rock)—which, incidentally, he carried by a 2-to-1 margin.[9]

Phoning opposition voters is generally considered a poor strategy. Thus, candidates are advised to choose voters from precincts that consultant Edward Schwartzman believes "research shows to be at least 60 percent favorable or undecided."[10]

Though I believe in the more orthodox techniques, occasionally a candidate will succeed when he or she flouts these rules. For such a case, let's go to the State of California. Prior to the 1972 gubernatorial election, Republican State Senator Bill Bond was unknown. He decided to ignore the rule that the telephone works well only for candidates with name familiarity, and that he should relatively start late so as to be fresh in the minds of the voters. He started his telephone campaign months before the election, and he hit everyone with the same fervor. Also flouting the rule that candidates should never raise or address controversial questions (because "you are bound to make someone mad"), he encouraged his operators to become involved in extended discussions. His volunteers routinely engaged in lengthy telephone conversations with prospective opposition voters, making frank and honest comparisons of candidates. His only concession to the orthodox was to ask the volunteers to evaluate each conversation and decide if the voters "would vote for us? Would they work with us? Were they undecided? Do they hate us? If so, which of our opponents would they vote for?"

Bond catalogued this information, and its early acquisition gave him plenty of time to target sympathetic voters with a mailer explaining his stand on major issues facing the State of California or, in some instances, to call the telephone subscriber and chat personally. In Bond's case, this unorthodox approach not only succeeded but, following his primary victory, was adopted by his local Republican organization. In about a month Bond's telephoners were able to call 21,000 and to recruit house-to-house crews that knocked on almost 50,000 doors in the last five days of the campaign.[11]

Target Traditional Support. Telephoning can be a powerful tool for increasing registration among voters who favor the candidate's views. Party activists target areas that have a tradition of supporting their party. They then phone subscribers in these areas and ask: "Mrs. Householder, this is Dorothy Solicitor. I'm your neighbor down the block, and I'm making a survey to find unregistered voters. Is there a convenient time to chat with you for a few minutes?" That last sentence makes an especially good impression. It allows busy people to stop the conversation politely. Then the volunteer can ask when it will be convenient to call again.

If the person is free to talk, the telephone solicitor then says something like "I am helping the Democratic or Republican party or John Candidate's campaign for Congress and want to be sure everyone is registered who may want to vote. Are you registered?" By putting it this way, they have not asked the householders to reveal their party affiliation, but they have provided an opening so the person on the other end may do so. If the prospect is interested but not registered, the caller explains registration details. If the campaign has the facilities, they arrange to have the unregistered picked up by car and taken to register. Or if the campaign organization has a deputy registrar who can be sent to the home, the registrations take place there.

Telephone Banks: Generating Phone Lists, Choosing Operators, Making Calls

The telephone bank—or "boiler room"—is simply a way of formalizing telephoning efforts on a large scale. This is how Texas Republican William D. Clements reached 17,000 voters a *day* in 1981 and became the first Texas Republican to hold the office of Governor since reconstruction.[12] The following discussion focuses on using telephone banks to recruit campaign volunteers. The principles apply as well to soliciting votes and monetary support.

Before embarking on a large-scale telephone campaign, candidates must evaluate its potential effect realistically. For example, when planning to recruit campaign workers via telephone, campaigns must keep in mind that the response to little-known, first-time candidates will be far lower than that for better-known politicians. Moreover, when measuring campaign recruits against the number of calls, the Republican National Committee calls a telephone project successful if it recruits one percent of those contacted.

After deciding to proceed, candidates must design the operation skillfully. First they must find or generate a list of phone numbers for each precinct identified. In some cases, as with doorbelling walking lists, the campaign can obtain lists from their political party, or purchase computer lists from firms that synchronize registered voters with telephone subscribers. Also valuable is a reverse telephone directory that lists telephone subscribers by address.

If these tools are not available or are too expensive, candidates must turn to a volunteer nucleus to compile the lists. Typically, they work in teams of two so one can look up the numbers while the other writes or types them on a list. (It's tedious work, so switching off is a good idea.) This same group then recruits or hires the initial bank of operators.

Amateur Versus Professional Telephone Solicitors. The office of Women's Activities of the Democratic National Committee asserts that telephone solicitors must have a high degree of motivation. Volunteer telephone campaigners are easiest to recruit when they are working in support of very liberal or very conservative candidates, or are part of a group embarked on a single-issue crusade.

In theory, professional operators work on an eight-hour shift (noon to 9:00 p.m.) with an hour out for lunch, but it is difficult to be polite and efficient when tired. Thus, the operator's day is usually split into 20- or 30-minute shifts broken by 5- or 10-minute breaks. Thus if candidates are to have a boiler-room operation, they will need more operators than there are telephones.

After a few days' experience, those managing the operation should set quotas of the numbers contacted per hour. In a city environment where more callbacks must be made, a good operator can complete from 20 to 30 calls an hour. In other situations, say election-day reminders to vote, operators can do considerably better. Operators are instructed to take at least two and no more than four minutes to deliver a short message—that is, unless the prospect shows interest.[13]

There are two schools of thought regarding the decisions of whether or not operators should mention the political party. Unless the prospects' affiliations are known, one school has the callers refrain. Those holding this view use an instruction sheet that goes like this: "Hello, Mary Voter, how do you do. Mr. John Candidate, who is running for Congress, has asked me to call you. John has an important request to make of you." Or the operator starts the message by simply saying they are calling for John Candidate, and asking that the person consider him because of his record or stand on some issue. Eventually, the prospect is asked if he or she can be counted on for help.

Those holding the other view would have the operators first ask those called if they are Republicans or Democrats. Then, using their predisposition, the operator says: "I am calling fellow Democrats" or ". . . fellow Republicans." If the prospects belong to another political party, the operators begin or end by complimenting them for showing open-minded fairness and responsibility as voters by listening to both sides. Either technique has a valuable side benefit. Even though the prospect might not be willing to work actively to support John or Mary Candidate, the operator can identify friendly supportive voters who can be targeted specifically as part of a later get-out-the-vote drive.

Most campaigns arm the operators with the candidate's biographical information and an issue sheet with previously prepared answers to questions that are most commonly asked. The operators' instructions must make it emphatically clear that any inquiry not specifically covered by this sheet will be referred to the candidate's campaign manager or staffer, who will call back at a later time. The instruction sheet should also tell the operator not to argue or hang up in anger. If the person called refuses to help, the operator might say something like, "Thank you, Mr. or Ms. Voter. I know John Candidate will understand. Again, thank you very much."[14] Above all, operators should be warned to be careful when making a reply and not to give in to any temptation that might annoy the voter. One operator did, when a voter replied to the request for help with, "Am I crazy or are you?" The operator replied in a voice dripping with sarcasm, "Sorry, but I do not have that information."

Experts also differ in how best to respond when prospects agree to help. Some telephone operators are given a range of prospective jobs to offer those who respond favorably, such as, are they willing to: (a) work in headquarters? (b) put up a yard sign or a bumper sticker? (c) send endorsement cards to their friends? (d) make telephone calls? (e) make a contribution?, etc. Most try initially to persuade the volunteers to work door to door in their own neighborhoods. If the prospect agrees to help, the operator takes whatever time is needed to clearly explain the necessary arrangements, and concludes with, "Thank you, Ms. Voter, John Candidate will be very pleased and very grateful when I tell him you are going to help us."[15]

Effective telephone soliciting requires call-backs. After operators have tried a second time and failed to reach the callers, a notation is made at the top of the call sheet. This sheet is set aside for the next shift, who are instructed to call the numbers the previous shift failed to reach. If, after several calls on two successive days the operators still fail to reach the prospect, another volunteer or staffer mails the prospect a form letter with a volunteer appeal card. See the nutshell (opposite) for a summary of effective telephone techniques.

Finally, candidates should not forget to send volunteers personal letters of thanks.

Caution: Hide the Boiler Room. Candidates who use telephone campaigns do run some risk of being equated with con artists, peddlers, dance studio hustlers, and roofing and siding salesmen.

In my opinion, the boiler room should not operate in general headquarters nor in any location open to the public. If a boiler room is used, a central location with suitable physical facilities for installation of a large number telephones must be ready at least 10 to 12 weeks before election day and will be in virtually constant use during that entire period. Further, only those having direct business with the telephone operators should be admitted to the work area. No doubt the opposition will be aware of the telephone operation, but why furnish them with precise information and an opportunity to take photographs of a large boiler room operation, which they might be tempted to use as a campaign issue?

I suppose it is fair criticism to say that a systematic telephone operation smacks of old machine politics. But being compared with the old machine doesn't upset political professionals like Matt Reese who (speaking of the vote-getting techniques of "I am the boss" Frank Hague), says with reverence: "He got there—by paying attention to the principle of personal contact."[16]

Expenses and Some Suggestions for Reducing Them

During World War II, the distinguished foreign correspondent, Quentin Reynolds, had the privilege of visiting President Franklin D. Roosevelt at the White House. While he was there, the President put through a transatlantic call to England's Prime Minister Winston Churchill. Shortly after the conversation got underway, Reynolds was startled to hear the President say, "I'll have to hang up now, my three minutes are up."[17] FDR would have been astounded at the costs and dimensions of today's large-scale telephone campaigns—starting from acquiring the prospect list and continuing right through to encouraging people to vote on election day itself. Edward Schwartzman points out, "Even with volunteers [telephone] campaigns involve [substantial] expenditures for rent, furniture, telephone installation, food, methods of development, and even miscellaneous items like transportation and babysitting.[18]

Recognizing that the boiler room is expensive, the National Association of Manufacturers campaign manual suggests that the candidate use what they call "Dial-A-Dozen." It starts with a personal letter from candidates to a select mailing list. It asks each person on the list if they are willing to dial one dozen friends and ask them for their votes. If they are, they are sent letters, self-addressed stamped envelopes, and tally sheets. Each volunteer is asked to record the names of those they call and to transmit to headquarters immediately those who show any interest in volunteering for the campaign.[19]

One gubernatorial campaign I am closely familiar with successfully employed an inexpensive and unorthodox telephone campaign. Although the woman candidate had never run for office, and lacked both campaign funds and an experienced political organization, she defeated two strong opponents: the mayor of the state's largest city and the county executive of the state's largest county.

Among the primary reasons Dixy Lee Ray upset the political pros and became Governor of the State of Washington in 1977 was that she had achieved substantial name recognition by virtue of previous appointments to prestigious positions and had accumulated an abundance of highly motivated volunteer supporters. To deploy them, her campaign aides simply ordered telephone books for every area in the state, then tore out the pages and assigned them to the volunteers. They, in turn, telephoned from their homes every subscriber in the state at least once and often two or three times.

Once the campaign commits to a boiler room telephone effort, it must address several management concerns. How these are handled can substantially impact both the effectiveness and cost-efficiency of the operation, and the person in charge would be wise to consult a telephone company for advice. Operators' headset-type telephones should be installed and operators separated by sound-absorbing partitions. To avoid conflicts with incoming personal calls or other business, the phones should be unlisted and out of sequence. Additional phones should be available for operators' and staffers' personal use.

Monitoring is necessary to ensure that calls are made and the proper sales message conveyed. As a rule of thumb, during evening telephoning, the supervisor can expect operators to initiate 27 to 30 calls and complete 18 or 19 per hour. When professionals are used, inefficient and ineffective operators should be identified and replaced. If they are volunteers, find something else for them to do.

Note that the only way to determine operator effectiveness is to keep a running daily tally, carefully computing the cost necessary to recruit prospects. The cost per call should include the prorated cost of preparing the list of telephone numbers, the telephones, postage, office rent, and labor if using paid operators as well as amenities for operators such as parking, coffee, or soft drinks.

Telephone Technique*

Note: Regardless of where or how telephone solicitation is done, supervisors must be sure the operator understands the basics:

1. The current belief is that women's voices are preferred as telephone solicitors, considered less likely to be a nuisance or threatening.
2. Normally solicitations should be limited to a single message, e.g., registration, organizing volunteers, getting out vote, soliciting support.
3. When canvassing rural voters, hours are more flexible because people are home more hours. In city, best call times are Saturday, Sunday daytime, or 6:00 to 9:30 p.m. weekday evenings.
4. Callers should first verify name of person contacted, then identify themselves by name. What happens next depends on call's purpose.
5. Script should be followed and presentation should be rehearsed until smooth and personal.
6. Callers should be monitored at first to correct mistakes and to weed out those whose telephone voices or manners are deemed unproductive.
7. Telephone operators should never waste time talking with dyed-in-the-wool supporters, unless they are willing to volunteer to work or contribute. To help terminate such conversations, the Women's Division of the Democratic National Committee suggests telephone solicitors say: "It's a pleasure to talk with such a good Democrat (or Republican). I hope we'll have a chance to talk some more later. Don't forget to go to the polls. Thanks a lot. Goodbye."
8. Solicitors are bound to run afoul of an unfavorable few. When this becomes clear, operators must remember that quarrels give the voters reasons to complain about the call to friends or neighbors, or to brag to others about how they told the operator off.

---

*From *Campaign Notebook*, Office of Women's Activities, Women's Division of the Democratic National Committee, Washington, DC, p. 6

In A Nutshell

Part 2

The Money Ritual

$ $ $ $ **WARNING** *$ $ $ $*

Today, campaign costs and contributions have soared beyond the wildest predictions. Though dollar amounts quoted throughout this book are historically correct and valuable as general percentage guidelines, dollar amounts more than two to four years old should not be depended upon for structuring campaign budgets.

Chapter 8

Drawing the Budget

> Never ask of contributions spent
> Where the candidate thinks it went,
> Politicians were never meant
> To remember or invent
> What he did with every cent.
> —Parody on Robert Frost's "The Hardships of Accounting"[1]

Campaign financing has come far since Thomas Jefferson ran for president and spent a total of $50. In all Democratic countries, candidates spend to publicize and popularize, and their expenditure depends on what they expect to raise—which, in turn, depends on what the campaign expects to spend.

Preliminary Rough Budget

The only thing worse than running out of money in the final days of the campaign is the plight of the loser who has no one to help him or her pay off a huge campaign debt.

Before I discuss the making of a rough preliminary budget, I must call your attention to other matters. These are so important that they can and often will make or break the campaign.

It is important that the candidate not stop with a preliminary budget. It must be reviewed periodically as the campaign progresses. Someone, usually the treasurer, should keep track not only of the expenditures to date but of all binding financial commitments made on behalf of the candidate or the campaign. And there should be regular finance committee or campaign committee meetings in which the amount of contributions, the rate of contributions, and future prospects are discussed. There should also be a careful analysis of how incoming and outgoing funds balance.

In many ways, today's candidates resemble compulsive gamblers. Once they launch their campaigns, they lose their perspective. They want to win and are tempted to spend more than they can afford. The only practical way to control expenditures and to carry out the responsibilities imposed by law is to look at each of the campaign components and budget at least enough to cover the essentials.

Although expense breakdowns vary in different campaigns, some ideas can be gleaned from the percentage allotment of funds taken from the 1968 Humphrey-Muskie campaign.[2]

It is helpful to prepare both a maximum and a primitive bare-bones budget. Both should be committed to writing so that fundraisers have a goal and so the candidate realizes their responsibility for the deficit in the event the election is lost.

The budget committee then works out a series of options. It is decided how the budget will be reformulated if funds are not raised on time. For example, it will need to be decided how planned last-minute mailings of literature to the voters or eleventh-hour newspaper and radio advertising will be cut back. The committee should also anticipate how best to spend additional money if it is raised.

Sample Advertising Agency Analysis

This is not as easy as it sounds. Typically, candidates and their managers and finance committees expect to raise and spend money on advertising and other campaign activities but have no idea of costs. Before they can act, a list of proposed costs must be prepared, followed by a preliminary budget proposal.

By itself, such a sketchy budget skips over a great number of necessary details. What is to be analyzed and how detailed that analysis should be will vary widely. There is no standard to guide the candidate during the early part of the campaign. It would take someone with miraculous foresight to determine what funds will be raised and what expenditures will be made.

However, even at this early stage the candidate or committee should isolate some if not all of the proposed expenditures and make a more complete analysis. For example, some necessary services may be donated, such as campaign headquarters, public relations, rentals, secretarial services, and travel or utilities. However, others, such as polling, party organizational expenses, management, and certainly advertising should be evaluated, and if such expenditures are to be made there should be a detailed—preferably written—analysis.

The need for polling should be evaluated. Candidates must decide if they can afford to spend anything. And if they can, they must decide when and how often polls are to be made, what the polling depth will be, and how much this will cost. Then they should ask who is going to do the polling. This of course involves a choice between in-house and

Item	Percentage
Advertising	62.3
Travel	8.2
Personnel	7.1
Communications	6.8
Field operations	5.4
Contributions to state and local candidates	3.7
Polls and surveys	2.5
Office	2.4
Miscellaneous	1.6

Table 2-1

professional polling, with or without professional analysis. Many of these and other questions that must be considered in a preliminary budget are discussed in greater detail elsewhere in the book.

In a large campaign one expenditure—advertising—will consume half the campaign budget, and this expenditure should be carefully analyzed. As an example of what advertising costs consist of, I offer these excerpts. They include staff comments and are taken from a 1977 staff memo designed to help the finance committee draw a campaign budget for a mayoral campaign in the city of Seattle, population 500,000.[3] (Note that costs have escalated since that time.)

Media Costs in 1977

Bus Signs: Cost $3,653, for 65 Super-Deluxe Spectaculars (big) for one month. If the Super-Deluxe is too deluxe, buy the smaller queen size for $2,500 per month.

Billboards: Cost $10,072. Some experts say a good deal of your money should be invested in billboards. Doing what the experts say is half the job in a political campaign, but still costs plenty. Staff question: Are they too expensive? Too ugly?

Radio: Cost $5,000. Radio is considered a cheap and effective medium for politics but can be quite the opposite. The little 60-second spot you hear on KIRO Radio on your way to work costs $64. (At KVI, 60 seconds costs $55; KIXI is selling its one minute at $44.) A minimum radio campaign, the experts say, is $5,000. Question: Are they effective? Staff comment: Yes, but costly.

Television: Unlike radio, television does not advertise its rates in 60-second units. It might frighten advertisers away. It advertises its rates in 30-second units, and the costs are sufficiently high anyway. "The Today Show," 30 seconds—$200. "Good Morning America," 30 seconds—$160. If you are interested in highly informed, politically interested audiences, you might try buying time on "60 Minutes," 30 seconds—$2,000.

Soapers during the day will go for approximately $80 to $400. If you are looking for the family audience, you must buy some prime time: "M.A.S.H.," 30 seconds—$1,500 to $1,800. "Mary Tyler Moore," 30 seconds—$1,100. Mariner's Baseball, 30 seconds—$1,000.

Staff Note: This listing doesn't include production costs, printing, or postage.

Fig. 2-1. Staff memo re media costs, 1977.

Public Relations

The budget writers should know that every major campaign will spend money on public relations. This includes writing and sending press releases and photographs, staging press conferences, and preparing radio tapes.

There must be money for expenses as well. West Virginia's Governor Jay Rockefeller spent $75,000 on Kentucky Fried Chicken to service the many political picnics that were given on his behalf.[4]

In some jurisdictions, money was spent by organizations such as New York's Tammany on men and women who picked up $20 to $25 a day getting out the vote, with the tacit understanding that the workers and their relatives would follow his or her political recommendations.[5]

Cost of Raising Money

When calculating income, the committee must recognize that campaign contributions are not net dollars. The budget must provide for the cost of raising money. Assume we have a campaign requiring $27,000. To raise this sum by conventional techniques, it is necessary to allocate 20 percent of any sum raised to cover expenses. This means that to raise the $27,000 in campaign expenses at least $33,000 must be taken in.

Fundraising expenses include such items as secretarial salaries, telephone, rent, and postage, all of which are necessary for direct solicitation. If a meal or drink fundraiser is used, there is the cost of food or refreshments, hall rentals, invitation printing, and programs. Even a simple cocktail party will require liquor, some food, hall rental, and the other expenses of hosting a reception.

In employing direct mail, the cost of raising money escalates. A successful program is likely to net only one-quarter of every dollar raised. It will cost about $90,000 to raise the $27,000.[6]

Tracking Expenditures

Constructing and refining a campaign budget so that it accurately predicts exactly what will be spent is very difficult. For one thing, the actual expenditure depends upon what is necessary to keep pace with what is spent by the opposition, and for another it is limited by the amount of money the candidate can raise. Figure 2-2 shows a sample campaign budget and Figure 2-3 shows one way to lay out a budget plan.

There is still another consideration. Campaign planners do not want to put the amount that must be raised so high that the troops become discouraged. At other times, they are afraid to let their opponent know what they secretly expect to raise. Thus, it often happens that the solicitors are not privy to the real goals.

The solicitor candidate—or the candidate's surrogate—must be a salesman. As such, he or she needs a norm by which to measure day to day success as the campaign progresses. Consequently, it is up to the candidate, the manager, or the finance chairman to set a short-term quota. The committee then projects a time frame by which the campaign can expect percentages of the goal. Again, a written plan is essential so that, at succeeding meetings, a running account can be kept of the progress toward meeting the projections.

Even if the campaign is going well, the candidate must temper daydreams of big advertising productions, lots of TV, radio, and newspaper ads, direct mail, and

POLITICAL CAMPAIGN BUDGET FORM

CAMPAIGN_____   DATE_____

CANDIDATE_____   MANAGER_____

I   HEADQUARTERS, GENERAL
    Rent (Main) $ *275*
    Rent (Outlying)   *500*
    Utilities   *175*
    Insurance   *175*
    Phones (Office only)   *700*
    Printing (letterheads, etc.)   *600*
    Signs, Decorations   *175*
    Office Supplies   *200*
    Equipment rental   *300*
    Misc.
                  SUB-TOTAL $ *3100*

II   PERSONNEL
    Management $ *3750*
    Secretaries   *1750*
    Fieldmen   *3500*
    Publicity   *800*
    Part-time Help
    Expenses
                  SUB-TOTAL $ *9800*

III   CANDIDATE, PERSONAL EXPENSES
    Travel $ *1000*
    Telephone   *350*
    Meals   *600*
    Misc.
                  SUB-TOTAL $ *1950*

IV   SPECIAL EVENTS & CAMPAIGN ACTIVITIES
    Coffee Hour Expenses $ *350*
    Sound Truck   *100*
    Meetings, rallies, etc.
    Special phone operations
    Contingencies
    Public opinion poll   *2500*
                  SUB-TOTAL
                                $ *2950*

V   PARTY ORGANIZATION ACTIVITIES
    Precinct $ *3700*
    Registration   *1000*
    Club Activity
                  SUB-TOTAL
                                4700

Fig. 2-2. *Ways to Win* (Wash. DC: Republican National Committee,
1968), p. 40. (This is a good illustration, fitting a campaign for a
small-town mayor, but note that it doesn't provide for advertising.)

giant billboards blanketing the district. When the dust settles, there is a limit as to
how much can be raised. Most contributors are going to react like Joe Kennedy,
multimillionaire father of President John and Senators Bobby and Teddy, when in
1958 he allegedly said to John in jest, "Don't buy a single vote more than
necessary. I'll be damned if I'm going to pay for a landslide."[7]
    Someone, usually the treasurer, should play the devil's advocate, constantly
reminding the candidate and his financial committee of the campaign's current

POLITICAL CAMPAIGN BUDGET FORM

		Brought Forward	$ 22,500
VI ADVERTISING AND PROMOTION			
Mailing			
___Republican, incl. postage	$ 5000		
___Democrat, incl. postage	1500		
___Special Letters, inc.postage	1000		
___Dear Friend cards incl. postage			
___Other	1500		
Billboards	2000		
___7 Sheets			
___24 Sheets			
___Snipe Sheets			
___Quarter Cards			
___Other			
___Production Costs			
Newspaper Advertising			
Weeklies	1200		
Dailies	2000		
Mets	500		
Production costs.	300		
Radio-TV Advertising			
Radio	3000		
Television			
Production costs	300		
Handout cards	600		
Brochures	1900		
Bumper Strips	300		
Special Printing	500		
Photography	500		
Mats and Cuts	200		
Misc. Advertising	200		
Other			
	SUB-TOTAL		$ 22,500
VII OTHER			
CONTINGENCIES		$ 5000	
(10 % of TOTAL)			
	SUB-TOTAL		$ 5000
	GRAND TOTAL		$ 50,000

Principle of Budgeting
"Spend half your budget on
media — and the other half
on people." Raymond U. Humphreys

Fig. 2-2. Continued.

financial status. The treasurer will often find himself or herself in the position of Secretary of the Treasury Henry Morgenthau. Someone said to him, "You must have struck gold." "I did," he grinned. "I've just figured a way to save the government three million dollars." "Wonderful! That should make the President very happy." "Oh," cried Morgenthau, "I can't tell President Roosevelt. On the strength of that savings of three million dollars, he'd go out and spend six million."[8]

Advance Money

Hubert Humphrey's campaign manager, Michael Berman, said, "It takes money to raise money." For this reason, when the candidate and finance committee

	6th Month Before Election	5th Month	4th Month	3rd Month	2nd Month	One Month Before Election	15 Days Before Election	Total Campaign Budget
PROPOSED BASIC CAMPAIGN BUDGET								
ADMINISTRATION								
Payroll (Hqs.)								
Payroll Taxes, etc.								
Office Rental (Hqs.)								
Equip. Rental (Hqs.)								
Stationery, Supplies, Postage								
Telephone & Telegraph (Hqs.)								
Travel (Hqs.)								
District-wide Meetings								
Miscellaneous								
Contingencies								
TOTAL ADMINISTRATION								
PUBLIC RELATIONS								
Publicity								
Travel								
Telephone & Telegraph								
Mats								
Release Sheets								
Envelopes								
Photography								
Postage								
Stencils								
Press Relations								
Contingencies								
TOTAL PUBLIC RELATIONS								

Fig. 2-3. Let's Talk About Running for Office (New York: National Association of Manufacturers, 1967), p. 44.

consider the financial requirements of a campaign, a pay-as-you-go policy won't work because there has to be seed money.[9]

At the outset, the campaign will probably not have the cash flow necessary to meet payroll, telephone, and advertising expenses or the candidate's travel expenses. The same is true of the preparation of public opinion polls, which requires printing questionnaires and hiring professionals to conduct the polling, then tabulating and evaluating the results. In the same vein, a campaign must have money to cover early emergencies. For example, a volunteer group may request a large shipment of materials for early distribution at a state fair.

Before any ads are prepared, money must be available for copywriters, radio and television spots, artists and print layout personnel, as well as billboards and posters. Budget makers should not be misled. Production costs will not be covered by the 15 percent rebate to the advertising agency by the media.

TV time and billboard space are limited, so if the candidate wants them, he or she must contract weeks and often months in advance of the election. Chances are they will not be available at the last minute. Payment for radio, newspaper, and direct mail advertising usually can be postponed until later in the campaign.

There is no formula for deciding how much the candidate should have in advance or can afford. But the candidate and the finance committee should understand that campaign advertising is most effective just before the electorate vote, thus there should be an advertising plan that will cause a spending peak just before the election.

This was the case in Robert Kennedy's successful bid for U.S. Senator from New York. His late-breaking television campaign constituted 75 to 80 percent of his campaign's thrust. Kennedy had wanted to buy heavily in the last six weeks, but his ad man, Fred Paper, argued that, "Nobody ever has enough money for that much television," saying, "If you hold back, it looks like more." They compromised and concentrated on the last five weeks, pouring out their heaviest fire in the final seventeen days.[10] Usually, such a plan provides for buying backward from election day.

The Strategy of Allocation

This spending is easier to track if records are kept on a worksheet that makes provisions for time. This is especially true at the end of the campaign when the impact of campaign advertising is magnified.

In summary, a preliminary budget and ongoing monitoring of contributions versus expenses are essential. See the nutshell below for a summary of the money ritual.

The Money Ritual

Overall considerations:
The preliminary budget
Cost of raising money
Tracking expenditures
Advance money
Allocation

Sources of Campaign Support:
Candidate, candidate's family
Supporters looking for a job
PAC contributions (will depend on
    whether candidate is likely to win and
    on positions likely to take)

Wise Men Bearing Gifts
Balancing the need for money with taint
    of supporters' money.

Carefully identifying contributor
Good old boys on main street

Selection and direct solicitation
Candidate is best fundraiser
Setting up

Salesmanship
Campaign pitch
Obtaining a contributor list

Direct mail
Ideology
Direct mail pros and cons
Package
Followup letter
Test marketing

★ ★ ★ ★ ★ **In A Nutshell** ★ ★ ★ ★ ★

Chapter 9

Facing the Gamble

It turned out to be one of my worst successes.
—Darryl Zanuck, movie producer[1]

My epitaph should read, "She paid all her bills."
—Gloria Swanson, early film star[2]

Never let that bastard back in—unless we need him.
—Jack L. Warner, movie producer[3]

Money Up Front

The candidate, the manager, and the finance committee must face the fact that much, even most, of the funds will not be raised until near the end of the campaign. As Dr. Hunter S. Thompson put it, "There is a fantastic adrenaline high that comes with total involvement in almost any kind of fast-moving campaign—especially when you're running against big odds and start to feel like a winner." If the campaign goes well chances are it will bring out contributions from sources that no one previously considered.[4]

So where does the campaign get the up-front money? In some jurisdictions there is an ongoing organization such as the Republican campaign committee in Los Angeles and some New York reform groups who lend money to attractive candidates firmly committed to their strong ideological point of view. But in most cases up-front money is the candidate's responsibility.

Recounting the difficulty he had raising seed money during his first gubernatorial campaign, Adlai Stevenson, Sr., summed it up this way: "Our campaign funds were so low that it became a joke around the house. Even my kids would take a look at me when I'd come home and say, 'Hi, Gov!,' and stick their hands in their pockets to protect their loose change."[5]

Sometimes there is an understanding bank who is willing to make the candidate a personal loan. If none of these work and the candidate doesn't have it, he or she must get it from a wealthy benefactor. Being realistic, the candidate who expects to raise money must heed the advice of then Republican National Chairman George Bush, when he advised prospective candidates of his party: "When the chips are down, if you are not willing to look at a big donor in the eye and ask for his support, then I do not see how you can ask people to vote for you on as broad a base as you need."[6]

In the past, payments to suppliers, landlords, media people, etc., often depended on the candidate's winning. The losers left them holding the bag. A reckless candidate could, and often did, go on spending blindly, expecting to be the winner of an election, and would receive a number of checks from people who "just forgot" to send them in before election day.[7]

Times have changed. If the money isn't contributed, other money will have to be found to sustain the drive. Usually this means one has to look to the candidate's ability to come up with cash or assets against which he or she can borrow. For example, when Colorado's U.S. Senator Gary Hart set out in pursuit of the Presidency prior to January 1984, his campaign had attracted only $125,000 in donations. The candidate kept the campaign afloat by taking a $45,000 mortgage on his house.[8]

Some candidates have wealthy friends who can be persuaded to make imaginative short-term loans. Early in September of 1974, Drew Lewis, who was later to become Director of Transportation in the Reagan cabinet, was the Republican nominee for Governor of Pennsylvania. He arranged two loans of $250,000. One was from Fitz Eugene Dixon, Jr., wealthy sportsman, and the other was from Richard Mellon Scaife, a banker and industrialist.

These benefactors accepted as collateral a written pledge that they would have first call on one third of the net proceeds of three planned G.O.P. fundraising dinners in October. Once the dinners were held, the proceeds were to be divided immediately into two equal shares, and they would be repaid with interest calculated at the annual rate of 14 percent. The agreement further provided that if they were not paid off within twenty days of the last dinner, the state Republican committee would assume the obligation.[9]

Very few candidates have rich backers reckless enough to risk thousands or a solvent party central committee willing to guarantee a deficit. But when the finance committee looks for guarantees it helps if the fundraiser has a sales pitch, such as Senator Barry Goldwater's "Gold for Goldwater" fundraising campaign. In that effort funds were collected in advance of the Republican convention, but it was guaranteed that Goldwater would return the money if he lost the nomination.[10]

The most popular way to raise funds is to have dinner or lunch with a few backers. At the outset, the finance committee should recognize that convincing an elite group of possible contributors to attend a reception to meet the candidate does not necessarily lead to contributions. In most cases, the candidate finds that even sincere individuals making pledges view them as good faith expressions of support but do not expect to be bound in the same manner as they are when they get a loan from the bank.

Don't Count Pledges Until They Are Cash

In 1964, the National Democratic Committee held several luncheons for major figures of the financial and corporate world in New York City. One luncheon at

Le Pavillion was erroneously reported to have raised $1 million. As it turned out, a substantial portion of the money "allegedly raised" was in uncollected pledges. Many of those making pledges intended to give part of the money themselves, but depended on friends and associates to raise the balance. The million dollars in pledges didn't materialize because others making pledges were dependent on that same group of friends.

Money pledged around the table, or by telephone, should never be turned down, but until the cash comes in, it is not safe to depend on it. The candidate, the manager, and the finance committee should be skeptical of vague early promises of help because expressions of interest and goodwill promises of contributions can't be spent unless they are actually received.

Pledges, even those made by a candidate, a relative, or a financial angel, must be in writing. It is even better if contributors go to the bank and guarantee a loan so that a line of credit can be negotiated after a banker examines the pledges or guarantees.

More often than not, early promises are contingent upon the campaign's future momentum. Even if they are going to contribute, methodical followup via personal telephone contact is necessary because most of these promised contributions will evaporate if the candidate does not look successful.

After evaluating the task of raising the money, the candidate and the finance committee may find themselves at their lowest ebb. As Prince Philip of England once put it, "After many years' experience, I have come to learn that the present moment, whatever it may be, is never a good one for raising money."[11] But this is not all bad. These realities force the money-raisers to expand their horizons, and make them less hesitant when asking potential contributors for money, because they know that the candidate must have money or they will struggle on from day to day not knowing where the next dollar is coming from.

A few campaigns, however, have succeeded in spite of such handicaps. In 1948, the odds makers, pollsters, and political insiders were convinced that Thomas Dewey would defeat President Harry Truman. As a result Truman had a terrible time getting credit to conduct his presidential campaign. At one point he scheduled a nationwide radio broadcast, but his campaign committee didn't have the $25,271 necessary to finance it. Cancellation was avoided when a bag of paper money in small denominations from Greek Restaurant owners in New York was rushed to the network just before air time.[12]

What should the desperate candidate do if he or she feels the contributions are not keeping up with the campaign as it escalates? I suggest the candidate examine the situation carefully, heeding a warning given by Arnold Steinberg in his book *Political Campaign Management*, where he recounts the story of a U.S. Senate campaign caught short of cash. An outside consultant called in to evaluate early pledges of support discovered only vague promises of help, many of which were made by those who had encouraged the candidate to run months before. Typical of the candidate's prospects was the Republican campaign committee. It could earmark $10,000, $20,000, or even $25,000 to the senate campaign. He knew that, like other promises, these were contingent upon the campaign's gathering momentum. What the outside consultant also discovered was a stalled campaign that reduced the candidate's prospects. He noted that there was a slight chance of receiving a token $5,000 from the candidate's campaign committee, but it was unlikely they would contribute anything because the congressional decision makers would see, as he did, that the campaign lacked structure, survey research, and momentum. The consultant also noted that the campaign was getting little publicity, especially from out-of-state media—something that was necessary if the candidate was to get out-of-state contributions.

He explained these facts to the candidate, who realized that, in spite of early promises of support, his campaign was bankrupt. Because his personal credit was nil, the candidate was forced to give up the race to stop further expenditures and had to pay the existing debt as best he could.[13]

Principle: Pledges are fine, but they are no substitute for cash.

$ $ $ $ WARNING $ $ $ $

Today, campaign costs and contributions have soared beyond the wildest predictions. Though dollar amounts quoted throughout this book are historically correct and valuable as general percentage guidelines, dollar amounts more than two to four years old should not be depended upon for structuring campaign budgets.

Chapter 10

Yes, Virginia, There Is a Santa Claus

> The year is 1887. "I am eight years old. Some of my little friends say there is no Santa Claus. . . . Please tell me the truth, is there a Santa Claus?"[1]

In direct answer, yes, there are Santa Clauses who contribute to political campaigns. Each of us is represented by a number of these different vested interests and has a stake in who is elected.

Even the most uncomplicated citizen lives in a specific geographical region. We all pay a variety of taxes. Most belong to a labor union or a farm, a business or professional group. We are a renter, a home owner, or a users' group of one sort or another. Most of us own a car and have children who attend schools.

Though most of us do not directly contribute to political campaigns, the contributing is done when we pay for breakfast food, banking services, athletic equipment, or medical fees because much of the money that comes to the candidate comes by way of a political action committee (PAC). (Perhaps this explains how PACs are made up—that is, local bankers, grocers, etc.).

Yes, Virginia, Just As You Suspected, Santa Claus Is One of the Family

This brings to mind the story of a campaign solicitor armed with a prospect's name and address on a card that also included a suggested contribution amount to request. He called at the home of a prospect and was greeted by the lady of the house. She didn't invite him in, but did call her doctor husband to the door. They stood together and listened as the solicitor gave them a canned speech. He outlined the candidate's platform and qualifications. Then, with some hesitancy, he asked for the amount suggested by the financial chairman.

The doctor exploded, "I don't agree with anything he stands for. I wouldn't give a guy with that philosophy one red cent." Then a quizzical smile crossed his face as he looked at his wife and said, "Unless he was my brother-in-law, and since he is, I'll write the check."

A 1974 Washington State Common Cause survey showed that self-help together with money from the candidate's family accounted for 13 percent of campaign spending.[2] Why do relatives contribute? The reasons vary. In some cases, having an office holder flatters family ego and has become a tradition.

The first Robert F. Wagner is remembered as a U.S. Senator and author of the Wagner Act. His son, Robert M. Wagner, served two terms as Mayor of New York City. In 1973, the third Robert M. Wagner followed his grandfather and father into elective politics. After he served as New York City Councilman, in 1977 he entered the campaign for borough president. In spite of the fact that his family was not thought of as having great wealth, his television coverage costs of $115,000 were financed largely by loans: $80,500 from his father, former Mayor Robert F. Wagner, and $45,000 from the candidate himself.[3]

Fat Cats and Wealthy Family Group Contributions

Prior to modern election laws that limit contributions, a few wealthy families had almost purchased elective offices. George Thayer writes that the Kennedy family spent $100,000 to elect John F. to the House of Representatives. It spent another $350,000 to $500,000 to put him in the U.S. Senate, almost $1.5 million to win reelection in 1958, and approximately $3 million of their own money to win the Democratic nomination and the presidency in 1960.

The family spent another $1.2 million to put Edward in the Senate in 1962, and similar amounts to reelect him in '64 and '70. About $1 million more was put in Robert's U.S. Senate race in 1965, and the family contributed another $3 million or so to his presidential race in 1968. This brought the Kennedy family contributions to Joe's sons' campaigns to a minimum of $14 million.[4]

The attitude was put into words by the patriarch of the Kennedy clan, Father "Joe." He reportedly told his sons, John, then President, and Robert, then U.S. Attorney General, when they raised objections to brother Edward's running for John's old U.S. Senate seat, "Look, I spent a lot of money for that seat. It belongs in the family."

The Kennedys are not alone. In his five campaigns, one-time Vice President Nelson Rockefeller benefited from his three campaigns for governor. The candidate's and family's contributions were $4 to $8 million each plus the $3 to $5 million he spent on two campaigns for the presidency. To this must also be added the three expensive campaigns conducted by Nelson's brother, Winthrop, who served for eight years as the first Republican Governor of Arkansas. Now in the fourth generation, the family has another with political ambition, Jay Rockefeller—who, incidentally, has the guts to spend his own money.

Of course, there are times when a candidate's money won't do the trick, which was the case with parking-building genius, self-made millionaire, and one-time New York assemblyman, Abraham Hirschfield. He put more than $1 million of his own money into two unsuccessful campaigns for United States Senate and spent lavishly on his campaign for New York borough president in 1977 without achieving success.[5]

The same has been true for other wealthy political aspirants: insurance man E. Clayton Gengras of Connecticut, actress Shirley Temple Black of California, businessman Sam Grossman of Arizona, drugstore chain owner Jack Eckerd of Florida, and Baggies tycoon Howard J. Samules of New York.

Yes, Virginia, Just As You Suspected, Santa Claus Is a Fat Cat or Groupie

As they sit at the desk, stand at the cocktail party or converse over lunch, politicians sometimes talk about men and women who have become symbols of those who give. Men like Stewart Mott, R. L. Hunt, Martin Pretz, and W. Clement Stone are donors who can be distinguished from political investors in that they seek no tangible reward. They fit Frank R. Kent's description: "Such men are known in political circles as fat cats."[6]

Prior to modern election laws that limited contributions in 1965, a congressional committee headed by U.S. Senator Albert Gore, father of present U.S. Senator Gore of Tennessee, found that family groups such as Dupont, Field, Ford, Harriman, Lehman, Mellon, Olin, Pew, Reynolds, Rockefeller, Vanderbilt, and Whitney have a tradition of contributing substantial sums. They found that these contributors favor establishment candidates, usually Republicans, in a ratio of approximately 10–1 to 20–1.[7]

Occasionally, contributors work against the candidates of their party when a candidate's views are deemed repugnant and the opponent falls heir to their political help. This is what happened in the Johnson–Goldwater race for President. In 1962, many rich contributors were opposed to their party's nominee for president—U.S. Senator Barry Goldwater. Because of his attacks on Eastern, mostly Republican, establishment men such as Henry Ford II, whose grandfather had been a candidate for U.S. Senator on the Republican ticket, they broke a standing family tradition and contributed $40,000 to Democrat Lyndon Johnson. The same was true of the prominent Wall Street family of Mr. and Mrs. C. Douglas Dillon, who had given $26,500 to the Nixon campaign and $59,500 to two Eisenhower campaigns. They contributed $37,000 to the Democratic candidate in 1962,[8] a considerable amount of money at that time.

Although there are exceptions among wealthy, old-line contributors, most "fat cats" enjoy a personal sense of power and importance. Typically, they like the notoriety they receive when their gifts are publicized and the boost in ego they get when they are treated to the attention usually reserved for a movie queen or a famous athlete.

Friendship can also play a big part in such political donations. Occasionally, a candidate can tap this source because he or she is a personal friend, as was the case of Drew Lewis in his unsuccessful 1974 Pennsylvania gubernatorial campaign. He attracted three fat cats. Richard Mellon Scaife, heir to a banking and industrial fortune, wrote checks totaling $42,000. Fitz Eugene Dixon, Jr., who maintained racing stables and owned 25 percent of the Philadelphia Flyers, contributed $21,000. And John T. Dorrance, Jr. (chairman of the board of Campbell Soup Company) gave $17,500.

Often friendship will overcome ideology. H. L. Hunt was a conservative who believed the rich should have more votes than the poor. He put up $150,000 in support of General Douglas MacArthur's presidential campaign in 1952. Most of his other political gifts were to right-wingers, but he is believed to have given $100,000 to the Kennedy–Johnson ticket in 1960, simply because of his long-standing friendship with the vice presidential candidate.[9]

Personal Friendship

Recognizing that friendship, prestige, and a sense of power have value, candidates have experimented with ways to flatter fat cats' egos. George Thayer tells of a southern California rancher who was invited to the White House twice every year that Eisenhower was President because of his campaign contribution. He boasted, "It was the best $1,500 I ever spent."[10]

For generations both parties used Governor Clubs, County Chairman clubs, and the like, designed to put big contributors and officeholders on a first-name basis. However, John F. Kennedy was the first president to do this on a national scale. He formally recognized those who had contributed $1,000 or more to the national Democratic coffers and promised these "fat cats" a little social prestige, a chance to meet the President at small cocktail parties, and possible invitations to formal White House dinners.

Under Lyndon Johnson, the members of the President's Club were assured that if they "wanted to talk to the President, the Vice President, or one of his assistants, they would only have to contact his office. Members will immediately be put in contact with whomever they want to reach."[11]

Republicans were not outdone. In 1965, substantial G.O.P. contributors were given a membership in the Republican Congressional Boosters Club and promised "intimate briefings" at "closed-door meetings with Republican congressional leaders." They were also supplied with special stationery so they would be recognized as big contributors when they wrote to members of Congress.[12]

Eventually, such clubs came under criticism. Although the nature of the criticism varied, most critics charged that the clubs were composed of "fat cats with axes to grind," who were getting preferential contracts in return for their contributions. A few political contributors, such as Paul Grindle, criticized the $1,000 sum needed to join as so small that it lowered the quality. "Hell," Grindle said, "You can't get into a golf club for that."[13]

When the clubs were abolished at the federal level, candidates had to find other ways to merchandise this sense of power and ego. When a candidate has charisma or can produce a glamourous guest, he or she might try what the Kennedys (President Jack, Senators Bobby and Ted) called the intimate dinner. This ego-flattering technique was chronicled in the *New West Magazine* by Susan Littwin. She described the exploits of a wealthy Californian, Hershey Gold, and his "parlor meetings," which we will discuss later.

Principle: Don't be intimidated by philosophy. Ask your friends to help.

Chapter 11

Yes, Virginia, Sometimes Santa Claus Is More Interested in a Cause, a Job, or the Triumph of a Party Than in Christmas

> Two percent of your salary is _____. Please remit promptly. At the close of the campaign we shall place a list of those who have not paid in the hands of the department you are in.
> —Letter to all State of Pennsylvania Employees, 1882[1]
>
> Do you contribute to campaign expenses?
> We do.
> To which party do you contribute?
> Depends upon circumstances.
> To which fund do you contribute in Massachusetts?
> The Republican.
> To which in New York?
> The Democratic.
> To which in New Jersey?
> I will have to look at the books. That is a doubtful state.
>   —Testimony by the head of the Sugar Trust when interrogated by the Senate committee at the turn of the century.[2]

Ideological Contributor

Yes, Virginia, there is a Santa Claus, and sometimes his interest is in a cause, not Christmas.

Scratch the political and philosophical surface and the ideological giver emerges. Pop singer John Denver contributed $25,000 plus all receipts from his 1976 Portland concert to support an Oregon ballot measure that advocated a ban on nuclear energy.[3]

Normally, such ideological contributors get no personal benefit. They use money as an instrument to accomplish objectives. When candidates take a strong ideological position, they usually find they have gained its zealots as friends. For example, in 1977 before modern campaign limitation legislation, Stewart Mott gave $100,000 to George McGovern because he wanted an anti-Vietnam War candidate elected President.[4]

Speaking of crusaders, history has shown that among those to whom political giving is an emotional experience, ideology often makes strange bedfellows. This happened to a wealthy young Congressman, John F. Kennedy, who took pride in his anti-left bias, when he strode into the House offices and asked to see a Republican colleague in 1957. After being informed that the congressman was out, Jack then suggested that he'd like to see his confidential secretary, who was William Arnold. When he and Arnold were alone, Jack pulled a check for $1,000 from his pocket and gave it to help Arnold's boss, Richard Nixon, who at the time was running for U.S. Senate against the left-leaning Democrat Helen Gahagan Douglas.[5]

When the ideological contribute to defeat a particular individual or point of view, they are not wedded to a candidate. If their champion should fall in the primary, these ideological "fat cats" unite using a primary election survivor to defeat those with whom they disagree.

Let's use a case history to explain. One day, after the August, 1974, Georgia primary, the wealthy contributors who had previously supported loser Bert Lance were systematically contacted by one of their social peers on behalf of George Busbee, a primary survivor who eventually became governor. Busbee won partly because contributors opposed the other survivor of that Georgia primary, segregationist, Lester Maddox. The state's financial disclosure report showed that thirty Atlanta blue ribbon contributors who had given Lance a total of $38,000 in the primary gave him $34,600 in the runoffs.[6]

Yes, Virginia, even in this age of cynical politics, there are a few sincere, earnest, and occasionally intolerant people who are engulfed in a single issue. Usually, they give through organizations led by political evangelists. Typical of those on the right who gather their own set of political barnacles are groups such as the gun owners of America, conservative Victory Fund, Committee for the Survival of a Free Congress, National Abortion Rights Action League, the National Rifle Association, the John Birch Society, and the Moral Majority.[7] A few of those across the liberal spectrum are the Americans for Democratic Action; Sierra Club; Planned Parenthood; National Organization for Women; Handgun Control, Inc.; The Wilderness Society; and the myriad organizations who profess concern for American civil liberties.[8]

Some contributions depend upon general political ideology, not on single issue organizations. The American Jewish community for example supported a Catholic, John F. Kennedy, as well as Protestants Harry S. Truman, Dwight D. Eisenhower, and Lyndon B. Johnson because of their sympathetic attitude toward Israel and their liberal approach to solving domestic problems. Barry M. Goldwater, whose grandfather was Jewish, got very little Jewish money because of his domestic and foreign policy views.[9]

Although they have their detractors, these political evangelists have redeeming qualities. They make contributions to political campaigns from the money they collect. Or often, they share with the candidates and organizations active in these individual causes who are often willing to contribute to a common political philosophy.[10]

When Earleen Collins embarked on her campaign for the Illinois State Senate, she built her campaign around the ratification of the Women's Equal Rights Amendment. Because of her fidelity to this cause, her largest contribution was from the "Women's Fund." This was started with a loan from General Motors heir, Stewart Mott. In 1974, it supported, with amounts ranging from $100 to $1,750, twenty-eight women candidates for state and federal offices, most of whom won.[11]

Job-Related Contributions

Yes, Virginia, there are Santa Clauses and sometimes they have a job to protect.

There was a time when financing a campaign depended on contributions from those who owed their job to political patronage. This has changed over the years and in the process has invoked vigorous philosophical debate. On one side, there are purists who support unionization or civil service laws which make most government jobs and promotions depend on the action of the bureaucracy, rather than on partisan political manipulation.

On the other hand, there are those who argue that government employees should not be entitled to any more protection than those who work in the private sector. Civil service purists respond to this argument by claiming that it is nothing more than a smoke screen used by those who believe, as did turn-of-the-century Tammany leader George Washington Plunkett, that "a political organization has to have money for its business as well as a church, and who has more right to put it up than the men who get the good things that are going."[12]

Turning from the philosophical to the practical, like any other facet of raising and spending campaign money, politicians have been slow to change. It wasn't until 1939 that Congress enacted the Hatch Act. This banned overt political activities by federal civil service employees and made it illegal to force them to make a political contribution. However, unless a state or local government voluntarily followed suit, it had no application to state or local employees.[13]

Responding to criticism from the media and pressure from unions representing government employees, most local jurisdictions have restricted the spoils system and the right to force contributions. Although the bare-knuckle approach has been fading, vestiges of the old spoil system still exist. David W. Adamany and George L. Agree contended as late as 1975 that in Chicago (Cook County), as well as in hundreds of other cities and counties, public employees were regularly asked to contribute a percentage of their salaries to the political party in power.[14] For example, in 1973, state employees in Indiana owed their jobs and two percent of their pay to a party organization controlled by the Governor.

Meanwhile, back at the federal government, the Hatch Act has undergone congressional and court modifications. As things now stand, any federal official or employee can make a voluntary contribution to a candidate or political party. However, it is still unlawful for any federal official or employee to solicit campaign funds from another employee on the job.

Thus far, we have discussed only exposed contributions. Like an iceberg, nine tenths of which is below the surface, employees even protect government employees, including teachers and college professors who participate in campaign financing. They contribute through employee organizations. These groups are anxious to create a favorable climate for wage and hour negotiations or they want to stop what they interpret as a threat to their job security.

Teachers seek better teacher salaries and benefits through organizations such as PULSE (a political arm of teachers' associations), so they contribute substantial sums. For example, teachers' organizations contributed $240,000 to California Governor Jerry Brown's first campaign.[15]

Aside from government employees who enjoy Civil Service or union protection, there remain top echelon positions. The Hatch Act, which was supposed to protect federal employees (similar to acts passed on behalf of state employees), did not apply to top echelon employees whose jobs were dependent upon their boss' political survival.[16]

Those who make political appointments take a position described by one-time Texas Governor Dolph Briscoe when he said, "I don't reward people just because they contribute, but don't disqualify them either." Another former Texas Governor, Allan Shivers, commented, "I took the position while I was in office that I would rather appoint my friends than my enemies."[17]

Solicitation techniques vary. In the 1975 campaign for Governor of Maryland, for example, the executive director of the lottery, the chief deputy comptrollers, deputy attorney generals, and public defenders were all saddled with blocks of tickets that they could either sell or pay for.[18]

We should not forget another source of campaign money that comes from the upper crust of the blue book of business and finance, those who serve on boards and commissions. I do not doubt that in most cases they first contribute because they want to see the politician succeed as a candidate. Still, they enjoy prestigious appointments. For instance, Washington State Governor John Spellman appointed a wealthy businessman, W. Hunter Simpson, to the Board of Regents at the University of Washington. True, Simpson was a UW graduate, the president and chief executive of an eight-hundred-employee firm, and president of the University's alumni association, but he also had another qualification. His $16,000 was the largest single contribution to the Governor's election campaign.[19]

Party Contributions

Yes, Virginia, there is a Santa Claus and sometimes he gets a present from party headquarters.

While it is not too important today, there was a time when this had a flip side—the era of the political machine and a powerful boss. They asked for—or in some cases demanded—a contribution for the candidate. Let's go to the late 1880s when Tammany bigwig George Washington Plunkett described a calloused, illegal procedure used in a Republican district when deciding who would win his party's congressional nomination. "Four men wanted it," Plunkett explains. At first the local boss asked for bids privately, but after some dickering he decided the best thing to do was to get the four men together in the back room of a saloon and have an open auction."

Then Plunkett says, "When he had his men lined up, he got on a chair, told about the value of the goods for sale and asked for bids in regular auctioneer style. The highest bidder got the nomination for $50,000."[20]

Even today, party support helps office holders who expect to climb the political ladder. Many still give a percentage of their salary, or at least a large contribution, to local party organizations. On the flip side of the coin, what can the candidate expect financially from the party? In most jurisdictions, the local party will contribute modest sums to a prestigious campaign, such as that for governor, Congress, or U.S. Senator.

Under the Federal Election Campaign Act, the national party can and does expend money an behalf of a federal aspirant within a limit that fluctuates by law using 1974 dollars as a base. This a limit has been raised over the years to keep pace with the inflated dollar. In 1982, a national party committee with funds could spend approximately $18,500 in a congressional campaign. Permissible contributions to senate contests ranged from a low of $37,000 in Wyoming to approximately $500,000 in California.[21]

Most candidates for federal office can also expect the party to supply indirect help. This does not involve a direct contribution as defined under federal law. For example, the party may pay the candidate's hotel bill or a state or local party can provide support by producing and distributing campaign materials. This activity is not considered a contribution as long as the materials are distributed by volunteers. But to stay within the limits, the party, not the candidate, makes payment directly to the vendor, and the candidate reports the expenditure as well.[22]

Further examination of federal law reveals that state and local party organizations may print and distribute sample ballots and other listings of candidates without having to register or report as long as the list includes at least three candidates and no advertising is used.[23]

Traditionally, the party organization is permitted—outside federal or state limitation—to spend funds registering, getting out the vote, and holding events that give a candidate exposure. Because it is given preferential postal rates, often the party makes mass mailings on behalf of individual candidates that it endorses.

It has been my experience that the Republicans do give their candidates some direct financial help, and both parties recommend their favorites to Democratic or Republican fat cats who are willing to kick in a few dollars.

Given an aggressive party organization, financial assistance can be very substantial. In 1974, the Ohio G.O.P. raised $2.9 million. Today, the Minnesota Democratic Farm Labor Party has over 8,500 regular contributors. It helps its party's candidates and, in some cases, fully finances their campaigns. These small to medium donations accounted for 10 percent of local campaign financing in 1952, but this source has steadily increased until today they account for 80 percent. Donors who contribute above a designated sum get membership cards and tickets to the annual Jefferson–Jackson Day dinner, which features a nationally recognized political speaker and is attended by over 2,500.[24]

In Congress, and in almost every state legislature, members are elected from a political party, so the sitting members have a vested interest in getting or maintaining a working majority. At one time, Democratic congressmen levied an assessment on themselves to help finance the party's candidates in tough campaigns. While this levy has been discontinued, both congressional caucuses have a fund they collect from vested interests which they use for the purpose of getting and maintaining a majority.

This practice has another side. Few recipients have any qualms in accepting funds when they are doled out from a central pot. In fact, most claim they are proud that the party officials have placed a stamp of approval on their candidacy. Nevertheless, it would be foolish to assume that either a Democratic or Republican party blessing purified the contribution. All too often, special interests use the party or the party's political caucus funds to eliminate the political stigma that might go with their contribution.

On some occasions, using these funds can result in failure. In 1974, there was a special election to fill a vacancy in the California State Senate. A Republican State assemblyman, Jerry Lewis (not related to the comic), took aim at the job. His public disclosures showed contributions of $144,736.70, over half of which came from the Republican State Senatorial Caucus fund, while his Democratic opponent, Reuben Ayola, wasn't that fortunate. Ayola's contributions from all sources totaled only $32,250.58 against expenditures of $40,031.86.

With no chance to match his opponent's spending, Ayola used a four-page tabloid to expose the source of the opposition money. His big, front-page headline read, "Republican Attempts to Buy Election January 15," but he did not just concentrate on the amount Lewis raised. He used the information gained from the

Republican Caucus public disclosures to "single out contributors to the caucus fund as the oil companies, pharmaceutical firms, Las Vegas gambling concerns, and big time real estate promoters whom he labeled as contributors to the Lewis–Reagan machine."

Lewis met the issue head on, saying the cost of being elected to public office is out of hand and that reform was long overdue. But for now the only thing a candidate can do is to tell the truth about campaign financing—"where it comes from and how it is spent." Judging from the results, the voters agreed that the money Lewis received from the Republican caucus fund subjected him to vested interests. He lost the election.[25]

$ $ $ $ WARNING $ $ $ $

Today, campaign costs and contributions have soared beyond the wildest predictions. Though dollar amounts quoted throughout this book are historically correct and valuable as general percentage guidelines, dollar amounts more than two to four years old should not be depended upon for structuring campaign budgets.

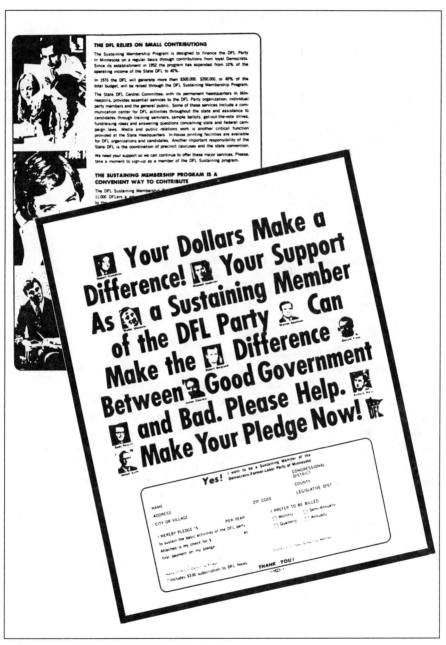

Fig. 2-4. Pledge solicitation, Minnesota Democratic–Farmer–Labor Party, State Central Committee Sustaining Membership Program, 1974.

Chapter 12

PACs and How They Get What They Want for Christmas

> The machine has got big expenses. If a corporation sends in a check to help the good work of the Tammany Society, why shouldn't we take it like other missionary societies? Of course, the day may come when we'll reject the money of the rich as tainted, but it hadn't come when I left Tammany Hall at 11:25 a.m. today.
> —George Washington Plunkett, Tammany Hall, 1909[1]
>
> Every Republican candidate for President since 1936 has been nominated by the Chase National Bank.
> —The late U.S. Senator Robert A. Taft2
>
> Walter Reuter has announced that labor was not wedded to the Democratic party. If this is true, we have been witnessing the world's most notorious case of living in sin.
> —U.S. Senator Kenneth Keating3

PAC Contributors

In 1970, American milk producers wrote President Nixon and protested his slowness in approving import quotas on ice cream and other dairy products. At the same time, they reminded him that they had contributed $135,000 to Republican congressional candidates and that they intended to channel $2 million to his reelection campaign. Within two weeks the quotas were approved.[4]

During most of the 19th century, the corporate giants, often using political machines to win, gave financial support to manipulating office holders. In the early part of the 20th century there was an adverse reaction. New laws restricting these powerful corporations and their political conspirators were enacted that applied to federal candidates as well as those running for local office. They restricted company officials' use of corporate funds and the ability to pressure their employees to give to political campaigns.

This slowed down but didn't stop the abuses. Corporations circumvented the law by permitting individuals to give on behalf of a company or a whole industry. For example, in the mid-1960s millionaire trucker Neal J. Curry acted as national political agent for truckers who wanted heavier trucks allowed on interstate highways. He had the individual truck officials make out personal checks which he, in turn, distributed in the name of the industry.[5]

This technique is still used even today by special interest groups. In the final days of the 1978 campaign, a few Florida State legislators were under fire because

PAC BUCKS: Who Gives, Who Gets

Top PAC Donors in 1983	To Federal Candidates	% Over 1981
Seafarers Union	$549,246	22
Natl. Assn. Of Realtors	467,592	10
Nat'l Assn. Of Home Builders	359,358	329
Marine Engineers Union	349,892	83
United Transportation Union	358,218	131

Top Cash Hoards

HOUSE		% of 1983 Donations from PAC	SENATE		% of 1983 Donations from PAC
Dan Rosten-kowski, *D, Ill.*	$612,834	80	Bill Bradley *D, N.J.*	$1,847,092	14
Stephen Solarz *D, N.Y.*	396,495	*	Alfonse D'Amato *R, N.Y.*	1,383,419	14
Henson Moore *R, La.*	466,671	41	Rudy Boschwitz *R, Minn.*	1,321,444	13
Joseph Addabbo *D, N.Y.*	431,411	30	Bennett Johnston *D, La.*	1,302,371	40
Bill Archer *R, Tex.*	426,011	*	Howell Heflin *D, Ala.*	1,058,463	32

*No fundraising in '83, cash left over from previous years.

Source: WSJ tabulation of records of Federal Election Commission

PAC Funds Flowing to Congress

Fig. 2-5. Note that funds contributed were in 1983 dollars. "PAC Funds Flowing to Congress," The Wall Street Journal, February 23, 1984. Reprinted by permission of The Wall Street Journal, © 1984 Dow Jones & Company, Inc. All rights reserved worldwide.

they had opposed the state's ratification of a national Equal Rights Amendment. The leaders of the Church of Jesus Christ of Latter Day Saints (known as Mormons) funneled some $60,000 in individual checks into four legislative campaigns. When contacted after the fact, a Mormon regional representative, J. N. Lybbert pointed out, "The structure exists where I can make 16 calls and by the end of the day 2,700 people will know. . . ." He added, "I just talked to a few of my friends."[6] Turning our attention to more familiar ground, high-ranking corporate employees, such as the chairman and presidents of organizations like United Airlines and Pacific Northwest Bell (now U.S. West Communications), contributed substantial sums.

Referring to this type of contribution, Bobby Baker, one-time intimate of U.S. Senate Majority Leader Lyndon Johnson and Senate powerhouse Robert Kerr, wrote, "Anyone not blind in both eyes and deaf in one ear can tell you that corporations have routinely circumvented the campaign funding laws. They grant their executives personal 'bonuses,' which just happen to coincide with the sum total of the money the corporations need to raise for political purposes. By a strong quirk of fate, these same executives decide to make 'personal' political contributions in the exact amounts of their respective bonus."[7]

We need not take the word of Bobby Baker. Even though Ohio law prohibits corporate contributions, a letter was written to out-of-state corporations and executives in the 1974 campaign on behalf of Governor James A. Rhodes. It asked that "your group give $1,000 in the form of 'personal checks' for 'each of your installations in Ohio'."[8]

Contributions from top corporate executives are easy to track compared to ferreting out the substantial contributions made by major stockholders and lesser corporate executives. These were detailed in a 1974 slander suit when a one-time San Antonio telephone company official testified that $1,000 a year salary increases were given company executive personnel with the understanding that the increases were to be used as political contributions. He said that Southwestern Bell executives were required to contribute $50 cash each month to select political accounts. Furthermore, he stated that a political contact man directed 142 telephone executives where to send an estimated $90,000 in personal checks.[9]

Prior to campaign reform legislation that was passed and modified during the early seventies, ring-wise contributors could decide to hide the source of their contributions. In 1968, money—or more accurately, the lack of it—hopelessly stalled Hubert Humphrey's campaign. It was finally able to sputter into motion because of loans arranged by Democratic National Treasurer Robert Short from two individuals, John (Jake the Barber) Factor and MCA President Lou Wasserman.

At the time, there was a $5,000 limitation on campaign contributions to any single committee supporting a candidate. This was easily side-stepped by the simple expedient of setting up committees.[10] Each loan was split and funneled through separate political action committees. When it was finally received by the candidate, it came from committees with names such as "Doctors for Humphrey and Muskie," "Dentists for Humphrey and Muskie," "Economists," "Conservationists," "Executives," "Sport Stars," etc. After the election, a *New York Times* editorial pointed out that there were 97 committees accepting donations for the Humphrey–Muskie ticket.

Humphrey was not alone. President Nixon conducted a similar campaign by creating such organizations as "Victory in 1968," "Tennessee for Nixon," and "Thurmond Speaks" (named for South Carolina's Senator Strom Thurmond).[11]

Following Watergate election reforms, there was an attempt by Congress to expose and limit contributions. A candidate for federal office could receive gifts of money and loans from friends, family members, or committees, subject only to reporting requirements and to monetary limits. Under this act, federal candidates had to disclose contributions, loans, and expenditures if they exceeded $200.[12] Primary contributions were limited to $1,000, but a donor could contribute a second $1,000 in the general election.[13]

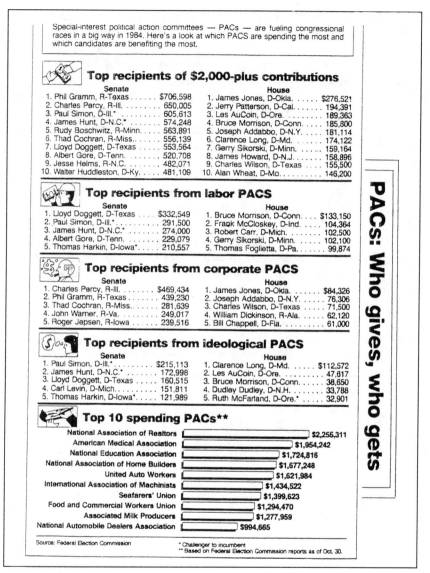

Fig. 2-6. "PACs: Who Gives, Who Gets," *USA Today,* Nov. 1, 1984. Copyright 1984, *USA Today.* Reprinted with permission. Note that sums are in 1984 dollars.

Probably the most significant thing the law did was to foster and promote corporate PACs. As the labor unions had done for a generation, the 1974 act now permitted the corporation to spend a limited amount of corporate money through political action committees, which was not legal until that time.

Actually, the PACs were not a new concept. This mechanism was first popularized by labor unions in response to restrictions imposed by the Taft–Hartley Act, which prevents unions from using dues money to help friendly candidates. Subsequently, labor had to use volunteer donations, which were distributed through PACs such as COPE (Committee on Political Education).

After federal law recognized corporate-sponsored political action committees in 1972, corporate America went for them in a big way. By January of 1979, United Press International found that there were 1,360 PACs contributing to Congressmen alone.[14]   And in 1983, the number had risen to more the 3,500. Today there are more than 4,000.

Federal law provides for several distinctly different types of PACs, for example, in addition to the in-house. Trade associations and multi-candidate national committees can receive contributions from other PACs.[15]

If these national or regional PACs are legally constituted as political action committees for multiple candidates, they can receive as much as they can collect. Multicandidate committees could contribute up to $5,000 a candidate in the primary and $5,000 again in the general election. This structure permits individuals to contribute up to $20,000 to each of the three national campaign committees: presidential, senate, and house. Other multicandidate committees can contribute up to $15,000 each to the national committees, and a national committee can contribute $25,000 to a single campaign.[16]

As one would expect, PACs have become a device for getting around the legal restrictions that prohibit corporate donations. This law permits corporations or individuals to make a contribution of $5,000 to one PAC in any one primary. It also permits them to contribute to a multi-candidate national committee which might be supporting a particular candidacy. The wealthy corporations can make contributions through their trade associations and, finally, executives or stockholders can give as individual contributors.

However, federal law does not recognize instant committees. Thus, a rich backer can't

"By golly, Edgar, you've done it.
It's not illegal, but it should be."

Fig. 2-7. C'Barsotti's People, *USA Today,* February 12, 1985.

organize single-issue PACs simply to increase his or her support of one candidate. Still, candidates or their supporters organize them for state and local candidates under some state laws. Even under federal law they can use this device if they start six months prior to making the contributions.

Banks

Beneath its marble exterior, the bank is vitally interested in where and how and under what conditions the millions in local tax revenues are deposited. Assume local government does not need the tax receipts for a few months or more. How much of the deposit is going to be in a checking account? Will the bank be expected to pay interest? If so, will the bank give the local government the same rate they would someone else making a similar deposit?[17]

At the state and national level banks are interested in regulatory legislation and how it is administered. For example, they are keenly conscious of the showing of need required for additional service made by a bank or savings and loan which applies for a new license. They are ready to fight any effort made by a legislative body to control the interest rate or legislation requiring them to write long-term mortgages with fixed interest rates.

Since the 1907 federal law, nationally chartered banks have been prohibited from contributing to federal campaigns. The laws in most states are even tougher. In general, banks cannot even use their profits to participate in political campaigns. However, if we look behind the marble front, we find they play a sophisticated but important political role.

Like any other corporate entity, banks have PACS with names such as First Associates (First National Bank), Evergreen Associates (Evergreen Savings and Loan Association), and Pacific Bank Political Activity Committee.[18] Their officers participate directly—nationally and regionally—through PACs such as the Mutual Bank Legislative Committee, the American Bankers Association, Community Banks, The Savings and Loan League, etc.

In 1974, bank officers and stockholders contributed heavily to the reelection campaign of U.S. Senator John Sparkman, the chairman of the U.S. Senate Financial Committee, because they feared that if he were not reelected U.S. Senator William Proxmire, who was frequently at odds with the banking community, would succeed to the chairmanship.[19]

This, of course, is only a small part of banks power. They can exploit their substantial economic ties. Bank directors have communications and other influential connections and some bank board members use their board meetings to devise ways to channel the personal contributions of large stockholders and executives of the institution itself. On occasion, contributions pass through their attorneys, who get it from the bank disguised as a fee.

Though banks don't make direct contributions, they do make loans. Under current federal law, if a bank loan is made to the candidate "in the ordinary course of business," it must be reported by the campaign committee. But nothing prevents a friendly banker from inflating a candidate's assets or accepting co-signers to justify a campaign loan. Of course, if the candidate loses and is unable to pay, the bank can foreclose. If the loser's assets are still insufficient, and there is no co-signer, the bank can write it off against their reserves as a bad debt.

Often, the candidate wants to hide the source of his or her campaign money, at least until after the election. This is difficult under federal law where the guarantee is reported like a contribution. For example, if a bank loans a candidate $1,000 and four individuals endorse the loan in equal parts, the money from each of those four individuals is reported at $250.

Under state and local contests, however, there are a myriad of techniques that can be employed to hide the contribution. In some jurisdictions, for example, candidates for state and local offices list loans, but it is not necessary that he or she mention that there is a co-signer. Or the bank can make the loan directly (if the candidate has resources), and need not mention it, even though they know the candidate has an understanding—even a separate contract—with a wealthy investor who will pay the loan if he or she loses the election.

In 1979, Congress tightened the law a bit, adding a requirement that bank loans to campaigns must be made "on a basis which assures repayment." So normally banks demand collateral for campaign loans. For example, freshman Republican Chester Atkins (D., Mass.) once borrowed $115,000 from banks to help finance his House race, but said the loans were backed up by several mortgages on his $450,000 house and on his collections of expensive antiques and original artworks. Similarly, Republican Alex McMillan, a wealthy North Carolina businessman who ran for the U.S. House in 1984, pledged corporate stock as security for $70,000 he borrowed to finance his successful race.

But the banks are not always that strict. "What you have in

Biggest Bank Loans To Campaigns

(Totals outstanding Dec. 21, 1984)

President	
Sen. John Glenn (D, Ohio)	$1,900,000
Sen. Gary Hart (D, Colo.)	1,240,771

Senate	
Sen. John Kerry (D, Mass.)	135,000

House	
Tommy Robinson (D, Ark.)	226,588
Chester Atkins (D, Mass.)	115,000
Mac Sweeney (R, Texas)	81,000
Alex McMillan (R, N.C.)	70,000

Fig. 2-8. *The Wall Street Journal,* April 1, 1985. Reprinted by permission of *The Wall Street Journal,* © 1985 Dow Jones & Co.y, Inc. All rights reserved worldwide.

effect are contributions by large financial institutions," says Daniel Swillinger, a Republican attorney specializing in election law. Democratic Attorney William Oldaker, former general counsel of the Federal Election Commission, says the commission's rules on loans are open to abuse.[20]

At least that is the way it looked when U.S. Senator John Glenn of Ohio borrowed $2 million from four Ohio banks with very little collateral to keep his Presidential campaign afloat. When Senator Glenn's presidential bid collapsed, his campaign still owed the banks $1.9 million. Glenn was not alone. Colorado U.S. Senator Gary Hart borrowed even more for his presidential race. Hart's bank loans totaled nearly $5 million, and were backed up largely by his predictions that new donors would flood the campaign with money in response to mass mailing appeals. But Hart's projections proved too optimistic and the banks were left holding unpaid loans totaling more than $1.2 million at the end of 1984.[21]

Fortunately, both U.S. Senators were able to conduct fundraising appeals to liquidate this debt. But a donor can no longer make a distinction between a donation and a private loan (unless the loan is from a bank and was made in a commercially reasonable manner), if there is a default, and if the bank used every effort (including litigation) to collect, then the debt could be written off by the bank against their reserves.[22]

This loophole is subject to abuse. Let me cite two examples involving congressional candidates. When Republican Congressman MacSweeney was a candidate, he was a poor prospect for a big bank loan. He hadn't drawn a regular salary for months, had few personal assets, and was in the midst of an uphill campaign for his first elective office at the age of 29. Yet Brooks Jackson, writing in *The Wall Street Journal*, pointed out that Mr. Sweeney was able to borrow $81,000 from three Texas banks, mostly without any collateral.

Meanwhile, in Arkansas, Democratic Congressman Tommy Robinson was borrowing $226,588 on his signature from local banks to finance his first bid for the House, although his job as Pulaski County Sheriff paid less than $37,000 a year. Brooks Jackson says "He [Tommy Robinson] publicly listed few assets and still had debts from his earlier campaign for sheriff, but with the help of the banks, he outspent his rivals."[23]

State Campaign Contribution Legislation

As we move to state campaign debt legislation, we find it has other facets used by "political predators." Following Watergate, Georgia State Senator George Busbee authored a watered-down public disclosure act which the state's attorney general interpreted as permitting contributors to quietly convert what was previously reported as a loan to a contribution after the election. During his campaign for Governor, Busbee made an issue of the loopholes in the law he had created by claiming his opponents were using them. Busbee attacked former Governor and Lieutenant Governor Lester Maddox, claiming that he had four loans totaling $225,000, all countersigned by local campaign supporters. Busbee also nicknamed another opponent—President Jimmy Carter's intimate, Burt Lance—"Loophole Lance," because he had borrowed $350,000 and put it into his own campaign when more than $200,000 of it was in overdrafts on a bank of which he was chairman.[24]

Federal banking regulators referred the matter to the election commission, which authorized a lawsuit against Lance for violating election law. But after years of legal maneuvers by Lance, the commission admitted it was stymied and voted 4-2 to drop the matter, partly on grounds that the evidence had become stale.[25]

Other Regulated Industries

Most state laws prohibit highly regulated industries such as telephone, insurance, and electric and natural gas utilities from charging rates that cover political contributions. However, they use money collected from allowable profits to support their legislative goals. Gas and electric utilities working through PACs such as the "fair competition council," are permitted to exercise their political muscle, while insurance companies act through affiliated groups such as the National Agents and Life Underwriters Political Action Committee.

The Appointee with Financial Connections

There is another philosophical question that is related to, though not directly connected with, campaign contributions. Often these regulated industries or professions are regulated by appointees who owe their power to the fact that they are selected from a business, trade, or profession. They use their positions to generate contributions from company executives and stock holders.

As far back as 1924, *The Washington Merry-Go-Round* described the seventh richest man in the United States, Andrew Mellon, as seeking to escape from the monotonous routine of his home, bank, and club by donating to hospitals, buying rare portraits, and seeing everything he touched turn to gold. In the book's words, "He yearned for new worlds to conquer, so it was not mere accident that found him at the top of the list of heavy contributors to the Republican campaign fund, who expected to realize far more than six percent on their investment by putting Warren G. Harding in the White House. He was rewarded with an appointment and he served for 12 years as Secretary of the Treasury." The *Washington Merry-Go-Round* also tells us Andrew Mellon "was one of the first to cash in on his investment. He paid himself $400,000, the largest tax refund ever awarded to any single individual."[26]

Big Labor, Small Labor and . . . Management

Labor has an interest in almost everything government does or fails to do. Their primary interest is to protect the right of unions to organize; strike; and bargain for higher wages, hours, pension, and fringe benefits. Labor also wants the right to include a provision which permits a closed or union shop. And at the state level they have an interest in industrial insurance and workers' compensation benefits.

Federal law prohibits labor's use of union dues to aid federal candidates. But most laws restricting corporate donations were passed before unions had become financial forces. Thus, only four states (Indiana, New Hampshire, Pennsylvania, and Texas) prevented unions from using dues in a state or local campaign.[27]

At the Federal level, the AFL–CIO works through a PAC. In addition, most national and many local labor organizations have their own political action committees. They distribute funds voluntarily collected from their members. For example, the nation's largest union, the Teamsters, has a political action committee called D.R.I.V.E. The machinists work through their non-partisan league. Also, the Maritime Engineers have what they call a Beneficial Association, and carpenters use a PAC titled The Washington Council of Carpenters Lobbying Fund.

This is only part of the story. Each state has a labor council representing the combined interest of the AFL–CIO, one or more Joint Council of Teamsters, as well as hundreds of local unions, who can and do contribute to campaigns in which they have an interest.

A novice at the task of raising campaign money may well assume that a candidate must choose between labor and management. This is not necessarily so. Often a candidate can get substantial contributions from both. During the 1950s and 1960s, California State Senator Allen Short of Stockton was a labor-leaning Democrat with a strong interest in construction and building legislation. Understandably, he received campaign contributions from the AFL–CIO and special help from unions such as the Operating Engineers, International Brotherhood of Electrical Workers, Building Trades Construction Council, and the Sacramento Central Labor Council. At the same time, he received contributions from the California Council of Professional Engineers, and Sheet Metal and Plumbing-Heating-Cooling Contractors. He also received campaign money from both industries and unions associated with motion pictures and TV productions. Employment agencies helped, as did the typographical unions. His contributions also included the Journeyman Barber Association, the Teamsters' Brotherhood of Railroad, the Airline Clerks, and the Cannery Workers Political Education Welfare Fund.[28]

While both labor and management political action committees can contribute separately, they cannot do so jointly. Federal law separates union and corporate

PACs in that it will not permit corporate political action committees to solicit funds from nonmanagement corporate employees, and labor PACs may not solicit from shareholders, executives, and administrative personnel.[29]

In theory, each political action committee is an independent entity that controls its own funds and makes its own choice of candidates. With labor there is little sham. They use their contributions to support union endorsed candidates. And when a PAC is composed of management personnel, it is reasonable to assume that these corporate officers know where the corporation stands. When they contribute to a campaign, they reflect the politics of the corporate board.

Laws restricting internal communications still permit corporations to spend their funds to communicate with their shareholders, executives, and administrative personnel and their families, which gives the corporation the opportunity to urge their support of a particular candidate. They are also permitted to carry out other political functions, such as professional hosting. For instance, in 1976, Coca Cola's political committee hosted a luncheon for 52 political "fat cats" at New York's exclusive 21 Club to hear a political pitch by presidential candidate, Jimmy Carter.[30]

But this only scratches the surface. Nothing limits labor's right to use dues to communicate to their members or their immediate families in support of a federal or state candidate,[31] as long as the communication is not deliberately designed to influence the non-union public.[32] For example, the union can set up a phone bank to urge its members to vote for its favorite candidate, or the candidate can attend a regularly scheduled event of the organization or even request contributions from the audience.

After the AFL–CIO endorsed former Vice President Walter Mondale in the 1984 presidential primary, the unions set up eighteen labor phone banks across the state of Iowa. In Sioux City, they paid members from union funds to burn up the phone lines calling their union brethren and their families. The thrust of the call was to identify Mondale supporters, whom they later urged to participate in Democratic caucuses. Using information culled from phone calls, the big computers at AFL–CIO headquarters in Washington, DC, spit out personalized follow-up letters. These used interchangeable paragraphs that came as close as possible to addressing voter concerns previously identified by phone.[33]

To see how potent this combination of union money and volunteer help can be, let us return to Mondale's mentor Hubert Humphrey. When he ran for President, labor printed and distributed 55 million pamphlets sent from Washington, plus 60 million more from local unions. There were telephone banks in 638 localities using 8,055 telephones, manned by 24,611 union men and women and their families. Another 72,225 were used as house-to-house canvassers, and on election day, 94,457 volunteers served as carpoolers, campaign literature distributors, babysitters, poll watchers, and telephoners.[34]

Chapter 13

Like Christmas Spirit the Gifts Improve with Prospects of Victory

> Winning is always more fun than losing except when fighting temptation.
> —Anonymous

To the Winner

The plight of the long shot was best described by finance chairman for Senator Stephen Douglas in his presidential campaign against Abraham Lincoln when he said, "If we could only demonstrate to all those lukewarm and selfish money-bags that we have a strong probability to carry the state of New York, we might get from them the necessary sinews of war."[1]

The desire for a winner extends to all contributors, even those with strong ideological views, and it prompts many prospective contributors to hold back until they see the candidate has a chance. For instance, when anti-war U.S. Senator Gene McCarthy was a Presidential candidate, he acquired hordes of anti-war activists and funds trickled in until after the New Hampshire primary. Following his strong showing in that primary, funds poured in. Then U.S. Senator Robert Kennedy entered the race and contributions momentarily slacked off. The Wisconsin, Nebraska, Indiana, and Oregon primary victories saw contributions climb. The death of Robert Kennedy sent them spinning. But McCarthy's surprising New York primary victory sent them climbing once more.[2]

What effect does the candidate's election prospects have on the political investor? In the real political world, so-called smart money follows the latest political polls just like its does the stock market. During his career, Democratic Congressman Albert Gore had sponsored of legislation that would curtail political action committees. When Republican majority leader Howard Baker announced his retirement, Gore sought his U.S. Senate seat, an office once held by Gore's father. During their careers, Gore and Baker got sharply different ratings from business. Mr. Gore, for example, got a 9-percent rating from business and industry political action committees and Senator Baker got 96 percent score. The U.S. Chamber of Commerce gave Senator Baker a lifetime vote rating of 76 percent on business issues, but graded Mr. Gore at 33 percent.

Nevertheless, a full year before the 1984 election Mr. Gore received $111,325 from 79 political action committees that had backed Senator Baker. One Gore $500-a-person reception brought in nearly $28,000 from business leaders, representing Chrysler Corporation, Boeing Company, General Electric Co., Northrop Corporation, and dozens of others. Brooks Jackson, writing in *The Wall Street Journal* summed up the reason: "If there's anything a business lobbyist likes better than donating to an incumbent, it's supporting a winner."[3]

There is no uniform way a political investor decides who the winner is going to be unless it is by looking at the latest polls. For example in 1974, First National Bank of Topeka (Kansas) organized two in-house political committees, the "Americans for Free Enterprise" and the "Citizens for Good Government." Two weeks after the primary, "Citizens for Good Government" gave the Democratic nominee for governor, Vern Miller, $750. A week later, on August 27, "Americans for Free Enterprise" sent the Republican nominee, Bennett, $750. Later, on October 8th, "Citizens for Good Government" sent $500 to Bennett.[4]

How PACs fared

PACS — special-interest political action committees — contributed heavily to House and Senate campaigns this year. Here are the PACs that backed the highest percentage of winners Tuesday:

Political action committee	Winners backed	Losers backed	Won-lost percent
Associated Milk Producers	199	9	.957
National Rifle Association	181	9	.953
National Right-to-Life Committee	80	5	.941
National PAC (pro-Israel)	76	5	.938
Handgun Control Inc.	72	5	.935
American Bankers Association	287	21	.932
Rockwell (industrial)	210	16	.929
National Association of Realtors	336	31	.916
American Medical Association	336	43	.887
Tenneco	128	19	.871
National Education Association	228	49	.823
United Auto Workers	196	52	.790
Fund for a Conservative Majority	75	24	.758
National Abortion Rights Action League	57	24	.704

Source: Based on contributions through Oct. 17 as reported to Federal Election Commission

Fig. 2-9. Election USA: How PACs Fared, *USA Today*, November 8, 1984. Copyright 1984, *USA Today*. Reprinted with permission.

Impact of the Polls

"A terrifically lopsided poll can kill a campaign by killing off the contributions," says Thomas "Tip" O'Neill. The Speaker of the U.S. House added his strong suspicion "that in some cases newspapers have rigged their surveys in order to stifle someone's candidacy."[5]

After a three-way battle for mayor of New York in 1969 in which Democrat Mario Procaccio's opponents were John Lindsay, a liberal independent, and John Marche, a Republican, Procaccio thought he was doing fine until a preference poll showed him 20 points behind Lindsay. After that the *New York News* gave Lindsay a front page endorsement. When this was picked up on by television, radio, and other newspapers, nervous investors jumped to Lindsay. Procaccio contends that Lindsay won because their money permitted him to mount a media campaign that literally drenched the citizens of New York City with advertising.

Following his defeat, in which he finished only four points behind Lindsay, Procaccio complained that the polls were rigged, then added, "If it had scientifically reflected voter's views, no doubt I would have won."[6]

In an election where everyone agrees there is no sure thing, an imaginative fundraiser will solicit those who support the opposition, asking them if they "want to buy insurance." This is effective with nervous Nellies, contributors who would rather brave complaints from the candidate they favor than be shut out by a winner-take-all victory.

In 1975, officials of the Monsanto Chemical Company had a political fund that was administered by an assistant to the president, James H. Lum, after he told reporters he chose the recipients "on the basis of ability." He was a little embarrassed when reporters asked why his group gave to both Democratic Senator Edward V. Long and his Republican opponent, Crosby Kemper. Lum replied simply, "It's one of those things."[7]

Chapter 14

The Ethics, The Wise Men Who Came Bearing Gifts

> As Zsa Zsa Gabor said, "Hotel tycoon Conrad Hilton and I had one thing in common. We both wanted his money."[1]
>
> "If you can't eat their food, drink their booze, screw their woman, and then vote against them you have no business being here."
> —Jessie Unruh, Speaker of the California Assembly[2]
>
> CAUTION: Many a candidate goes into politics with a fine future and comes out with a terrible past.
> *NY Trade Composer*[3]

Separating Life from Myth

Let's play cynic. For openers, we should understand that Santa Claus, St. Nicholas, and the Bishop of Myra were all the patron saints of pawnbrokers. During the 18th century, pirates emblazoned St. Nicholas' likeness on their flags. He was considered the spiritual protector of many other practitioners of picturesque vocations such as thieves and gangsters. The "Knights of St. Nicholas" was another name for the light-fingered gentry.[4]

Hubert Humphrey once described the money collection ritual as "the most disgusting, demeaning, disenchanting, debilitating experience of a politician's life. It stinks. It's lousy. I just can't tell you how much I hated it."[5] Still, it is a real and usually crucial part of getting elected and we may as well look at its legal and philosophical implications.

Since most campaign contributions are made by those who have a special interest, this poses a question. Can a candidate succeed without accepting campaign money? There are a few successful politicians who take a very strict position. One-time U.S. Senator Margaret Chase Smith of Maine and present U.S. Senator William Proxmire of Wisconsin said they refuse most, if not all, contributions from vested interests. They adopt the lofty attitude espoused by Governor Frank Lausch in his 1944 Ohio gubernatorial race. He spent only $27,162.75, while loser Mayor James G. Stewart of Cincinnati spent $988,000. The head of his ticket, President Franklin D. Roosevelt, lost the state by 11,500 votes, while Frank Lausch, who also ran on the Democratic ticket, won the governorship by 112,000.[6]

When the political action committee of the CIO offered Lausch $1,000, he turned the money down. When his campaign was still $8,700 in debt, the Democratic National Headquarters telephoned him in New York, volunteering to pay off his bills if he would accept their check, which was to be funneled through the local party. Lausch refused the money.[7]

It is simply a fact of life, however, that tainted or untainted political contributions finance most campaigns. The attitudes of Senators Margaret Chase Smith, William Proxmire, and Frank Lausch toward campaign contributions do not represent the usual reality.

Add to this another fact of life. As political writer and former congressional aide Richard Larsen stated, "Citizens are strangely skittish about making a contribution to a candidate."[8] When a pioneer of New York's Tammany Hall, Aaron Burr (later Vice President of the United States), ran for Governor of New York, he conducted a house-to-house canvass of "little people" in search of contributions. He was defeated in part because he failed to collect enough to match the bankers, led by Alexander Hamilton.

The Socialist and Labor parties in England, Australia, and Canada depend on mass solicitation. Except for the modern Minnesota Democratic Farmer Labor Party and the Nonpartisan League of North Dakota,[9] other parties, such as the "Do Nothings," "Free Silver," "Populists," "Prohibition," "Socialist," "Labor," "American," "Communist," and "Progressives," have withered or been losers from day one.[10]

Most modern politicians find the drudgery of collecting small contributions an unprofitable, time-consuming use of campaign effort. They know because they have tried. In recent years there have been efforts by both parties. Milton Shapp, a Pennsylvania millionaire who became Governor, personally financed most of his first two runs. Once elected, he decided to use small contributions to finance his reelection campaign. He chose his best grass roots organizers and supplied them with a prospect list meticulously compiled from those who gave to previous campaigns. After they used direct mail and telephone solicitations to seek small contributions, still they experienced failure. They experimented in Allentown, Pennsylvania, with door-to-door solicitation and they "raised only $300."[11] After that the Shapp committee felt they had to rely on contributions of $500 or more.

Reality and the System

Contrary to the picture conjured up by rabble-rousers in their stump speeches, big political contributors are usually represented by respected men and women. They come from labor, agriculture, business, or the professions. They participate in a system that veteran editor Ross Cunningham describes as "subtle" and "legal." They admit that what the politician does is important to them, and their lobbyist is not ashamed of his calling or their motives. They attend fundraising dinners to make sure that the interests they represent get credit.[12]

I know it's hard for an outsider to grasp a system in which hard-headed businessmen and -women donate thousands of dollars to a political candidate without a clear understanding of what they are to get in return, let alone say with a straight face that there are no strings attached to the contributions, but this is reality.

Let's look at this problem in perspective. Philosophically, it is not special-interest money itself that's evil. It is the fact that it might influence a candidate once he or she is elected to public office. Of course, this can and does happen. So the real question is, how do the candidates and the contributors square contributions and their influence upon a potential decision? Those who support "the system" argue that, in the final analysis, we are governed by an imperfect democracy. Within its parameters, there is a constant struggle pitting people who have special interests against one another.

Although it may be even harder for an outsider to understand, it is rare that the candidate sees the contributor's ultimate goal as one that involves a moral or ethical question. To illustrate, during the 1950s and 1960s in Southern California there was a struggle for the right to develop large offshore oil fields. The fight found its way into the political arena. State Senate leader Hugh Burns was a friend of "Big Oil" companies such as Standard and Shell, while Lieutenant Governor Glenn Anderson had close ties with the independent operators. The liberal speaker of the State House of Representatives, Jesse Unruh, could see no liberal versus conservative issues hidden in the middle. He felt he was simply balancing one special interest against another; Unruh chose the independents.[13]

And, yes, in a democracy, political and economic forces use campaign contributions to make friends and allies. Those who do so argue money is only one of the forces that shapes political conduct. They agree with Ross Cunningham when he said, "It would be wrong to assume that because a politician grants a contract or votes down the line in a way that pleases his financial bankers he had, ipso facto, sold his soul. In all likelihood, he would have voted that way in any event."[14]

I know that to outsiders this sounds like the preacher who says, "God said it, I believe it, and that settles it," when it's hard for a nonbeliever to understand how the preacher knows what God said. So let's approach this question of morality from a different perspective. The realist asks, "How does the politician achieve public office?" Traditionally, politicians are rewarded with high public office because they make promises or because they have a proven track record upon which all of us with special interests of one sort or another can make a judgment. As Kansas newspaper editor William Allen White, when speaking of then Vice President Charley Curtis, said, "For 35 years he [Curtis] has been depositing favors in the political bank and today he is drawing checks on them."[15]

This raises a practical question that is ignored by the pious hypocrite and the unsophisticated reformer. How does the politician who refuses to take campaign contributions react when asked for a vote by their party or any organization that speaks for a gender, race, religion, union, chamber of commerce, or geographic region? The realist says, "Let's not look at campaign contributions in isolation, but rather how the politician stands up in the local media or chamber of commerce to organizations representing the interests of labor, business, veterans, women, elderly, or consumers. Do those who argue that special interest money is tainted say the same thing about special interest votes?"

The Right of a Special Interest to Impact the System

Certainly the candidate must admit their support is contingent on favoring a particular point of view. So they are asked, "Is it any more moral to be influenced by these political minorities because they represent thousands, possibly millions, of votes?"

In recognition of this question, our imperfect democracy has recognized the right of narrow special interests to collect money from their stockholders or employees, or draw on their profits to give in the name of their industry or

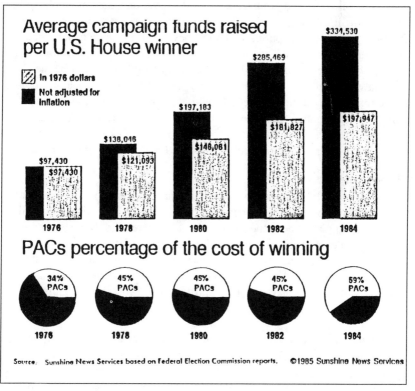

Fig. 2-10. Edward Roseder, Special Interest Contributions to Congressional Races Soar, *Seattle Times/Seattle Post-Intelligencer*, June 30, 1985.

professions. In practice, our political system condones many Santa Clauses: Big Labor, businesses, even special interests. Their participation in politics is consistent with the objectives of democracy, which is that everyone, including vested interests, has a right to impact political decisions. If those with only money to offer were denied this access, government would be the province of mob psychology. We accept the fact that a candidate needs money, and we accept the present system as a fact of life. Accepting special interest campaign money, then, is rationalized or justified on the theory that any policymaking office holder is only relatively free, and that is when he or she has many Santa Clauses.

Still there is the practical problem of deciding which sources the candidate will solicit or accept contributions from. Looking for an explanation—or if you prefer rationalization—it is easy to say that the candidate should decide from whom the money should be solicited and from whom it will not be accepted. However, in the real world, this is almost impossible. Many groups pursue more than one objective. When this is true, it is entirely proper for a candidate to accept a contribution when the two groups are in conflict over one, but not all objectives.[16]

By way of illustrating, assume a jurisdiction where optometrists, who are not MDs, cannot write prescriptions. Suppose they favor a change of law that allows them to use the same eyedrops to dilate the eyes that MD ophthalmologists use when they fit glasses. Even though the MDs might vigorously oppose the changes in the law sought by optometrists, the candidate might decide to accept contributions from both optometrists and AMPAC (the political arm of MD doctors that represents ophthalmologists). The candidate can accept and disagree with the MDs on this particular issue because he or she expects to agree with the MDs on many other objectives dealing with the broad subject of health care.

Sorting Out the Differences

To be honest, when it comes to campaign financing no one raises political cash without personal or political leverage. The legality of accepting a contribution versus accepting a bribe depends on the candidate, the contributor, and the candidate's state of mind. It is illegal if the contribution is intended to buy something. However, this doesn't happen very often. Editorial writer Ross Cunningham explains, "The politician is very, very rare who would say, 'I'll do this for you if you'll make a good contribution.' Most political investors and candidates do not exchange specific promises. This is too close to cash on the barrelhead."[17]

Using the same reasoning, contributions are legally acceptable if money is given to elect an official who, for his or her own reasons, will be favorably disposed toward the contributor. Unsophisticated contributors do not always understand this distinction. Consequently, most prosecutors and politicians overlook innocent offers that are made by those who don't understand. In 1972,

United States Senator Edmond Muskie of Maine was the early frontrunner in his party's presidential primary when he was approached by a man who offered $200,000 for his campaign. However, the contribution had a catch. If Senator Muskie was elected president, he had to promise that the contributor would be appointed to an ambassadorship. As Muskie describes the conversation, the potential contributor said, "Not a big country like France of England, you understand. I couldn't afford those anyway. But can you give me a little one? Switzerland or Belgium?" Senator Muskie, of course, refused the contribution.[18]

The vast majority of contributions are legal because most politicians and contributors carefully observe this imaginary line. And often their reasons have nothing directly to do with being legal or moral but rather both the candidate and the recipient are fully conscious that it hurts their self-image to do otherwise. As Texas lobbyist Stacy Bracewell put it, "most politicians are pretty idealistic and sincere. I don't think they would put up with contributions with ties. Naturally, contributors expect a better entree to present their case. They establish a rapport with the person being helped."[19]

Then, you may ask, what does a special interest expect to gain by contributing? Bracewell answers, "People do business with their friends. Politicians can't help rationalizing a controversial matter in favor of their friends. They do it unwittingly."[20]

To see how this works, let's look at a typical case. In most jurisdictions, architecture is considered a matter of art, and the selection of the architect for government buildings is made without competitive bidding. In 1974, architectural firms that received lucrative contracts for designing state buildings were the subject of inquiry. A senior partner of one state firm, Perry Johanson, made this pious statement, "Our firm has never made contributions to any state political campaign. Principals of the firm have made contributions on a personal basis. . . . We have felt this to be a part of a general responsibility which includes contributions to other worthy causes such as the UGN." On closer scrutiny, his partners admitted to a total of $5,090 in contributions to state officials from members of that firm. $3,500 of this money went directly to the current governor. Another $1,300 in contributions went to the Republican Central Committee, which the governor controlled. Only one Democrat received anything—$180, which was given to another architect, a personal friend who was a candidate for State Representative.[21]

A very small minority of candidates though use the campaign as an excuse to collect money not intended for the campaign. Under most state and federal laws, the candidate who does so can be prosecuted for fraud. Even where there is no specific law, the candidate can expect not only bad publicity but harsh treatment from his colleagues when the matter is exposed by the news media. These colleagues may feel that such conduct affects their credibility when seeking contributions for their own campaigns.

This happened in 1968 when U.S. Senator Thomas C. Dodd, Sr. (father of the present senator) of Connecticut took the floor of the United States Senate arguing against a motion censuring him for conduct "contrary to accepted morals." He was trying to justify funds received for campaign purposes when there was no campaign, and which far exceeded his unreimbursed costs of office. Though Senator Dodd said these funds were collected to liquidate old campaign debts, he could not show ongoing political accounts, debts, creditors, or loans from his earlier campaign and he had no answer for his accusers who said he paid personal bills with $116,083 collected from supporters at political dinners. The outcome was a 92 to 5 vote for censure.[22]

When contributors are pressured, candidates are not always responsible. Occasionally, pressure is applied by the political party, labor, or other contributors. Theodore H. White reported this happening in the 1960 campaign. The State Chairman of Connecticut's Democratic party, John Bailey, a loyal Kennedyite, informed former U.S. Senator William Benton, who had already given Humphrey $5,000, that if he gave Humphrey more, he would never hold another elective or appointive job in Connecticut at least as long as he [Bailey] had any say.[23]

Although there is no clear rule that covers how to deal with pressure from contributors, I suppose the best rule of thumb is that the candidate and his supporters should recognize that no matter who applies pressure, it is dangerous. If exposed, it can cause the loss of the election even if no law is broken.

In summary: Subtle understandings make this area of political activity subject to confusion and misinterpretation, but a few things are clear:

- If money is given to or taken for an office holder (and in some jurisdictions a candidate), conditioned on a promise to vote or to give an economic advantage, it is not a contribution. It is a bribe and is a violation of criminal law.
- If money is solicited for a campaign with the clear intention of using it personally or for something other than the campaign, the act is fraud and, in most jurisdictions, it is also a criminal offense.
- Subtle arm-twisting is a two-way street. Candidates twist arms to get campaign money. Contributors twist arms for a commitment to issues they favor.
- The use of political pressure to collect campaign money or force a public official to vote a certain way is often immoral or dangerous and is usually illegal.
- It may happen that the candidate has no knowledge or, if he or she has, they have no power to stop the pressure that is applied to get campaign contributions.

Campaign Contributions—A Look at Disclosure Information

No matter how they explain it, contributors—especially investors—are not innocents. No one gives very often unless the candidate's philosophy and personality or actions are compatible.

In a jurisdiction where campaign contributions are a matter of public record, past disclosure information includes the names and recent history of politicians and how they are viewed by special interests. If the focal point is an executive— governor, mayor, county commissioner, comptroller, etc.—those who do business with that office recognize the importance of having a friend in power.

This is apparent when looking at past disclosure information. The candidate running for mayor, governor, or county commissioner can expect to see contributions from those who contributed to others who have stood for a similar office, interests that sell uniforms, food, janitorial supplies, and services such as financial consulting, banking, and architectural engineering.

Such contributors will give almost automatically when asked because they are vitally affected by government regulation and enforcement. This was the case in the 1974 campaign for Florida state comptroller, when the incumbent received substantial contributions from those to whom his office granted charters and regulated, such as small loan companies, cemeteries, and banks.[24]

Businesses licensed and regulated by other departments range from race tracks to barber shops and are subject to state or local regulation. For instance, in Maryland in 1973 liquor regulation was controlled by twenty-four divisions. Each was managed by its own board, which was composed of members appointed by the governor. In the 1973 gubernatorial campaign, eighty liquor dealers gave the incumbent $27,000 through their state trade association. And one hundred individual dealers also found reason to be generous.[25]

There are a few regulated industries that involve gambling. Some states allow parimutuel betting. To some this is the sport of kings. Others believe it fosters a degrading form of sin. Track operators want friends among those who have life-and-death control over their continued operation. In 1973, the incumbent Maryland governor was considered a friend. As one would expect, the industry contributed $28,000 toward his campaign.[26]

The executives of an administration make large purchases that range from road equipment to janitorial supplies. When an office performs an administrative function, there are a variety of ways in which those in control of government can do business. For example, even when the law requires competitive bidding, government officials have the power to define the product or the service in a way that gives some firms a competitive advantage.

Public projects such as buildings, roads, dams, or airports are financed by floating bonds. While the bonds themselves are subject to competitive bid, they cannot be sold unless there is an engineering feasibility study—which may not be subject to competitive bid. It is not surprising that in the 1973 Maryland gubernatorial campaign, Kaiser Engineering of Oakland, California, and Irving F. Mandenhall of Los Angeles, who had $22 million in consulting contracts, were listed as contributors.[27]

In most jurisdictions, a financial advisor is employed to help public entities market their bonds and make sure they are getting the best interest rate. A bond issue must also be approved by bond attorneys before a regional or national brokerage house will market them. Again, in most states, public bond council and financial advisors, being professionals, don't bid.

Tim Carrington reported in *The Wall Street Journal*, "Some high-ranking executives of finance houses are political liberals, and others tend to contribute to both parties as a means of hedging their bets and remaining in the good graces of both major parties, because many Wall Street Executives contend that it's almost impossible to obtain much underwriting business without making campaign contributions to state financial officials."[28]

Aware of this, most states require firms holding non-bid government contracts to report separately the political contributions made by their top officials.[29] This doesn't prevent them from contributing. A stock brokerage firm contributed $20,000 to a fundraising dinner, and a partner in the firm bought $6,000 in tickets to pay off the campaign debts of one-time Illinois Governor, Daniel Walker. In the same month, that firm was retained as advisor to the state on a $100 million bond issue with a fee estimated at $75,000 to $100,000, in 1974 dollars.[30]

Investing, Influencing, and Impacting Legislation

Presidents, governors, mayors—all control departments that recommend new legislation. Legislators have the power to propose and reject. Executives have the power to veto legislation they oppose.

Both legislative and executive officials receive campaign contributions from political action committees (PACs). The interests involved cover a wide spectrum. At the congressional level, for example, legislation can affect industries such as steel and the automobile, which are concerned with the effect of Japanese imports. At the state level interests are concerned with the minimum wage and the imposition of taxes on utilities, entertainment, and businesses and occupations, etc.

Before giving, contributors evaluate the influence legislators have on their interests. In Congress this usually depends on committee memberships.

The Seafarers International Union PAC, for instance, gave $449,000 to 215 members of Congress in 1976. $102,563 of this money went to 29 of the 40 members of the House Merchant Marine and Fisheries Committee.[31]

There are also other considerations. When the candidate is a legislator, organizations and individual contributors have political obligations that they incurred when the incumbent gave them a vote when they needed it.

For example, let us look at the 1.8 million teachers in the National Education Association. When their PAC distributed some $250,000 in the 1980 congressional campaign, they had their memories fixed on those who supported their "number one" bill, which provided for the creation of a Department of Education. This bill cleared the United States House by only four votes.

At that time, the NEA PAC raised some eyebrows by making $2,700 in contributions to several Republicans who supported the bill, although some of them opposed most liberal education measures favored by teacher organizations such as the Equal Rights Amendment and labor law revision that would have made it easier for its employees to join a union.[32] It's not surprising that a typical survey of investor contributions shows incumbents received 71 percent as opposed to the challenger's 53 percent, and that 71 percent of their money, as opposed to 54 percent for challengers, came from outside the legislative district they represented.

Generally, when investor contributors give to nonincumbents, it is in districts where the incumbent is not seeking reelection. Thus, most incumbents can truthfully say, as Florida State Senator Guy Spicola did in 1974, that campaign contributions (in his case over $13,000) come unsolicited. In the same campaign, State Representative Don Halextan could explain that, "Most of the contributions just came in the mail and I turned them over to my accountants."[33]

Identifying What the Contributor Wants

Federal and some state public disclosure laws, such as those in Pennsylvania, require reports covering all campaign contributions and expenditures be recorded in the commonwealth secretary's office.[34] Not all public disclosure laws are open to public scrutiny, but attempting to identify the motives of those who contribute is like playing Twenty Questions.

PACs representing doctors, dentists, and lawyers are among the most generous when it comes to legislative and congressional campaigns. Doctors are interested in the regulation of fees by Medicare and welfare, and they are interested in the laws regulating insurance companies that guarantee payment for their services. The names of their PACs do help, as in the case of the American Medical Action Committee and the Washington Dental Political Action Committee. The Bar Association and the American Trial Lawyers work through political action committees such as IAMEAC. They contribute to congressional and legislative races to aid those who oppose changes in tort and products liability laws.[35]

In identifying business investors, let's look at the most basic need: food. The complex food industry takes a lively interest in politics through their national agro-business groups, such as the Wheat Improvement Association of Manhattan, Kansas, or the National Corn Growers Association of Boone, Iowa.[36] Supermarket chains operate through trade organizations like the Food and Marketing Association of Chicago; Grocery Manufacturers of America, Inc., of Washington, DC; and the Western Association of Food Chains of Pasadena, California.[37]

Prior to modern limitations on campaign contributions, U.S. Representative Wilbur Mills was chairman of the House Ways and Means Committee, which wrote tax legislation important to dairymen. During that period the dairy cooperatives contributed more than $50,000 to his bid for the Democratic presidential nomination.[38]

I don't think it would be hard to identify the interests of other business contributors, such as the Realtor's Political Active Committee; the Southeast Committee organized for the trading of cotton; the Alaska Skies Association, which is the political arm of Alaska Airlines; and the Burlington Northern (railroad) Employees' Voluntary Good Government Fund.[39] Nor would it be hard to identify labor contributors, which include PACs representing the United Automobile Workers, United Mine Workers, International Union of Operating Engineers, and the United Steel Workers of America. Santa Claus could represent packing houses, the allied workers organizing fund, or the PACs of national unions of retail clerks.

There are PACs for all kinds of special interest groups. For instance, REDEMs represent the Washington Association of Automobile Dealers; PULSE stands for Political Unity of Leaders in State Education, an arm of the Washington Education Association; and the Fair Competition Council is an organization contributing to candidates who see eye to eye with private electric utilities.[40]

Simply knowing the name and even the nature of the contributor's business may not identify what the contributor's interests are. Fred Taylor was one of Georgia Governor Busbee's earliest and most devoted financial angels. It was easy to ascertain that Taylor was in heavy truck equipment sales. It required someone with insight to guess that he wanted the weight limits raised on multiaxle trucks. A new regulation could represent a bonanza in truck sales, benefiting men like Taylor who owned truck dealerships.[41]

It also took an insider to know that the political contribution of the National Asphalt Paving Association might be dependent upon the candidate's position in its fight against the transfer of federal highway dollars to mass rail transit.

The same is true of the Tacoma Fund, alter ego of the Weyerhaeuser Corporation, whose business is growing and harvesting timber. It would take an insider to know that their congressional contribution is affected by the congressional candidate's reaction to legislation restricting log exports to Japan.[42]

The Good Ol' Boys Who Do Business on Main Street

Most candidates will never enter a large expensive contest. They simply "do their thing" at the local level. This brings to mind a statement from a publication designed to serve candidates, *Campaign Insight*: "Politics is a much bigger business in the United States than it is given credit for. The number of elective offices in this country is slightly above the 522,000 mark. In even numbered years, there are as many as two million candidates for offices in the United States. In odd-numbered years, it settles down closer to the million mark."[43]

At the local level, contributions can decide who sells heavy road equipment, who gets the city or county light-bulb-replacement account, who does the government printing, and who provides computer facilities. This applies also to the purchase of insurance, office equipment, and the auto agent interested in providing local government police and other cars.

From years of experience, I know that at the local level it is easy to use hypocrisy to cover political contributions. The contributor and the local candidate are on a first-name basis. They belong to the same golf or bridge club, church, or political organization. Donations are often split using relatives, business associates, or employees to hide the actual contributor. This is especially true where there are statutory limits on contributions. In the 1983 campaign for governor of Maryland, most observers believe real estate developer Jerome D. Kay legally and properly circumvented the $10,000 individual limit on the size of a campaign contribution by splitting it between himself, his brother, and his wife.[44]

The so-called "local interests" are hard to categorize because the investors are anything but one monolithic group. For example, a candidate for sheriff would draw different political investors than a candidate for treasurer or mayor. In his book, *Who Shakes the Money Tree?*, George Thayer relates a time in Alameda County, California, when funeral directors found it profitable to contribute to a race for coroner. The result was that the coroner then appointed favored funeral directors as deputy coroners, which entitled them to be paid for every body they removed from the scene of death. Thayer, speaking in generalities, says: "This type of thing still goes on today not only in California, but in all states where these types of jobs are elective."[45]

Again, George Thayer observed, "In the City of New York, the H. J. Heinz catsup account runs more than $100,000 a year. Coincidentally, one member of the Heinz family makes sure he is listed each year on the mayor's list of contributors."[46]

Most residents agree that there should be industrial plants, shopping centers, high rise apartments, garbage dumps, and sports arenas. However, they argue that they should not be located in their neighborhoods. The wise developer wants officials who can withstand local opposition and approve controversial zoning.

For this reason, builders, contractors, and developers have political action committees, such as B.U.I.L.D., which seeks (among other things) modification or repeal of density regulations plus uniformity/simplification of building codes and safety regulations.

$ $ $ $ WARNING $ $ $ $

Today, campaign costs and contributions have soared beyond the wildest predictions. Though dollar amounts quoted throughout this book are historically correct and valuable as general percentage guidelines, dollar amounts more than two to four years old should not be depended upon for structuring campaign budgets.

Chapter 15

Selection, Direct Solicitation, and Seduction

> Before Huey Long, politicians may have been scoundrels, but they were always gentlemen.
> —*Time* magazine quoting Louisiana aristocrats, 1940[1]
>
> Seduction, defined as "The difference between rape and rapture."
> —*Playboy*[2]

The Mechanics

Now, let's turn our attention to the mechanics of asking for the campaign money. Hank Parkinson, in his book, *Winning Your Campaign*, says, "When all the elaborate plans and nebulous dreams have been exhausted, and the smoke has settled, do what one of Iowa's all-time top fundraisers, Thomas E. Murphy, advises: "The best way to get money is to ask for it!"[3]

As Thomas E. Murphy suggests, most personal fundraising efforts fall short not because the need is lacking or because there is poor accounting. They fall short because the candidates do not devote enough of their time and effort to planning and executing the task of raising the bucks. As Murphy puts it, "The more people you ask, the more money you're going to get. Take in hand your fundraising chairman, and the budget you've prepared, and start making the rounds of your top social and economic contacts. Then, start on his. When these two lists are exhausted, start knocking on the doors of potential contributors whom you feel should support your views."[4]

Direct solicitation is particularly effective late in the contest when the campaign is running out of money. At that point, most campaigns find it more profitable to simply resolicit those who have given rather than consider another fundraiser. It conserves volunteer effort desperately needed for other campaign chores and avoids costs that must come off the top for staging a dinner or some other event or sending off a direct mailing.

Potential contributors are divided roughly into two categories: the political investor and the contributor who gives for one of the many other reasons already explored. When soliciting the political investor, realists often follow the suggestion of investigative and political reporter for the Honolulu *Star Bulletin*, Toni Coffman: "Sit down and figure out where the leverage is. Then, do not abuse it, but certainly work it thoroughly."[5]

Pressure to make a political contribution can be and often is immoral, illegal, and dangerous. Leverage does not mean that solicitors break either the law or the contributors' arms. If the politician is an incumbent or the election favorite, the prospective contributor may feel the leverage, even though nothing is said. Leverage must be so subtle that it can honestly be said that all contributions are voluntary.

The best way to clarify this is by using the explanation of the man who was responsible for bringing together an informal group that helped Franklin Roosevelt win the presidential nomination in 1932. New York political boss Edward Flynn explained the effect of political contributions when he said, "They are used to cement friendships and to justify a more or less tacit expectation that, whenever possible, the donors' interest will be taken care of."[6]

Translated into action, this means businesses that operate by virtue of government franchises and those requiring permits or licenses usually contribute to the candidate likely to be in a position to exercise or influence decisions that affect them. When the governor of Maryland filed for re-election in 1973, the nursing homes contributed $7,800. Perhaps they hoped that state welfare payments would be high enough to eliminate carrying the losses they claimed to have suffered when handling state cases.[7]

This brings to mind a quip from a colorful wheeler dealer who served over twenty years in the Washington State Senate. On one hot spring morning Augie Mardesich walked by the rostrum in a new white suit. The Secretary of the Senate, Sid Snyder, who mentally compared him to Colonel Sanders of Kentucky Fried Chicken, quipped, "Good morning, Colonel." "Snyder," Mardesich said, wiggling his eyebrows, "There's one big difference. The colonel deals in chickens. I deal in pigeons."[8]

After the candidate has exhausted the political investors, it's all salesmanship. Most campaign solicitation starts with what investigative political reporter for the Honolulu *Star Bulletin* Tom Coffman calls "goodwill."[9] Solicitation succeeds when it puts potential donors in a position where they give not only when they have something to gain, but because they want to, they are flattered, or in some cases they find it embarrassing not to.

The Candidate Is the Best Fundraiser

In most cases, but not all, the person best able to put prospects in the giving frame of mind is the candidate. Drew Lewis is a man of varied political experience who served as treasurer and chief fundraiser for the Republican party of Pennsylvania. Then he filed for governor.

Lewis's campaign itinerary was carefully set to provide for six days of campaigning, with a seventh day spent personally concentrating on large contributors and organizing the other "nuts and bolts" of fundraising.[10] This facet has become so important that former finance chairman of the Democratic Party,

Joseph Cole, estimated that during the last twenty years of this century, "candidates spend up to half their time seeking campaign funds."[11]

In the 1974 campaign for Governor of California, this attention to fundraising was carried one step further. The winner, one-time Governor Jerry Brown, let money dominate his daily schedule. Reporters discovered that except for media events his appointments were mostly dinners with potential donors. Brown's campaign manager, Tom Quinn, said that during the 1974 primary 80 percent of Brown's time was allocated to fundraising. The remaining 20 percent went to traditional campaigning.[12]

It is considered best if a local peer introduces the candidate to the potential donor when they are not already on a first-name basis and asks for the help. For example, before the New York Presidential primary, I. Hershey Gold and his money-raisers had their candidate, U.S. Senator "Scoop" Jackson, stayed in a hotel suite for two days. At the same time Gold and his most able regional money-men took turns at the hotel-room phone bank, calling lists of possible contributors all over the United States. The typical conversation went roughly something like: "Lou, I'm here in New York with Senator Scoop Jackson, and he'd like to talk to you." Senator Jackson then took the phone, explained the seriousness of the situation, and asked Lou if he could help out.

This effort raised more than $300,000 because, as Susan Littwin commented, "It is hard for a dermatologist in Detroit, or a tool and die manufacturer in Akron, to say no to an old friend and a presidential contender."[13]

I. Hershey Gold also organized "nineteen parlor meetings and netted $855,000" on behalf of Jackson's presidential candidacy.[14] Such intimate dinners were of two types: those paid for in advance and those in which the candidate simply gambled that once the contributors were exposed they would be persuaded to leave a substantial check. Typically, there are thirty or forty guests that may include a suburban dentist, real estate broker, accountant, etc., whose previous exchanges with politicians have been as TV viewers. They are sold an aura of exclusiveness over a few drinks, a chance to meet and chat with the candidate and to socialize with other well-heeled supporters.

After a short talk, followed by an open question and answer period and a "thank you," supporters are asked to donate time and money. When he was running for President, Senator Jackson took in $3,000 to $4,000 at a typical party. But the relationship had only begun. The donors were "targeted" with a barrage of follow-up phone calls and letters seeking more contributions, which more than doubled the original take.[15]

Occasionally, the demands of a national race make it impossible for the candidate to attend the intimate party. The local elite will have to be satisfied with a substitute. I. Hershey Gold solved this problem by having his presidential candidate, Senator Jackson, stay in Washington and talk to his cocktail party supporters over a two-way telephone public-address hookup. In his 1968 large-gift fund drive, President Nixon used closed-circuit television to communicate with guests at twenty-two dinners held on a single day.[16]

Where the candidate is running for a less-important position, he or she might try an old-fashioned pledge party. This differs slightly from I. Hershey Gold's "parlor meetings," in that it does not depend upon those who want a little flattery. The invitees are friends, ideological sympathizers, and political investors who expect to give and that their pledges will be made in front of the other guests.

However, pledge parties are parlor parties in that they start by inviting the potential contributor to a free event, hoping that once he or she has broken bread or had a drink with a candidate, they will contribute. This technique works best when the candidate has affluent friends, dedicated peers, or if his or her views correspond with the contributor's strong ideological loyalty.

When an outspoken liberal, Judge Norm Ackley, filed for Congress, his finance committee persuaded a very prominent supporter to lend his name and house for such a party. Invitations were sent to people who, it was theorized, shared the candidate's liberal persuasion. There was a careful follow-up by both telephone and in-person contact to assure attendance. When the guests arrived, there were talks by the campaign manager and the candidate. Then the finance chairman told the group that unless they contributed, the campaign would not get off the ground. As the result of a carefully planned suggestion, they went around the room and asked each potential contributor for a pledge. Again by advance arrangement, this started with a guest who pledged a sizable amount. When they finished, $30,000 had been pledged.

Setting Up the Finance Committee

Although candidates may be the best fundraisers, in most campaigns they can't afford to spend all of their time in search of campaign dollars, rather than votes. With this in mind, a veteran of many campaigns, as both finance chairman and campaign manager, Michael S. Berman says, "Fund raising should be a full-time activity for someone in the campaign and that person should not be given responsibility for door belling, direct mail, or some of the other activities."[17]

Ideally, that person is prominent, aggressive, and clearly understands the necessity of getting the job done. If a person with these qualifications is not available, the candidate may want to split the job, using as figurehead a person with a good reputation. With or without the title, there should be someone with energy, time, good reputation, and lots of gall to run the money-raising show. This may mean recruiting a person with more time who is given the task of organizing and/or making the contacts.

The Finance Committee

Usually, the "fundraiser" works through a finance committee. At its first meeting, a treasurer should be selected to set up the bank account and a plan for a bookkeeping system, as the laws require a single bank account and accounting and control system. The law in most jurisdictions makes the candidate responsible for honest records of the campaign's financial activities and the debt itself. It is necessary that the committee follow cash flow and report to the appropriate state or federal disclosure agency, so it helps if the treasurer is a lawyer, accountant, or banker. That way, his or her secretary can spend, say, an hour a day on the books.

As a part of the first meeting, the committee should decide the time and how often they will meet. Then usually the chairman or coordinator is made responsibile for calling and reminding each member of the meeting. Organizational meetings are best scheduled at breakfast-time, 7:00 to 9:00 a.m., or in the late afternoon. The most successful volunteer fund solicitors are busy, successful people from business and the professions, and they object to late, after-dinner meetings.

After setting fundraising goals, the chairman, the candidate, or the campaign manager should lead the discussion of the nuts and bolts of direct solicitation. As Henry Walther, Director of Membership Services for the National Right to Work Committee, reminds us, "You have to not only look at the number of responses, but the dollars," meaning that the campaign must also consider how much each of those who responded gave. For instance, if the goal is $25,000, the entire amount could be financed by two pledges of $12,500 each or the money could come from seventeen $1,500 contributors. Most campaigns will be financed by a few large and a number of small contributors.[18]

During finance committee meetings, major sources should be identified, discussed, and categorized according to potential. After the committee determines a class, individual, group, or PAC they want to approach for a contribution, they should identify the peers of the persons or group at the top. During this process, the finance committee should be on the lookout for supportive peers with the contacts. These should be asked to join the finance committee.

The best fundraisers socialize in the board room or country club—men such as Max Fisher, a legendary millionaire who raised money among the Jews; Willard Marriott, a Mormon with access to other Mormons; and J. Clifford Folger, who seemed to specialize in Republican, White, Anglo-Saxon Protestant contributors.[19]

Most fundraising is not at this level. A few people who do fundraising are experienced with local contacts, but most are enthusiastic volunteers with little or no experience. If the candidate is a Republican, the committee might seek out a local activist, say the owner of the local hardware store, and persuade him or her to put the arm on fellow Chamber of Commerce club members. If the candidate is a Democrat, the candidate might recruit the union activist who can persuade those in his or her circle to contribute, as well as persuade the union to remember the candidate when they distribute their PAC money.

Even a few unlikely, untrained fundraisers can be successful. For example, a high school government class was split into groups, which were given the assignment to design their own version of political ads supporting a real candidate. One of the groups got so enthusiastic, they decided to print their ad. They collected $5.00 apiece from their friends, whom they asked to be sponsors. After the election, the class surveyed those who contributed. They found that though most contributors had never donated to a political campaign before, once they contributed $5.00 and lent their names they too got caught up in the contest. Not only did they vote, but most of them persuaded their families and friends to join them.

Sources

After discussing sources, fundraising goals and how the committee intends to meet their goals, the fundraising committee should have some idea of what kind of support the candidate can expect. When the names of key prospects are decided on, their addresses and phone numbers are recorded on cards. The prospects are then matched with a solicitor who, hopefully, knows them on a first-name basis.

How much should the candidate ask for? Categorizing the potential contribution becomes a team effort in most campaigns; there is input from the finance committee, the candidate, and the campaign manager. The trick is to get the maximum contribution while using caution not to ask for so much that the potential giver is turned off. One technique uses five stars—for the best giver (highest contributor or top two), four-star giver (very large, generous), three-star (good size, medium giver), two-star (average to modest), and one star (small).

If a large donation is contemplated, the contributor should be researched and the solicitor briefed as to the contributor's past history of giving and a feeling for his or her capacity to give. Another reason for getting the best information the candidate has available is that, when balancing a number of different circumstances, one needs to determine whether or not the prospect will be asked to give again at a later date.

The Pitch

The solicitors or the candidate should do more than tell the prospect how important their contribution is to the total effort. They should be prepared to answer some tough questions, one of which is a cardinal rule of fundraising—have you given yourself?

When dealing with big investors who handle large sums of money, the solicitor will frequently find that the "fat cats" act like bankers. They want to evaluate the candidate's chances. The candidate or finance chairman should be prepared with a scenario that shows the candidate winning. For example, they point to the polls if they are favorable. If the polls are bad, he or she is ready with reasons why they are inaccurate or reasons for believing public opinion will change before election day.

The big investor may also wait to preview the campaign budget to see how money is being spent. For such a contributor, I suggest using a pocket-size card outlining some of the actual campaign costs for campaign materials that must be paid in advance.

The card might look something like that shown in Figure 2-11.

If more detail is desired, the card might also show the actual cost of printing and mailing brochures or campaign letters to the district (even when volunteers are used to stamp, address, and stuff the envelopes). It might detail the cost of materials to be used in doorbelling and the number of volunteers it will take to reach each home.

All of these functions can be combined in a clever brochure, such as the one circulated by a very energetic ex-Mayor, Mike Parker, of Tacoma, Washington. He made up a 16-page "Investment Portfolio, Mike Parker for Congress," which he introduced with the words, "The following is the case for investing in Mike Parker's Campaign for Congressman. . . ."

The brochure included reproductions of letters supporting his candidacy that he had received from labor and business. The prospectus featured the results of an opinion poll that found him leading his closest opposition. Parker displayed his party credentials by pointing out that he had been elected to three terms as Chairman of the State Democratic Platform Committee. Parker presented his campaign forecast:

- A seven-day-a-week headquarters,
- A phone bank designed to reach every registered voter in the district,
- A volunteer direct-mail and letter-writing kit,
- A doorbell program designed to reach 86 percent of the homes in the district,
- A plan to put up 16,800 signs,
- A handout of 50,000 balloons and 14,000 bumper stickers, and
- A professional mailing program to cover the entire district.

Price per column inch for newspaper ads_____: One 2x5 in each newspaper_____, one quarter-page ad in each newspaper__
Cost per radio spot_____: Number times_____, number planned_____
Cost per TV spot_____, number times_____, number planned_____
Brochures_____
Bumper strips_____
Letters to voters_____

Your contribution will help us elect _____ by giving [him, her] the materials to put on a campaign of which we can all be proud.

Fig. 2-11. Sample pocket-sized card outlining materials costs.

Finally, using a campaign flow-chart, Parker described and explained how he intended to orchestrate the campaign so that it would peak on election day.[20]

A wise finance chairman protects the candidate by instructing those soliciting campaign funds not to use overt pressure when talking to prospective contributors. Solicitors should be warned in advance to be prepared to retreat rather than pressure opinionated people, including those who may refuse to contribute because they are unhappy with the candidate. Pressure can create a disaster if the unhappy person reports it to the press, the public disclosure commission, or criminal authorities.

If, before making his or her contribution, the donor pressures for a commitment on a pending issue, the solicitor should answer that the money will be appreciated, but never that the money will influence the candidate's acts as a elected official.

The pressured solicitor might tell the story of John M. King, who in 1968 gave Nixon $250,000 for his presidential campaign. Even this sizable contribution did not protect King when he was later charged by the Internal Revenue Service, which slapped tax liens totaling more than $5 million on his property.[21]

Instructions for Collecting Campaign Funds

Checks should be made out to: C. P. Dollar, Treasurer, or John Candidate for Congress Committee.

Accept all checks made out from individuals in federal campaigns. Do not accept checks made out from a corporation. (Look at local law. In some states this is not necessary in state and local races.)

Personal contact is best. If impossible, phone or mail. Just "ask 'em." You'll be surprised at the number of people who want to be asked to contribute.

What to ask for. Have a definite amount in mind or something in lieu thereof. If the contributor does not want to give money, perhaps he or she would be willing to give any of the following: stamps, postcards, signs, newspaper ads, radio and/or television time, billboards—or help putting up signs or passing out cards, envelopes, or office supplies or might provide printing, secretarial or clerical help.

Get funds early; it is easier. Now is the time to start.

Record of contribution. Please help us keep an accurate list of those who contribute. Merely list on the enclosed form and mail to C. P. Dollar, Central City. He will detach the receipt at the bottom of the form and return it to you.

All individuals, including federal employees, can lawfully contribute to a political campaign.

Fig. 2-12. *Let's Talk About Running for Office*, National Association of Manufacturers, 1967, p. 45.

If the solicitor is the prospect's peer and in the same line of business, they can use leverage to explain why it is in the contributor's best interest to give. For example, assume during a congressional campaign that the contribution is being solicited from a private pilot. The solicitor for an incumbent might be armed with arithmetic attesting to the benefit provided by the U.S. Government. In the statistical abstract headed, "Subsidy Programs of the Federal Government," it was reported that the federal government spent about $160 million annually to service private and business aircraft. Only four percent of this money came from aviation and gas taxes. Calculated per capita, those who operate private planes received about $5,000 per plane per year subsidy from the taxpayer.[22]

Solicitors are hesitant to ask for money unless they have some sort of a standard approach. As a model, the finance chairman might use the instructions from the National Association of Manufacturers shown in Figure 2-12.

The kit also should include some simple forms, tickets, letters, telephone instructions, etc. For an example, see the one published by the National Association of Manufacturers shown in Figure 2-13.

Beyond general instructions, the solicitor should be informed that he or she is the only individual designated to collect funds from that prospect.

It is wise not to overburden solicitors. At first they should be given a limited number of prospects and instructions that they are expected to report at the next meeting. If the solicitor does not report, contact should be made. If the solicitor does not intend to pursue the prospects, the name list should be given to someone else.

See the following nutshell for a summary of fundraising activities.

Recognizing and Encouraging the Financial Soldiers

Unfortunately, the solicitation of funds is one area in which campaign workers do not share the camaraderie that welds workers together, so it is not surprising that members of the finance committee sometimes revolt or lose interest. While it is not realistic to let them control the campaign strategy or organization, if they want to be on the inside, they can be encouraged to join the planning with those who work on a sign crew or run a political rally, coffee hour, etc. Fortunately, most only want attention, not control. To satisfy this desire, the candidate and a finance chairman should spend time and effort encouraging them doing anything within reason to keep their spirits and interest high. This can take the form of almost daily contact by baiting, cajoling, and gentle prodding with lunches, telephone calls, person-to-person talks, and thank-yous.

No-Nos

Both the candidate and the solicitor should be alert to the fact that fundraising is subject to federal and state laws. For example, while laws place no limit, current federal law prohibits the solicitation of contributions in federal elections from people who have a contract with the United States or a matter pending before a federal regulatory agency. Non-resident foreign nationals may make a contribution to most local and state candidates, but they cannot give to one running for federal office unless the alien is a permanent resident of the United States; then they can contribute on the same basis as citizens.[23]

Make Checks Payable to: "SMITH FOR CONGRESS COMMITTEE"

PLEASE PRINT OR TYPE

Name of (County or Designated Area)

Name of Contributor (Print)	Address (Print in Full)	Amount

SEND TO: A. P. Henry, Treasurer
              Center City

Signature of Sender

Address

Date

- -

R E C E I P T

I hereby acknowledge receipt of the sum of $_____ from _____

County as contributions to the Smith for Congress Committee sent in by _____

A. P. Henry, Treasurer
Smith for Congress Committee

Fig. 2-13. *Let's Talk About Running for Office*, National Association of Manufacturers, 1967, p. 44.

Fundraising Specifics

Note: The candidate one-on-one is the best fundraiser; his or her phone call is second best.

Budget/Legal Requirements
Finance chair.
Treasurer.
Fundraising budget.
Required reports for disclosure commissions.

Preliminary
Make calendar of fundraising activities/events.
Recruit committee members.
Decide who will do asking (candidate, finance chair, or campaign chair) & how fundraising is to be carried out: One-on-one in person, one-on-one by telephone, direct mail
Open bank account (two signatures).
Set up record-keeping system.
File with state and other authorities as required.
Prepare a preliminary budget.
Decide on startup amount needed.
Identify key dates money needed.

Identify Contributors
Major individual & organizational donors
In-kind donors: services, printing, signs, other

Prioritize
Major or minor effort with (a) individual contributors, (b) organizations, PACs?
Dollar limit on organization contributions?
Start early; tie down dates.
Which appeals to use with: individuals, organizations.
Is candidate to appeal by direct mail? To which groups?

Materials
Candidate fact sheets, brochures
Pledge/endorsement/volunteer cards, envelopes
Campaign stationery
Rubber stamp with committee name & address
Potential contributor letters
Direct mail materials
Door prizes

Activities List
Personal contacts by candidate, committee members
Events (e.g., receptions, luncheons, dinners, coffees)
Auctions, dances, garage sales

★ ★ ★ ★ ★ **In A Nutshell** ★ ★ ★ ★ ★

A wise candidate or finance chair consults with someone who is familiar with the law and how it applies to a campaign finance and then follows the laws. (A few more details are found in Part 8.)

If a request from a contributor for commitment on an issue comes after the contribution has been made, most candidates politely ignore the request and send the contributor a noncommittal thank you note. If the contribution is large, or the individual or organization is politically important, the candidate should try to satisfy the contributor's desire for recognition with a personal telephone call or a luncheon.

If, after listening to the donor explain his position, the candidate can't honestly support the contributor's cause or he or she waffles, the candidate should return the money. If, on the other hand, what the contributor wants is consistent with the candidate's conscience, then the candidate should still refuse a private commitment based on the contribution, but say that, quite aside from the money, he or she favors the contributor's position.

What happens when a candidate takes money and ignores the donors' pleas and pressures once elected? Most donors don't want publicity, so those in the business of influencing governmental decisions will not even remind the candidate of the contribution, but will probably refuse to contribute to the next campaign. Of course, there is always a chance that, once elected, the official will be attacked publicly as an ingrate. The simplest answer is that the candidate was not then, nor is now committed, and can still return the contribution.

As an alternative, the candidate might do what United States Senator Richard Schweiker did when a wealthy Pennsylvania contributor pressured him to vote to confirm President Nixon's nominee for a United States Supreme Court Justice. The contributor said, "Damn it, I gave you $10,000 for your campaign [1968 dollars]." Schweiker's reply was reported to have been, "Look, I bought $10,000 worth of your stock, but I don't tell you how to run your business."[24]

$ $ $ $ WARNING $ $ $ $

Today, campaign costs and contributions have soared beyond the wildest predictions. Though dollar amounts quoted throughout this book are historically correct and valuable as general percentage guidelines, dollar amounts more than two to four years old should not be depended upon for structuring campaign budgets.

Chapter 16

Salesmanship . . . Via Direct Mail

> Some people have their names perpetuated in stone or cast in bronze, but most of us are perpetuated on mailing lists.[1]

The Basic Concept

We live in a society where the businessman opens his mail almost as soon as it arrives. The private resident is more than a little interested in what the postman leaves behind on his daily trip, so the wise candidate uses direct mail to collect political funds.

First of all, though, direct mailing is more than a device to raise money. In most cases, it's real political thrust is to gather votes. Sometimes the two functions are intermingled. The Rhode Island Biden for United States Senate campaign, New Jersey's Bryne for Governor campaign, and the Michigan Vander Veen for Congress campaigns all had something in common. Advertising specialist Ekeliel Payne used a solicitation letter and a return envelope attached to a campaign tabloid. Although they didn't raise enough to finance its mass distribution, they did raise a significant sum.[2]

The same thing can be done with a campaign letter. "I was really surprised that it brought in about $6,000.00," reflected Majority Whip of the U.S. House, Congressman Tom Foley, when commenting on the results of his district-wide announcement letter. He used a standard letter with a card enclosed asking for workers and other campaign help. It also told of the cost of campaigning, asking for a dollar or more to help cover the cost of mailing.[3]

The Candidate's Own List

Those who have raised money via direct mail have a saying: "No list out-performs the candidate's own," which means that the top prospects are friends and supporters. A good example of this featured King County Councilwoman Bernice Stern. When she first filed for office, she sent out formal announcements titled, "You're not invited to a Fund Raising Cocktail Party." These were personally addressed to prominent members of her party, to her bowling team, and to local members of the Seattle branch of the National Council of Jewish Women, of which she had been president. The announcement raised $9,000.[4]

Mrs. Stern's percentage of returns was phenomenal, a lot better than that of professional fundraisers. This was due, at least in part, to her personal charm, her wide range of affluent friends, and to the fact that some of them took this opportunity to pay her back for all the times over the many years she had contributed large sums to other worthy causes.

Of coures, Mrs. Stern did not have to depend on mail contributions to finance her entire campaign. There are several reasons a direct mail fundraising campaign should not be expected to raise all the necessary campaign funds. The most common is that the prospect list isn't large enough to cover the enormous up-front costs of a mail campaign, which include printing, postage, and the cost of the mailing list plus original design, typesetting, sorting, stuffing, and business reply envelopes.

The Ideological List

How does the candidate go beyond the candidate's friends and acquaintances? Let's look at the plight of U.S. Senator George McGovern when he was nominated for president in 1972. At the time McGovern's party, the Democrats, were both broke and desperate, and he was written off by virtually all the known political investors, who were supporting President Richard Nixon. On the plus side, he had an almost fanatical following among the young, those who opposed the Vietnam War, and others who leaned mildly to the political left.

McGovern took his problem to one of the largest direct mail firms in the world, Rapp, Rollings, Stone and Alder of New York. Together they decided to try mass mail fundraising. First, they borrowed or rented lists of those who shared McGovern's outlook and added them to the donor lists the party already had. Using these names, they managed to finance a respectable campaign.[5]

A second, but less effective, alternative is to use computers to select prospects from city directories, driver license files, or telephone books—or use census information, which allows the experts to do imaginative things. For example, the candidate can direct personal letters to areas where older individuals live in relatively wealthy neighborhoods in the hope that, since their children have completed college, those with motivation have money to give.[6] This technique has been used and has worked, but only in a presidential campaign or in one where there is an ideological crusade. Most candidates find they can only raise big money if an issue group considers leadership essential.

A right-wing candidate might work through organizations that want to protect the right to own handguns, those who promote the liberty amendment, or those who oppose abortion. Liberals might find a rich vein in members of organizations that espouse the protection of civil liberties, the advocates of gay rights, Common Cause, or the Equal Rights Amendment.[7] When working single-issue groups, candidates should not expect to get the organizations' mailing lists, but may persuade the organization to mail the candidate's appeal to their membership list if the campaign agrees to pay the costs.

The Direct Mail Pros

Direct mail fundraising experience in the presidential campaigns of Senator Goldwater, Senator McGovern, and George Wallace have led adventuresome individuals to make political mail fundraising a commercial enterprise. To do this, these ideological evangelists set up organizations supporting views that are either single-issue partisan or strongly favor the political left or right.

In 1982, the top ten money-raisers were the National Committee for an Effective Congress, Dallas Energy Political Action Committee (DALENPAC), National Conservative Political Action Committee, Americans for Constitutional Action (ACA), Citizens for the Republic, Louisiana Energy National Political Action Committee, Business Industry Political Action Committee, HOUPAC, and Citizens Concerned for the National Interest.[8]

Among those of liberal persuasion is Roger Craver, who gained experience raising money for Common Cause and has since formed his own firm, which claims to have a mailing list of about five million politically liberal donors.[9]

On the other side of the political spectrum, we find the "Wizard of the Right," Richard Viguerie. He first gained national experience when he raised millions for Governor Wallace's presidential campaign. Today this millionaire boasts of having the largest conservative mailing lists in the country.[10]

These professional fundraisers maintain an ongoing list of conservative or liberal contributors and are able to choose from among hungry candidates. Typically they ask the candidate or their campaign organization if they can advance the substantial sums necessary to cover up-front costs. Before they become serious, they measure the candidate's chances and then screen the candidate's ideology to make sure it is in sync with their contributors.

If John or Mary Candidate passes these tests, they may either rent the professional's list for so much per name, or the fundraiser may accept them as a client. When they do, most want payment of expenses plus a flat fee off the top of whatever is raised. Some insist on the right to select the printer and data processing facilities, which they own or from which they have arranged a rebate. Unless there is a prior arrangement to the contrary, the professional adds the candidate's personal donor list to the prospects they use in other campaigns.

However, there are exceptions. Richard Viguerie, for example, raises money for candidates who sympathize with his right-wing philosophy, but his services are not for sale in the usual sense. Instead he chooses his candidates like his causes. When he makes a choice he takes all of the risks, then splits the money raised.[11]

Quite aside from their sincerity and financial integrity, these money raisers are, to say the least, controversial. Candidates who place themselves in their hands subject themselves to potential political attack from those who claim their views are the same as that of their backers.

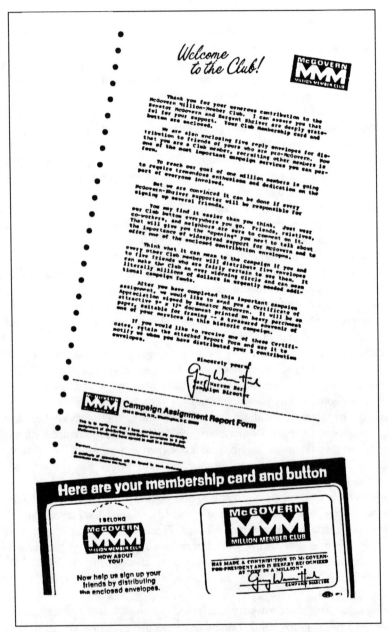

Fig. 2-14. Tom Collins, "The Political Battle in the Mail: McGovern v. Nixon," *Direct Marketing*, November 1982, p. 28.

The Direct Mail Package

Soliciting political funds is done with a package that includes a list of names and addresses, a letter exhorting those who contribute, a pledge form or card, and a reply envelope. As is true with any fundraising appeal, success or failure depends on the psychological impact of a number of related factors. At the outset, it is best to hire a professional to write copy. However, in most campaigns, it is done by an amateur. Thomas Collins sets out the following principles of good copy, which I've annotated:

Timeliness. The copy writer should be on the lookout for headline issues because political fundraisers find it pays to ride a crest of feeling. For example, this was the opening statement taken from a 1972 letter sent by Congressman Jerry Waldie to known liberals to solicit funds: "You will remember me as a Congressman and as author of the resolution to impeach Richard Nixon."[12]

Appreciation. The letter should give the donor sincere appreciation. The writer emphasizes the importance of the donor and the value of the contribution.

Cultivation. "Give them appreciation and information," says Thomas Collins. He continues by saying, "Treat your donors right and they'll treat you right." One method is to have an appropriate letterhead, good copy and artwork, along with any other device/gimmick which will make the contributor open his or her purse.

Urgency. Stress the importance of sending money now, instead of next week or next month. To do this the fundraising letter should tie in the need for funds with the approach of specific campaign events. Some fundraisers send Western Union Mailgrams to the donor list to achieve this sense of urgency.

Authenticity. The effectiveness of the package depends on the contributor's reaction to an appeal letter, so the appeal should be or appear to be a real letter, not simply a piece of political literature. One way this is done is by individually typing or renting printers capable of producing high-quality personal letters. Speaking to this point, Carl Bender follows what is almost the mailing industry's Holy Writ, saying, "Personalize and flatter the contributor's ego."[13]

Authority. The copywriters should take the position of the recipient and ask "Who is writing me? Is it someone I respect and care about and will listen to? If the letter is not signed by the candidate, then use the prominent sponsors and list their names on the letterhead. Typically, the letter is signed by a person of substance, a leader with a committed following, or a banker with a reputation for integrity and care in handling money.

Length. As Abraham Lincoln once said, "Like legs, it should be long enough to reach the ground." A fundraising letter is aimed at committed people. There is no hard rule governing the length of copy, but don't attempt to make it short.

Conviction. The copy should have a sincere ring.

Importance. The letter should give the potential donor assurance that a contribution will make a difference. Conviction and importance is best expressed where views are polarized and the contributor can be persuaded to react against someone the solicitor can identify as a common enemy.

Hope. Here the potential donor is given reason to believe the contribution will not be wasted and that, with help, the campaign will be successful.

Concreteness. To build a solid foundation for claims and to provide a specific campaign use for contributions, the copy should use concrete facts. In 1973, there was a confrontation in California between the Western Growers' Association and United Farm Workers. The Republican nominee for governor, Houston Flournoy, expected no support from Cesar Chavez and his United Farm Workers. He created an "Agriculture for Flournoy Committee," which was headed by cattle rancher Wes Sawyer. Sawyer sent letters addressed to dairymen and farmers who opposed Chavez that combined conviction, importance, hope, and concreteness.

First he claimed that Mr. Flournoy's opponent, Jerry Brown, "had consistently supported the Cesar Chavez movement. . . ." Later he said, "We are fighting for our way of life, for the future of our families, and for the future of agriculture." Then he appealed for television time, which was needed then to ensure a victory on election day. The letter worked. Flourney wound up with more than $100,000 from agribusiness interests.

Involvement. Thomas Collins advocated giving donors something to do—a monthly installment coupon book, a phonograph record they could play for friends, a special pin to wear, or an acknowledgement letter with a "get a friend form" enclosed.[14]

If the candidate is seeking a state or local office in one of the nineteen states that do not prohibit corporate contributions, it is important that the candidates' solicitors or direct-mail effort say so. In a letter Sawyer wrote to California ranchers on behalf of the Republican nominee for governor, he stated, "Your contribution of $50, $100, or more would be a tremendous help and greatly appreciated." This appeal contained the reminder, "Corporate checks are acceptable under California law."[15]

The McGovern for President campaign used a fundraising package even more specific designed for contributors of lesser means. It attempted to persuade contributors to pledge at least 10 dollars a month in four allotment checks. The fundraising package included check forms that the fundraisers hoped would be signed and returned. The checks were post-dated and potential donors were assured that the checks would not be cashed until the due dates shown on their faces—for example, August 1, September 1, October 1, and November 1.[16]

Ideology, Urgency, and Targeting

Early in the 1976 presidential campaign the Democratic front-runner was U.S. Senator Scoop Jackson, a solid, reasonable, middle-of-the-roader. His organization hired Morris Dees, one of Senator McGovern's direct-mail geniuses of four

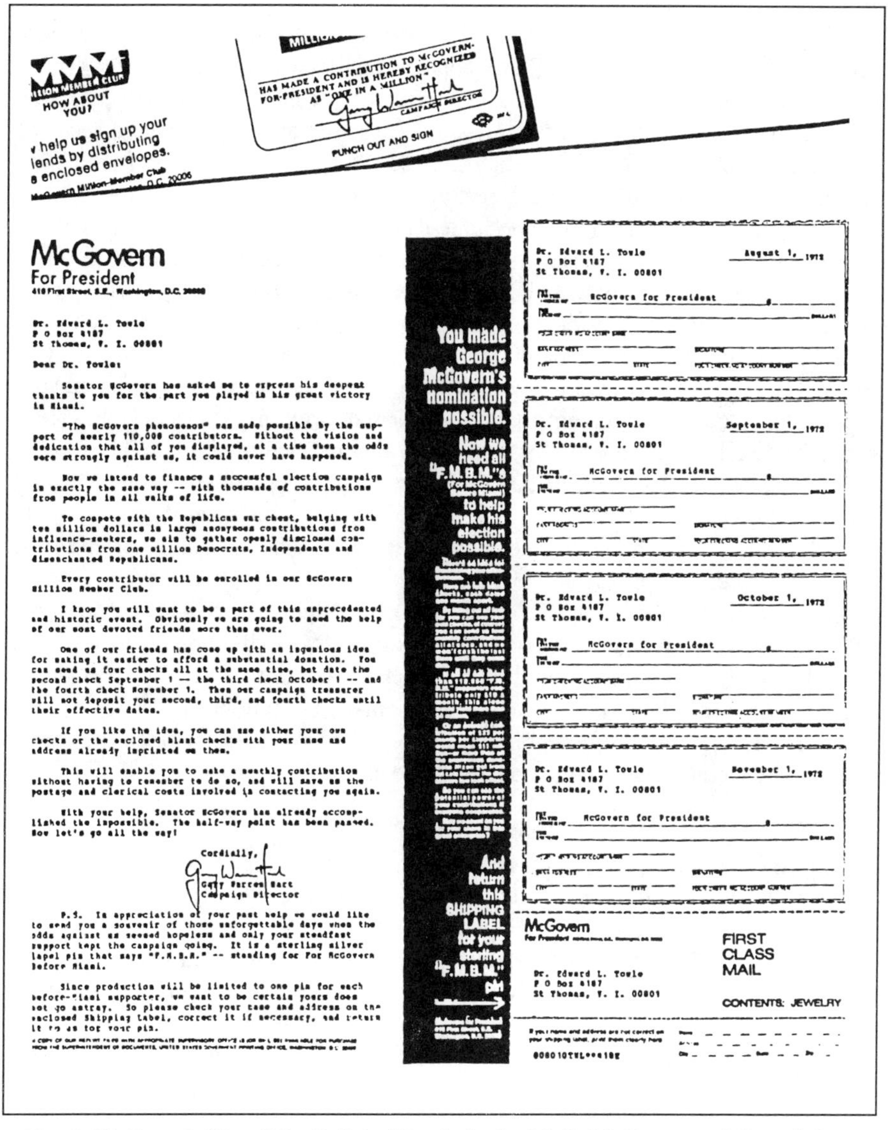

Fig. 2-15. Tom Collins, "The Political Battle in the Mail: McGovern v. Nixon," *Direct Marketing*, November 1982, p. 28.

years before. Dees and Jackson were both disappointed when the initial mailing costs of paper, postage, and printing came to $431,000 and the amount raised was $600,000, in spite of the fact that he was a front runner.[17]

Scoop Jackson's experience is cited by direct mail fundraisers to prove that historically it takes an emotional and controversial cause or candidate to turn on most mail contributors. Although Jackson ran in presidential primaries, he was never actually nominated. For this reason, he was not able to generate a sense of urgency, which Tom Collins, who handled Senator McGovern's fundraising campaign in 1972 noted is strongest just before the presidential election.

Those most successful in raising huge sums by mail have found that the bulk of their contributors are dissatisfied with so-called middle-of-the-road political figures. For example, when U.S. Senator Barry Goldwater, a committed conservative, ran for President of the United States, his campaign activated 650,000 individuals, about 560,000 contributing $1,000 or less. Goldwater was the first presidential candidate to employ direct mail extensively as a fundraising device. His late surge of contributions surprised everyone. Indeed Goldwater's strategists were so unprepared for this money that by the time it materialized they had actually canceled much of his television advertising, something they would not have done had they been able to accurately anticipate the last-minute contributions.[18] Though Goldwater raised one and a half times as much in direct mail funds as the Democrats, he lost the election.[19]

Of course, there are unusual circumstances. Highly motivated contributors often choose a bland alternative as the lesser of two evils, hoping to defeat a candidate with whom they strongly disagree. For example, nominally Democratic contributors sent donations to anti-Viet Nam-war Republicans such as U.S. Senators Mark Hatfield of Oregon and Charles Percy of Illinois, when they were opposed by Democrats who took a harder line on the Vietnam War.[20]

Follow-Up

One of the principle figures in direct-mail advertising, Carl Bender, put it bluntly, "In most cases, the original letter is designed to identify the contributors. Early contributions do little more than pay the costs of computer time, printing, and postage." They do, however, identify potential contributors. "But to make them worth the cost of finding, they must be mailed often enough to establish an almost personal relationship." This is follow-up. Professional fundraiser Bruce Eberle calls that relationship the "in-house phase," which he describes as a phase ". . . when costs of going back and asking previous contributors, raises $2 or $3 for every $1 of costs."[21]

Sample Letter

Few solicitation letters embody all the qualities of conviction, importance, hope, concreteness, etc. But one comes close. It was written some years ago on behalf of a man who since that time has achieved notoriety as a major Watergate figure. Unlike the other defendants, he earned both condemnation and grudging respect when he served five and a half years in prison and refused to implicate others in his misdeeds. Although he is remembered for his silence, there was a time when Gordon Liddy did a lot of talking. In 1967 he asked the people of Poughkeepsie, New York, to send him to Congress. At that time, he used the kick-off letter signed by his campaign treasurer shown in Figure 2-16.

Test Market the Appeal

All professional fundraisers say that they design more than one direct-mail package and test them on small samples of the contributing public. Democratic nominee for President, U.S. Senator George McGovern, followed this procedure. In his 1972 direct-mail fundraising campaign, several direct-mail packages were drafted and assembled. Each package consisted of a letter, a coupon, an eye-catching envelope, and some copy. Before Tom Collins decided on the letter he finally used, each version was mailed to randomly selected samples of from 2 to 5 percent of the total mailing list. The fundraising results were carefully monitored and the package that received the best response became the choice.[22]

One Last Comment

The candidate should guard last-minute campaign mail about to be sent out because if anything happens to destroy it the campaign can't duplicate it overnight. To illustrate, here's the story of a race for State Senator that took place in Spokane, Washington, during the Eisenhower election year of 1954.

Just five days before election day, a six-foot-tall, middle-aged, pot-bellied man with a cigar in his mouth, an "I Like Ike" button on his hat, and a "Vote Straight GOP" bumper sticker on his truck banged at the locked door of headquarters of a Republican candidate for State Senator. The elderly lady volunteer in charge seemed a little confused when he said, "I'm from Republican headquarters to pick up the mail." She stood aside as he proceeded with a burglar's gall to take full charge of a mountain of letters that were addressed, packaged, and held for a last-minute appeal. He loaded approximately 70,000 pieces of hand-addressed mail into his pickup truck and left. The lady in charge phoned her candidate, who then called Republican headquarters. They said they did not have the mail and had not given instructions to pick it up. The frantic candidate was beside himself. The party was furious, but that was the last anyone ever heard of the mail. And the candidate lost the election.

LIDDY TO CONGRESS Committee

35 Market Street . Poughkeepsie, New York 12601 . Telephone: 452-2540

Chairman
John P. O'Shea, Jr.

Treasurer
Vincent J. Cuccia

Public Relations Director
Raymond W. Tyson, Jr.

Research Director
Miss Carolyn R. Dexter, PhD.

Adviser on Education
Richard C. Kuralt

Chief Counsel
Peter L. Maroulis

COMMITTEE
James E. Carroll
Mrs. Joseph Conley
Mrs. Helen Crooksten
Hon. Joe E. Daniels
Mr. & Mrs. William S. DuBois
Mr. & Mrs. William H. Fissell, Jr.
Paul C. Carrell, M.D.
Mr. & Mrs. Paul H. Goldberg
Mrs. Joyce Greber
William Hanson
Carl Hildebrand
Anthony A. Ingoglia
A.D. Robert Jones
E. Ralph Kulseng
Mr. & Mrs. John C. Luber
Mr. & Mrs. Theodore Overbagh
Rev. Armand Padula, S.T.D.
Miss Ann Purcell
Miss Loretta Purcell
Mr. & Mrs. William A. Reed
Mrs. Duane Rooney
Geriaco M. Serino
Dayton R. Stemple, Jr.
Miss Margaret Toomey
Robert Trotta
Mrs. Ruth P. Wildman
(partial listing)

Fellow Republican:

How much did you pay in taxes last year? $1,000? $2,000? $5,000? More?

Most Americans paid <u>nearly 1/3 of their income</u> in taxes to cover the spiraling costs of government. Now, President Johnson wants to add a 10% "surtax" on top of the already staggering Federal income tax.

Let me ask you another question: "<u>How much have you contributed to help candidates who will work to lower your taxes?</u>"

Have you considered that such a contribution would be an investment that could pay high dividends . . . for you, your family, and every other American taxpayer?

I ask you this because there is a candidate for Congress in New York's 28th District <u>who feels strongly that both government taxes and spending must be cut</u> . . . that our military commitments must require the Federal government to cut back on the non-essentials.

<u>He's Gordon Liddy.</u>

Gordon Liddy is, today, Assistant District Attorney in Dutchess County. The remarkable work that he has done to curb the peddling of dope and LSD has been well-reported by the newspapers . . . his real interest in frugal and clean government is not be taken lightly.

Gordon told me recently:

"Vince, I am honestly convinced that the Johnson Administration's proposed 10% surtax clearly points out what I've been saying all along. The Democratic Party in control there in Washington has a cynical disregard for the hard-working, tax-paying American who simply lives an honest and "unprotesting" life. <u>These are the people who pay the bills but get the short end of the stick . . . everytime.</u>"

Today, almost <u>one out of every three</u> dollars you and I earn is taken to support government through taxes. Income taxes . . . property taxes . . . excise and sales taxes . . . inheritance taxes . . . gasoline taxes . . . cigarette and liquor taxes . . . gift taxes . . . <u>And now the President wants to TAX TAXES!</u>

WHERE WILL IT END?

Fig. 2-16. Lynn Mueller, "Political Direct Mail Can Be Useful Candidate Tool," *Direct Marketing*, February 1971, p. 31.

In 1966, the Democrats won this District with a very narrow 50.3% of the vote. This presents an excellent opportunity for a candidate of Gordon Liddy's caliber. With your help, Gordon will be elected to Congress in November.

I am supporting Gordon Liddy because he is extremely well-qualified for the office.

- He is a former FBI agent and supervisor.
- He has earned a Bachelor of Science Degree from Fordham University and an LLD Degree from Fordham University Law School.
- He served as an officer in the U.S. Army during the Korean War.
- He is an attorney by profession who has been admitted to practice law before the Supreme Court of the United States.
- He is Assistant District Attorney of Dutchess County.
- He is a man of impeccable honesty.

The current Congressman is Democrat, Joseph Y. Resnick. He's an extreme "liberal" who has been a Congressional "rubber stamp" for virtually every LBJ "spend" program since he was first elected in 1964.

In 1967, Resnick voted: for increasing the appropriations for Rent Subsidies; for increasing the National Debt to an overwhelming $358,000,000,000; and is on record favoring additional funds for the "War on Poverty".

If the Democrats maintain control of this Congressional seat in November, 1968, they may become so well-entrenched that we will find it impossible to dislodge them for the next decade.

That's why a Republican victory is so important now, in the 1968 election. Gordon Liddy needs less than 7,000 additional votes to carry the 28th District for the Republican Party this year.

But if Gordon Liddy is to win in 1968, he needs your financial support. The most important contribution in a political campaign is the EARLY one. Until this money is received, a campaign staff cannot be assembled, literature cannot be printed, campaign buttons and bumper stickers cannot be ordered.

Your contribution of $130 will pay a month's rent for his campaign headquarters; $95 will pay a week's salary for a secretary; $23.50 will buy a desk; $15 will install a phone; $8 will buy 500 campaign brochures.

Please, ACT NOW to restore a fiscal "common sense" to government! Your contribution, today, can help elect a dynamic Republican who cares about the American taxpayer.

Sincerely,

Vincent J. Cuccia

Vincent J. Cuccia
Treasurer

P.S. Remember, EARLY money is vital. Please send us your maximum contribution today!

Fig. 2-16. Continued.

Chapter 17

Cash, Calories, and a Slice of Heaven

> When dinners run out, the luncheons begin, and when the luncheons run out, the breakfasts begin. We may all meet next week to get the campaign out of the red with a midnight brunch at $85 a person . . . and I will be there.
> —President John F. Kennedy, 1960[1]
>
> I've never been able to understand how the Democrats can run those $1,000-a-plate dinners at such a profit, and run the Government at such a loss.
> —Ronald Reagan, Dallas, October 26, 1967[2]

Today Thomas McClusky is remembered not because he was a wealthy Philadelphia contractor (which he was) and not because he was a long-time treasurer of the National Democratic Party, but for rather unusual reasons. Today he is remembered because, in 1934, he held four luncheons to persuade those who attended to join with him to form a "100 Club." The club's purpose was to recruit one hundred affluent Democrats who would support the local party by paying $100 once a year to attend a fundraising dinner in honor of the patron saint of the Democratic party, Andrew Jackson.[3] Soon the Republican party, too, adopted the idea with their Lincoln Day dinners.

Publicity Featuring a Luminary

Since that time, the idea has been expanded and customized. Today this format has become a political institution. Candidates hold these events to raise money and to give the donor a chance to meet in person the individual for whom the dinner is being held as well as to visit with others who are in politics or at least interested in politics.

Assume the decision is made to sponsor a dinner or cocktail party. In most cases, the media will not recognize a political fundraiser as a newsworthy event, with the result that there will be very little pre-event publicity to stimulate ticket sales—unless the sponsoring committee can capture a luminary. Make no mistake, the presence of big-name guests helps raise money. Speaking of this, one fundraiser expert put it this way: "The president—you have to have him! Unless, of course, you don't want to raise money." Speaking of how he used the president in his campaign, he said "$1,000 per person gets a picture with the chief (signs), a reception (where the picture is taken) and dinner." Then he added, "$500 includes dinner only."

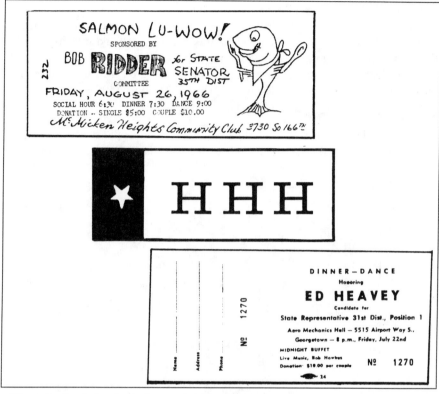

Fig. 2-17. Fundraiser invitations and tickets, Ridder for State Senator, 1966; Heavey for State Representative, 1964; Hubert Humphrey reception, 1978.

"Towards the end, we had to stop selling tickets (so we called everyone who had bought a ticket to see if they were coming; if not, we sold their ticket again). Incidentally, we tried to increase the numbers by having long banquet tables, as opposed to round ones for eight; the Secret Service objected, so we squeezed nine or ten at tables for eight."

It is important to remember that negotiating with the White House staff to arrange this is not easy. Of course, it would take a U.S. Senator of the President's party to carry off such a feat. So what of the candidate who can't get the President? She or he might try the Vice President, or a presidential contender. Maybe one of them will be willing to add the fundraiser to the 200,000 miles they must go. However, there is a hurdle if such a luminary is to add another fundraiser to his campaign agenda. Normally, it must be sponsored by the local party or the candidate must be that party's nominee for a major statewide office.[4]

The Flip Side: Avoiding Publicity

Of course, fundraising publicity has a flip side. When Senator James Hartke of Indiana was chair of the Senate subcommittee handling rail and trucking legislation, his enemies charged that he held his 1970 function not in his constituency but in Chicago to avoid fundraising publicity focusing on the railroads and rail unions, trucking industry, and Teamsters, who bought most of the tickets.

Setting the Ticket Price

Once the decision is made to hold a fundraiser, there is the sticky question of price. This depends on the prominence of the candidate, the office, and type of event planned.

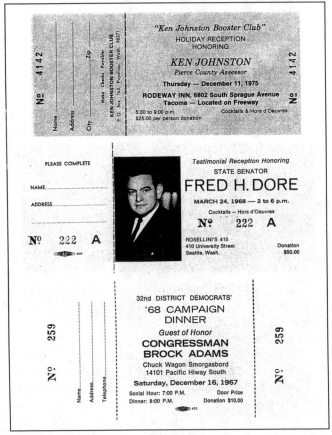

Fig. 2-18. Fundraiser invitations and tickets: Johnston Booster Club, 1975; Dore testimonial reception, 1968; Brock Adams campaign dinner, 1968.

Rudy Boschwitz, a Republican U.S. Senator from Minnesota, discussed this sensitive aspect of fundraising during his 1984 campaign. He said, "You'll get articles written about your fundraising (the press is consumed by money in politics). . . . I raised $6 million plus and got three or four (maybe even five) stories and cartoons that irked me and lots of questions from outlying (and metropolitan) journalists. . . . In retrospect, I'm glad I had the money."

Candidates must try to keep the ticket price small, but they may reconsider after examining the cost of meals, hall rental, advertising, telephone, etc. This is overhead that Michael Breman, who managed Hubert Humphrey's senatorial campaigns, cautions will run approximately 18 to 23 percent, in some instances as much as 50 percent, of the money raised.[5]

Special Event Publicity

Decision-making
Decide when and under what circumstances campaign wants publicity:
    Some fundraising events do not encourage publicity.
    If there special interests are represented, probably won't want publicity.
    If candidate attracts a big-name speaker, then publicity is desirable.

If publicity is desired:
Plan publicity/advertising program and schedule: news releases, ads, etc.
Media list, including deadlines and contacts.
Name lists for publicity releases: VIPs, special guests, entertainers, speakers(s), volunteer organizers.
Initial news release announcing event: date, time, place, purpose, VIPs, program, volunteer organizers.
Additional news releases.
Invite media with phone calls to editors: date, time, place, purpose, VIPs, program, time candidate or speaker(s) will talk.

If the candidate or speaker is important enough:
Ask radio, TV, and newspaper editors if they want pre-event or followup stories/pictures.
Provide followup stories/pictures for media not present.
Call reporters the day before the event to remind them.
Assign greeters to assist reporters/photographers.
Plan photo coverage for campaign use: color.
Coordinate plans with other event personnel and others involved in campaign (event chair, master of ceremonies, etc.).

★ ★ ★ ★ ★ In A Nutshell ★ ★ ★ ★ ★

In general, $150 is the maximum per plate charge for any dinner below a major regional or state-wide office. Many political local-candidate fundraising events are priced from $50 to $100. If these prices seem too high, the committee settles for $50 a person, then tries to sell the tickets in pairs. Occasionally, there is a fundraiser where the admission cost is low. With these, most ticket sales are made in books of perhaps five $10 tickets. The committee increases the take by going out and soliciting donations of liquor, food, etc. Occasionally money can be raised to augment the dinner income by selling chances on a side of beef or some other object or by selling advertising in the program to other candidates or entities.

In 1970, when State Supreme Court Justice Fred Dore was a State Senator, he had a successful sit-down fundraising dinner. He kept the price at $10 because he had a donated hall and volunteers prepared the spaghetti. When the guests paid for their own drinks, he made a profit on his no-host cocktail bar. For the basics of fundraising and for ideas re financing special events consult the accompanying nutshells.

★ ★ ★ ★ ★ ★ ★ ★ ★ ★ ★ ★ ★ ★

Special Event Finances

It takes money to raise money
Seed money available? If not, loans to campaign from candidate, family, backer
Allot a sum for the event, to be reimbursed by:

Ticket sales	Campaign budget
Partially financed outside backer	Other_____

Event money-handling
Pledge cards for hospitality committee table.
Boxes for contributions.
Ticket program.
Gifts, prizes, other fundraising items.
Time in program to ask for contributions.
Single out early contributors to get the action started.
Read rules regarding cash contributions (FPPC federal, also state).
Tabulate contributions; safeguard them, turn over to treasurer.
Coordinate plans with with other events and with others in campaign (event chair, master of ceremonies, publicity chair, campaign manager, candidate).
Mail thank-you letters to contributors immediately as contributions come in.

★ ★ ★ ★ ★   In A Nutshell   ★ ★ ★ ★ ★

Fundraising Event Basics

Note: This page is designed to help the candidate handle a special event without the expense of a catering service, be it a reception, luncheon, dinner, or cocktail hour. If food is to be servec, the candidate or staff must decide whether it will be sit-down or buffet. *Remember:* Fundraisers should be fun.

Purpose
Fundraising
Publicity
Other

Audience
Contributors
Public
Target group

Timing
Weekday/Weekend
Midday/Afternoon/Evening

Location
Indoors/Outdoors
Private/Rented

Dress
Formal/Informal/Costume

Invitations
RSVP
Mail/Phone
Publicity/Advertisement

Food & Service
Snacks
Buffet
Sit-down meal

Catered
Volunteers

Beverages
Open bar
No host bar
Champagne, Wine
Beer, Whiskey/Gin, etc.
Punch (alcoholic, plain)
Soft drinks
Coffee/tea

Program
Live music
Records/tape
Entertainment
Guest speaker
VIP introductions
Master of Ceremonies

Financing
Ticket sales
Campaign budget
Outside host/sponsor

Chair: _____

Budget: $_____

In A Nutshell

Staging a Big Sit-Down Dinner

Shirley Polikoff of Baltimore, Maryland, has organized several million-dollar sit-down events recognized as Cadillacs among political fundraisers, where the contributors dress up and become the elite for the evening. She has been so successful with her fetes that she has become a legend in her native state of Maryland.

Here is one Shirley Polikoff anecdote: Shirley died and went to heaven, where she met St. Peter at the Pearly Gates. He said, "Shirley, there has been a computer error. You died a little ahead of schedule, and we don't have room for you up here just yet. I want to apologize because I will have to send you down to the other place till we get your place prepared here in Heaven." Then St. Peter, being a busy man, went on managing Heaven. In a couple of weeks, he got a frantic telephone call from Satan, asking him to make room in Heaven for Shirley, to which St. Peter replied, "This is most unusual. What's up?" Satan answered, "You've been so busy with Heaven, you don't know what this woman is doing to hell? She has staged dinners, cocktail parties, and other fundraising events, until she almost has enough money to air-condition this place!"

As Shirley explains it, the dinner committee's job starts with scheduling. When choosing a date, it is necessary to balance the campaign's need for early money against the fact that money is easiest to raise when the intensity is greatest, just before the election. And the committee should check with other candidates for possible conflicts because a competing event can kill ticket sales.

Experienced fundraisers disagree on where a fundraiser should be held. One theory is that every dollar paid for food, drink, or entertainment lessens the amount that goes into the campaign. This was the reasoning of U.S. Senator Rudy Boschwitz, who put it this way: "I used a reputable hotel to be sure, but it was also the oldest and cheapest one in town. They charged the dinner committee $6-$10 a plate." Boschwitz continued, "Don't waste money on food and facilities. Big donors will understand and like you for it." See the nutshell for more tips on special event facilities and decorations.

However, the conventional view is that if the campaign is selling tickets with a big price tag, guests should get the feeling that they are getting something more than a drink and a $6.95 blue-plate special. The place, the host, the distinguished guest, the invitation, and the ticket should impart elegance.

Figure 2-19 shows the ticket used to invite patrons to "An evening with the Jacksons" (U.S. Senator and Mrs. Scoop Jackson). The invitation size, design, paper, and lettering all heralded quality. Also note the technique of publicizing prominent guests, by naming U.S. Senator and Mrs. Warren G. Magnuson as co-hosts.

Just as for direct-mail or person-to-person solicitation, finding prospective ticket buyers is always a chore. The National Association of Manufacturers

★ ★ ★ ★ ★ ★ ★ ★ ★ ★ ★ ★ ★ ★

Special Event Facility and Decorations

Note: When selecting the site, consider a possible in-kind contribution by holding it in a supporter's home or a restaurant that is not open that day (say on a Sunday).

People
Appoint a chair
Recruit volunteers
Sign up speakers, entertainment

Site
Select site. Consider location, price
Check availability, effectiveness of:
     Refrigerator
     Stove
     Cooking & serving utensils
     Dishwashing facilities
     Restrooms (clean & stocked with supplies)
     Controls for light, heat, air conditioning
     Emergency procedures
     Chairs, tables, etc.
Get necessary keys

Decorations
Choose theme in conjunction with planning committee.
Borrow decorations.
Recruit volunteers.
Decorate:
     Entry way, doors
     Walls
     Head, sign-in, other tables
Ideas:

Bunting/ribbons	Banners	Pictures
Tablecloths	Flowers	American flag
Balloons	Place cards	Campaign signs

★ ★ ★ ★ ★ **In A Nutshell** ★ ★ ★ ★ ★

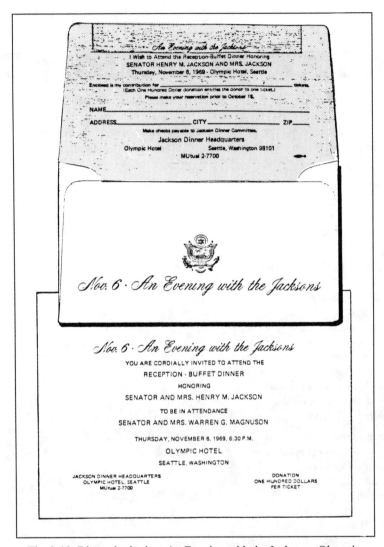

Fig. 2-19. Dinner invitation: An Evening with the Jacksons, Olympic Hotel, Seattle, Washington, November 6, 1969.

suggests a very elaborate ticket committee with several ticket sales chairmen. As they see it, a major campaign should have a commerce and industry chairman to sell tickets to major industries and to teachers, government employees, doctors, etc. There should also be a special gifts chairman to direct a sales force that personally contacts major donors to political campaigns.[6] While this may seem a little pretentious, it sells tickets. (See the nutshell on invitations for more ideas.)

Normally, the dinner committee starts making a list of prospective donors, including personal friends, political investors, party people, etc. Senator Tydings' 1970 dinner committee's prospect list included the contributors to the 1968 Salute to Tydings' committee, those who had contributed to Tydings' deficit dinner in 1969, and those who had given to Hubert Humphrey's campaign for President in 1968.[7]

Looking again at the National Association of Manufacturer's suggestions, it is a good idea to sell blocks of tickets to major contributing groups. They should be seated together and be identified by signs on tables or by the speaker.

Such fundraisers may be a slice of heaven to the candidate, but there is no miracle in how blocks of tickets are sold. In most cases, these blocks are sold only after the candidate or solicitor persuades "someone," perhaps a union leader, corporate officer, or president of a local trade association, to apply internal persuasion. This starts with a solicitor contacting that "someone."

Special Event Invitations

Have a planning meeting for candidate, campaign manager, event chair, hospitality committee, publicity chair.

 –VIPs and special guests
 –Elected officials and other community leaders
 –Media: editors, reporters, journalists, announcers
 –Campaign committee and volunteers

Be sure invitation designs state:
 –Time, place, date
 –Type of event
 –Purpose of event if it has special purpose (e.g., birthday)
 –Dress
 –Cost (if any)
 –RSVP instructions

Print invitations.

Address and mail invitations.

Keep an acceptance or RSVP list.

Make follow-up calls to nonresponders and send reminders to those who responded.

Coordinate with the campaign publicity chair (VIP list, special features, etc.).

★ ★ ★ ★ ★ **In A Nutshell** ★ ★ ★ ★ ★

Shirley Polikoff drafted the letter in Figure 2-20 which she uses as a fast, efficient way to make the first contact.

Dear Mr. Jones:

    On Sunday, October ____, _____ will be honored at a dinner at the Civic Center in _____. The guest speaker for the evening will be _____. The dinner is being given under the auspices of the _____ Salute to Senator _____. Co-chairs of the committee are _____ and _____.

    I have been asked to contact several individuals in connection with this dinner. Tickets for the dinner are $_____ per person, or $_____ for a table of ten. I hope that you will be represented at such a memorable and important evening.

    I will telephone you within the next several days and arrange to make the reservations you require. In the meantime, if you have any questions, please do not hesitate to call me at _____.

Sincerely,

Fig. 2-20. From Shirley Polikoff, Speaker, National Conference on Political Fund Raising, University of Chicago, Dec. 15-16, 1976.

Though it is the custom to a send an informational letter, it is a very poor way to close a $100 sale. Most tickets will be sold by telephone with a personal call, which is even more effective. Calls will stimulate sales to people who might not otherwise attend, especially those who would be embarrassed not to buy.

To help inexperienced salespersons, Shirley Polikoff drafted the instructions shown in Figure 2-21—appropriate for either an in-person contact or for the telephone squad.[8]

When the sale has been made, someone, usually the coordinator, mails the tickets with a letter signed by a campaign dinner official. See Figure 2.22 for an example of this type of letter.

Then a designated person, usually the committee secretary or coordinator, assigns tables. If the sponsors want to go first class, The National Association of Manufacturers suggests that there be a reservations chairman who is responsible for seating arrangements and special tables. Meanwhile, the chair continues to keep in contact with the committee members, see that the tickets are paid for, and that all monies collected are deposited with the campaign treasurer.

Most importantly, just before the event, there should be what fundraisers call a telephone "body check." What this means is that all of those whom the committee has reason to believe might be coming must be contacted again if they have not

---

Instructions for the Telephone Squad

If you are calling a first contact list, after you reach the person on your list:

1. Introduce yourself.
2. State that you are calling on behalf of the Maryland Salute to Senator Joseph D. Tydings Committee.
3. State that the committee is planning a dinner:
   a. Civic Center
   b. Monday, October 27, 1969
   c. 6:30 p.m.
   d. Tickets-$100 per person
4. State that the committee hopes they will be interested in purchasing tickets.
5. If answer is yes, please mark phone sheet appropriately.
6. If person called states he has already purchased tickets, try tactfully to find out from whom.
7. If answer is no, please mark phone sheet appropriately.
8. Make any notations or any changes in reference to names called.
9. Please leave no messages.
10. Do not identify yourself and committee until speaking to person called, if possible.
11. Apologize for any duplication.

Please be polite at all times, for you represent the Salute Committee.

Fig. 2-21. From Shirley Polikoff, Speaker, National Conference on Political Fund Raising, University of Chicago, Dec. 15-16, 1976.

paid for their tickets. When making a body check Shirley Polikoff gives the stock instructions shown in Figure 2-23.

The call will remind the donor to send money. It will also identify the no-shows. Eliminating them will save money because there will be no need to pay the caterer for food and liquor intended for people who do not attend. And it will let the committee know if they have sold enough tickets to make a respectable showing. If not, it gives the candidate a chance to save face by distributing enough complimentary tickets to fill the hall with friends and supporters.

These formal events are subject to variation. In 1970, one politician held a $25-a-couple cocktail party at a Virginia estate. It was attended by political investors, the party faithful, and many friends from the worlds of entertainment and business. About 4,000 people turned out for cocktails. This was followed by a more exclusive $125-a-plate dinner. Five hundred stayed for dinner, and after the main event there was a little gathering that grossed another $125,000. The turnout

---

Maryland Salute
to
SENATOR JOSEPH D. TYDINGS
Civic Center, Baltimore, October 27, 1969

Co-Chairmen

Irving Blum
P. McEvoy Cromwell
Victor Cushwa Jr.
Dominic Fornaro
Robert H. Levi
C. William Pacy
George L. Russell Jr.
Fredrick L. Whier
Martin L. Weil

> **Please reply to:**
> 201 North Charles Street
> Baltimore, Maryland 21201

Treasurer
J. Hardin Marion

September 15, 1969

The Honorable Julian Bond
361 Lee Street Southwest
Atlanta, Georgia   30301

Dear Mr. Bond:

A large group of my friends from throughout Maryland have formed a "Salute to Joe Tydings" committee and they are planning a fund raising dinner in my honor at the Baltimore Civic Center, at 7:00 p.m., on the evening of Monday, October 27, 1969.

The salute committee has asked me to invite you to be a distinguished guest at the dinner. The plan is not to have a head table, but to have some of my Senate and other friends strategically placed at different tables throughout the hall. Your name should appear on the program (unless you indicate otherwise) and you would be introduced.

As I am sure you understand, this dinner will be the big "show" on my behalf prior to November, 1970, and the success of it is tremendously important to me. I would be highly honored if you would agree to join us.

Please respond to the attention of Mrs. Shirley Polikoff by October 1, 1969, if at all possible. Mrs. Polikoff also can furnish additional details (AC301/962-3300).

Sincerely,

Joseph D. Tydings

JDT:am

Fig. 2-22. First-contact letter, Maryland Salute to Senator Tydings, Baltimore, Maryland, October 27, 1969.

Last-Minute-Call Instructions for Phone Squad

1. Introduce yourself.
2. State that a phone squad is calling the entire _____ committee for the following information:
   a. How many tickets have they sold?
   b. Has the money been sent to _____?
   c. Have they purchased their own tickets?
   d. Has that money been sent in?
   e. How many tickets should be sent to them?
3. Please enter reply to phone call on yellow card.
   a. Sold _____ number of tickets.
   b. Money in for _____ number of tickets.
   c. Amount to come in $_____
   d. No sale.
   e. If you receive any other message, please make note of it on card.
   f. Have you checked to see if the ticket purchaser intends to attend? If so, please notify this office. If not, we also want to know so we will be able to estimate the needed quantities of food and liquor.

Fig. 2-23. From Shirley Polikoff, Speaker, National Conference on Political Fund Raising, University of Chicago, Dec. 15-16, 1976.

was probably helped by the fact that the candidate was U.S. Senator Ted Kennedy.[9]

Such events all have this in common. When contributors pay a big price to attend a major political fundraiser, they assemble for more than food and drink and to listen to a succession of prominent political personalities. Just as important, ticket holders attend to dress up and mingle with the personalities that they have seen on TV or read about in the newspaper.

With this in mind, Shirley Polikoff makes an effort to impress local guests, as well as the investors, by getting powerful, instantly recognizable figures from politics, entertainment, and business to attend. Planning this facet starts early. She has the candidate sign a letter extending an invitation to prospective guests that fit this description. It requests they attend as personal non-paying guests. Of course she starts early. The best draws must be booked long in advance. See Figure 2-25 for her sample checklist.

Not only does Shirley Polikoff have the candidate issue a personal invitation, but she is careful to follow it up by phone, and she keeps track of those who accepted prior to the night of the event. To avoid any slip-ups, she sends "Directions for Distinguished Guests," Figure 2-26.

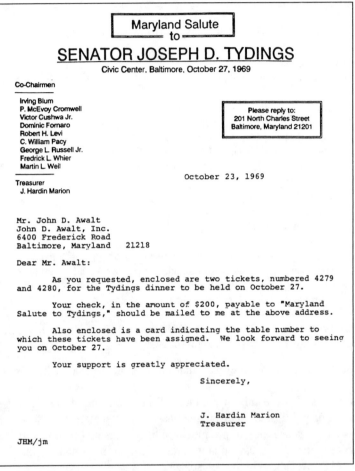

Fig. 2-24. Follow-up letter, Maryland Salute to Senator Joseph D. Tydings, Civic Center, Baltimore, Maryland, October 27, 1969.

It's a good idea to follow up by phone to be sure guests understand the directions. Often Shirley goes so far as to arrange for the transportation of her VIPs to and from trains and planes. Most sit-down dinners feature formal speeches with placecards for the head table personnel. But this is not the way Shirley Polikoff does it. She is anxious to see that all luminaries share a sense of importance, so when displaying personalities from the political, theater, and sports worlds, she makes these special arrangements for the night of the dinner:

1. She provides the press with access to the distinguished guests, using a special entrance with separate bar (tickets marked).

2. She provides the VIPs with a separate entrance (hostess assigned escorts them to private reception area accessible to press).
3. She provides a hostess to escort VIPs to their assigned tables.

If VIPs come, it is common courtesy and good politics to be sure the audience recognizes them. Although she arranges for short speeches by three VIPs and the candidate from the stage, not every luminary can be billed as a speaker. But their presence, including those who come as paying attendees, should not be overlooked. To avoid this embarrassment, some knowledgeable person is assigned to locate the luminaries who are in attendance and to be sure they are introduced. When Polikoff sets it up, she eliminates the head table and substitutes a moving spotlight. This requires a lighting director with a cue sheet to identify them as they are introduced. Since VIPs and spouses are introduced during the meal by categories, she coordinates with the caterer to stop serving courses temporarily. (See the master of ceremonies nutshell for more ideas.)

Distinguished Guests Invited to Maryland
Salute to Senator Tydings,
October 27, 1969

Name/Position	How Contacted	Reply Yes/No	Use of Name on Program?	Ticket Number
Barbara Bain	call			
Russell Baker *New York Times*	letter	yes	no	042
Al Barkan National Dir. of COPE	call			
Mike Bass Wash. Redskins	call	yes	yes	088
Betty Beale	call			
Warren Beatty	call	yes	yes	065
Joseph Beirne International President, Communications Workers of America	letter			
Harry Belafonte	letter	yes	no	133

Fig. 2-25. From Shirley Polikoff, Speaker, National Conference on Political Fund Raising, University of Chicago, Dec. 15-16, 1976.

To cover such details as the menu, ushers, and special arrangements, Shirley Polikoff suggests a committee with responsibility for:

–Menu (see food and drinks nutshell)
–Table decorations
–Printed program (with paid ads)
–Hostess (chairperson hostesses) (good place to use young people)
–Usher (also good for young people)
–Entertainment
–Lighting
–Publicity
–Floor trouble-shooters
–Seating arrangements
–Transportation
–Research for VIP introductions
–Coordination with orchestra to play appropriate background music for each VIP
–Arrangements for ample police coverage inside and outside
–Cleanup (see nutshell)

Directions for Distinguished Guests for Maryland Salute to Senator Tydings

The Baltimore Civic Center is located at Baltimore and Howard Streets.
Please use the Howard Street entrance marked W-6.
Go directly to the VIP room across the corridor from the above entrance, which is marked Bullets VIP Room, where your hostess will be waiting.
Please try to schedule your arrival for no later than 7:00 p.m.
If interested in transportation from the Washington area, please call Mrs. Melville Locker at _____.

Fig. 2-26. From Shirley Polikoff, Speaker, National Conference on Political Fund Raising, University of Chicago, Dec. 15-16, 1976.

★ ★ ★ ★ ★ ★ ★ ★ ★ ★ ★ ★ ★ ★

Special Event Master of Ceremonies

Preparation
Obtain a list of people to be introduced.
Assemble information and details for introductions.
Coordinate with others involved.
Compile information for introducing entertainers/speakers and event chair, campaign manager, etc.

At event
Study sign-in sheets for people to be introduced.
Have spotters help with identifying them.
Arrange head table seating plan.
Ask for: financial assistance, volunteers, after-event clean-up crew.

★ ★ ★ ★ ★   In A Nutshell   ★ ★ ★ ★ ★

Special Event Food and Drink

Note: Use this list after it has been decided whether to have the event catered, or to have volunteers put on the event.

People
Recruit volunteers.

The food
Plan the menu.
When using volunteers:
 –Purchase and prepare food
 –Arrange for disposal of surplus
  (local food bank, etc.)
 –Arrange for disposal of garbage

Meal preparation
Food storage area
Refrigerator
Stove, hotpads
Cooking dishes and utensils
Serving dishes and utensils
Dishwashing facilities and supplies

Meal service
Supplies:
 –Plates, cups, saucers
 –Knives, forks, spoons
 –Napkins
 –Salt/pepper shakers
Arrange for collection of meal tickets

The bar
When using volunteers:
 –Plan the list of drinks
 –Get serving supplies: glasses,
  napkins, towels
 –Purchase beverages and supplies
 -Plan for disposal of surplus
 –Set up money-handling procedures

★ ★ ★ ★ ★ In A Nutshell ★ ★ ★ ★ ★

Special Event Cleanup

Assemble supplies:
 –Garbage bags for paper/dry trash
 –Plastic bags for wet garbage
 –Soap, scrubbers, towels
 –Boxes to carry utensils, bottles,
  equipment
 –Put lender's name on loaners.
 –Cleaning cloths, brooms, dust pans
Arrange for later disposal of surplus
 food and beverages.

Stack tables, chairs; take down
 decorations.
Wash, scrub, sweep.
Collect left-over campaign materials,
 take lost-and-found items back to
 campaign headquarters, etc.
Turn off the lights, other switches;
 return keys.
Return all loaned items.

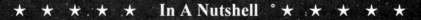
★ ★ ★ ★ ★ In A Nutshell ★ ★ ★ ★ ★

The candidate must remember that the event is more than a rare chance to bask in the warm glow of campaign praise. Many of the guests are there to be seen by the host and appreciated, so it is essential that the candidate and his or her spouse spend time visiting and chatting with those who attend. Typically, the candidate stands by the door and greets the guests.

There are other techniques. Long-time United States Senator Jacob Javits of New York was not one to sit at the head table and limit communication with the audience to a few minutes via the hotel public-address system. He attempted to personalize fundraising by eating before he arrived at the dinner. Then while it was in progress, he started at the back of the hall, visiting every table before being called on for his formal remarks.[10]

The Cocktail Party

Many successful cocktail party fundraisers are held in a luxurious home, plush restaurant, or cocktail lounge. Commercial establishments are usually used on a Sunday or any other time the facilities can be donated or rented cheaply because they are closed or because business is slow. Another variation is the wine-tasting party. This event is not only novel, but often a local winery can be persuaded to donate samples as part of their sales program.

★ ★ ★ ★ ★ ★ ★ ★ ★ ★ ★ ★ ★ ★

Special Event Hospitality Committee

Before event
Recruit volunteers.
Make sign-in book with space for names, addresses, and phone numbers of guests.
Set up a table for sign-in book and campaign materials.
Provide chairs for volunteers.
Make name tags for guests.
Bring pens for sign-in, felt-tips for name tags, pins to attach tags (if needed).
Assemble campaign materials (pledge cards, brochures, etc.).

At event
Lay out campaign materials (pledge cards, brochures, etc.).
Ask incoming guests to sign in.
Provide name tags.
Introduce guests to candidate.

After event
Sign-in book/sheets go to campaign manager.
Collect surplus campaign materials, name tags, etc., and return to campaign manager.

★ ★ ★ ★ ★   In A Nutshell   ★ ★ ★ ★ ★

Most of these events are drop-in affairs, conducted in an open-house fashion between 4:00 p.m. and 8:00 p.m. They feature a wide choice of format. A function put on by the President of the Seattle City Council, Sam Smith, drew 500 people. He treated them to a full orchestra and dancing.

All have a common ritual. As the guests arrive, they are greeted by attendants sitting at a table a short distance from the door, where their names are checked against a list of persons who have purchased tickets or who have been sent complimentary passes. If the paying guests have not yet contributed, they are asked if they wish to pay now or be billed later.

Another volunteer writes the guest's name on an adhesive-backed nametag, which is fastened to the attendee's clothing. These tags must be clearly written so the candidate can pick up the guest name from the tag and won't fumble trying to recall the name of the old schoolmate he hasn't seen for twenty years. After the guest is greeted at the door by the candidate and his or her spouse, then, as in any conventional cocktail party, they circulate. As the candidate circulates, guests are encouraged to go to the bar and order or are served cocktails by a wandering waiter. As a rule, most of these events feature only hors d'oeuvres, but occasionally there is a buffet supper.

As is true in any fundraising event, it helps if prominent persons attend even if they must be given personal invitations and complimentary tickets. Typically, there is a point when a master of ceremonies introduces these distinguished guests, who often say a kind word or two about the candidate. Then the candidate is introduced, who tries to keep remarks light, cordial, and full of optimistic gratitude. Typically, there are comments on the huge turnout and the presence of so many distinguished guests, and the workers—who are really the backbone of the campaign—are thanked.

Those in charge of planning should always be on the lookout for an interesting idea or bit of entertainment. In one area, there is a social worker by day, Enid Mcaddo, who is also a talented vocalist. She is highly prized at such events because she can weave attending political personalities, campaign events, victories, and even disasters into her songs.[11]

A different sort of surprise was provided by super fundraiser I. Hershey Gold when his gilt-edged guests assembled at plush surroundings for a $250 cocktail event. He ushered them over to say hello to the star for the evening, U.S. Senator Moynihan from New York, where a photographer took their pictures with Moynihan. Shortly after the event, they received an 8 x 10 glossy, signed by Moynihan "with warmest regards."[12]

See the nutshell for an overview of setting up a special event.

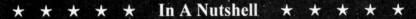

Special Event Quick Overview

Before event

Does event call for music? meal? reception? table decorations?

Does campaign want entertainment? speaker? presentations?

If there is a need, check public address system, get projector and screen, podium with light.

Contract with speaker and/or entertainer. (Are they free or will someone have to pick up the hotel or travel expenses?)

Coordinate event with others in campaign

At event

Information to M.C. who is to make introductions.

Locate light controls, fuse boxes.

Assign greeters.

Treasurer write check(s) to pay for entertainer/speaker.

Post event

Candidate sign thank you letters.

Return borrowed equipment.

In A Nutshell

Chapter 18

Adding a Touch of Imagination and. . . .

> I want you guys to tell me candidly what's wrong with
> my ideas even if it means losing your job.
> —Sam Goldwyn, movie producer[1]

Ridiculous But It Worked

Of the many variations designed to give donors something for their money, a most expensive, exotic, and unusual fundraising event was a party given by Louisiana Governor Edwin Williams. It raised slightly more than $5 million, liquidating $4.4 million in campaign debts, by taking 616 people for a week to Paris, France. Some paid $10,000. Some simply accepted the trip and forgot what they had lent the campaign. A few friends, journalists, and legislators were given reduced rates, ranging from $2,100 to $2,500.

To make sure the event was properly kicked off, the Paris-bound contributors were bugled aboard one of two 747s, either a TWA jet named Gabriel or an Air France jet named Evangeline. To do it up with style, Governor Williams employed Harold Dejan's Olympia brass band, led by a prancer in a bowler and spats.

When they arrived in Paris, the Louisianans were spread among four luxury hotels. After that, their week included an $85,000 black-tie dinner—where the band played "Dixie at Versailles"—plus side trips to Monte Carlo and Brussels. As the junket played out, *Time* correspondent Gregory Jaynes reported, "The sole complaint, from the Governor on down, was that too many stops had been jammed into the itinerary."[2]

Assorted Innovations

Returning to less expensive events, there are those that the contributors want to attend for social reasons. When television commentator Charles Royer first decided to run for mayor of Seattle, he had instant public recognition but no bankroll and little contact with the interests who traditionally financed candidates for that office.

However, Royer was fortunate in that he attracted a group of young activists. They came up with innovative ways to raise campaign money. One of these ways was a series of tea dances held at Seattle's older, but recently refurbished, hotels. Delighted with the chance to show that their facilities had been completely redone, the hotels made them a special deal. One such event was held at the

Camlin Hotel, and attended by more than 200 people.[3] The invitation is shown in Figure 2-27.

An exclusive night at a movie was responsible for one imaginative fundraiser. A front-runner for governor who had local theater and exhibitor connections purchased the first local showing of what proved to be a second-rate movie. The event was billed by the theater as a première. The evening started with the candidate and his wife going to an intimate dinner party hosted by a wealthy

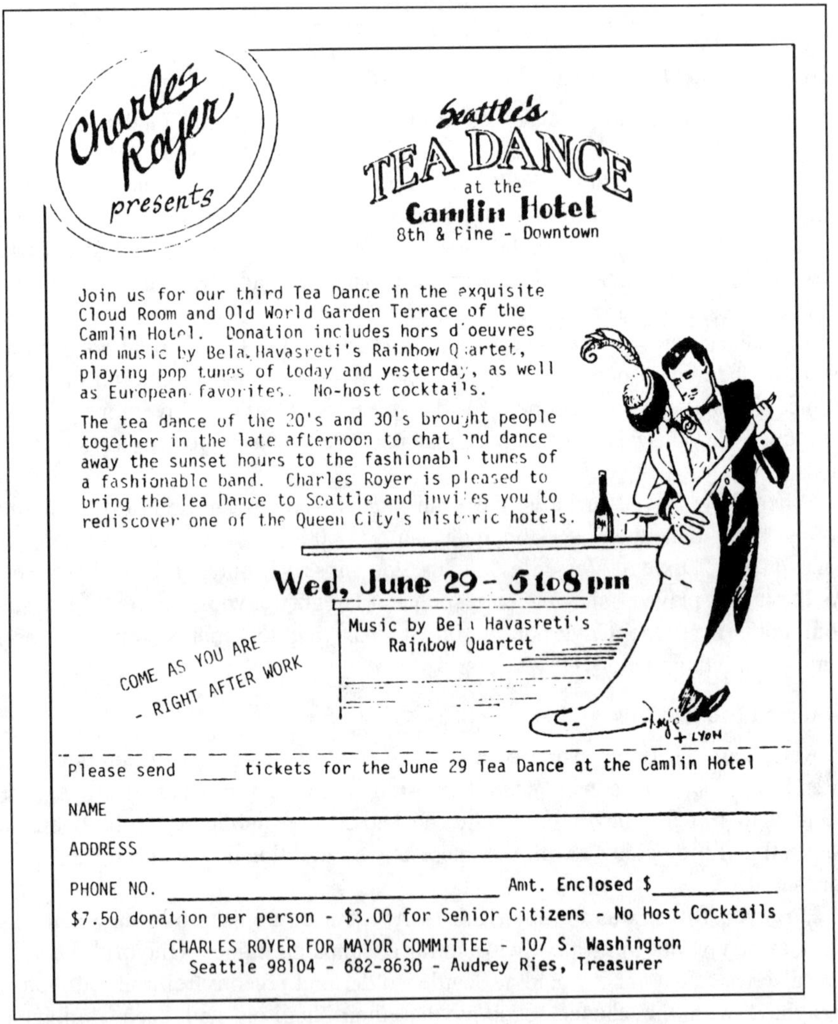

Charles Royer presents

Seattle's TEA DANCE at the Camlin Hotel
8th & Pine - Downtown

Join us for our third Tea Dance in the exquisite Cloud Room and Old World Garden Terrace of the Camlin Hotel. Donation includes hors d'oeuvres and music by Bela Havasreti's Rainbow Quartet, playing pop tunes of today and yesterday, as well as European favorites. No-host cocktails.

The tea dance of the 20's and 30's brought people together in the late afternoon to chat and dance away the sunset hours to the fashionable tunes of a fashionable band. Charles Royer is pleased to bring the Tea Dance to Seattle and invites you to rediscover one of the Queen City's historic hotels.

Wed, June 29 – 5 to 8 pm

Music by Bela Havasreti's Rainbow Quartet

COME AS YOU ARE - RIGHT AFTER WORK

Please send ___ tickets for the June 29 Tea Dance at the Camlin Hotel

NAME ______

ADDRESS ______

PHONE NO. ______ Amt. Enclosed $______

$7.50 donation per person - $3.00 for Senior Citizens - No Host Cocktails

CHARLES ROYER FOR MAYOR COMMITTEE - 107 S. Washington
Seattle 98104 - 682-8630 - Audrey Ries, Treasurer

Fig. 2-27. Tea dance invitation, Charles Royer for Mayor Committee, Seattle, Washington, July 10, 1976.

friend, which featured a star of the movie who was flown to town for the occasion. This raised enough to pay for the evening's overhead. After the dinner, they all went in separate cars to a small plush theater that had been rented for that evening. The entry was lighted by giant searchlights, and they were met by a street crowd of campaign supporters as the cars with a few local celebrities drove up in front of the theater.

First to alight in formal dress were local figures, then the star, whose studio permitted him to appear to promote the show, and finally the candidate and his wife. Those who attended the opening did so at a cost of $50 per person. After the show, there was a third fundraising champagne party featuring both the star and the candidate, which cost an additional $100 each.[4]

Another device used occasionally to raise money is an auction in which prominent political supporters or business figures are persuaded to donate their time to a dinner, a golf game or other event. The personality and the event are auctioned or raffled off to raise money. Unfortunately, this can have an embarrassing side, as was the case when a private lunch with the governor and a game of golf with the state attorney general were auctioned off at a benefit for the Minnesota opera. The high bidder was Rebecca Rae Rand, a convicted prostitute and madam.[5]

Using an Event as a Springboard

When Charles Royer first ran mayor, some of his imaginative fundraising events gave him a chance to show at least a symbolic interest in racial minorities. For example, he bought out the house and then sold tickets to a double bill at a local Japanese language movie house, the Toyo. Another of his benefits was a jazz cabaret. This was sponsored by a committee under the chairmanship of the city's leading black, the Reverend J. W. DeWitty, who persuaded his son, Gordon, one of the best jazz organists in the country, to fly in from California for the event and to perform with local jazz musicians who had donated their services.[6]

Joel Pritchard was a popular Republican member of the state senate, who used events as springboards in his first congressional campaign. He met with twenty boosters who agreed to be "table captains." Each persuaded at least one prospect and friend (190 in all) to attend a pledge breakfast to kick off his congressional campaign. Political writer Richard Larsen reported that "the event raised $19,000 minus the cost of the breakfast.[7]

The candidate's birthday, wedding, or anniversary while in office can also provide a springboard for fundraising parties. Cake, favors, and appropriate jokes can give the event a festive ambiance. Figures 2-28 and 2-29 provide examples.

Washington State Senator Ray Van Hollenbeke purchased crab and beer by the barrel and put on a crab and beer feed. Then he augmented the event's income by having volunteers sell chances on a side of beef.

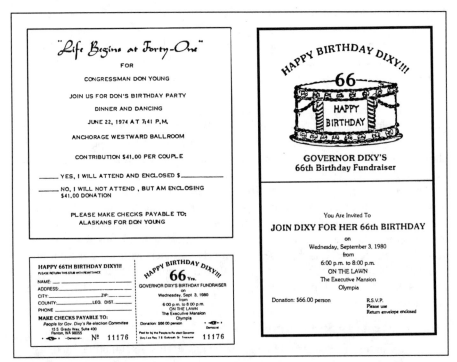

Fig. 2-28. Birthday invitation, *How to Raise More Money Than You've Ever Raised Before . . . for Your Candidate, Cause or Campaign* (Hadlock, Washington: C. Montgomery Johnson Associates, 1981).

In another case, a public high school teacher running for the legislature combined an event with person-to-person solicitation. He and his campaign committee, composed mostly of high school students, decided to hold a rummage sale to raise funds. First they collected rummage from friends and relatives, then to get patronage and to avoid any political stigma, they used the name of a non-political entity they had organized. They used its name as a sponsor when they advertised the event in the newspaper and on the radio.

On the morning of the sale, the committee found a long line of people (those who generally go to rummage sales) waiting at the door with shopping bags and even wagons. Once customers actually got into the building where the sale was being held, the youthful workers running the sale forgot the non-political title used to promote the sale. In fact, the shoppers were surprised to find the sales personnel wearing campaign hats, campaign buttons, and handing out campaign literature with purchases, etc. But this didn't dampen the profit, which was almost $2,500.[8] Later, a deal was made with the Salvation Army to clean up the hall for the balance of the unsold items.

Soliciting Person to Person

When this device is employed, the campaign committee purchases promotional materials in bulk imprinted with the candidate's name and sells them to supporters. For example, one might purchase political buttons at 15 cents each and sell them at $1 to generate money.

Sales are easier if promoted by enthusiastic young supporters. These supporters might dress in straw hats and sweatshirts or vests featuring the candidate's name or use ribbons across the worker's chest that say something like, "Volunteers for Bob Ritter," or "Wallace Workers," or "Kennedy Girls."

**CHIP
MARSHALL
FUNDRAISER
PROMISES
TO BE
TOPS OF
SEASON**

A fundraising bash on Sunday, July 31 at 8:00 P.M. shows all
the signs of being the most enjoyable party of the political season.
Music by Junior Cadillac, the atmosphere of the unpretentious
Central Tavern, and the mixture of lively folks expected
to attend all make the party a must for anyone interested in the
leading candidate for the open seat on the City Council.
Admission is $5 at the door. For more information, call the
campaign headquarters, 633-0675 or 633-0676.

P.O. Box 12659, Seattle, Washington 98111   Telephone 633-0675/0676
CHIP MARSHALL FOR CITY COUNCIL CAMPAIGN COMMITTEE John Caddock, Treasurer

Fig. 2-29. Fundraiser invitation, Chip Marshall for City Council Campaign Committee, Seattle, 1977.

When Florida Congressman Dante B. Fascell first ran for the state legislature, he had a special book of simulated stock certificates. These were sold at five dollars each to his friends whom he urged to "Ring the bell for Dante Fascell and buy a share of good Government."

Fundraising Imagination

Some campaigns have been financed in part by selling items of value, for example a cookbook featuring favorite recipes of prominent political people. This was used by Democratic National Committeeman Bobby Pafford in his race for the Georgia Public Service Commission.[9]

U.S. Senator Goldwater cut off some big donors when he made the "liberal eastern financial establishment" a target during his 1966 run for the Presidency. To compensate, the Goldwater campaign came up with several very imaginative fundraising ideas. Among them was the printing and sale of a handsome book of photographs entitled "The Faces of Arizona," taken by the candidate himself. Several thousand copies were snapped up by large contributors at $1,500 each.[10]

President Kennedy and his brother, U.S. Senator Bobby, sold specially designed campaign trinkets such as charm bracelets and pendants at their candidate teas and coffee hours. Candidates going this route should do it with flair. That is exactly what Nevada Governor (now U.S. Senator) Paul Laxalt's campaign organization did. It produced a distinctive sorority-type pin, "Pledged to Paul," complete with chain and engraved with the year—'66. For the men, he had a lapel pin or tie clasp manufactured with the initials PAL to designate 'Pals for Paul." "Believe me," Laxalt said, "this became a major item financially. The college girls and all our ladies throughout the organization gobbled them up. They were all over the State."[11]

The ultimate in imagination was used by U.S. Senator Mark Hatfield of Oregon in 1978. He made it possible for his supporters to take part in a (non-existent) $100-a-plate fundraiser. He simply took their $100 and sent them a specially manufactured plate featuring his autograph as a memento.[12]

Using Sports to Add a Touch of Imagination

Before the football season started, when seats were still available, Speaker of the Michigan house, Bobby Crimm, purchased a block of 300 seats to the Michigan State versus Ohio State football game. Then he used this event as a reason to stage a fundraiser. On the day of the game his guests were treated to a reception, a brunch, football tickets, transportation to and from the game, and a special cushion that said, "Bobby Crimm Buckeye Bash."[13]

During the course of his first campaign for mayor of Seattle, Charles Royer had firm support from the leaders of Seattle ethnic and racial minorities. He was aided by his wife, Roseanne, who was active in the city's Slavic community, a group that included some of the city's most avid and active soccer fans. During that election, there was a memorable soccer match between the Seattle Sounders and the New York Cosmos, which featured the last Seattle appearance of the world renowned soccer player, "Pele" (who was playing for the New York Cosmos but was about to retire to Brazil).[14]

Royer made an advance purchase of a block of tickets to this match. Then using the Slavic community as a base, his campaign committee sold Royer's

Fig. 2-30. Campaign solicitation, Charles Royer for Mayor Committee, Seattle, July 10, 1977.

supporters a soccer package. This consisted of a buffet and cocktails at a restaurant within walking distance of the stadium, and a chance to purchase cocktails after the game (see Figure 2-30).

Some candidates have used golf, including Brian Lewis (in his campaign for Congress), State Senator Ray Van Hollenbeke, and County Councilman Tracy Owen. The Lewis and Van Hollenbeke guests got a breakfast and a round of golf on a course they rented for a specific time.

The invitation to the Tracy "Owen Open" was a little different. It featured a map of an imaginary golf course where each hole was in the shape of one of the nine county council districts. On the invitation, Owen used the names of incumbents to label them. In doing so, he poked fun at his colleagues of a different political faith, describing their holes as the Lowry Dog Leg, the Greive Gulch, the Mooney Marsh, the Chow Chow Bogies, and the Stern Sandtrap.

Fig. 2-31. Campaign solicitation, Committee to Re-Elect Tracy Owen to County Council, Seattle, April 27, 1977.

"The Poor Man's Alternative"

When the event concentrates on volume, it is kept at popular prices. Like its expensive counterparts, format is limited only by imagination. One of the best is the pancake breakfast, which has become a stable fundraiser for churches, Chambers of Commerce, and service clubs.

As the 1976 Minnesota Democratic Farm Labor Campaign Handbook states, "There are always fresh ideas and when combined with the necessary enthusiasm, they will succeed. They can be moderately complicated, such as progressive dinners, pool parties, potluck suppers, bean feeds, tours, ice cream socials, boat cruises, square dances, or hay rides." The handbook further states, "These fundraisers can also be very elaborate dinner dances, all-day picnics with games and prizes, or auctions."[15] In some areas, a refreshment stand at the county fair featuring hot dogs, coffee, and pop may be sponsored by the candidate.

One candidate, his family, and his supporters used a youth walk-a-thon to raise money. His youthful supporters persuaded adults to pledge 75 cents a mile. Altogether, they walked almost 3,000 miles.

Speaking of unusual events, one was billed as a Poor Man's Alternative. It was intended not only to raise money but to embarrass an opponent who was holding an expensive testimonial at the same time. It started with the candidate renting a local hamburger drive-in for a late Sunday-afternoon bash. During the pre-event sales hype, his theme was, "Let's make with volume what the opponent's fundraiser makes from the wealthy few."

On the day of the event, campaign volunteers sold or collected pre-sold $5 tickets when they admitted the early arrivals to the sit-down portion of the restaurant. As the candidate expected, supporters soon filled up both the drive-in and its parking lot, with most guests staying in their cars. As the overflow guests arrived, they were given a printed apology and a map that directed them to alternate parking sites, where he had already arranged for additional space at two nearby supermarkets to accommodate the overflow.

For communications, the candidate installed radios with loudspeakers in the restaurant's seating area. For those in the parking lots, his volunteers gave them a sheet of paper on which was printed a menu and a request that they tune in their car radios to the least expensive radio station in the area on which the candidate had rented time. Then campaign workers visited the parked cars where they took orders, turned them in, picked them up, and served the guests hamburgers, coffee, French fries, Coke, and milk shakes. The candidate, his wife, the campaign manager, and other known political personalities first shook hands inside. Then they walked from car to car introducing themselves and chatting with the parked guests.

The radio station had made the candidate's campaign committee a package deal, arranging for remote coverage of the event. They ran their usual non-political radio commercials, requiring the candidate to pay only for time he used promoting and publicizing, for example, time used introducing the candidate and other political personalities, making impassioned pleas for additional campaign funds, and publicizing guests who had contributed or pledged substantial sums.

The candidate scored a public relations triumph. The "poor man's" alternative got the candidate not only the radio exposure but was so unusual that it was picked up and publicized in the local press.[16]

In 1932, the Governor of Louisiana, Huey Long, was "the King Fish." He said, "We (the Democrats) have all the votes and no money . . . the best thing we could do is to sell President Hoover (a Republican) a few million votes for half of what he is going to pay to try to get them. We can spare the votes, and we could use the money."[17]

Though these words were spoken in jest, such a situation actually took place during the 1964 presidential primary when a Goldwater for President supporter, Robert T. Gaston, was the leader of the Young Republicans of California. After Gaston's inside sources told him that Rockefeller was going to get the signatures anyway, he mobilized local young conservatives and persuaded them to collect signatures that helped qualify New York's Governor Nelson Rockefeller for the California Presidential ballot. The $3,500 they collected was donated to Rockefeller's presidential rival, U.S. Senator Barry Goldwater.[18]

This is not the only time volunteers have made a profit for their favorite by doing a campaign chore for someone else. Cooperation between two candidates who do not oppose each other is not uncommon. For example, candidates can put on a joint fundraiser. This is especially beneficial when one has the financial contact and the clout to sell big blocks of tickets, while the other can get free food, hall rental, etc., or can furnish volunteers to put on a function. Occasionally, a candidate furnishes his or her volunteers to make, assemble, or put up signs for another candidate (who is running for a different office) and is repaid with a substantial campaign donation.

Chapter 19

After the Votes are Counted: Winners, Losers

> After the ball is over, After the break of dawn, Many a heart is broken. . . .
> —Composer Charles K. Harris, "After the Ball," 1890s era
>
> When a man needs money, he needs money, not a headache tablet or a prayer.
> —William Feather

Your Check: Did It Just Arrive Late?

President Harry Truman was embarrassed during his 1948 cross-country campaign train trip when, as the incumbent, his campaign ran out of money just as his railroad car reached Oklahoma. Then-Governor Roy Turner and wealthy banker W. Elmer Harber of Shawnee threw a fundraising event held in the President's private railroad car. It was attended by local fat cats who contributed enough to pay for the rest of the trip.

However, the day after Truman's unexpected victory the worm turned. A blizzard of predated checks arrived at Democratic headquarters, many of which were followed by telephone calls from eager donors lamely explaining why their check had been mislaid.[1]

Winners with a deficit usually hold some sort of reception, testimonial, or other fundraiser to pay off the campaign debts. President John F. Kennedy held five post-election dinners and grossed between $1.4 and $1.5 million. As a matter of public relations, the campaign chairman should be sure to let the candidate's supporters know before election day that he or she has a deficit. This will alert them to the probability that they will be called back at least one more time.

When the contributors are investing in a winner, the campaign can usually expect repeat contributions from friends who feel flush as well as money from contributors who were supporting the opposition but who are now anxious, though late, to be aboard.

Assume a contributor makes a voluntary pledge and the candidate spends, relying on that commitment. A realist relying on this form of campaign financing must plan to pursue the uncollected pledges, even at the risk of some misunderstanding. For example, when Dr. Ruth Farkas was nominated Ambassador to Luxembourg in February 1973, she had to explain to senators why her contributions arrived after the president's election. She said that she had pledged $300,000 to Nixon's presidential campaign before his election, but had simply waited until afterward to obtain a better price for the securities she and her husband sold to pay it off.

Book of Campaign Memorabilia

On occasion, the campaign committee publishes and sells campaign memorabilia books. In these books, the candidate and staff put together pictures, letters, and newspaper articles, along with text, and have it printed or reproduced on a copier.

Keep in mind that what contributors are buying at a highly inflated price is a boost to their ego. The expensive individual copies include one-of-a-kind personal letters of thanks to the contributor from the office-holder with the pages juggled to put special emphasis on the more prominent contributors. These deluxe copies are often bound by a commercial binder and may have the contributor's name imprinted in gold on the cover, and are usually personally delivered by the candidate, who tells how important they were in liquidating the debt.

The same book, without the expensive binders and special flyleaf pages, can be sold at a lesser price to less affluent supporters or given free as a thank you to campaign volunteers. In some cases, the memorabilia book is used as a gimmick to bring aboard contributors who have been with the opposition.[2]

Use Someone Else's Prestige

Losing campaigns often end with deficits, which losers have to liquidate personally as best they can—that is, unless the loser holds another political office or has enough political clout to stage a deficit fundraiser. Those who use this device usually call on all previous contributors to help them stage one last fundraising effort as soon after the election as possible. The most successful fundraisers usually appeal to strong liberal or conservative issue-oriented individuals and organizations that respect the candidate who fought for "their issues."

Losers who are not strident, issue-oriented candidates and no longer hold an office might use someone else's prestige. This is what a very clever political veteran did. Reading the letter of invitation, which is reproduced in Figure 2-32, one would assume that it is a simple testimonial sponsored by friends and neighbors who wanted to thank the politician for his years of service. Sophisticated political investors knew that the people who were sponsoring the event included the Speaker of the State House of Representatives; the mayor of the state's largest city; a television commentator who appeared on the state's largest station; the most powerful lobbyist in the state; the editor of the local Teamsters' paper; the state's attorney general (of the opposite political faith), who was the former minority leader of the State House and the political writer for the state's largest paper; and one of the state's most powerful labor leaders.

Durkan Committee
(Address, Date)

Dear Friends,

How do you tell Martin J. Durkan that you love him? Well, we asked some close friends who know him well, and their answer? "You can't, he won't let you." So, we decided to tell him we don't, and we're putting on a "Roast" in his honor to tell him lovingly.

On Sunday, May 22, friends of Martin Durkan are going to spend a few hours (3:00 p.m.-6:00 p.m. specifically) expressing appreciation and gratitude for the years of leadership that he has provided.

There is a deficit from this "Best Hurrah" that we would like to see reduced, which is one reason for this testimonial. However, we feel that it's time to let Martin know that his years of public service have not gone unnoticed.

These are some of the friends who are clamoring to lend their oratorical talents to this "bash":

Bob Austin	Tom Hujar	Charley Royer
John Bagnariol	Dick Larsen	Barbara Shinpoch
Jerry Buckley	Harry B. Lewis	Jack Tanner
Ed Donahoe	Rita Matheny	Wes Uhlman
Jenny Durkan	Peggy Maze	Arnie Weinmeister

(all this for only $25.00 for two)

We would like to receive your acceptance as soon as possible. We will be calling in a few days with a gentle reminder.

For further information or additional tickets, call (206) _____.

Paid for and authorized by Durkan for Congress Committee/Jerry Farley, Treas., P.O. Box _____, Seattle, WA 98___. A copy of our report is filed with and available for purchase from the Federal Election Commission, Washington, DC 20463

Fig. 2-32. Durkan testimonial invitation, 1977.

According to the news story, the once powerful state legislator, Martin Durkan, who had tasted two defeats for governor and one for congress, used humor to entertain, to cushion the loss, and to recoup financially from a crowd the news media stated to be about 200. This did not include the many who contributed but did not attend.

Republicans and Democrats turned the whole evening into one of fun as they took turns needling a grinning Durkan. "He's better at losing than I am," said Seattle Mayor Wes Uhlman, "He's simply had more practice."[3]

"A fund raising political event should be exciting, and the losers are usually not," says political consultant Jill Buckley of the campaign consulting firm of Rothstein and Buckley, Washington, DC. She went on to tell of a defeated Denver candidate who, after the primary, used Halloween night to throw a $25-per-person haunted house fundraiser.

It began with the candidate and his campaign manager persuading a supporter to donate the use of a very large old house for the party. The attendees who came after dark on the night of the event were given options. They could go directly to the party in the basement or follow a step-by-step horror tour, in which they groped through dark halls and creaking steps. They were greeted with sudden moving objects, squeaky doors, and noisy chains. Each of these Halloween "horrors" was a clever play on political personalities and issues, such as "Smear Monster," the "Cooked Candidate's Goose," etc. Once the contributor had proceeded through the horror route, he or she too reached the gaily decorated basement where each guest was handed tickets good for three drinks of Halloween cider, beer, or cocktails and where additional drinks could be purchased. At the party, the guests were entertained by the more adventuresome who paid a dollar to bob for apples. The successful ones got the apple, applause from onlookers, and their dollars back.[4]

Always **Say Thanks**

"Always say thanks" is an important rule of human behavior, and is applicable to any fundraising—charitable, civic, or political. Usually, though, the candidate has more than appreciation on his mind. As President Harry Truman once put it, "There is no gratitude for things past. Gratitude is always for what you are going to do for people in the future."[5] Truman was speaking of an ulterior motive best expressed in these words from La Rochefou: "The gratitude of most men is but a secret desire of receiving greater benefits."[6]

Applying this rule, as fast as contributions come in, letters or phone calls should be dispatched thanking the giver. Futhermore, after the fundraiser, the Chairman of the Finance Committee should go through the records, carefully noting people who contributed and worked on the fundraiser and they should be thanked again. This applies even to the small contributor.

When the campaign is over, the thank-yous are a part of the wind-up. The candidate or the finance chairman should make a list of the financial "angels." The important ones should, at a minimum, get a phone call, if not from the candidate, then certainly from the chairman of the finance committee. When the contribution is large or the contributor controversial, thanks should be given at a private lunch or dinner. Or wait till after the election, then invite the investor, along with the campaign wheelhorses, to a free, intimate thank-you cocktail or dinner party.

In the flush of victory, the successful candidate should be careful not to put him- or herself in the pocket of a special interest, as happened in 1970 to

Chairman of the U.S. Senate Labor Committee Harrison Williams when he addressed a key group of labor leaders, and said, "I owe everything to you. What you want, you've got. I owe that much."[7]

Even though both the candidate and the contributor understand that they are not purchasing a vote, still "thank you" notes in the wrong hands can prove embarrassing. Such a statement, even if only in a letter, is particularly damaging if it is in response to a contributor who was previously unfriendly, or who is currently doing business with the public entity with whom the candidate (now an officeholder) has a control.

The candidate must also realize and remember that words that seem to fall short of a political commitment may appear differently to the less sophisticated. Let me explain. A mass membership organization speaks through a president, an executive secretary, or a finance chairman, who often try to enhance their position with the members by flaunting thank you letters. Later when issues affecting their organization come up, a thank you can leave the candidate in a dilemma he or she has to answer to organization members who have their own interpretation of what the thank you letter means.

In some elections, there is no safe written thank you, so the candidate must settle for a simple acknowledgement such as the letter shown in Figure 2-33. This style is okay for a jurist, as most people understand that a judge has to be above influence. However, his letter is hardly adequate for political office.

A search through books, articles, and campaign manuals in an effort to see how others have handled this matter, revealed no gracious yet noncommittal letter. But here is a technique that has been successful over the years. The finance chair writes an internal letter conveying to the candidate the money was collected without incurring any obligation, but was given because the contributor "understands your views," "appreciates your record," and "wants to help with your candidacy," etc. Upon receiving this letter, the candidate writes a simple thank you note in his or her hand at the bottom on a copy of the letter, expressing his personal thanks. Then the finance chairman sends this copy with the note to the contributor.

This still leaves the candidate with the problem of what to say. Because this is awkward, here are some standard (non-political) texts in language that conveys warmth and feeling in non-specific terms: "As soon as I opened your letter, I felt that I must sit right down and tell you. . . ." ". . . to indicate, in a small measure, my gratitude for your cooperation (kindness, friendship, courtesy). . . ." "You were kind to send a gift. . . ." "Your substantial gift came this morning. . . ." "Sidney and I were overjoyed with the. . . ." "I find an ordinary thank you entirely inadequate to tell you how much. . . ." "It was most thoughtful and generous of you to send the. . . ."

Further samples were, "I appreciate very much your. . . ." "I realize that the task took a great deal of sacrifice. . . ." "Thank you for doing me a real favor. . . ." "Your generous spirit of cooperation. . . ." "You may be sure that I appreciate. . . ."[8]

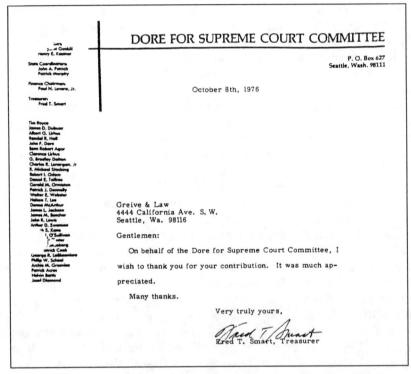

Fig. 2-33. Campaign thank-you letter, Dore for Supreme Court Committee, Seattle, Washington, October 8, 1976.

$ $ $ $ **WARNING** $ $ $ $

Today, campaign costs and contributions have soared beyond the wildest predictions. Though dollar amounts quoted throughout this book are historically correct and valuable as general percentage guidelines, dollar amounts more than two to four years old should not be depended upon for structuring campaign budgets.

Part 3

Polling

IF GOD WANTED US TO
VOTE . . . WHY DIDN'T HE
GIVE US BETTER
CANDIDATES?

Chapter 20

The Political Poll

> Election day is a solemn occasion when millions vote to
> determine . . . which of the political poll takers was right.
> —Robert Orben[1]
>
> Don't worry about polls. But if you do, don't admit it.
> —Rosalyn Carter[2]

Old-Fashioned Horse Race Poll

"As you know, come November 6th, we will be voting to fill many state offices here in Utah. I am going to read you the names of the candidates in each of several races. For each race, please tell me how you would vote if the election were held today." (Races and candidates were then listed.)

This is the hallmark of an American horse race. Such political polls have been used by newspapers, radio, and television. They are designed to create news, rather than provide candidates in-depth information, and have helped sell newspapers since the 1824 presidential campaigns.

At that time two newspapers, the Harrisburg *Pennsylvanian* and the Raleigh North Carolina *Star* asked their readers to choose between Andrew Jackson, John Quincy Adams, and Henry Clay. Both papers predicted Jackson would win the popular vote (which he did), but no one got a majority of the electoral votes.

As provided by the United States Constitution, the selection was left in the hands of the United States House of Representatives. Clay threw his support to Adams, who became the sixth President of the United States. Incensed, the Jackson forces continued to organize and campaign; they were victorious in the next election.[3]

Exit Polling

Today's news media have modernized and updated this type of poll. For example, in recent years the television networks have spent millions on exit polling where they ask the voters how they have voted after leaving the polls.

As David Halberstam sees it, exit polling is more evidence that television dominates big-time politics. He says, "In 1976 it was a complete media campaign to the end. Often before the polls closed in the Western United States, the major television networks had already projected the winner. . . ."[4]

Since that time there has been strong adverse political reaction, especially in the western United States, to such early announcements. Chicago columnist Mike

Royko even came up with a unique tongue-in-cheek solution to this problem. He urged voters not to give the press an honest answer. "If enough lie," Royko predicts, "the entire nation will be treated to chaos in the newsrooms, network executives will try to cut their wrists, and anchormen will have nervous breakdowns before our eyes."[5]

This cynical reaction has been met by the television networks who claim their right to exit polling is protected by the freedoms of speech and the press.

Polling as a Marketing Tool

Public opinion polls have many diverse functions beyond creating news. A private poll taken during a campaign can be used to monitor public reaction to the candidate and/or to his or her advertising theme, television commercials, and public position on controversial issues.

In the 1984 presidential campaign, President Reagan carried private polling—or shall we call it market research—to new heights. During his nationally televised debates with ex-Vice President Walter Mondale, Reagan's staff assembled a cross-section of the voting public which they used as a sounding board. Each held trace copy testing equipment registering their second-by-second reactions to statements made by the candidates.

The results revealed that one of the biggest negatives was Mondale's reaction to the President's offer to make a theoretical missile defense system available to the Russians in return for a disarmament agreement. As Reagan's strategists viewed it, the Democrats compounded the mistake when they used clips from the debate that emphasized Mondale's reaction in a television commercial.[6]

This was just one of several polling efforts. During the same presidential contest, Reagan's advertising people used in-depth interviews to fathom the voters' concept of President Reagan. After sifting through the research, his people decided on the theme "Leadership that is working," which they incorporated into television commercials.

As the commercials were completed, Reagan's advertising people tested them in three small markets. One of the most successful commercials started off showing a bear rambling through the wood. In the background a voice asks, "Will this bear turn vicious and attack or just amble on its way?" The voice

'I TAKE IT, THEN, YOU'RE NOT WILLING TO BE PART OF OUR EXIT POLL...'

Fig. 3-1. AUTH © The Philadelphia Inquirer. Reprinted with permission of Universal Press Syndicate. All rights reserved.

goes on saying, "If it proves to be mean, it's best to be prepared to defend yourself—Mr. Reagan is the personification of preparedness."

After showing "the bear" on the air in these small markets, the public was polled. The commercial tested so favorably that it was strategically released nationwide just before the election.[7]

Private polling is often designed to find the best way to allocate campaign resources. In 1971, after studying the polls, United States Senator Albert Gore, Sr., father of the present United States Senator and his campaign strategist, were convinced that his reelection hinged on the right-wing voters who supported presidential candidate George Wallace. After locating the Nashville precincts in which Wallace had run strongly in his presidential race, they bombarded them with special mailings.

Though defeated, the incumbent Senator fared far better in these precincts than expected. Indeed, after the election, Gore's Nashville manager declared that, "If we had done the same thing statewide or even only in the three other metropolitan areas, he'd have won the reelection."[8]

There are still other ways in which politicians use polling as a marketing tool. Some polls taken by mail or by campaign workers seem like public opinion polls, but they are actually designed to measure and persuade the voters that the politician commissioning the poll is interested in their reaction.

A prestigious veteran of many political wars, Stephen Shadegg, advocates this type of poll. After admitting the questions are not designed for the sophisticated voter, he says, "A man or woman who is willing to spend five minutes recording his or her opinion of a candidate has moved several steps closer to commitment."

In this type of poll, the voter is first flattered by being told that they are representative of thousands and that their opinion is important. When evaluating the candidates, the voter is asked questions such as: "Do you believe the people of Vermont associate Senator John Incumbent as a strong advocate of economy, as an intelligent spender, as a middle-of-the-roader, as a conservative, or as a defender of constitutional rights?"

Shadegg explains: ". . . in several campaigns we have had as many as 20 percent of the voting population respond to this type of questionnaire."[9]

On rare occasions political polls masquerade as smear pieces where inflammatory labels and associations are used to turn opinion against an opponent. This is the tack that Judge Bryon Arnold of the San Francisco Superior Court found in ruling against Richard Nixon's campaign committee when Nixon was running for U.S. Senator.

After hearing the evidence, the Judge held that Nixon's committee had created a dummy organization, "Committee for the Preservation of the Democratic Party in California," and used this organization to send out hundreds of thousands of questionnaires written in such a way that they intimated that Nixon's opponent, Congresswoman Helen Gahagan Douglas, sympathized with the Communists.[10]

Such tactics have brought official wrath. The West German Parliament has banned publication of candidate preference polls during the two weeks prior to election day. And in British Columbia private unpublished polls are legal, but publicizing opinion is not permitted during provincial elections.[11]

Thrust

Most political polls are factual surveys and the questions are designed to get information. For example: Did you vote in the last State Senate election? Do you plan to vote in this year's election? Do you plan to vote for Mary Incumbent or John Challenger?

In a true opinion poll, the questions are designed to uncover the voter's opinions. Interviewers ask questions such as, "What is your opinion of the city's plan to permit highrise buildings at the Alaska Street junction?" When surveys probe motivation, the interviewer uses 'why' questions to probe into why a person thinks or behaves in a certain way. To see this, let's go back to the turbulent Depression years.

The 1938 California election is remembered for a very colorful, controversial, and irresponsible pension initiative with the slogan, "The Ham and Eggs for Californians, Life Pension Begins at 50, $30 Every Thursday." This scheme enlisted thousands of pension-seeking volunteers who turned out in huge numbers for rallies where they heard spellbinding speeches and sang, "Glory, Glory, Hallelujah, While We Go Marching On."

Out on the campaign trail, supporters displayed religious fervor as they went door to door and covered bus stops, train depots, and business districts with leaflets. An alarmed business establishment raised huge sums and financed a massive media campaign against the initiative, reasoning that such a pension plan had to be paid for and this one was designed to soak "business."

Early polls showed that the voters were brushing off business protests against increased taxes and, further, that they were not impressed with the argument that, if the initiative were enacted, it would bankrupt the state. However, the survey did show that the majority of voters feared that after the initiative's passage they would have to support millions of oldsters who would come to California to reap the initiative's benefits. With this information, the businesses switched their advertising message to, "Don't Encourage Outsiders to Retire at Your Expense." This new strategy stopped the trend toward the "$30 Every Thursday" initiative.[12]

What Can a Poll Tell the Campaign?

To see how these political factors affect each other, let us take a real candidate's support and voter reaction when the candidates are matched against each other. For example, a survey taken from the *Boston Globe* released approximately two weeks before the 1982 Massachusetts general election matched the Democratic nominee and eventual winner, Michael Dukakis, against the Republican nominee, John Winthrop Sears, after Dukakis had beaten the incumbent Governor Edward J. King in a bitter primary.

While the poll was sponsored by a newspaper and was not superficial, it didn't focus on subjective voter motivation. Thus, it did not explore the factors that created the candidate's image, but it did have enough depth to give some insight as to how voters were reacting to the candidates.

The poll highlighted Republican Sears' low visibility. Twenty-nine percent said they did not know Sears well enough to have an opinion of him. Of those who did know him, Sears scored well, having a seventy-five percent favorability rating. Dukakis had a seventy-two percent rating.[13] The *Boston Globe* poll also looked at internal switches between candidates as the campaign progressed. Their results showed Sears' voter retention level was not as good as that of Dukakis. Ten percent of those who voted for Sears in the primary said they now would support Dukakis, while only two percent of Dukakis' supporters indicated they are now with Sears.

Analyzing the results, the *Boston Globe* explained that several things had gone as the Republican nominee Sears hoped. He retained substantial support from the voters who voted for all three Republican candidates in the primary. In addition, he seemed to have achieved a key goal by winning the support of a majority who voted for defeated Democratic Governor Edward J. King in the party primary. Persons who said they had voted for Governor King were broken down as follows: Forty-three percent for Sears, thirty percent for Dukakis, six percent for minor party candidates, and twenty-one percent undecided.

In a race where the turnout is going to be light, the outcome may well depend upon a handful of party voters who are concentrated in loyalist precincts, but this was not the case. Looking to the one third of the registered voters who did not vote in the primary, fully fifty-four percent did expect to vote in the final. Of those who intended to vote, 32 percent said they were leaning toward Dukakis, 18 percent toward Sears, and 6 percent were for minor party candidates.

Another goal of in-depth polls is to provide an analytical tool permitting candidates to measure the public's reaction to his or her image or to issues. Demographically the *Boston Globe* poll found Republicans and conservatives supported Sears and that he did better among Protestants and those with high incomes and better education than he did among the electorate as a whole. The poll also found that this was not enough to make the race tight because Dukakis showed unusual strength among young voters, liberals, and Jewish voters.

Looking at the results by gender, male respondents were for Dukakis by 49 to 31 percent, while women favored him by 57 to 19 percent.

The only referendum item that could be correlated with the governor's race was capital punishment. Candidate Mike Dukakis opposed reimposition of capital punishment, while candidate John Sears supported it.

When attempting to measure the influence of the issue, the poll found that those polled were in the same category as an elderly New Englander, who when interviewed for a public opinion poll, hemmed and hawed over every question, finally apologizing to the interviewer by explaining, "I'm not so much of a 'no opinion' as I am a 'couldn't care less'." Because the death penalty was not a major factor when the majority made their choice for Governor, twenty percent had no opinion on the issue. Those favoring the death penalty supported Dukakis by forty-six to thirty-two percent, while those opposing the death penalty were overwhelmingly for Dukakis by seventy-four to fourteen percent.

As in all elections, there are voters who researchers Lazerfeld, Berleson, and Gaudet say tend to belittle the whole affair or are undecided because they subconsciously enjoy their status, the attention, and the sense of power it brings. Looking at these undecideds, the pollster made an effort to interpret their mood. Nineteen percent of them said they were not leaning in any direction and, when pressed, Dukakis got forty-seven percent, while Sears got only twenty-one percent, with four percent going to minor parties.[14]

Telephone Interviews

The telephone is the cheapest and quickest method of survey, yet most professional pollsters have found telephone conversations too short to pursue voter opinion in depth. Also, adjustments must be made for the eleven percent of the population without telephones who lean toward the Democrats, as well as for those with unlisted numbers, who have a tendency to be Republicans. Further adjustments must be made for new voters, many of whom are on telephone companies' waiting lists because in some areas their telephone cannot be installed for some period of time. (See Chapter 5 for details on setting up the telephone bank.)

Taking Polls by Mail

Some pollsters use a return postcard or a postpaid envelope in an attempt to gauge political opinion by direct mail. The problem with this is that experience has shown that mail gets returned from the committed who may not be typical voters and it is useless as an analytic tool unless the pollster has some way of determining a political profile of those who answer.

Person-to-person interviewers have instructions that tell them what to do in cases where the selected person isn't home. They are instructed never to go to anyone's home for a personal interview after dark, unless an appointment has been made by telephone. If the person at the door refuses to cooperate or gives a "smart" answer, which the interviewer often gets when the front door is answered—such as, "I gave my opinion at the office"—the voter terminates the interview. If the interview is terminated before it is completed, the interviewer is told to be friendly and courteous and never argue with the voter.

Protecting the Client

When taking an in-depth poll, the interviewer, like a baseball pitcher, starts with a warmup. When the poll is for a political client, the pollster does not reveal the client. Instead, the person being surveyed is told that the poll is being conducted for a professional polling or research firm.

There are two reasons for refusing to reveal who has commissioned a poll. First it would be impossible to get an unbiased result if the client were known. Second, the candidate, after measuring public reaction, might find it embarrassing if it becomes necessary to adjust his or her campaign strategy.

This was the case in a 1966 poll when it was discovered that seventy percent of the voters in outspoken Liberal Congressman Henry Helstoski's district opposed his attacks on the bombing of North Vietnam. Seeing the poll results, Helstoski temporarily stopped harping on that issue.[15]

Even though the interviewer refuses to name the client, this does not stop a curious voter from trying to guess for whom the pollster is working. To combat this curiosity, the Democratic National Committee suggests that the pollster gather information on several races at the same time.[16]

Sample Section

The cost of conducting polls is almost prohibitive unless a few voters reflect the view of many. How large should the sample be? Experts answer that it isn't the size, but the distribution and random selection of the voters in the sample that determine the poll's accuracy.

These experts point to a 1936 *Literary Digest* poll that encompassed two million people and mistakenly predicted that presidential candidate Alfred Landon would get fifty-seven percent of the vote. Instead, President Franklin Roosevelt received sixty percent. The error lay in the poll's sampling criteria. All of those surveyed had either a telephone or a car, which left out tens of thousands of Depression-year voters.[17]

When a survey covers a wide area, the pollster breaks the sample into regions. A few suburban, rural, or city precincts are chosen by lot to represent the vote in each sample area, and they become sampling points. A number of interviews are conducted in each sampling point.

A systematic selection procedure is used to be sure that the sample reflects the voting population. This means comparing the sample to this population to make sure the voters chosen represent the same race and income that statistics show live in the sample area.

How samples are selected varies from pollster to pollster. Seldom are their secrets revealed, but they must follow a standard procedure. For a national survey, the Gallup organization first selects sampling points and uses fifteen hundred interviews. Gallup used to assign ten interviews in each of one hundred fifty nationwide sampling points to get its fifteen hundred samples. It now assigns clusters of five interviews for each of more than three hundred sampling points, to achieve even greater dispersion.[18] This means there might be as many as ten points in California or New York, and it is possible that no one will be interviewed in Alaska or Hawaii because of their size and distance from the more populated areas.

Another pollster, Marvin Field, polled 1,217 (708 Democrats and 429 Republicans) when he conducted a statewide poll of California's 20 million residents.[19] For other polls, campaign specialist Edward Schwartzman suggested the ranges shown in Table 3-1.[20]

Scientific sample results should be adjusted to account for luxury apartments with security arrangements that make their residents hard to reach. Results should also be adjusted to account for times when no one is home during the day in ghetto areas, because chances are there will be no follow-up solicitation at night because the interviewer may be afraid.

In the 1968 Presidential contest, the mid-October Gallup poll showed Nixon leading Humphrey by 44 to 36 percent with the rest undecided call-backs. Utilizing call-backs, the Harris poll found many of these not-at-homes were Black and ethnic voters who favored Senator Humphrey. This reduced Nixon's lead from 8 percent to 5 percent. After seeing the Harris results, the Gallup organization corrected their error in a subsequent poll (released just before the election).

Although all private polls are not alike, they have much in common. The validity of a poll depends on a whole host of preliminary judgments. For example, turnout can make a substantial difference. In 1972 when Senator George McGovern ran in the Democratic presidential primary in Massachusetts, he picked up 42 percent of the vote cast in a split field, and got all of the convention delegates.

Voters at Large	Sample Size
Under 10,000 voters	150
10,000 – 24,999 voters	250
25,000 – 49,999 voters	400
50,000 – 99,999 voters	500
100,000 – 249,999 voters	750
250,000 – 499,999 voters	1,000
500,000 and more voters	1,500

Table 3-1

Turnout and Falloff

In this election, one third of those eligible to vote were not registered and, of those who were, only nine percent voted. Of course there was also a Republican primary, so the forty-two percent that McGovern polled in the presidential primaries represented about three percent of all eligible voters.[21]

Admittedly, this represents an extreme, yet accuracy in predicting election turnout can depend on the techniques used when selecting the sample. While this is particularly true in a primary, the same principle holds in general elections though the pollster must also consider the fact that most of those eligible to vote do not exercise that privilege in non-presidential years.

The same principle of selecting the sample impacts polls taken during presidential election years. There was a 62.8% turnout in 1960 of the registered and unregistered, and the electorate narrowly elected the first Catholic in United States history. Then voter turnout slipped to 61.9% in 1964, to 60.6% in 1968, to 55.5% in 1972, to 54.3% in 1976, and to 52.2% in 1980. There was a slight increase in the 1984 Presidential race, but this barely halted the slide in voter participation.[22]

Even when voters go to the polls and vote, the number of those casting their ballot falls off as they move down the ballot to the less prestigious offices.

Commenting on both turnout and falloff together, the eminent psychological researcher Ernest Dichter, speaking of the registered voters selected for interview in most races, said, "Out of every 100 people you interview in the perfect sample, forty to fifty have to be eliminated."

Turnout statistics show that race, age, education, marital status, and residency affect voter participation. Strategists want to track down the effects of these factors not only on their voter participation, but on their voters' preferences. After examining statistics, Dr. Dichter said, "The people who don't vote aren't like the people who do vote."[23]

This difference between those who vote and those who stay home was studied in the 1970 Michigan gubernatorial election. A part of that effort was a poll taken concentrating on voter preferences of the undecideds in the dying days of the campaign. It showed the undecided vote had moved to Republican Governor William Millikan by a ratio of two to one over his opponent.

However, the same study found that, if all who were eligible but did not vote had gone to the polls, the situation would have been reversed. The nonvoter undecideds favored his Democratic opponent, Sandra Levin, by a three to one margin.[24]

To overcome this chance for error, the pollster looks at the past history of the election in question. If the poll is designed for primary voters, the pollster selects a sample from those who have a history of voting in that primary election before making a selection. Then the pollster goes further and asks who is likely to vote and who is likely to stay at home.

There are several question designs used to get the voter's intention. In one technique the phrasing goes something like this: What are your chances of voting in this election? Will you probably vote? Are the chances 50-50 or are the chances very slight that you will want to vote in this particular contest?[25]

No matter what technique is used, those polled are often ashamed to admit they are not interested in candidates of lesser importance. Supposing the pollster only wants responses from people who intend to vote in the state Senate elections, the best way is to just ask, because the pollster must also separate out those whose interest is stimulated because they are being polled.

Instead of asking direct questions, the interviewer substitutes a question like this: Some people don't pay much attention to minor political campaigns. How about you? Or the question might be: Would you say that you usually follow lesser political campaigns with very much interest, some interest, or not much interest?[26]

Whatever technique is used, there is an instruction to the interviewer that goes like this: All respondents must indicate that they are almost certain to vote or that they will probably vote in the upcoming election and in the client's political race; otherwise, terminate.[27]

Asking Sensitive Questions

If pollsters want to measure the responses from people with certain characteristics, they use screening questions to determine how they are perceived by the various population segments such as male, female, married, divorced, single, poor, wealthy, middle class.

However, the voter considers these personal questions and the interviewer doesn't want to frustrate or anger the voter and cause him to prematurely terminate the interview. So—they don't ask their screening questions right off.

Most pollsters put interesting and easy to answer questions at the beginning. They leave the tough and personal questions until after the interviewer establishes a friendly relationship, which is usually at the end of the interview.

At the end of the interview, in order to get sensitive personal information that inquires into the voter's racial and ethnic heritage, interviewers might try asking: "Now, just to make sure we have a representative sample of everyone, may I ask, what is your race?" Or the interviewer may state:

> Most people classify themselves as white, black, Hispanic, or Asian. How do you classify yourself: White male___, white female ___, black male___, black female___, Hispanic male___, Hispanic female___, Asian male___, Asian female___, other___.[28]

In the state of Hawaii, which is a blend of several races, ethnic heritage plays a significant part in the political process. Here, cultural leanings must be explored in greater depth. For example, the inquiry will have to go beyond simply Asian. The pollster will want to know if the voter is native Hawaiian, Japanese, Chinese, Korean, Vietnamese, or Filipino.

Political analysts have always recognized the importance of white voters' ethnic heritage, and to get this needed ethnic information, some pollsters ask:

> Most people think of themselves as Americans, but also as very close to the country where their grandparents or parents came from. What about yourself? Do you feel close to some nationality other than American? American/English___, Irish___, Italian___, Polish___, French Canadian___, Russian___, East European___.

If the potential voters establish themselves as Hispanics, the interviewer then asks if they consider themselves Puerto Rican/Cuban___, South American___, Other_____ (write in).[29]

Somewhere in the questions a professional pollster will bury a question that probes another sensitive area, age, by asking "What age group do you fall into: 18 to 24___, 25 to 34___, 35 to 49___, 50 to 64___, 65 and up___?"

"Well, Happy Birthday, Doris. . .And welcome to the 49-to-55 demographic group."

Fig. 3-2. Stein, Editorial Viewpoint: "To Bury the Hatchet," *Advertising Age,* May 10, 1982.

Questions concerning personal economic conditions can also be sensitive. Economics has played a major part in every national election since William Jennings Bryan was nominated for president on an anti-gold platform and, incidentally, was defeated when establishment forces led by United States Senator Mark Hanna mobilized the voters of the commercial trading and manufacturing states east of the Mississippi and north of the Mason-Dixon line.[30]

When setting campaign priorities appealing to support groups, a political candidate should target different economic segments of the population, and develop appropriate campaign issues, campaign literature, budget, and allocation of advertising dollars. Interviewers approach this delicate subject with:

> Now we would like a little background on you and your family. Are you presently: employed outside the home___, employed in the home___, unemployed___, retired___, a student___?

Then interviewers ask: "What is the occupation of the wage earners in your household_____?" (If retired, get former occupation.)

Most pollsters conclude with a question like:

> I would like to read some groups and have you tell me approximately what your total income will be this year for yourself and your family, before taxes: Under $3,000___, $3,000 to $6,000___, $6,000 to $12,000___, $12,000 to $25,000___, $25,000 and over___?31

Before the pollster makes use of an interview, the entire sample needs to be re-examined and measured against census demographics to make sure the race, ethnic origin, family size, income level, etc., of the model approximately reflects the voter population surveyed.

If the pollster is not convinced that a group of polling samples reflects party registration, sex, age, income level, etc., the pollster discards some interviews or gives some classifications more weight than others. If this is impossible, the candidate must do as national pollster Elmer Roper did; he had to abandon a randomly selected national sample when he found that there was only one point representing the entire west coast (which turned out to be Death Valley), and the state of Texas was represented by the King Ranch.[32]

For a checklist of survey or polling tips in a nutshell, see below.

Overview of Polling

Note: Seek help from a professional when determining information to gather. If such help is not available, reread chapter on polling.

Purpose for conducting poll:
Determine status of name recognition
Identify support of candidate or
    opposition
Find out candidate popularity ranking
Identify issues
Determine importance of issues
Find out voters' evaluation of a
    candidate's image

Basic information for all polls:
Age, sex
Ethnic group (if appropriate)
Religion (if appropriate)
Educational background
Income level
Occupation
Time lived in community
Homeowner/renter
Marital status
Stands on issues
Whether participant intends to vote in the
    election; if not, discard sample

Survey methods:
Telephone interview

Personal interview (conduct "surveys" of
    constituency: walk door to door with
    a clipboard and questions)
Direct mail questionnaire

Sampling (taken from constituency)
Random sampling
Targeted group/area (e.g., community
    leaders only)

Structure
Short/long
Open/closed questions

Timing
Time of day (different for working
    people vs. retired)
Days of week
Number weeks before election_____

Use of results
Planning
Drafting message of campaign materials
Distributing to news media
Emphasizing issues
Assessing voter's evaluation of
    candidate's image

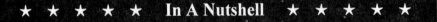

In A Nutshell

Chapter 21

Measuring Name Familiarity and Performance

> Many a man forms his opinions only after submitting them to his preconceived ideas.
>
> Some people never change their opinion because it's been in the family for generations.[1]

Name Familiarity

A political poll may be a good way to evaluate the President but, realistically, most voters do not know lesser candidates. In fact, with these candidates exposure and persuasion are often the same, and the pollster runs afoul of the candidate's ego.

Candidates are wrong to assume that the election was or will be won because he or she is known by everyone in the city, county, state, etc. Surveys show that voters often do not recognize even those who seek major office.

Just two weeks before the 1972 election, a New Jersey poll reported that only five percent of the electorate could identify the Democratic candidate for the United States Senate, Paul Krebs, and his opponent who was running for a fourth term, Republican Senator Clifford Case.

To get this information, the pollster uses recognition questions, such as: Do you know Joan Candidate? Do you know her personally? Have you met her once or twice? Have you seen her, but never met her? Have you ever seen her or met her? Have you ever heard of her?[2]

When the candidate is a challenger who has little or no name familiarity, the pollster must mobilize those who don't like the incum-

"I have no answers, mister — just questions."

Fig. 3-3. Hagglund. *Campaign Insight,* July 1973, p. 7.

bent. To do this, a candidate may want to identify voter dissatisfaction. Pollsters use questions such as: Now I would like to ask you to rate the job performance of a few public figures. (List several names, one of which is the candidate for whom the information is sought.)[3]

If the candidate is an incumbent and the poll wants to test voter impression, the question might be: How would you rate the job Gerald Ford is doing as President? Excellent___ Good___ Fair___ Poor___.[4]

If the voter answers this type of question, the pollster may go further, asking how the voter views the candidate's leadership abilities.

Image

Ambrose Gwinnett Bierce tells of a candidate who attended a Chamber of Commerce meeting. When the candidate rose to speak, there was an objection to his continuing on the grounds that he had nothing to do with the Chamber.

"Mr. Chairman" said an aged member, "I believe that the objection is not well taken. The gentleman is a commodity, which makes his connection with the Chamber close and intimate."[5] He was right. High-image candidates are sold like commodities. For that reason, it is crucial that they identify unimportant and even ridiculous traits that create an impression and influence a substantial portion of the voting population.

In-depth polls ask forced-choice questions to measure reaction to both the candidate's and opponent's image, such as: strong/weak___, compassionate/ uncaring___, and intelligent/dull___.

When asking image questions, pollsters try to uncover the impact of image traits or stereotypes to determine how the voter sees the candidate and how this image contrasts with that of opponents. With this information the strategist can decide what perceptions should be reinforced or minimized.

United States Senator Rudy Boschwitz of Minnesota took a series of in-depth polls prior to and early in his 1964 re-election campaign. He said: "Our polls showed a very common disease for first term senators. People liked me but didn't know why or what I had done." To prevent a "What's he done?" kind of attack, they ran a series of sixty-second ads regarding Boschwitz's involvement with social security, small business, agriculture, and veterans that also helped to discourage potential opponents.[6]

Because answers are subject to suggestion, particularly when the questions are of a sensitive nature, the pollster usually solicits information indirectly using questions such as:

> I'd like to read you some of the kinds of leadership qualities and personality traits people tell us candidates have. Now I'm going to read you a list of personality traits. Which, if any, of these traits do you feel applies to senatorial candidate Richard Ottinger, Democrat___? Charles Goodell, Republican___? James Buckley, Conservative___?[7]

If the interview takes more than ten minutes, the professional pollster includes an open-ended question designed to find out what, if anything, is bugging the voter. Here both the pollster and the candidate should be prepared for impressions that defy intelligent analysis. Pollster Michael Wheeler tells of a poll taken in 1966 which showed that in Milton Shapp's campaign for Governor of Pennsylvania, his image was hurt by a habit of wearing maroon socks.[8]

When traits are identified, they are studied further to find out how much they influence voter conduct. Then politicians try to conform to what the voting public wants, even when it involves changing or modifying personality traits.

This type of change occurred after hard-working, back-slapping, extrovert Massachusetts Governor John Volpe commissioned an in-depth political poll. After he received the results, he substituted a quieter, relaxed, and more soft-spoken style because his poll revealed that the voters reacted unfavorably to his loud, extroverted political stereotype.[9]

Party

The interviewer always asks about party preference as well as the strength of the voters' party preference because it affects the way the voter reacts to issues and even to the candidate.

Researcher Richard H. Schweitzer describes those who term themselves as independents as "ticket splitters" who frequently show independence from their normal party viewpoint in their voting behavior. As a matter of fact, 45 percent of Republicans and 47 percent of Democrats vote a split ticket. However, Schweitzer says that does not mean these voters are independents. Most are partisan centrists with weak political loyalty who most of the time are party voters that can be counted on to vote the party line.[10]

Knowing how the ticket splitters—especially the undecideds—lean, the strategist can estimate what will happen in the late stages of the campaign, when the undecideds tend to return to the party that normally claims their allegiance.

To get this information, the pollster asks questions such as: "Which political party do you generally feel has the best position or is more likely to correctly solve the problems you mentioned? Democrats___, Republicans___, Both___, Neither___, Don't know___."[11] Hopefully, the answers to these questions iden tify those who have toyed with the idea of voting with the opposition.

Trends

Candidates are frequently carried to victory or drowned in a political tide, so political polls include questions designed to probe for more than known issues or personality traits. The answers are used to chart political trends and just how much the trend affects a particular campaign.

When the only black in the United States Senate, Edward W. Brooke of Massachusetts, ran for re-election in 1966, he hired the Opinion Research Corporation to conduct continuous state-wide surveys. Initially, Brooke held a lead of 66 to his opponent's 23 percent, but then aggressive blacks all over the U.S. mounted a nationwide protest. An adverse white reaction followed, making it difficult for any black who had to appeal to predominately white voters. Following these protests, Senator Brook watched his support erode, falling from 59 to 49 percent in August and to 37 percent in September. At that time his analyst noted that, among the least racially prejudiced, Brooke's race did not seem to hurt, but among those with some prejudice, his support had slipped. This substantial rise in the popularity of the lesser-known candidate called for action. Brooke, who till then had ignored the racial issue, changed tactics. In mid-October he shrewdly captured national attention when he spoke out on television, condemning violence as a means of gaining civil rights, while simultaneously speaking out against white racists. The decline was reversed and Brooke won by a margin of 61 to 39 percent.[12]

Speaking of trends and how they affect the vote, the pollster and the strategist find that we humans are an incredible mass of conflicting motivations. For this reason they use in-depth polls to sift through inconsistent attitudes, which often show that voter backlash outweighs the gains the candidate makes by advocating a particular program or ideological point of view.

The existence of such cross-pressure was apparent in the 1964 presidential campaign. The Republican nominee, Barry Goldwater, assumed that the middle class was fed up with the liberal establishment that had been in control of the country through both the Democratic and Republican administrations for the past 10 years. He relied on his gut feeling that the electorate was about to vote against those who advocated anything they considered liberal. When measuring the pulse of the American voter, pollster Oliver Quayle found that, true enough, there was a bipartisan 8 percent who were anti-liberal. Had Goldwater held his party's vote, this would have won most elections, but the backlash to Goldwater's extreme conservatism turned off the liberal Republicans. Twenty-five to 30 percent of them deserted the party and voted against him.[13]

Fig. 3-4. Kathleen Hall Jamieson, *Packaging the Presidency* (New York: Oxford University Press, 1984), p. 182.

Chapter 22

In-Depth Polling

> We are more like doctors than anything. We must sit down with the candidates and ask: Where does it hurt? and then we tell them how to fix it.
> —V. Lance Tarrance, Pollster for President Reagan[1]

> Winning elections today is a science, not an art form, and I believe that 10% of any campaign budget should be spent up front on public opinion studies—to make sure the other 90% is not wasted.
> —Richard Richards, Past Chairman of the Republican National Committee[2]

As we have seen, voters are individuals who are influenced by logic, perception, and emotion, with the result that accurately collecting and evaluating polling information is not easy.

In-depth polls depend on and go beyond who is ahead during a campaign. They seek to gauge the effect one issue or personality trait has on another. Before

Fig. 3-5. Horsey, *Seattle Post Intelligencer*, November 4, 1984. Reprinted courtesy of the *Seattle Post-Intelligencer*.

we touch on analysis of an in-depth poll, let us remember that no poll can be better than its basics, which we have discussed separately, so let's look at them all together.

Typically, analytical surveys use two types of questions: open-ended questions that allow voters to answer in their own words questions that give voters possible answers from which to choose. Closed-ended questions are answered with a simple yes or no, or a multiple-choice format is used in which the voter selects one or two choices on a graph or a scale. Some polls also give the voter a list of alternative choices such as: Yes, I think so; I don't know; I don't think so; and No.

These surveys probe to find if voters recognize the candidate's name and then ask if in their minds the candidate has a recognizable political image. Then the surveys try to quantify voters' loyalty to a political party and determine how strong that loyalty is.

Finally, in-depth surveys look for measurable factors that influence the vote in a particular political contest. However, the questions on these surveys aren't always clear and can unreasonably influence the answer or embarrass the voter.

To avoid error, the pollster tries to assure that the question itself avoids distortion—or, in other words, so it accurately gauges voter reaction and doesn't influence the voter's answer. Before sending interviewers out into the field, pollsters pretest the questions on a representative sample of voters. Even after the analyst has the information, it must be determined why the voter chooses one candidate over another.

"Next question...it's not me who's crazy, it's the rest of the world that's crazy, true or false?"

Fig. 3-6. Cheny, *Saturday Evening Post,* March 1985.

The value of the information produced depends on the design of the poll. This, in turn, depends on circumstances. For example, private political polls can be designed to get information but be used to aid in increasing name recognition or help undecideds make up their minds in favor of a particular candidate.[3]

In-depth polling is designed to do more than find out who the voters favor at the moment. It also gives the candidates a window into the mind of the voter and tests voter reaction to particular issues, attacks, or strategies, and how these reactions affect the outcome.

For example, in 1988 Los Angeles pollster Patrick Caddell was hired by California U.S. Senator Alan Cranston in his non-presidential-year reelection campaign. This senatorial race was a feature attraction, a contest likely to draw the intermittent voter. At that time, Democrat Cranston faced a young, self-made millionaire, Ed Zschau. Zschau was a liberal moderate Republican with good looks that created a very attractive TV image, contrasting with Cranston's bald, elderly image.

After careful polling, Caddell drew several conclusions. First, that the odds favored Republican Zschau because of the nonorganizational votes he was attracting, votes not attached to either party, though this type of voter was easily discouraged from participating in the election.

Second, after further examining the core support among the regular Democrats and Republicans who were most likely to vote, Caddell concluded that Cranston had made a good impression, especially on the Democratic-leaning elderly, the handicapped, labor, and other special groups, and he had both a better organization and a larger hard-line following among those who were certain to vote.

After considerable thought, Caddell advised Cranston that if the voters' turnout were low enough, Cranston had a chance of pulling through. Then Caddell specifically advised him to run a negative campaign designed to drive voters away and "Piss them off with politics."[4] Following this advice, Cranston launched an all-out negative campaign and Zschau responded in kind. At the urging from Cranston, special interests entered the fray, which prompted much response from the newspapers.

The result was a low vote in which Cranston won by a mere 2 percent.

Pre-campaign Polling

An in-depth poll can be taken before a campaign in order to make an educated guess at what is bugging the constituents.

To illustrate, go back to 1961, when university professor John Tower became the first Republican United States Senator since reconstruction. He was elected to fill then-Vice President Johnson's unexpired term in the United States Senate, and he upset a 100-year Texas tradition.[5]

Sixteen months prior to Tower's campaign for re-election, he employed the services of the John F. Kraft polling organization. In an in-depth survey, Tower was matched against three possible Democratic opponents, Governor John Connolly, Congressman James Wright, and Texas Attorney General Waggoner Carr.[6]

This pre-campaign poll revealed that Senator Tower was well known, but he was handicapped by his outspoken, conservative ideology. With this information, Senator Tower strategically moderated his aggressive promotion of volatile conservative issues. Although there was no hope of his being endorsed by labor, he chose not to arouse its leaders by discussing right-to-work legislation. He even attempted to soften their opposition by adding job security as an issue, and he emphasized his efforts in the United States Senate to control the cost of living.[7] This strategy won Tower his victory.

Where the candidate is unknown, opinion polls can't gauge voter reaction because they have no pre-existing image to which the voter reacts. But another problem plagues an over-exposed front runner.

To illustrate, assume there is a race for Governor. The front-running candidate has served as state representative, run twice for United States senator, and is currently the state's crusading Insurance Commissioner. The polls show him with high name recognition among voters, three times higher than any of his major opponents. Also assume a hefty percentage of his high name recognition is negative.

The interviewer might ask: What does the name John Candidate mean to you? A majority of those interviewed probably have heard the name, and the interviewer must assume the name conjures images either of a tireless consumer advocate or a political opportunist.

After weighing this information, the analyst must decide the impact of the people who think the candidate is an opportunist. And the analyst must decide if John Candidate, who looks strong early on because thirty percent of those questioned say they are going to vote for him, will be able to move beyond that thirty percent. Analysts find that often it is harder for a controversial front runner to move from thirty to fifty percent than it is for an unknown to move from fifteen to fifty percent.

If this is true, then well-known candidates might want to make a few image changes, yet a complex pre-existing image may prevent the candidate from finding out how the voter will react to a new campaign theme or to an image change.

No-name Polling

Pollsters have created polling innovations to solve problems of being either unknown or overexposed. One innovation is the use of what consultant Gary Nordlinger calls the "Q-vignettes" technique. Paul Harstead of Peter D. Hart Research Associates calls it "hypothetical candidate" polling.

Actually, both consultants use a technique in which the pollster uses fictional candidates, measuring voter reaction to personal characteristics such as race, sex, age, past experience, education, marital status, and occupation as well as positions on various issues. This type of poll also measures voter reaction to candidates who have a combination of these characteristics and then matches these characteristics against other candidates with different backgrounds.

This technique is particularly helpful early in the campaign where a candidate is unknown because it may be necessary for the candidate to shape basic approaches such as a theme that will turn voters on.

This type of polling was used by pollster Patrick Caddell in the 1984 presidential primaries. Caddell showed Senator Hart the results of polls he had conducted in Iowa and New Hampshire indicating substantial support for a fictional "Senator Smith" whose characteristics resembled what later became United States Senator Gary Hart's theme: "A new generation revitalizing America."

In another example, Beth Bogart, writing for *Advertising Age*, describes a Colorado congressional race where no-name polling explored nine criticisms being leveled at a Democratic incumbent by the challenger. The poll found the only criticism doing any damage was that he was not from the western slope. Although the incumbent could not say he was from the western slope, he did use geography and won by running ads emphasizing that he was the only native Coloradan in the race.

"No-name" polling, though, does not work late in the campaign when advertising has reached its peak and a candidate has a better than fifty percent level of name recognition. Under these circumstances, voters easily guess who the candidates are and resent what they perceive as the efforts of the pollsters to play games with them.

Continuous Tracking

How the poll is disguised depends on who is using it. Often after a campaign is in full swing, strategists want to know more than the relative candidate standings. They want to know how switches in voter sentiment affect the candidate.

For example, if two candidates are running neck and neck, it makes a difference if the gains are from the uncommitted, if the leaders are gaining at the expense of a third candidate, or if the principle opponent is draining votes from the leader.

Because strategists are as interested in who is losing and in gaining as much as they are in where the votes are coming from, like bookkeepers they constantly track losses and gains in public support as well as which part of the public the losses and gains came from.

Issues

Political issues can be sobering, educational, and controversial. They satisfy curiosity and stimulate the imagination. But what the candidates commissioning private political polls want to know is whether the issues can be translated into votes.

To get issue information, the pollster asks questions such as: "In the election for United States Senator, the candidates are [list candidate's names]. Which of the three candidates do you feel can best deal with the following list of issues? If you do not know the candidate's positions or have no preference, just say so."

To get more definite information, the pollster can list the issues and the candidates one by one and then ask the voter who, in their opinion, can best deal with them.

There will be situations where the candidate will want to pursue this with further questions and answers. For example, when a campaign seems to be floundering, a private poll can be designed to search for a key issue.

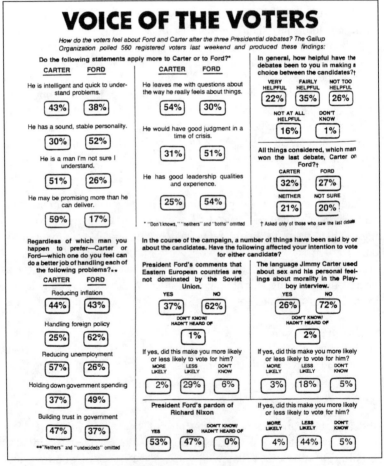

Fig. 3-7. Richard Steele with James Doyle, Thomas M. DeFrank, and Eleanor Clift. "Decision Time," *Newsweek*, November 1, 1976.

To get this information, the pollster might take a different tack by asking the following: "Which one issue concerns you the most: Morals in America___, the environment___, street crime___, or student and educational disorders___?"

Where discontent is suspected, pollsters try to isolate the reason. One question asked during the last days of Nixon's Presidency might have been: "Since the Watergate incident, I'm afraid to trust any politician who has been in office very long: Agree___, Disagree___, Don't know___."

Other questions might be: "Gas and oil companies are the most blamed for the current energy crisis because they probably knew about it ahead of time: Agree___, Disagree___, Don't know___." "We should not have sold our United States wheat to Russia and mainland China: Agree___, Disagree___, Don't know___."

Whatever the questioning technique, once the key issue is identified, the pollster can go into greater depth. Interviewers might even use a probability scale to quantify the voter's support or opposition to an issue. One such scale has two values ranging from ten percent for "no chance" to ninety percent for "certain, practically certain."[8]

For a checklist of practical tips on telephone polling, see the next page.

★ ★ ★ ★ ★ ★ ★ ★ ★ ★ ★ ★ ★ ★

Telephone Polling

Note: Seek help from a professional when determining procedures and interpreting poll results. If such help is not available, at least reread polling chapter.

	Target Date	Date Compl.

Survey procedures

	Target Date	Date Compl.
Use updated voter lists. Mark numbers to be called (e.g., every 25th or every 1000th name).	_____	_____
Prepare script, instructions, response forms, and tally sheets.	_____	_____
Recruit and train volunteers.	_____	_____
Select phone sites.	_____	_____
Designate a supervisor to be available to callers.	_____	_____
Make up a schedule for callers.	_____	_____
Distribute supplies: e.g., rulers, pencils, erasers.	_____	_____
Draft & field test.	_____	_____
Revise questionnaire and go for it.	_____	_____
Tally results.	_____	_____

Hints

As most jurisdictions close registration 4 to 5 weeks before election and it takes time to update and print the lists, it is best to use lists available at filing time and then supplement with updated information.

Best calling time is early evening, Monday through Thursday.

Have callers ask for voter by name on precinct sheet; interview spouse only if also a registered voter.

Allow five rings before hanging up.

Callers should complete entire list before going back to busy or not-at-home numbers.

Pollsters should not deviate from the script or procedures.

Pollsters should be nice even if rebuffed; these are your potential voters.

Carry on this time-intensive task in conjunction with another candidate; surveyors might alternate, or do five from one list, five from the other.

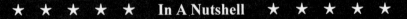

★ ★ ★ ★ ★   In A Nutshell   ★ ★ ★ ★ ★

Chapter 23

The Pitfalls of Evaluation

> The most spectacular defeat was suffered by the institutes of public opinion.
> —Francoise Giroud, Former French Minister of Culture[1]
>
> It's not my place to run a train, the whistle I can't blow.
> It's not my place to say how far the train is allowed to go.
> It's not my place to shoot off steam, nor even clang the bell,
> But let the damn thing jump the track and see who catches hell.
> —Anonymous

The Possibility of Error

As pollsters make their calculations, politicians must be constantly aware of possible error because in spite of the most elaborate precautions many scientific polls prove no better than unscientific surveys in predicting the election outcome.

One of the more notable unscientific polls was the 1948 "chicken feed" poll conducted by a Kansas miller. Unlike the scientific Gallup or Roper polls, he correctly predicted President Truman's victory when he offered his customers feed in bags that were illustrated with either a donkey or an elephant.

Then there was the Belvins poll which asked movie theater patrons to choose between popcorn boxes decorated with the pictures of presidential candidates. This poll came within 3.3 percent of predicting the exact percentage of President Kennedy's victory in 1960.[2]

Yet millions are spent each year on "scientific" polling. *Time* magazine estimated that in 1981-82, United States Senate and House candidates spent roughly $100 million on polling, an increase of about twenty-five percent over 1980. *Time* went on to say, "When races for governor and state legislative posts are added in, the grand total may hit a half billion dollars."[3]

To the research professionals, political polling is only the financial tip of the research iceberg. A few well-known names in political polling find that the majority of the polling professionals' income is from private corporate clients for whom they do market research.

Unlike election surveys, most commercial surveys have no foolproof verification, so pollsters must sell these customers by conveying the impression that their accuracy is assured by mathematical tables and random selection, while they try to forget that in 1948 the polls chose Dewey to beat Truman.

In spite of improved techniques, thirty years later in Great Britain the polls mistakenly predicted the defeat of Edward Heath's Conservative Party by the Labor Party of Harold Wilson. The fact is that polls are not always accurate.

Back to the United States: On election night immediately after the voters cast their ballots in 1982, ABC television and radio network, employing the results of exit polling, were on the air with poll results showing Democrats would pick up thirty seats. CBS foresaw a thirty-four seat gain, while the venerable Gallup poll put a wet finger to the wind and projected a Democratic surge in the House that translated to a gain of thirty-three seats.

In the same election, the Chicago *Tribune*'s final weekend poll had Republican Illinois Governor James Thompson with a fifteen point edge over challenger U.S. Senator Adlai Stevenson III. One pollster predicted defeat for Democratic incumbent United States Senator John Stennis of Mississippi as the "upset of the year."

But none of these predictions was accurate. True, Governor Thompson won, but it was in a neck-and-neck squeaker that the Democrats picked up 26 house seats, which was six to eight less than expected.[4]

How do we account for the difficulty pollsters have predicting voter reaction? For one thing, polling involves political judgment, which is colored by the fact that voters give even the most popular of politicians a mixed review.

In January 1984, when reporting on President Ronald Reagan, market research firm Louis Harris and Associates found that by three to two the voters gave Reagan credit for the economic recovery, as contrasted with earlier opinions that Reaganomics was a failure. Reagan's strongest issue was the decline of inflation and the steady decline of unemployment. A big majority (sixty-one percent) thought he was a superb communicator and that he had the leadership ability a President needs.

However, those polled were critical of his foreign policy. A sixty-one percent majority was worried that he would get the United States into war. Most of those polled perceived Reagan as favoring the rich at the expense of the poor. In fact, a seventy-two percent majority didn't think the budget could be balanced if he stayed another four years. And the poll found Reagan was found lacking in the eyes of those who placed emphasis on women's rights and environmental issues.[5]

Mixed reviews influence poll results and are affected by the way pollsters use issues. This was demonstrated during a lull in the 1984 Presidential primary. Polls matched Republican President Ronald Reagan and one-time Democratic Vice President Walter Mondale. One showed Reagan and Mondale tied, another showed Reagan ahead by three points, and a third showed Reagan ahead by sixteen points.

When the polltakers compared notes, they found that in the poll that showed the President was ahead by sixteen points, the Reagan-Mondale question had been asked first. When the voters were asked their opinions on issues like taxes, the deficit, and the mess in Lebanon, more of them leaned toward the Vice President.

In the poll that showed the candidates running neck and neck, the voters were asked to decide between Reagan and Mondale but only after they had been subjected to a whole barrage of questions about the deficit, foreign policy, etc.[6]

Other factors besides question sequence affect the validity of the conclusions pollsters reach, such as how the data is interpreted. For example, during the 1971 Presidential campaign, George Gallup reported that the Democratic party held a marginal lead over the Republicans (fifty-three to forty-seven percent) because the voters believed the Democrats could better handle the problems they considered to be most important.

This is not what the voters actually told the interviewers. Thirty-four percent thought the Democrats were more competent, twenty-eight percent favored the Republicans, but the largest group, thirty-eight percent, either said that there was no difference between the two parties or did not express any opinion.

Although no one knew how that thirty-eight percent would react without probing further, when reporting the results, Gallup simply discarded the thirty-eight percent, arbitrarily allocating half of the group to the Democrats and half to the Republicans.[7]

And there are other problems. For example, the evaluation of the poll results must take into account that a percentage of the voters may be unwilling to give the pollster their true preferences. This circumstance is likely to happen when those interviewed are ashamed to admit that they intend to vote their prejudices.

In the 1972 Presidential primaries segregationist Governor George Wallace invariably got a much higher share of the vote than was predicted by pre-election polls. In the Indiana primary, for example, Wallace got forty-one percent of the vote rather than the predicted twenty-two percent he received in the polls. In the Florida primary he got forty-two percent, not thirty-four percent; in Wisconsin, twenty-two percent instead of fifteen percent; and in Massachusetts, nine percent, not four percent. Not only did the pre-election surveys underestimate Wallace's true electoral strength, but the election returns proved that even the exit polls misled the interviewers.[8]

Similar discrepancies between the polls and actual votes often plague the pollster who is using the voter's past performance as a baseline for predicting future conduct. For example, a survey was conducted after the Watergate scandal and Nixon's resignation as President of the United States in 1973. Pollster Pat Caddell asked the voters in California whom they had voted for in the presidential election.

If taken at face value, his poll showed that McGovern really didn't lose California by forty percent (which he did), but would have carried it by an eight point margin. When informed of this phenomena, Caddell, who had been active in

McGovern's campaign, sent the Senator a tongue-in-cheek telegram, telling him to demand a recount.[9]

Candidates and issues are often combined in the person of popular leaders. Politically these leaders have a coattail effect that impacts lesser candidates. Their personality or a key issue they stand for polarizes the electorate and becomes a political force powerful enough to both persuade and dissuade voters who give their allegiance within that political party.

To get information concerning candidates and issues, technicians carefully design questions that do not suggest an answer. For example, when dealing with an issue, the interviewer might say: "Here is a list of items prominent in the news. Could you please tell me whether you approve or disapprove of each?"

Occasionally the issues are popular, but the candidate who advocates them is not. When this happens, a poll is needed to determine why the popularity will not carry over to the political aspirant. If the candidate can isolate the cause, sometimes remedial action can be taken.

This was the case in 1968, when researcher John Maddox, using such open-ended questions, discovered that Americans perceived Richard Nixon as lacking in personal warmth. Nixon and his strategists then hired Paul Keys, a writer for the popular "Laugh In" program, to give Nixon's presentations a sense of humor.[10]

When a controversial leader or cause polarizes an election, candidates for other offices must be realistic. When measuring their chances, they need to use polling to assess the cost in votes of having their fate linked with a popular—as well as an unpopular—leader, cause, or political party.

The coattail effect

The GOP gained at least 10 seats in the House of Representatives Tuesday.* The party holding the White House lost House seats in only one of the last five elections in which presidents were returned to office.

Year	President	Seats gained/lost
1944	Roosevelt	+21
1948	Truman	+75
1956	Eisenhower	-2
1964	Johnson	+38
1972	Nixon	+12

Source: *Congressional Quarterly*   *five races still too close to call

Fig. 3-8. *USA Today,* November 8, 1984. Copyright 1984, USA Today. Reprinted with permission.

Chapter 24

Balancing Image and Issues

> Public opinion is like the castle ghost; no one has ever
> seen it but everyone is scared of it.
> —Sigmund Graff in *Die Weltwoch,* Switzerland[1]

During most campaigns a large percentage of the voters are an unstable mass that leans toward a particular candidate, but is constantly shifting as the campaign wears on. Tracking and evaluating these voters is a process of weighing and balancing a number of forces.

When considering the political impact, there should be added a large constituency of voters who, for one reason or another, fit the description given to the interviewer by the lady of the house when she said, "In my opinion, whoever is elected . . . my husband will be furious."

The pollster must be able to recognize and allow for the fact that voters have what can be called political schizophrenia. For example, citizens who generally want lower taxes and believe in cutting the fat out of the budget are like the resident who explained why these congressmen get re-elected: "Oh, I don't blame Congress. If I had $600 billion at my disposal, I'd be irresponsible, too." Still voters re-elect those who qualify as spenders with respect to parity for farmers, road repair, or "pork-barrel" projects.

Voter perception of issues and how they relate to candidates is further complicated by the fact that most major political figures are neither pure barn-burners nor pure hunkers. Stated more accurately, candidates all believe in issues, but are wise enough not to commit political suicide.

Fig. 3-9. Ben Wicks, *The Province,* Vancouver, B.C., February 7, 1980.

Before taking a strong position regarding a controversial issue such as the legalization of marijuana, forced school busing, stricter gun control laws, legalized abortion, reinstitution of the death penalty, or life imprisonment for drug pushers, candidates try to calculate voter reaction by using polls.

There is still another complication. Issues have a synergistic effect on each other. A voter may not be persuaded by the candidate's stand on a single issue, but will be persuaded when taken with what the voter perceives to be a good or poor image or a favorable or unfavorable party preference. So it is important that the strategist sees how these factors affect each other.

To pick up meaningful information, the voters' answers must be cross-referenced and categorized. Before undertaking the tedious job of assimilating this information, the Democratic National Committee suggests each question and answer be given a code number.[2]

Tabulating is easier if a computer is available to track the results. Computer software includes telemarketing packages that can be adapted to campaigning. There are analytic packages specifically designed for the IBM and Apple computers like AIDA (Action Research Northwest), Survey Tab, and Tabulyzer.[3]

When a computer is not available, the Democratic National Committee suggests that cross-tabulation be carried out as illustrated in Figure 3-10.

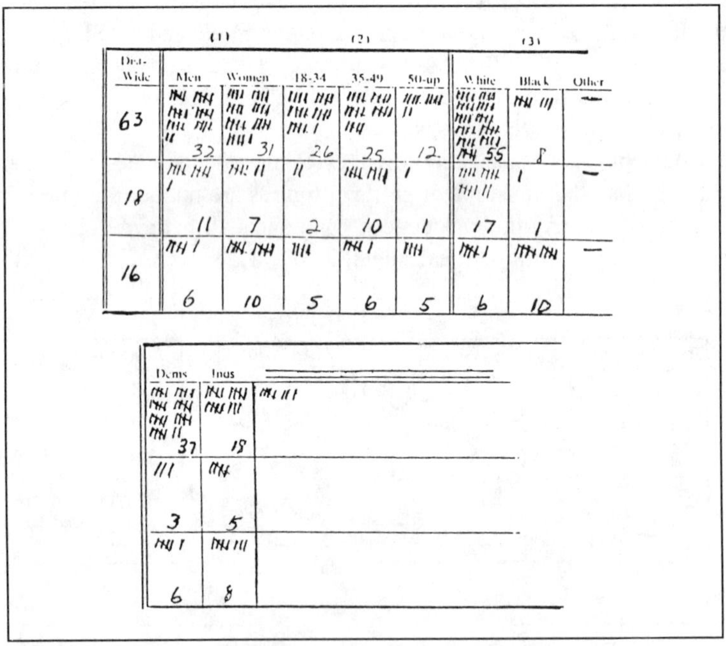

Dra-Wide	Men	Women	18-34	35-49	50-up	White	Black	Other
63	32	31	26	25	12	55	8	—
18	11	7	2	10	1	17	1	—
16	6	10	5	6	5	6	10	—

Dems	Inds	
37	18	
3	5	
6	8	

Fig. 3-10. "Cross-tabulation of polling results." "In-house Polling," *Target '76* (Washington DC: Democratic Natl. Comm., 1976), p. 18.

Chapter 25

Is Polling Really Worth the Cost?

Professional polls are expensive.
—Edward Schwartzman, campaign pollster[1]

As campaign professional Edward Schwartzman points out, professional polls are expensive. Costs include overhead, profit, training, supervision, interviews, questionnaire design, sample design, sample selection, coding schedules, cross-tabulation or computer-program development and testing, data entry, computer operation, preparation of final tables, analysis, and presentation of final results as well as consultation with the candidate and campaign staff.

Schwartzman adds: "In large-scale, professionally conducted campaigns, five to ten percent of the total amount available can reasonably be budgeted for research. The dollar research cost of such polling can be almost the same for a smaller contest, and, because it takes a much larger share of their smaller campaign budget, it is often skipped."

Even worse, for most campaigns, the expense must be incurred early when the campaign also needs the money to reserve billboard space or television time. Thus, the run-of-the-mill campaign either goes without polling or it commissions one early poll to set the campaign's course.

Let's return for a moment to the confused candidate as he or she attempts to conduct a volatile campaign. We know in-depth polls are expensive, but this is even more disturbing when poll findings can be wrong. It is obvious there is even a greater chance polls can be wrong when attempting to measure the impact of the voter to a pre-existing image, a new campaign theme or a controversial leader or issue.

Because polling results fluctuate and are occasionally wrong, some prominent men and women refuse to put their confidence in them, such as the father of Governor Jerry Brown, former California Governor Edmund (Pat) Brown. Although he used polls, he said: "I'd give at least equal weight to my own sensing of how things are going, developed primarily from conversations with people I meet during the day's campaigning."

But the problem with the "sensing" approach is that candidates and their close supporters are usually their own worst enemies. When it comes to campaign predictions or analysis, they are blessed more with optimism than cold realism. They find it hard not to become mesmerized by the support they inspire. It is hard to undo the damage done if they lose sight of a majority of the voting public who may not care about or be aware of their position on an issue. So, in spite of inevitable errors, careful in-depth polling is still the best way to interpret voter reaction and track public opinion during a political campaign.

The candidate should keep in mind, though, that the voter is fickle. Information collected in any given poll is only valid at the time the poll is taken because people's attitudes and opinions change.

Charles Roll and Albert Cantril illustrate this fickle attitude in their book, *Polls*:

> When Truman came into office in 1945, the Gallup poll showed he had an eighty-seven percent approval. By October of the next year, his rating was down to a favorable thirty-two percent, and it bobbed up and down thereafter. On coming into office in 1953, Dwight Eisenhower had a sixty-eight percent approval. His popularity stayed around the seventy percent mark until the end of 1957, when it fell to sixty percent and then to fifty-five percent. After that it never really recovered its earlier heights.
>
> President John Kennedy's early ratings were in the low seventies and they dropped to fifty-nine percent just prior to his assassination. Lyndon Johnson was initially buoyed by a rating of seventy-nine percent and then eighty percent when he inherited the Presidency at a time of crisis. However, by 1966 his standing had dropped to the fifties and by the time the 1968 election came along they were in the lower forties.[2]

Politicians who have had experience with these surges in public sentiment encourage well-heeled campaigns to provide for multiple polls to track the campaign's progress and to acquire the information necessary to shape political images and sharpen sales pitches.

Another reason why candidates benefit from continuous polling is that a sizable portion of voters do not make up their minds until late in the campaign. For this reason the political landscape is strewn with the "corpses" of candidates who failed to pick up on late popularity shifts.

Typical of these was former United States Senator Thomas McIntyre of New Hampshire. He was the overwhelming favorite against a 38-year-old Allegheny Airlines pilot, Gordon Humphrey, in the early 1978 polls. Indeed, McIntyre thought he was so far ahead he quit polling and permitted his opponent's commercials on Boston television (which covered most of New Hampshire) to go uncontested, while he relied on radio, print, and personal handshaking. Many experts believe this miscalculation cost him the election.[3]

This brings us to the alternatives to continuous polling. When less-affluent campaigns try to balance the cost of knowing how the campaign is progressing against other demands for campaign funding, some try shortcuts to save money. In a few cases they skip the research necessary to select a new panel for subsequent polls. Instead, they split up the original sample into smaller panels and re-interview the originally selected voters as the campaign progresses. Most pollsters warn their clients that re-using the same voters is dangerous since the original interview has already stimulated the sample voter's interest.

However, almost any professional poll beats using volunteer pollsters to conduct a candidate's "do it yourself" survey. An accurate opinion poll requires expert question design, supervision, training, coordination, testing objectivity, sample selection, and verification. Untrained volunteers find it hard to cope with unfavorable results and some lose heart. Others, being friends and admirers, change the results to protect the candidate from the facts. And because most volunteers do not fully understand polling, they skip some of the tedious details that make the poll accurate.

After the Campaign

Speaking of campaign polling and its value, victory is not the final chapter. In most cases the candidates, and certainly their party will conduct future campaigns. Without an updated poll, they can only guess what persuaded voters to vote the way they did.

Even after an election, the question remains as to how undecideds voted. Did the pollster accurately assess the undecided voters who claimed no partisan preference? Did he or she divide undecideds among the candidates in the same percentages exhibited by the voters who had decided? Did the pollster take into consideration the fact that the voters who took a position on issues had little political motivation?

A wise political organization or candidate can design a poll for use after an election. This is what George Romney did when he was Governor of Michigan. Questions were specifically designed to find how the campaign techniques and strategies worked. His poll asked: What was the most effective kind of advertising? What were the most appealing issues? How did the organization function?

Chapter 26

Reaction to Polls

> I must follow the people. Am I not their leader?
> —Benjamin Disraeli, British Prime Minister[1]
>
> A man who is influenced by the polls or is afraid to make decisions which may make him unpopular is not a man to represent the welfare of the country.
> —President Harry S. Truman[2]

The Impact of Polling Information

There is no question that the use of political polls has increased politicians' dependence on what happens to be popular at the moment. Understandably, pragmatic candidates want to use polling information to control their strategy. Polling results may also determine the thrust of the candidate's advertising and the nature of the campaign attack.

Polling and the candidate's reaction to the polls have often become so important that, rather than simply measuring public opinion, polls have almost taken on a life of their own. Clearly the media has so publicized the results that polling does more to an election campaign than simply track voter reaction. Favorable polls spread enthusiasm among supporters and encourage voters and financial investors who want to support a winner.

Some newspaper endorsements even follow poll results. In 1981, the New York *Post* ran a "coupon questionnaire" asking readers whether Mayor Edward Koch should run for governor. A majority of those answering thought he should. A short time after the highly touted results were in, Mr. Koch announced his candidacy and received support from the *Post*.[3]

Poll results can also create a political climate and thus have a political impact. When asked by the media to comment on a favorable poll, most candidates are cautious, exuding confidence and avoiding comment because of the potential shift in poll results.

Understandably, candidates are even more reluctant to comment when the poll results are bad. They often rationalize and play down the results saying something like, "Did you know that if the pre-election opinion polls had been right, both Presidents Franklin Roosevelt and Harry Truman would have lost?"[4] Avoiding comment is comparatively easy where the poll is private and the press has only a rumor to go on. Where the poll is conducted by newspapers, television or radio, the candidate must roll with the punches.

Polls are so important that occasionally a candidate's success can create a pollster. This happened in 1975 when presidential candidate Jimmy Carter was running in Florida's primary against a crowded field, which included George Wallace of Alabama. When searching for someone with expertise, he found a young bachelor, Pat Caddell, who gained his knowledge of Florida and southern politics by research for his senior thesis at Harvard. Carter won that primary, and thereafter Caddell became the pollster for the team that swept Carter into the White House.[5]

Some office holders carry polling beyond the campaign. One-time Michigan Governor George Romney approached polling as the efficient captain of industry he was before becoming Governor. After he was in office, he continued to use in-depth polling. For example, Romney's pollsters, DeVries and Currier, knew what Michigan voters thought about civil rights in 1962 and in every year thereafter, and how it affected conceptions of and attitudes towards issues, parties, and candidates.[6]

Romney based not only his campaign strategy on the polling results but much of his conduct after he was elected. For example, if the voters rated Romney's ability high and the party's more conservative image low, they advised him to keep his party out of it. If the opposite result was obtained—that is, a high rating for the party, a low rating for Romney—he was advised to switch the strategy around and emphasize the party and play down the individual character of his candidacy.[7]

The tendency that politicians have to follow, rather than lead, has prompted intellectuals such as Allan Brownfield to ask, "How can our society restore faith in its institutions and in its ability to cope with the complex problems of this technical age?" He answered his own question saying: "It cannot be done by men who are busy making television commercials and running for office on the basis of their image, rather than their programs."[8]

Mythical Political Poll—1776

This prompts these intellectuals to speculate on what would have happened if a public opinion poll had been taken by the leaders of the American Revolution just prior to 1776. Humorist Art Buchwald puts the question and answers in his own way. "If there had been political pollsters," Buchwald says, "This is how the results might have turned out":

> When asked if they thought the British were doing a good job in governing the Colonies, this is how a cross section of the people responded: British doing good job—63%, Not doing good job—22%, Don't know—15%. Next question: Do you think the dumping of tea in Boston Harbor by militants helped or hurt the taxation laws in the New World? Hurt the cause of taxation—79%, Helped the cause—12%, Didn't think it would make any difference—9%. What do you think our image is in

England after the Minute Men attacked the British at Lexington? Minute men hurt our image in England—83%, Gave British new respect for Colonies—10%, Undecided—7%. Which of these two Georges can do more for the Colonies— George III or George Washington? George III—76%, George Washington—14%, Others—10%. (It is interesting to note that eighty percent of the people questioned had never heard of George Washington before.)

Next question: Do you think the Declaration of Independence as it is written is a good document or a bad one? Bad document—14%, Good document—12%, No opinion—84%. (A group of those polled felt that the Declaration of Independence had been written by a bunch of radicals and the publishing of it at this time would only bring harsher measures from the British.) When asked whether the best way to bring about reforms was through terrorism or redress to the Crown, an overwhelming proportion of Colonists felt appeals should be made to the King. Reforms through petition—24%, Reforms through act of terrorism—8%, Don't know—66%.

The pollsters then asked what the public thought was the most crucial issue of the time. Trade with foreign nations—65%, War with Indians—20%, Independence issue—15%. The survey also went into the question of Patrick Henry. Do you think Patrick Henry did the right thing in demanding "liberty or death"? Did a foolhardy thing and was a trouble maker—53%, Did a brave thing and made his point—23%, Should have gone through the courts—6%, Don't know—8%.

Buchwald, tongue in cheek, then commented, "On the basis of the results of this mythical poll, the militant Colonials decided they did not have enough popular support to form a revolution and gave up the idea of creating a United States of America.[9]

Of course, there are those who oppose this philosophical view. They point out that we live in a democracy and if public opinion is to control, what better way is there to know what the public wants than by sampling the electorate.

Politicians Have Always Exploited Issues and Philosophies

Beth Bogart gives the typical reply of those who employ these types of polls saying, "Most pollsters defend their profession and hypothetical polling in particular by saying that, although the techniques may shift a campaign's emphasis, it does not affect a candidate's values."[10] Those who make this argument remind us that long before there were modern, in-depth political polls, politicians were opportunists and ready to exploit trivial nonessentials that might help their cause.

Shortly after the turn of the century, Tammany Hall dominated the Democratic Party in New York City. Then-Congressman William R. Hearst (the renowned publisher), a candidate for mayor, opposed a Tammany man and son of Civil War General George B. McClellan, who also had a following among the upper income voters with British ties.

Fig. 3-11. David Seavey, *USA Today,* January 31, 1984.
Copyright 1984, USA Today. Reprinted with permission.

When McClellan dined at the British Embassy, it hurt him politically with the anti-British Irish who constituted a substantial part of his New York constituency. Hearst, speaking through his paper, the New York *Journal American,* accused McClellan of being a hireling of Great Britain.

Then McClellan got word that a British-American squadron, commanded by Prince Louis of Battenberg, was about to make a courtesy visit to New York City during the campaign. At this prospect, McClellan was beside himself. While he felt politically obliged to join the greeters, he could see a cartoon of himself on the front page of the Hearst newspaper scraping before "his highness." Faced with this dilemma, McClellan moved heaven and earth to be sure that the visit was postponed until after the election. This was probably wise because he beat Hearst by less than 3,000 of the approximately 600,000 votes cast.[11]

Those who use philosophy to justify modern in-depth polling argue that it is necessary if the politician is to have perspective. They add that without polling candidates become advocates with fixed and often erroneous ideas as to how voters are reacting. For example, in the 1968 New Hampshire presidential primary, United States Senator Eugene McCarthy was distinguished from other Presidential candidates opposing President Lyndon Johnson. He ran a single-issue, peace-dove or anti-Vietnam war campaign, while President Johnson supported the United States involvement in the Vietnam War. McCarthy came from nowhere in the public opinion polls to get a stunning forty-two percent.

After the New Hampshire primary, there was a post-election survey to determine the reason. These studies showed that McCarthy benefited from the minority who opposed involvement in Vietnam, but that did not account for his showing. The Democratic voters of that state saw the primary as a two-man race. This diverted the Democratic anti-Johnson vote from the other anti-administration hopefuls.

Indeed, the University of Michigan Survey Research Center found that most of McCarthy's votes were not pro-McCarthy, but anti-Johnson, and, even more surprising, it showed that three out of five McCarthy supporters in New Hampshire believed that the Johnson administration was wrong on Vietnam, not because it was too hawkish, but because it wasn't hawkish enough.[12]

Part 4

Advertising

$ $ $ $ **WARNING** $ $ $ $

Today, campaign costs and contributions have soared beyond
the wildest predictions. Though dollar amounts quoted
throughout this book are historically correct and valuable as
general percentage guidelines, dollar amounts more than two to
four years old should not be depended upon for structuring
campaign budgets.

Chapter 27

Political Advertising Techniques

Hail to B.B.D. and O. It told the nation how to go
It managed by advertising to sell us a new President.
Eisenhower hits the spot, one full general, that's a lot.
Feeling sluggish, feeling sick? Take a dose of Ike and Dick.

Philip Morris, Lucky Strike,
Alka-Seltzer, I like Ike.
  —Marya Mannes[1]

You sell your candidates and your programs the way a
business sells its products.
  —Leonard Hall, National Republican Chairman during the
  late 1960s[2]

Exposure

Hal Every, Los Angeles public relations man, says: "Eight percent of the people don't even know the name of their congressman. Ninety-nine percent of the people don't know whether an incumbent running for reelection has kept his earlier campaign promises. Almost one-third of the people eligible to vote don't even register. Many of those who register don't vote, even though news media exhort them repeatedly to go to the polls."[3]

J. V. Steward's Harvard Business School study entitled, *Repetitive Advertising in Newspapers*, in which he tested newspaper advertising for new products on different segments of the population, found people making choices just because they were exposed. The first rule not only of political merchandising but of advertising is that, in a vacuum, neutral exposure and persuasion are the same.[4]

Most political campaigns involve advertising and even conventional merchandising. But campaigning is a process in which paid merchandising and advertising and are integrated with the existing political environment. This includes political news coverage, media editorials, staged and unplanned events, all of which are non-commercial public relations. Together, they create a persuasive force so powerful that Marshall McLuhan described it as the "greatest teaching system devised in the history of the world."[5]

In most political contests the better-known incumbent has name familiarity— but there is a flip side. Invariably they have had exposure, but it has not always made them popular. When Arizona Senator Barry Goldwater went to New Hampshire to begin his 1964 presidential campaign, a hostile media painted him

Fig. 4-1. Advertising used by presidential winners.

Fig. 4-2. Goldwater billboard courtesy Metro Media, Seattle; remainder from Gary Yanker, *Prop Art* (New York: Darien House, 1972), pp. 90-91.

as advocating voluntary Social Security. It ridiculed him as ignorant, scoffing at his alleged statements that he didn't know a single state with more Negro discrimination than New York, home of his principal opponent, Governor Nelson Rockefeller. At the same time Rockefeller's popularity was sagging because he was just emerging from a highly-publicized divorce and remarriage to a woman many years his junior.

Up stepped a group of college students. They hastily organized an alternative—a write-in campaign for Henry Cabot Lodge, the United States Ambassador to Vietnam. Lodge swept the Republican primary, even though he didn't come home to campaign.[6] Obviously, this illustration does not apply to run-of-the-mill candidates where advertising—or more accurately merchandising—depends on the candidate's ability to pierce the voters' stream of consciousness.

Those fighting in the political trenches soon find out, as Professor Dan Nimmo puts it:

> ... exposure is not easily won. Each candidate's appeal competes for the voter's attention with the exhortations of other candidates and with non-political sources—product advertising, the day's news, documentaries, live coverage of men circling the moon, variety entertainment, each radio station's 'Top Forty Tunes' and sundry other communications bombarding the human senses.[7]

Savvy candidates try to be creative. For example, U.S. Senator Robert Dole has been elected to two terms in Congress, twice to the United States Senate, and has served his party as Senate majority leader, as its national chairman, and as its candidate for vice president. When he was unknown, he sought his party's nomination for Congress in a twenty-six county district in western Kansas. He had spirited opposition from a candidate who had come within a few votes of winning an earlier primary, and from another candidate whose last name was Dale. Robert Dole handed out thousands of cups of Dole pineapple juice to associate his name with Dole of Hawaii.[8]

Just how effective is candidate exposure? Imagine a television camera zeroing in on a still photo of three Boy Scouts at a flag raising. The camera moves in on one of the Scouts, young Jerry Ford. *"Announcer:* 'He was an Eagle Scout. He was an honor student.' " The camera shows hands holding a football. The camera pulls back quickly, revealing Ford as a college-age student crouched over the ball. *"Announcer:* 'He was the most valuable player at Michigan.' " The camera shows a large group photo, then closes in on Ford. *"Announcer:* 'He was graduated in the top third of Yale Law School, while holding a full-time job.' " The camera focuses on a still photo of Ford in a military uniform. *"Announcer:* 'He served courageously in World War II.' "

Then the camera picks up Ford on the floor of Congress with Speaker John McCormack. *"Announcer:* 'He led his party in the Congress.' " TV shot of President Ford in oval office, working at a desk. *"Announcer:* 'And in two short years as president, he has brought us peace, helped turn the economy around, and helped make us proud again.' " The screen fades to Ford's profile, looking thoughtful, and the camera slowly moves up close. *"Announcer:* 'Gerald Ford has always been best when the going was toughest. Let's keep him in charge.' "[9]

This is a typical campaign television commercial. It capably marshaled the evidence and touted the qualities of a very prestigious person—the President of the United States. Strategically, such a commercial may have been necessary early in Ford's reelection campaign. Its only weak point is that, from its first moment, it is recognized as a political commercial. This fact alone can psychologically turn off A viewing audience, even making them change channels. For that reason, it lacks something—call it creativity, message flash, or style.

To be effective, all pieces of advertising, including political gimmicks, must compete to impress the voter. What is the nature of that competition? Leo Bogart, Executive Vice President of the Newspaper Advertising Bureau, answered that question when he calculated the number of messages that companies send and that consumers see or hear every day. Bogart found that in 1982 the average consumer was exposed to 323 messages daily in the four media—television, radio, newspaper, and magazines—compared with 271 in 1967,[10] and that figure has increased way beyond 323 by now.

Even more difficult than the overall competition is that the political piece must attract voters who demonstrate something less than enthusiasm for what it has to sell. In the 1978 presidential election, the three networks in the New York election coverage were shunned by 70 percent of the TV viewers; 31 percent preferred watching a rerun of the movie, *The Pink Panther*. According to nationwide figures for the 56 primetime shows aired during the week of that election, CBS coverage ranked 54th and NBC's four-hour "Vote 1978" ranked dead last.[11]

Then how can an ad persuade when it touts a candidate and looks like a campaign spot? Let's move to another obviously political TV commercial—a little surprise that conveys a more sophisticated presidential image. The television camera focuses on President Jimmy Carter in a meeting. He says, " 'My own inclination is to get the nose of the federal government out of local affairs and out of state affairs whenever they can be handled in a state or in a community.' "

The camera focuses on others around the table, reacting to his comments. President Carter is seen from behind two people across the table, listening to someone make a point. *"Announcer:* 'He used to be a full-time farmer. He does a different kind of work today, but it's still work—long hours of hard work.' " Carter looks down and fidgets, preoccupied, then speaks softly, saying, " 'I'll make a decision on it today.' "

Jimmy Carter walks down a hallway into the Oval Office. He walks briskly to his desk, on the way lightly touching a world globe beside his chair. He leans over his desk and reads a paper. *"Announcer:* 'His decisions reach out to touch the lives of millions. In the course of any day, he focuses on every vital issue facing the nation.' "

President Carter is seated next to HEW Secretary, Patricia Harris at a conference table, along with several others. He comments, " 'Our comprehensive nationwide health program has been presented to the Congress. For us to depart from those two basic documents is a serious mistake.' " Then the TV camera shows a shot of the President gesturing from a podium standing in front of various military charts. He emphasizes, " 'My number one responsibility is to defend this country, to maintain its security.' "

The camera shows people applauding and President Carter shaking hands with members of the audience. *"Announcer:* " 'It's nothing at all like being alone in a Georgia field, driving a tractor for ten hours in the hot sun. Yet no other candidate can match his work experience or his life experience. President Carter—a solid man in a sensitive job.' " White letters appear against a green background, " 'RE-ELECT PRESIDENT CARTER in the Democratic Primary April 22.' "[12]

Building Name and Image Recognition

Note: The candidate should decide whether there is time to plan for a long-term effort, or must settle for the short-term, and proceed accordingly. (If the candidate has declared early, many of these strategies can be used even before filing.)

Make a list of important local, regional, and national groups or constituencies, with
    identities of the leadership. For example:
    –Businesses, Chamber of Commerce
    –Professional employment groups (e.g., unions or medical associations)
    –Voting segments, e.g., seniors (e.g., AARP) and ethnic or religious organizations
    –Community councils
Evaluate: Does support already exist or will it need to be developed? Take steps to
    increase visibility, e.g., increase publicity.
Prepare speech. Practice, practice, practice. Let friends, associates, and program chairs
    know you're available. Volunteer to speak to local groups.
Volunteer to write a weekly column for the local house organ, community newspaper,
    etc.
Look for opportunities to speak out on popular issues.

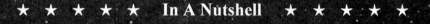

In A Nutshell

Chapter 28

What Distinguishes the Image of Mickey Mouse From Other Mice?

> The citizen does not so much vote for a candidate as make a psychological purchase of him.
> —Joe McGinnis[1]

Selling an Image

Selling a candidate is like selling a product. As one-time Governor of the State of Florida Fuller Warren put it, "advertising should concentrate on the image of the candidate himself, the public service he has rendered, his integrity, qualifications, etc. Sell the man or woman, not how he will vote or act on individual causes."[2]

Before today's modern communications, word-of-mouth and print were used to merchandise a candidate. President Martin Van Buren came from New York and the dominant Democratic Party, yet he was defeated by the candidate of a new party—the Whigs.

One newspaper editorial said that the Whig candidate, General William Harrison, was unfit to govern the nation because he was more at home with poor frontiersman than the people he would have to deal with as President. But instead of giving General Harrison (dubbed "Tippecanoe" because of his Indian fighting) a negative image, it gave him a positive political image tied to developing the west.

Seizing the initiative, the Whigs republished and circulated the editorial and composed a little ditty tying Harrison to log cabins and cider, western staples of life at the time:

"Oh, let them talk about hard cider - cider - cider,
and log cabins, too.
It will only help speed the ball
For Tippecanoe and Tyler, too.
For Tippecanoe and Tyler, too.
And with them we'll beat Van - Van - Van
Oh, he's a used up man.
Yes, with them we'll beat Van - Van - Van."[3]

Communications have come a long way since "Tippecanoe and Tyler, too." Tony Schwartz, author of more than five thousand radio and television commercials, explained one of the most important psychological goals of modern mass persuasion: "If the advertisers evoke human feeling and human experience in relation to a product, there is a good chance it will evoke the associations experienced with the commercial."[4]

In the hands of knowledgeable commercial pros, even inanimate objects take on human qualities. Let's look at the best known of such synthetic images—one of the most loved characters in American folklore—Mickey Mouse. What makes Mickey Mouse different from other mice? He's different because Walt Disney created an image and gave it personality. The same is true in politics; the success of most political candidates does not depend on the voter's memory of individual promises or acts, but rather on the total impression or image.

The political importance of this quality has been enhanced by television, where from the beginning early studies conducted by such distinguished researchers as Lazarsfeld (1940); Stouffer (1940); Lazarsfeld, Berelson and Guadent (1948); McPhee (1953); and Bogart (1965) found that television permitted the performer to project a personality much like a face-to-face friendship.[5]

During Eisenhower's first campaign, he shared the national ticket with a young U.S. Senator from California, Richard Nixon. As the campaign unfolded, the Democrats publicized the fact that the Republican nominee for vice president, who at that time was a junior senator, had after his election established an ongoing source of office money made up of contributions from wealthy citizens of his state. This he used to defray political expenses which at that time he felt were beyond the means of a United States Senator.

While his was not the only fund of that type, when the Democrats made it a major campaign issue, it was rumored that Ike would drop the young senator from the ticket. That was before a fascinated voting public watched Richard Nixon take his case to the nation via television. During that speech Nixon impressed the TV audience as a young man of very limited means—a man who was almost overcome with emotion and ready to burst into tears as he defended his reputation, the reputation of his wife and her "cloth coat," and even the reputation of his dog Checkers. He convinced the public that he was an official whose income was not adequate to serve the voters of a huge state.

The "Checkers" speech not only changed millions of minds, but caused Nixon to emerge with a new saleable public personality—one that equated with the thousands of other young men who had just come out of the service and found it hard to compete financially with those who had stayed behind.[6]

When personalizing the product—or candidate—the advertising professional sees the candidate's background, education, economic success, and family appearance as props that can be used to create a new image or the image perceived by the voter. The television commercial is so short that it is used to emphasize a single quality at a time. For example, the camera focuses on a candidate in an

Fig. 4-3. Excerpts from President Nixon's "Checkers" speech. Used by permission of L. Patrick Devlin, Curator, Television Political Advertising Collection, University of Rhode Island.

upcoming Presidential primary, ex-Governor Jimmy Carter. Expression serious, he stands in a dark blue suit before pale green curtains. He says, "I have tried to speak for the vast majority of Americans that for too long have been kept on the outside looking in. I have no obligations to those whose only interest in this campaign is to stop the people from getting control of your government."

A panel flashes on the screen, white letters on blue background: "Jimmy Carter June 8." He continues, "I'm running for president because I have a vision of a new America. A different America. A better America. If you share that vision, help me fight for it." Announcer: "Vote for Jimmy Carter and his delegates, June 8."[7]

Four years later another ex-Governor used his television personality when running for President. Ronald Reagan had the same concern with the public's perception and in his television debate with President Carter gave highest priority to projecting himself as sensible and safe. His debate strategy memorandum said, "The major debate task turns on enhancing Ronald Reagan's perceived trustworthiness. If more voters believe he is more worthy of their trust after the debate than they did before, his vote support will expand and strengthen."[8]

How Reagan succeeded was reported by author and political analyst David Halberstam, who confessed that prior to his election as President, nationwide reporters "under-estimated President Reagan's appeal because they fastened too literally on what he said, missing instead his true appeal, which was subliminal: the fact that he seems a comfortable, reassuring man," unlike the image of him projected by his opposition as a threat to peace.[9]

The Voter Likes Variety

There is considerable evidence that the public likes variety in the figures who prance across the political stage. To illustrate, in 1960, two-term Republican congressman John Lindsay successfully ran for mayor of what was considered a Democratic bastion, New York City. In that campaign his advertising presented him as a handsome, smiling young man striding down a busy street, using the caption: "He is fresh when everyone else is tired."

Once in office, John Lindsay, like Robert Wagner before him, found being mayor meant dealing with tough, controversial problems that required unpopular decisions. He was rejected by the Republicans in the primary when he filed for re-election, but, thanks to New York's unique party structure, his name still appeared on the final election ballot as the nominee of two splinter parties.

Lindsay's advertisers had the task of finding a new message that would appeal to tough, sophisticated New Yorkers, most of whom owed their loyalty to the Democratic Party. Lindsay did it by using what the national advertising trade journal, *Advertising Age*, calls "Incredible Honest Ads." In them his message remained the same. He admitted his failures and pointed to his strong points. One of his commercials featured a tieless, short-sleeved Lindsay, who looked straight into the TV camera and said, "I guessed wrong on the weather before the city's biggest snowfall last winter (for which the opposition alleged the city was not prepared), and that was a mistake. But I also put 6,000 more cops on the street, and that was no mistake."[10]

Another piece showed Lindsay saying, "The school strike in which the opposition alleged we should have settled went too far—and we all made some mistakes; I fought for three years to put a fourth platoon (of police) on the streets and that was no mistake; and I reduced the deadliest gas in our air by 50 percent and forced the landlords to roll back unfair rents; and we didn't have a Newark, a Detroit or a Watts [cities that experienced race riots that year] in this city—and those were no mistakes. When things go wrong, then this is the second toughest job in America. But when things go right, they make me want it."[11] Lindsay won again.

For another more graphic illustration of voters being drawn to variety, let's look back to the late 1920s when the State of Washington was governed by terrible-tempered Roland Harley, who enjoyed being the center of bitter controversy. Periodically, he went to the state Senate, which was controlled by his enemies, and make headlines as he told the senators what he thought of them. On one occasion, he violated protocol and appeared unannounced, instead of asking for an invitation.

Seeing the governor inside the outer chamber, the dean of the body, Oliver Hall, raised a point of order that no one was allowed in the state senate chamber unless he had the prior permission of the body. The governor's faction in the senate tried and failed to get the body to approve it. A public spectacle was created as the sergeant of arms escorted the governor out of the chamber. While this was taking place, Hall and Hartley got into an argument. An infuriated Hartley promised that next election he would go into Hall's district and tell his constituents what kind of S.O.B. he really was. The elderly Hall, voice cracking, fists clenched, let the Governor know that not only did he welcome the challenge, but he promised that if the governor came to his county, he would tear his political hide off.[12]

Next election both men filed for re-election to their respective posts. When the governor came to Hall's district, they shared the same election platform. As they traveled from town to town, Grange Hall to Grange Hall, their vitriolic debates were a box-office smash that drew record crowds as they accused each other of assorted real and imaginary misdeeds. When the votes for that county were counted, these bitter antagonists had not only beaten their respective opponents, but they shared the highest vote ever recorded in that county for both offices.

Again, the candidate must remember the first rule of merchandising: Where a political vacuum exists and there is no other over-powering issue or condition, exposure and persuasion are the same.

Moving from Exposure to Creating an Image

Often in a political contest, especially one for lesser office, the winner is decided primarily by name familiarity. Under these circumstances a candidate is ready to seize on any handy crutch that will give him or her exposure. One winner in a 1980 Oakland, California, city council race won because he decided that people were tired of hearing gloom and doom. He emphasized that there were some good things about Oakland and let people know what they were. With a smile, he said, "Hey, we've got some good things too. Let's see about making more good things happen." The voters chose him and rejected his opponents, who had offered the public another dose of doomsday served up with a frown.[13]

*"I'm sure our firm can handle your campaign, Senator, but first we
have to answer the question 'Who are you?' "*

Fig. 4-4. Drawing by Lorenz; © 1978 The New Yorker Magazine, Inc.

Incumbents usually settle on a message, such as one used by one-time House minority leader, John Rhodes. Billboards pictured him full length, moving with briefcase in hand, with the words, "He Knows *Your Way* Around Washington."[14]

Now shift to a different challenger, a different medium, and a different image problem, where a small-town Republican chief of police was running for sheriff in a strongly Democratic county. Did he emphasize his party? Did he promise to clean the Democrats out of the sheriff's office? No! There would have been a Democratic call to arms. He wisely decided to play down his party (except to identify it as required by state law) and project an image emphasizing his reputation as a tough cop (see Figure 4-5).

Even candidates for mayor look for an identification hook to distinguish their message from the thousands of others competing for attention every day. Typical of those who needed name familiarity was the 1978 Republican nominee for governor of New York. Though he was a fishing fleet tycoon and the state senate majority leader, Perry Duryer was not widely known. To familiarize the voters with Duryer, one of the nation's leading political consultants, John Deardourff, concentrated on image making. He used TV to show Duryer riding on one of his lobster boats, piloting his plane, and speaking on the floor of the state assembly. After Deardourff established the image, he used films taken of Duryer sitting in the study of his home in Montauk, Long Island, talking about crime, taxes, inflation, and education.[15]

TOUGH!

★ THE "DOPE PUSHERS" AREN'T VOTING
   FOR CHIEF AL GLANDT
★ THE "HOODLUMS" AREN'T VOTING
   FOR CHIEF AL GLANDT
★ ORGANIZED CRIME WILL NOT BE VOTING
   FOR CHIEF AL GLANDT

BECAUSE CHIEF GLANDT IS A

TOUGH COP

and a FAIR COP!

NOBODY ever got a "bad shake" from Chief Glandt–BUT no lawbreaker ever got an ounce more than he deserved, either. Chief Glandt is a DEDICATED LAW OFFICER, who believes women should be able to walk the streets without fear of personal harm. Police officers have a right to enforce the law without fear of physical harm. Chief Glandt is dedicated to these causes. In the e times of unrest, you will feel a lot more comfortable with a trained, experienced, CAREER law enforcement officer who is FAIR– but TOUGH! Check his record . . . ask anybody in the city where Al Glandt has been the Chief Law Enforcement Officer for 11 years. Ask the law abiding citizens of Lynnwood what they think of Chief Glandt.

VOTE FOR

Chief
AL GLANDT FOR ★ SHERIFF ★ REPUBLICAN

PAID POLITICAL ADVERTISEMENT BY DEMOCRATS FOR GLANDT — JAY RATT — CHAIRMAN 33431 794 W. EDMONDS

Fig. 4-5. Democrats for Glandt. Jay Ratt, Chair, *The Everett Herald*, October 31, 1970.

If the candidate is older, he or she usually emphasizes experience and wisdom, mature understanding of problems, and extensive background of coping with events. U.S. Senator Warren Magnuson was a case in point. For forty years "Maggie" climbed the seniority ladder to become chairman of the appropriations committee. There, he gathered so much federal money for his state that he was touted at home as the state's "fourth largest industry."

When he filed for re-election in 1974, this fat, aging politician was challenged by a man in his late thirties who jogged three miles a day. Senator Magnuson's TV commercials didn't avoid his image. Instead, he used television spots in which a commentator spoke of him as old, fat, and wearing a rumpled suit. Then using the affectionate term, "Maggie," the announcer said, "There comes a time when every young senator shows that he's putting on years. Senator Magnuson, there comes a time (sure as fate) when slim senators assume a more impressive stature. So when youth is gone, once dash is gone, what can you offer the

Fig. 4-6. George Lois and Bill Pitts, *The Art of Advertising* (New York: Abrams, 1977), p. 106.

voters of the State of Washington?" (Maggie reflects and then knowingly taps his forehead). Voice-over: "Let's keep Maggie in the Senate."[16]

Stereotypes

As much as politicians would like to believe that they are unlike commercial products, they have created political stereotypes that help the public distinguish between political personalities.

One stereotype young candidates play on is the fact that all voters are consumers conditioned by advertising to demand new models, new discoveries, and new improved everything. These candidates use advertising to sell the majority the need for a new order, new techniques to meet new challengers, and the need for change and youth.

When Franklin D. Roosevelt was a rash young political aspirant, he was selected not by the party of his famous uncle (Republican President Theodore) but by the opposition—to stand as candidate for state senator from a district that had not gone Democratic in fifty-four years. He resurrected the latent image of his uncle, President Teddy Roosevelt, and combined it with the brashness and energy of youth.

In that campaign Franklin D. Roosevelt projected a new image. In that day most of the people of the area used carriages, so Roosevelt rented an eye-catching red Maxwell touring car, which he decorated with flags and nicknamed the "Red Peril." He demonstrated a fresh, energetic image by traveling 2,000 miles (mostly over rough dirt roads) to meet trains, attend rallies, and meet and shake hands with thousands of farmers who lived in his three counties. In ten speeches a day and in newspaper advertising, he condemned the existing political machines and told the voters, "I am pledged to no man, to no special interest, to no boss." "I want to represent you people in these counties and no one else."[17]

Maybe F.D.R. was elected because the Republicans were overconfident. Or maybe he was elected because he bore the name and in a way reflected the image of his famous uncle Teddy. Or maybe he was elected because the voters wanted a new man who was the enemy of both the Tammany-run Democratic machine that ran New York City and the Republican machine that controlled up-state New York. Whatever the explanation, the Roosevelt image sold.

Of course, F.D.R. had more than fresh energy. He spent more than five times as much as any other candidate had spent in that district. But there was no denying he ran far ahead of his party's ticket, winning by 1,140 votes of the more than 30,000 cast,[18] and launching one of the most successful and controversial political careers in the history of the United States.

Younger politicians continue to use this stereotype. In the 1984 California Presidential primary, U.S. Senator from Colorado Gary Hart used a TV commercial to talk about new ideas, concluding the spot with footage that showed him frolicking with bare feet on a California beach with a voice-over saying, "How are we going to save this natural beauty for our children?" Another TV commercial used the sound of a faint heartbeat in the background and the theme, "New ideas for the heartbeat of this nation's future."[19]

Another stereotype is the typical challenger technique. Usually the challenger criticizes the opponent in hopes of selling a change. For example, when John Kerry ran for lieutenant governor of the State of Massachusetts, his TV spots ridiculed the way past incumbents had performed. "Ever wonder what Lieutenant Governors do?" the voice began. Then, behind a plaque reading, "Lieutenant Governor," the ad showed a balding, middle-aged actor "unfolding paper dolls, talking to a stuffed duck, and staring at the phone wistfully, awaiting an assignment from the Governor." The announcer went on to laud Kerry's accomplishments "as an antiwar activist and as a criminal prosecutor," concluding: " 'John Kerry really made something out of those jobs, and he'll make something out of this one.' "[20]

Aggressive challengers also run a risk, though. If he or she emphasizes the need for new programs, new ideas, or a new coalition, these proposals must not be so radical that they scare the middle-class voter. For example, when prize-winning novelist Norman Mailer ran for Mayor of New York City in 1969, he deliberately chose a radical image using the campaign slogan, "Vote the Rascals In—The Other Guys Are a Joke."[21] Mailer also advocated that New York City leave the State of New York and apply to the United States Congress to become the fifty-first state.

Mailer received the admiration and support of some of the nation's best-known radical personalities and attracted lots of volunteers. He articulated well, receiving good newspaper, radio, and television coverage. He campaigned hard and was helped by the fact that the conventional vote was split three ways. But he was soundly beaten. This demonstrates that voters are wary of radical ideas and candidates. New proposals must make sense and a challenger must be able to explain and defend them against criticisms.

Chapter 29

Image Weak, Dull, or Unpopular?
Change It or Use Someone Else's

> The man who never changes his opinion never corrects his mistakes.[1]
>
> This is the first time I've heard a party campaigning on the slogan, "Throw the rascals in."
> —Adlai Stevenson, when speaking of Eisenhower endorsement of Senators Joe McCarthy, Henner, and vice versa.[2]

The New Image Need Not Be Substantive

After an in-depth poll the candidate will want to know the things most likely to influence the vote. Assume the polls show the voters are not reacting favorably to the candidate's message, record, or image. Being practical, politicians will want to change.

No doubt, an image change can trigger an attack. Sometimes it hurts the campaign, but people's memories are short. For example, surveys of the general public show only 9 percent recalled the events of World War I; only 17 percent remembered Lindbergh's solo flight across the Atlantic; only 30 percent can remember the great Depression of the thirties; only slightly more than one-third can identify with World War II; and only six out of ten actually recall Kennedy's assassination.

Changing a political image is made easier because the new image need not be substantive. Giving an established political figure a new image is like repackaging a product. It's putting a different face on reality, just as one of the pioneers of modern advertising, Claude Hopkins, did when promoting Van Camps canned milk. At that time, before modern refrigeration, the canning process produced milk with a "scalded taste." When discussing a way to overcome this defect, one of his associates, Albert Lasky, observed that it tasted a little like almonds. Hopkins exploited this reality. He persuaded the public to purchase Van Camps canned milk because it had an almond taste, though in fact it had neither almonds nor almond flavoring.[3]

Usually candidates do not have to completely abandon their images. Instead, they can modify and humanize their earlier images. For instance, during the 1984 Presidential primary, U.S. Senator Gary Hart's image was that of an innovator with new ideas. When he looked to Ohio in a last-ditch effort to win a hard-hit industrial state, his ads showed that he was also a traditional politician interested in the economy and in getting Ohio's unemployed back to work.

To give the common touch to Senator Hart's new image, he was shown in three of his Ohio TV ads wearing worn work clothes and standing in the mud with a clump of laborers outside a steel mill near Youngstown. In two of these ads, Hart never said anything. Instead, he listened intently while the grim workers said things like, "We've had Mondale. We don't need him again."[4]

Fig. 4-7. Nick, *Advertising Age*, September 28, 1981.

When a candidate must cope with an unflattering, preconceived public image, those skilled in political packaging don't allow the advertising to dwell on these aspects. Instead, they attempt to change the public's perception. When President Jimmy Carter's media advisor, Gerald Rafshoon, was faced an image of Carter as a weak leader, his television commercials flashed through scenes of Carter with the Emperor of Japan, Pope John II, Israel's Menachem Begin, and Egypt's Anwar Sadat. They showed the President returning to the White House at night, a solitary light burning in his oval office. Then an announcer compared the complexities of the modern presidency to the simple task it was during Lincoln's day.

Most successful politicians have found it profitable to change some aspects of their public image. Abraham Lincoln grew a beard after he became president because it gave him a fatherly appearance. Chief Justice of the Supreme Court Charles Evans Hughes trimmed his beard drastically just before he ran for president in 1924 to give himself a modern image. Former speaker of its assembly, California's Treasurer, "Big Daddy" Jesse Unruh, "lost ninety pounds and kept it off" because an in-depth poll showed obesity gave him the image of a political boss.

Of course an image change can trigger opposition criticism, so before making image changes, candidates must carefully weigh the pros and cons in terms of votes. Mostly, though, changes in image don't affect public sentiment.

Harold Washington Anti-Byrne Commercial, 1983

"She's hired some New York media experts to give her a 'new image'."

"But when the election's over, we'll be stuck with the same old Jane Byrne and the same old problems piling up.

Fig. 4-8. Used by permission of L. Patrick Devlin, Curator, Television Political Advertising Collection, University of Rhode Island.

Well-known political figures actually gamble on the fact that voters' memories are based on their most recent impressions. A case in point is the change the Ted Bates organization made of "Ike" in the first Eisenhower presidential campaign. The organization secured the mailing list of the *Reader's Digest* Corporation, and from this list selected a cross-section of 10,000 voters. The voters were divided into ten groups. Each voter then received one of ten letters, each promoting a different image. As a part of the package, each voter got a questionnaire and a return envelope that asked for a contribution, but the real thrust of the letters was to help Ike decide on an image.

As things worked out, there were two over-powering choices: Ike could become Mr. Reform and go after the deep-freeze, fur-coat scandal, which had plagued the latter years of the Truman administration, or he could do something to end the Korean War. The "end the Korean war appeal" had drawn two-and-one-half times as many responses.

Eisenhower's image makers had a real military hero who had no diplomatic image and didn't want to run the risk of undermining the military or interfering with any ongoing diplomatic efforts of the State Department. On the other hand, Eisenhower was a candidate for president. The polls showed his opponent, Adlai Stevenson, gaining in the closing days of the campaign. Politically, the circumstances were right for the most successful soldier in a generation to change his image. So he was touted as a man capable of bringing peace, promising, if elected, "to go to Korea." The new image was promoted using an ad in the news media and a campaign mailing of twenty million letters.

Apparently, the voters imagined that Eisenhower's promise would somehow miraculously end the Korean War. Although his personal diplomatic efforts were not able to stop the Korean War, most observers believe that this image change and the promise to go to Korea stopped a rising tide of support for his opponent and created an Eisenhower landslide.[5]

Some changes in political image are easier to make because the political personalities have more than one image to choose from. Let's go to a time when there was no television and look at the political image of the first Irish Mayor of Boston, James Michael Curley. To some, Curley was the man who got the Irish scrub women of City Hall off their knees by insisting they be given long-handled scrub brushes. He was the man who fought Boston's commercial business interests and accused them of abusing "the poor Irish." To others, he was a man of legendary charm.

During Curley's time as mayor, a woman I know had occasion to go to his office. There she saw him immaculately dressed and smiling, seated behind an enormous desk surrounded by pictures and mementos. She was impressed by the pictures showing him with important people and overwhelmed by this little speech: "Every woman should be charming, beautiful and wealthy. It is obvious to me that you have achieved the first two." Then he reached into his desk drawer and handed her a newly-minted silver dollar and said, "In pursuit of the third, please accept this with my compliments."

Though corny—and sexist by today's standards—many of Curley's poor Irish constituents accepted that little speech as a demonstration of his interest in them as individuals. The recipients, including my friend, repeated and repeated the story the rest of their lives. Curley's willingness to fight vested business interests and his concern for the poor Irish, plus his courtly manners, created a favorable image, for which his constituents rewarded him by electing him to several terms in Congress, three times mayor of Boston (at one point mayor and congressman at the same time), and one term as governor of Massachusetts.

However, James Michael Curley had other images, which he gained as the result of two criminal convictions—one for mail fraud, for which he served a prison term. Because of his fiery temper and his high-handed use of administrative power, he had an old-fashioned-machine political image which was emphasized when he was vilified by the press and so-called "good government groups." These negative images caused him to be beaten once for Congress, twice for governor, once for the United States Senate, and three times for mayor.[6]

In spite of two prison terms and his many defeats, James Michael Curley's courtly manner and caring image became legend. In 1945 when he was seventy-odd years, his Boston constituents paid him one last tribute by again re-electing him mayor.

Endorsements

Most political endorsements go something like this: "I am supporting Ed Heavey for State Attorney General because his record proves he is the candidate who will provide the leadership we need in this most important office."[7] Although this is good standard language, it isn't exciting. It draws little attention from voters who, as consumers, are besieged by advertisements. So there are many devices candidates can use to enhance the effect of their endorsement.

When a candidate gets an important endorsement, he or she might arrange a press conference featuring the person or organization making the endorsement. The endorser can personally issue a publicity release and call it to the attention of local newspapers, radio, and television. The candidate can use a photograph or tape in which he or she appears with the person making the endorsement. In 1968 U.S. Senator Robert Dole of Kansas used a television commercial that included footage taken at the party's Miami convention, where Dole appeared with the vice president as a part of Nixon's welcoming committee. The commercial featured a closeup showing the vice president's arm around Dole's shoulders as Nixon arrived at the convention to accept his party's nomination.[8]

John Gilligan used a creative twist in one of his endorsement spots during his 1970 campaign for governor of Ohio. The camera opened showing an older man saying, " 'I've watched him get elected to city council six times. I've seen him elected to Congress—in fact, I was there the day he took his seat. I know that he's familiar with the problems of the older citizens of Ohio, because he and I have discussed them many times. And so I'm going to vote for Jack Gilligan for governor of the State of Ohio. I think I should, because, after all, I'm his father.' " The camera then shows Gilligan and his father laughing. "We did it mainly because we were having trouble with the elderly," said his ad-man, David Garth. "Also Jack Gilligan was perceived as a kind of cold fish. He wasn't, but that's how he came across."[9]

Another way to create interest is to have the endorsement message tailored to the individual making the endorsement. Sometimes this can be done with a flourish, as composer Richard Rogers did with an endorsement for Governor Rockefeller. Rogers, speaking of Governor Rockefeller, said, "He has the right sound."[10]

Candidates might also use small newspaper bullet ads featuring the endorser's signature, commercials in which the endorser personally delivers the endorsement, or commercials in which the endorser delivers a personal message.

Like any other communication, an endorsement can have a political bite, such as one television commercial for Gerald Ford. The camera showed a screen with

Fig. 4-9. Arnold Fochs, *Advertising That Won Elections* (Duluth, MN:
A. J. Publishing Co., 1974), p. 99.

white letters against a black background: " 'Those who know Jimmy Carter best
are from Georgia. That's why we thought you ought to know.' " A photo of Gerald
Ford appears and remains underneath. New words appear on the screen,
accompanied by the sound of teletype:

"The Savannah, Georgia, *News* endorses Gerald Ford for President. The
Augusta, Georgia, *Herald* endorses President Ford. The Atlanta, Georgia,
Daily World endorses President Ford. The Marietta, Georgia, *Journal* endorses
President Ford. The Albany, Georgia, *Herald* endorses President Ford. The
Augusta, Georgia, *Chronicle* endorses President Ford. The Savannah, Georgia,
Press endorses. . . ."[11]

The spot fades out mid-sentence, suggesting more papers to be named. Most of the newspapers mentioned in the commercial were small in circulation, and they had been endorsing Republican candidates for President for some years. The commercial didn't mention, of course, that the state's major paper, the Atlanta *Journal Constitution*, had endorsed Carter. Still, this was a clever way to use the smaller newspapers' endorsements against Governor Jimmy Carter, who was a home-grown product.

Using Actors for Political Endorsements

Generally, politicians are communication amateurs. Real communications professionals are the actors who appear in movies and on television and radio. For years advertisers have exploited loyal fans and have benefited from the artificial light given off by show-business personalities.

Charlie Chaplin sold Old Gold cigarettes. Charles Lindbergh advertised watches. An aspiring actress, Nancy Davis, promoted Deltak simulated pearls. That was before she married Ronald Reagan, who posed for Van Heusen shirt ads (Figure 4-10).[12] This practice reached a milestone of sorts in 1982 when a leading brewery paid actor James Coburn $250,000 per syllable for two words he uttered in their television commercial.

The participation of prominent personalities from the movies, radio, or TV in a political contest increases exposure and creates excitement. Early in a contest for U.S. senator from the State of Virginia, the state Republican party rejected the bid of millionaire businessman-turned-politician John W. Warner in part because Warner was the current husband of movie actress, Elizabeth Taylor. Instead, the Republican party nominated Richard Obehganin. But when Obehganin was killed in a plane crash, Warner received the nomination. The politicians were in for a surprise because instead of being a liability because she had been married several times before, Liz Taylor turned out to be good political copy. This was good news for Republican Warner who overcame Virginia's Democratic voting tradition to take a seat in the United States Senate.[13]

Occasionally, candidates get response by changing the pace in their advertising. This is what New York Mayor John Lindsay did when he used an endorsement delivered by the man audiences recognized as the television character Archie Bunker—actor Carroll O'Connor. This appeal was aimed at New York's liberal sophisticates who loved the way O'Connor satirized bigoted Archie Bunker's right-wing views. In the commercial, actor O'Connor made fun of Bunker, then stepped out of character and delivered a serious message.[14]

Here's another technique that was used to pep up an endorsement. On the television screen is a single figure standing before a huge audience under a sixty-foot banner that reads: "Mr. Smith goes to Washington 1946, Mr. Reagan goes to Washington 1976." Looking closer, we see James Stewart, the actor who starred

Fig. 4-10. Advertisement, *The Saturday Evening Post*, September 26, 1953.

in the film, *Mr. Smith Goes to Washington*. His sincere, instantly recognizable voice says: "I'm working for Ronald Reagan because he's my friend. But more than that, I'm working for Ronald Reagan because he is a man who is showing genuine concern for the security and well-being of the United States."

Jimmy Stewart was not alone at election time in California; several stars came out to shine. Actress Candace Bergen made this endorsement: "I'm responding to

Jerry Brown, and you should respond to Jerry Brown; and together we will elect him President."[15]

Movie personalities are not the only ones with a following. Thousands of fans are influenced by the opinions of popular sports figures. When Vice President Agnew was first elected Baltimore County Executive, he got acquainted on a first-name basis with several local sports figures. During his first campaign for Governor of Maryland, his campaign manager got testimonials from the stars of the Baltimore Colts (pro football) and Orioles (pro basketball). Here is how he used their support on radio:

"Hi, this is Johnny Mackey, No. 88 of the Baltimore Colts. You know, it isn't too often that you'll find folks like us getting involved in political campaigns, but this time it's so important that it would be wrong for us to keep quiet. So I want to join guys like Tom Matte, Jim Parker, and Brooks Robinson, and tell you how urgent it is that all decent people in Maryland get together and really make sure that Ted [his nickname for Agnew] is elected our next Governor. We've got to work, and we've got to work hard. We've got to tell our friends and our neighbors that every single vote counts, and that every vote must be for Ted. . . . Ted Agnew is beyond a doubt the qualified man in this election. He's carrying the ball for every decent citizen. Let's not let him down. Join John Mackey and other Colts and Orioles. Get out to vote for Ted."[16]

Chapter 30

Comprehension, Targeting, Repetition, and Momentum

> *Comprehension:* "No one ever went broke under-estimating the taste of the American public."
> —H. L. Mencken[1]
>
> *Targeting:* "The candidate is smart when he finds a message that appeals to half of the voters . . . and brilliant when he pleases the right half."
> —Anonymous
>
> *Repetition:*
> "If you wish your cause to advance,
> Your merits you had better enhance.
> You must strut it and stump it
> And blow your own trumpet.
> Or trust me, you haven't a chance."
> —W. S. Gilbert[2]

Be Sure the Voter Comprehends

To persuade, a message must do more than simply gain attention. All voters must comprehend it, and so ideas or concepts must be understood even by those who have only seventh to eighth grade educations.

In the 1980 presidential race, the Republicans ran an effective television spot featuring a man walking through an idle factory in Baltimore, who said, "If the Democrats are good for working people, how come so many people ain't working?" Two years after President Reagan won and the Republicans gained control of the United States Senate, the economy worsened. The Democrats then persuaded the same factory worker to make a television spot for them saying he was wrong, that the same plants were closed and that the economy was in even worse shape. The man concluded with a strong personal endorsement, saying that he wasn't being paid for making *this* television commercial, though he had been paid by the Republicans.[3]

Political messages are aimed at voters of many educational levels. Typically, copywriters look at candidates' drafts, then rewrite following the advice of one of the most respected men of advertising, David Ogilvie: "Copy should be written in the language people use in everyday conversation." He believes it pays to write short sentences and paragraphs, avoiding difficult words.[4]

Fig. 4-11. Richard L. Gordon, "Political Shift," *Advertising Age*, September 1, 1980.

The political career of Adlai Stevenson, Sr., illustrates what happens when a candidate doesn't keep things simple enough. Stevenson was recognized as a man of perception, wit, and wisdom. His speeches, writing, and observations were some of the finest in American political history. Yet, although he was twice Governor of Illinois, twice his party's nominee for president of the United States, and his country's spokesman in the United Nations, surveys showed that the average voter found Stevenson's articulate and complex analyses difficult to follow. His beautiful phraseology and style is cited as a contributing reason for his overwhelming defeat in 1952.

In keeping with simplicity, political television commercials typically do not emphasize issues. If the issues are numerous or complex, as they often are, candidates should heed the advice of Harvard psychologist George A. Miller, who contends that "the average mind . . . cannot deal with more than seven units at a time."[5] Senator Bob Dole says no more than five; campaign specialist Hank Parkinson says no more than three.[6]

If the strategy calls for multi-issue statements, the candidate should seek the advice of advertising professionals. Most recommend that candidates avoid radio and television, because they run the risk of boring a substantial voter segment. Candidates should concentrate on a print piece that readers can skim, concentrating on an issue or issues that interest them.

Headlines That Deliver

Only about 10 to 24 percent read the body of advertising copy and those 24 percent are those most vitally interested. So the best copywriters don't depend on voters reading their copy. Instead, to pierce the voter's stream of consciousness, they use punchy headlines to convey the message, even to those who are not inclined to read the body. For this reason an issue-packed print piece should be divided into sections, so the voter can pick out a subject he or she is interested in without having to read it in full.

Ogilvie's record is better than anybody's promises.

When Richard Ogilvie ran for governor, he said he'd get the tough jobs done.

He was elected for guts, not glamour.

And he performed.

He performed in a job that's no place for somebody whose independence has been surrendered to a political machine.

Ogilvie brought courage and character to the office of governor. He brought an approach to government that faced up to the problems of all the people of Illinois.

When he saw that only a state income

State aid to grammar and high schools doubled.

tax could solve the state's financial crisis, he proposed one in the face of prophecies of political disaster.

"I'd rather be right," he said. And then he went to work and got his program passed.

Ogilvie has managed the affairs of government so well, there will be no new taxes this year. And no increase in the income tax or other state taxes.

He faced up to the problems of education. By doubling the state's contribution to grammar and high schools. Increasing funds

45,000 acres of new state park lands acquired.

for colleges and universities by 64%. And providing scholarships for 70,000 college students this fall.

He faced the problem of Illinois' lagging

mental health facilities by ordering construction of seven new residential care centers for the mentally retarded. By eliminating the emergency waiting list for admission of retarded children. By reducing patient population at over-crowded state hospitals. And by increasing the mental health budget significantly.

These are statewide problems. But the

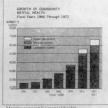

Massive support for mental health.

Ogilvie approach to government goes deeper than that.

What has the governor done for rural and small-town Illinois?

He's introduced legislation to completely eliminate the personal property tax on farm machinery, inventories and livestock. He worked to obtain nearly $109 million in federal funds to expand rural electrification.

The governor is with farmers on property tax reform, according to Jim Thomson, Editor, *Prairie Farmer.*

He led in efforts to solve the Gulf Coast dock strike, which was costing Illinois farmers millions of dollars. And he has improved more than 3000 miles of Illinois roads to make them safer, and to speed the farm-to-market flow of agricultural products.

His anti-pollution bond issue made it possible for the state to help build badly needed sewage treatment systems for 600 communities in the state.

What has Ogilvie done for city and suburban residents?

He proposed and signed the toughest anti-pollution laws in the nation. He has ex-

panded the state's park and recreation facilities—acquiring 45,000 new acres of park and recreation land, most of it close to urban population centers.

His comprehensive transportation pl —first of its kind in the nation—is supporti mass transit services in cities and suburbs all parts of Illinois. And the plan will i prove suburban commuter service as well key inter-city passenger trains.

He has developed a drug abuse progra that's had great success in taking addicts the streets and helping them cure themselves. And he's initiated a new system corrections in Illinois that stresses educati and rehabilitation—a system that's be successful in lowering the number of parol

Highway improvement program has saved more than 600 lives.

prisoners who return to crime by more th 30%.

Detached observers have classed Ogil as one of the best governors Illinois has e had.

And that's why you should ask fo Republican ballot at the primaries, Tuesd March 21, and cast your vote for Ogilvie.

Governor Ogilvie ought to be re-elect not on the basis of promises, but on the ba of his record. That's the real promise – dedication and performance.

That may sound simple.

But before you vote, ask yourself:

How many Illinois governors have be as good as Ogilvie?

☒ Ogilvie
Republican

Sponsored by Citizens for Governor Ogilvie
Committee, Henry L. Pitts, Chairman
John C. Parkhurst, Campaign Manager
77 West Washington St., Chicago, Illinois 60602
200 South Second Street, Springfield, Illinois 62701.

Governor Ogilvie is a good governor. And they're hard to find.

Fig. 4-12. "An Outstanding Ad Takes on an Unpopular Issue," *Campaign Insight*, May 1972.

Target Advertising

Targeting is not confined to a commercial message, media, or technique. Sometimes targeting means a candidate finds a way to get votes by reaching a market in which no one else has bothered to solicit votes. Former Senator Butler of Maryland used several popular bakery supply men to send a letter to other bakery men, stating their approval of Senator Butler's candidacy. The letter was designed to impress the small Baltimore bakers and influence them to speak favorably of the candidate to the first and second generation immigrants who had not forsaken the bread of the old country for the cellophane-wrapped supermarket product.[7]

No question the media giants can effectively deliver a message. Yet often the constituency is so small that the advertising cannot be justified by the expected contribution in votes. Or the constituency may be broad, but the voters are divided and the advertisement will hit only a certain segment of the market. Either way, it is only necessary to convince the people who are likely to vote.

At the local level the candidate has to use what he or she has at hand to "pierce the voters' stream of consciousness." In this situation candidates must often ignore metropolitan newspapers, television, or radio stations and instead use direct mail and local radio and newspapers. If, on the other hand, the candidate happens to be a multimillionaire willing to spend with abandon, all kinds of options are open. This was true when Governor Jay Rockefeller ran for re-election in West Virginia. He spent $800,000 of his own money and reached millions in the Pittsburgh area of Pennsylvania who could not vote for him, just to reach a few thousand constituents in West Virginia. He did the same in Maryland and in the District of Columbia.[8]

Targeting has other applications. Sometimes income level, geography, or occupation determine the voters who are interested in a particular message. When Jimmy Carter was running for the Presidency, he used radio ads to target different constituencies. On black-oriented stations, his commercials emphasized his views on civil rights. On white country stations south of the Mason-Dixon line, he used this piece:

> *Announcer:* "On November 2 the South is being readmitted to the Union. If that sounds strange, maybe a Southerner can understand. Only a Southerner can understand years of coarse, anti-Southern jokes and unfair comparisons. Only a Southerner can understand what it means to be a political whipping boy.
>
> "But then, only a Southerner can understand what Jimmy Carter as President can mean. It's like this: November 2 is the most important day in our region's history. Are you going to let it pass without having your say? Are you

going to let the Washington politicians keep one of our own out of the White House? Not if this man can help it."

Carter: "We love our country. We love our government. We don't want anything selfish out of government, we just want to be treated fairly. And we want a right to make our own decisions."

Announcer: "The South has always been the conscience of America—maybe they'll start listening to us now. Vote for Jimmy Carter on November 2."[9]

Repeating the Message

"Please, Bill, don't try to please the press by saying something new all the time. Keep saying what works." These are the words of one of the most successful vote-getters of our time, Richard Nixon, when instructing his speech writer William Safire. President Nixon was accepting the fact that 90 percent of what candidates say in most successful campaigns is constantly repeated in slightly altered form in speeches, newspaper releases, and campaign pieces.

Eventually a candidate can expect pressure from well-meaning advisors who want a change. After all, repetition may bore those who closely follow the campaign, but those hounding the candidate for changes should be reminded of the observations of presidential candidate Tom Dewey, who said, "You have to tell people something at least four times before they remember it." When Abraham Lincoln gave his house-divided speech, which brought him to the attention of the leaders of the press and party prior to his nomination, he was delivering a speech that he had given at least one hundred times before.[10]

When it succeeds, repetition does more than attract attention. It gives a candidate the chance to build the impression that their candidacy represents a majority consensus, simply because the voter has been temporarily surrounded with his or her own advertising.

One of the best applications of this principle was in the early days of Alaska television, when a candidate could still afford a considerable amount of television time. Mike Gravel conducted his first campaign for the U.S. Senate at a time when he was riding a string of successes that started when he went to Alaska and became a real estate developer. He was elected to the State House of Representatives and became its speaker. Then he filed for the U.S. Senate.

Early opinion polls showed the incumbent, Ernest Gruening, had a commanding lead. Gravel shrewdly staked his chances on what at that time was a novelty, a fifteen-minute documentary. It depicted his beginnings in the Great Depression and how he worked his way through Columbia College as a taxicab driver. The film spiced up his story, claiming that he worked with the French underground as an intelligence officer in the U.S. Army during World War II— pure fiction, since he would have been only eleven years old when the U.S.

entered the war. The rest of the film portrayed Gravel coming to Alaska without funds, starting at the bottom and working his way up the real estate ladder, then finished with highlights of his political career.

The campaign piece was shown twice a day on all the TV channels for a week, as well as on airplanes to and from Alaska. Prints and a projectionist were even flown to remote Eskimo and Indian villages.[11] This novelty elected Mike Gravel U.S. Senator.[12]

Momentum and Peaking

This analysis deliberately skips lightly over the important element of momentum and peaking, which are often not present in commercial advertising campaigns. See Part 7, "Political Strategy," for more details. Briefly, momentum and peaking are necessary because a political campaign is pointed at a single day when voters must choose between those who offer themselves for public office. And there is no tomorrow.

A political campaign must influence voters, most of whom are only vaguely aware of the issues and candidates and thus not committed at the beginning of a campaign. Voters take sides as the campaign progresses and find the reaction of others a powerful influence when they vote. So a carefully orchestrated campaign tries to give the impression that it is gaining momentum as election day nears.

Momentum has another facet. Stated simply, most successful campaigns try to bring their advertising to a boil. To do this, they step up their advertising, pulling out all stops in the last day or two prior to the election. It is so hard to make an impression in a minor campaign—and in some major ones—that the candidate usually sticks to repeating a simple message, using as tools such things as clever political signs to blanket a local area (e.g., those in Figure 4-13). Their aim is to catch the voter's attention and to repeat their message as often and in as many places as possible.

Some adopt and repeat a theme, such as "Stay Cool with Coolidge" and "Two Chickens in Every Pot with Hoover." This approach can be used over and over with different advertising formats and is particularly popular with those who merchandise candidates by radio or television. The message, like that for a commercial product, can be delivered like a punchline.

For example, when California's U.S. Senator, Alan Cranston, was running for president, the punchline distinguished his otherwise routine television commercial, which depicted Senator Cranston at a radio microphone during his youthful stint as foreign news correspondent, Senator Cranston, then speaking at a peace rally with anti-nuclear banners waving in the background, then pressing a point at a session of the Senate Foreign Relations Committee. The screen goes dark and then fills again, this time with the words: "For Peace. For Jobs. For President. Alan Cranston."[13]

Fig. 4-13. Yard signs: Willard Crow for Washington State Representative, 1950; Gwynne Page for Salt Lake County Commissioner, 1946; Harry Cain for U.S. Senate, State of Washington; Smathers for Florida U.S. Senate, 1946; Biden for U.S. Senate, 1976; Mike Lowry for U.S. Senator, State of Washington, 1983. Gary Yanker, *Prop Art* (New York: Darien House, 1972), p. 93.

Chapter 31

Brochures, Pamphlets, or Tabloids

> Putting pen to paper will light more fires than matches ever will.
> —Malcolm S. Forbes[1]
>
> Politicians stroke platitudes until they purr like epigrams.
> —Anonymous

Name, Face, and. . . .

Biased, stilted, egotistic as they may seem, brochures, pamphlets, or tabloids are handed out by all candidates. In many cases candidates hand them out door to door, but others find it advantageous to use them as a mailer or as a weekly or daily newspaper supplement. They are not cheap. Indeed, one study made in San Francisco and Oakland areas showed that such material accounted for 26 percent of all expenditures made by congressional candidates.

The typical brochure is printed on good paper using high quality photographs and is designed to fit with a letter into a number ten envelope. Alternatively, it could be four to eight pages and become a tabloid. This resembles the Sunday newspaper supplements in that it is printed on news stock. It has space for more photos and more copy to develop issues. If the tabloid is to be mailed close to election day, it's wise to leave the front page design until the last minute, so the candidate can pep up the tabloid face by emphasizing something that is in the current news, or perhaps refuting an attack.

There are differences of opinion on whether to use the brochure or the tabloid. Those supporting brochures argue that the tabloid format looks cheap and smacks of sensationalism. It is awkward to enclose with a campaign letter, and so is usually sent open and thus can be immediately spotted as an advertisement. Some even argue that the ink rubs off on hands and clothing, and its large size makes it awkward for door-to door use.

Layout

Because candidates are selling themselves, all brochures concentrate on the candidate's name. In fact, when the political piece is thrown into the air and let fall, it is designed so the candidate's name jumps out no matter which way it falls. That way the voter sees the name even if the piece is doomed to the garbage or recycling bin without being read.

Those planning the campaign piece should also keep in mind these words once used by Burma Shave: "His future is his face. It's his best advertising space."[2] At first glance the photograph of a middle-aged politician is about as exciting as a

Fig. 4-14. Brochure, Committee for Bob Honts, Travis County
Commissioner, Precinct 2, Austin, Texas.

kitchen sink. But the same is true of the pictures of most advertised products. But
a picture not only humanizes the candidate, it takes advantage of the candidate's
wide circle of acquaintances. Some voters may not know the candidate by name,
but will vote for them because they recognize their face. So the candidate should
have someone with skill take the picture. With good angle and lighting, a clever
photographer can make an asset of even the most "experience worn" face.

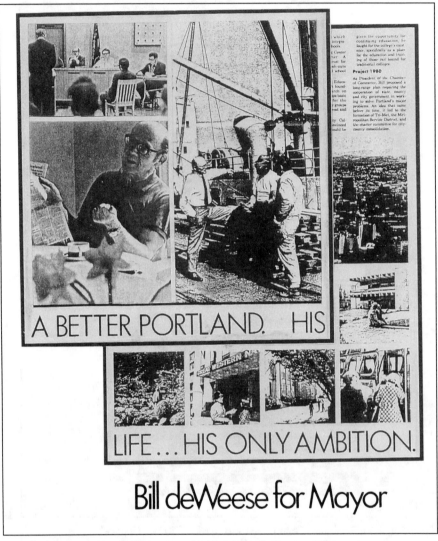

Fig. 4-15. Bill deWeese for Mayor tabloid, Portland, Oregon, 1976.

As with any advertising, a good brochure should have a simple theme. This approach was used by Huston Flournoy when he ran for governor of California. Flournoy's theme emphasized his background as a political science professor and his legislative experience, which he contended constituted a special set of qualifications for office: "If there were an academy to train men for high office, it would include the kind of training Hugh Flournoy had. . . ."[3]

As it is with other pieces of advertising, when laying out the tabloid or brochure the message depends on the candidate and the political wares they want to emphasize. If the issue is local, the candidate examines it, dramatizes it, and tries to persuade a substantial portion of the voting public that he can do something about it. See how Don Underwood used the issue of road repair when he sought to become county commissioner (Figure 4-16).

Fig. 4-16. Don Underwood for County Commissioner, Underwood Campaign Committee, State of Washington, 1960.

Impression, Technique, and Political Corn

The campaign piece should feature some biographical information. A good rule of thumb is to make the candidate fit William Allen White's description of President William McKinley: A kindly, dull gentleman, who tried to be all things to all people. Should the candidate expect the voters to swallow this political corn? Yes and no. But the important thing is that this advertising can be a success even if the constituents don't believe it. For example, during his congressional campaigns in the 1940s and 1950s, Clarence Cannon (no relation to Uncle Joe Cannon), chairman of the U.S. House Ways and Means Committee, published the "Clarence Cannon Courier," an eight-page tabloid that gave detailed accounts of his alleged exploits. It featured such enthusiastic headlines as "Cannon and the Atom Bomb" and "The World's Greatest Parliamentarian."[4]

Since nothing bores the casual voter like a page of text, multi-issue print advertising should be broken into blocks with sub-headlines so readers can select segments that arouse their interest. Also to break the monotony, the candidate should illustrate the piece with action photographs. A good campaign piece includes shots taken at different angles under various conditions, as in Figure 4-17.

When United States Senator Richard Schweiker of Pennsylvania sought re-election, he used a 3.5-inch by 6.5-inch, twenty-four-page booklet featuring photographs of himself receiving or presenting awards or talking to people in his office, and a picture of his family and the pet dog. The booklet had 105 sequences with the last one reading, "He stood up for us long before Watergate."[5]

One of the best action photos on a brochure came from California's State Superintendent of Schools, Wilson Riles, Sr., when he ran his first campaign. He was shown standing in the door of a school, smile on his face, arms open, while a horde of school children rushed toward him.[6]

A candidate running for office between June and September can be portrayed campaigning with his coat off. Maybe it is slung over his shoulder, displaying shirt and tie. Or if the candidate is a woman, a casual cotton dress might be appropriate. Occasionally, a brochure can show the candidate wearing a hard hat inspecting an industrial plant.

A brochure might also feature a day with the candidate. The piece may show the candidate at recreation—say jogging in the morning, playing a game of handball, fishing, hunting, golfing, or playing tennis, mingling with crowds, or talking to young children. Incidentally, the latter is effective particularly when race is involved. Even the most bigoted voter is not turned off by a candidate mingling with a group of children of different races.

The candidate must also be depicted as a person of depth and perception. He or she may be shown discussing problems with elderly people or studying reports at a cluttered desk. A family picture is a must, in part because some voters feel empathy with officials who have a family. Also, the spouse or other members of

Fig. 4-17. Dolores Sibonga for Seattle City Council Position Two, Citizens for Sibonga Committee, 1979.

the family also have friends who might feel empathy for the family. And usually the brochure includes a few political endorsements, which are especially effective with voters who do not have a deep interest in elections or a clear concept of the candidates and their stand on issues.

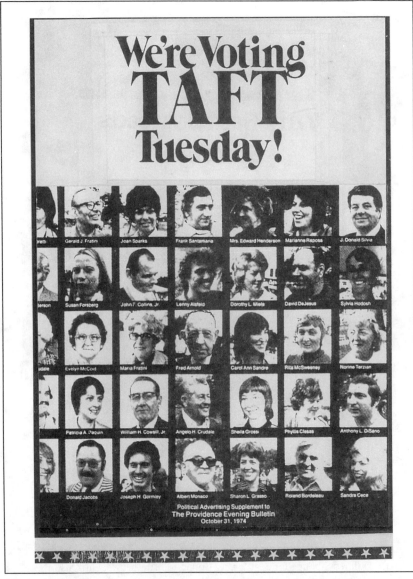

Fig. 4-18. Taft ad, *The Providence Evening Bulletin*, October 31, 1974.

The candidate can pep up a campaign piece in several ways. He or she might offset an opponent's endorsement or show the community how others in the constituency are reacting. For example, see the cover from a tabloid insert for Mayor Taft of Providence, Rhode Island (Figure 4-18).

Color Art and Photography

A combination of art and photography is preferable to either art or photography alone, and a large, full color, deluxe tabloid often warrants the extra cost.[7]

As a rule, a multi-colored piece is more eye-catching than a black-and-white piece. California U.S. Senator S. I. Hayakawa used an unusual brochure, printed in black and green ink on egg-yolk yellow paper when he won his seat in 1976.[8] When selecting colors for advertising, people should be conscious that colors have subliminal effects. Generally, red is thought to be revolutionary; red, white, and blue to be patriotic (or by some conservative); and green and blue to be restful.

The candidate should insist on seeing a printer's proof. There may be mistakes in the copy, and sometimes colored pieces have technical problems, such as wrong placement of color. Generally, slick-paper brochures should be of slightly heavier stock, but not so heavy that a fortune is paid out in postage.[9]

When designing the format, a clever candidate plays on what semanticists call identification. In 1964 John F. Kennedy's press secretary, Pierre Salinger, sought the Democratic nomination for the U.S. Senate. He was handicapped by the fact that he had spent little time in California and had never held an elective office. He capitalized on his association with the Kennedys by distributing a pamphlet that contained a black-framed picture of the late President, Jack Kennedy. It carried a plea to support his candidacy, "In the tradition of our martyred President."[10] He won the primary, but lost in the finals.

It is helpful if a tabloid or brochure has a theme that sets the tone and is carried throughout. To illustrate, when McKinley first campaigned for president, his campaign literature described him as the "Advance Agent of Prosperity." When he ran for re-election four years later, it claimed, "McKinley Stands for the Full Dinner Pail." The theme was updated to "A Chicken in Every Pot and Two Cars in Every Garage," when Herbert Hoover used the same theme in his campaign for President in 1928.[11] Even after we were caught in the Great Depression of the 1930s, Hoover tried the theme again, with "Prosperity is Just Around the Corner."[12]

The nutshell below can start the candidate thinking about print materials development and cost.

Print Material Planning

Note: This list is designed to start the designing/planning process. As there are so many possible designs, the candidate is best served by hiring a professional to assist, or at least get the help of an experienced printer or a successful candidate.

Factors: There will be separate costs for typesetting and graphic design. Production costs will vary depending on paper size, color (e.g., normal bond colors or bright hues), and type (glossy or flat, thick or thin); the number, kinds, and colors of inks; whether there are to be photographs (requiring half-tone printing); and the number and type of folds. To compare prices, use older brochures as models. After obtaining estimates, may want to reduce number to be ordered, use a cheaper paper, or reduce the number of colors.

Also ask how much lead time the printer will need and decide if printing must carry a union label (obtain prices with and without).

Options

Brochures, per 1000:
    8½ x 11 $_____   8½ x 14 $_____   1 side $_____   2 sides $_____
    normal bond $_____   colored paper $_____   colored ink $_____   folding $_____

Single-sheet flyers, per 1000:
    8½ x 11 $_____   8½ x 14 $_____   1 side $_____   2 sides $_____   folding $_____
    normal bond $_____   colored paper $_____   colored ink $_____

Letterhead, per 1000 $_____   Envelopes, per 1000 $_____

Rubber address stamps (various sizes) $_____

Bumper stickers, per 100   1 color $_____   2 colors $_____

Posters/signs: Paperboard $_____   Plastic $_____   Wood $_____

Yard signs, per 100:
    Sign: 1-color $_____   2-color $_____   Stakes $_____
    Double-sided/foldover $_____   Backing if not double-sided $_____

★ ★ ★ ★ ★ **In A Nutshell** ★ ★ ★ ★ ★

Chapter 32

Persuasion Via the Printed Word

> Advertisements contain the only truths to be relied on in the newspaper.
> —Thomas Jefferson[1]

Newspaper Advertising

When we think of print advertising, most of us picture the general-circulation daily newspapers. They have played a major role in electing and defeating candidates for over 150 years. General-circulation newspapers are more than a vehicle for carrying daily news and advertising. Like a department store, they are designed to appeal to the reader interested in sports, business, politics, religion, and a host of other features.

An industry group operating on behalf of newspaper publishers, The Bureau of Advertising, claims that, "On the average weekday, four out of five men and women (18 and over) read at least one daily newspaper, and 71 percent go through a standard metropolitan daily newspaper page by page, from front to back. The others go through a newspaper quickly scanning its contents, using it to supplement television or radio."[2]

Print advertising is not limited to newspapers. Magazines base their readership claims on studies conducted by Foote, Cone and Belding, and Needham, Louis and Brorb, Audits and Surveys. These studies compared people who observed ads in magazines with those who watched television. They reported that the readers of *Time*, *Newsweek*, and *U.S. News and World Report* could recall 95 percent of the weekly ads, while about 70 percent could recall television ads.[3]

Specialty Publications

We all have an occupation, a community, a racial heritage, and—most of us—a religion. Normally, these interests are serviced by specialty publications. In the trade, these are referred to as "house organs." Sophisticated campaign technicians use house organs to target different voter classes. Most students, for example, read the campus newspaper on a regular basis but only occasionally read the general circulation newspapers from their home towns.[4]

The campaign realist recognizes there are other reasons for advertising in programs or bulletins published by their political party, church, union, etc. The powerful forces in charge of civic events and church factions get some advertising because their followers might be offended if the candidate does not participate.

Before sending out a provocative appeal, the candidate's staff should be sure that it has the candidate's approval. Otherwise, the aspirant may be placed in a position where he has to deny something sent by his own organization. Under some circumstances, the organization may be wise to do what was done in 1958, when there was a bitter conflict between Barry Goldwater and the Arizona labor unions. Organized labor refused the candidate an audience at their meetings and had their publications reject his ads.

Persuasion Via the Printed Word

Those who sell print advertising argue that they are more persuasive than other media because, unlike television and radio, readers make the effort to purchase the magazine and newspaper. They also note that newspapers provide reader interest because they express opinions, that a newspaper or magazine may be picked up and read several times, and that newspapers lend themselves to the use of explanatory charts or graphs that help show, for example, that taxes have risen or that a particular bridge has improved traffic flow, etc.

Print advertisers also contend that a large segment of the public has become immune to television and radio advertising, with the result that they fail to penetrate the audience's stream of consciousness. They insist newspaper advertising is the media of choice for those trying to reach active people, especially the young, who are less likely to stay home and watch television during prime time. In addition, Nielsen ratings show that the number of hours spent watching television has declined with the "increase of working women."[5]

Using Newspapers to Target a Specific Area

When planning a print ad, candidates must be aware that, to be effective, ads must reach their constituency, which means that they should be aware of their districts' boundaries and compare them with the newspapers' circulation boundaries. This isn't difficult, because nearly all daily and weekly newspapers have their circulations broken down by zones or areas. Some publish regional editions. In any event, the candidates or their advertising advisors should ask for a rate card listing rates by size and placement, for both Sunday and daily circulations.

Size, Placement, Layout, and Copy

Ads must vie for attention, not only with opponents' ads, but with all other ads in that publication, so it's advisable to "think big" in every phase of preparation: Both type and illustrations should be big and eye-catching.

While Governor Nelson Rockefeller of New York used full-page newspaper ads (Figure 4-19) when he sought the presidency of the United States, some advertising people prefer using a number of small ads because they believe

Why I Run.

America cries out for a leader.

Events overwhelm us. Change outruns us.

Headlines deliver us our daily jolt.

"Things are in the saddle, and ride mankind"—this warning we have let come true.

I run for President because I do not believe this must happen to us.

I believe we can recapture control of *things*.

I believe we can end the drift, the doubt, the division.

I intend to say how, here, in this newspaper. I intend to write what course I believe America must follow.

My beliefs will not be tailored to please the voters of this region or that. What I believe in New York, I believe in Nebraska. And I will answer for it throughout the campaign.

I do not take my case to Republicans alone. It is a nation and not just a party which needs leading, healing, uniting.

I begin tomorrow, on a subject that has tormented us like none other in our recent history: Riot.

NELSON A. ROCKEFELLER

To burn or not to burn.

The British burned Washington in 1814. The Americans burned it in 1968.

Detroit, Newark, Watts, which once blazed on our TV screens, smoulder now in our minds. What do these people want?

In the ashes of Washington, a slum child answered: "I would like my street to look like a brand new neighborhood with changed people who are friendly to others no matter what color."

Now I say that is a decent dream, and we can help make it real.

I am accused of raising "false hopes" by men who raise no hopes. No, I raise *real* hopes. Because I have been doing real things.

One real thing: A program in New York State that will attract as much as 5 billion dollars in private money, to rebuild the slums.

Another: A fund to help small businessmen in the slums get loans. Another: a frontal assault on narcotics addiction, a major source of crime in the slums.

So I say that our cities can be saved. But they will not be saved by a gospel of do-nothing.

They will not be saved by men who read rousing speeches about crime control—and say not a word about gun control.

They will not be saved by men who choke hope in the name of law and order—and then turn to undermine our highest court of law.

Our cities will be saved by men who say it *is* possible to build "a brand new neighborhood with changed people who are friendly to others no matter what color."

And this faith is one reason why I run for President.

NELSON A. ROCKEFELLER

Fig. 4-19. "Sink or Swim: Rockefeller Push Gets Underway," *Advertising Age*, June 17, 1968.

repetition attracts attention. The next few figures show a variety of techniques employed by politicians to attract attention to small newspaper ads.

Prime time determines the number of listeners a TV or radio program attracts, and so does placement of an ad within a newspaper. Even the casual headline reader can't miss the front page. Given two ads of comparable size and layout, the front page ad has the greatest chance to catch the reader's eye. Generally, readership decreases as the reader moves inward. However, most daily papers will not sell ads on the front pages, and even if they do there is little space for the message. Savvy candidates design their advertising for a specific section of the newspaper, where their ad targets those who read that section.

When the sections are being evaluated, candidates should depend upon research and be wary of myths that have sprung up about who does or does not read particular sections of the newspaper. For example, some political figures have shied away from advertising next to the comic pages because they fear that persons reading comics material may be too young, unlikely to vote, or poorly educated. But this runs counter to reality. Most comics aren't funny, and they deal

Fig. 4-20. Ad, Committee to elect Fascell for state representative, *Miami Herald*, August 25, 1946.

with real-life situations. Research shows the median age of the adult comics reader is 41.7, slightly less than the average voter in the United States. Comics readers approximate the national educational average: 65.4 percent of those comics readers have graduated from high school and 27.5 percent are graduates of colleges.[6] Speaking of the comics, Figures 4-20 and 4-21 illustrate how two nonincumbents used cartoon motifs to distinguish their candidacies.

Distinctive theme layout and design are so important to the success of the ad that it is not recommended that candidates without advertising experience draw their own ads. Every candidate should employ an advertising agency and follow their advice. Of course this means advertising costs more money, but it's worth it. Candidates can also consult others from their party with some experience or seek advice from a newspaper advertising department. Most newspapers will accept typed copy and set it into print at no extra charge. For those that require camera-ready copy, the campaign must find a graphic artist.

Creating the Headline

When designing eye-catching advertising, specialists assume that only about 5 percent of the newspaper readers will read the copy, so, as we have seen, they lay great emphasis on an attention-getting headline. (Some examples are shown in Figures 4-22 and 4-23.) Advertising great David Ogilvy said, "The two most powerful words an advertiser can use in the headlines are 'free' and 'new'." Both words have been on the political scene for generations. In 1856, the Republican Party used its first slogan, "Free Speech, Free Press, Free Soil, Free Men."[7]

Another giant of modern advertising, John Caples, recommends that the copywriter begin the headline with the word "now." For instance, "Now with Medic 1 you have around-the-clock protection" or "Now the manufacturer will have to print the truth on the package label." He suggests also that the copywriter put a date in the headline. For instance, "Since 1979, all dangerous substances must be labeled."[8]

Advertising pro John Sackheim extends the list of key words to include: "magic," "quick," "wanted," "easy," "challenge," "advice to," "the truth about," "offer," "compare," "bargain," "hurry," and "last chance." Other clichés recommended in the advertising community are words such as "improvement," "important development," "amazing," "sensational," "remarkable," "revolutionary," "startling," and "miracle." Many of these may seem corny, but Sackheim concludes with this sage advice: "Don't turn up your nose at these cliches. They may be shopworn, but they work."[9]

Fig. 4-21. Ad, Jim Stephanis, in Arnold Fochs, *Advertising That Won Elections* (Duluth, MN: A. J. Publishing, 1974), p. 107.

Color and Other Attention Getters

Those who deal in print cost tell us that one color costs approximately 19 percent more than black and white and three colors cost 30 percent more. David Ogilvy says that when the candidate's ad is the only piece with color on the page, "on the average, they are 100 percent more memorable."[10] Other split-level recognition studies have shown an increase of 58 percent when one color is used, and 78 percent for full color.

Candidates can use a column format similiar to that shown in Figure 4-24 to appeal to newspaper readers, who are in the habit of reading columns. In the copy itself, the candidate can explain programs or make or rebut charges. For example, a candidate for the legislature might run a "Senator John Papajohn Answers," or a "Letters to Vince Higgins" column, using questions developed from letters and personal appearances to keep reader interest. This is particularly effective when the candidate poses tough, provocative questions and keeps the answers short and to the point.

Fig. 4-22. Gary Yanker, *Prop Art* (New York: Darien House, 1972), p. 122.

Fig. 4-23. Winning Ideas For Political Advertisers (New York: Bureau of Advertising, n.d.), p. 122.

As is true with other advertising, newspaper advertising should have a theme. If a candidate is to identify with an issue, he or she should keep it simple because as legendary advertising genius Maxwell Sackheim said, "The thought must reach the brain through a series of intricate mental switches, cams, gears, springs and motors, which are poor conductors of an idea." Again, if an ad must explain a complicated idea or feature a number of criticisms, most political advertisers favor newspapers as the vehicle.

The information in the nutshell on the opposite page provides a jumping-off place for planning newspaper/magazine advertising.

★ ★ ★ ★ ★ ★ ★ ★ ★ ★ ★ ★ ★ ★ ★ ★

Newspaper & Magazine Ad Planning

Advance preparation

Publication name_____   Contact Person_____

Ad size_____   Cost $_____

Date of appearance _____   Camera-ready copy deadline _____

Typesetting/graphics help available? _____   Kind? _____

Preparing the camera-ready copy (if candidate/staff must do):

Type faces and sizes _____   Mark photos for size and screen _____

Proofread:

    Check names, places, dates, spelling, numbers

    Scan for appearance and clarity, typos

Write work order; deliver with layout and copy

Make copies for files

Proofs ready (date) _____   Final corrections made _____

Legal

Candidate's name, address included? _____   Chair/treasurer name included?_____

Type size for sponsoring committee per public disclosure requirements?_____

Financial

Request reprints (number_____)___   Make arrangements for payment____

Costs for newspaper ads

per column inch $ _____   1/4 page $_____

1/2 page $ _____   full page $ _____

Costs for other print media

per column inch $ _____   1/4 page $_____

1/2 page $ _____   full page $ _____

★ ★ ★ ★ ★ **In A Nutshell** ★ ★ ★ ★ ★

a new face with clean hands

where he stands:

1. TAXES

JIM NELSON, *unlike his opponent*, believes that Texas doesn't need any new taxes. He is convinced the state is already taxing its people too heavily, and that it should learn to live within its income, like the rest of us.

Jim knows there is a lot of duplication and waste in the state budget. He also knows two studies have shown that as much as $110 million in tax revenue has been lost to the people of the state because of laxity and special favors.

Jim pledges to see that Texans get all they should from the government for their tax dollars. He wants to find ways to save, not spend.

2. ETHICS

JIM NELSON, *unlike his opponent*, believes Texas needs a tough new ethics law making it a felony offense for state officials and lawmakers to betray their public trust.

Jim believes people have a right to know about any financial entanglements which might sway your senator's vote. He would require that all state officials file a *complete* financial disclosure each year.

Jim would also make it a crime for any legislator to sell his services to private clients by representing their interests before any state board, agency or commission ... which his opponent has so often done.

3. WELFARE

JIM NELSON, *unlike his opponent*, believes we owe aid to those who can't help themselves. He feels we owe *nothing* to those who are simply unwilling to work for a living.

Jim wants a major legislative drive to clean up the welfare rolls. He thinks a law requiring able-bodied welfare recipients to take a job or enroll in a job-training program would be a step in the right direction.

4. BUSING

JIM NELSON, *unlike his opponent*, believes that busing school children out of their own neighborhoods simply for the purpose of achieving racial balance is a major threat to our public school system.

Jim thinks the real issue is quality education for *all children*. He pledges to work to improve all schools, while fighting to preserve the neighborhood school concept with local control over education.

5. ECOLOGY

JIM NELSON, *unlike his opponent*, believes it's time to get the politicians out of pollution control. He feels action must be taken now if we're to save our natural resources.

Jim wants a central state environmental protection agency to take care of the problems. He thinks all the various pollution control groups should be combined into one strong arm with the proper tools to do the job.

Jim, as a man who has worked on environmental problems in our space program, knows the problems and knows what needs to be done.

6. NEPOTISM

JIM NELSON, *unlike his opponent*, **believes the job of a state senator is to represent the people, not get his relatives on the state payroll.**

JIM NELSON THINKS LIKE YOU DO.

Fig. 4-24. Arnold Fochs, *Advertising That Won Elections* (Duluth, MN: A. J. Publishing, 1974), p. 253.

Fig. 4-25. *Background:* "Newspaper column format," Winning Ideas For Political Advertisers (New York: Bureau of Advertising, n.d.); *Foreground:* newspaper column, *Miami Herald*, April 12, 1950, p. 23.

The Case for McCUTCHEON for Prosecutor

EXHIBITS A and B

Crime up, Convictions Down, Costs Up

Between 1966, the last year John G. McCutcheon served as Pierce County prosecutor, and 1970, the number of major crimes reported nationwide in the FBI Index of Crime increased 55 percent. That's bad enough, but in Pierce County, in the same period the increase was an alarming 130 percent. What's even more disturbing, while crime skyrocketed, convictions declined—a full 50 percent in just two years. In 1968, for example, there were 249 robberies committed in Pierce County. The incumbent prosecutor filed charges in 33 cases. He obtained 11 convictions, dismissed 11 and had 11 pending at year's end. Eleven out of 249—a 1 to 25 ratio of convictions to robberies in 1968. Is it any wonder that the number of robberies soared—to 444—in 1969?

Between 1966, the last year John G. McCutcheon served as Pierce County Prosecutor, and 1970, the amount budgeted for wages and salaries in the Prosecutor's office almost doubled—from $186,220 to $343,833. During that time, the crime rate in Pierce County more than doubled while the conviction rate declined dangerously. Crime may not pay, but the taxpayers do. Twice over, as a matter of fact. Once, for the Prosecutor they elected and once for the lawyer he hired to tell him how to run his office. This lawyer is on the payroll as special counsel, at $22,000 per, which is in addition to the salaries paid a full complement of assistant and deputy prosecutors. In other words, the taxpayers are getting two for the price of two, when only one should be needed.

EXHIBIT C

Daniel J. Evans, being first duly sworn, on oath deposes and says: that he is the duly elected, qualified and acting governor of the state of Washington and makes this verification as such officer; that he has read the foregoing complaint, knows the contents thereof and believes the same to be true.

Subscribed and sworn to before me this ____ day of ____, 1969.

The Governor's Oath

Do you believe the Governor of the State of Washington under oath? He is authorized to ask the Attorney General to preempt a Prosecuting Attorney if he "has failed or neglected to institute and prosecute violations of criminal laws." RCW 43.10.090. This was done in Pierce County in September, 1969, the first time in modern history that a Governor has stripped a Prosecutor for what we can only conclude is incompetence. The Governor and Attorney General filed a complaint against amusement machine operators on September 11, 1969, in Pierce County, completely bypassing the incumbent Prosecutor, and alleging his failure to act. State ex rel Evans and Gorton vs Amusement Assn, Pierce County No. 191006.

EXHIBIT D

Remember the Rack and Q?

Lakewood residents do. They beseeched the incumbent to put a stop to the extracurricular activities taking place there, he failed to and so did just as he failed to stop the drug abuse at Eatonville. Just as he has failed to stop it elsewhere. In 1968 he managed to obtain only one conviction for every three narcotics charges he filed. It will take a prosecutor with ability and determination to rid the county of the drug pushers who continue to operate here.

Restore Competence to the Prosecutor's Office

Elect John G.

McCUTCHEON

DEMOCRAT

Fig. 4-26. Advertisement, *Tacoma News Tribune*, October 31, 1970.

Chapter 33

Politics Versus the Business of Broadcasting

> Nothing is certain but death, taxes, and a commercial
> having no substance, no sex, no owner, and a message of
> importance to every voter.
> —Henry V. Wade[1]

Reaching the Voter

The extent to which the electronic sales message has permeated our society can best be expressed in the story of the three small boys who were playing cops and robbers. "All right," said the oldest to the second boy as they started, "the next time I'll be a cop, you be the robber." The youngest joined in, saying, "And I'll be the commercial."

Television and radio share a problem common to all mass media: A campaign message is only effective if it reaches the candidate's constituency. Fortunately, this can be determined by superimposing a circulation graph over voting areas. These graphs can be obtained from representatives of radio and television stations and are called "coverage maps." Circles on the maps indicate the areas where signal can be heard or seen (Figure 4-27).

Demographics

When analyzing radio or TV audiences, candidates and media advisors should keep two things in mind. First, the viewer or listener doesn't tune in for the advertising. Ads are designed to influence an audience that has already been attracted by a particular program. The cost of a commercial spot on radio or television is calculated on the basis of the number of viewers the station has at the moment the commercial is aired.

Commercial desirability depends upon what the stations call prime time. Both radio and television have prime times, but these differ, although what constitutes prime time (the most expensive hours) for each is determined by station ratings, the time of day, and the activity of the competition. In most markets, the cost is less after 11:00 p.m. Television and radio stations have to fill an entire day, which includes listener peaks and valleys. Both sell commercials singly or in packages. The "spot package" involves the use of a given number of spots spread through the broadcast day.

The cost-effectiveness of any package depends on station programming. The ideal package is designed to reach everyone in the day's audience. For example, in 1972 an expensive package consisted of eighteen 60-second and twelve 30-second

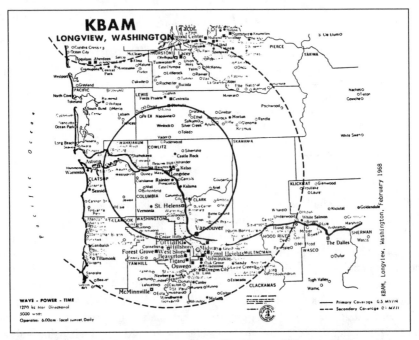

Fig. 4-27. Rate card, KBAM, Longview, Washington, February 1968.

spots on KNBC-AM radio in Los Angeles. The package cost $1,200, but it reached an estimated 1,117,000 people![2]

Candidates who want to buy radio or television time should watch the survey estimates of the station audience at the hour their ads are aired. For information about television audiences, candidates should look at the Nielsen ratings. The Nielsen Company is employed by the television industry to monitor and determine the number of viewers at any given time. Neilsen maintains both ongoing daily monitoring and also collects demographic data by three mammoth "sweep weeks" of 190,000 television households each year.

The Right to Purchase Broadcast Time

When modern electronic communications became big business, those who invested in them as a commercial enterprise wanted to limit competition. Congress agreed and made electronic communications companies the subject of federal licensure and regulation. In the beginning, this presented little problem. It was a buyer's market, permitting Tom Dewey to buy 15 minutes of each network hour on NBC radio to answer questions from persons recruited from the street the weekend preceding the 1948 presidential election.[3]

In local markets, a candidate with big bucks could buy a radio exclusive. This was the case in the 1950s when a bitter battle raged between incumbent Arkansas Governor, Sidney McMath, and the local power and light company owned by Middle South Utilities.

Just before McMath filed for reelection, there was a minor scandal in the state administration and, although it did not involve the incumbent personally, it made headlines. This encouraged the power company leading the anti-McMath forces into action, who threw their support to the candidacy of an honest, but obscure, county official, Francis Cherry. To publicize Cherry's candidacy, the utility took over a radio station for 10 to 12 hours a day for the week preceding the Democratic primary, where he answered listeners' phone questions.[4]

Since then, the desires of politicians and the business of broadcasting have collided. Commercial radio and television stations see broadcasting as a profit-making enterprise. They contend that the political advertiser is a customer who is competing for their time, which is subject to the laws of supply and demand. In their view, political ads have no right to interfere with nonpolitical programming that has been contracted for months in advance. Because politicians demand special treatment, stations have insisted that they pay a premium. Politicians, on the other hand, consider television and radio to be public service communication tools and the access to air waves an essential ingredient to twentieth century democracy.

For years, the broadcaster had the upper hand, and candidates were at the mercy of the stations. Then, in 1972, the politicians struck back. Congress enacted a bill governing the sale of political radio and television time. These regulations did not give the candidate an absolute "right" to purchase, but they took away the absolute right of the broadcaster to make programming decisions.

Burt Schorr, writing in *The Wall Street Journal*, summarized the effect of this legislation: "It really becomes a balancing act."[5] A station cannot have a blanket rule against all local or state contests, but it can limit its advertising to certain races. The legislation provides rules that govern radio and TV rates during the period 45 days before the primary and 60 days prior to a general election or runoff. During this period, candidates are legally entitled to "the lowest rate charged any advertiser. And this is true even though regular advertisers may have received a volume discount rate."[6]

Critics of this legislation argue that these regulations work a financial hardship on TV stations. But these critics also say that the hardship is less pronounced in small or medium-size markets where local stations never sell out their inventory. It is felt more by regional and local giants in the radio and TV industry. "These stations actually wind up losing money," says Craig McKee, General Sales Manager for WLS (AM-FM) in Chicago. Chris Corson, general sales manager of

KQV-AM in Pittsburgh, explains: "Political advertising eats up your inventory at bottom rates while your steady commercial advertisers get blocked out."[7]

As the result of legislation, regulation, and court decisions, a fairness doctrine has evolved. If one candidate secures a substantial block of air time, it is up to the Federal Communications Commission (FCC) to apply the fairness doctrine, requiring that time be made available to an opponent.

In the Oregon Presidential Primary of 1976, U.S. Senator Frank Church asked for prime time. After the stations refused, he was forced to appeal to the FCC. They ordered the stations to permit him to purchase half an hour of prime time. Some authorities believe the FCC's decisions could be stretched to include the requirement that free air time be made available to any bona fide opponent. In 1976, this was the reason the stations gave for refusing the request of Pennsylvania's Democratic nominee for the U.S. Senate that fifteen television stations set aside four and one half hours between 10:00 p.m. and 3:00 a.m. for a campaign telethon.[8]

There are several other regulations governing political TV and radio ads. One is that candidates must acknowledge their advertising is a paid message. This has prompted the media specialists to look for a device to minimize the negative effects this has on listeners or viewers. Although the Federal Election Commission doesn't like it, imaginative consultant Tony Schwartz advocates that candidates not close with a sponsoring committee name like "Committee for Election of Senator Woodall." He suggests using a name like "A Committee of Lots of People Who Want Perry Woodall in the State Senate."[9]

In order to qualify for political rates, a candidate must also have his or her voice somewhere in the spot. To solve this problem, the candidate can record the entire spot. They can say, "Hello, this is Francis Hadden Morgan. Please vote for me on April 3rd." Or they can simply read the required disclaimer at the end of the commercial that tells who paid for the ad.[10]

Candidates may find radio or television formats attractive, but it is not accurate to say that only supporters are interested in what is said. A whole host of special interest groups representing the opponent are monitoring, recording, and preparing to use what candidates say against him.

Radio Versus Television

Despite today's obsession with television, those who plan, run, and manage major political campaigns can't afford to ignore radio when making their advertising plans. Usually television coverage is accompanied by a substantial number of radio ads, with the result that, for every two dollars spent on television, one is spent on radio.

Eighty-two of every hundred Americans over the age of twelve listen to radio sometime during the day, and 96 percent listen, if only briefly, during the week.

Like television, radio has prime time, but unlike television, it is not 6:30 to 11:00 p.m. A high percentage of those who drive follow the news by radio. This is especially true in an area such as Los Angeles, where per capita car ownership is high and prime time equals "drive time." Next in radio's order of importance are specialty times. For example, a sports event may be covered by a radio station and not televised because the promoters don't want to diminish gate receipts.

After drive time and special events, the most expensive radio time is that aimed at retired people and housewives. Sixty-two percent of those 18 and over have a radio on as they go about their daily household tasks.[11] Others keep the radio on to follow local news because they get it while it's fresh.

Most politicians use the radio. As Judy Trabuolski, media buyer for Consultants '84, explains, "Part of the reason candidates do not ignore radio is that often you have to buy a television spot in an adjacent market, which makes for some waste. In buying the local radio station, there is no waste."[12]

Financial constraints were the key reasons for the increased use of radio advertisements in the 1984 New Hampshire presidential primary. A prime 60-second radio spot that reached 10,000 people in the Manchester, New Hampshire, area in 1982 cost about $30 to $50. A 30-second spot on Boston television, with the potential to reach seven million viewers (the vast majority in Massachusetts), reached more people, but only 30 to 40 thousand people lived in southern New Hampshire. In 1984 this 30-second TV spot cost about $2,500 during evening prime time.[13]

Radio is also the most flexible of mass communications. Even when the candidate cannot justify the use of television because the constituency is small, he or she may use radio because it is localized or targeted to a particular segment of the population. Local radio permits a major candidate to target his or her appeal to the voter's legitimate regional loyalty and to exploit a popular "home town" issue. Note this Washington State radio commercial:

Announcer: "Two years ago ... when California made a bold attempt to steal Columbia River water ... Senator Henry Jackson stopped them cold. As Chairman of the Senate Interior Committee, Jackson threw his full weight against the scheme. Result: The Senate voted a ten-year ban on water diversion, said the *Tacoma News Tribune*."

Different Voice: "Jackson's astuteness in calling the right plays helped prevent the California-Southwest team from running off with the Columbia River."

Original Announcer: "In times like these, it's good to have the common sense and uncommon courage of Senator Henry M. Jackson."[14]

Appealing to a local market is not the only way radio is used. In many areas television goes off the air between 1:00 a.m. and 6:30 or 7:00 a.m. But not radio. As the Radio Advertising Bureau says, "Insomniacs vote," and so do "night owls,"[15] to say nothing of those who work these shifts.

Radio is also an effective way to reach a segment of the voting population whose average age is less than 25 years. On a rock radio station, a large percent of the audience is between 12 and 16.4 years old. So a candidate pays a premium to target. Nevertheless, the few who can and do vote might decide a tight race. In the hands of a competent professional, radio advertising can create the impression that a candidate is "interested in us," because he or she is advertising on a station that is "playing our music."

Any segment of a voting population might decide a close race. Radio can be— and often is—used to target other special audiences. For instance, consultant Tony Schwartz once took advantage of a very humid Labor Day weekend to aim campaign spots at thousands of listeners who were cooling off at the beach.[16]

When President Gerald Ford succeeded to the presidency, the image of his party was marred by President Nixon's resignation and the Watergate scandal. Ford spent the early part of his campaign separating his identity from that of the Nixon administration. Thus, his strategist looked for something positive to carry him the rest of the way. Surveying the public mood, Ford's ad people concluded that his best reelection chance lay in going along with the prevailing spirit of patriotism and well-being in the United States, which was celebrating its 200th Birthday. His ad people came up with a happy song, "I'm Feelin' Good About America":

> "There's a change that's come over America
> A change that's great to see
> We're livin' here in peace again
> We're going back to work again
> It's better than it used to be.
>
> "I'm feelin' good about America
> I feel it everywhere I go
> I'm feelin' good about America
> I thought you ought to know
> That I'm feelin' good about America
> It's something great to see
> I'm feelin' good about America
> I'm feelin' good about me!"[17]

The song was used as background for a television commercial, but its best and most frequent application was on various radio stations, where it was arranged and played as a ballad with mixed chorus, as a rock piece, as a march, and with a Latin beat. The campaign advertisers targeted rural constituencies with a country-western rendition, and even arranged it with full orchestration to target upper income radio listeners. In a few metropolitan markets, special arrangements and radio stations were used to reach particular cultures.[18]

A musical parody may have legal restrictions. Candidates should be wary when music is suggested as a prop for a political pitch, unless the tune or the words are original or the music is old enough to be a part of the public domain. If not, usually a small fee will acquire the owner's permission to use a song.

Imaginative sounds can also be employed on radio. The picking of a guitar, the sound of a whistle or a siren, and the roll of a drum have all been used to distinguish the candidate's message. For example:

> (*cash register rings*) How much is experience worth?
> It's worth an awful lot of money. (*rings*)
> Senator Don Talley fought hard to keep your tax ceiling. . . .
> Sure, real estate taxes are higher. . . .
> But not nearly as high as some people wanted.
> Twelve long, tough years in our state senate has created and molded a man for our times. (*rings*)
> This is worth an awful lot of money
> Take time to think twice
> Then think Talley. . . .
> Your state senator for twelve good years.
> Be sure to vote Don Talley, November 5th!!![19]

Sound effects and gimmicks will not fit every campaign, however.

As a rule, radio commercials are constructed around the same themes used in television, often using the same words, but since radio spots run longer than television spots, radio can be used to expand a campaign's theme. Most radio commercials run a full minute and sometimes a candidate can purchase five minutes or more. Media pro Charles Guggenheim says in comparing radio and TV advertising, "Television should be used to convey the candidate's personal qualities, compassion, involvement, sincerity and the way he relates to people, and use radio to convey facts, figures, and issues."[20] Refer to the following nutshell for a worksheet to use when calculating radio and television advertising

Radio Techniques

The added length of radio ads without the distraction of pictures makes a good environment for the testimonial ad. For insurance, candidates can buy ads to reinforce and spread the effect of endorsing newspaper editorials.

Radio helps an issue-oriented candidate. This view is consistent with that of old political pros like ex-President Richard Nixon, who argued that a well-stated radio commercial could at least get a hearing, while only a small percentage of voters will read through a newspaper ad.[21] Radio is also the logical place for the interview technique pioneered by the talk-show stations. This format gives an advantage to better-informed candidates and those who have a fixed position on issues, and it holds public interest better than a formal speech.

★ ★ ★ ★ ★ ★ ★ ★ ★ ★ ★ ★ ★ ★

Electronic Media Ad Planning

Note: Viewers and listeners will compare the candidate's radio and TV ads with commercials for other candidates as well as commercial products, so most candidates need professional help with scripting, lighting, etc.

Research market area prime time; see market share and then focus on a particular market. Must reserve space in advance. Must pay for electronic ads in advance. Pay for media first if possible, then raise money for other campaign functions.

Radio Advertising
Production cost $_____
Cost for time:

Station	No. minutes	Time of day	Amount
_____	_____	_____	$ _____
_____	_____	_____	$ _____
_____	_____	_____	$ _____

Television Advertising
Production cost $_____
Cost for time:

Station	No. minutes	Time of day	Amount
_____	_____	_____	$ _____
_____	_____	_____	$ _____
_____	_____	_____	$ _____

★ ★ ★ ★ ★   In A Nutshell   ★ ★ ★ ★ ★

Let's look at a hot 1968 Texas primary. Nine were vying for the Democratic gubernatorial nomination. The well-heeled contenders made extensive use of radio and television commercials. Candidate Wagner Carr, a former state attorney general, didn't have money for television ads, so he spent his advertising dollars on radio, where he answered questions phoned in by listeners for periods ranging from one hour in small towns up to four hours in larger cities. The programs were promoted in advance by radio spot announcements and newspaper ads. In all, Carr used 58 radio stations to talk to people in 62 cities and towns. Wagner Carr's use of radio moved him ahead of candidates who had more to spend, yet he didn't win

Fig. 4-28. Excerpts from President Ford's "Feelin' Good" television spots. Used by permission of L. Patrick Devlin, Curator, Television Political Advertising Collection, University of Rhode Island.

the election. Most of his supporters felt that with a larger budget he could have won.

Radio presents less of a problem than television to politicians who seek a smooth, professional style. President Nixon preferred radio because he could wear his eyeglasses. For the candidate who finds any public appearance difficult, radio commercials can be prepared and taped by the radio station's staff announcers or by a free-lance performer. These individuals advertise in a variety of trade journals, such as *Roll Call* (see Figure 4-29), a newspaper dedicated to the activities of Congress.[22] However, the candidate needn't go to Washington D.C. Any advertising agency or any radio station will be glad to supply the names of qualified announcers.

Radio is valuable because it permits immediate reaction to surprises that inevitably turn up in a hard-fought campaign. As Judy Trabuolski, media buyer for Democratic presidential candidate Walter Mondale, explained, "You can go into the studio one night and literally have your spot on the air the next day."[23] Usually the candidate can also buy local radio and use it to flood the air waves during the crucial days before the election, restating positions or using simple memorable slogans to shake the uncertain.

Call

JAMES CARLETON

He has the voice for your radio / TV
political spots.

(999) 123-4567

MEMBER AFTRA/SAG (AFL-CIO)

Fig. 4-29. Modeled after ad in *Roll Call* (Capitol Hill newspaper, Washington, DC), September 23, 1976.

Chapter 34

Television

> Television gives voters a chance to see Presidential candidates close-up, almost to the bone.
> —President John F. Kennedy[1]
>
> I ask ad men not to confuse candidates for the Presidency with a deodorant or the White House with an armpit.
> —John O'Toole, President of the Belding Advertising Agency[2]

TV Demographics

Today, in the last part of the twentieth century, approximately 97 percent of American households have at least one television set, 68 percent have color sets, and 41 percent have two or more sets. In 1978, the Nielsen Company took all of the television viewers together and divided them, to get a weekly viewing median. This included the young who can't vote and those who don't vote along with those who do. They found that weekly viewing averaged 24 hours and 54 minutes for men, and 31 hours and 52 minutes for women.[3]

Fig. 4-30. Brickman, The Small Society, *Seattle Times*, March 5, 1970.

Because television has such a huge audience, it also attracts political advertising. Recognizing television dominance, Pulitzer Prize winning author David Halberstam summarized the relationship between big-time national politics and television, saying, "The sad lesson . . . of television's participation in national politics is that it is not television which has adapted itself to the norms of politics, but politics which has adapted itself to the norms of television."[4]

Sixty- and 30-second commercials sandwiched between regular programs date back to 1952 when advertising specialist Ross Reeve suggested, "Why not merchandise Eisenhower as you would any other household product?" He reasoned that not only could these TV spots be purchased at will, but they were short and could be rehearsed.[5] Even though candidates find the 30-second format frustrating and inadequate for most serious messages, these TV spots have become a standard election-year staple. In fact, campaign specialist Edward Schwartzman tells us that of the millions spent for political radio and television, 92.5 percent was spent on commercials of less than three minutes.[6]

The preference for television advertising is reflected in dollars. In 1976, political candidates spent $50.8 million on TV advertising, more than twice the amount they put into newspapers. In the 1980s, that difference grew. The $90.6 million spent on air time for television commercials by candidates represented more than three times the total spent on newspaper advertising.[7]

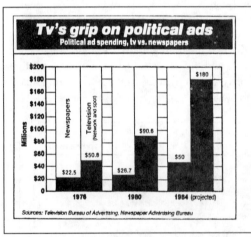

Fig. 4-31. Stuart Emmrich, "Newspapers Actively Seeking Politicians' Vote—For Ad Buys," *Advertising Age,* December 12, 1983.

Techniques and Perception

Advertising research reveals that viewers form their perception within the first 30 seconds of a 60-second message. And a 30-second spot is brief enough to discourage viewers from getting up to change channels.[8] Most commercials feature the candidate facing the TV camera as they give a pitch (e.g., Figure 4-32). This technique has been used by President Bush, President Carter, U.S. Senate minority leader Howard Baker, former Texas Governor John Connally, and U.S. Senator Teddy Kennedy.

A few commercials add another element. In a commercial for Los Angeles Mayor Tom Bradley, the camera shows a running track. In the distance Tom Bradley walks toward the camera (Figure 4-33). A runner goes by. Then Bradley says:

"When I was running track here at UCLA, I couldn't have dreamed that someday I'd be running for mayor. But it was possible, because of the kind of city that Los Angeles is. It's a city that respects a man who makes it on his own, who works hard and who doesn't ask for favors. After twenty-one years on the Los Angeles police

Fig. 4-32. Jacques Neher and Richard Gordon, "Iowa Airwaves Fill with Presidential Drives," *Advertising Age,* January 14, 1980, p. 2.

force and ten years on the city council, I think the people of this city know where my heart is. I love this city. I want to keep fighting to make it better. That's why I'm running."

A caption saying " 'ELECT TOM BRADLEY' " quickly changes to " 'LOS ANGELES NEEDS A WORKING MAYOR.' " After Bradley finishes talking, the image fades.[9]

Fig. 4-33.Used by permission of L. Patrick Devlin, Curator, Television Political Advertising Collection, University of Rhode Island.

Commercials can have imaginative themes, including a scenario, actors, background music, even animated characters. When Jerry Brown ran a poor third in the 1980 presidential primary, Wisconsin was make or break for the California governor, so Brown staked his all on television spots featuring cartoons. One illustrated inflation by showing a dollar bill being squeezed through a pair of washing machine rollers until it was only a tiny version of the original. Another featured a slowly turning wedge of apple pie. As it turned, shots of an imported car, wristwatch, shoe, and television were flashed on the screen. When the back crust faced the camera, it revealed a sticker: "Not made in the U.S.A." These commercials drew rave reviews, and although Governor Brown didn't carry Wisconsin, he managed to get nearly three times the percentage he had achieved in any of the other primaries in that election.[10]

A less expensive spot with an equally imaginative theme was used during the 1984 Presidential primary. A red telephone similar to the one designated for use by the president in the event of a nuclear attack was the centerpiece of a theme used by Vice President Mondale. In that spot a narrator emphasized Mondale's experience in foreign affairs, which he argued was superior to that of Mondale's opponent, concluding with, "The Presidency is the most awesome, powerful responsibility in the world. . . . The idea of an unsure, unsteady, untested hand is something to really think about."[11]

Occasionally, television commercials are used to ridicule. A 1980 Republican commercial depicted the Speaker of the House—or more accurately it pictured an actor who looked like Democratic House Speaker Tip O'Neill—who ignored warnings by an aide, so that his limousine ran out of gas in the middle of nowhere. "The Democrats are out of gas," said the announcer. "We need some new ideas."[12]

Avoiding a Huckster Image

Drawing on experience, David Garth and Associates uses a controversial technique, which many candidates and TV consultants claim produces an inferior commercial. In these commercials the candidate speaks directly to the TV audience. Garth argues that there is a danger in most slick TV scenarios where candidates sound as though they are hucksters.

To better understand his concern, let us go back to 1966 when one of Garth's clients, John Lindsay, was elected mayor of New York City. In the process Lindsay gained the reputation of being a media huckster, who could work miracles via television. When he used the same slick commercials that succeeded in New York City during the Florida and Wisconsin presidential primaries, TV consultant Robert Goodman said, "All that happened was that he insulted the voters," and fell flat.[13]

Since then David Garth has gone to great lengths to avoid a huckster image. Now Garth candidates speak directly into the camera but concentrate on statistics. At the bottom of the TV screen his commercials feature type repeating the specifics of what the candidate claims, for example, how many policemen were hired and exactly how much tax money was cut. If the candidate claims credit for attracting industry, the television spot includes names of newly opened plants and their locations. Admitting they look amateurish and bland, Garth rationalizes, "Our commercials are designed for the long haul. We know that people are going to be seeing them 10 or 12 times during a campaign, and we want to keep them interested. We want to leave them with a little bit more of the message every time they see it."[14]

This technique has drawbacks, as most candidates are not actors and are often nervous as well as unfamiliar with lighting or camera techniques. For example, California Governor Edmund Brown (Jerry Brown's father) served his state in many capacities, including attorney general and governor. He knew the issues and could speak fluently on them. In his second reelection campaign his television budget matched, if it not exceeded, his opponent's. However, his television personality offered little compared to the personal style and the accomplished performance of his successful opponent, one-time movie actor, Ronald Reagan.[15]

So candidates look for alternatives to Garth's look-into-the-camera technique. For instance, a candidate who does well on the political stump, working the crowd, or meeting constituents on the street can have a television crew follow as he or she goes through the familiar litany of a political campaign. The odds are that every so often the television crew will hit a political bullseye that can be lifted out and used as a commercial. For example, though Senator George McGovern lost his bid to be president in 1972, he made a very effective television commercial. The camera crew, following McGovern, filmed him wearing a red shirt while visiting a factory and giving this answer to a factory worker's question, "You know, politics is my profession, and I'm embarrassed when it doesn't work. . . . While I don't expect you to agree with everything I say, you're gonna know that when I say something, it is what I honestly believe." Then McGovern added, "There will never be a time when I go sneaking around advocating something in secret behind closed doors that I'm ashamed to defend in public."[16]

Issues and Television

Some candidates use opinion surveys to determine what issues should be emphasized and how the voter perceives them (see Polling). During the early part of his first campaign for governor of California, Jerry Brown focused on his role as Secretary of State, where he had championed election reform—that is, until after market surveys showed that the public perceived his as a "one-issue candidate."

To broaden his appeal Brown developed several other issues to show his concern about oil, air pollution, the environment, transportation, and economic needs. He did several 30-second capsule speeches. One on education dealt with public school students and advocated the distribution of state money for schools on a "more nearly equal" basis. A post-election poll showed this was the only clearly identified position most voters could remember. They liked his stand on education, which was expressed only in his television ads.[17]

Beware of Association

Often, other ingredients affect the viewer's perception of a candidate's commercial. Coverage of a commercial is measured by the ratings of the show during which it is shown, but the type of program also affects the audience's perception. Psychologists explain that during some television shows, the viewing public confuses the political advertiser with the show, and this can affect the candidate's image, either positively or negatively. For example, the candidate may be lumped with a comedy show's characters that appear to be dimwitted or slow. For this reason, television specialists, such as Gerald Rafshoon who masterminded Jimmy Carter's rise, prefer a spot before or after the evening news, sports programs, or family programs.

Governor Millikan of Michigan used audience psychology to his advantage. His hard-hitting, prime-time television commercials discussed drugs and crime and were placed next to newscasts and other shows with appropriate police themes such as "Mod Squad" and "Hawaii 5-0."[18]

Chapter 35

Shake Hands With Every Voter
Through the Mail Box

> It is bad enough if a campaign piece is marked as second-class matter . . .
> the real loser is the fellow who receives junk mail with postage due.
> —Mrs. Elsa Lanstrom[1]
>
> Some people have their names perpetuated in stone or cast in bronze, but
> most of us are just on mailing lists.[2]

Direct Mail Power

In spite of the power of electronic media and the high-speed press, direct mail still has a very real place in political life. Unlike other forms of advertising that involve a lot of guess-work, major market surveys have determined that 75 percent of the recipients at least glance at their mail.

To illustrate how powerful direct mail can be, I offer this glimpse of a most interesting character among the many who have shot across our nation's political horizon. An eccentric millionaire, George Holden Tinkham, was elected in 1918 to Congress as a Republican from Massachusetts. He was bearded when fashion dictated that a man's face be smooth. He was a bachelor when having a wife and family was considered a political necessity. He was aloof at a time when his contemporaries were back-slapping extroverts. He excelled as a big-game hunter, which required his absence for long periods. He made twenty-seven trips to Europe and twice went around the world. As a Congressman he authored no major legislation and rarely made a speech on the floor. Through the years, his constituency changed, with redistricting. At one point Roosevelt carried his district by a 21,000 majority. Yet this eccentric Republican managed to survive until he died in office on May 21, 1941.

The secret—and there had to be a secret—of Tinkham's success was the skillful way in which he plied his constituency with personal mail. Although he never formally campaigned, after every election he sent a postcard of gratitude to all the faithful in his district. Tinkham believed that men paid no attention to greeting cards, but women did, so his dedicated staff sent a Christmas card to 77,000 women each year. The staff also noted every birth, death, and graduation and used the mail to notify individuals when legislation they were interested in was being considered by a Congressional committee. In all, Tinkham's staff sent as many as a million pieces of literature a year to the people of his district.[3]

Most campaigners make no pretense they depend on what the trade terms "junk mail." These campaign pieces range from three to six panels or foldouts on slick paper to eight-page tabloids, printed on newsprint. The origin of this type of mail can be traced to 1900 when a telegraph clerk in a Minnesota railroad station, Richard Sears, conceived of the idea of selling to other telegraph operators by mail a consignment of watches refused by a local jeweler. Once he sold the originals, he made arrangements to purchase more from another watch supplier. His success led him to leave his job, and, with the help of mail advertising, he created the largest retailer in the United States, Sears and Roebuck.[4]

Why does the recipient react favorably to so-called junk mail? One theory is that even "junk" political mail is personal to the extent that it has been stamped, addressed, and sent to an individual. And such mail must work because, despite rising postage, paper, and printing costs, direct mail plays an ever-increasing part in both commercial and political advertising.

Most campaign mail consists of a letter and an enclosed brochure that extols the candidate's virtues and outlines his or her sales pitch. Like other forms of political advertising, campaign mail has to be an attention-getter and attract readership to make it worthwhile. Occasionally it has an attention-getter on the outside of the envelope, such as the phrase, "Your Polling Place May Have Changed!" Then inside it states the exact address of the polling place.

The Gimmick Mailer

Often direct-mail pros gain attention with a gimmick. A group in California sent a simulated IBM card with "Are your property taxes paid?" printed on one side and a message about taxes and the high cost of living on the other. Campaign craftsman Edward Schwartzman favors an envelope with a campaign insert that looks like a machine-printed telegram. He cites the results of a New Jersey study comparing a standard computer letter with a simulated telegram in which the recipient's name was filled in by computer. It was found that the telegram format was 9 percent more effective because voters open it thinking it might be a telegram.[5]

Folding techniques also make a difference. Odd shapes help the mailer stand out. However, before taking a chance on an odd-shaped self-mailer, candidates should check postal service regulations on sizing as well as other requirements.

Occasionally the candidate can use a teaser campaign. These are of two types, one consisting of two or more letters mailed in a series. The other, more common, is a one-shot mailer where the recipient cannot determine the nature of the message from the outside. It must be opened to delve into its contents. See Figure 4-34 for an example.

Fig. 4-34. Mailer, Washington State legislative report from Senator Lowell Peterson, 1972.

Chapter 36

The Magic of Personalization

> There was no substitute for the personal touch, and there never will
> be unless the Lord starts making human beings different from the
> way he makes them now.
> —James A. Farley, Chairman of the Democratic Party, 1932[1]

Campaign Letters

The campaign letter has much in common with other mail advertising, but it has an important distinguishing feature: It is a personal form of communication that the sender expects to be read. One of the greatest of the political professionals, former Postmaster General Jim Farley said, "A letter is maximized when it makes the receiver believe it is intended for him personally and no one else in the world." The campaign manual of the Public Affairs Department of the National Association of Manufacturers warns against using mail addressed to "Postal Patron" or "Boxholder" unless the sender is prepared to enclose a dollar bill to attract attention.[2]

When candidates use equipment that automatically types in recipients' names (e.g., a computerized form letter), a personal letter can be mass-produced "in-house." However, if candidates can afford it, they can employ a direct-mail firm with high-speed printers equipped with typewriter-emulating fonts. Some printers are capable of up to 2,200 lines a minute. With such sophisticated equipment the voter's name can appear not only in the salutation, but one or more times in the body of the letter. The addresses are printed on continuous form envelopes.

On occasion the candidate can use a mailing technique employed by former United States Representative Bella Abzug. Six months before her 1970 congressional contest, she prepared hundreds of kits consisting of 25 voter names and addresses and a supply of letterhead, envelopes, and brochures. The kits were given to volunteers who were asked to write a personal letter supporting Bella, choosing their text from one of three form letters. The instructions on the outside of the kit made it clear that after the writers had finished and addressed 25 handwritten letters, they were to hold them for pickup. A week later Bella's campaign staff collected the letters and the writers were asked to work up another kit, which the majority were happy to do. All completed letters were held until five days before the election, then mailed en masse. This avalanche of mail helped Bella upset an entrenched old guard.[3]

There are several ways the recipient's name can be used to personalize a piece of mail. Some direct-mail campaigns use cellophane windows as part of a specialty mailer. This saves addressing cost, because it permits them to fold the letter so the address can be seen through a cellophane window. Following Jim Farley's reasoning, it is important that the letter do more than use the recipient's name. It should be enclosed in an envelope with a stamp rather than a machine imprint.

Personalization doesn't stop there. The name and address should look as it would if a secretary had typed it. Mail houses often program their computers to automatically type words from abbreviated components. Figure 4-35 illustrates the difference between raw and final mailing lists.

Original List	Final List
J Smith	Mr. Joseph Smith
20 N Parklane Ave.	20 North Parklane Avenue
Garden Cy NY 12530	Garden City, New York 12530
E Hanson	Mrs. Elenore Hanson
3522 St. Anne St	3522 St. Anne Street
Western Hills CA 91366	Western Hills California 91366

Fig. 4-35. Raw address list compared with typed.

Jim Farley also reasoned that in addition to using the recipient's name in the salutation, his letter should have a personal mark. He decided that his letterhead should be one color and the signature another. Over the next 40 years in his political and commercial careers with the United States Gypsum and Coca Cola companies, he sent hundreds of thousands of letters signed "Jim" in green ink.[4] In Farley's day, personalization meant signing several thousand letters at a sitting. Today, machinery can simulate a signature that looks reasonably genuine.

Another way to test the effectiveness of a political letter is to ask, "Does it come from someone the recipient believes to be important?" Apparently Jim Farley's letters were deemed important. "I know," he said, "because I have seen them time and again, frayed, soiled and tattered, and being exhibited on a thousand different occasions, but still holding together somehow or other." The letter in Figure 4-36, from Robert Kennedy, provides a fine model.

The Mailing Target

What makes mail advertising competitive is the ability to reach voters with special interests. One candidate who did this was one-time Governor Orval Faubus, when he dominated Arkansas politics. During the first Catholic presidency of the United States, John Kennedy found Faubus insulting. Yet after Kennedy's death, Faubus made a hit with thousands of Arkansas Catholics. He sent them special letters canceled in Boston that had Kennedy memorial stamps

KENNEDY *For President* *HEADQUARTERS*

2000 L Street, Northwest - Washington, D.C. 20036

June 2, 1968

Mr. Robert P. Grieve
5116 S.W. Hudson
Seattle, Washington 98116

Dear Mr. Grieve:

I need your help and your support in my campaign for
the Presidency of the United States when you meet in your
District Caucus this month.

In the past ten weeks, I have travelled to many parts
of this country -- in the north, south, east and west. Everywhere I have found people concerned about what is happening
in our country, as I found in Seattle when I visited there
on March 26th.

I, too, am concerned. I am concerned about the future
of our country -- about restoring peace among the family of
nations, about preventing organized crime and crime on the
streets, about giving our family farmers their rightful share
of our national income, about halting the pollution of our
national resources, and about turning back the pressures of
inflation.

If you share my concerns, and my hopes for the future
of this country, I will need your help and support when you
meet at your caucus and your State Convention.

I hope to be in Washington again before too long, and I
hope we have the opportunity then to discuss the issues so
vital to our future.

With warm regards.

Sincerely,

Robert F. Kennedy

Fig. 4-36. Letter from Robert F. Kennedy to author.

affixed to the envelopes. In the text Faubus commented he was proud that when
President Kennedy visited Arkansas there was no unpleasantness.[5]

Compared to other means of communication, direct mail has financial and
tactical advantages. Most small campaigns and even some fairly large ones can't
afford city newspaper, radio, or TV coverage. Most congressmen or assemblymen
running from Los Angeles or New York constituencies can't afford the mass
media, where nineteen of every twenty listeners, viewers, or readers do not vote in
their contest.

If the candidate is going to use a mailing list, especially a general one such as that of all registered voters, breaking the list down geographically increases response and saves paper, postage, labor, and the cost of personalization. How extensively the list can be segmented depends on how detailed the local election department information is. All jurisdictions show newly registered voters and those that have moved from another address.

Most official voter files categorize the voter by sex and age. This makes it easy to reach young and elderly voters with special mailings. For example, a candidate might pull out all the people between the ages of 25 and 35. This group—Robert Beuhler, Director of Public Affairs for the National Association of Manufacturers, observes—could be the key to victory, because "younger people as a rule do not receive a great deal of mail."[6]

Everyone understands that voting records are limited to registered voters, but most candidates don't realize that they can select those who vote in primaries—or, in some instances, voters with a history of going to the polls in a certain type of election campaign.

Where official records show voting histories, the campaign organization can determine who is likely to vote. If the race is a primary in a state where the voters must declare their party, the candidate may want to concentrate on getting his or her message in the hands of those who will vote in that primary.

Even in a state where voters don't register by party and the election department does not keep track of how often the individuals voted, candidates are given access to voter poll books and voter statistics. They can use past election statistics and then concentrate on precincts with a history of voting for candidates in their party's primary.

All organizations have membership rosters. Most keep them up to date so they can send their members periodic bulletins. These members are usually turned on by an issue that affects their interests. If the organization makes endorsements, the candidate might try to get one, but with or without an endorsement a wise candidate concentrates on getting mailing lists from organizations with political interests, such as the Chamber of Commerce, unions, granges, veterans, churches, and lodges.

One politician who creatively used direct mail was a wealthy Republican who in the early 1960s performed many generous and public-spirited deeds for his adopted state, Arkansas. Then he decided that he wanted to be governor. During the campaign he had to overcome the fact that Arkansas was by heritage a one-party state that had not elected a Republican since the days of reconstruction.

Pursuing the governorship, Winthrop Rockefeller established a nerve center in the Tower Building in Little Rock. His staff coded information supplied by volunteers who went door-to-door and canvassed by telephone. These paid professionals put the coded information on the computer. In the process they

Fig. 4-37. Brant Parker and Johnny Hart, The Wizard of Id (Chicago: Field
Enterprises, 1978). By permission of Johnny Hart and Creators Syndicate, Inc.

collected almost 200,000 names and addresses in a special interest file. Then they
used direct mail and modern computer technology to target the voter on the basis
of occupation, sex, income level, geography, race, and age. Almost overnight, the
technique worked. Thanks to these files, Winthrop Rockefeller could mail to
members of various trade and professional groups.[7]

Creating a Mailing List

Candidates should ask supporters with diverse contacts to acquire rosters from
as many organizations as possible, but this is sometimes difficult because most
organizations pride themselves on being nonpolitical and have rules restricting the
use of their membership lists. In practice, though, many groups with a political
interest are willing to surreptitiously make a list of their members available to a
friendly candidate, especially an incumbent with a record they consider favorable.
Also, direct mail houses make a business of collecting and selling commercial
mailing lists. While these can be used politically, the cost per name is so great that
they are beyond the capability of most campaigns.

Telephone yellow pages can be used to compile lists of those who follow a
business or profession. However, using the phone book has some drawbacks:
Often individual voters are missed because the telephone book uses company
names, and in a metropolitan area, tradesmen and professionals do not necessarily
live and vote in the district where their business is located. To solve these
problem, a campaign organization can also use a city directory.

For candidates who are interested, public records show recently naturalized
citizens and the country of their origin. In some jurisdictions a candidate has

access to other government records, such as licenses issued to businesses or professions. In my state at one time there were 639 categories, ranging from abortion clinics to x-ray device approvals. Candidates with access to this information can send letters to nurses, medical doctors, lawyers, chiropractors, beauticians, barbers, contractors, real estate sales people, etc. To avoid embarrassment, the candidate should double check the law to be sure these licenses are public record and can be used to solicit support in political campaigns.

In almost every case, the candidate can get names of individuals involved in specific occupations from public records, for example, police officers or other county, city, or school employees. Of course, home addresses may not be available, but even without them, a creative campaign can find a way. For example, teachers can be reached at the school where they work, and the same technique can be used to reach policemen and firemen.

If generalized information such as income or race is desired, the candidate might purchase United States government census information. It will list family size, race, age, average income, whether the residents of an area are rural or urban, and whether they live in an apartment or a single-family dwelling.

If the circumstances are appropriate, the general voter list—or better yet names selectively taken from a city directory—can be synchronized with census information to build a mailing list of racial or ethnic voters. This technique was used by U.S. Senator Jacob Javits just prior to his 1974 campaign when the New York Republican mailed 700,000 messages targeted to specific race and ethnic voters designated as "official business."[8]

It is only fair to warn anyone who decides to follow this procedure that there are inherent problems. Allowances must be made for a margin of error, say 15 to 50 percent, when targeting voters of a mixed race or of a different race or ethnic origin than their neighbors. Campaigners who try to use names to identify ethnic origins can be misled. For example, in Hispanic areas of New York City, some change their names and some women, when they marry, acquire surnames that do not reflect their ethnic origins.

Some candidates use a general voting list in combination with the telephone. They conduct a phone survey to more accurately segregate the voters, then use the results to target various facets of the population. During one campaign, workers from New York Governor Nelson Rockefeller's headquarters made questionable calls to all phone subscribers in the Democratic wards of New York City. They represented themselves as public opinion pollsters, asking people how they intended to vote. The results showed that some of the Democratic households called were leaning toward Rockefeller. The pro-Rockefeller voters were reinforced by letters from the Governor or a letter from individuals endorsing the Governor's candidacy. When the canvassers located undecided voters, they identified their political concerns and broke them down into half a dozen categories. These concerns were addressed by a letter in which Rockefeller explained his views.[9]

A Message

When voters receive political mail, the first few seconds are critical. This is when they decide to read it or throw it away. Effectiveness, of course, usually depends upon how the text strikes the reader. If the letter is more than one paragraph, the copywriter should ask: (a) Does the first paragraph grab the reader? (b) Does it hold the reader's interest? (c) Does it close with a bid for action?

If the letter is more than one paragraph and the first one doesn't catch the reader's attention, there is a strong possibility the reader will never finish reading the letter. Usually the reader's attention is gained by mentioning something that he or she interprets to be in their self-interest. In some cases the recipient's interest will be so strong that no urging is needed. For example, in each of his election years, Orval Faubus, Governor of Arkansas, sent each welfare recipient a personalized letter that arrived just before the primary explaining to some 80,000 why they were getting a $5 monthly increase.

If a campaign letter were to be sent to those who teach or to those who have children in the public schools, the candidate might catch attention with an opening such as: "The public schools are in trouble. As a state Senator I see evidence of the causes—some of which I believe can be corrected by legislation."

A candidate who wants to capture a doctor's attention might open with: "Fantastic legal judgments increase your insurance premiums. If the present malpractice claims trend continues, it may be impossible to obtain any protective insurance."

A candidate who wants to hold the attention of real estate developers and building contractors might begin by showing concern for old-fashioned restrictive building codes and archaic zoning and materials requirements, which reduce their efficiency and turn profit into loss. A candidate might go on to explain a legislative plan to solve their problems.

The Special Interest Message

Candidates welcome and encourage endorsements, but few want to project themselves as being captives of an organization's special interest. A letter directed to a special interest should be supportive, yet noncommittal, and end with a request for suggestions and comments. An example is found in the letter shown in Figure 4-38, sent to registered nurses during a campaign for Governor of Florida.[10]

Where there is no overpowering issue, letters to voters traditionally include endorsements from other politicians or members of an organization. To give endorsements punch, candidates often depend on the recommendation of someone

Dear Friend:

As you know, I am a candidate for Governor, subject to the Democratic primaries in May. Because I believe we have a mutual interest in the welfare of the state, I am writing to solicit your vote and active support.

You, as a member of the nursing profession, are aware of how much remains to be done in the field of public health. I am certainly no advocate of socialized medicine. On the other hand, I am conscious of the great need for expansion of the state's public health program, particularly in the area of prevention of childhood diseases and the eradication of sources of infection.

I assure you that as Governor, I shall be ready to cooperate in progressive measures aimed toward the achievement of these ends.

My experience as a businessman and as a member of the Legislature qualifies me, I believe, to serve the people of the state aggressively and constructively. You, as a member of the profession dedicated to serving humanity, understand the need for unselfish public service in governmental affairs. Any suggestions or comments you may care to offer will be greatly appreciated.

Fig. 4-38. Sample special-interest letter; from Fuller Warren, *How to Win in Politics* (Tallahassee, FL: Peninsula Publ., 1964), p. 128.

they know. This technique, as already discussed, was used by one-time congressman Bella Abzug. The copy does not have to be elaborate and, if it is personalized and handwritten to someone the writer knows personally, a few lines are adequate.

In the 1972 Presidential primary Jimmy Carter's New Hampshire campaign headquarters supplied postcards bearing a black and white photo of Carter in a work shirt, leaning on a fence, apparently at his Georgia farm. His supporters were encouraged to copy one of the seven sample postcard messages[11] shown in Figure 4-39 in their own handwriting and mail them to friends.

Where there is a split in the opposition, the same thing can be done using some of their prominent members. For instance, in 1970, New York Republican Governor Nelson Rockefeller formed "Democrats for Rockefeller." A major effort was made to recruit prominent Democrats, and computerized letters were sent over their signatures to areas where they had followers.[12]

However, if the candidate has neither the money nor the volunteers to fill in the recipient's name or change names, addresses, etc., to personalize thousands of letters, they can use creativity. Print might be combined with handwriting in a two-color piece, such as the letter I once sent with a sample ballot (Figure 4-40); the handwriting was printed in a different color.

- I met Jimmy Carter the other day at Yoden's. Jimmy makes sense. I hope all of us in the Portsmouth area will support him on February 24.

- Jimmy Carter is a businessman like us and has common sense ideas about making federal government efficient. We need someone down there who has run a government. Hope you'll vote for him.

- Jimmy Carter did a great job straightening out the government in Georgia. I think he could do the same thing in Washington. I hope you'll support him February 24.

- Jimmy Carter had a great record on environment as Governor. He'll do the same thing as President. I hope you'll vote for him February 24.

- I'm going to vote for Jimmy Carter. He's a hard worker and does what he thinks is right. That's what we need in Washington.

- I just met a guy who's running for President, Jimmy Carter. He's really different. He's one of us. Vote for him.

- Jimmy Carter is really an honest guy who would be a great President. I hope you'll vote for him. (Kathy) and I will.

Fig. 4-39. Sample postcard messages from Jimmy Carter campaign.

★ ★ ★ ★ ★ ★ ★ ★ ★ ★ ★ ★ ★ ★ ★

"Dear Friend" Cards

Note: "Dear friend" cards are mailed by the candidate or volunteers and friends of the candidate to their friends (for example, those on their Christmas card list) just before election day.

Design and have cards printed?
    One sided _____   Two-sided _____   Number to print _____

Mailing:
    First class_____Third class (bulk) _____
    Does campaign pays postage?_____Or does sender pay?_____

List names of people who will sign (campaign coordinator mails cards).
Establish a control sheet.
Make up packets: Instruction sheet_____   Cards in batches of 25 _____
Distribute packets to volunteers.
Have senders hand write the message following sample messages which candidate has
    provided.
Have signers mail them out about 5 days before the election (less if first class, more if
    third).

★ ★ ★ ★ ★   In A Nutshell   ★ ★ ★ ★ ★

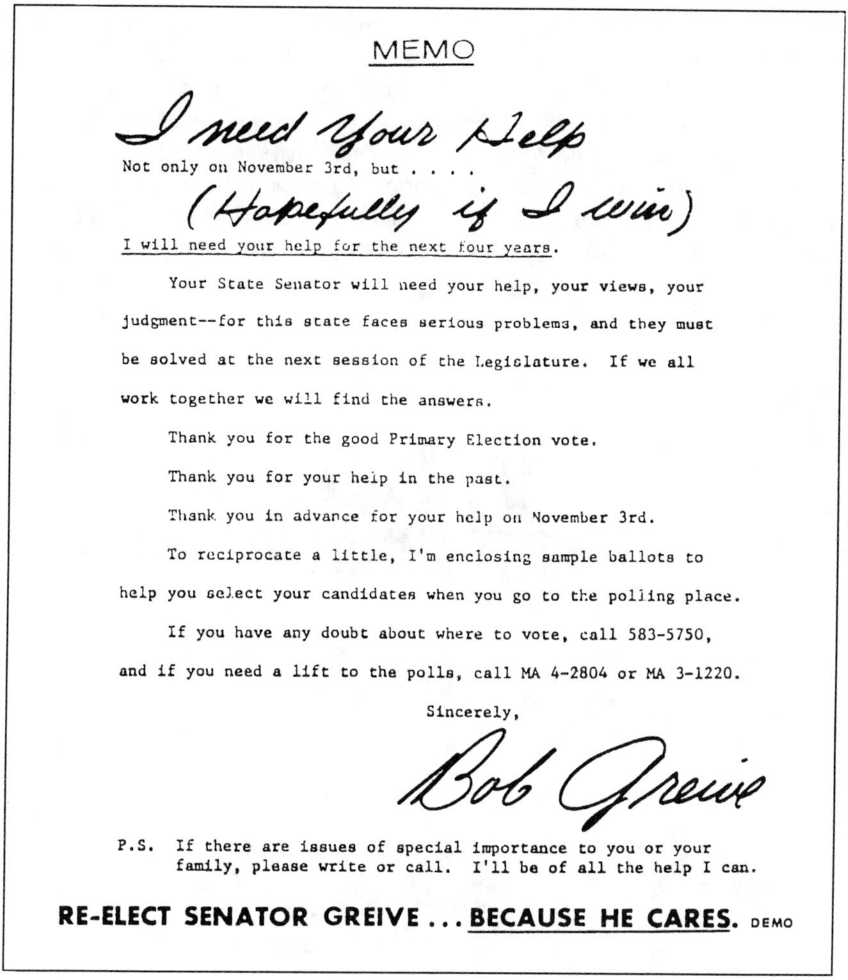

Fig. 4-40. Mailer, Reelect Senator R. R. Bob Greive, 1968. Note that the handwritten material was printed in a different color.

Getting the Mail Recipient to Participate

In his book, *How to Win Friends and Influence People*, Dale Carnegie used the following story to illustrate what social scientist Joseph T. Klepper describes as a conversion, which, Klepper explains, is intensified under the conditions of audience participation:[13] On the day of a big presentation the sales engineer for a large fabric manufacturer was unable to speak. He had to write on a pad of paper: "Gentlemen, I have lost my voice; and I am speechless." At that point the president of the company said, "I'll do the talking for you." When he took over, all the salesman did was smile, nod. "As a result," the salesman said, "I was awarded the contract which called for over half a million yards of upholstery fabric at an aggregate value of $1,600,000 . . . the highest order I ever received."[14]

Applying this psychology to an election contest, in 1946 two promoters elected a virtual unknown, Carl Ziedler, as Mayor of Minneapolis by simply mailing and receiving the results from thousands of double postcards which told the voters, "You write my platform."[15] Ruby Chow, King County (Washington) Councilwoman, also used this psychology. She turned her routine newsletter to her constituents into an "opinion poll" with what may be a record for brevity (Figure 4-41).

Fig. 4-41. "Budget polling piece," King County Councilwoman Ruby Chow, 1980.

Special Letter From the Spouse

In November 1967, former President George Bush made his first Texas campaign for Congress. Two days before the election, several hundred thousand women voters in Houston received a letter from his wife. The recipient's name was not filled in, and the letter was a printed reproduction of one written in her hand. As Bush put it, "She has one of those Ivy League, womanly scrawls. It was on a feminine-looking piece of paper, and it used commemorative stamps instead of a postage meter."

Bush relates, "The letter did not talk about . . . the United States or the John Birch Society or the ACLU. My wife simply wrote that her husband was a good guy and that she would appreciate the recipient's vote for him. You should have seen the response we got to this personal approach."[16]

This letter has many variations. In Seattle, there is a version nicknamed "Uhlman's Blue Letter" (named for former mayor Wes Uhlman). It is a reproduction of a typewritten letter addressed to all women voters. It uses blue paper and includes a recipe from his wife, patterned after the one for coffee cake used by Nelson Rockefeller's wife "Happy," in the New York Governor's campaign.[17] When I used it, my wife Barbara's recipe was for "Hamburger Soup." Laila Uhlman's was for "Quick Party Bread" (Figure 4-42). In his 1973 campaign, Uhlman used the back of the recipe card for a picture of his family.

The Closing

Normally, a campaign letter should close with a bid for action. It might conclude with, "I would appreciate it if you would fill out the enclosed questionnaire and include any comments, suggestions, or facts that you wish to pass on to me. I need them if I am to do the job you want at the state level."

A campaign letter to retired public employees—who usually live on a pension and have an overpowering fear of inflation—might discuss legislation the candidate has or might sponsor that would provide automatic cost-of-living increases in public employee retirement programs. The letter might conclude with, "I intend to keep watching for your needs. Please remember me when you exercise your right to vote on _____."

Another good way for a candidate to wind up a personal appeal for votes is with a closing such as, "I urge you to vote in the primary election on September 15, and I hope my past record or program for the future merits your support in my campaign for reelection."

Voters don't like a vendetta, so if a candidate wants to use names and make comparisons, it is best to use a committee composed of members of a target group. For example, a letter sent out in the name of a property owners' group might say, "We have evaluated the records and positions of both candidates for State Representative in the 44th district and feel the voters should be advised of their stand on property taxes." Or "We urge you to vote for Mary Candidate. She has strongly taken the position of general tax reform as the answer for meeting the needs of state government, instead of continuously increased property taxes. Her

Laila Uhlman
6040 Thirty-fourth Avenue N.E.
Seattle, Wash. 98115

Dear Neighbor,

Managing a household is similar to serving in public office; both require a watchful eye on rising prices.

Each penny of our household dollar is important. Since nearly every trip to the grocery store means higher prices, I am sure you share the concern both Wes and I have for stretching our household and tax dollars as far as possible.

During the last four years Wes has worked to ensure effective and efficient city spending. Our special concern has been to make Seattle a safe city, particularly for women. Did you know that more than half of the city budget is spent for police and fire protection? Crime has been decreased 26% since 1969. No wonder Seattle has become one of the safest cities in the nation!

As you know, Wes is now seeking a second term as mayor of Seattle. Our service has been a family affair. I have been fortunate in sharing Wes' efforts and hopes to continue to make Seattle a safer and better place in which to live.

Sincerely,

Laila Uhlman

A FAVORITE FROM THE UHLMAN KITCHEN

QUICK PARTY BREAD

1 Cup Sugar	⅓ Cup Applesauce
⅓ Cup Shortening	½ Cup chopped Nuts
2 eggs	peel of 1 small orange, grated
1¼ Cups Flour	TOPPING:
½ teaspoon Salt	¼ Cup Sugar
1 teaspoon Baking Powder	juice from 1 small orange

Cream together sugar and shortening; add lightly beaten eggs. Sift flour with salt and baking powder; add flour mixture alternately with applesauce. Stir in nuts and grated orange peel. Pour into well greased loaf pan, bake 1 hour at 350°. Meanwhile, prepare topping; thoroughly mix sugar and orange juice. When bread is removed from oven, make holes in the top with a toothpick; immediately pour topping over bread. Cool in pan before serving.

enclosed one of our family's favorite will enjoy it.

Fig. 4-42. Mailer, Reelect Wes Uhlman for Mayor Committee, 1970.

opponent, William Opposition, voted for EHB 978 in the last session which increases regular property tax levies."

When someone else writes the letter, the approach is slightly different. If the letter is to be used by a taxpayers' association, it might go like this: "We urge you to join with us to elect John Candidate as our State Representative from district 32 next Tuesday, because we feel that the time has come for you to elect legislators who will vote to spread the burden of state government more fairly to all taxpayers, rather than to those who own property."

If the group consists of independents attempting to persuade those who share their philosophy to support a candidacy, the letter might close with this: "As independents, we are proud to ask for your support in helping keep Senator Rubin Knoblauch as our man in the State Capitol."

Occasionally a candidate can persuade an individual or organization that already has the confidence of the voter to write a letter stating his or her position. For example, chiropractors have used the political process to force medical insurance plans that are either administered by or have close ties to conventional medicine to pay their bills. When mailing to their patients on behalf of a political candidate, a letter might close with a bid for action by saying, "We are writing to you, a chiropractic patient, asking that you join in our efforts to end the refusal of M.D.-controlled insurance companies to pay for your treatment."

No matter how hard it is to get out the vote, there is always one group that is on hand to cast their ballots. Workers who staff the polls make a good target, especially for a judicial candidate or a holder of some other non-partisan office. To persuade these partisans to support his or her candidacy, I would suggest a note: "Dear _____: Just a note to let you know that I join thousands of other citizens in appreciating the important public service you will perform on the Election Board next Tuesday."

Using the Postal Service to Advantage

The U.S. Postal Service does not insist that first-class mail be sorted. In most cases, first-class mail need only be in the mail 24 hours prior to the delivery date. If the mail is sorted by zip code using mail tags available at the post office, local first-class mail can be scheduled for the next day's delivery.

Substantial discounts are available for presorted mail, termed third-class or bulk mail. There is a minimum charge for third-class mail, determined by weight. Those making the mailing need a permit imprint, which must be purchased and renewed each calendar year. There must be at least 200 pieces of mail of identical size, weight, and configuration to get this rate. When mailing third class, a form must be filled out showing postage and the number of pieces in the mailing. There must be an advance payment account which is set up when the permit is granted, and deposits must be made in advance to cover the postage. Third class campaign pieces are not forwarded or returned to the sender unless special arrangements are made (see below). Check with the postal service for any changes in requirements.

Politicians often get political allies to make a mailing for them, because mail sent by and in the name of a political party qualifies for a greatly reduced special rate. The same is true of political mail sent in the name of a union or its political action committee to its own members.

The Computer and the Message

Third-class envelopes have to carry a "Third-Class" notation, but, contrary to what many believe, the post office does not require a bulk-rate imprint be used. A bulk-rate mail stamp can be used, or the sender can use a regular postage meter impression. Then "Third Class" typed in the lower corner will do.

If the candidate wants the letter to look personal, the "third class" imprint should not be used. Enough people will notice this designation to destroy the desired person-to-person effect. This is true even when it is small and in the lower left hand corner of the envelope. However, campaigns are often short of money, forcing a candidate to compromise.

Addressing and preparing mail can be done manually at headquarters or left to workers recruited to help in their own homes. When calculating the number of volunteers necessary, as a rule of thumb it takes one hour for five people to fold, stuff, seal and stamp a thousand letters. Also, it takes good organization to truck, pick up, and deliver the mail when the candidate decides to let volunteers perform these tasks at home.

An affluent candidate might turn this responsibility over to a mailing bureau, which would have advanced addressing technology. In some cases, the candidate can obtain and furnish the agent a mailing list that is on a computer disk or tape. Some typed mailing lists can be electronically scanned. Most mailing houses have machinery that automatically addresses or glues computer-produced labels onto envelopes at a fixed cost per thousand.

Once on the computer a mailing list can be programmed to accept updated information. For example, the members of a family are often combined to avoid duplication when mailing to a single household. Also, names and addresses can be continually updated without destroying the tape or disk. Furthermore, professional direct-mail houses often have machinery that automatically folds, inserts, and stamps as well as trucks that make regular runs to the post office.

Updating the Mailing List

When the candidate wants to target a select group of voters or contributors, caution should be taken when using a mailing list that is several years old. Both money and embarrassment can be saved by eliminating those who have died or no longer live in the candidate's jurisdiction, those who may not vote in a particular type of election, and those who are known to be hostile.

This should have been done before a letter signed by California Governor Ronald Reagan was mistakenly sent to his Democratic predecessor, Edmund G. (Pat) Brown. Reagan received this reply from Brown:

Dear Hon. Reagan:

In today's mail I received a letter from you recalling the days of the Brown-Unruh clique. I am very interested in your record of increased taxation, increased welfare costs and property taxes.

I really believe that Edmund G. Brown, Jr., will do a far better job than your hand-picked candidate, Houston Flournoy. I must, therefore, refuse your kind invitation to contribute to the Republican State Central Committee.

Sincerely, Edmund G. Brown
(former Governor of California; father of Edmund G. ("Jerry") Brown, Jr.)

Of course this was brought to Reagan's attention, and he sent this reply:

Dear Pat:

I just thought that you might be ready to do penance.

Sincerely, Ronald W. Reagan18

It is wise to update the list of registered voters even though the official list is updated every four years. There is a substantial loss, which can amount to 40 percent in a big city. Even if the mail is sent first-class and is forwarded, the voter may have moved, died, or re-registered in another jurisdiction.

A number of these problems can be avoided if the campaign organization can use first-class mail, which is either forwarded or returned. Mail undeliverable at the third-class rate is marked and destroyed unless the sender agrees to the payment of a premium for each piece returned. If a candidate contemplates multiple mailings, he or she should arrange to buy back the returned non-deliverable third-class pieces by applying for a postage return guarantee permit. Candidates can then use the returns to correct the mailing list, which will save postage, time, paper, and printing when making subsequent mailings.

Getting Out a Mailing

All third-class mail must be sorted and when there are ten or more individual pieces for an area, they should be bundled and marked by city zip code, rural carrier, or sectional center facility. Bulk-rate or third-class mail can take as long as seven days to arrive at its destination, so it should be mailed up to eight days in advance of delivery date. In most local post offices though, election-eve mail gets immediate delivery.

If there are any questions, the campaign manager should check with the post office. Mistakes are easy to make, as when Richard Nixon was running for Governor of California. His campaign organization used the abbreviation L.A. for Los Angeles, which the post office interpreted as Louisiana. Thousands of letters were sent there by mistake.[19]

Another facet of third-class mail is that it can be used when mailing what politicians call the "computer letter." This letter is electronically personalized, giving the receiver the impression that it was destined for them alone. Often the extra cost of personalization is justified, because even with the recipient's name filled in, it can be mailed at a bulk postal rate. However, unlike first-class, the bulk-mail envelope must be designed to be opened so post office personnel can be sure it complies with regulations. Postal regulations provide that those who use computer letters can disguise the fact that they are not first class by using special envelopes that are partially sealed.

For more direct mailing tips, refer to the following nutshell.

Test Marketing

One device employed by mail advertisers is test marketing, which involves making up several different direct-mail appeals that invite the voter to participate by return mail or postcard. Each test-marketing package should include a returnable reply card for recruiting volunteers or soliciting money. The packages are mailed to different small cross-sections of the market, and then the numbers of responses are compared. From these samples one appeal is chosen for an area-wide mailing. If the candidate's mailing is too small or for some reason a candidate cannot test-market, he or she can rely on someone's generalized direct mail studies.

When measuring typical responses, mail specialist Bob Stone reports that colored inks on an envelope or the corner of a postcard generally solicit more responses than black. A letter printed in colored ink on colored stock is usually more effective than one printed in black ink on white stock. When colored paper is used, blue has proven to be better than yellow or green. Specially designed letterheads tailored to fit the message outperform a standard letterhead. It has been the experience of those in the direct mail business that two-color letterheads are usually more effective than single-color letterheads, and that the appearance of a change of pace in letterhead increases response in a series of mailings.[20]

One note of caution: Don't mail the voter a piece that was left when door-belling or given out to voters on other occasions. A fresh new piece of advertising is always worth the cost.

Be Provocative and Expect a Backfire

Undoubtedly, candidates will want to target a particular segment of the constituency and say something provocative. When this temptation arises, the wise candidate will heed this warning of the National Association of Manufacturers: "Politics is a rough game. Don't say anything in a letter going to more than two people that the candidate would not want exposed in public print the next day."[21] Otherwise, a candidate may be left with no answer for a hostile news media.

★ ★ ★ ★ ★ ★ ★ ★ ★ ★ ★ ★ ★ ★ ★

Planning a Direct Mailing

Note: Like other forms of advertising, the candidate's materials must compete not only with the opponent's but also with others using the mail to persuade. Professional advice is advisable.

	Target Date	Date Compl.
Be sure someone knows postal requirements.		
Consult with the mailing agent/post office on the configuration of the proposed mailing.		
Purchase appropriate mailing permits from post office.		
Obtain precinct/district mailing or other lists. Check availability of computer tapes or label sets.		
Investigate tradeoffs between using the services of a mailing agent or a volunteer crew.		
Print flyer; deliver to mailing agent or volunteers for folding, labeling, and sorting.		
Have mailing delivered to the post office, after filling out appropriate forms.		

Costs and timing

Bulk mail center address_____ Phone _____

Permits: Bulk mail $_____ 1st class $_____ 3rd class $_____

Rates: 1st class $_____ 3rd class $_____ Post cards $_____

Postcard sizes: Mininum_____ Maximum _____

Mail prep. lead time_____ Third class delivery time _____

★ ★ ★ ★ ★ **In A Nutshell** ★ ★ ★ ★ ★

Chapter 37

Billboards

> Beyond the Alps lies Italy, and lest we forget, behind the
> billboards lies America.
> —Anonymous[1]

A Tradition

The billboard has been used to propagandize and to sell since merchants cut messages in stone and placed them along public roads in the days of Egyptian pharaohs. During the American Revolutionary War, an outdoor poster, known as a "broadside," publicized the Boston Massacre. Broadsides were used to help organize the Boston Tea Party and to spread the word about Bunker Hill. As can be seen from the samples from the United States, Great Britain, and Canada shown in Figure 4-43, posters are used the same way today.

Use of the modern commercial poster was started in the latter part of the nineteenth century by P. T. Barnum, who used them to advertise his circus when he traveled throughout the country by train. Before the circus came to a town or city, he carefully prepared the local populace by sending his advance men ahead to placard the area with posters touting the "Coming of the Greatest Show on Earth." These posters told the locals to "Wait for Barnum," which, of course, was the Barnum & Bailey Circus. Over the years they used and reused the same locations, which the circus advance men called billboards.

It wasn't long before politicians were also taking advantage of this means of communication. Just prior to the 1896 nominating convention, Ohio Governor William McKinley promoted his candidacy by traveling in a private railroad car from Maine to Minnesota. The legendary Mark Hanna, who masterminded that campaign, sent advance agents ahead to contact local politicians. With their help, bills or posters were tacked on the sides of buildings and fences, heralding the coming of McKinley, "The Advance Agent of Prosperity."[2]

Of course, all of this was early in this century when posting was left to local ingenuity. Then came World War I and the family automobile. During the late 1920s and the 1930s, outdoor posters evolved into commercial billboards, and they increased in size so that they could be seen from a moving car. Billboards continued to change to service a growing market—the American motorists, who drove a total of 458 billion vehicle miles by 1950. This tripled by 1973.

Fig. 4-43. Great Britain Conservative Party, 1968, p. 20; Canada, New Democratic Party, 1969, p. 128; Great Britain Conservative Party, 1968, p. 116; Gary Yanker, *Prop Art* (New York: Darien House, Inc., 1972): USA, Committee to Help Unsell the War, 1971, p. 177.

The Cost, Compared with Alternative Media

By the late 1970s, 270,000 sign structures provided advertising space on a rental basis in some 9,000 U.S. communities, each owned and maintained by a billboard company on land usually leased by the company. For political purposes, these signs are used to carry out the first rule of advertising—in a vacuum, persuasion and exposure are the same.[3]

Statistics gathered in the 1970s showed that in the United States this visual media, when taken as a whole, "reaches its audience at less than 30 cents a thousand. This is quite inexpensive compared with costs of $1 to $3 per thousand for network television, and as much as $50 per thousand for popular magazines."[4] However, in spite of its efficiency and economy, this media is only able to attract a little over one percent of total advertising expenditures, since most money is spent on newspapers, magazines, radio, and television.

Further evidence shows that billboards have been instrumental in achieving a wide variety of election victories. For example, in May 1976, an unusually heavy turnout of concerned citizens went to the polls of 33 voting precincts in the recently enlarged city of Roanoke, Virginia. Their objective? To choose in a special election an entire slate of municipal officials. The winners were seven independent candidates, including Roanoke's first black mayor and first woman vice-mayor, who all invested well over half their campaign budgets in outdoor advertising.[5]

Billboard Strategy

How do billboards compare with other advertising? The message delivered by a political ad in a newspaper is usually reduced to a headline. Even a television commercial is 95 percent entertainment and 5 percent sales message. The sales message lasts only a few seconds, but usually features the product and slogan.

After an issue is explained by television, radio, or newspaper, the political poster can be used to reinforce the voters' memory of the more complicated original explanation. Of course, the message must be short, simple and direct, such as "No Third Term," "Save Your Church," "Dictators Hate Religion," or "Hitler Was Elected the First Three Terms." All of these barbs were used against President Franklin D. Roosevelt when he sought a third term. Those who supported Roosevelt's third term used slogans such as "Wall Street Wears a Wilkie Button, America Wears a Roosevelt Button," and "Roosevelt's Way is the American Way."

Not only do billboards deliver a message, but they can be used to deliver thrusts and counterthrusts in a campaign. When the bright, articulate Congressman, John F. Kennedy, was challenging U.S. Senator Henry Cabot Lodge, he dotted the state with billboards that said, "Kennedy will do more for

Fig. 4-44. Billboard, Henry M. Jackson for U.S. Senator, 1964; Chris Livesay and John O'Connell billboard mockups, *Campaign Insight*, January 1973; Richard Daley for Mayor, 1971.

Massachusetts." Not to be outdone, his opponent's billboards countered with "Lodge has done—and will do—the most for Massachusetts."[6]

The Mechanics of Exposure

Typically, the effectiveness of outdoor advertising depends on auto traffic patterns. As is true in any commercial advertising medium, research has determined the success of billboard coverage. In general, 10 to 20 percent of the streets and highways carry 80 to 90 percent of vehicular traffic, and billboard companies see to it that outdoor boards are placed along these high-density thoroughfares.

Billboards are sold singly or by what the advertising companies describe as 100-percent showing or 50-percent showing. A showing refers to industry studies of the viewing audience in a 30-day period. A full 100-percent showing of a commercial outdoor billboard reaches at least 89.2 percent of all adults in a market area, and it is seen an average of 31 times per person in that 30-day period.[7]

A 1959 public awareness test conducted in New Jersey provides a dramatic example of billboard effectiveness. Prior to posting the billboard message, the research firm asked 500 adults in four counties to name the 30th President of the United States. Only 4 percent correctly identified Coolidge. After 170 billboards were used to deliver the message "Calvin Coolidge was our 30th President" for 30 days, another sample of 500 different adults was asked the same question. This time 39.8 percent correctly identified Coolidge.[8]

Fig. 4-46. *The First Medium* (New York: Institute of Outdoor Advertising, 1974), p. 17.

Still, seeing a billboard does not guarantee that the message has come across, as a young John F. Kennedy discovered. During his first senatorial campaign he and a friend happily observed a huge billboard blazoning forth "John F. Kennedy for U.S. Senator" over a restaurant. They decided to stop. After gulping down a

Fig. 4-45. Background: "Campaign Posters of Both Parties Plaster U.S. Walls," *Life,* November 4, 1940, p. 36; Foreground (Evans, Tower, Hart): courtesy of Foster & Kleiser, Seattle.

Fig. 4-47. Cooney and Odegaard are unused billboard mockups; the remainder are courtesy Foster & Kleiser, Seattle.

chocolate milk shake, Kennedy paid his check, stuck his hand out and said, "Hello, I'm John Kennedy."

The man behind the cash register looked at him vaguely, "Who?"

"John F. Kennedy, running for United States Senator."

"Oh, John Kennedy, running for what?"

Kennedy walked out, took another look at the sign, and drove on in silence.[9]

Variety, Types, Placement, and Techniques

The standard billboard is 24 to 30 sheets in size. This designation goes back to a time when presses were smaller, and it actually took 24 to 30 sheets to cover a billboard. Today's standard billboards are covered with 10 to 15 paper sheets, which are glued to the board.[10]

Most political billboard sheets are printed locally using the silkscreen process, rather than lithograph. While the silkscreen process can be used to reproduce either drawings, photographs, or pictures, the quality is not as good as that of lithograph, so most silkscreen boards concentrate on name alone.

When a candidate wants to zero in on a target, in some areas large, oversized single billboards can be leased. These measure 141 by 481 feet and are painted by individual artists from designs supplied by the advertisers.[11] The single boards differ from other billboards in that they usually use a rotary plan where an advertiser buys several designs for a year and the billboard company shifts them periodically.

Moving Billboards

A commercial billboard can also be reproduced in a size appropriate for use in a number of different settings, such as on public transit, taxicabs, and trucks. (See Chapter 40 for discussion of signs especially for automobiles.) The effectiveness of public transit advertising is emphasized by David Ogilvy who tells us that "on a New York subway the average rider is exposed for 21 minutes, while only 15 percent of the passengers carry anything to read."[12]

When poster space is located on public property and controlled by political entities, the courts have invoked constitutional provisions to insure free speech. During the Vietnam War, members of the New York members of Students for a Democratic Society went to court to force the New York Public Transit Authority to rent them poster space on the walls and platforms of the subway stations after they had been refused the right to display a poster depicting a child with scarred back and arms bearing the following inscription: "Why are we burning? Torturing? Killing? The Children of Vietnam." The court overruled Transit Authority objections and ordered the public agency to treat the students as they would any other customer to whom they rented space.[13]

Fig. 4-48. Billboard photos courtesy Foster & Kleiser, Seattle.

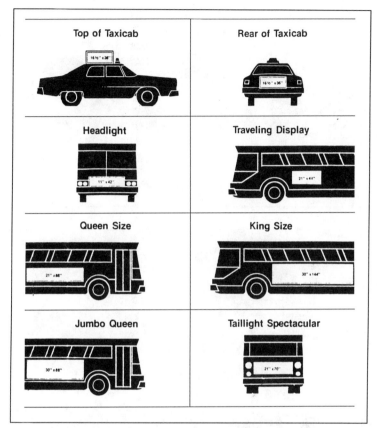

Fig. 4-49. Advertising in Motion Throughout the West (San Francisco: Transit Ads., Inc., 1975), p. 38.

Design

When planning a billboard display, advertiser David Ogilvy recommends using "strong pure colors with never more than three elements to the design."[14] The brand name (which in the candidate's case is his or her name and the sought-for office) should be set in the largest possible type for visibility from a distance. However, advertisers often violate these parameters to attract attention and to surprise. They use teasers and other revolutionary techniques. In 1970, the Sprague for Congress Committee commissioned an innovative advertiser, who designed the eye-catching billboard shown at the top of Figure 4-50. In mid-campaign they substituted an even more revolutionary piece, a poster designed by his nine-year-old son (shown at the bottom of the figure). These posters caused a great deal of comment and even generated television coverage.

Fig. 4-50. Gary Yanker, *Prop Art* (New York: Darien House, 1972), p. 70.

During Spiro Agnew's first campaign for Governor of Maryland, his advertising man, Robert Goodman, noted that Agnew's opponent's campaign had racial overtones. As Goodman put it, the opposition was appealing to the "fears of our people with their campaigns of hate and prejudice." In the dying days of the campaign, Goodman ordered strips (like giant bumper strips) printed with, "Come to the Aid of Maryland" in orange and green (University of Maryland colors). They conveyed an almost subliminal message when they were plastered across Agnew's billboards.[15] Such strips have a dual effect. They convey a message to those close enough to read, and they revitalize interest in signs voters have become used to seeing.

Economics

Unfortunately, the candidate must contract with billboard companies months in advance to get saturation coverage. And once a billboard is ordered, the candidate is stuck for its cost. When Dave Ceccarelli ran for Secretary of (Washington) State, he reserved a statewide show of outdoor billboards. Later the court declared him ineligible to run because he had been a member of the legislature when it increased the Secretary of State's salary. Dave was able to cancel his other advertising, but was still stuck with the cost for the billboards.

Chapter 38

Yard and Roadside Campaign Signs

> If you don't know whose signs these are,
> You can't have driven very far.[1]

Attempting to Control the Political Environment

The principal role of political signs is to place the candidates' names and possibly their pictures before the public. They can also be used to surround and control the political environment so that, when the voter thinks of the office, he or she thinks of one candidate—just like McDonald's means hamburgers, Sanka means decaffeinated coffee, and NBC, ABC, or CBS mean television.[2] Of course, this only happens if the competition permits it. When several competing candidates pursue the same goal, the sign campaign can escalate until it becomes ridiculous.

Outside Seattle is the township of Tukwila. In 1979, when Tukwila was a sleepy little town of about 15,000, pro-development Mayor Frank Todd was able to wrest the office from a man who had beaten him four years before by fewer than 50 votes. Four years before that, he won the mayor's race by 43 votes after having been beaten for mayor in the preceding race by a single vote. During these hard-fought campaigns the candidates and their supporters tramped door to door, soliciting sign locations. Each successive campaign saw more and more yard signs. Indeed, the process reached a climax in the 1975 campaign when almost one-third of the houses had political signs in their yards. And they were not just single signs for a single candidate, but five signs each for a slate of candidates.[3]

The Poor Man's Medium

Political signs, seen again and again, are often equated with the expenditure of big money, but in reality they are the cheapest form of mass communication. For this reason, earlier in the political history of the United States, signs were particularly popular with less affluent candidates.

This can be seen in signs shown in Figure 4-51 of men who made their reputations as crusading liberals. One sign was for Bert Wheeler, who as a young man ran for vice president on the Progressive ticket with fighting Bob LaFollett of Wisconsin. Another was for Congressman Charles A. Lindbergh, father of the pilot who was first to fly across the Atlantic. The senior Lindbergh started as a radical Republican and eventually became one of the founders and leaders of the

Non-Partisan League, which evolved into the Minnesota Farm Labor Party.[4] The third sign was for future Vice President Hubert Humphrey.

Fig. 4-51. B. K. Wheeler for U.S. Senator Committee, 1946; Charles A. Lindbergh for Congress, Minnesota Historical Society; Gary Yanker, *Prop Art* (New York: Darien House, Inc., 1972), p. 91.

Making the Sign Distinctive

When selecting colors, candidates should avoid pastels and go for bright, loud solids. It helps if signs are immediately distinguishable from that of the competition. In some jurisdictions, such as Canada, color is predetermined on both the national and provincial levels. The voter chooses a single provincial or parliamentary representative who runs in ridings or districts. Each party adopts a color scheme so the motorist can recognize the candidates and their party instantly in a given province. The Conservatives might use red, white, and blue, the

Liberals green and blue on white, and the new Democratic party possibly black and white on orange.

Wise candidates also attempt to distinguish their signs by selecting an unusual typeface or script, or by using an unusual shape, as shown in Figure 4-52.

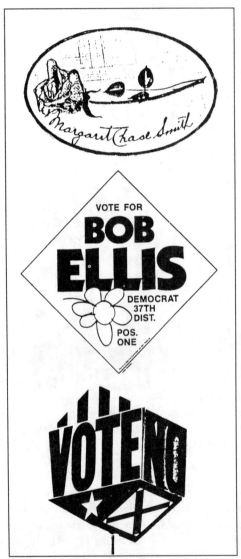

Unfortunately, shape is usually controlled by the material from which the signs are made and it can be very expensive to depart from standard sizes. However, a square sign, say a 4- by 4-foot sheet, can be stood on end to form a diamond with a candidate's name running across the center. Alternatively, painted designs permit candidates to distinguish their signs by use of a circle, a scroll, or some other imaginative design.

After the signs have been up for several weeks, some candidates add a strip message to convey an extra punch (as shown in Figure 4-53). For example, if a candidate receives a prestigious endorsement from organized labor or a citizens' committee, he or she can have a special piece printed or silkscreened and placed across the signs to publicize this. Another effective use of this technique comes after a hard-fought primary, when the successful nominee adds a simple "Thank you" to his or her signs.

For the candidate who already has name familiarity, another method of distinguishing a sign is available: Using fewer, larger words, as shown in Figure 4-54.

Among the imaginative ways to use a political sign is the technique used in the 1930s by successful Depression-era Republican State

Fig. 4-52. Examples of unusually shaped yard signs or buttons.

Fig. 4-53. Examples of yard signs with last-minute add-ons:
Return Claude Pepper, U.S. Senator, Florida, 1950; Retain Hugh
J. Rosellini, Superior Court Judge, Pierce County, Wash., 1956;
Elect Ferguson for Legislature, Dade County, Florida, 1950; Elect
Nicholas for State Representative, Dade County, 1950.

Representative Charley Moran. During the years when everyone was broke, he
survived the Democratic tide by billing himself as the "poor man's champion." He
hired a man to go to the city dump and pick up old cardboard boxes, cut them into
appropriate sign sizes, and then stencil on Moran's name and the office for which
he was running, to emphasize his poverty. According to Moran, his homemade
signs cost more than printed ones, but he contended they were worth it because
they helped him empathize with the common man.

Fig. 4-54. Examples of signs from candidates who were well-known prior to their campaigns (for example, "Jeb" is President Bush's son). Note the minimal amount of information included and also that the signs are designed to be folded.

The Clutter Issue

Signs are unpopular among some citizens, who view them as clutter. These citizens periodically join newspapers and radio and television stations to condemn the use of signs, but still, plastering signs over the landscape does not seem to hurt the candidate, as the following illustration suggests.

In 1970, two evenly matched incumbents were thrown together by redistricting. One was State Senator Fred Dore, who eventually became Chief Justice of the Washington State Supreme Court. The other was State Senator Richard Marquardt, who later became Washington State Insurance Commissioner. As the campaign started, Marquardt drew favorable statewide press by pledging not to use political signs. He got raves from some environmentalists when he sent out a letter to all those running in that election urging them to follow suit. A skeptical Dore went ahead posting his political yard signs. The outcome gave local politicians reason to ponder. Not only did Dore win the election, but every candidate who followed Marquardt's advice lost.

Still candidates need to be sensitive to those who resent political signs by at least pledging to take down all political signs after the election. State Representative Gene Lux of Washington gained favorable publicity by recruiting friends and a truck and conducting his version of a sign cleanup drive the day after the election. When Lux or his crew saw a sign in a yard, one of them went to the door and asked permission to pick it up. They retrieved not only Lux signs but, with the householder's permission, a number of others. They kept their own and returned signs to other candidates who wanted them. Materials from the unwanted signs were reused or recycled.

Aspirants Can Make Their Own

In May and June of 1968, one million French partisans staged a general strike. Sympathetic students seized the University of Paris buildings. Approximately thirty of them occupied six rooms, where they used the silkscreen process and a very small materials budget to turn out 120,000 handmade posters designed to rally support for their cause.

The same thing can be done by any campaign crew that chooses to make their own silkscreen signs. In almost every campaign there is someone who enjoys doing this type of work. Considerable detail is included here (and in Figures 4-55 and 4-56) because the information is not readily available.

Before beginning, it is important to understand that both sides of the sign are made at one time, creased at the top for ease of folding (see examples in Figure 4-54). Also, the process described here is for silk-screening on cardboard, the least expensive method. (Modern sign shops usually silk screen on plastic.)

I advise hiring or recruiting a professional or a talented amateur to make the screens. The process starts by stretching the cloth screen, usually silk, over a wood frame. This frame is attached to a table by a hinge that permits it to be raised or lowered. Then the sign painter uses special opaque paint or a commercial film with a paper back to cover the screen. When an opaque film is used, a design is cut and then adhered to the screen. After that, the paper backing is peeled.

There are various techniques, but all use opaque materials to block out the portions of the silk that are to be blank on the finished sign. Printing is then accomplished by pulling a rubber squeegee over the

Fig. 4-55. J. I. Biegeleisen and Max Arthur Cohn, *Silk Screen Techniques* (New York: Dover Publications, 1942), p. 164. Used by permission.

sign, forcing a special paint or ink through the areas of silk onto whatever is below that is not blocked out. This leaves an image on the paper, plastic, wood, or cloth placed below. The frame is then raised and the sign is removed and replaced with another blank piece of paper, plastic, or wood. If a multicolor sign is to be produced, the crew applies the lightest color first so that, when a subsequent darker color is applied, it can be superimposed on the original background color.

As the printed signs are removed, they must be dried. Usually this is done by laying them out around the room or yard, stacking them in a specially prepared rack, or, in the case of cardboard, using spring-type clothespins to hold them on a steel clothesline. When drying conditions are good, this takes about three hours. If a second color is needed, another screen is prepared; and the same process is repeated to apply the second color. Once the set-up is prepared and in place, even an untrained crew can silkscreen several hundred single or multicolor signs within a few hours.

When completely dry, the signs are waxed to make them waterproof.

Whether candidates buy or make their own signs, they should remember to never use cheap materials. It takes more effort and money to post a sign than to make it. Flimsy paper tears, and the sign falls. Cheap colors run or fade. A poor grade of cardboard will split or separate when it rains.

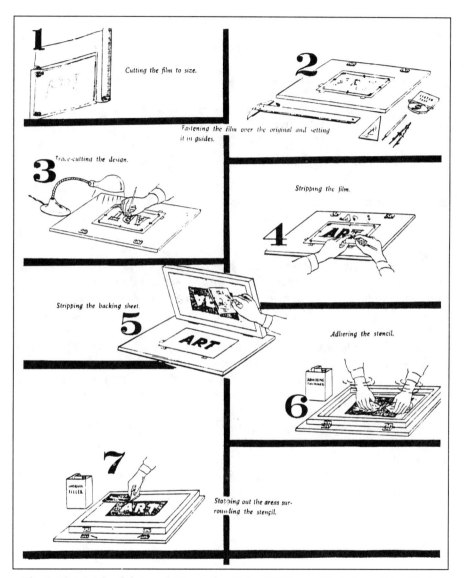

1. Cutting the film to size.
2. Fastening the film over the original and setting it in guides.
3. Trace-cutting the design.
4. Stripping the film.
5. Stripping the backing sheet.
6. Adhering the stencil.
7. Stopping out the areas surrounding the stencil.

Fig. 4-56. J. I. Biegeleisen and Max Arthur Cohn, *Silk Screen Techniques* (New York: Dover Publications, 1942, pp. 92-96. Used by permission.

Chapter 39

Posting Signs

> Slow down, Pa, sakes alive
> Ma missed signs four and five
> —Burma Shave[1]

Equipment and Materials and the Question of Durability

Yard and roadside signs are usually assembled in advance and transported by car, trailer, or truck to the place where they are posted. Making and mounting the original signs requires space, but usually the use of a basement, garage, barn, or warehouse can be borrowed, along with a hammer, nails, knife, and saw. A commercial stapler is helpful (this can be rented or purchased).

An 11- by 14-inch posterboard (cardboard) sign requires a one- or two-inch piece of staking lumber, which is presharpened or pointed and cut in three- or four-foot lengths. Large-head nails or a heavy-duty, hammer-type stapler are used to fasten the poster or cardboard to a wood crossbar at both the top and bottom. The sign-maker nails the wood cross-arms to the presharpened stake.

Changes in weather conditions should be kept in mind when assembling yard signs. In the summer months before primary elections the preparation in most climates is different from that in the fall when the materials must withstand wind and rain. The easiest way to protect a posterboard sign from the rain is to have it waxed before it is fastened to a wood frame. To do this send the signs to a large commercial sign shop or to a paper box factory where they can be dipped in wax. As an alternate, when rain is contemplated, an extra piece of lath can be fastened across the top so that the cardboard sign is held firmly between it and the top cross-bar. This prevents a rain-soaked sign from pulling through the top tacks or staples and falling before it has a chance to dry out.

The candidate can use manufactured sign board made of wood, paperboard, plywood, or plastic for large signs. To cut costs, the candidate might try shop-grade masonite. However, both masonite and plywood are porous so should be sealed with a protective coat of paint on both sides before screening.

Peaking and Other Strategies

A candidate should adopt a sign-posting strategy. Traditionally, challengers start erecting signs early because they need voter recognition to overcome the incumbent's built-in name familiarity. In some cases, the strategy is simply to order signs and get them posted. If the candidate runs out of signs, more are ordered. Another strategy is to post half of all campaign signs the first two or three weeks, reserving the rest to replace destroyed signs and to place in new locations.

Some candidates use sign posting as part of their peaking strategy. For example, they might create a massive psychological impression by holding a huge supply of their signs for simultaneous posting at a strategic time. Before Oregon's Robert Packwood became a United States Senator, he was chairman of the Oregon Republican Party. In that position he used this sign strategy as part of his effort to wrest control of the legislature from the Democrats. Early in that campaign, his party had signs printed for Republican candidates, but did not post them right away. Instead, Packwood had the signs assembled and stored in warehouse bins. After Labor Day the party released the signs to their legislative candidates; it seemed as though they covered their legislative district overnight.[2]

As effective as this delayed sign strategy may sound, it won't work unless the locations are committed in advance. This is difficult, because most residents are reluctant to place a sign in their yards and then only give permission to the first to ask. Then the candidate must persuade the tenant or owner to protect a good sign location not only the from opponent, but from solicitors for other offices who will try to get it.

As soon as permission is given, candidates pursuing the delayed strategy should send confirming letters, which are individually typed, then signed by the candidate or person to whom permission was given. The letters should stress that posting will be delayed and that the candidate expects the resident to protect the location.

Some candidates find it profitable, vote-wise, to use signs as part of a last-minute push. They stockpile a supply of signs and conduct a last-minute blitz or use new signs to flood their strongholds on election day with a number of "Vote Today, Courtesy of Sally Candidate" signs. Since signs posted the night or day before the election will soon be obsolete, they are often put on public parking strips and intersections, even though the signs will be taken down by state, county, or city road crews.

Posting Techniques

The novice thinks of telephone poles and highway right-of-ways when posting, which violates the law. Most jurisdictions have fines for those caught tacking signs on poles or posting in public areas or on private property without permission. So candidates in suburban areas must concentrate on getting permission to post in private yards or buildings, especially at intersections or in an urban area along a city bus route where traffic stops or at least travels more slowly. Most candidates secure permission to post signs through friends, neighbors, the political party, club members, etc. But an effective technique is door-to-door solicitation of the areas where the campaign signs are needed.

Other campaigners make phone calls using a reverse telephone directory that lists subscribers by street address. If the local telephone company doesn't publish a reverse directory, the phone numbers must be looked up, but once names are secured, candidates can systematically call and ask permission to post signs at addresses on heavily traveled streets.

Another popular technique is to send announcement letters with self-addressed postcards asking friends and other politically active people for help in the campaign. One form of help is permission for a sign to be placed in their yard. Following his successful primary election, State Senator John Cooney used a slight variation of this technique. He sent a letter to all voters of his district, thanking them for their support. In lieu of a campaign contribution, he asked them to call him with a sign location. The mailing produced 1,400 responses. Of course, this was far more than he needed or expected, but since he had solicited the locations, more signs were made to be sure that he took up every offer—even those on dead-end streets.

When pounding the vertical stake for a sign into hard dirt or grass surfaces, it is wise to have a steel bar and small sledge hammer so that a hole can be made in the ground before driving the stake. Also, the crew should follow the example of professional billboard companies and post the signs at right angles to oncoming traffic. I discovered the importance of this when I first ran against an incumbent with many years of political experience. Both of us started with small signs, which were replaced by larger signs as the campaign escalated. During the final weeks of the campaign, I noticed that the large signs that my crew had posted at right angles to the highway were being turned so that they were parallel to the road. After that, we inspected the signs regularly and turned them back so they could be viewed at right angles.

A sign can be doubled to serve two-way traffic. Sometimes a sign is tacked to both sides of a stake and cross-arm. On other occasions two signs can be placed in a three-cornered "V" design so that the motorist can see them from either direction.

Occasionally candidates turn political posters into yard signs by using staples to tack two posters together, back to back, then sliding the posters over the stake and stapling them to the stake. This doesn't make a very durable yard sign, but works for a short time when the election is near.

Inner City Signs

The sign crew will find when posting signs in the inner city that there are few yards and no vacant lots. Occasionally, signs are stapled to wooden window frames or wired to fire escapes. And although I don't recommend it, signs can be

Fig. 4-57. Campaign signs: Fluent for Governor, State of Washington, 1948; Langlie for Governor, State of Washington, 1984; Georgette Valle for State Representative, State of Washington, 1984. Re-Elect E. J. Stiglich, Dan Richie for Mayor taken from Political Americana Campaign Catalog (Political Americana, Asheville, N.C., 1969), p. 3.

printed on heavy paper and glued on masonry or concrete walls or tacked into mortar between bricks. So the best alternative is window space. Here we see an exception to the rule that limits pictures to billboards, large plywood signs, and window cards. The candidate's picture can be viewed by pedestrians in the city shop windows or on walls in the big city where people walk or use public transportation.

Fig. 4-58. Campaign signs: Re-elect Senator Allan Bible Nevada, 1954; John Spellman for Governor, State of Washington, 1984; Mondale/Ferraro for President/Vice President, 1984; Vera Ing for Washington State Representative, 1984; Rosellini for Governor.

Fig. 4-59. Gary Yanker, *Prop Art* (New York: Darien House, Inc., 1972), p. 83.

When a candidate or his/her sign manager begin posting signs in a city, they should identify tenants and/or owners of vacant commercial buildings, then contact the tenant, owner, or real estate firm handling window space rental and ask if its use can be donated until after the election. Any agreement should include the provision that, if a vacant building should be rented prior to the election, the signs will be taken down. In any case, it is always wise to promise that signs will be taken down after the election.

Rural Areas

In less-populated areas, the sign crew tries to find fences, vacant lots, and undeveloped wooded areas where posting signs is permitted—or, more accurately, tolerated. On rural roads where the sign crew can post at will, it is popular to post on all four corners of rural road intersects.

State Senator John Cooney found that when he posted on all four corners of an intersection, the opposition systematically destroyed his display. To remedy this problem he had his sign crews go to the intersection, then go back, say, a quarter of a mile in each direction from the place where the roads intersect, to do the posting. When Cooney did this, he found the opposition left destruction pretty much to chance because, as he explained, they couldn't fathom his posting strategy.

Where a candidate has small signs or large signs with a picture or where the name is in print so small it is hard to read from a moving car, sign-posting pros use a repetitive technique in which several signs are lined up to impress those riding in the automobile much as a moving picture would. Although this repetitive technique is usually rejected because it requires too much energy to (a) find enough locations and (b) keep the opposition and kids from destroying the display, the added attention is often worth the extra effort.

Local Laws Regarding Sign Posting

When posting campaign signs, the candidate may find that many jurisdictions limit how large a sign can be. Many do not permit signs on 4 x 8 or even 4 x 4 sheets of plywood, and some restrict the number of days that a sign can be posted before a primary or general election, although most permit a successful primary candidate to leave his or her signs up through the general election. A few jurisdictions insist that a sign be taken down within ten days following the election.

Some local ordinances provide that no political sign can be posted on private property without written permission, and the sign has to be taken down within 72 hours if written permission is withdrawn. Every jurisdiction has restrictions that apply to signs on public property, and typically they provide that a political sign must be placed 20 feet off the right-of-way.

Some sign ordinances restrict the use of flashing signs and placing signs on automobiles, and most jurisdictions will not permit candidates to use telephone poles. As a practical matter, except for posting on telephone polls and public property, most sign ordinances are ignored. Often they are only enforced when local authorities want to give the side they favor an advantage or when the opposition candidate insists on enforcement.

Repair and Replacement

There is nothing that causes more hard feeling at campaign headquarters than an opponent who systematically tears down a candidate's political signs. No doubt the opposition could have night wrecking crews equipped with special poles with hooks for knocking down signs. But the whole situation should be calmly and realistically assessed before the candidate or his supporters lose their tempers and react. When sign destruction occurs, the opposition may not be at fault. Frequently, the person in whose yard the sign was located has changed his mind

Fig. 4-60. Effective use of multiple signs; Mark Skolsky, illustrator, "The Candidates and the State of the Presidency," *Fortune,* December 3, 1979.

and quietly gotten rid of it. There may also be wholesale destruction of signs by bands of youngsters at Halloween.

Even when candidates believe the opposition is guilty of destruction, they may have a problem proving who is responsible. Instead of retaliating and running the risk of being caught tearing down opposition signs, the best alternative is to grin and bear it and to replace damaged or destroyed signs within a short time.

The campaign booklet published by the National Association of Manufacturers advises the candidate to establish a sign repair operation to be used throughout the campaign. For this, the candidate will need a fresh supply of new signs, hammers, nails, scrap wood, staple guns, wire, and masking tape.

If candidates are faced with wholesale sign destruction, in most cases, alerting the police is all they have to do to scare off the opposition, so the candidate might ask property owners to notify the authorities. This is especially effective if the police visit opposition campaign headquarters and ask if they have any information that will help catch, publicize, and prosecute these midnight marauders.

During one campaign the culprits were observed going boldly into private yards, uprooting hundreds of signs, throwing them into a red pickup, and driving off. Though several householders told the victim candidate, none were willing or able to make a positive identification. The enraged victim waited until nearly all his signs were destroyed then sent a mailing to every voter noting that his opponent's signs were very much in evidence, while during the same period all of his signs, most of which were on private property, had disappeared. He said that he intended to replace his signs and asked the voters to take note and fix the blame if they disappeared again. His signs remained miraculously untouched during the rest of the campaign.

The best way, though, to get the attention of the public media and stop destruction is to catch an opposition worker in the act or have some other documented evidence. Then a formal complaint can be made to a local fair campaign practices committee. If the candidate is only able to state that his signs are being systematically torn down while his opponent's remain standing, such charges are bound to spark vehement denials and countercharges.

Signs

Note: Most signs are silk-screened on wood, heavy paper, or plastic.

Legal
Check with city and county for sign
 ordinances, usually in public works
 departments.
Pay any required fees or deposits.

Creation
Select color theme.
Try to get a legible but distinctive design.
Compare production costs for various
 kinds of materials.
Compare costs, volunteer vs. professional
 production.
Decide how many are needed.

Where, How to Distribute
Personal request by phone or letter.
Ask building and business owners to
 display them as posters

Solicit homeowners for lawn display.
Instruct volunteers regarding posting
 rules (e.g., don't post on utility poles
 unless legal).
Recruit volunteers to post most of them.
Personally distribute a few to businesses
 or homeowners.

Strategy
Try to get them posted 30-45 days before
 election.
Replace damaged signs as needed.
Have a rerun of signs during last 10 days
 to pick up campaign pace.

Post election
Have volunteers promptly remove signs.
Get deposit refunded from city/county
 agency.

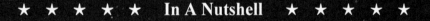

Chapter 40

Automobile Signage

> Politicians' names, like their faces, are often seen in public places.
> —Anonymous

Bumper Stickers

The most common way candidates use space on automobiles to advertise is the bumper sticker. Its function has changed with the times. When things went bad under Eisenhower's administration, the Democrats used a strip that said, "Don't blame me, I voted Democratic." During Nixon's campaign for governor of California, one strip carried an unflattering picture of the vice president with the words, "Would you buy a used car from this man?" During Goldwater's campaign for president, it was alleged that he advocated the use of atomic weapons in Vietnam. Opposition bumper stickers said, "Help Goldwater stamp out peace," and there were others that paraphrased his campaign slogan, "In your heart you know he's right," saying, "In your gut, you know he's a nut."[1]

However, the question is: Do negative or derogatory bumper stickers get votes? Assessing the advantages and liabilities, I believe the disadvantages far outweigh the benefits. To begin with, bumper stickers are hard to distribute; even sympathetic car owners refuse or are reluctant to put one on their car. Sarcasm always makes other voters feel sorry for the opponent, inspiring retaliation. In a nutshell, bumper stickers got partisan laughs in the past, but today sarcastic humor is not worth the backlash.

Getting the Strip on the Cars

The best way to get strips on cars is to ask the owners. Most candidates have success soliciting drivers as they park to go to work, the doctor's office, or the grocery store. Old-fashioned door-to-door soliciting works too.

Exploring other alternatives, the candidate can start solicitating during summer months when the drivers attend ethnic, community, church, union, and/or political club picnics. However, most of those who politely take the strip will conveniently forget to put it on the bumper, so if a car owner says yes, the candidate or one of the workers should immediately put the bumper strip on the car.

When Governor Barry Goldwater of Arizona challenged United States Senator Ernest McFarland, Goldwater's campaign manager, Stephen Shadegg, ordered 250,000 white bumper stickers printed with blue letters saying "I'm for Barry." Then his campaign organization mailed a letter to every registered Republican voter in the state. After thanking them for everything they had done in the primary, the letter asked, "Would you please put one of these stickers on your car and ask a friend to use the second sticker?"

Fig. 4-61. Bumperstickers: Re-Elect Senator Sarbanes, Maryland, 1982; Les Miller, Congress, Arizona, 1980; Ray Van Hollebeke, State Senator, Washington, 1968; Harley Hoppe, King County Assessor, Washington, 1983; John Ahearn, Insurance Commissioner, Arizona, 1980; Richard Daley for Mayor, Chicago, 1974; Dore, Mayor, Seattle, 1969; Hughes/Curran, Governor and Lieutenant Governor, Maryland, 1982; Re-Elect Satriale, New York Assembly, 1970; John O'Connell, Governor, Washington, 1972; Republican You Bet, Vermont, 1966.

Shadegg said, "The campaign was so hot that ten days after we distributed the stickers, these 'I'm for Barry' stickers on cars created a rising tide that lasted through election day." And he continued, "I had a count made . . . when the reports of the day were totaled, we found 43 percent had Goldwater stickers and that 28 percent of the cars had McFarland (opponent) stickers, 29 percent of the cars didn't have any sticker at all. . . ."[2]

One candidate for Congress thought he had a great idea. He had his campaign crew place bumper stickers on all the cars while their owners were at his party's political meetings. At first, the strategy seemed to work because a fair percentage of the car owners left them in place. That was until his primary opponent tipped off the press, then mounted the platform and made an issue of the fact that the bumper stickers had been placed on cars without permission. That evening the situation got even worse when a humiliated candidate and his campaign crew were filmed by the local television news removing the strips.

Cartop Signs

This type of sign has proven effective for years. In their candidate's pamphlet, the National Association of Manufacturers points out that an automobile with a cartop sign can be parked in locations from which all other signs are barred and can be seen by hundreds of people in areas where large groups gather.

The problem with cartop signs is that they are dangerous unless securely fastened, and the structure must be able to withstand both wind and weather. The National Association of Manufacturers suggests that the candidate look for help from someone with the skill to make cartop signs and approach a friendly lumber dealer for donations of wood. As an alternative, there are several firms that manufacture reusable cartop units that can be purchased. These may be made of steel, plastic, or tempered hardboard.

The National Association of Manufacturers further suggests asking a used-car dealer to let the candidate use a few old second-hand cars as traveling sign boards during the campaign, asking loyal supporters from two-car families for the use of their second car as a moving billboard on certain days.[3]

One successful thing I did in a political campaign was purchase the cheapest second-hand car I could find that was both licensed and in operating condition. Then, without further preparation, I had it spray-painted gold. Although it was an old Ford, we painted on its side the words, "The Solid Gold Cadillac," the title of a stage play and movie popular at the time. Then we attached a two-way, 4- by 8-foot, hand-painted political sign to its bumper. As we moved the "Solid Gold Cadillac" to various locations, the relic gained considerable attention and even some press comments. I used the stunt once more, only we used purple paint and called it the "Purple People Eater" after a popular song. This gimmick wasn't expensive, and I even recovered part of the cost when I resold the cars to an auto wrecking firm.

There is no limit to ingenuity when it comes to putting campaign signs on cars, trucks, vans, and in some instances campers and mobile homes. Anything capable of carrying a sign will do the trick. When George Wallace first ran for governor of Alabama, he purchased 150 war-surplus airplane wing tanks. Then he had them lettered with, "Win With Wallace," and decorated with the Confederate flag. They made fine signs when they were mounted on his and supporters' cars.[4]

Fig. 4-62. Election Ideas Co., Ottowa, IL, 1978, p. 7; *Test-Proven Vote Aids* (New York: J. Friedes Co., 1980); *Campaign Be-Sure-to-Vote Materials* (Waseca, IL: Roberts, 1964), p. 40.

Chapter 41

The Idea File

Master political strategist Ed Schwartzman, separating creative advertising from the other elements of the campaign, said, "It is responsible for almost five percent of the votes in most campaigns."[1]

Creativity is the life blood of effective advertising, and most creative advertising evolves from someone else's early idea. Keeping this in mind, it is helpful if candidates or their media advisors keep an idea file. In time, such a file will include campaign folders, political ads, campaign announcements, campaign slogans, notes describing TV or radio commercials and publicity stunts, and anything else that might capture voter attention. It is not important whether the original user of the materials won or lost; the ideas are still valid.

Fig. 4-63. Committee for Brian Lewis for Congress, *Argus,* July 31, 1980, p. 5.

Fig. 4-64. Pass, Brian Lewis, Congress, 1970; Voter Identification Card, State Senator Bob Greive, 1950; Bob Strong, "Graphics That Grab You," *Campaign Insight,* September 15, 1974 and August 1, 1974; Stimson Bullitt for Congress, 1974.

Contradictory statements were the centerpiece of an attack upon the integrity of 1968 Republican nominee for President Richard Nixon. The Democrats dramatized their attack with a television commercial featuring a weathervane in the shape of a Pinocchio-nosed Nixon facing west, north, east, then south. In the background a voice says, "Did you ever notice what happens to Richard Nixon when those political winds start to blow." The voice-over continues as the weathervane turns: "Take the nuclear test ban treaty. First he was against it; then somehow he was for it. Education—Sure he favored quality education for every child, but he voted against nearly every education bill he could. The open housing law—he was for it, but when those hot southern winds started up, he turned against it. Which way will he blow next? If you'd rather not find out, vote for Hubert Humphrey on November 9th."[2]

Four years later the Republicans used the same weathervane television commercial, although the issues and the message were different. This time the commercial criticized the Democratic nominee for President, United States Senator George McGovern.

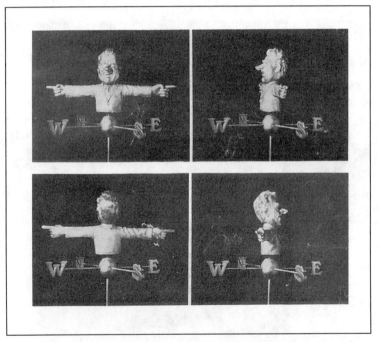

Fig. 4-65. Don Grant, "Did '68 Anti-Nixon Spot Inspire Anti-McGovern Ad?" *Advertising Age,* October 9, 1972.

When candidates need an idea, they can choose from many techniques. In 1969 advertising consultant George Lois packaged incumbent Democratic Mayor Lee Alexander of Syracuse, New York, with showmanship and style. When Alexander filed for re-election in 1973, the traditionally strong Republicans launched an all-out effort to recapture the position. As the campaign began, Alexander tried the standard themes, claiming he had modernized the fire department, built new schools, and promoted low-cost housing and parks. However, public-opinion polls showed that none of these accomplishments were making the voters forget their Republican traditions.

George Lois began looking for a new appeal. He noted that Alexander had been elected by his peers as Chairman of the National Conference of Mayors. After some thought, Lois decided to use this honor, dubbing Alexander "one of the six best Mayors in the United States." To make the claim creditable, the television commercial featured not only Alexander, but said something about the other five: Mayor Alioto of San Francisco, who increased services, but lowered taxes; Mayor White of Boston, who brought city government back to the people; Mayor Massell of Atlanta, who skillfully guided the fastest growing city in the south; Mayor Maier of Milwaukee, whose sensible curfew defused a riot situation; and Mayor Landrieu of New Orleans, whom the commercial claimed preserved the French Quarter.

This clever theme put Alexander's opponent and any unfriendly press in a difficult position. When they argued that Alexander didn't deserve to be rated as one of the six best mayors in the nation, the voter was left to believe that even if he were not one of the six best, he was good. How good was merely a matter of personal perception. The theme convinced 60 percent of the voters that Alexander was worthy of reelection.[3]

Using Music

If the candidate is using radio and, to a lesser extent, television, he or she can creatively attract the public with music. Music was a part of campaigning long before the days of radio or television. In 1909, for example, young Edward Crump beat the entrenched political machine that ruled Memphis, Tennessee, by a 79-vote margin and went on to build a political machine of his own that ruled the city and Shelby County for four decades.

In Crump's original campaign the anti-reform forces attempted to ridicule him.

Fig. 4-66. George Lois and Bill Pitts, *The Art of Advertising* (New York: Harry N. Abrams, 1977), p. 103.

A composer who was a jazz musician and played in a local brothel set these words
to music:

Mr. Crump won't 'low no easy riders here,
Mr. Crump won't 'low no easy riders here,
I don't care what Mr. Crump won't 'low,
I'm gonna barrel house anyhow,
Mr. Crump can go and catch himself some air."

Rather than being offended by the song, Crump adopted it as his theme, even
employing its composer, William C. Handy, and his band to play it on street
corners where the crowds who heard it whistled and cheered. Later the "E. H.
Crump Blues" was renamed "Memphis Blues."[4]

Stephen Shadegg described a candidate for sheriff in rural Arizona where
posting space was no problem. This candidate split up his message and spaced it
one sentence at a time, about 150 feet apart. They read like this:

Ain't no cowhand. . . .
nor politician. . . .
But when crooks pop up. . . .
he's in there pitchin'.
Roach for Sheriff!

A second jingle read:

Fourteen years a deputy. . . .
trained by the F.B.I. . . .
His record shows to you and me. . . .
for Sheriff he's the guy. . . .
Roach for Sheriff!"5

A Sample Ballot

Campaign strategist Edward Schwartzman insists that "the only [advertising]
piece that is mandatory two days before the election is the sample ballot." He
suggests it should not harangue the voter, but should make a special reference to
where the candidate's name appears on the ballot.[6]

A sample ballot is especially appreciated when the candidates are numerous.
This was the case in one New York election, where the ballot was so complex that
people took ten minutes to vote even though the legal maximum was three.

Using Dramatic Events

The political advertiser can also use dramatic events and/or news stories to
create advertising. Here's a commercial that illustrates this advertising technique:
There is a sound of three gunshots—outdoor crowd noises—siren of an
ambulance as it pulls away, then a the radio voice: "On November 6, 1963, a
Boston policeman was shot to death in the line of duty. He left a wife and four

Fig. 4-67. Sample ballot, Don Talley for Washington State
Senator, 1976.

children. At the time of his death, his Boston police take-home pay, after
deductions, was $76.22 per week. Help the police! Vote 'yes' on question eight!"
(Political announcement disclaimer).[7]

Using Humorous Issues

All political themes need not be volatile. Occasionally candidates can use a
change of pace or even comedy to attract attention, but they must recognize the
potential danger of appearing ridiculous.

Despite pitfalls, once in a while a candidate wins by focusing on less abrasive and even humorous matters. In Marg Fong's campaign for California Secretary of State, she ignored other issues and concentrated on one over which the office she sought had no control, but was dear to the hearts of all: pay toilets. She decided that pay toilets were the scourge of California, and anyone who could never find a dime at the right time (which is almost everyone) agreed with her. Although Ms. Fong had her serious side as well, she claimed that the public identified her as a "one-tissue candidate." She had found a subject that was a sore point with everyone.[8]

Placing Ads on Sports Schedules and Bags

In a sports-conscious area, a candidate might use a sports schedule to advertise on, so anyone who uses the schedule cannot help but associate it with the sender.

Paper or plastic shopping bags bearing candidates' names are effective, since shopping bags go places where other advertising is not acceptable. Shopping bags have a subliminal effect because, as in the case of the yard sign, others assume that those with a shopping bag personally endorse the candidate. Additional "points" can be scored with voters by choosing bags made of recyclable materials.

Several of the bags depicted in Figure 4-66 originated in New York State, where shopping bags had become an obsession in the 1972 Democratic primaries. 150,000 Bronx primary voters received 2.5 million shopping bags given out by candidates. One Bronx voter told the press he had so far collected 1,200 political shopping bags, and that when he had 5,000 he intended to have his name put on them and run for office himself.[9]

Any medium is open to experimentation—campaign buttons, combs, balloons, hats, wooden nickels, pens, pencils, matches, etc.—but when evaluating ideas remember that times and public tastes change. Eva Roman of Campaign Communications Institute of America, New York City, reported that the popularity of certain gimmicks was changing. For instance, potholder sales were down because they represented a symbol of domesticity insulting to some women, lollipop sales were off because they caused cavities, and matchbooks weren't moving because of the smoking-cancer relationship.[10]

Fig. 4-68. "Test-Proven Vote Aids," J. Friedes Company, Ad-Caser Line, Political Arena, 1980.

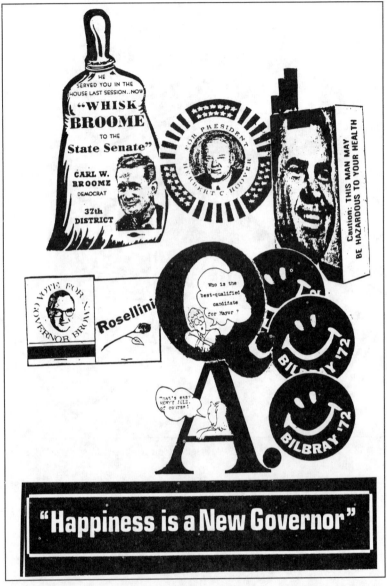

Fig. 4-69. Campaign gimmicks: Carl Broome for State Senate, Washington, 1946; Hoover for President, 1928; anti-Nixon ad, Trahey/ Wolf Advertising Co.; Pat Brown for Governor, California, 1964; Albert G. Rosellini for Governor, Washington; Jols for Mayor Q & A from Arnold Fochs, *Advertising That Won Elections* (Duluth, MN: A. J. Publishing, 1974), p. 30; Jim Bilbray for Congress, *Advertising Age*, June 1972.

Part 5

Anatomy of a Smear

Chapter 42

Fairness: Motivation and the Political Predator

> If you can't answer the opponent's arguments, all is not
> lost. You can still call him vile names.
> —Albert Hubbard[1]

Legitimate Ways to Justify Attacking Another Candidate

One legitimate way to justify attacking another candidate is to expose a corrupt administration, such as the government of Kansas City, Missouri, when Tom Pendergast held power in 1940. Columnist Westbrook Pegler, describing conditions of that era, said that saloon keepers had to buy their liquor from Boss Tom Pendergast's firms, contractors had to deal with Pendergast cement companies, and cops on the beat had to give 10 percent of their salaries to the Pendergast machine. As evidence of payoffs, Pegler cited a well-known restaurant that featured waitresses stripped to their high heeled shoes.[2]

Occasionally there is an issue that deeply divides the voting public. Those who disagree with the opposing candidate's position can legitimately use attacks to illustrate their contrasting view. This happened in the 1984 presidential campaign when the Democratic nominee for vice president, Geraldine Ferraro, privately opposed abortion while publicly supporting free choice for those who wanted to abort an unborn child. A religious fundamentalist group, Christian Voice, bought $250,000 worth of television time to air three ads featuring the 1980 Miss America, Cheryl Prewitt Blackwood, playing "God Bless America" softly on the piano. "I love America," she said in one ad. "That's why as a Christian woman I can't support Geraldine Ferraro. . . . Ms. Ferraro says she would not kill her own unborn child through abortion. Yet the pro-abortion forces give her a perfect voting record for supporting their position on 16 separate abortion votes."[3]

A Matter of Strategy

Unlike the above examples, most opposition candidates' attacks are not designed to expose corrupt conditions nor are there many disagreements on fundamental issues. Most candidates attack their opponents because they are behind by a sizable margin or because "the attack strategy is necessary to undermine the status afforded by incumbency, which consistently produces favorable attitudes among voters regardless of the incumbent's actual performance,"[4] or often attacks are used to get media coverage, since the media like to publicize campaigns in combat terms.

Most successful attacks deliberately manipulate facts to maximize their lethal political effectiveness. One of the most interesting attacks took place in 1950 when politicians could still be elected or defeated on the basis of stump speeches. In the Florida election, voters were treated to a verbal duel between two of the best stem-winders of the day. The winner, George Smathers, treated rural north Florida to a ridiculous piece of flim-flam. He said with a straight face, "Are you aware that U.S. Senator Claude Pepper is known all over Washington as a shameless extrovert. Not only that, but this man is reliably reported to practice nepotism with his sister-in-law, and he has a sister who was a thespian in wicked New York. Worst of all, it is an established fact that Mr. Pepper, before his marriage, practiced celibacy."[5]

The Political Predator

Much as smears are despised, they often succeed. This is especially true when smears are made by otherwise respectable citizens who are willing to rob an opponent of his or her good name for purely tactical reasons. Such individuals are political predators. The candidate against whom the attack is directed is the political "prey."

Some quibble with this harsh assessment. They have their own way of rationalizing. For example, campaign consultant Jeff Wainscott, stated, "I don't like to use things which even faintly resemble smear tactics or character assassinations." Then Wainscott got down to the nitty-gritty: "If it's factual, if the man is indeed a slum lord, or if he has voted and it's on public record, in some way that obviously favors him personally or a vested interest, that is factual information and should be used. It impugns his personality, yes, but it is a matter of public record and should be exposed."[6]

In 1965 John Lindsay, running for mayor of New York, made an issue of the real or imaginary problems of the previous mayor, Robert Wagner. Though he had been a part of that administration, his opponent, Abraham Beame, didn't want to meet the charges head on. Instead he claimed that, although he was a part of the previous administration, he was a minor official with "no real decision-making authority." About two weeks before the end of the campaign, Lindsay called a press conference. Using a huge chart entitled, "The Odds are 15,312 to 4 That Abraham Beame is Just Another Wagner," he detailed the similarities between the Wagner and Beame records.[7]

More often than not a smear is just a smoke screen used by a political predator to justify an attack based on alleged facts or on public records.

U.S. Senator Joseph McCarthy of Wisconsin is one of the best-known predators of the twentieth century. His reputation stemmed from his appearance before the U.S. Senate Armed Services Committee, where amid great publicity he claimed to hold in his hand a list of 205 disloyal (Communist) Pentagon employees. After examining the facts, the committee, speaking through its chairman, U.S. Senator Millard Tydings, concluded that McCarthy had no list. Instead, what he had in his hand was a "three-year-old letter from former Secretary of State, James Byrnes, informing a Congressman that permanent tenure for 205 unnamed state department employees might be denied on various grounds, including drunkenness." In its formal report, the Tydings' committee characterized McCarthy's charges as "representing perhaps the most nefarious campaign of half-truths and untruths in the history of the Republic."

This drew a response from the Washington *Times-Herald* that was later blown up to a full page printed in red. This anti-Tydings tirade was circulated throughout the state of Maryland, where Tydings was running for re-election. It said, "Why is there all the talk about your keeping parts of the hearing out of the official record? Why didn't you ask Secretary of State, Dean Acheson, to testify about loyalty?"[8]

Historians criticize McCarthy because he took advantage of the sensitive nature of the information and the secrecy necessary to conduct foreign affairs, as it would not have been appropriate for Secretary of State Dean Acheson to comment. McCarthy's attack is now generally condemned because of the circus atmosphere, the partisan nature of the charges, and the damage it inflicted on innocent State Department employees.

Often, the political effectiveness of a predator's attack is measured purely by its ability to pierce the voter's stream of consciousness. Even when a fact is true it can be distorted by a political predator that uses strong and sometimes wild rhetoric. As an illustration, a Los Angeles-based media consultant created a television spot showing a man wearing a gas mask alleging that, when the Defense Authorization bill was on the floor in 1984, Congressman Rod Chandler voted for continued protection of chemical weapons and nerve gas.

While it could be argued that this was factually true, it was a vicious distortion. The United States already had nerve gas and there was no question but that it was going to continue to have nerve gas. The amendment, which Chandler opposed, was to delete the funds for creating a new binary system of nerve gas to replace the old system. What Congressman Chandler voted for was not that the United States should have nerve gas, but that the current already mixed stock be replaced by the less hazardous binary system, which uses an artillery shell containing two liquids that do not mix until the shell hits the ground and explodes. This would be a safer system for the people who manufacture the gas and for the soldiers who handle it.

When Showmanship Conflicts with Being Fair and Factual

A candidate may be justified in attacking an opponent in the name of showmanship. For instance, the source of an opponent's campaign contributions. The predator may be justified in dramatizing differences in campaign assets, as

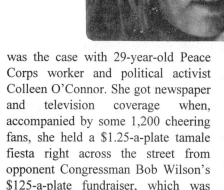

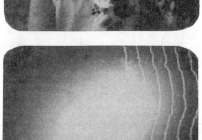

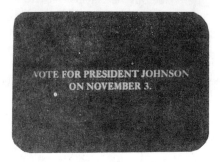

was the case with 29-year-old Peace Corps worker and political activist Colleen O'Connor. She got newspaper and television coverage when, accompanied by some 1,200 cheering fans, she held a $1.25-a-plate tamale fiesta right across the street from opponent Congressman Bob Wilson's $125-a-plate fundraiser, which was attended by some 400 well-heeled backers.[9]

In most cases, the predator is not motivated by the desire to be fair and factual, and if he or she is, it has been overshadowed by the desire for showmanship. The 1968 presidential race is remembered among other things for a TV commercial that was sponsored by a Democratic front organization. The commercial showed a little girl plucking the petals of a daisy using the words, "Will he or won't he?" and when the last petal was plucked the commercial showed an atomic blast (Figure 5-1). Was that an attack or was it simply showmanship?

Fig. 5-1. President Johnson 1968 campaign ad.

Although the opponent was never mentioned or seen, the viewer was left to draw his or her own conclusions. It could argued that the commercial was fair and factual because it mentioned no names and the information it contained was factual. I'll leave it to the reader to draw their own conclusions.

The Question of Persuadability

Are smear pieces effective? Commercial advertisers seldom use the negative hard-sell, so there is little commercial research to guide the candidate who seeks to determine the effectiveness of the smear as an instrument of mass persuasion.

Now let's look at the law. If attacks are really unfair or libelous, the candidate under attack might resort to legal action to persuade the voter they are false. This is what Los Angeles Mayor Fletcher Bowron did when his opponent, Sam Yorty, accused him of being the candidate of the downtown machine. Bowron, overreacting, called a press conference and the media recorded the following dialogue:

> *Mayor*: This is ridiculous. There is no such thing as a downtown machine. There is just a group of prominent downtown businessmen. They are individuals who support me. I'm glad they do. My opponent wishes they'd support him.
> *TV commentator*: But there must be something in it. Who backs your opponent?
> *Mayor*: If he can say I'm backed by a downtown machine, I could say with just as much truth that he is backed by an underworld machine.
> *TV commentator*: Would you say he is backed by an underworld machine? (The commentator was baiting an exasperated, overwrought man.)
> *Mayor*: Yes.

Following this charge, the challenger, Sam Yorty, got great publicity when he sued the mayor for $4 million. After that, Yorty used the suit to put the mayor on the defensive during the final weeks of the campaign, only to drop the suit after he won the election.[10]

In spite of the fact that this lawsuit helped Yorty, most candidates find it best to ignore libelous statements. An election campaign can't wait for prosecution, lawsuits take time and money, and usually the opponent's insurance doesn't cover libel, so there is little likelihood that monetary awards can be collected. Far more important, in *New York Times v. Sullivan*, the U.S. Supreme Court provided that even though statements or attacks are in error, there is no cause for action unless the victims can prove malice, which has been defined as knowledge of or reckless disregard as to the statement's falsity.[11]

Defamation of Character Lawsuits and Other Efforts to Control the Predator Usually Fail to Persuade

This was the experience of ex-President Theodore Roosevelt who, after his defeat on the Bull-Moose ticket, took a Pennsylvania publisher to court for calling him a liar, a drunkard, and a poor loser. Following weeks of publicity and ridicule, the court threw out most of the allegations. Roosevelt's action had to rest solely on the falsity of the allegation that he was a drunkard. During the trial he admitted that he was not a total abstainer, but he contended the article was "very blasphemous." He got the jury's verdict for the grand sum of six cents, plus a comment that he could carry his liquor like a gentleman.[12]

Defamation of character lawsuits are not the only approach. Radio and television stations have federal licenses that make them subject to regulation. So, occasionally, a candidate will ask the Federal Communications Commission (FCC) to stop "false and deceptive" commercials. This happened in 1984, when Republican U.S. Senator Jesse Helms tried to stop political opponents by filing a formal complaint against station WBT, Charlotte, North Carolina. He charged the radio station with "abusing the public interest" by carrying inaccurate commercials sponsored by the North Carolina Democratic party. In 1972, Governor Ronald Reagan of California tried to use the FCC to stop broadcasters from carrying "false and deceptive" ads. In both cases, the FCC informed the complaining public officials that it was not the commission's province to protect one side or the other with respect to alleged false and misleading statements.

In Senator Helms' case, his action was a minus. When he lost his appeal, another Democratic spot touched on Senator Helms' efforts to disrupt the campaign: "You are about to hear something on this radio station that some people don't want you to hear—the truth about Senator Jesse Helms' voting record in Washington. You wouldn't think that a voting record which is a public record would cause such a stir. After the North Carolina Democratic party began airing radio ads about Senator Helms' voting record, his campaign threatened legal action against any radio station that ran them, and a few stations didn't run them. Makes you wonder what Senator Helms doesn't want you to hear. Senator Helms doesn't want you to hear that on July 23, 1982, he switched his vote and voted to double the cigarette tax. He doesn't want you to hear that on May 11, 1982, he voted for a proposal for a $40 billion cut in Social Security. Jesse Helms is going to a lot of trouble and expense to make sure you don't find out about his voting record, but if he didn't want you to hear this, maybe he shouldn't have voted that way."[13]

Chapter 43

Packaging the Smear

> He [Lloyd George, one-time British Prime Minister] could not see
> a belt without hitting below it.
> —Margot Asquith[1]

Political Attacks Come in Endless Variety

In this segment, I will review some of the more common attacks, such as those that revolve around where the opposition gets its funds. Today's voter is sophisticated and this attack rarely succeeds unless predators can tie tainted campaign money to the opposition in a specific way.

Assuming there is a police tolerance policy toward vice, a predatory attack might succeed by emphasizing the fact that the opposition is getting its money from some unsavory businesses. True or untrue, the public often reacts favorably to this attack, because in years past criminals have contributed heavily to political campaigns. For instance, when the eighteenth amendment prohibiting the sale of liquor was in effect during the 1920s, "Scarface" Al Capone, the most celebrated bootlegger of that era, was one of America's leading political contributors. It is alleged he contributed $200,000 to the first campaign of Chicago Mayor William Hale. In 1925, it is said he gave $275,000 to James Walker in his race for Mayor of New York City, and it is estimated he gave several times that amount to judges and other lesser politicians.[2] Today, if contributions were made to a candidate by a shady character such as Al Capone, a political opponent would have plenty of ammunition for a political attack.

Campaign Money the Subject of Attack by Innuendo

The predator might launch a successful attack on a big contributor who gets preference in government business, or who contributes to officials who are lax when dealing with those the public servant is supposed to regulate.

As the 1974 Florida campaign began, Gerald Lewis was but one of twelve aspirants for state comptroller. He melodramatically demanded that the current officeholder meet with him and debate the propriety of his previous campaign contributions, most of which Lewis charged were from small loan companies and others whom the incumbent was charged with regulating. When the incumbent refused, Lewis rode to victory with a series of what he called "empty chair" debates. This feat was accomplished in spite of the incumbent's two-to-one campaign spending advantage.[3]

Fig. 5-2. Cartoonist Doug Marlette, *The Charlotte Observer*. Used by permission.

When the candidates spend their own money, political predators may resort to innuendo, charging foul. On rare occasions a rich, free-spending candidate such as millionaire Elisa de Pont, wife of Delaware's Republican Governor, Pierre S. de Pont IV, falls victim to such an attack. When she opposed incumbent Congressman Thomas Carper, he responded to his wealthy opponent's lavish campaign spending, saying, "In Delaware, we win elections the old-fashioned way. We earn them, we don't buy them."[4]

Vested Interests

Under normal circumstances, attacking a candidate for contributions from vested interests does not pay off. More often than not, voters themselves are members of groups that have vested interests. That is, they belong to a union or are members of the Chamber of Commerce. They may be teachers, nurses, state and local government employees, doctors, lawyers, accountants, social workers, and chiropractors, to name a few. All have reason to contribute through their professional industry, trade, or labor organization.

Fig. 5-3. *Roll Call* [Capitol Hill newspaper, Washington, DC], May 12, 1977.

Highlighting Incompetency

Newspaper journalists who have covered local politics for years know there is often an abysmal lack of knowledge on the part of nonincumbent candidates.[5] First-time aspirants should not become so intent with the mechanics of planning

Fig. 5-4. Gary Yanker, *Prop Art* (New York: Darien House, 1972), p. 99.

dinners, attending rallies, and shaking hands that they overlook study. During the campaign, these candidates must display some grasp of the issues and specifics of administration because as they compete for public attention, the voter compares their sales pitches. Even candidates for president, governor, the U.S. Senate, and other major offices should be sure to study, despite their large staffs of researchers who pour over records and newspaper files, collecting and digesting information.

The political mileage gained when opponents fail to understand issues and duties is obvious when journalists poke fun at candidates who have a poor grasp of the issues or of administrative details. Candidates can also suffer when the opposition demands they tell the public how they intend to pay for their "pie-in-the-sky" promises.

Occasionally research will fail to show that the candidate has done anything of note. Then the predator can highlight the incumbent's "lack of public service," as was done in a television spot for John Kerry (Figure 5-5) when he ran for lieutenant governor of the State of Massachusetts. The ad showed the incumbent cutting out paper dolls and holding a duck.

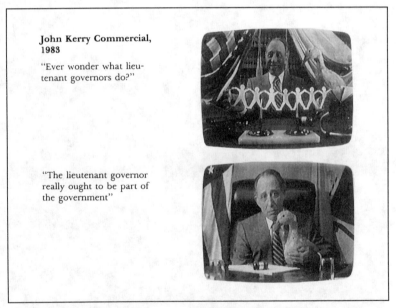

John Kerry Commercial, 1983

"Ever wonder what lieutenant governors do?"

"The lieutenant governor really ought to be part of the government"

Fig. 5-5. Used by permission of L. Patrick Devlin, Curator, Television Political Advertising Collection, University of Rhode Island.

Comparing Qualifications and Anything Else

When candidates with superior qualifications and experience attempt to make their learning or experience an issue, they often appear to be overbearing. So how does the predator project his superiority? Assuming qualifications and experience are a legitimate tool for attacking their opponents, he or she does so with subtlety.

One technique is illustrated in the campaign ad used by Phil Noel when he ran for Governor of Rhode Island (Figure 5-6). Another technique is demonstrated by a brochure used by Governor Albert D. Rosellini of the State of Washington when he ran for reelection in 1964 (Figure 5-7). In that election, both the governor and his opponent had public records. Rosellini's opponent had been a state senator before becoming Superintendent of Public Instruction. The governor's researchers went through the records of the two men and published a comparison of their positions on key issues.

The next illustration (Figure 5-8) is from 1972 when Rosellini was challenged by Daniel Evans, the man who succeeded him as governor. Evans' staff found the worst picture of Rosellini in existence

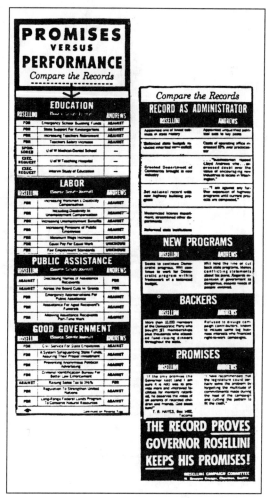

Fig. 5-7. Brochure, Rosellini Campaign Committee, Washington, 1964.

and then, contrasting it with a good photo of Evans, used favorable editorial comments to compare Evans and the incumbent governor.

The Incumbent's Attendance Record

Though U.S. Senator Griffin distinguished himself by blocking the nomination of Abe Fortas as President Johnson's nominee for Chief Justice of the Supreme Court and in managing Gerald Ford's nomination for President, he was defeated because he had no answer to his opponent's, Levin's, charges of poor attendance.

Fig. 5-6. Arnold Fuchs, *Advertising That Won Elections* (Duluth, MN: A. J. Publishing, 1974), p. 225.

TUESDAY'S ISSUE:

The qualities of two men

"The real issue in this '72 campaign involves the quality, class and competence of a man for the future; one capable, for example of innovative approaches such as the 'Washington Future' bond issues devised by the Evans administration, and which Al Rosellini does not even seem to understand."
Yakima Herald-Republic

"If there is one outstanding emphasis in the Evans program, it is in people. Nearly every position, every act and every step taken by the Governor is in behalf of helping people."
Tacoma News Tribune

"The central key is more likely to be found in Evans' adherence to John F. Kennedy's profile about a man having to do what he feels he has to do—which is a rare virtue in politics and may well account for the governor's spectacular success in public life."
The Seattle Times

"If anyone has a record of 'unkept promises' it is Albert Rosellini. He strains the public's gullibility by trying to pass himself off as the man who can bring 'spending reform' and 'savings' to the taxpayers. He had his chance and the trail of red ink he left behind speaks for itself. Dan Evans, on the other hand, has ended each biennium of his tenure with a surplus in the state treasury."
Longview Daily News

"When Rosellini talks about two faces, you are listening to an expert and a piker. He has a million of them himself."
The Washington Teamster

"When all the Rosellini campaign rhetoric is sifted, it easily comes out that Gov. Evans is by far the best choice for Washington voters. At age 39, Evans was the youngest man ever elected governor, and it might be added that after eight years he is possibly the best governor the state has ever had."
Portland Oregonian

\n honest today, a better tomorrow
Re-Elect Governor Dan Evans
Evans Campaign Committee, 1516 5th Avenue, Seattle 98101, Jay Gibson, State Chairman, REPUBLICAN

Fig. 5-8. Advertisement, 1972 Dan Evans for Governor campaign.

Levin didn't invent this line of attack. When newspaper publisher—and later congressman—William Randolph Hearst ran for governor of New York, Secretary of State Eliha Root traveled to New York to point out that Congressman Hearst had been absent for 160 of 185 roll calls.[6]

Liquor and Political Fallout

If there is any one weakness that seems to afflict politicians, it is liquor, but the predator who wants to attack an opponent who drinks excessively must find some way to exploit the candidate's drinking without offending the millions that reject the proposition that liquor is inherently evil.

To appreciate this dilemma, let's go back in time to when the Democrats nominated Al Smith for President. Harrison William Villard, editor of *The Nation*, wrote: "I am reliably informed that he [Al Smith] drinks every day, and the number of his cocktails and highballs is variously estimated at from four to eight."[7] Today this attack probably would not be worth using, at least not by an opponent. Millions might doubt its authenticity, and others would react sympathetically toward Smith and against such smear tactics. However, when we realize that the statement was made in 1928, it is quite a different matter. Then the manufacture and delivery of liquor was illegal. Millions agreed with newspaper editor William Allen White, who asked, "How does he get his liquor? He must either be violating the law or know someone else that does. If this is true, he is not a fit man to be either Governor or President."[8]

Even today a political predator can exploit the opponent's use of liquor. The problem is how to attack while maintaining good taste. There is no universal solution, but George Wallace did it in 1962 when he was running for Governor of Alabama against Big Jim Folsum. Folsum not only drank to excess, but, even worse, did it in public.

Wallace annihilated the Folsom candidacy by launching what amounted to a temperance campaign. He denied that he ever drank and stated that no member of his family drank. When asked to speak at graduations, he emphasized, "Now, you don't have to drink to be a man or a lady." When Wallace requested an entertainer from the Grand Ole Opry to brighten up his campaign, he issued a news release in which he stipulated that they send him a teetotaler. Also, Wallace vowed there would be no liquor in the mansion as long as he was Governor.

Exploiting Issues

Occasionally, a candidate can attack an issue instead of an individual during a campaign by aiming at an interest group that stands for a certain issue. For instance, candidates for the state legislature or school board might attack high spending. If they do, they might take a pro-taxpayer theme. However, they should not attack the schools—and certainly not the kids—for using too great a share of the tax dollar. Instead, the candidate might attack poor teaching curriculum, or top-heavy administration, or the fact that Johnny can't read or spell.

Candidates might take advantage of the issue of dealing with criminals. During his 1966 reelection campaign, Governor Nelson Rockefeller of New York found himself opposed by the district attorney from Queens, who would have been expected to get the "law and order" vote. However, unlike most prosecutors, O'Connor was a liberal with deep civil rights convictions, and for this reason had been the only prosecutor in the state to oppose Rockefeller's tough narcotics laws.

In the closing days of that campaign, Rockefeller, the winner, flooded the state's television channels with hundreds of TV spots. The most frequent spot showed a police car, lights flashing, cruising down a dark street, with the sound of footsteps in the background, and a voice saying, "If you walk home at night, or if there is a teenager in your family, you should be worried. Governor Rockefeller is worried. As much as half the crime in New York is caused by addicts. That's why the governor has sponsored a tough new law that can get addicts off the streets." This was followed by a picture of Rockefeller before a battery of microphones, saying, "If you want to keep crime rates high, O'Connor is your man."[9]

This same technique of targeting an issue was used in the 1984 presidential primary, when a radio commercial sponsored by those supporting the candidacy of former Vice President Fritz Mondale suggested, "If you really care about the nuclear freeze, you should know the facts." The commercial claimed that Mr. Mondale supported the freeze almost a year before his principal rivals in the primary. Then, speaking of that rival, the commercial said, "Gary Hart has shifted his position on the nuclear freeze seven times. That kind of uncertainty is something to really think about. It will take experience and a firm grip to reach the nuclear freeze we all want."[10]

On occasion, the shoe is on the other foot. In the early part of this century, Hiram Johnson served as governor and as United States Senator from California. During his heyday, Johnson was a leader in the Progressive Movement and a candidate for vice president on Teddy Roosevelt's third-party Bull Moose ticket. At that time, the California Progressives were part of a loose nationwide alliance that pursued reforms such as the eight-hour work day and the open primary. But they had areas of disagreement with progressives in the Midwest, who held a different view on free trade and tariff.

As one would expect, Johnson's California critics accused him and his progressives of not looking out for local citrus growers in Southern California. Johnson didn't answer. Instead, he chose to divert attention, charging that after the protective Lemon Tariff had been raised in 1909, 25 Western railroads, led by Southern Pacific, raised their rates, more than wiping out the advantages granted in the tariff legislation.[11]

Directing the Attack at Someone Other Than the Opponent

Occasionally, the predator tries to escape criticism by attacking a third person or organization. This approach has been the favorite of some prominent and respected leaders. Probably the most memorable illustration in modern politics was touched off at the 1948 Democratic National Convention. Polls showed the popularity of the prospective Democratic nominee for president at an all-time low. Left-leaning Democrats were already publicizing their plans to hold their own convention, where they intended to nominate Henry Wallace. Southern conservative Democrats planned to nominate the governor of South Carolina, Strom Thurmond.

Things were so bad on the Democratic convention floor that the chairman, who was one of the nominee's staunchest friends, did not dare to call for the traditional vote to make the nomination unanimous. Then, at 1:45 a.m. on the 15th of July 1948, wearing a crisp linen suit and a big smile, President Harry Truman was escorted to the rostrum to accept the presidential nomination. His first words were, "Senator Barkley [the vice presidential nominee] and I will win this election and make those Republicans like it . . . don't you forget that."

For the next twenty minutes, Truman unleashed a violent attack, not against the man whom the opposition had nominated, Governor Thomas Dewey of New York, but against the first Republican Congress in sixteen years, which he accused of attempting to turn back the clock to a time before President Franklin D. Roosevelt's New Deal. The partisan crowd, who up till that moment had little to cheer about, warmed up. Truman concluded by saying:

> On the 26th day of July, which, out in Missouri, we call Turnip Day, I am going to call Congress back and ask them to pass laws which they are saying they are for in their platform to halt rising prices and meet the housing crisis. Now, my friends, if there is any reality behind that Republican platform, we ought to get some action from a short session of the 80th Congress. They can do their job in 14 days if they want to do it. They will still have time to go out and run for office."[12]

Truman's attack electrified the convention delegates. And he continued to use it throughout his winning re-election campaign.

Concentrating on a Prominent Scapegoat

In a national or statewide campaign, everything depends on media coverage. Attacking a third party has little effect unless it attracts media attention, so the predator must select a prominent scapegoat. This requires that the predator be resourceful and have a tough hide.

To illustrate, let's go back in history just after the Civil War, to the origin of the phrase "the $64,000 question," where we find one of the boldest, cleverest uses of a third-party scapegoat in U.S. history. The chief actor in this drama was one-time Republican Speaker of the House, James G. Blaine from Maine. When the Democrats took control of the House, Blaine learned that a Union Pacific railroad director was about to expose the fact that while Blaine was Speaker, he had accepted a $64,000 loan from the railroad, when matters affecting the railroad's interest were before the House. A Union Pacific director was going to allege that the money was a bribe disguised as a loan. Blaine knew the alleged bribe would be aired before a congressional committee chaired by a southern Democrat.

Blaine found a scapegoat in former President of the Confederacy Jefferson Davis, hidden away in a bill pending in Congress to grant amnesty to former Confederate officers. Blaine offered an amendment to exclude Davis from the amnesty bill. He made an emotional, highly publicized speech in support of the amendment that has since taken its place in history as the "bloody shirt appeal." It was designed to inflame the passions of Congressmen, most of whom had been soldiers in the Union Army.

Shortly after his amendment was adopted, the $64,000 drama took a new twist. Blaine learned that the chief witness against him was a bookkeeper who possessed letters from one of Blaine's partners showing his participation. Before the witness could testify, Blaine went to the bookkeeper's hotel room and managed to secure possession of his letters. Claiming they were his property, he boldly left with them.

When the bookkeeper complained to the committee and the press, there was massive public reaction. Then Blaine took the floor of the U.S. House and raised a question of personal privilege, a parliamentary procedure that takes precedence over all others. When he got the floor, he displayed a large packet, which he claimed were the letters involved. Then he read selected passages to defend his conduct in taking the $64,000 loan. After this prelude, he launched a counterattack. He accused southern congressmen and, in particular, the committee chairman who was to hear the testimony against him, of attempting to retaliate for Blaine's position in persuading the house to refuse to grant amnesty to Jefferson Davis.

Not only did Blaine escape prosecution or censure but a few years later Colonel Robert G. Ingersoll, speaking before the Republican convention, interpreting Blaine's conduct, described Blaine as an "armed warrior, like a plumed knight, marching down the halls of the American Congress, who threw his shining lance full and fair against the brazen forehead of the defamers of his country and maligners of his honor. . . ." After saying, "Republicans do not demand that their candidate have a certificate of moral character signed by a Confederate Congress," he concluded, "In the name of those who perished in the Skeleton Clutch of famine at Andersonville and Libby [Civil War battles], whose sufferings he so vividly remembers, Illinois nominates James G. Blaine for the Presidency of the United States."[13] Blaine got the nomination and came within 25,000 votes of being President of the United States.

Chapter 44

Innuendo and Affirmative Ridicule

> Opinion is ultimately determined by feelings and not by intellect.
> —Herbert Spencer[1]

Innuendo

Another technique that deserves notice, but not admiration, is attack by way of the innuendo. Here the predator uses words and circumstances to convey an impression without actually putting the accusation in cold print. When accused of hitting below the belt, the predator says "You're all wrong. I didn't accuse the opposition of anything."

For example, during the McCarthy era, a time in the United States when the political world was sharply divided between left and right, a young congressman, Richard Nixon, gained name familiarity from notoriety he received by discovering a discrepancy in Secretary of the United Nations Alger Hiss's testimony before the U.S. Senate. That discrepancy eventually resulted in Hiss's being indicted, going to trial, and being convicted of perjury.

In his next election campaign, Nixon launched an underdog campaign for U.S. Senator from the state of California against his opponent, Congresswoman Helen Gahagan Douglas. In that campaign, Nixon emphasized his national image as a Communist fighter. Although Nixon didn't accuse his opponent of being a Communist, he conducted a campaign clearly designed to make her appear to be a Communist sympathizer. His advertising used a bold headline to ask, "Is Helen Gahagan Douglas a Communist?" It answered no, but in small print. Then the ad used this opportunity to make a comparison of voting records, in which Nixon claimed that Mrs. Douglas' record paralleled that of New York's Congressman Vito Marcantion, who the Nixon ad accused of following the Communist line.

Nixon went further. He billed the election "as a contest to determine whether the voters shall continue to tolerate the Communist conspiracies, persist in condoning the bureaucratic profligacy and appeasing totalitarian aggression." He circulated a piece called the "Pink Lady" printed on pink paper, featuring quotes he claimed Mrs. Douglas made. She said they were taken out of context, but the innuendoes stuck. Nixon became U.S. Senator, while Mrs. Douglas faded into political obscurity.[2] While "red baiting" is no longer fashionable, the innuendo is not dead. Some examples are shown in Figures 5-9 and 5-10. Note the ways in which print is used to dramatize and exploit vague feelings of discontent.

"You know what they'd say about something strong and solid, they'd say it was 'sound as a dollar' "

"But it has been changing, hasn't it?'

Fig. 5-9. 1972 McGovern versus Nixon "dollar" commercial. Used by permission of L. Patrick Devlin, Curator, Television Political Advertising Collection, University of Rhode Island.

Another example of innuendo is McGovern's effort to portray the reelection of President Nixon as somehow threatening to the future of democracy and free elections, the Irish Labor Party, the Canadian New Democratic Party, and finally the Republican party of the United States, which was dissatisfied with the incumbent Democratic administration following World War II in 1946.

Affirmative Sarcasm

Attacks may use both humor and innuendoes to muffle their shrillness. When Richard Nixon was running for governor of California in 1960, the opposition circulated his picture with the caption, "Would you buy a used car from this man?"[3]

In 1968, the Democrats felt they had the stronger of the two vice presidential candidates—U.S. Senator Edmond Muskie. They used a TV ad (Figure 5-11) to ridicule the candidacy of the Republican nominee, Spiro Agnew. The commercial opens with the camera showing the upper right-hand corner of a TV set, with knobs and a small part of the screen visible. The camera slowly pulls back to

Fig. 5-10. "Had Enough?" poster, Washington State Republican Committee, 1946; "No's": the Ireland Labor Party, and the Canadian New Democratic Party: Gary Yanker, *Prop Art* (New York: Darien House, 1972), p. 78 and p. 62, respectively.

show the screen, on which is lettered: " 'Agnew for Vice President?' " Throughout the entire spot is heard "raucous, uncontrollable laughter." Then black letters appear against a white background stating, " 'This would be funny if it weren't so serious.' "[4]

In 1980, a Carter television commercial featured the president's empty Oval Office with a background voice asking, "When you come right down to it, what kind of a person should occupy the Oval Office? Should it be a person like Ronald Reagan, who has a fractured view of America?"[5]

Humphrey "Laughter" Spot

Sound of raucous, uncontrollable laughter

Laughter continues

Humphrey "What Has Nixon Done For Me" Commercial

"Medicare? No, that was Humphrey's idea"

Fig. 5-11. Humphrey "laughter" and "What has Nixon done for me" spots used in 1968 Nixon versus Humphrey campaign. Used by permission of L. Patrick Devlin, Curator, Television Political Advertising Collection, University of Rhode Island.

When the Predator's Supporters Attack

Then in politics there is what billiard players call bank shots. The candidate pretends they aren't an attack at all. One way is to circulate, promote, and publicize a rumor. Another is to do the same thing with a funny story designed to emphasize or keep alive something the opponent wants the public to forget, such as Gerald Ford's habit of falling down. Of course there is a great deal more latitude with the humorous story as it's perceived as simply a funny story rather than a serious attack.

Let's look at a more serious example. By 1970, U.S. Senator Ted Kennedy had inherited the mantle and image from his assassinated brothers. In that year, he joined a drinking party at Chappaquiddick in which his wife was not present. This was attended by several of his youthful volunteers. Late that night, the Senator was driving an attractive young female member of his staff back to her hotel when his car went over the side of a small bridge. The woman drowned. The senator survived, but he waited nine hours before reporting the incident to the police. This tragedy turned on a flood of news articles, features, commentaries, and speculations. However, investigation turned up little hard evidence. Kennedy was convicted and paid a fine for negligent driving and for failure to immediately report the incident to the police.

The opposition exploited the tragedy in an effort to ruin Kennedy's image. One technique was to circulate a tongue-in-cheek fabrication of a mythical telegram from the Irish Government to the U.S. State Department. It started by saying that at the time of Chappaquiddick, the Irish government, who had great reverence for the Kennedy family, decided to comment on the tragedy via this diplomatic cable to the United States Government and to simultaneously make it public to the Irish people. It read:

> God Bless Senator Kennedy, that sainted son of Irish heritage, who was taking that fine Catholic girl to Midnight mass when the tragedy of Chappaquiddick occurred. Noble man that he was, he remained at the scene of the accident for nine hours in devout prayer before telling anyone. The American government would be well advised to find the Protestant bastards who built the bridge.

The use of political rumor or innuendo is still prevalent today. In Salem, Massachusetts, the city infamous for its witch trials in 1600s, one contemporary candidate for mayor found it necessary to deny a rumor accusing him of being a warlock (a male witch). After Robert Gauthier publicly said the rumor was directed at him, and it was denied, the accusation took a bizarre turn. Laurie Cabot, a local business woman who wears a long, dark cape and is a familiar figure in Salem, claimed to be a real witch, and she too requested a candidacy application for mayor.

Chapter 45

Opposition Research

> Though the predator may be bored with his opposition's
> accomplishments and uninterested in his troubles, he is certainly
> interested in his sins. . . .[1]

A Successful Attack Needs Specifics

It is not as difficult as it might seem to obtain specifics. Experienced political investigators claim that careful research will turn up damning evidence against any officeholder. As proof, consider this statement spoken by a candidate for the United States Senate from Illinois: "I am not, nor ever have been, in favor of bringing about in any way the social and political equality of the white and black races."[2] Would you believe this man was Abraham Lincoln?

If the predator is seriously interested in making an attack, and if the campaign is one that merits newspaper coverage, the candidate should buy the services of a newspaper clipping agency. These organizations employ professionals who read all current newspapers and other publications daily. They are paid a fee for clipping out and sending the subscriber copies of items the subscriber is interested in. This might be anything the opposition says or does that is carried as either news or advertising in those publications.

Fig. 5-12. Brant Hart and Johnny Parker, The Wizard of Id (Chicago: Field Enterprises, May 16, 1976). By permission of Johnny Hart and Creators Syndicate, Inc.

Reading the press accounts of the opposition's day-to-day activities and looking at their ads, the researcher might find statements that are intended for one area, but would be embarrassing when published in another. Such a situation was reported by one-time Florida governor Fuller Warren. During the early 1930s, his state's vote was split between the traditional Southern "crackers," who believed in states rights and segregation, and the more liberal south Florida population, most of whom had moved there from northeastern metropolitan areas like New York City.

One candidate for governor tried newspaper ads designed to appeal to the residents of north Florida. He appealed to them to defeat the opponent to protect themselves from the residents in the southern part of the state. His opponent adroitly circulated reprints of this ad in south Florida, then rode their massive indignation vote to victory.[3]

It saves immeasurable time and hard work if when researching the opposition the researcher can access a newspaper, radio, or television station "morgue." A morgue is a file of newspaper articles, magazine articles, photographs, and often confidential notes kept for future reference on most public figures. The researcher might find statements made in past campaigns that could be very embarrassing when considered in today's light.

Author Myles Martel relates a dramatic instance that occurred during the 1968 Oregon U.S. Senate race between a young Republican challenger, Robert Packwood, and an aging four-term Democratic incumbent, Wayne Morse. Throughout the campaign, Morse emphasized his "twenty-four year seniority." Shortly before the election there was a televised debate between the two. Then Packwood confronted Morse with his own statement made fourteen years earlier. "Never confuse seniority with ability because when you go to the mat ability will win every time. When you've got a chance to replace an incumbent U.S. Senator, even if he is a committee chairman, with a dynamic young legislative leader, take that opportunity."[4]

In Search of an Opponent's Secret Achilles Heel

In most campaigns searching for opponents' weak points isn't an intelligent way to use limited campaign resources. As a master in the field of candidate consulting, John Deardorff, says, "For every usable nugget the researcher comes up with, he or she will have to turn down a hundred items which they cannot use."[5] I don't recommend extensive candidate research because normally there are better ways for candidates to spend their time, assets, and volunteer effort. However, some candidates, being natural predators, will want to build a smear file.

How is it done? The answer is, slowly and meticulously—treating what is found with great skepticism. As campaign expert Steven Shadegg said, "In one campaign we developed enough information to fill three standard size filing cabinets. This collection of newspaper clippings, photographs, and confidential memos on our opponent and his close associates was indexed and cross-indexed. When the campaign was over, and we were ready to dispose of the material, I had it weighed—it was 123 pounds. I estimated that we had used it in a specific way only seven times."[6]

If the opposition is prominent and has held office before, the researchers can go to the public library, where past issues of local newspapers are kept, to search for articles that deal with the opponent. This is what John Deardourff did when he was working on behalf of New York Governor Nelson Rockefeller. He was sent to get some dirt on Rockefeller's opponent, Brooklyn District Attorney Frank O'Connor. While combing through old newspapers, he ran across the fact that some years earlier, when O'Connor was a state legislator from Brooklyn, he had been the leading opponent of the New York State throughway. As Deardorff tells it, at the time "it was probably a wise (political) decision (for a Brooklyn legislator) to oppose that highway." But when he was running for governor it placed O'Connor in the embarrassing position of having opposed a project regarded by the upstate voters of New York as one of the great gifts of all time.[7]

There may be no legal requirement that an office holder (a congressman) live in the area he or she seeks to represent, yet we live in a democracy where most of the electorate believes their office holders should be one of them. With this in mind, one of the first things an investigator should check is how long his opponent has lived at a particular address, and what other addresses he may have had.

From there, the investigator might go to the courthouse (or courthouses) where the opponent has lived, first checking voting registration to see how often he or she voted. Then an investigator should look at the official criminal index, just to see if the opponent has been accused or convicted of a criminal offense. After that the opponent's name should be traced through the civil court index on the chance the opponent has been sued.

When U.S. Senator Robert Jepson of Iowa filed for re-election, he was known as a "born-again Christian" and champion of the conservative "new right." Upon investigation, it was found that he had applied for membership in a leisure spa and health club some seven years before it went bankrupt. Checking further, it was also discovered that the leisure spa and health club offered nude encounters and nude rap sessions.

When the story broke, Jepson's morality was the issue. In the 1984 re-election campaign, to his credit, the Senator didn't lie. He took a full-page newspaper ad in which he admitted his guilt and pointed out that this was before he was a "born-again Christian." During the campaign he counter attacked his opponent, Democrat Congressman Tom Harkin, as a liberal, and described him as a "slick-

REPRESENTATIVE

TOM SMITH.... WHERE WERE YOU WHEN THE ROLL CALL VOTES WERE COUNTED?

THERE IS A TIME FOR WORK AND A TIME FOR PLAY... AND OUR SENATOR DAN JOLLY KNOWS THE DIFFERENCE

Fig. 5-13. Examples of using opponent's record against them: Jaques Neher, "Ad Charges Spark Illinois Campaign," *Advertising Age,* November 6, 1978, p. 2.

talking lawyer." But most observers say he lost simply because the race pivoted on the issue of Jepsen's character, which Harkin exploited with a slogan: "Tom Harkin: A senator Iowans can be proud of."[8]

Along the same lines, one candidate for prosecutor found a divorce action in which the incumbent's ex-wife had petitioned the court for temporary support. In her affidavit, she listed among her husband's income $200 a month he was receiving from a firm that controlled the pinballs that were operating illegally in local taverns.

The researcher should also check the records of the opponent's real estate holdings to see if he is delaying payment of his real estate taxes until threatened with a tax sale. This is often done so the taxpayer can collect a higher rate of interest on his money by investing it elsewhere. It is likely that the public would be reluctant to support someone who is not doing his share to support government.

The researcher should try to gain access to the opponent's credit ratings. This means getting a copy of what is on file about the opponent with Dunn and Bradstreet or other firms that specialize in credit information. Here the researcher will often find a record of past financial transactions plus other pertinent personal information bearing on whether the opponent is a good financial risk.

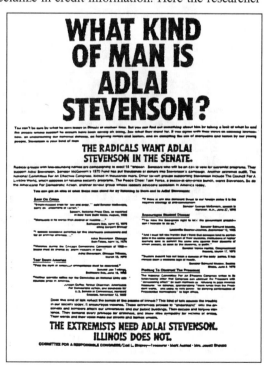

Checking Out the Opponent's Official Record

When the opposition is or was an office holder, his or her public voting record should be scrutinized. When Brooklyn District Attorney Frank O'Connor was campaigning for the governor of New York and John Deardourff was working for the incumbent Nelson Rockefeller, Deardourff sat for five days with ten volunteers in the New York Public Library, wading through old newspapers and other documents, analyzing O'Connor's voting record.

Fig. 5-14. Another example of using opponent's record against them.

Their search went back to the time O'Connor was a state legislator. Commenting on that task, Deardourff said, "It was not an easy job. Whenever we found a vote that looked as if it might be even a little bit useful, we had to find a copy of the appropriate bill."[9]

If the opposition has already held office, thorough research calls for checking his or her payroll allowance and expense accounts. I suggest the researcher see how the opponent was reimbursed for car expenses and travel, and how much he or she spent for meals and hotel accommodations when attending conventions, etc. The candidate should not be dissuaded by the fact that the opponent is a person of good moral character. The researcher may be surprised at what he finds. When Lincoln first came to Washington as a congressman, like others of that era, he charged the government for traveling 1,626 miles, which we are told is about twice the number of miles that he would have taken had he used the shortest route.[10]

A serious researcher should examine any legitimate but irregular way the officeholder reimburses himself. Congressman Randall Hermon was defeated when an opponent pinned the moniker, "Front Porch Hermon" on him because he charged the government $100 a month for a district office he maintained in his home.[11]

Occasionally the officeholder is padding a payroll. So the researcher might make a check of the office holder's employees. This was the accusation against one-time New York congressman Adam Clayton Powell, who put his wife on his Washington, D.C., office payroll when she lived and presumably worked in Puerto Rico.[12]

Fig. 5-15. Still another example of using opponent's record against them.

Making Opponents Eat Their Words

When an opponent has been prominent or held office, it is in the predator's best interest to review accounts of political battles the opponent has participated in. Occasionally the opponent has written or been quoted in a newspaper, or, more importantly, a magazine or periodical with an extreme liberal or conservative point of view.

During the early years of this century, all of Montana's daily newspapers were dominated by the Anaconda Copper Company. During this time Burton K.

Wheeler was Anaconda's gadfly. When he was still a rising young politician, Anaconda's candidate defeated him for governor, and once for the U.S. Senate. Then, in spite of their opposition, Wheeler was elected to the U.S. Senate. After some years of opposing each other, Wheeler and the Anaconda Company came to an understanding.

Then came World War II. Prior to the Japanese attack on Pearl Harbor, Wheeler was the leading opponent of U.S. intervention. In 1946 he came home to campaign in spite of the fact that when the war was over he found there was an adverse reaction to his pre-war isolationist stand. Though weakened politically, re-election odds were still in his favor. Then, as fate would have it, the state's leading newspaper, the Anaconda-owned Montana *Standard*, endorsed Wheeler and ran his picture on the front page.

Wheeler's opponent in the primary, Montana Supreme Court Judge Leif Erickson, went on the radio to remind the voters of Wheeler's words when as a young politician he had opposed Anaconda Copper: "If you ever see my picture on the front page of a company paper, you will know I have sold out to the company." Erickson, Anaconda's new gadfly, led Wheeler by a narrow margin when the primary ballots were counted. However, it was a hollow victory. The campaign had become so bitter that Erickson was defeated when much of Wheeler's support went to the Republican nominee.

When an opponent is prominent, the predator should go to the library and check the author index. Occasionally a predator can make an issue of the type of publication a candidate has written for. This happened to California Congressman Will Rogers, Jr., when he ran for United States Senator. Researchers working for his opponent, U.S. Senator William Knowland, discovered that Rogers had been a guest columnist and had written under his own by-line in a newspaper that was owned by the Communist Party.[13]

Campaign consultant Jeff Wainscott advises that it is not unusual for a candidate to get carried away by an audience's special interests.[14] He says, "Have someone who can get into opposition meetings and look for contradictions."

The predator should comb the opposition's past and present campaign literature for contradicting statements or promises. Nick Thimmesch, syndicated columnist for the Los Angeles *Times*, claims that millionaire Governor Jay Rockefeller of West Virginia was against strip mining and for gun control, legalized abortion, and unionization of state employees when he ran in 1972, but reversed these stands when he ran for re-election in 1976.[15]

Old campaign promises can present the candidate with a problem. During the early New Deal years, Samuel I. Rosenman wrote speeches for a number of eminent Democrats. He recalled that President Franklin D. Roosevelt had opened his 1932 campaign in Pittsburgh with a speech calling for a balanced budget. Four years later, the government was deep in red ink from spending millions to overcome the effects of the Depression. Roosevelt asked Rosenman to write a speech that Roosevelt could use when opening his re-election campaign. Roosevelt wanted to deliver it in the same city, in the same ball park, and in exactly the same spot where he had pledged a frugal administration.

Roosevelt specifically asked Rosenman to find a convincing explanation of his earlier balanced budget position. Rosenman carefully read and re-read Roosevelt's 1932 kickoff speech. He then called on the eagerly waiting President. "Mr. President," Rosenman said, "the only thing you can say about that 1932 speech is to deny categorically that you ever made it."[16]

Off-the-Record Tips

When checking what the opposition has done, the researcher will find politics is a huge stew combining friends and enemies with conflicting ambitions and ulterior motives in the same pot. Every officeholder depends on a staff and often department heads to carry out orders. On the surface, those who work for an officeholder must at least pretend to agree. But ex-staffers are not always loyal to their ex-boss.

Even those still employed may not be satisfied with their boss's personality, their orders, or their pay. Nevertheless, if they want to remain employed, they cater to the officeholder's whims. Clarence Cannon ruled the House Ways and Means Committee like a feudal king during the Truman administration. His dissatisfied staff often described him as: "God . . . with the limitations of Clarence Cannon." Those who felt his wrath were said to comment, "Being Cannonized may help to get one to heaven, but it does nothing whatsoever to advance one's career on the Appropriations Committee."[17]

Frequently, one or two staff who have been fired for insubordination or other reasons are willing to supply damaging "on or off the record" information, as are those who supported the opponent's competition in the primary. When Republican John Tower first ran for U.S. Senator, his general election opponent was a conservative Democrat, Wagner Carr. Carr had fought his party's liberals when he served his State as both speaker of the House and as attorney general. After the primary, in which Carr was the Democratic nominee, Peter O'Donnel, chairman of the Texas Republican Party, approached the defeated liberals who had supported Carr's primary opponent. These Democrats agreed to tell the Republicans everything bad they knew about Wagner Carr. They justified their position saying that they would rather have Republican conservative John Tower represent his party's conservative objectives as a United States Senator than Carr, who they felt would also fight their liberal Democratic objectives.[18]

Chapter 46

Backlash

> If you play a pig, they think you are a pig.
> —Marlon Brando[1]
>
> Once the candidate starts throwing mud . . . a good image
> doesn't just fade away, it drops dead.
> —RRG

During the 1979 primaries, Gerald Greenberg, the media-time buyer for the George Bush for President Committee, hit the nail on the head when he said, "You are dealing with an environment when you place a TV ad, an environment that reflects positively or negatively on a candidate."[2] A predator must not forget that it does little good if he or she damages or destroys the opponent's image if the backlash then costs the election.

In 1982, Republican Robin Beard used a TV spot attacking incumbent U.S. Senator James Sasser of Tennessee in which the camera showed a wooden crate labeled "U.S. Aid," with hands holding crowbars prying the lid open. Hands grabbed for stacks of dollars as the announcer said:

> "When it comes to spending taxpayers' money, Senator James Sasser is a master. Take foreign aid. While important programs are being cut back here at home, Sasser has voted to allow foreign aid to be sent to committed enemies of our country— Vietnam, Laos, Cambodia, Marxist Angola, and even Communist Cuba. You can bet James Sasser is making a lot more friends abroad than he is here in Tennessee."

Then an actor dressed as Fidel Castro held up a flaming dollar bill, used it to light his cigar, and said, " 'Muchissimas gracias, Senor Sasser.' " This distortion was criticized by the news media and the backlash helped Senator Sasser get reelected.[3]

Attacks on the Opponent's Personal Life

Attacks on a candidate's personal life sometimes succeed but more often backfire because they offend the voter's sense of fair play. This was the case when the enemies of Andrew Jackson charged him with being the son of a prostitute, and when James K. Polk was accused of buying and branding a slave.[4]

If a personal attack is launched, the predator must expect the opposition to bounce back with counter charges. Then the campaign can become a bloodbath. This happened during the campaign for president between Governor Grover Cleveland and former Speaker of the House of Representatives and Senator from Maine, James G. Blaine.

When Blaine was speaker of the U.S. House some years before, legislation that affected the Union Pacific Railroad was before that body. Blaine had received from the Union Pacific $64,000, which his opponents said was a bribe disguised as a loan from the Union Pacific Railroad. To secure the loan, Blaine had pledged nearly worthless collateral consisting of bonds in the insolvent Little Rock and Fort Smith Railroads. The embarrassing details of the incident were documented in a series of letters from Blaine, one of which ended with, "Burn this letter."

Such disclosure would have been enough to destroy a lesser politician, but not Blaine. He not only was an accomplished orator, but he had the skill of a great actor and managed to gloss over his involvement, claiming that the accusations against him were the work of "unregenerated rebels," former Confederate soldiers.

Cleveland too had a moral shortcoming, but of a different nature. Opposition newspapers made much of the fact that, prior to taking office as president, that although he was a bachelor, Cleveland had fathered an illegitimate child.

As the campaign drew to a close there were torchlight processions and political rallies in which the partisans marched and chanted. The Democrats chanted, "Burn this letter! Burn, burn, oh, burn this letter!" and "Blaine! Blaine! James G. Blaine! The con-ti-nen-tal liar from the state of Maine!" The Republicans countered with the chant: "Ma, Ma! Where's my Pa? He's gone to the White House. Ha! Ha! Ha!"[5]

The Fickle Nature of Public Preference

A predator candidate contemplating an attack should realistically examine the fickle nature of the public's preferences. Some candidates succeed when they project a new image and some don't. Sometimes the electorate is tired of the brand they have on the shelf and may be captivated by a previously unknown personality.

An example of this occurred in one prominent Massachusetts race. In 1962 Ted Kennedy ran for the U.S. Senate seat vacated by his brother John. In the Democratic primary, his opponent was the state's attorney general, Edward McCormack, the nephew of another Massachusetts luminary, Speaker of the U.S. House of Representatives, John B. McCormack.

The campaign, involving members of two of the most prominent Democratic families in the nation, became a media event. There was extensive national coverage when the candidates met in a series of debates. Late in the campaign, during one of these debates, when the polls showed McCormack trailing, he took a desperate gamble. After saying, "Let's keep the families out of it," McCormack tried to make it clear that he stood on his own two feet and on his record of almost a decade in elective office. He stated that he had not started at the top, but had worked his way up the political ladder. Then he let Ted Kennedy have it, saying:

Since the question of names and families has been injected, if his name was Edward Moore, with his qualifications, his candidacy would be a joke, but nobody's laughing because his name is not Edward Moore. It's Edward Moore Kennedy, and I say it makes no difference what your name is. In a democracy you stand on your own two feet and you say to the people, you have the right to vote. You go behind that curtain, and you vote without fear, without favor, and you vote for the candidate whom you feel is the qualified candidate, and I place my case in your hands.

Looking directly at Kennedy, McCormack then continued:

You never worked for a living. You have never run or held an elective office. You are not running on qualifications. You are running on a slogan: "You Can Do More for Massachusetts." . . . and I say, "Do more, how?" Because of experience? Because of maturity of judgment? Because of qualifications? I say no! This is the most insulting slogan I have seen in Massachusetts politics, because the slogan means: Vote for this man because he has influence, he has connections, he has relations. And I say no.[6]

Despite McCormack's eloquence, Ted Kennedy won the primary and went on to beat two opponents in the general election. The attack failed in part because McCormack owed his own rise to the office of attorney general in the state of Massachusetts to the fact that his uncle was the speaker of the U.S. House. But, even more important, McCormack verbalized the reason thousands of voters of Massachusetts wanted to support Ted: His brother Jack was president, and his brother Bobby was U.S. Attorney General. This made them rightfully believe Ted would have more influence than his opponent.

While there is little to be admired in a political attack, a stand-up predator is at least to be respected when he or she does not shadowbox but stages an attack in his own name.

Calculating the Impact

Attacks are more effective when there are only two viable voices and the voters must choose between two predators. The intelligent predator must calculate the impact of a third opponent, holding rhetoric in check, because voters have an alternative choice.

"Be careful you don't elect an advertising campaign," was the headline for a full-page newspaper ad that pictured thirty television screens, all of which featured the millionaire the Democrats nominated to the United States Senate, Congressman Richard Ottinger. The copy underneath read:

Don't laugh. There's evidence that two million dollars just won the Democratic nomination for the U.S. Senate. The winner had nothing different to say. But he had enough money to say it 20 times as often as his opponents. Nobody heard the other guys, because he simply drowned them out. Now he's going to use the same tactics in this election, only it looks like he's going to spend even more. . . . Just to even things up, why don't you send Senator Goodell a contribution so he can tell people what he's done. It won't make him a television star, but that's okay. He'd rather be a Senator.

The winner of the election was neither Congressman Ottinger nor U.S. Senator Goodell but the candidate of a third conservative party, James L. Buckley, who ironically spent more than either Congressman Ottinger or Senator Goodell.[7]

Not all attacks and counterattacks rise to great emotional heights. However, they are controversial and like any fight the thrust and counterthrust attract a disproportionate amount of publicity. Misstatements or small incidents can give the candidate a chance to use an opponent's attack as a launching pad to justify his or her own predatory conduct.

When Congressman Jim Jones of Oklahoma filed for reelection, his opponent was U.S. Attorney Frank Keating. Early in the campaign, Keating unleashed a television commercial his supporters dubbed the "Rocky spot." In it, Mr. Keating was pictured in shirt sleeves standing in a boxing ring, where he said, "I've been in tough fights before." Then, looking directly into the camera, he told the TV audience, "Jim Jones has met his match."[8]

But in the ad, Mr. Keating stretched the truth when he claimed that, "As a Tulsa prosecutor, I won every case I tried." That might have been true in 1971 when Mr. Keating was an assistant county prosecutor, but, in 1982 and 1983, when he was Tulsa's U.S. attorney, he had lost two major county commission kickback cases. Jones responded with a TV ad of his own. After detailing those losses, the ad concluded: "In Oklahoma, we believe a man is only as good as his word." Public opinion polls showed the counterpunch scored, and this incident turned the voters against Frank Keating.

Even the Most Successful Predators Risk Overkill

Politicians, like actors, are in show business. Public approval or disapproval of their careers depends on their public images. If the voting public views the attack as bullying someone who is innocent, their images can change and their attacks are perceived as overbearing.

Again, one predator who seemed to thrive on the give and take of controversy was U.S. Senator Joseph McCarthy of Wisconsin. In the 1950s, he labeled the Secretary of State as "The Pied Piper of the Politburo"; the Chief of Staff during World War II, General C. Marshall, as, "An instrument of the Soviet Conspiracy"; and Professor Owen Lattimore of John Hopkins University as, "The number one movie spy in the United States."[9]

His impact on U.S. history was so great that the years from 1950 to 1954 are known as the McCarthy era, which has been defined as: "(1) The political practice of publicizing accusations of disloyalty or subversion with insufficient regard to evidence, and (2) the use of methods of investigation and accusation regarded as unfair, in order to suppress opposition."[10]

One McCarthy incident comes up again and again. To understand the incident, it must be remembered that as Joe McCarthy's political power grew, so did his gall. After accusing an ever-widening list of people of being Communist sympathizers, McCarthy found his charges were becoming stale. To keep the public interest, he and his staff opened a new front against an institution older than the nation itself, the United States Army.

The army counterattacked, bringing formal charges against McCarthy's Senate staff aide, Roy Cohen, before the United States Senate. They charged that Cohen had wrongfully used his official position in an attempt to gain favors for a millionaire friend who had been drafted as a lowly private. The charges were aired before a senate committee and the whole controversy was televised. A fascinated nation followed the ruckus like a continuing soap opera.

At first McCarthy seemed equal to the battle. He diffused the attack by labeling the accusations as a cheap attempt to blackmail him into calling off his investigation into the army's protection of subversives within its ranks. Then an unlikely star emerged—short, balding Joseph Welch, soft-spoken trial attorney of the old school. In his quiet way, he got under McCarthy's hide. As a nation watched, McCarthy retaliated, singling out Welch's young assistant, Fred Fisher, whom he accused of being a member of the left-leaning Lawyers' Guild, which McCarthy claimed was a haven for Communist sympathizers.

It was then that Joe McCarthy learned that predators are like an infantry wandering through a minefield. They must be on guard because they never know when public opinion is going to explode beneath them, when the person or interest under attack begins looking like an underdog.

McCarthy's personal attack on Fisher shocked and enraged Welch and touched off this historic exchange:

Mr. Welch: "I said, 'Fred [Fisher], I just don't think I am going to ask you to work on the television and it will hurt like the dickens.' So, Senator, I asked him to go back to Boston. Little did I dream you could be so reckless and so cruel as to do an injury to that lad. . . . It is, I regret to say, equally true that I fear he shall always bear a scar needlessly inflicted by you. . . . If it were in my power to forgive you for your reckless cruelty, I could not do so. I like to think I am a gentleman, but your forgiveness will have to come from someone other than me. . . .

Senator McCarthy: "May I say that Mr. Welch talks about this being cruel and reckless. He was just baiting, he has been baiting Mr. Cohen here for hours.. . . . I just give this man's record and I want to say, Mr. Welch, that it has been labeled long before he was a member, as early as 1944.

Mr. Welch (skillfully refusing to be deterred): "Senator, may we drop this? We know he belonged to the Lawyers' Guild, and Mr. Cohen nods his head at me. I did you, I think, no personal injury, Mr. Cohen."

Mr. Cohen: "No, sir."

And then Mr. Welch continued:

> "Let us not assassinate this lad further, Senator. You have done enough. Have you no sense of decency?"
>
> *Senator McCarthy*: "I know this hurts you, Mr. Welch, but. . . ."
>
> *Mr. Welch*: "Mr. McCarthy, I will not discuss this with you further. You have sat within six feet of me and could have asked me about Fred Fisher. You have brought it out. If there is a God in heaven, it will do neither you nor your cause any good. I will not ask Mr. Cohen any more questions. You, Mr. Chairman, may if you will call the next witness."[11]

First there was an awkward silence. It took a few seconds for it to sink in that the mild-mannered Welch had struck the bully. Then the committee room rocked. For the first time in the memory of Washington observers, even the press photographers were so moved that they dropped their cameras and joined the thunder of applause.

Feeling the hostility from the spectators and reporters, but puzzled by it all, the mighty Joe McCarthy slouched in his chair and asked, "What did I do wrong?" At that moment, history records that McCarthy's grip began slipping, although polls still showed nearly one third of the nation supporting him. His political enemies were no longer petrified by fear and came out of hiding to begin the attack. Indeed, they eventually brought McCarthy's censure by the United States Senate.

Chapter 47

Looking Piously Toward Heaven While Raising Hell

> [Irish agitator Daniel O'Connor is] a systematic liar who has
> committed every crime that does not require courage.
> —English Prime Minister Benjamin Disraeli[1]

Rationalizing Predatory Conduct

When predators decide to do their own dirty work, they normally rationalize
their conduct in an effort to explain and thus soften the backlash that follows the
attack. Usually the predator stands up boldly and insists that the public has a right
to know. To illustrate, I include the outrageous full-page ad used during the 1950s
to persuade voters that an opponent was a Communist sympathizer (Figure 5-16).
The prey was a distinguished educator—one-time president of the University of
North Carolina and the incumbent United States Senator, Dr. Frank Graham. The
attack was made by a man thought to be the picture of conservative
respectability—one-time president of the American Bar Association, Willis
Smith.

When North Carolina Governor Scott Kerr characterized the accusation as
slanderous and inaccurate, Smith replied, "I have made an honest effort to be
absolutely factually accurate in every statement I have made about Dr. Graham's
record. . . . I thought the people of North Carolina ought to know the record. I
determined that Dr. Graham's record of leftist associations should not be hidden
by a commercially advertised halo, and should not be obscured by the smoke
screen of the cry of smear."[2]

Typically, the predator justifies an attack by claiming that it was necessary to
compete with the opposition's low tactics, saying the opposition asked for it. The
predator might say, "I didn't start it, but now that you have brought it up. . . ." In
the 1977 New York City campaign for mayor, Mario Cuomo, then New York's
Secretary of State, was beaten for the Democratic nomination in the primary by
Congressman Edward L. Koch. But Cuomo's name remained on the final election
ballot as the nominee of the New York Liberal party. At the time, Cuomo used an
undercurrent of gossip to indicate that Koch was a homosexual by saying, "It is
absolutely untrue that I brought up the issue of homosexuality." At the same time,
Cuomo attacked the Gay Activities Alliance, which endorsed Koch. He pointed to
a homosexual rights bill before the City Council, saying, "If elected, I will insist
on a public hearing to resolve the sensitive question of homosexual teachers."[3] In
answer to those who objected to his making this an issue, Cuomo cleverly

TRUE OR FALSE

Dr. Frank Graham made the following statement in Dunn, N. C., on March 24, 1950: "I have never been . . . a member or supporter of any organization known or SUS-PECTED by me of being controlled by Communists or Socialists."

☐ **TRUE** or ☐ **FALSE**

FACTS OF RECORD ON WHICH TO BASE YOUR ANSWER:
Frank Graham belonged to many Communist Front Organizations.
Let us examine one of them which he can hardly avoid "suspecting" was Communist or Socialist controlled.

The Southern Conference for Human Welfare (SCHW)

1938—The "Daily Worker" (Communist news and propaganda newspaper) announced the forming of the SCHW and gave its whole hearted approval.
—Earl Browder (Head of Communist Party) vigorously supported forming of SCHW.
1944—U. S. House of Representatives Committee on Un-American Activities branded the SCHW as a Communist Front Organization.
1945—"Raleigh Times" newspaper said the key man of the organization was a man who stands publicly accused of dealing with sinister Communist groups.
1947—"Raleigh Times" editorial said Dr. Graham has the burden of washing his hands of the SCHW which might well change its name to the "Conference for SOVIET Welfare" or submitting strong evidence that the group has no Communist leanings.
—"News and Observer" said "an official report" hung the "Red Tag" on the SCHW.

AMONG THE CHIEF OBJECTIVES OF DR. GRAHAM'S SOUTHERN CONFERENCE FOR HUMAN WELFARE WERE: ADOPTION OF BOTH STATE AND FEDERAL FEPC LAWS, ABOLITION OF SEGREGATION, SOCIALIZED MEDICINE, AND SOCIAL EQUALITY AND ASSOCIATION FOR WHITES AND NEGROES.

Dr. Graham was an organizer, first Chairman, and Honorary President of the SCHW.

HE NEVER RESIGNED FROM SCHW!
HE NEVER PUBLICLY DENOUNCED SCHW!

Is it possible that Doctor Graham did not "SUSPECT" that SCHW was being "CONTROLLED" by Communists or Socialists?
Did he ever report it to the Department of Justice?

The Record Speaks the Truth

The Only Political Party Willis Smith Has Ever Been Affiliated With
in Any Way is the Democratic Party.

SUPPORT WILLIS SMITH FOR U. S. SENATE!

Fig. 5-16. Newspaper ad, Committee to Elect Willis Smith U.S. Senator, North Carolina, 1950.

justified his position: "I will never submit to heavy-handed pressure by people professing the highest moral concerns, but in reality promoting another candidate they have endorsed."

Occasionally, the predator rationalizes that "politics is politics" or "all is fair in love, war, and politics." U.S. Senator Wendell Ford was referring to this when he said, "There's nothing to worry about in a good old Democrat primary fight. It's like when you wake up in the middle of the night to the sound of cats fighting. . . . When you wake up in the morning, there will be more cats . . . and there will be more Democrats, too." This justification is rare during the heat of the primary campaign, but is routinely used after the primary when the general election nominee attempts to unify the party.[4]

The "politics is politics" tack was also tried in 1950 when the Democratic voters of the state of Florida had to choose between two ex-friends, the incumbent United States Senator, Claude Pepper, and his former protege, Congressman George Smathers. After absorbing weeks of abusive attacks from his opponent and a hostile press, Pepper publicized embarrassing handwritten letters written to him by his hypocritical opponent (Figure 5-17). The problem was that Pepper waited too long to make his counterattack; he couldn't get the evidence distributed. Nearly all of the state's newspapers already strongly supported Smathers and refused to recognize the letters either as news or as paid advertising. Pepper had to circulate the evidence door to door. Even here his efforts were thwarted by the Smathers' campaign. Paid college students and other campaign workers followed those circulating the material and picked it up from the doorsteps.[5]

Hiding Behind a Third Party

It is not unusual for candidates to use third parties to attack political opponents. Nor is it unusual for them to lie and say that they have had no part in the dirty deed. Knowing this, voters have a tendency to discount political razzle dazzle and seek verification from independent sources. Sources can be the news media, something the target has said inadvertently, or something that has been said by another opponent in an earlier campaign.

A 1972 television commercial attacking "The McGovern Defense Plan" video shows a table full of toy soldiers, planes, and ships, and a voice says:

"The Democratic presidential nominee, U.S. Senator McGovern, would cut the Marines by one-third [portion of toy soldiers is swept off the screen], "the Air Force by one-third" [a portion of toy planes were swept off the screen], "the Navy fleet by one-half, and carriers from sixteen to six," [portion of toy ships were swept off the screen].

Then the commercial quotes an acknowledged leader of the opposition party, Senator Hubert Humphrey, as saying during the primaries that U.S. Senator George McGovern's proposal, "Isn't just cutting into the fat, it isn't just cutting into manpower, it is cutting into the very security of this country." The commercial closes with Republican nominee President Nixon aboard a naval ship

READ FROM
ᴛʜᴇ LETTERS
OF THE MAN
(In His Own Handwriting)

WHO WANTS
TO BE YOUR
UNITED STATES
SENATOR➡

Fig. 5-17. Campaign letter, Claude Pepper for U.S.
Senator, November 1950.

moving through the sea. The voice says, "President Nixon doesn't believe we should play games with our national security. He believes in a strong America to negotiate for peace from strength."[6]

Using Media News in a Smear Campaign

Occasionally, the public media will conduct a smear campaign of their own. In 1934, for instance, muckraking novelist Upton Sinclair won the Democratic nomination for Governor of California by promising to end poverty in California. He promised state help to the millions who had moved to California in the prosperous 1920s and were without jobs during the Depression. To pay for his program, he proposed an increase in taxes on the wealthy and special taxes on movie studios.

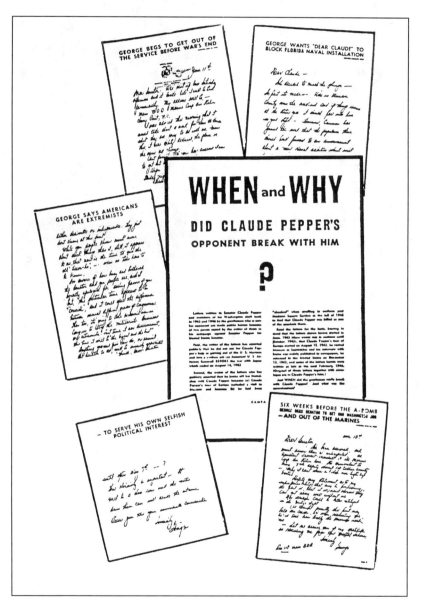

Fig. 5-17. Continued.

Nixon Anti-McGovern Spot

"The McGovern defense plan. He would cut Marines by one-third. The Air Force by one-third."

"He would cut interceptor planes by one-half . . . and carriers from sixteen to six."

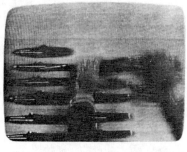

Fig. 5-18. Used by permission of L. Patrick Devlin, Curator, Television Political Advertising Collection, University of Rhode Island.

Alarmed studio executives united in backing the Republican candidate, Frank F. Merriam, and portrayed Sinclair as a supporter of the Bolshevik menace. MGM Studios, run by arch-conservative Louis B. Mayer, took the lead. A sham newsreel titled "The Inquiring Reporter" was produced and exhibited throughout the state. Although it pretended to represent California voters' attitudes toward Sinclair, neatly dressed persons that did not support Merriam were edited out of the film. Sinister men with beards and foreign accents were found to praise Sinclair; they were depicted as vagrants who were supposedly flocking to California to enjoy welfare payments that would increase if Sinclair won.

Shortly before the election, the *Los Angeles Times* ran what was purported to be a picture of hoboes riding the rails to California. Later it was learned that the so-called news photograph was actually a movie still taken from a Warner Brothers movie, "Wild Boys of the Roads." Commenting on the election, the *New York Times* observed, "Political leaders attribute Sinclair's defeat to the splendid work on the part of the screen moguls."[7]

When predators have the help of the news media, they end up with written material they can recirculate, including articles written by investigative reporters who have explored facets of an embarrassing incident or reprints of slanted feature articles, editorials, or cartoons. Voters should always be suspicious when the media break stories just before elections, and especially skeptical when a third party does the dirty work while the predator stands back and claims to have had nothing to do with the political carnage that follows.

Let me use two re-election campaigns conducted by former Washington state Governor and U.S. Senator Dan Evans to illustrate how candidates and their supporters seem to conspire to defeat candidates for public office and in the process often ruin political reputations. After serving his first term as governor of the state of Washington, Evans was running for reelection. His opponent was the state's attorney general, who, as things turned out, had a weakness for gambling at Nevada casinos. Evans had an early lead in the polls, which had begun to slip. Less than a month before the final election, the opponent had risen to 46 percent against the governor's 48.

The state's largest newspaper ran a front-page series in which it alleged that Evans' opponent had a $10,000 line of credit with a Las Vegas gambling casino. The newspaper followed up with a photocopy of one of his personal checks made out to the casino. The charges were picked up and used by the rest of the news media.[8] In the circus atmosphere that followed, voters didn't seem interested in the fact that no one explained how the information, especially the photocopy of the check, fell into the newspaper's hands. While the controversy raged, Evans was interviewed and contended that he had nothing to do with the attack.

A sequel occurred four years later when Evans sought a third term. Again, less than a month before the final election, the same newspaper broke another sensational story, alleging that Evans' opponent, former Governor Albert D. Rosellini, had made a telephone call to a vice detective in Honolulu on behalf of a man with an Italian name who was a reputed crime figure. The story dominated the headlines for several days. Bumper stickers appeared that said: "Washington state does not need a godfather."[9]

The truth, as it finally emerged, was that early in his law practice, Rosellini had represented truck farmers of Italian ancestry who happened to be the crime figure's parents. At their request he had made a call to the Honolulu Police Department asking why the application of the crime figure's younger brother for a nightclub license had been delayed. The local authorities found that his behavior was totally proper, and the application was later approved. The source of the information about the phone call turned out to be an unauthorized state attorney general's investigation, which was paid for in part by the Governor Evans reelection committee.

When Rosellini made an issue of the method by which the information was obtained, the person in charge of the investigation, the chief deputy state attorney general, admitted breaking the story and resigned. Shortly after Evans won the election, the chief deputy was quietly appointed legal counsel to the National Governors Conference by its chairman, Governor Evans.[10]

The Fringe

In addition to those who operate from the mainstream, there are those who speak from what has been described as the "lunatic fringe." Sometimes voters recognize their motivation and discount their messages, as in 1928, when a Catholic, Al Smith, was nominated for President. John Roach Staton, minister of the Calvary Baptist Church in New York City, said that Smith was "The nominee of the worst forces of hell."[11]

Early in his career, publisher William Randolph Hearst was a reform politician. He spoke through his flagship newspaper, *The New York Journal*. The *Journal* not only attacked politicians but it engaged in a running battle with fellow publishers and most of the other forces that controlled New York politics. It fearlessly vilified the one-time Democratic nominee for President, calling him "a political cockroach from under the sink." The *Journal* also commented that both Judge Alton Parker, New York Governor, and President Theodore Roosevelt were "One who has sold himself to the devil and will live up to the bargain." But these were just warmup pitches. The newspaper's big guns were reserved for New York City's regular Democratic organization, Tammany Hall, and its leader, Charles F. Murphy, who Hearst alleged had become wealthy dispensing patronage and public contracts.[12]

Hearst didn't depend on his newspaper alone. Of course there was no radio or television, but Hearst spoke through his reform-minded supporters, who marched, sang, attended rallies, and created what radio and television advertising people of today would call a "production spot." As they marched, they sang a parody designed to ridicule Murphy, which was put to the tune of a popular song of that day, "Everybody Works but Father." In part, the words of the parody went like this. "Everybody works but Murphy, he only rakes in the dough. . . ." then continues in typical Brooklynese, "Hoist, Hoist, he is not the woist; we are for the Hoist, last and foist."

This may have pleased Hearst at first, but as time went by he found that these vicious, unflattering comments continued to live on in the memory of the recipients. When Hearst sought higher office after being elected to Congress twice, he was defeated for both mayor of New York City and later state governor by the combined efforts of those he had castigated: New York's Republicans, opposition newspapers, New York City's Democratic organization, and Tammany Hall, which all either openly or covertly assisted his opponents.[13]

Chapter 48

Reducing the Target or . . .
The Fine Art of Being a Cautious Jellyfish

I have never been hurt by anything I didn't say.
 —President Calvin Coolidge[1]

The secret of managing is keeping the five guys who hate you away from the five guys who haven't made up their minds.
 —Casey Stengel, Baseball Manager[2]

I've heard so much about you, I would like to give you a chance to tell your side.[3]

What kills a skunk is the publicity it gives itself.
 —Abraham Lincoln[4]

Reducing the Size of the Target

The 1991 Louisiana governor's campaign was one of the most bitter in modern history. Everyone in the state was familiar with three-time governor Edwin Edwards, a Democrat who had been indicted but acquitted of bribery before his previous defeat, and his opponent, David Duke, who had been wizard of the state Ku Klux Klan and a founder of the National Association for the Advancement of White People, and who had been accused of being a Nazi sympathizer.[5] Duke's previous affiliations enraged both mainline Republicans and Democrats. In fact, George Bush, the Republican president of the U.S., said that if he could vote in Louisiana he would vote for the Democratic ex-governor. During the closing days of the campaign, at a game played by the New Orleans Saints football team in the New Orleans Superdome a huge banner was displayed that read "Edward Ain't No Saint. But He Ain't No Nazi Either."

When we explore profound, brilliant, and penetrating defenses, explanations, and excuses used by politicians under enemy fire, we find a practical drawback. Most of those making brilliant replies are nevertheless defeated—because the answer further publicizes the attack. With this in mind, smart politicians consciously say nothing, reducing the size of the target, and follow President Calvin Coolidge's advice to become "cautious jellyfish."

U.S. Senator Everett Dirksen of Illinois was the master of this technique, earning himself the nickname of the "Wizard of Ooze." When this cautious jellyfish first ran for Congress, his constituency was split on the repeal of the 18th Amendment (prohibition). During most of the campaign he carefully avoided the subject. Just about the time it looked like he was going to get away with it, a partisan demanded that he take a position at a public meeting. Then Dirksen answered:

> Only last night while my wife was finishing up a needlepoint of the American flag, we had a long talk on this very subject. Here is what I said with no hesitation or qualification to her, and I say to you. "Some of my friends are for prohibition, some of my friends are for repeal. I say, let the chips fall where they may . . . I stand by my friends."[6]

While today's voter is too sophisticated for such an obvious cop-out, other techniques can be employed when a constituency is split and the cautious jellyfish wants to avoid controversy. During prohibition, Al Smith was the Democratic nominee for president, and because Smith was a Catholic and in favor of loosening up prohibition and permitting limited legal consumption of beer, the Democratic South was leaning toward Hoover. Democrats supporting Al Smith then used a prominent dry Protestant, United States Senator Carter Glass of Virginia, to counterattack. Glass offered $1,000 "if anyone would come up with a single categorical 'dry' statement that Hoover ever made. . . ." Amid the controversy, the Republican nominee, and winner, Herbert Hoover, played the part of a cautious jellyfish and simply ignored the issue.[7]

Exaggeration, Fantasy, Campaign Rhetoric, and News

Cautious candidates don't place themselves in a position to be the target of a counterattack. They use their skill to reduce the size of the target. Frequently, candidates organize so-called independent committees to support their candidacy, then invisibly control and coordinate the activities of these committees. Control starts by carefully selecting committee names. As U.S. Senator John Chaffee once advised his fellow Republicans, "I think having Hunters for Jones is fine, but you want to be careful because sometimes hunters are associated with special interests. And Riflemen for Jones connoted some rather special interests which you may want to avoid."[8]

A cautious candidate will retain veto power over what these so-called independent committees say on his or her behalf. One of the best methods of insurance is to allow nothing to be mailed until after it is okayed by the candidate or the campaign manager, and by having campaign headquarters type and reproduce all statements. Further, when preparing a political campaign piece, the candidate or staff should assume that the opposition is critically examining the candidate's speeches, ads, and brochures.

After serving on the Seattle City Council, Wayne Larkin gave up his seat to run for mayor. When a council position opened up following his defeat, Larkin staged a comeback. As part of his effort, he issued radio reports that claimed to be a daily commentary on the progress of the campaign. His opponent, Norm Rice, who had been a television commentator, went to the radio station and found that the daily reports had all been prerecorded on a single day. Rice was able to make the news when he charged that a particular commentary was made eleven days before it was aired, saying, "That's the kind of politics Seattle voters have continually rejected as unworthy of their elected officials."[9]

Some candidates attempt to appeal to special interests to sidestep attacks by the opposition. Public statements designed to appeal to special interests should not only avoid reckless rhetoric but include a paragraph emphasizing civic pride, patriotism, and citizen responsibility.

A candidate should also carefully avoid situations that lead to quibbling and bickering over nonessentials that give the predator an excuse to attack. Let me illustrate with a campaign initiative to ban nonreturnable bottles. In the voter's pamphlet, supporters used statements by officials of leading soft drink firms taken out of context. Thereafter, the opposition, including these soft drink manufacturers, avoided the basic issue—is it or is it not wise to enact a law that bans nonreturnable bottles? Instead, they cleverly made an issue of the use of the soft drink executives' statements, claiming th executives were misquoted.

Recovering the Candidate's Fumbles

In the highly charged campaign atmosphere, almost every candidate fumbles sometime during a campaign. When this happens, the cautious "jellyfish" candidate doesn't enlarge the issue, which gives the opposition a chance to keep it alive. During an interview with the Associated Press in the 1976 presidential campaign, Jimmy Carter suggested that, if elected, he would try to shift the tax burden, saying that taxes should be boosted on Americans earning more than the "mean or median level." Gerald Ford leaped into action, calling Carter's statement "an incredible position" and arguing that this meant higher taxes for most voters who earned more than $14,000 a year. Carter charged his opponent with distortion, claiming that he had made it clear that he had not yet worked out his tax program.[10] Usually, however, the best course of action when recovering from a fumble is to say nothing. (For more on this, see the following section, Answering When the Predator Strikes.)

Blessed Are the Self-Righteous

In every campaign, there are some donors from whom a wise candidate should not accept campaign contributions, not because they are evil, but because acceptance would give a predator an excuse to attack. For example, in a period of rising gas and oil prices, a candidate might refuse campaign contributions from the executives or political action committees representing Atlantic Richfield of California, Shell Oil of Houston, or Union Oil of California. Or he or she might

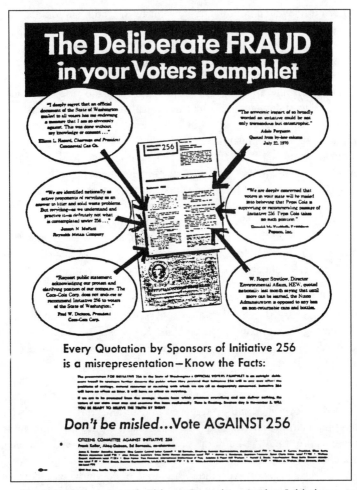

Fig. 5-19. Newspaper ad, Citizens Committee Against Initiative
256, *Tacoma News Tribune,* October 20, 1970.

be unwilling to take money from the Dallas Energy Political Action Committee
because this committee supports deregulation and higher natural gas prices.

However, most candidates take the money. If the source of the candidates'
campaign funding is attacked, they look pious and proclaim that, as far as they are
aware, the contributors expect absolutely nothing but good government for their
money. Then, playing the cautious jellyfish, they call a press conference
explaining that, no matter how carefully the finance chairman watches, there will
be inadvertent mistakes. Then they admit that the contribution was accepted,

explain that, although they respect the contributor, they disagree with their objectives or the way they do business, and then return the money.

President Teddy Roosevelt loved to crusade against John D. Rockefeller and Standard Oil, whom he assailed as the worst of the one-eyed monsters. Yet before it was illegal for a federal candidate to accept corporate gifts, Roosevelt took substantial contributions from several big businesses, including $150,000 from banker J. P. Morgan and Company, $100,000 from Frick Steel interests, and $148,000 from New York Life Insurance Company.

But you can imagine Roosevelt's embarrassment when, in his 1904 campaign, he learned shortly before election that his finance committee had accepted a $100,000 contribution from Standard Oil. In typical Teddy Roosevelt style, he took immediate action by directing a self-righteous letter to his campaign treasurer, which, of course, he released to the press. In it he stated, "I have just been informed that the Standard Oil people have contributed $100,000 to our campaign fund. This may be entirely untrue, but if true, I will ask that you direct that money be returned to them forthwith." As Roosevelt was dictating, the Secretary of State, Elihu Foot, walked into the room and commented, "Why, Mr. President, you can't send that letter. We not only got the money, but we spent it and there is nothing left in the campaign treasury to pay it back," to which Roosevelt replied, "Well, the letter will look well on the record anyway."[11]

Frequently a cautious jellyfish can ward off an attack by documenting some dirt on the opposition and letting news of its contents be discretely communicated to the opposition, who then keeps the campaign clean because of fear of retaliation. Ohio Governor James Cox was criticized by Democratic insiders when he ran for president in 1920 for refusing to concentrate on the "moral issues." In their opinion Cox should have made an issue of the fact that the previous Republican President Warren Harding had both a wife he lived with and a long-time mistress. Historians speculated that Cox refused because he was afraid the Republicans would exploit the details of his own divorce.[12]

Preparing for the Expected

Finally, a cautious candidate should prepare in advance to cover some of the most obvious places vulnerable to attack. Previously made inflammatory statements need to be refuted. Just how the cautious jellyfish squares explanations with the facts or how he or she manages to satisfy his conscience is a highly personal decision, but the techniques used require knowing exactly what was said on previous occasions.

Barry Goldwater is an example of someone who kept track of what he said on previous occasions. When he was in the U.S. Senate, he was in the minority from a small state, and being a conservative without heavy responsibility, he felt free to test public reaction to mildly radical ideas. He called the Tennessee Valley

Authority a "socialistic octopus with a death-like grip on the area it served," and he advocated giving control of atomic weapons to field commanders in the Vietnam War. Most of these trial balloons went nowhere. However, when Goldwater ran for president, one of his first acts was to catalog his past statements, so that in seconds his staff could find a microfilm of anything he had ever said on any topic[13] when it was necessary to either deny, rationalize, or reinforce his current position.

Of course this is only the first step. In the give and take of most major campaigns there will be explanations, redefinitions, and denials, which is why the National Council of Teachers of English has instituted the annual Doublespeak award for inaccurate assertions made during a political campaign. In 1980, President Ronald Reagan was named the winner of the award. William Lutz of Rutgers University, who chaired the Committee on Public Doublespeak, noted eighteen untrue or inaccurate public statements by Mr. Reagan. He also cited a *New York Times* article as saying Reagan's "speeches are peppered with omissions, exaggerations, and reinterpretations of his experience both as Governor of California and as a candidate. It should not be surprising, however, that in the same year they awarded his opponent, President Carter, second place."[14]

Answering When the Predator Strikes

The cautious jellyfish knows there is risk in answering a personal attack. Chances are the answer itself will create controversy and further expose an attack that has not been widely publicized.

The classic example of such a backfire occurred shortly after the turn of the century when U.S. Senator Mark Hanna of Ohio served as both U.S. Senator and a spokesman for big business. Hanna was lampooned regularly by cartoonist Homer Davenport, who always showed him wearing a suit covered with dollar signs because Hanna collected and distributed big business money to "deserving" Republican candidates. These attacks were made by the Hearst Press, who at that time favored Democrats.

On the stump, Hanna attempted to counteract Hearst by offering $100 to anyone who could find a single dollar mark on his suit. One day an anonymous heckler from way back in the audience made national news with a comment that got a place in political history books when he shouted, "Of course we can see 'em, they're branded on yer hide."[15]

Most answers to attacks are dangerous because they draw attention to the original attack. However, before assuming that silence is the only possible response, the candidate should look at one of the following options: (a) ignore the substance of attack, then avoid a direct answer, or (b) point out the predator's hostility and ask the voters to consider the source.

Usually there is a distinction between a question from an inquiring reporter and an inquiry from a live audience. The audience is more likely to ask an embarrassing question than to make a personal attack. Such questions are usually made on the spur of the moment and have no follow-up. If politicians feel a need to respond to such questions, they should keep a cool head. The audience usually appreciates give and take and imaginative answers.

The Rehearsed "Off-the-Cuff" Reply

In the late 1960s a white Republican Mayor, Lawrence F. Kramer, of Patterson, New Jersey, found it necessary to face some black, mostly Democratic, constituents. As he stood on the back of a truck and advocated changes he knew they wanted and deserved, a black in the audience asked, "Why should I vote for a candidate who runs in the party that nominated Barry Goldwater?" Republican Mayor Kramer imaginatively replied, "It is just as silly for you to vote for me because that party also nominated Abraham Lincoln."[16]

Sometimes a candidate's answer can ignore charges with a flip comment that says nothing. In August 1966, California's state Democratic Chairman, Robert L. Coate, called a news conference in Los Angeles where he accused gubernatorial candidate Ronald Reagan of being an extremist. Coate claimed that Reagan had collaborated with the top leaders of the super-secret John Birch Society. As proof of Reagan's endorsement of the society's projects, Coate used public documents that showed Reagan had obtained substantial contributions from conservatives, men whom Coate called the "rightist brain trust," the financial mainstays of the right wing.

Reagan assumed his voting constituency was more interested in a whole range of other issues than in his right-wing friends, so he ignored Coate's evidence, replying, "It's absolutely not true that I am in the power or influence of extremist groups, but it never occurred to me to give a saliva test to the people who supported me."[17]

U.S. Senator Robert Dole used TV to carry out a variation of this technique. In one of his commercials, the TV screen featured an announcer detailing Dole's overstated version of charges his opponent, Congressman Rob Roy, was making against him, while in the background a hand was defacing one of Dole's campaign posters. Then, taking advantage of the natural adverse reaction of the audience, the background announcer ridiculed the attacks and praised Dole.

Asking Voters to Consider the Source

When an attack is made by a political opponent, it is easy to ask the voter to consider the source. New Hampshire's largest daily newspaper and its late publisher, William Loeb, had a reputation for nasty criticism. These are excerpts from his paper, the Manchester, New Hampshire, *Daily Union Leader*:

Fig. 5-20. Don Grant, "Bob Dole a Big Ad User in 13 Election Victories," *Advertising Age*, October 11, 1976, p. 68.

Dwight D. Eisenhower, President of the United States: "Dopey Dwight," "That stinking hypocrite," "Playboy President," "Fake Republican," "As much backbone and substance as a ribbon of toothpaste," "Fatuous—fat-headed," "A slick general on the political make."

Ralph Flanders, U.S. Senator from Vermont: "All the sap isn't in the trees," "Fatuous Flanders."

Gerald R. Ford, President of the United States: "Jerry the Jerk."

Lyndon B. Johnson, President of the United States: "Snake Oil Lyndon."

John F. Kennedy, President of the United States: "Calamity Jack," "No. 1 Liar in the U.S.A."

Rev. Dr. Martin Luther King, Jr., Civil rights leader: "A pious, pompous fraud."

Richard M. Nixon, President of the United States: "Keyhole Dick," "Tricky Dicky," "The Great Devaluator."[18]

Of course, a candidate can always say "consider the source" and then counterattack, but a cautious candidate should avoid the publicity that flows from the continuing controversy that may result.

The candidate may want to use the "consider the source" argument without identifying the accusers. Instead, the candidate may refer to "the opposition," "the opposition machine," "the dissidents," "a group of people," or "the alter ego" of his opponent, etc., while still emphasizing the critic's hostility and claiming that the attack is motivated by a desire to get even.

Chapter 49

Change-of-Pace Ridicule

> The gentleman is indebted to his memory for his jests and to his imagination for his facts.
> —Richard Brinsley Sheridan, speaking of the Earl of Dundas[1]

Using Ridicule to Highlight the Counterattack

The ridiculing counterattack must come after some attack, rumor, or innuendo has been impressed on the voters. Then the voters are interested in how the prey will answer to the charges. In 1944, months before President Franklin D. Roosevelt was to run for a fourth term, some Republican congressmen spread the rumor that on his way home from Alaska the president discovered that his Scottie dog, Fala, had been left behind and that at a tremendous cost in public funds Roosevelt sent a United States naval vessel back to retrieve his dog. The story was repeated and became the subject of editorial comment in a number of anti-administration newspapers.

Roosevelt, spotting this as a potential political jewel, forbade any administration source from answering, saying he wanted to save this for himself. Shortly before the November general election, Roosevelt began a speech to a group of labor leaders at the Statler Hotel in Washington, DC, by making fun of his opponent's—Thomas E. Dewey—charge, that he was a "tired old man" saying, "There are millions of Americans who are more than eleven years older than when we started in to clear up the mess that was dumped in our laps in 1933." Then the president accused the Republicans of attacking labor only to change their tune just before election day every four years when votes are at stake.

Conscious of the fact that his speech was delivered in the midst of World War II, he accused his opponents of switching labels and of no longer being against preparations for defense that he began as far back as 1939. Then he said they were attempting to blame the Democrats for the "Republican depression" of 1933. As he concluded his speech he said:

> These Republican leaders have not been content with attacks on me, or my wife, or on my sons. No, not content with that, they now include my little dog, Fala. Well, of course, I don't resent attacks, and my family doesn't resent attacks, but Fala does resent them. You know, Fala is Scotch, and being a Scottie, as soon as he learned that the Republican fiction writers in Congress had concocted a story that I left him behind on the Aleutian Islands and had sent a destroyer back to find him—at a cost to the taxpayers of two or three, or eight or twenty million dollars—his Scotch soul was furious. He has not been the same dog since."

Continuing the serious tone, which he maintained despite the laughter and applause of his audience, he said:

> I am accustomed to hearing malicious falsehoods about myself—such as that old, worm-eaten chestnut that I have represented myself as indispensable. But I think I have a right to resent, to object to libelous statements about my dog.

Aware of the impact the "Fala" speech had made on the public, the Democrats made a radio spot of just that part of the President's speech, introduced with the tune, "They Gotta Quit Kickin' My Dawg Aroun'," and spent substantial

Fig. 5-21. Newspaper ad, Faulk for State Senate Committee, *Tacoma News Tribune*, October 27, 1970.

Democratic funds playing the spot on the radio. Then, instead of ignoring the "Fala" speech, Roosevelt's opponent, Governor Dewey, made the mistake of changing his prepared speech the next day and attacking the president for being humorous about his dog while our boys were dying. This prompted Paul Porter, who was managing the Democratic campaign, to write a memorandum that ended, "We have a new slogan in headquarters now—the race is between Roosevelt's dog and Dewey's goat."[2]

Keeping a Cool Head: Answering with Dignity and Style

Candidates often see failure to answer an opponent's charges as an admission that the charges against them are true. They fret that failure to answer will have an adverse effect on their supporters and leave a cloud of allegations hanging over the campaign. They feel overcome by what one-time U.S. Senator Margaret Chase Smith described as the "Four Horsemen": Fear, ignorance, bigotry, and smear. But there are viable ways the candidate can answer allegations. Three options are to: disagree and take exception, become a martyr, projecting righteous indignation, or cry smear.[3]

Most of those under attack insist on answering point by point, and different techniques are available. Let's consider a typical attack and answer. The following two figures depict print ads from an era when the political tide was running strongly against the far right. The first volleys were fired on two occasions by a predator who held the chairmanship of the local Democratic Party organization. As you can see (Figure 5-22), this blistering attack was followed by a disagreement and response by the Republican incumbent (Figure 5-23), who used righteous indignation with the cry of smear before counterattacking.

When Mayor Tom Bradley was in his second campaign for Mayor of Los Angeles, this black policeman and city councilman didn't dwell on the fact that most observers attributed his previous defeat to a racist campaign mounted by a predator incumbent, Sam Yorty. Instead he spurned sympathy and chose dignity. Facing the camera, Bradley said, "The last time I ran for Mayor, I lost, probably because a lot of people weren't sure of what I stood for. Maybe you were one of them. Maybe you wondered whether I'd treat all people fairly, or whether I'd only listen to the problems of the blacks. Frankly, I couldn't win this election with only one block of voters. . . ." The commercial then featured a voice saying, "He'll work as hard for his paycheck as you do for yours."[4]

When one-time State Representative Mary Ellen McCaffree was stung by political attack, her print piece used different techniques. She reprinted the predatory mail-out and used written interlineations to answer the accusations point to point. It ended on a positive note, with reprints of favorable newspaper editorial comments.

Fig. 5-22. Newspaper ad, 34th District Democratic Precinct Organization, *West Seattle Herald*, October 1964.

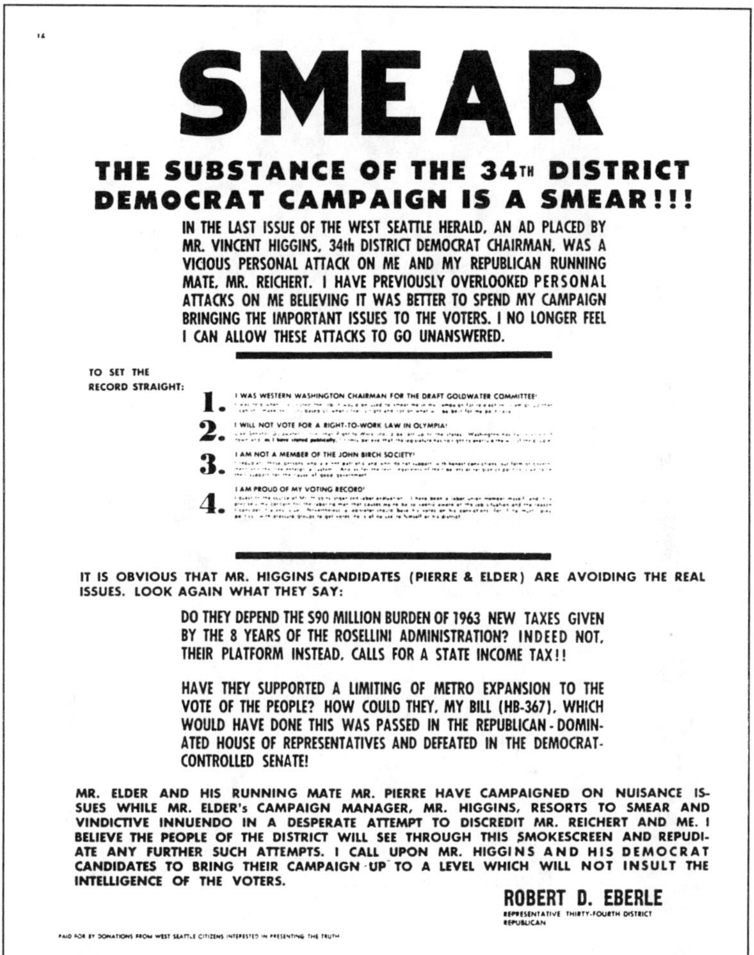

SMEAR

THE SUBSTANCE OF THE 34TH DISTRICT DEMOCRAT CAMPAIGN IS A SMEAR!!!

IN THE LAST ISSUE OF THE WEST SEATTLE HERALD, AN AD PLACED BY MR. VINCENT HIGGINS, 34th DISTRICT DEMOCRAT CHAIRMAN, WAS A VICIOUS PERSONAL ATTACK ON ME AND MY REPUBLICAN RUNNING MATE, MR. REICHERT. I HAVE PREVIOUSLY OVERLOOKED PERSONAL ATTACKS ON ME BELIEVING IT WAS BETTER TO SPEND MY CAMPAIGN BRINGING THE IMPORTANT ISSUES TO THE VOTERS. I NO LONGER FEEL I CAN ALLOW THESE ATTACKS TO GO UNANSWERED.

TO SET THE RECORD STRAIGHT:

1. I WAS WESTERN WASHINGTON CHAIRMAN FOR THE DRAFT GOLDWATER COMMITTEE!

2. I WILL NOT VOTE FOR A RIGHT-TO-WORK LAW IN OLYMPIA!

3. I AM NOT A MEMBER OF THE JOHN BIRCH SOCIETY!

4. I AM PROUD OF MY VOTING RECORD!

IT IS OBVIOUS THAT MR. HIGGINS CANDIDATES (PIERRE & ELDER) ARE AVOIDING THE REAL ISSUES. LOOK AGAIN WHAT THEY SAY:

DO THEY DEPEND THE $90 MILLION BURDEN OF 1963 NEW TAXES GIVEN BY THE 8 YEARS OF THE ROSELLINI ADMINISTRATION? INDEED NOT. THEIR PLATFORM INSTEAD, CALLS FOR A STATE INCOME TAX!!

HAVE THEY SUPPORTED A LIMITING OF METRO EXPANSION TO THE VOTE OF THE PEOPLE? HOW COULD THEY, MY BILL (HB-367), WHICH WOULD HAVE DONE THIS WAS PASSED IN THE REPUBLICAN - DOMIN-ATED HOUSE OF REPRESENTATIVES AND DEFEATED IN THE DEMOCRAT-CONTROLLED SENATE!

MR. ELDER AND HIS RUNNING MATE MR. PIERRE HAVE CAMPAIGNED ON NUISANCE IS-SUES WHILE MR. ELDER's CAMPAIGN MANAGER, MR. HIGGINS, RESORTS TO SMEAR AND VINDICTIVE INNUENDO IN A DESPERATE ATTEMPT TO DISCREDIT MR. REICHERT AND ME. I BELIEVE THE PEOPLE OF THE DISTRICT WILL SEE THROUGH THIS SMOKESCREEN AND REPUDI-ATE ANY FURTHER SUCH ATTEMPTS. I CALL UPON MR. HIGGINS AND HIS DEMOCRAT CANDIDATES TO BRING THEIR CAMPAIGN UP TO A LEVEL WHICH WILL NOT INSULT THE INTELLIGENCE OF THE VOTERS.

ROBERT D. EBERLE
REPRESENTATIVE THIRTY-FOURTH DISTRICT
REPUBLICAN

PAID FOR BY DONATIONS FROM WEST SEATTLE CITIZENS INTERESTED IN PRESENTING THE TRUTH

Fig. 5-23. Newspaper ad, West Seattle Citizens Interested in Presenting the Truth, *West Seattle Herald*, October 1964.

The Political Prey as Martyr

Projecting righteous indignation requires fancy political footwork, asking for sympathy while maintaining dignity. Let's look at a few concrete examples. The most powerful congressmen are middle-aged or older and benefit from the legislative seniority system, so younger challengers often attack the seniority system by belittling the aging leaders who benefit from it. When the one-time chairman of the U.S. House Appropriations Committee, Clarence Cannon, was confronted with an attack on the seniority system, and on himself in particular, he quoted St. Peter, "Likewise, ye younger, submit yourselves unto the elder." He also answered:

> Between the ages of 70 and 83, Commodore Vanderbilt added $10 million to his fortune. . . . Oliver Wendell Holmes at 79 wrote his *Over the Teacups* and Tennyson, at 83, wrote "Crossing the Bar.' . . . the [critics] badger men grown old in honored service, men who have made the supreme contributions to the nation in the most critical period in human history with the taunt: 'Yeah, you're getting old!' Closing with the philosophy of the aboriginal; the culture and finesse and good taste of the jungle. . . . Let them serve for a time as seamen before the mast before assaying to push the admiral off the quarterdeck."[5]

Fig. 5-24. Mailer, Mary Ellen McCaffree for Washington State Senate Committee, November 1970.

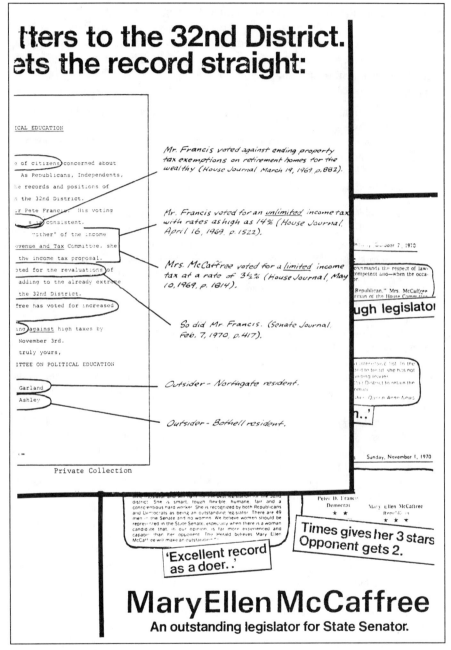

tters to the 32nd District.
ets the record straight:

ICAL EDUCATION

e of citizens) concerned about

As Republicans, Independents,

he records and positions of

n the 32nd District.

r Pete Francis. His voting

s is consistent.

"other" of the income

evenue and Tax Committee, she

the income tax proposal.

oted for the revaluations of

adding to the already extreme

the 32nd District.

free has voted for increased

ing against high taxes by

November 3rd.

truly yours,

ITTEE ON POLITICAL EDUCATION

Garland
Ashley

Mr. Francis voted against ending property tax exemptions on retirement homes for the wealthy (House Journal March 19, 1969, p.882).

Mr. Francis voted for an underlined income tax with rates as high as 14% (House Journal, April 16, 1969, p.1522).

Mrs. McCaffree voted for a limited income tax at a rate of 3½% (House Journal, May 10, 1969, p.1814).

So did Mr. Francis. (Senate Journal, Feb. 7, 1970, p.417).

Outsider – Northgate resident.

Outsider – Bothell resident.

Private Collection

commands the respect of law-
competent and—when the occa-
r.

Republican," Mrs. McCaffree
rman of the House Committee

ugh legislator

district to return the

Queen Anne News

n..'

Sunday, November 1, 1970

district. She is smart, tough flexible, humane, fair and a
conscientious hard worker. She is recognized by both Republicans
and Democrats as being an outstanding legislator. There are 49
men in the Senate and no women. We believe women should be
represented in the State Senate, especially when there is a woman
candidate that, in our opinion is far more experienced and
capable than her opponent. This Herald believes Mary Ellen
McCaffree will make an outstanding...

Peter D. Francis
Democrat
★ ★

Mary Ellen McCaffree
Republican
★ ★ ★

Times gives her 3 stars
Opponent gets 2.

'Excellent record
as a doer..'

MaryEllenMcCaffree
An outstanding legislator for State Senator.

Fig. 5-24. Continued.

There is another way to project a martyr image. The candidate can make conscience and strength of character the issue rather than the original charge. Following is a classic letter to the editor. It is an old-fashioned martyr appeal, published in 1937. It is too long for most letters to the editor, but then its author was the governor of the state of North Carolina:

Dear Saunders,

This is a strange picture you paint of me—as a man indifferent to the opinions of his fellows.

I know of no one who craves agreement with his fellow more than I do—nor do I know one who more highly esteems their applause and goodwill; no one is more tempted than I to cater to popularity; no one more averse to going against the tide of public opinion. It is the hard way, and like all men, I would have for myself the easy way.

But there are other considerations: I remember one Pontius Pilate. He pleased his crowd—and let them slay their best friend. He went the easy way. So he held the governorship. I do not admire him, but he was a hard politician.

I remember one Peter—a fisherman, who declared to the people demanding that we agree—we ought to please God rather than men. He went the hard way. They tell me he lost his life on a cross, but I admire him.

I remember Christopher Columbus, the majority of whose sailors demanded that he turn back, but he nevertheless pressed on. He went the hard way, but he was most unpopular with his crew. But he discovered America. His sailors discovered that they were cowards.

I remember Moses, who chose to dwell in the tents of the wandering tribes of Israel rather than the palaces of the Pharoahs. He went the hard way. He died in the wilderness, but God gave him a mountaintop to die on; and he is still on the mountain!

I remember Him (Christ) who said to the Pharisees—"Your fathers stoned the prophets and you build monument to them!" He knew the hard way. He died on the instrument of the slave's torture, but all men looked to him on that Cross. Unlike Pilate, they went against the tide of public opinion.

You say I rely on the past. It was Patrick Henry who said that he had no light to guide him save the light of the past. If you know of any other, tell me what it is and where to find it. That and the inner light which we are told God kindles within one's soul—these only are known to me, but if there is yet another, tell me the way to find it, for I know I need every possible light.

Do not think that I do not know the easy way. Do not think that I could not choose the easy way. Do not think that I do not see around me men who have successfully made a business of holding office, and who all their lives have held office by finding the course that pays the best—in votes—and "Going for it baldheaded." They do not have to contend. All they have to do is to deceive, but I have deliberately chosen not to go that way. I am determined to do the best I can for the people who have trusted me, whether it pleases them at the time or not. I am thinking of their children no less than of them. I may be wrong, but if I do my duty as I see it, I shall at any rate have the satisfaction of a good conscience.

We all admire Henry Clay for saying that he would rather be right than President. Why do we so often tell public men that it is better to be popular than right? Shall we reverse the story and say that Henry Clay was a fool?

It may pay to pander to the multitude, but is it fair to them? Is it right? Am I here to serve myself or the people? And if here to serve the people, shall I seek to do the popular thing and get the popular applause and hold on to my office, or shall I seek to do the right? You cannot answer these questions for me. I have answered them within my soul! I shall do my duty—not for my own ease or interest, but for the people who have trusted me and honored me.

Very truly yours, Josiah W. Bailey[6]

The Prey Cries Foul

As an alternate, the candidate can both disagree and take exception to the martyr techniques. Typically those using this approach let the predator take his shots, then they counterpunch by concluding that the predator is striking below the belt.

In 1974, United States Senator Robert Dole of Kansas faced a hard re-election campaign. As the campaign began, opinion polls showed Dole was far ahead of his Democratic opponent, Congressman Dr. Bill Roy. Roy brought out his heavy artillery, accusing Senator Dole, who was an ex-Chairman of the Republican party, of being an apologist for the Nixon administration during the Watergate scandal. Roy claimed Dole was against Social Security and in favor of cutting the budget and the school lunch program.

By September, the attack had succeeded. The polls showed that Dr. Roy had overtaken Dole, and by mid-October he had a substantial lead. It was then that Dole came up with a television commercial designed to make an issue of the predator's dirty campaign and spread the impression that Roy was at best stretching the truth, and at worst lying. Dole's television commercial showed a campaign poster of a handsome, smiling Bob Dole (Figure 5-25). Then several gobs of mud hit the poster as the narrator declared, "Bill Roy says that Senator Bob Dole is against the farmer . . . against cutting the federal budget . . . against the school lunch program." When Dole's face was covered, each accusation was answered and the action was reversed as little by little the mud came off the poster. The commercial ended with the narrator observing, "All of which makes Bob Dole look pretty good . . . and Bill Roy look like just another mudslinger."[7]

Another comparatively safe technique was used more than thirty years ago in Miami, Florida, by an incumbent city commissioner, Leslie Quigg. The text of his newspaper ad (Figure 5-26) was nothing but affirmative campaign material, yet it ridiculed and answered his opponent's charges without repeating them.

Fig. 5-25. "Mudslinger Television Spot for Senator Dole," *Advertising Age*, October 11, 1976, p. 68.

If the candidate is not afraid of publicizing the original charges, ridicule might be used to mimic and poke fun at the original attack. The forces supporting President William Howard Taft used this technique during their party's 1912 Chicago Convention, when they circulated this spurious flyer making fun of opponent ex-President Teddy Roosevelt.

> At 3 o'clock on
> Saturday afternoon
> Theodore Roosevelt
> will walk on the
> waters of Lake Michigan.[8]

Taft also used this parody of a Teddy Roosevelt campaign speech: "The bestial nature of the indecent horde of pirates, second story men, porch climbers, gunmen, and short card dealers who oppose me is now perfectly manifest."[9]

Sometimes the prey can brush an attack aside by accusing the predator of being guilty of the same sin. This is what Ronald Reagan did when he was governor of California. In one reelection campaign Reagan's Democratic opponent was the Speaker of the Assembly, Jesse Unruh. In a previous campaign, Unruh had been widely quoted as saying, "Money is the mother's milk of politics." When Unruh accused the incumbent of accepting money from special interests and complained that he didn't have the money to compete with the governor's lavish advertising budget, Reagan used Unruh's words spoken earlier, replying, "For someone who says, 'Money is the mother's milk of politics', you've never seen a baby who has so much squawk about where the milk comes from."[10]

Making the Attacker a Political Buffoon

In a political campaign, strategy depends on what is popular or unpopular at the moment and on pre-existing public attitudes and prejudices. It also is

Fig. 5-26. Newspaper ad, Re-elect H. Leslie Quigg, Commissioner,
Miami Herald, November 1, 1950, p. 22A.

influenced by opportunities. On rare occasions an attack is so ridiculous the prey can portray the attacker as a political buffoon.

In 1916, Sidney J. Catts became governor of Florida. He owed his success to his loud public opposition to the Catholic church and the Pope, who he claimed "planned to lead the Catholics to political power in the United States." After serving one term, he was prevented by state law from succeeding himself. After waiting out the one term in 1924, Catts again ran for governor and attacked a different opponent, John W. Martin, "for being so in league with the Pope." Tongue in cheek, Martin told the assembled throngs, "My friends, you gave your support once to Catts on his promise to run the Pope out of business. Did he accomplish this promise? No. While he was governor, mind you, and supposed to be looking after this promise he made you, one Pope died and he let them appoint another without raising a finger to stop it."[11]

Responding to Political Paper Tigers: Looking Through the Smoke Screen

Although there are exceptions, frequently political attacks are made by predator candidates who are not willing to stand toe to toe and slug it out. They use an individual or a front organization to plant derogatory news stories. These committees are usually hastily organized, with prominent spokesmen who call news conferences and perform what some newspapermen call a "Charley Michaelson." This is a formula named for the publicity director of the Democratic National Committee during the 1930s. Michaelson wrote political attacks on the opposition, then fed them to Democratic Senators and Congressmen, who made them front-page news.

The same technique is used with advertising. The predator attempts to preserve his or her good image, while encouraging and often conspiring with a "paper tiger" who does the dirty work. There are even organizations of politicians who attempt to ruin political reputations without encouragement from opposition candidates. For example, attacks can be motivated by political extremists of the right or left wings. Figure 5-27 depicts the work of two organizations that make a business of political assassinations. They are the right-wing National Conservative Political Action Committee (NCPAC) and the liberal-leaning Progressive Political Action Committee (PROPAC). These organizations function independently of political parties or candidates and collect millions of dollars by mail to support smear campaigns.

In most cases though, the attack is part of a conspiracy that includes the opposition candidate. One way to respond to an attack by a third party is to connect the attacker with the opposition predator candidate. Vice President Alben Barkley did it with this story. He told of a man who resided in a small town in western Kentucky who bought a bill of goods from a wholesale merchant in Paducah. Six months after purchase, he had not paid, and the concerned seller

Fig. 5-27. Newspaper ad, Committee to Replace Jim Jones, *Baltimore Sun*, July 14, 1982, p. 4; Newspaper ad, Progressive Political Action Committee, Arlington, Virginia, January 1982.

wrote letters to the station agent checking to be sure the goods had arrived, to the president of the local bank inquiring about the purchaser's credit, and to the mayor of the small town, asking him for the name of a good lawyer in case he had to bring a lawsuit.

In a few days, he got this reply:

Dear Sir:

    As station agent, I am glad to advise you that the goods were delivered. As president of our local bank, I have the honor to inform you that my credit is good. As mayor of our town, I am compelled to say that I am the only lawyer here; and if it were not for the fact that I am pastor of the local church, I would tell you to go to hell."[12]

Before the target answers charges by looking past the paper tiger and involving the opponent, they should keep the future in mind. This is especially true when a political attack is leveled by a newspaper or a radio or television station. Initially, the candidate must decide if the attack threatens his or her political survival. If not, the candidate should look at whether or not he or she has political plans that extend beyond a single campaign—seeking re-election or another more prestigious office in the future. In this case, charges should be ignored because it is generally unwise to escalate the fight.

Under some circumstances, if the candidate decides to escalate the fight, the candidate or his supporters can demand to know why the third party is doing the predator's dirty work or how sensational facts have been obtained. When possible, they should exploit the third party's connection with the predator and attempt to have the predator's connection and methods judged along with the target's guilt or innocence.

When Estes Kefauver first ran for the U.S. Senate, the campaign was marked by a bitter verbal attack on Kefauver by a man who had dominated Tennessee politics for forty years, ex-mayor of Memphis, Edward Crump. When Crump accused Congressman Kefauver of being a Communist sympathizer, Kefauver replied:

> You, Mr. Crump, are not running for the Senate. Your candidate, Judge Mitchell, is. I say, let Judge Mitchell meet me in Memphis in open debate, and if the audience then thinks I am a communist, I will quit the Senate race. If they decide I am not, I'll not ask you to leave the state, but I think it might be a good idea.

When Judge Mitchell did not reply, Kefauver's challenges continued. They were ignored. Kefauver followed his opponent, often appearing on the same platform, where his remarks went something like this: "You people have just been hearing Judge Mitchell call me some very ugly names. Now the Judge is a hit-and-run speaker. I challenge him to stay here and in open discussion repeat the things he has said behind my back."[13] Interestingly enough, the judge always found another engagement. Kefauver won.

Using Character Witnesses

Often the political prey can divert an attack and spread its base by making the voter believe the attack is aimed not at him or her alone, but is, in reality, an attack on his or her party or a popular political idol. In its simplest form, the prey tries to wrap himself or herself in the idol's image, by, for example, calling himself a "Roosevelt Democrat" (see Figure 5-28) or claiming that she is a Republican in the tradition of Ronald Reagan. The thrust of this technique is to imply that the attack is really not against the candidate, but against the Truman administration or the principles espoused by Gerald Ford, etc.

Fig. 5-28. Pamphlet, Re-elect DeLacy to Congress, First District, Seattle, 1946.

This character-witness technique was also in operation under different conditions in Denver, Colorado, in 1908. Like hundreds of other turn-of-the-century cities, it was run by an easy-going mayor (Mayor Speer, in this case) who got on well with businessmen whose income depended on wide-open vice. When a reform element, led by a blue-nosed corporation lawyer, Horace G. Phelps, and two of the city's newspapers, *The Rocky Mountain News* and *The Denver News*, zeroed in on Mayor Speer's tolerant attitude toward the flourishing red light district, Speer chose to rise above the battle and let his surrogates vouch for him.

One of Speer's supporters, N. Walter Dixon, an ex-judge, reasoned with audiences, saying, "Vice exists, not because laws are not made nor do they exist because laws are not enforced. They exist because of the infirmity of human nature." Then the judge went on to say, "Mayor Speer has never been a hypocrite about anything. . . . He has set the standard of morality as high as it can be carried out. . . . I defy any man who has a sense of decency about him, to say that during the last four years, there has not been a constant uplift from year to year."

The Denver Post, a newspaper loyal to Mayor Speer, counterpunched with editorials and feature articles ridiculing the reformers. It said they were poisoning minds of women and children—who at the time did not even have the right to vote—by gathering them on the capitol building's lawn to listen to the dramatic vile descriptions of the habits of the scarlet women, who were being used as playthings by evil men.[14]

In the last quarter of the twentieth century, this character-witness technique was perfected in a mailout by Citizens Committee for Fair Campaign Practices in support of former state senator Wes Uhlman in his campaign for Seattle mayor (Figure 5-29).

Slugging It Out: Counterpunching

Since most voters do not follow the details of a political campaign, there is a good chance they have not read, heard, or seen the original attack. Also, the candidate who counterpunches must realize that if he or she throws mud back, it will not close the matter. A reply encourages another volley, which keeps the controversy ablaze and gets more publicity from the media, who use it to create news. TV producers especially like to design their political stories around accusations because they are lively.

If the candidate, after considering these possibilities, decides to counterpunch, he or she should try to reach the same audience that heard the original attack. Any delays increase the chance that the reader, listener, or viewer will not be familiar with the original attack, so the best way to counterpunch is to have the reporter include it as part of the story publicizing the original attack.

The simplest way to get this type of coverage is to be prepared when the press asks for a reaction. If the prey has any idea that an attack is imminent, he or she should have some pithy comments ready. These comments should be short and should be so sarcastic that no red-blooded reporter can ignore them. If at all possible, candidates should avoid making reference to the charges. Here are some general samples:

"The opponent is shooting from the lip."

"He should be in the Olympics, the way he jumps to conclusions."

"He can compress the most words into the smallest ideas better than any man I ever met." (Abe Lincoln)[15]

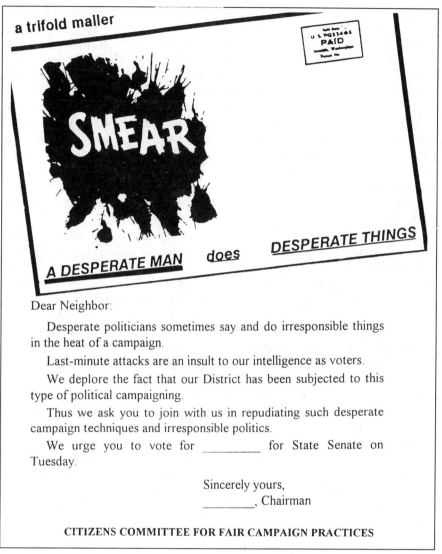

a trifold mailer

SMEAR

A DESPERATE MAN does DESPERATE THINGS

Dear Neighbor:

Desperate politicians sometimes say and do irresponsible things in the heat of a campaign.

Last-minute attacks are an insult to our intelligence as voters.

We deplore the fact that our District has been subjected to this type of political campaigning.

Thus we ask you to join with us in repudiating such desperate campaign techniques and irresponsible politics.

We urge you to vote for _____ for State Senate on Tuesday.

Sincerely yours,

_____, Chairman

CITIZENS COMMITTEE FOR FAIR CAMPAIGN PRACTICES

Fig. 5-29. Campaign letter, Citizens Committee for State Senator Wes Uhlman, November 1, 1964.

If the candidate is not afraid of publicizing the fight and wants the answer to be carried by the news media, he or she should use language that makes an impression and hopefully the news. In 1877, when old standpatter, U.S. Senator Roscoe Conkling, was placed in what the questioner thought was an embarrassing position of opposing reform, he made the news by counterattacking with this answer: "Their vocation . . . is to lament the sins of other people. Their stock in trade is rancid, chanting self-righteousness. They are wolves in sheep's clothing. Their real object is office and political plunder. When Dr. Johnson defined patriotism as the last refuge of a scoundrel, he was unconscious of the then undeveloped capabilities and uses of the word 'reform.' "[16]

Occasionally, a counterattack will stop the predator's assault, but this is usually limited to situations where the attack comes from someone who is guilty of the same or a more serious political sin. In the 1978 Florida Democratic primary for governor, one of the candidates in the run-off primary, Attorney General Robert Shevin, attacked his opponent, State Senator Robert Graham, for being a big spender while he was a member of the legislature. One of Shevin's TV spots showed "an adding machine spewing out tape, while a voice-over told of Graham's big-spender votes."

When the polls showed that Graham's lead was slipping, Graham's media man, Bob Squier, produced their own version of an adding machine. It was visually identical to Shevin's spot. They focused the camera on the "adding machine punching out long tape." The announcer said, " 'Bob Shevin is an expert on spending the taxpayers' money. Year after year, Shevin would dip into the general fund to bail out his office. We'll never know how much Shevin would have spent, because finally the legislature stepped in and put a stop to it. We couldn't afford Bob Shevin as attorney general. Imagine what he would cost us as governor.' " Graham's "adding machine" spot ran for three days, until Shevin's went off the air, then Graham withdrew his.[17]

When the prey chooses to counterattack, he or she may choose what is almost standard operating procedure: Praising the target and counterattacking the predator. Occasionally the target might even capitalize on the predator's words to demonstrate that the charge is false or unfair.

In 1982, challenger Bruce Morrison of Connecticut cast his rival for Congress as an opponent of social security. His TV commercial showed the candidate seated next to an elderly woman. As he began talking about the problems of the elderly, the woman interrupted him and lashed out at the incumbent Republican, Lawrence J. DeNardis. She said, "I've got a few choice words for you, Congressman DeNardis. Too bad I can't say them on TV." She concluded by shaking her finger into the camera and scolding, "You ought to be ashamed of yourself, Lawrence J. DeNardis." Throughout the spot, candidate Morrison looked on, silently and haplessly.

Morrison won that election, and two years later there was a rematch between the two candidates for the congressional seat. Former congressman Mr. DeNardis retaliated in kind. His ad opened with an elderly looking woman who peeled off her stage makeup wrinkles and her wig. Then she described the 1982 ad as "a trick by Bruce Morrison that cost us a very good congressman," and concluded, "Bruce Morrison, it's you that should be ashamed."[18]

For a summary of the attack and counterattack techniques discussed in this and the previous chapter, see the nutshells below.

Anatomy of a Smear: Planning the Attack

Note: The first question in the voters' and candidates' mind is always fairness and motivation.

Reducing the size of the target
Think carefully twice before attacking or even answering.
Adapt the fine art of being a cautious jellyfish.
Don't attack unless behind.

Opposition research:
Get facts straight.
Candidate or trusted confidante check opponent's record with ex-staff members, ex-opponents.
Check and make opponent eat his/her words.

Looking piously toward Heaven while raising hell
Rationalize; claim opponent struck first.
Justify.
Necessary to expose opponent's record.
Constitutents have right to know.
Hide behind third party.
Use media and the fringe groups.
Reduce the target.
Exaggerate fantasy.
Campaign rhetoric.

Focus the attack:
Reveal campaign money sources.
Expose attendance record, incompetence.
Reveal personal habits, e.g., liquor, sexual misconduct, etc.
Attack someone other than the opposition candidate, e.g., puppet of prominent supporters.

Conflict between showmanship and fairness:
Balance damage that it does to the attacker's image against impact of the information.
Avoid attacks on opponent's personal life. Such attacks should come from the press or someone else.

Backlash:
The political predator becomes known as a character assassin.
Danger that public will resent.
Overkill.

★ ★ ★ ★ ★ **In A Nutshell** ★ ★ ★ ★ ★

Anatomy of a Smear: Response Options

Counterattack:

Use innuendo and/or affirmative ridicule.

Use ridicule to highlight counterattack.

Rehearse reply in advance.

Point out opponent's hostility.

Admit in part.

Disagree and take exception.

Keep a cool head: Answer with dignity and style.

Play political prey, martyr junior grade.

Characterize attacker as political buffoon.

Cry foul and say attack is smokescreen to hide real issues.

Respond to paper tigers.

Use character witnesses.

Counterpunch.

Cite something the opposition doesn't want exposed.

Consider ignoring the attack:

Discussing it in detail only spreads it further. If the candidate answers, the opposition will reply and further emphasize the original charge.

★ ★ ★ ★ ★   **In A Nutshell**   ★ ★ ★ ★ ★

Part 6

News as a Political Tool

Chapter 50

The Media

Their favor is the pole of the tent . . . without it thy house will fall.
—Omar Khayyam[1]

Media Influence

In the days of iron men and wooden ships, no clipper ship or other fine sailing rig was complete without a hand-carved masthead as part of the flag boom. These mastheads were carvings of human heads and the ships were often named for the person represented. So it is in the world of politics: Campaigns are identified by a candidate's name and face first and then by the issues and the office sought.

Ninety five percent of all Americans watch television at least once a day . . . 85 percent of all Americans listen to radio once a day. Most of what the public remembers of a major political campaign comes to them from half-hour TV news segments, only 22 minutes of which are devoted to actual news. Candidates for major office observe a political rule of thumb named for Ed Guthman, a Pulitzer Prize-winning newsman, press secretary for Attorney General Bobby Kennedy, and editor of the Philadelphia *Inquirer*. "Guthman's Law" goes like this: "Three minutes on the early evening news program [is] worth any amount of exposure on any other medium at any time of the day."[2]

In addition to local television coverage, almost every locality has newspaper coverage. Here local officials can tell a story and explore issues of interest to the voter. And every campaign can use specialty publications to target racial, ethnic, or religious minorities. Distinguished scholar Austin Ranney used the 1976 presidential debate between President Ford and challenger Jimmy Carter to illustrate how influential this local media coverage can be. When Ford gaffed, claiming that Poland, unlike other Eastern European nations, was not under Soviet domination, Ranney noted, "Opinion polls taken immediately after the debate reported few viewers were turned off by the remark, and 53 percent thought Ford had won the debate." "However," Ranney continues, "when the opinion polls were taken later that week, they reflected the views of commentators who felt that Ford had committed a terrible boner. Then 58 percent of the people thought Carter won and that Ford's statement on Eastern Europe was the main reason."[3]

Reporters, columnists, and editorial writers, like everyone else, make an extra effort to make their favorite candidates look good. One politician who enjoyed such support was Governor, and later United States Supreme Court Justice, Earl Warren. In his memoirs, he points with pride to the fact that from the day he declared his candidacy for the Governorship of California he enjoyed the support

Fig. 6-1. "Punchcard Voting," *Modern Voting Machines*, September 15, 1992.

of virtually all the Republican-leaning newspapers. The few that favored the Democratic, such as the Los Angeles *Daily News*, were at least willing to give him a fair shake.[4]

Friendly reporters can ignore boring rhetoric and make news of a candidate's comment or the appointment of campaign committee heads. Reporters can also turn out speculative stories that keep a prospective candidate's name in the news: "John Incumbent keeps acting more and more like a candidate, but still hasn't made his intentions known," or, "Insiders say Mary Challenger will make the

Fig. 6-2. Edward Schwartzman, *Campaign Craftsmanship* (New York: Universe Books, 1973), p. 193.

race." Coverage from a friendly media can include stories about a candidate's home, family, hobbies—things that make the candidate interesting as a human being. On one occasion, ex-U.S. Senator Charles Percy saw a group of young men engaged in Indian wrestling. Percy, who had done this as a youngster, joined them, and a friendly newspaper ran a photograph of them.[5]

Newspapers

During the 19th century, most newspapers relied on subsidies from political parties; this was reflected in the way the news was written. Later, advertising assumed the burden of support. Many of today's publishers are successful corporate enterprises with stockholders more interested in advertising and making money than in preconceived political ideas. Yet newspapers still carry a powerful political punch. Though radio and television are now the primary news sources, newspapers consider it their privilege to generate political support among those who share their views and follow their advice. Newspapers are not hampered by broadcast doctrines nor by so-called "fairness" or "equal time" restrictions. Most make formal endorsements that are picked up and used by candidates as a part of their advertising. However, newspaper participation doesn't stop there. Support can often go beyond editorials and endorsements.

Early Newspaper Coverage

Newspaper coverage early in a campaign establishes the political atmosphere even while the electronic media pursue other news. Mary Ellen Leary, speaking of the 1973 race for governor of California, noted that from June 5 to September 2 the electronic media virtually ignored the contest. Meanwhile, major newspapers covered the campaign so industriously that they ran one third of all their 260 stories about the race.

Why didn't the electronic media cover the contest? Most television editors agreed with the Los Angeles broadcast news editor who said, "My feeling is voters don't make up their minds until the last minute. They aren't much interested until the last week. That's when we give the election attention."[6] It comes as no surprise that television ran one quarter and radio ran one third of all their campaign stories in the final week. Although the final week's newspaper stories occupied a greater proportion of news space than in any previous single week, they accounted for only 14 percent of the political stories.

Early newspaper coverage creates an advantage for candidates whom the press establish as front runners. By the time electronic media start taking an interest the news consists of voters choosing from the candidates the newspapers have established as front runners. As media consultant Bud Arnold put it, "There is a kind of interaction among the media, so the TV news editor suddenly sees a guy

Fig. 6-3. Nice way to highlight portion of a newspaper article, from Joe King Campaign for Washington State Governor, 1992.

picking up ink in the paper and he's going to start taking him more seriously and cover him. . . ."[7]

Another reason newspapers exercise influence is that they give politics extensive coverage. Unlike broadcast reporters, most newspaper journalists covering politics make it a business and have years of specialized experience. Ellen Leary found that radio reporters were just as likely as their television counterparts to lean on newspaper coverage. Television anchor Jess Marlow of KNBC has commented: "Broadcast news relies on newspapers for backgrounding and often extracts material directly from them for newscasts. One late-night programmer in Los Angeles occasionally reads items from the first edition of the *Los Angeles Times*."[8]

Television

Nearly two thirds of the American people say that their main source of news is television. Then come newspapers and radio.[9] George Reedy, Professor of Journalism at Marquette University and one-time press secretary to President Lyndon Johnson, observed, "An appearance, even a 30-second one on the evening news, has far more punch with the voter than any campaign commercials."[10]

Television anchorman Jess Marlow explains, "Television news gives the viewer something personal. He can make his own assessment. It lets him watch the candidate actually saying it. If he declines to answer a question, or evades, the viewer can spot that, as non-answers are revealing."[11] For this reason the polls tell us that over twice as many people trust television news more than what is reported by newspapers, radio, or magazines.

Some in the industry argue that television is many different things—and it's certainly not all wrapped up in the evening news. Every station devotes substantial time to public service, to round tables and candidate debates. Unfortunately, such programs are rarely aired during prime time, and when they are their ratings are low. Major political forums are reserved for the superstars—presidential, gubernatorial and senatorial front runners—or, during a legislative session, for the speaker of the state house or majority leader of the state senate, while all the local candidate can ask for is a brief mention on television news.

How the Shift in TV's Priorities Has Changed Its Political Coverage

When television took over as the number one news source, TV stations decided to go after larger audiences and higher ratings. They increased the length of their newscasts and their advertising revenue. The quest for ratings brought competition. *New York Times* television writer Les Brown wrote that any station that climbs six or seven rating points can boost its advertising charges and "improve its profits by millions of dollars."[12]

Television executives directing news coverage have dramatically increased the news program audience by using a light, fast-paced style. Triggered by an ABC station in New York City, this brought a wave of program changes and a phenomenon known variously as "action news," "eye-witness news," and "happy talk."

These formats necessitate news stories that tell the story photographically. KNXT's bureau chief at Sacramento, Howard Gingold, noted this: "The emphasis these days is on visuals. We can't get into anything that takes a lot of explaining." The phenomenon also makes TV editors suckers for political events that are both dramatic and visual, such as when Congressman Ottinger dramatized the New York pollution crisis by taking a dive and a brief swim in the filthy Hudson River.[13]

The new TV broadcasting look also places greater emphasis on the anchorman's visual attractiveness, chatty manner, and light pleasantry. This phenomenon affected all television. As Michael Wheeler, in *Lies, Damn Lies and Statistics*, explains, "TV news directors live or die according to the ratings their shows draw. No matter how high the quality of the production, if the ratings are low, the director will be let go."[14]

The impact of this trend was felt in San Francisco when KGO-TV, which had been trailing in market share, hired audience-building consultants. Following their advice, the station started broadcasting "action news," which was promoted on billboards, in newspapers, and on buses. It dressed newscasters in costumes and presented them as "happy people" everybody liked. As KGO-TV's audience grew, convulsions swept the newsroom at top-rated rival KPIX. It began revamping. Its new format did not require political specialists and political reporter Rollin Post expressed his concern: "It is very difficult to do a 20-second or a 30-second story that tells anything. It's just got to be superficial."[15]

An example of "major" campaign television coverage follows in this excerpt from KGO-TV on October 9, 1973:

> Both candidates for Governor [of California], Jerry Brown (Democrat) and Houston Flournoy (Republican), were here in San Francisco today to pick up what political support they could get. The Republican candidate's most influential backer, Governor Reagan, joined him at a luncheon at the Fairmont Hotel today, which was a fundraiser. The main topic, as you can imagine, was the economy.

Then came a 15-second quote from Flourney and a five-second summary of his views by a reporter. The next item began:

> The elderly of San Francisco are here every day, in the basement of the First Congregational Church—one of the few places where they can afford lunch. It is only 50 cents. They don't have much money, but they do have a block. And the elderly are a powerful voting block in this city. Edmund G. Brown Jr. knows it, and he came here today. . . . He promised more aid for the elderly, and compared the philosophies of Republicans and Democrats.

There followed three sentences from Brown's remarks.[16]

Emphasis on the superficial is only one of the problems associated with a lighter news style. In addition, candidates for public office have to compete for TV attention with hundreds of other events. Speaker of the California Assembly,

Bob Moretti, complained that during his run in the gubernatorial primary one television station interviewed him and ran one minute of the interview, while on the same newscast four minutes were devoted to "togs for dogs." A different station ran a few seconds on his campaign remarks and six minutes on a frog-jumping contest.[17]

Television anchorman Jess Marlow contends that the public should not choose between television and newspapers. "To be well informed, you need both." Marlow adds, "There are too many races we haven't covered at all, and some of our coverage is shallow. On many issues, we just don't have time for an explanation. If I were going to have to make a choice I would go for newspapers."[18]

But in the real world of elective politics, success is measured in votes, and campaign consultant Arnold Steinberg, in his book, *Political Campaign Management*, argues that television exposure is invaluable. He applies a formula to television coverage: Every repetition of the candidate's name on television is equivalent to a 10 percent increase in the value of his or her prior visuals. Other political strategists also have to admit that TV coverage appeals to millions of voters who are not politically involved. After citing the first rule of politics, that "in a vacuum, exposure and persuasion are the same," strategists say television coverage fills the vacuum.[19]

Radio

The ratio of news time to time devoted to an election by radio is almost identical to that of television. Looking at the two-month radio coverage of the 1973 California election, 25 percent of its coverage was in the last week of the election; 17 percent came opening week. As with television, their coverage was superficial. Here is a typical 20-second morning news report on KCBS radio: "Flourney will be passing through town later today as part of a week-long campaign tour, and Brown will be speaking to a group of his supporters here in Sacramento later this morning."[20]

However, speed of dissemination and flexibility distinguishes radio election coverage from television. For example, a reporter with a portable microphone can ask questions as he or she walks alongside the candidate, and two minutes later (or even immediately) broadcast the results. Also, most radio stations have more local programing than television, so they are looking for variety. Potential candidates with something interesting to say prior to filing can often prevail on disc jockeys who conduct interviews with prominent people. Many candidates find it advantageous to stake out a controversial position, then have someone on their staff find a spot on an interview program.

In a major market, radio stations specialize. The audience of a rock radio station might be interested in a rock rendition of the candidate's campaign song. Most youth-oriented stations can be persuaded, as part of their news coverage, to air a candidate's views on lowering the drinking age or plans to put a student on the board of regents at a state university. A classical music station might be interested in the candidate's classical music preferences or plans to help establish a local opera or symphony.

Radio stations find that serious panel discussions have a side benefit. They satisfy a radio and television licensing requirement that stations set aside a portion of their time for the discussion of public issues. However, after the candidates make their official announcements, the rules change. Then, except for legitimate news, time is paid for. In addition, Federal law requires radio and television stations give all sides equal time.

Most markets, especially small ones, have a local station that provides general programming aimed at its total listening audience. This station publicizes visits by major candidates and local campaigns as part of its news coverage, along with sports events and feature stories. Occasionally, these stations may even feature a debate between local aspirants for county commissioner or the state legislature. Some local stations have a telephone talk show that permits candidates or their supporters to call and comment on issues.

Drive time is another way in which radio is distinguished from TV. Although it may have little impact in a central city or on the east coast where most commuters use public transportation, drive-time news and commercials can be crucial for candidates who want to reach those who live in suburbs. These commuters drive to and from work every weekday morning between 6 and 9 a.m., and early evenings between 4 and 6:30. During this time commuters cannot read a newspaper or watch television, so 63 percent of their car radios are tuned to the news.[21]

Professional campaign manager and media consultant Joe Cerrell, with 15 years of political experience in Los Angeles, dismissed the importance of the written press by arguing that it reaches the fewest people. After he gave his opinion on TV news, which he described as the most persuasive, he added, "Don't overlook radio. Not in this commuter paradise, Los Angeles."[22]

Efforts to reach this prime-time radio audience became an issue in the 1976 Presidential primary, when a heated battle broke out between a New York time buyer, Ruth Jones, representing California Governor Ronald Reagan, and a number of Texas radio stations. That issue was based on the limit the radio stations placed on the number of commuter-time spots they were willing to make available for political purposes. Mrs. Jones appealed their arbitrary restrictions to the Federal Communications Commission. There the matter was settled quietly when FCC staff informally advised the stations to grant most of the spots the Reagan campaign had budgeted.[23]

Chapter 51

Publicity Mechanics

> People say that whenever I have a picture coming out I always start a controversy about something that gets into the papers. Well, in all sincerity, I want to assure you that as a general proposition—there's not a single word of untruth in that.
> —Sam Goldwyn, movie producer[1]

The Announcement

Announcing a candidacy and the act of filing are news. Every candidate should prepare an announcement and send it to newspapers and radio and television stations. This news release should state what office the candidate is running for, what the candidate's qualifications and past experience are, and what he or she perceives as the major issues. The news release should also mention impressive endorsements, if any. In some instances the candidate will want to predict how much money will be raised and what kind of campaign will be run.[2] Refer to the News Releases nutshell for some ideas.

If a candidate announces too early, there may be no interest and little media coverage. A candidate who files too late runs the risk of being lost in a sea of other filings. Three to five days before filing closes is usually a good time to make the announcement. If the office is important the candidate occasionally uses a kick-off breakfast or luncheon or calls a news conference to make the announcement. Sometimes candidates for major offices spend "announcement day" meeting and talking to the press. Some fly from city to city discussing their candidacies at a series of highly publicized press conferences.

Endorsements

Nothing lends credibility to a candidacy like endorsements. The press considers them second only to money in determining media coverage. Endorsers include elected officials, leading community figures, neighborhood groups, and local clergy—anyone with a wide basis of support.[3] Not all candidates publicize their endorsers up front. Some deliberately hold onto prestigious endorsements that they have had from the beginning, then feed them to the press at strategic times to give the impression that everybody is getting on the bandwagon.

Getting Publicity From the Stump Speech

Merely having a reporter present does not insure that there will be coverage. Stock speeches filled with trite pronouncements get little media attention, so it is

★ ★ ★ ★ ★ ★ ★ ★ ★ ★ ★ ★

News Releases

Note: A news release must say something of interest or it will not be news. Tailor the release to a particular audience/media (e.g., radio, television, newspapers, community service newsletters).

	Target Date	Date Compl.

Planning:
With campaign committee, choose topic(s).
After studying issues, visit local editor or reporter covering politics. Candidate should not be afraid to ask for his or her views or advice.

Technical Details of Preparation
Schedule release date.
Prepare distribution list; tally number needed.
Type double-spaced, one side of paper.
Indicate enclosed attachments at end of story.
Have copied or printed.
Caption any photos, including committee name, address, etc.
Check all for accuracy of names, facts, dates, etc.
Assemble packets (send with background material if appropriate).
Address the envelope even if delivering by hand.
Plan to deliver in person if possible; otherwise send by mail.

Additional requirements:
Opening sentence should be designed to get reader's attention.
First paragraph should state who, what, when, where, how, why.
Opinions should come from named people.
Use quotations for emphasis.
Have friends and staff review before release.

★ ★ ★ ★ ★   **In A Nutshell**   ★ ★ ★ ★ ★

up to candidates to provide color, drama, or humor as they explore ideas, propose solutions, or comment on events.

Occasionally, a clever candidate gets coverage by providing a bit of showmanship. The leader of the anti-Long ticket, James H. (Jimmy) Morrison, took a leashed monkey which he called "Earl Long" with him when he stumped the state. Morrison delighted the partisan crowds as he apologized for Earl, saying that the monkey shouldn't be blamed for anything it said or did because it was only doing what his master required of him.[4]

Getting Publicity From Campaign Events

Few people remember what President Carter said in his inaugural address, but millions remember that immediately after he delivered the address, he broke tradition by walking hand in hand with his wife down Pennsylvania Avenue in his own inaugural parade.[5]

From the television producer's point of view an interesting gesture is news. As Vick Biondi, KNBC Sacramento political reporter, says of television, "Local television does not offer background stories on politics or anything else, that require more than the optimum 90 seconds air time to explain. But they do delight in the candidate who can take advantage of the old saying 'If dog bites man, it isn't news, but if man bites dog it makes the front page'."[6] For example, when Elliot Richardson ran for Lieutenant Governor of Massachusetts, he carried his hand-shaking campaign across the border to Connecticut. His official explanation was that he wanted to "meet and talk to Massachusetts voters who worked there." But most observers saw it as a successful gimmick designed to make news, particularly television news, as he was photographed shaking hands with Connecticut voters.[7]

Fluff, Showmanship, and Publicity

It's hard to say what will catch the media's fancy. To illustrate, a picture was published on front pages in 1924 featuring a stern-faced man in a high celluloid collar and pin-striped suit wearing a massive eagle-feather Indian headdress, which trailed down his back to his ankles. This picture was news because the man smoking a peace pipe in a circle of leather-faced Indian braves was obviously out of place, but no one cared. He was Calvin Coolidge, campaigning for re-election to the Presidency of the United States.[8] South Dakota Congressman Larry Pressler demonstrated similar showmanship in his campaign for the U.S. Senate when signed on as a worker for a day with a meat-packing plant, as a beekeeper, and as a grocery bagger.[9]

Commenting on the use of these fluff pieces, television anchorman Vick Biondi says, "The consultants have turned television news into mere entertainment.[10] In fact, media men, such as Los Angeles-based Joe Carrell, brag that they stage-manage events. Carrell explains that he got coverage for gubernatorial candidate Joseph Alioto by having Alioto visit Grand Central Market in Los Angeles and stop to commiserate with a grocer about the price of pinto beans. Richard Bergholz put it on the front page of the *Los Angeles Times*. "Now, Alioto didn't have to go to Grand Central Market to learn about the high cost of rice and pinto beans," Carrell stated. "I could have told him about it." Carrell further stressed, "It's a game. You need a gimmick. While he was there, I had Alioto lunching on a huge sandwich because it makes good television."

Sometimes candidates have carried fluff pieces to great lengths. One-time Governor of Florida Rubin Askew and Tennessee Governor Lamar Alexander walked the entire lengths of their states to dramatize their candidacies.[11] As these candidates walked, the publicity may not have been spectacular, but their trip became a media event. The voters saw and heard them because they were covered on television, radio, and the local press on their brief passage through towns. They left in their wakes a ripple of stories and pictures of them shaking hands, being presented keys to the cities, and, on occasion, rubbing tired feet.

Fluff pieces do require preparation. As one-time California Congressman Jerome Waldie put it: "You don't just go out and walk. It's a major logistical operation. You have five or six people working full time in preparation."[12] Local news personnel must be notified as to when and where the candidate will be. Television must be alerted to meet the arrival at a busy corner where the candidate can be seen chatting with townspeople. The appearance has to be scheduled early enough in the day to allow processing for the local station's evening broadcast and the appearance in town should be timed to take advantage of local radio talk-shows. Candidates also need to be prepared to enliven radio programs with remarks regarding local issues.[13]

There are hundreds of other imaginative ways to create fluff pieces. The candidate of Irish ancestry might invite the press to make the rounds of the pubs on St. Patrick's Day, but the candidate should not drink. Charles Percy got publicity during his first campaign for the U.S. Senate by sponsoring an all-black Little League baseball team. He even went to a game and pitched a few practice balls.[14]

Another publicity piece might feature handicapped people, who roll a precinct in wheelchairs instead of walking a precinct as they campaign. This is great coverage for the candidate and the handicapped.[15]

Experienced media personnel apply different rules to publicity pieces than to straight or hard news. While publication depends on the nature of the event, in most cases rivals are not upset if the candidate invites only one television and one newspaper or magazine reporter to a staged event.[16]

Mr. or Mrs. Big and the News

If political personalities are important enough, or if a campaign catches the eye of nationwide news, correspondents will be assigned to cover all or part of the race. Then even a routine campaign will make local news. During the Johnson-Goldwater campaign of 1964, President Lyndon Johnson was able to generate news by flying to the Columbia River Basin to sign a Canadian treaty, to El Paso to meet the Mexican President, and to Oklahoma to dedicate a dam. Johnson then combined politics and showmanship in Salt Lake City, where he made a visit to 91-year-old David McKay, patriarch of the Mormon Church.[17]

President Jimmy Carter used the three-hour difference between time zones at the end of his 1980 presidential race to make local news in several states. The day before the election Carter started with an early news conference in Washington, DC. Then he made stops in Detroit, Michigan; Akron, Ohio; Granite City, Illinois; and Springfield, Illinois. After a news conference and a change of clothes, Carter flew to Los Angeles. From there he went on to Portland, Oregon, and Seattle, Washington, departing at 11 p.m., Pacific Standard Time, for Plains, Georgia, where he cast his ballot. He then took a plane for the White House, where he spent election day awaiting the returns.[18]

Smart candidates are ever conscious of their images when they create fluff pieces. U.S. Senator John Kennedy went to plant gates to shake hands with workers at 5 o'clock in the morning. In answer to aides who told him he could use the same time to expose himself to twice as many people in other places, Kennedy replied that he was at the plant gates because he wanted the TV image of an active man hustling votes.[19]

The fact that Mr. or Mrs. Big makes local news should not be lost on candidates for minor office. Knowing that local media follow national, regional, or state-wide personalities, local candidates attempt to appear with them and share in the publicity they generate.

Fresh Ideas

Rudy Boschwitz, a Minnesota Republican, used family members to help generate news. Speaking of his 1984 campaign Boschwitz stated: "The Family were great campaigners. There are 300 weekly newspapers in Minnesota and about 120 radio stations. My two younger sons (together) during seven weeks of the summer went to 240 of those smaller towns, spent 30-90 minutes in town (seldom more than an hour), got the local editor to take a picture of them 'Mainstreaming,' and gave them a news release about themselves. To make sure it was printed, we put a nice-sized ad into the paper the preceding week, announcing they were coming!"[20]

Political professionals thrive when the public and media are fascinated by new ideas, plans, and proposed projects. When New York's U.S. Senator, Patrick Moynihan, was a junior cabinet member in the Kennedy administration, he captured national attention with an endless stream of visionary ideas, which he supported, as observed by Michael Wheeler, with "obscure studies of rural elections in India, or (would) insist that it was impossible to understand the Third World without reading a particular Ph.D. study, which exposed the influence of the London School of Economics on African heads of government."[21]

Of course, few political aspirants have Moynihan's mental equipment or education, but with study and imagination all candidates can generate interest in something new. For example, governmental reorganization may be justified in the interest of efficiency, and candidates seeking posts at the national level can demand decentralization to meet the needs of the citizenry.

However, the visionary approach has its flip side. Though candidates can usually interest the media and catch public attention, there is a risk. New proposals and trendy images may succeed in one constituency and not in another, or with changes in times and public tastes they can go sour. This was demonstrated by one-time California Governor Jerry Brown. In his first campaign for Governor of the State of California, he used the campaign slogan "A New Spirit." He avoided concrete solutions to current problems and always talked about the future.[22]

After Brown was elected governor, he captured media attention with a series of eccentric but attention-getting gestures. He drove an aging blue Plymouth rather than a state limousine and took up residence in a comparatively inexpensive apartment in lieu of the "Taj Mahal" that California supplies its governors. Brown further captured publicity by exuding a "mod" image as he chummed around with one of America's leading rock groups, the Eagles, and singer Linda Ronstadt.

In 1980, flushed with success, Jerry Brown went national in pursuit of the presidency. Now Brown was attempting to appeal to a different and more conservative constituency far from his native California. What seemed fresh and trendy in California two and four years before was viewed in a different light.

Brown's one-time campaign press secretary, Charlotte Perry, described how Brown failed. She said, "He sought to interest the voting public in what he conceived to be serious, thoughtful—yes, even visionary proposals. In an era when Americans wondered how they would be able to purchase a home, Jerry Brown talked about the colonization of outer space. As the people of New Hampshire fretted about the energy shortage and how they could afford to heat their homes through the winter, he talked about beaming solar energy to the earth from a space platform. As the average person begged for simple, decent and affordable medical care, Brown preached the virtues of whole grains and holistic health."[23]

Reaction Makes News

Reacting to events and statements is another way to create news. Some prominent candidates make themselves accessible, others seek out local press, hoping that their reaction to events will merit news coverage. This attention is usually reserved for office holders who have a flair for news. President Ronald Reagan had such a flair. While governor, he served on the Board of Regents of the University of California. Speaking of Reagan's conduct during that period, a liberal Democrat, Fred Dutton, said, "We would have long, intense meetings and argue fiercely among ourselves. Governor Reagan would seem, at best, barely interested in what was happening—mostly bored." But as we would walk out of the room and the television cameras would be lined up, when they asked him for a comment he would come alive. He was very good at it."[24]

For a worksheet of ideas on how to use the news media as a political tool, see the nutshell on the opposite page.

Attack Psychology

So far, news as a political tool has been discussed in light of positive coverage. Yet candidates, consultants, and politicians consider negative political attacks just as capable of generating news coverage. Mary Ellen Leary, monitoring the media in the 1973 California governor's race, found in both primary and general campaigns that the media viewed the contest in combat terms, strongly focusing on criticisms, slurs, bitter words, and exchanged recriminations.

During this campaign Dick Rodda, political editor of the *Sacramento Bee*, observed in one of his columns, "There was a tendency among newsmen to lean on the attack. It was significant that the uncomplimentary phrase, the sharp jibes, were picked up more than the substance of the criticism. If for no other reason the reporters wanted a good strong verb in the news story lead." These attack references or rejoinders were reported with such journalistic zest that they dominated more than half of both the press and broadcast stories. Lee Fremstad, the *Sacramento Bee* capitol bureau chief, said he was astonished at the speed with which "instant rebuttal" erupted after a candidate attack, almost as though the mimeographed press release had been prepared in advance.[25]

During a campaign the media tend to pick up whatever a combatant says even if the candidate's statements confuse, blunt, or destroy the opposition. But there are tradeoffs. Throwing mud while staying popular requires luck and genius. Those without this genius often arrange with a supporter or conspirator to light the fuse of controversy. This may not help the candidates directly, but they benefit when the attack turns off those who might otherwise support the opponent. When the alter ego of Florida's big industries, Ed Ball, set out to defeat U.S. Senator Claude Pepper, he persuaded Congressman George Smathers to file for Pepper's seat. Then Ball organized news fronts with names such as the "Anti-Pepper Campaign Committee of Volusia" and "Democratic Club of Duval," whose only purpose was to pass resolutions opposing Pepper. Ball circulated these statements among anti-Pepper daily newspapers throughout the state,[26] and his tactics met with success: Pepper was defeated.

★ ★ ★ ★ ★ ★ ★ ★ ★ ★ ★ ★ ★ ★

News as a Political Tool

Pre-filing publicity (challenger)
Become informed about issue(s).
Visit local editors (newspaper, radio, TV) personally to let them know candidate is running.
Solicit their ideas and view of campaign and issues.
Let them know how important their support is.
Make appointments in advance.
Look for some controversy or other newsmaking event to be involved in.
Weigh value of publicity (will it do more harm than good?)

The announcement
Write it out and get it down pat, but best to speak off cuff.
Choose strategy: Early vs. late or last minute.
Where to make: Reception or news conference?
Add endorsements.

Getting publicity from stage-managed campaign events
Try attaching candidate to Mr./Mrs. Big (coattails).
Invent fresh ideas.
Create new proposals.

Use trendy images (popular songs, movies).
Know that reaction makes news (if opponent makes statement, be prepared with immediate reaction, usually written in advance).

Special sources of coverage:
Contact political columnist(s).
Write letters to editor(s).

Organize public relations
Hire or designate a press agent.
Prepare handouts for all media.
Hold news conferences.
If controversial have sufficient backup of written material along with oral presentation.
Be sure event is worthy of coverage.
Call assignment editors on the news desk and/or political editors or columnists.

Perils of Provocation
Know the perils of a forthright position.
Use experienced PR judgment.
Watch for hostile press; make effort to overcome.
Emphasize person to person.
Don't attack the media.

★ ★ ★ ★ ★ In A Nutshell ★ ★ ★ ★ ★

To gain publicity, a few candidates have initiated public service lawsuits, for example, charging a major manufacturing company or a public utility with polluting a river. No doubt such gestures catch media attention, but the candidate runs the risk of being labeled a demagogue. And such lawsuits can turn out to be a minus rather than a plus, especially if the suit is dismissed as frivolous in the middle of a campaign.

Attacking an alternate target is another way a candidate can get publicity. For example, here's a 1972 TV commercial: "Hello, I'm Ogden Reid and I'm running for reelection to Congress from Westchester. I'm demanding a public explanation from the Public Service Commissioner. Mr. Swidler (an official of the New York rate commission), how can you justify handing the telephone company a $361 million increase and other special favors at the expense of the New York phone user? Sure, the telephone company has problems modernizing and making ends meet, but so do the people. When are you going to start working for the public?" The ad generated news and follow-up stories. Nationally syndicated columnist Jack Anderson even reported that, after viewing the spot, phone company executives contributed money to Reid's opponent.[27]

Newspaper Columns

There is an old saying, "Opinions are not news, unless they are coming from the Supreme Court." This isn't true. The public reads columnists who make a career of stating their opinions. In fact, millions read the newspaper just for the columns or op-ed pages and read little else. If a candidate says or does something clever, someone should report it to a favorite political or feature columnist. And when an opponent makes a faux pas, that should be leaked to the local gossip columnist too.

Some columnists accept tidbits over the phone. When a candidate or P.R. aide contacts a reporter with this kind of information, authors Toni Delacorte and Judy Kimsey suggest they should make it clear that it's off the record after making sure that the reporter is one that honors off-the-record statements.[28]

Letters to the Editor

On occasion a candidate can generate free publicity by using one of the best-read sections of the newspaper, the letters to the editor. What is required to get letters to the editor into a newspaper will vary, but being prominent helps.

One-time Florida Governor Fuller Warren was a regular letter-to-the-editor writer. Warren claimed that he never pulled any punches, saying: "I wrote what I thought and in the strongest language I could put together" (see Figure 6-4). Letters frequently create controversy and generate more publicity when other readers write rebuttal letters.[29]

Editorial-page editor Herb Robinson follows these rules when making his choices: "Editors are always looking for pieces carrying a punch. So everything on the editorial pages, including the letters, should have a point of view." He likes strong verbs, colorful adjectives, and crisp, short sentences. Robinson adds that those with a fresh viewpoint and humor are always welcome. Robinson prefers "letters dissenting from views published earlier, especially our editorials and signed opinion pieces." He is not impressed with abstract essays or general

THE PUBLIC PULSE

ANTI-SALES TAX

Dear Journal:

The people of Florida need to be alerted and aroused to the actual meaning of the slogan, "Broaden the Tax Base." Nearly every time one of the growing multitude of self-styled "experts" on taxation "gives out" on the subject, he ends up by pontifically declaring, "We must broaden the tax base."

This is just a sly way of saying the tax burden should be further shifted to the low-income citizens of Florida. Specifically, it means that a sales tax should be saddled upon the already over-taxed taxpayers of this state.

No new taxes of any kind should be imposed upon the people of Florida until the wanton waste of several million dollars a year is stopped by the passage of an act creating a central purchasing commission for the state. If, after this is done, additional revenue is absolutely essential to the proper administration of state government, the extra money should be raised by a severance tax (a tax on phosphate, limerock and other minerals), and by some of the several methods advocated by the Citizens' Committee on Taxation. A sales tax should not be imposed under any circumstances now conceivable.

To prevent a sales tax from being rammed through the 1949 legislature, the citizens of every Florida county should see to it that every person elected next year to the legislature is irrevocably and unconditionally pledged to vote against a sales tax. And they should go one step further by seeing that the man elected governor is likewise pledged and committed. Citizens' protective committees should be formed to wait upon each candidate and demand such a pledge.

FULLER WARREN.

Fig. 6-4. Fuller Warren, How to Win in Politics (Tallahassee, FL: Peninsular Publishing, 1949), pp. 54-55. Used by permission.

philosophizing and favors reactions to issues and/or people in the news. He sorts through a heavy flow of mail repeating the same theme and selects a representative sample. Robinson rejects letters containing demonstrable untruths as well as "libelous statements and other forms of tasteless personal attack."[30]

In their book, *The Candidate's Handbook for Winning Local Elections*, Harvey Yorke and Liza Doherty suggest that additional publicity may be gained after a candidate writes a letter to the editor, by "encouraging friends to respond commenting on the original letter to the editor saying, in effect, 'The candidate's letters make sense.' "[31] But editorial page editor Robinson disagrees. He states that he is not impressed with "self-serving communications from, or in behalf of, politicians or other public figures who have their own access to the regular news columns or letters addressed to other individuals or publications." Finally Robinson notes, "All newspapers are leery of unsigned letters and those lacking writers' home addresses and telephone numbers."[32]

A word of caution: Newspapers are infuriated if they find they have been manipulated. An extreme example of this happened during the 1979 Provincial election, in the Canadian Province of British Columbia. Jack Kelly, a public relations man for the ruling Social Party Credit party, distributed a press packet that included canned letters to the editor. These letters were intended for use by the party faithful. The press was especially upset because Kelly suggested the party fool the editors by having party workers sign the letters with the initials and addresses of real people taken from the telephone directory who had not given them permission to sign them.

The scheme first came to light when the newspapers called some of the residents whose initials were used by the party faithful. The residents denied that they had written the letters on which their initials were forged. The newspapers complained to the province's Attorney General, and an investigation was ordered. After this ploy was exposed, Kelly defended himself, claiming that "when . . . the future of the province is at stake we'll meet the opposition N.D.P. [New Democratic Party] at their terms." This exposure generated headlines and embarrassed the party, and Kelly was forced to resign.[33]

★ ★ ★ ★ ★ ★ ★ ★ ★ ★ ★ ★ ★ ★ ★

Getting Your Name and Image in Print

Note: A news release must say something of interest or it will not be news. Tailor the release to a particular audience/media (e.g., radio, television, newspapers, community service newsletters).

	Target Date	Date Compl
Use candidate's contacts or get introduced by friends		
Make the public aware of potential candidate's views through letters to the editor (i.e., support or opposition on community problems and issues).		
Get friends to write follow-up letters supporting your views.		
Seek unusual ways to get press coverage:		
After the candidate has studied the issues and has been carefully briefed, contact political reporters.		
Later contact editors who are likely to make endorsements.		
If only one contact is possible, seek out the editor(s).		
On anniversaries, special achievements, condolences, etc., write letters to editor(s).		
Expand the candidate's holiday greeting card list.		
Make card file for individuals, tracking group membership, your common interests, and their leanings on issues.		

★ ★ ★ ★ ★ **In A Nutshell** ★ ★ ★ ★ ★

Chapter 52

Organizing Public Relations

> The fool touts himself; the wise man hires a press agent.
> —Anonymous

Taking Inventory

When organizing public relations, candidates should pick two or three issues. Then they should do all they can to get the pubic to identify these issues with their candidacies, so early in the campaign, a wise candidate takes a media inventory, listing every newspaper and radio and television station in the area. Then they rank the media by political importance to the race. Although TV may dominate big-time politics, local candidates may not give it a high priority because the audience is vast and may have little interest in the candidate's office. All candidates, however, including those running for local office, should set out to become acquainted with the key staff of the news media. A personal visit not only flatters the news personnel, but permits the editor, columnist, or reporter to explore issues and ask personal questions. While visits are helpful, though, they don't guarantee coverage, and candidates should avoid media staff resentment of the type generated by President Richard Nixon when, in 1972, his managers offered candidate Nixon for extended interviews, but only to the chief news executive of the local radio and TV stations.

Different media have different editorial structures, so it is often difficult to know which news media staff member a candidate should see. In a small news operation, it is safe to say that candidates should see the editor in charge. In a large newspaper or at a television or radio station, a candidate should seek out the political editor and/or political reporter if one will be assigned to cover their campaign.

Candidates should talk to editorial writers and political columnists if there are any because they frequently inject their views in editorials and "interpretive" stories. Candidates should also get acquainted with both the sports and society editors if they can find a reasonable opening. If a newspaper or TV station sends a reporter out to interview a candidate, he or she should cooperate. If the media also sends a photographer, the candidate or P.R. person should let the photographer select the pose and the settings.

Candidates should keep in mind that a P.R. person may be needed to ferret out unwritten ground rules. For example, a newspaper, radio, or TV station may favor the candidate who buys its advertising. Or the competitive situation may be so

Fig. 6-5. Patrick Oliphant, © 1983 Universal Press Syndicate. Reprinted with permission. All rights reserved."

bitter that it is difficult for one of the media to be friendly to a candidate favored by a rival.

Straight News

If a candidate uncovers graft and corruption in city hall, and can prove it, or has a significant role in an important event, or can bask in reflected glory because of an endorsement by a big-name celebrity, the candidate is entitled to "straight" news coverage. This differs from a fluff piece.

But how does the candidate release a significant story? Kathy Bushkin, press secretary for U.S. Senator Gary Hart during his '84 presidential campaign, said of the media, "You can't give tips, and you can't play favorites."[1] P.R. professionals say not to grant an exclusive, but incorporate the story into a speech, issue a news release, or hold a news conference. However, the difference between TV and newspaper deadlines can produce conflicts. The morning paper will be satisfied with a late story while the evening newspaper must pick up a story and complete it by noon. Television wants both story and pictures. Their deadlines usually depend on the time necessary to process film and they prefer a morning news briefing so they can be ready for the 5 or 6 p.m. newscast. A candidate needs expert P.R. advice and must realize that he/she isn't going to be able to please everyone.

As for radio editors, the stations need fresh news every half hour, so they want to report it within minutes. Robert Zimmerman, manager of radio station WPRW,

Manassas, Virginia, takes an extreme view, saying: "If the candidate has already given the story to the newspaper and it has appeared, he or she need not turn around and give it to the radio." He continues: "We in radio feel if it is read, it is dead. If it is heard it is news. One thing we cannot do, of course, is show pictures, so give the picture and details of the event to the newspaper and TV . . . but let us break the story." Before the candidate follows this advice, he or she should discuss this with an experienced P.R. person. Even Zimmerman admits, "Most newspapers and some television people are very narrow-minded about this."[2]

Handouts

Former newsman, and editor of *Campaign Insight*, Hank Parkinson tells candidates to use their imagination. He says, "We advise candidates to ask themselves, '[What] have I just done, or am I about to do . . . that I can envision as an item in the paper?' "[3]

Assuming the candidate has something newsworthy to say, a complete well-written handout is helpful. Some P.R. professionals say the candidate should provide the media with a biography, or information sheet. A candidate might offer a friendly newspaper or TV station a selection of photographs it can use.[4]

In a major statewide campaign Hank Parkinson advises the candidate to make up and give a professional packet to each television outlet, consisting of:

- A page with a brief summary of his or her campaign pitch or program.
- A set of 35-mm color slides with one full-face of the candidate, one of wife or husband, one of family, and a variety of action shots at political meetings or showing the candidate engaged in outdoor activities.
- A videotape color film clip (no sound, 30 to 60 seconds) of the candidate at a press conference, in an outdoor setting, or with family.[5]

When a speech or news release is used to convey newsworthy information, the P.R. person, who understands the importance of advance information, will, if possible, arrange to distribute copies. The assignment editor, having seen the speech, will know whether to assign a reporter or a TV camera to cover what the candidate has to say. Handouts help reporters zero in on what is important and give a print reporter the information needed to write the story in advance to meet a deadline.

To illustrate the importance of advance handouts, Mary Ellen Leary, in her book, *Phantom Politics: Campaigning in California*, refers to "A bright young Congressman, Jerome Waldie," who aspired to be Governor of California, but almost never wrote out his speeches. John Laird, Waldie's district assistant, who traveled with him and did his scheduling, said, "At the Democratic State Convention other candidates for governor, (George) Moscone had a release of his speech, (Bob) Moretti of his, (Joseph) Alioto of his. Jerry Waldie got up and told what he did on Nixon's inaugural day: He went to visit a Veteran's Hospital in

Washington instead of attending the inauguration." His words were spontaneous and from the heart but nothing was written out from which we could generate an advance press release. So, Laird says, "The *Los Angeles Times* went to press next morning with remarks from the other three speeches. Waldie might as well have not been there."[6]

There are still other reasons for a handout, even one that describes what has been said or done after the fact. Newspaper and radio and television stations have limited staffs. They may be willing to use a story but may not think it is important enough to cover themselves. Former assistant to the Republican National Chairman, Clarence I. Townes, Jr., says minority media often suffer from extreme budget limitations. If a candidate delivers a well-written news release that features a story of interest in time to make the deadline, it stands a good chance of being used. It may make the front page of a minority newspaper if it is accompanied by a picture of the candidate doing something that includes a member of the minority.[7]

When calculating the chance that a news release will be used, former editor of the New York *Herald-Tribune*, Tom Grayson, stated that some news people are lazy and like to get their information without too much work. He illustrated with this story: Early in his career when Grayson was working for a news service, he was sent out to cover a collision between a Navy fighter plane and an airliner near Fort Dix. After he arrived at the scene with a photographer, he filed his story. But the editor wanted periodic updates for later editions. This meant Grayson had to collect accounts from eyewitnesses, then jog back more than a mile to the nearest farmhouse and phone in. After the third trip, a friendly old reporter from one of the New York newspapers pulled Grayson aside. "Why wear yourself out, son?" he asked. "You heard one eyewitness report. Try to add a few fictitious remarks to go along with them." Grayson took his advice. His imaginary accounts of the eyewitnesses was so good that he received an official commendation from Associated Press headquarters in New York.[8]

When writing a news release, ex-newsman Hank Parkinson sets out guides to help the media release writer. First he insists the story itself shouldn't draw any conclusions or point out a moral. This would invade the right of the newspaper, radio, or television station to present its opinions as editorials. He lists other guidelines:

- Make sure the release carries a name and phone number in case additional information is needed.
- Include release instructions such as whether the editor should hold it for a day or two or use it immediately.
- Include plenty of white space between the release instructions and the copy start, so a headline or instructions to the back shop can be jotted in.
- Keep the margins wide.

- Double-space. (Never turn in a release that isn't typed.)
- Never continue a paragraph from one page to another. (Use the word MORE when continuing a story to a second page.)
- Keep the lead paragraph under 30 words in length. (Never use more than three sentences per paragraph.)[9]

If possible the candidate should take the release personally to the editor or reporter, and, if the news media are to be contacted one by one, care should be taken not to give the editors duplicate copies. Each contact needs a rewrite. For example, Clarence L. Townes, black assistant to the Republican National Chairman, advised, "Never send the minority newspaper the same news release that you sent to the white press. Do not distort, but rewrite. Try to pull out a lead that would be of interest to a Black." Or better yet, the candidate or P.R. person might look for stories with special appeal to the minority community.[10]

News Conferences

The news conference should be reserved for when the candidate has something important or at least provocative to say. It is helpful if the candidate can get P.R. advice so the conference is arranged at a time when the media are not meeting deadlines. It is also helpful to call the editor or assignment editor and explain briefly what is going to be said so that they can determine whether the subject matter has sufficient news value to warrant staff time.

Two interwoven news conferences were held by candidates in the 1977 campaign for president of New York's City Council. Assemblyman Herbert F. Stein held a press conference in front of the home of Soliman Schraf in which Stein told the assignment editors that Schraf was alleged to be a manufacturer of home adult movies. To get coverage, the news media was told that Stein intended to challenge Schraf to admit or deny that he had hosted a meeting of those connected with the "adult movie industry" and that at this meeting financial contributions were solicited and made to the campaign of Robert Wagner, Jr., Stein's opponent.

Schraf saw the TV cameras and refused to come out and meet Stein, and an hour later Councilman Robert Wagner called his own news conference at his Madison Avenue residence. Wagner denied that he had received or expected to receive or would accept any money from the adult movie industry.[11]

A news conference is no love feast, of course. Governor of the State of Oklahoma Henry Bellmon suggested the candidate study, if possible, before even calling a news conference. He and his staff would compile a list of questions the reporters might ask. Then he spent several hours, sometimes days, going over them, figuring out the best answers. Then he was able to give consistent and intelligent answers regardless of where the reporters probed.[12]

When preparing for a press conference, press aides help with details like introducing the candidate to the press. They also know that there will be embarrassing moments, especially when a candidate is called on to refute or explain. P.R. persons can't stop reporters' embarrassing questions, but they can advise candidates on how to answer. Lynn Nofziger, veteran director of communications for President Ronald Reagan, advised, "The candidate should not only be prepared to meet tough questions but to say the positive things first instead of the negative in replying to questions or responding to situations."[13]

Most P.R. people have contacts among the media that they use to plant enough friendly questions to bring out the points that the candidate wants to cover. When the news conference will appear on television, the candidate should keep replies to the reporters' questions short and easy to follow to enable television news editors to pull a short segment out of the news conference.

There is no magic method for determining if the candidate is issuing enough releases or calling enough conferences, but a clipping service can be employed so the candidate can determine how often materials are used by the print media. To track electronic media, a candidate or staff members must monitor radio and television.

Advice: TV Appearances

Occasionally the press aide has to impress on the inexperienced candidate that TV is an intimate medium that favors a warm, relaxed delivery and that being on TV is not the same as being on the political stump.[14] More than two decades ago both political parties recognized the need for competent television advice. In 1970, the Democratic Congressional Campaign Committee gave out copies of a book on techniques of television campaigning, and invited its members to attend seminars on the subject. The Republican Senate and House Campaign Committee did even better. They hired a television consultant, Lee Bowman, whose full-time and year-round job was to coach their party's senators and congressmen on the use of television.[15]

To begin with, Bowman advised his charges on dress and makeup. For instance, it was his opinion that the blue television shirt, which is traditional dress, was wrong. Instead he said to wear a "nice, clean white shirt which underlights the underside of the face," adding that, "generally clothes should be conservative and shouldn't be distracting."[16]

Like any good television director, Lee Bowman permitted the candidates to rephrase their television script using their own words. A typical example of a candidate using his own words in a television commercial is President Nixon in his 1972 campaign. As the camera zeroed in, the President said to an aide in the oval office, "What's the matter with these clowns? The whole purpose of this is to get property taxes down, not to increase the budgets for local officials to continue to raise property taxes?" The aide replied: "That's what we thought you'd say." Then Nixon added, "Unless you put the heat on these local officials they'll just take the money and pour it into all their pet projects. That's not the way it's going to be."[17]

Bowman warned his GOP politicians that viewers have seen too much television and too many good performers, so if a candidate is artificial, pompous, or patronizing, they recognize it. For this reason, candidates should avoid cliches, though orators have used cliches for generations when addressing live audiences—such as "this great state of Ohio." Also, Bowman advised his prominent pupils to forget the makeup, adding "Most of them don't have time for it and these men [and women] aren't in a beauty contest anyway."[18]

However, there are exceptions. Some men have a five o'clock shadow and need to shave before appearing on television. Other candidates must discard tinted glasses that may cause a sinister look. Bowman also advised that candidates appearing as the main attraction in a major campaign setting, such as a big auditorium, may be subject to the glare of lights and need to apply light makeup.

Bowman, being a realist, was inclined to tolerate most personal mannerisms, explaining that television is a conversational medium and that if candidates start worrying about mannerisms they can become self-conscious. Bowman believed that television directors should only interfere when politicians respond to questions too glibly or give "frozen" responses.

Nervousness often causes the candidate to appear untrustworthy on the television, and in extreme situations the P.R. person must advise the candidate not to accept a television invitation at all. However, most experienced television coaches try to help their candidates overcome their nervousness. Consultant Lee Bowman often invited his political pupils to a television-equipped hotel-suite studio. He believed that a candidate's apprehension could be greatly reduced if he or she could visualize the TV equipment and how it functions, and how they were going to look on camera. For practice, Bowman would ask a controversial question then ask the politician to give part of the answer looking at him and part of it looking directly into the camera. Then Bowman played back the sequence.[19]

Special Public Relations Duties

Even if an event merits no general news coverage, it pays candidates to have their own P.R. persons cover their appearances before organizations and take photographs that are appropriate for reprint in the organizations' house organs or club bulletins. P.R. people are also responsible for providing the news media with accurate schedules. They are expected to tip off reporters when major candidates intend to make policy statements, and to make sure the interview, rally, or event is scheduled so reporters have time to meet deadlines. And if the campaign is large enough, the P.R. staff does even more. They take care of hotel and airplane reservations, seats at banquets, press tables, telephones, typewriters, and transportation.

To understand the enormity of this task, let's look at a three-day swing by presidential candidate Senator John F. Kennedy when he stumped Ohio. As his plane circled the airport, there were last-minute briefings and name checks. When the candidate alighted, there was a flurry of introductions and handshaking from receiving parties holding candidate signs.

After a few words for the local television and radio reporters, Kennedy got a fast ride into town behind the wailing sirens of a police escort. A staffer was left behind to handle the confusion of bags, coats, and briefcases. Once in the car, At the hotel there was a more leisurely interview with local reporters, and a short TV appearance in which he was asked the inevitable questions: "Do you think a Catholic can be elected President? And what is your present stand on Senator Joseph McCarthy?"[20]

Within a few hours, a crowd was rising and applauding as Kennedy and his party entered a formal fundraising dinner. After introductions, snatches of conversation, and the scrawling of autographs, Kennedy gave a speech. This was heard not only by the attending faithful but over a statewide radio hookup. Once the event was concluded, the local Kennedy organization hosted a private party. In attendance were local bigwigs and Kennedy delegates to the National convention. After that there were individual huddles with visiting Governors, U.S. Senators, and local party chairmen.

By midnight, candidate Kennedy was in a hotel room. After conferring with his local advisors, he had a look at the next morning's newspapers, before going to bed. His next days were similar, except for an appearance before 60,000 at a steer roast in Texas.

The number of people required to schedule, coordinate, and advance such campaigns depends on what is planned. When choosing schedulers, candidates should select diplomatic, even-tempered people who can communicate well, since they must adjust and readjust schedules. If a rally must create the illusion of campaign momentum, schedulers should choose dates and times when voters can get off work to attend and they should carefully choose a hall too small for the numbers planned.

An advance team should be responsible for publicity and setting up a telephone committee to turn out a crowd by purchasing ads or distributing leaflets to pedestrians or to residents near the rally site. They must make sure that the media people have advance notice of and access to the event. In addition, the advance team must find people to supply transportation, decorate rally sites, and clean up after the events.

Occasionally, candidates or their strategist(s) may decide on stunts. A political parade of private cars decorated with candidates' signs is common. During his campaign for Governor of the State of Louisiana, Jim Morrison held a truck parade. Each truck carried a cage holding a volunteer in prison garb with a sign indicating that he or she represented appointees of the incumbent Governor who at the time was under indictment on charges of corruption.[21]

When organizing a car or truck caravan, the advance team is responsible for consulting local police before setting the route. Police have valid reasons for not wanting caravans to use certain streets at particular times. After the route decision is made, the advance team has to make sure the route is carefully outlined and that participants meet at a designated place. They should also know what action should be taken if the caravan is interrupted by a red light or a traffic hazard.

Being a publicity stunt, such a caravan only succeeds if it attracts attention. Horn blowing should be discouraged since it angers a great many people, but those in charge may want to hire a band. In most cases, the advance team arranges for a sound truck to broadcast a message and to supply music. Mile-long auto caravans were staged on successive nights when both major candidates for U.S. Senator from the State of Florida wound up their campaigns with rallies at Miami's Bayfront Park. Those in charge of arrangements for then Congressman George Smathers used both a band and a sound truck. Those for his opponent, then U.S. Senator Claude Pepper, bought radio time on a local radio station and had everyone in the auto caravan tune in.

At rally sites there should be advance coordination with a local leader who acts as master of ceremonies, and recognizes local dignitaries in the audience. Arrangements must be made to give the candidate an appropriate introduction. Whoever is in charge of arranging the program should be sure that comments from local VIP's and other guests are kept short.

Because local campaign generals are going to quarrel over scheduling jurisdictions, who sits at the head tables, etc., it is equally important that schedulers search for creative ways to keep factions happy. President John Kennedy deliberately scheduled events involving car travel so he could chat with local politicians during long drives through the country while being trailed by two or three cars full of reporters. After a brief talk, questions, and a receiving line, he was accompanied by different leaders as he drove back to the city.[22]

The planning team should be prepared with diplomatic excuses when the candidate refuses to cater to the whims of important supporters, who want to enhance their own prestige by displaying a candidate at their local club functions, or when the candidate feels it necessary to move quickly through areas they expect to carry by substantial margins. Often local candidates feel that a joint appearance with the candidate will help their ticket, and they must be mollified.

Finally, everyone should know that no formula will satisfy people who have arranged appearances at political clubs or coffee hours that must be canceled or interrupted. This occasionally happens when the candidate, who is the star of the event, must meet with someone else who has more political clout, such as the executive board of a union or the editorial board of a newspaper.

Lynn Nofziger, who served Governor and later President Reagan as press secretary, advised candidates to obtain an exclusive P.R. spokesman who knows the answers when the press requests information. This spokesperson should be involved in all policy-making and decision-making.[23] In a major campaign P.R. expertise can be so valuable that it is desirable to boost a press aide's ego by giving him or her a title. Before doing so candidates should decide just how much authority will be given to the press aide. As Jane Mayer wrote for *The Wall Street Journal*, "Most press secretaries are neither loved nor praised by reporters."[24] As official mouthpieces, their words can actually become barricades between the candidate and the media.

Where does this leave local candidates who do not have high-powered press aides? They can consult friends with political experience or agencies handling campaign advertising. Most of them have press know-how. Another possibility is to seek out the advice of friendly reporters or volunteers who are familiar with editorial coverage.

Chapter 53

The Perils of Provocation

Candidate: "I thought this paper was friendly to me."
Editor: "So it is."
Candidate: "I had a news conference last night and you didn't print a word."
Editor: "Well, what further proof do you want?"[1]

If you want a place in the sun you have to expect a few blisters.
 —Movie Star Loretta Young[2]

The Peril of a Forthright Position

Political activists are often unhappy when candidates won't take forthright positions. That was the reaction of Agar Jacks, one-time chairman of the San Francisco Democratic Party and producer of an early morning talk show at KGO-TV in San Francisco, who showcased a number of the gubernatorial candidates on his program in 1973. After listening to the candidates' cliches, Jacks commented, "You rarely see politicians who will commit themselves frankly on any position at all, unless they are extremely courageous or extremely intelligent." He continued, "The people who are exciting to listen to are vehement young advocates for causes today. . . . They articulate their positions with passion and conviction."[3]

This may be true, but saying or doing something provocative has a flip side. It may get publicity, but does it get votes? The media can paint the publicity seeker as a clown, as they did to Mayor Edward Hanna of Utica, New York. This strong-willed political figure rejected the traditional political parties, creating the local Rainbow Party and issuing an order to remove the door from his office to demonstrate his openness and accessibility to constituents. His administration decided to string banners from light poles, and to plant 2,500 trees on voters' lawns, which he said was to improve the ecology. The media was particularly critical of Hanna's decision to distribute coloring books to school children that favorably depicted him and his administration.[4]

Experienced P.R. Judgment

All of this, again, underscores the need for experienced P.R. personnel who understand that candidates must be factual and consistent and deliver the message in a professional manner. P.R. people know that "off the record" comments and in-house jokes that sound witty during an interview can appear deadly in print.

A good press aide constantly reminds candidates that anything said to a reporter (even before and after a "formal interview") may be used. For example, President Ronald Reagan took the microphone in Santa Barbara in 1983 and made this humorous quip while doing a sound check several minutes before a radio address: "My fellow Americans, I am pleased to tell you I have signed legislation to outlaw Russia forever. We begin bombing in five minutes." Everyone present laughed. When his opponents and some of the media took issue with the comment, he had to apologize.[5]

Although there are exceptions, when candidates' positions are critical, most P.R. professionals seek outside reactions from the campaign manager, from friends, and/or from other advisors. Margaret Heckler, who served eight terms as a Massachusetts Congresswoman prior to becoming Secretary of Health and Human Services, waited to give the press her reaction to controversial ideas or statements until she called various friends. She did not finally make up her mind until she got a wide range of reactions from Republicans, conservatives, liberals, and moderates.[6]

But what about the damaging statement after it has been made? In cases of small slips, they can simply apologize, as Reagan did, but in most cases candidates want to immediately deny false allegations and they must keep a cool head. There are circumstances, though, when denials may be unwise. One such situation took place when U.S. Supreme Court Justice Earl Warren was first campaigning for Governor of California. At that time there were several candidates for lieutenant governor. The conservative advertising agency that was handling his campaign, Whittier and Baxter, attempted to get him to run as a team with a candidate for another office who was the favorite of the people who were putting up most of Warren's money, but Warren steadfastly refused.

Then, the weekend before the primary election, without authorization, Whittier and Baxter announced Warren's endorsement of this candidate. Though Warren was furious, he was in a dilemma. If he made a public issue, he risked the loss of a substantial segment of his own support. After consulting with his press aide, he let the statement stand, but seething with anger he quietly telephoned the agency and ordered them to withdraw from his campaign.[7]

Bad Press

Even a simple unscheduled event can hurt a candidate. They are covered by the media because, like a fire or an earthquake, they are news. In 1980 the incumbent Democratic Governor of Washington State, Dixie Lee Ray, mailed out several hundred thousand brochures. Then she found that her advertising violated state law in that it failed to include her political affiliation. This made news and had political impact in part because the Governor was already in trouble with the Democratic faithful. Some even blamed the error on her very savvy campaign

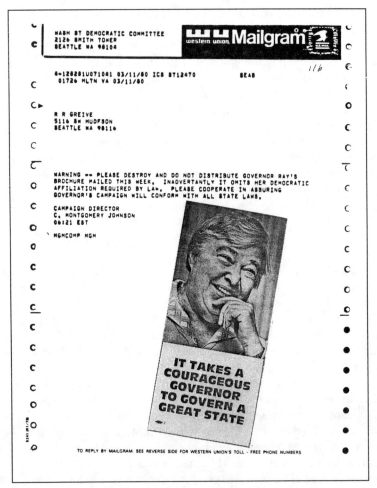

Fig. 6-6. Mailgram, Re-Elect Governor Dixy Lee Ray, Washington
State Democratic Committee, March 11, 1980.

manager, who had been a former Republican State Chairman. When he dispatched
thousands of explanatory telegrams publicly acknowledging the mistake (see
Figure 6-6) he made more news.

News gathering, publishing, or broadcasting is done by individuals, and their
final product reflects their ideas, feelings, and consciences. Right or wrong
individuals of the news media may dislike a candidate's policies or they may
believe he or she is not qualified for the office. They may be suspicious of a
candidate's motives, politics, or financial dealings.

Every candidate or public official who has received bad press is in good company. "Probably no man in American history suffered more than George Washington," according to historian James Thomas Flexner. Newspapers revived old lies and concocted new ones. They questioned Washington's integrity in foreign-policy matters and charged him with deception, deceit, perfidy, and fraud in caring for the nation's financial affairs. They found fault with his personal style and manner, and they denounced him as "full of ostentatious professions of piety."[8]

In 1795, a New Jersey paper criticized what they called Washington's ascent to the imperial presidency: "He holds levies like a King, receives congratulations on his birthday like a King, receives ambassadors like a King, makes treaties like a King, answers petitions like a King, employs his old enemies like a King, shuts himself up like a King, shuts up other people like a King, takes advice of his counselors or follows his own opinion like a King . . . swallows adulation like a King. . . ."[9]

U.S. Senator Huey Long, Presidents Franklin Roosevelt and Harry Truman, and U.S. Senator Wild Bill Langer were among the few modern public officials who were able to capture the public's fancy while under attack from the news media. Since then public perception of the news media has changed.

Governor Pat Brown of California referred to this reality in a memo to his successor, Governor Ronald Reagan, before he took office. Brown cited a passage from the book *War and Peace*, in which a young military officer, the toast of elegant farewell parties, gallops off on his first cavalry charge. He finds real bullets snapping at his ears, and for the first time realizes that, "They're shooting at me, whom everyone loves."[10]

When Someone in the Media Holds a Grudge

Though they compete among themselves to dish out criticism, the news media is very thin-skinned and protective of its position, rights, and privileges. They resent the politician who fights back, and they don't forget if the politician publicly plays one medium against another.

This brings us to probably the most memorable political news conference of our time. It was called in November, 1962, by Richard Nixon, who had just been defeated for Governor of the State of California, He started the conference saying, "As I leave you, I want you to know how much you're going to be missing." Then he picked up the tempo, saying, "You won't have Nixon to kick around anymore because, gentlemen, this is my last press conference in which . . . I have the opportunity to test wits with you." As he concluded his remarks, Nixon threw his Sunday punch: "I think it is time that our great newspapers have at least the objectivity, the same fullness of coverage television has. You and I can only say, "Thank God for television and radio for keeping the newspapers a little more

Fig. 6-7. Masaelly, Jefferson Communications, Inc., distributed by Tribune Company Syndicate, Inc., Seattle Times, January 14, 1984. Used by permission.

honest."[11] This, of course, was not Nixon's last news conference, and the news people never let him forget his bad-tempered remarks, even when he went on to become the President of the United States.

Singling out a reporter, an electronic medium, or a newspaper for attack has disadvantages. Candidates must say enough to make the attack newsworthy. Candidates aiming at a prominent target must realistically expect the target of the attack to retaliate. One newspaper publisher and politician, William Randolph Hearst, took on his contemporaries and came out second best. During Hearst's bare-knuckled battle with contemporary publishers he used the flagship of his publishing empire, the *New York Journal-American*, to call rival newspaper publishers Joseph Pulitzer of the *New York World*, a "coward, a traitor, and a sycophant." He described Oswald Garrison Villard of the New York *Evening Post* as ". . . sued by his own sister," for allegedly trying to rob her of her share of her father's estate. James Gordon Bennett of the *New York Herald* was described "as lately indicted for printing obscene and indecent advertising," and William Laffan of the *New York Sun* was pictured as "the mortgage menial of Morgan."[12]

These publishers had their revenge. They joined with the political establishment in viciously attacking and narrowly defeating Hearst, first when he ran for mayor of New York City and then for Governor of the state. Hearst's experience only reinforces the advice given by California Governor Pat Brown in his memo to incoming Governor Reagan, "Never to get into an argument with a newspaper unless you own it. A newspaper fails to get in the last word only if it goes broke in mid-debate. Politics is strewn with the defeated who tried."[13]

Good public relations requires that regardless of how they feel about reporters, candidates or their agents return media calls promptly and answer questions honestly. Candidates are foolish to fib. Jeff Greenfield states in his book, *Playing to Win*, that it was fibs to the press that caused the crumbling of President Lyndon Johnson's credibility. He tells of small incidents, for example when President

Fig. 6-8. Ben Wicks, The Province, February 10, 1980. Used by permission.

Johnson denied that Richard Goodwin was writing his speeches—after the reporter had just talked to Goodwin about the speeches Goodwin was working on—or when, after making extensive preparation, the White House canceled a press stop in 1966, saying that it had never intended to make such a stop. "These 'little lies' helped solidify the press' sense of Johnson as a dissembler." Thus the media was far more willing to listen to the argument that anything he said was not the whole truth.[14]

Media people emphasize that it is foolish to "stonewall it," as President Nixon did in the Watergate scandal. Most of those with press experience advise candidates to voluntarily face the music early and make full disclosure, thus avoiding the need to be evasive, pretentious, or antagonistic. If the press digs up facts themselves, there may be sensational exposure. This was the case with one-time Alabama Governor "Big Jim" Folsom. He acquired the title "Kissin' Jim" because he always kissed the beauty queens he crowned at civic celebrations. Then the press found out that he had been sued by a young lady who claimed he was the father of her child without the benefit of matrimony.[15] After that he quit kissing beauty queens.

When candidates do own up, they need not give all of the facts. "You have to be honest," Kathy Bushkin advised press secretary for U.S., Senator Gary Hart, during his presidential effort. Then she said with a smile, "But you don't have to answer every question."[16]

Sometimes the media—or more accurately a particular newspaper radio or television station—is unfair. Some of them even relish barbed attacks. For example, the newspaper, *New Hampshire Union Leader*, characterized Wesley Powell, Governor of New Hampshire: "Wesley One-Note," "too big for his britches," "peculiar, vindictive, highly egotistical," and "dog in the manger." The same newspaper characterized Nelson A. Rockefeller, Vice President of the United States, as a: "wife swapper," "home wrecker," "Kennedy's alter ego, errand boy and all-round flunky," and "Nelse the Knife." Margaret Chase Smith, U.S.

Senator from Maine, was depicted as "Moscow Maggie" and "State of Maine's liability," while Harry S. Truman, President of the United States, was called "the little dictator," "reign of ignorance," "General Incompetence," and "The Maharajah of Washington." Barbara Walters, co-host of the NBC-TV "Today" show got called "a shameless huckster" and "a hussy."[17]

If candidates are faced with such killer journalists, they should take a cue from President Calvin "Silent Cal" Coolidge, when a reporter asked:

"Have you anything to say about Prohibition?"
"No."
"About the farm situation?"
"No."
"About the upcoming senatorial campaign?"
"No. And don't quote me."[18]

Under such circumstances radio and television journalist Jeff Greenfield says, "Do not be intimidated by the threat that, 'We want to be able to get your side of the story'." Rather, depend on the fairness of the public, who will at least wonder why an inaccurate or biased presentation does not state the candidate's point of view.[19]

Part 7

Political Strategy

Chapter 54

Examples of Strategic Technique

> Political strategy is a little like a clandestine love affair . . . conceived in
> secret . . . relished in anticipation . . . painful in experience.
> —Anonymous

Defining the Objective

Political strategy consists of a plan or method marbled within a campaign that is used to meet the opposition in political combat. In most cases, strategy consists of calculating the political options and, after weighing them, making a choice. It affects everything that happens in a political campaign, and its application is important enough to be treated separately. This section consists of a number of stratagems that I believe merit special attention.

Scare Strategy, For Example

Sometimes incumbents or other candidates attempt to scare a substantial segment of the voting public by accusing the challenger of being a radical, a Communist, or an irresponsible spendthrift, or they argue that, if the opposition succeeds, they will take away voters' benefits. For example, fear is instilled in older voters by accusing the opposition of intending to cut social security benefits. On other occasions, an incumbent can instill fear in parents, students, and alumni by saying a candidate who intends to cut the school budget will cut out high school sports.

When plotting political strategy, the candidate should keep in mind the words of Arnold Steinberg, who warns candidates that they must understand ". . . victory at the polls is the overall goal; not educating the electorate; not dramatizing a particular issue; not criticizing the opponent; not attacking the incumbent President or Vice President."[1] When Richard Nixon ran for president against John F. Kennedy, the transcripts of their first televised debate do not reveal why Kennedy won—or Nixon lost—in the eyes of the voting public. But veteran political image maker Steven Shadegg contends Nixon made errors in strategy. Nixon's first error occurred when Kennedy, with a deep tan and better television appearance, was offered makeup and promptly said "no." Nixon looked sick and pale because he had recently been confined to the hospital. When the makeup was offered to him, he let his pride, not reality, prompt him to refuse. During the confrontation, Vice President Nixon's image suffered, not only because he looked sick, but because the cameras showed that he was visibly shaken by Kennedy, who sat confident and poised.

Shadegg argues that Nixon should have recognized his sickly appearance and refused to debate. In any event, Shadegg believes the election could have been saved if the Nixon camp had issued an advance news release portraying Nixon as the underdog and stressing his willingness to get out of a sickbed and go on TV so as not to disappoint the public. Even when the debate was over, Shadegg argues Nixon's publicists could have strategically made an asset out of Nixon's solid homey appearance, while damning the slick movie-star image exuded by Kennedy.[2]

Strategy Is But One Element of Victory

Political strategy is only one of the factors contributing to political victory. Often other forces are in control. For example, a wealthy candidate is able to use a personal fortune to buy advertising and overpower the opposition. Simple desire and willingness to work and to sacrifice can overpower other considerations. And ambitions that fuel a political career can manifest themselves in various ways. For example, from the age of seventeen, Mildred Millier was determined to marry a man who would someday be president. It was largely through her efforts after marrying William Howard Taft that he became President and later Chief Justice of the United States Supreme Court.[3]

Outside forces may create or destroy the best of political strategies and unforeseen circumstances can upset the best-laid plans. In December 1944, a little-known reformer was running for Mayor of Minneapolis. Most prognosticators gave him no chance of winning. Then a local scandal sheet published an article headlined "Mayor Kline [the incumbent] is a hypocrite and a liar, and the Kline administration is the most corrupt regime in history of the city." Following this, the editor of the scandal sheet was murdered and the reformer, Hubert Humphrey, rode to victory on the backlash against the incumbent mayor. This started a career that catapulted Humphrey into national prominence as a U.S. Senator and later Vice President of the United States.[4]

Front-Runner Strategy

If a candidate enters the campaign with a decided advantage—such as superior party registration or incumbency status—classic strategy calls for him or her to avoid controversial issues and to entrust his or her election to party identification, superior visibility, and whatever record of constituent service he or she can point to.[5]

At the same time, the word "reelect" is used as part of the "let's stick with the brand we have been using" strategy to emphasize the incumbency. When the incumbent candidate uses "return" or "keep" as a part of advertising, it may

Fig. 7-1. Campaign posters: Keep Sparkman, County Commissioner, King County, Washington, 1950; Retain Earl Coe, Secretary of State, State of Washington, 1950; Re-Elect Everett Dirksen, U.S. Senator, Illinois, 1956.

indicate that the incumbent was appointed to fill out an unexpired term, rather than having been elected in his or her own right (see Figure 7-1).

Using the Power and Stature of Incumbency

Frequently, an office-holder uses the stature of his or her incumbency to exude an image of power and competency. For example, a television commercial depicts Barney Frank as a heavy-set, fortyish man with black-rimmed glasses. He is wearing a softball jersey and is standing at home plate. After he swings the bat to limber up, Frank hits the first pitch, throws down the bat, and runs. The camera cuts back and forth between Frank running the bases and an outfielder chasing the softball across the grass. Then the camera shows Frank standing up quickly and jogging, the catcher trying to tag Frank as he slides into home plate. His teammates cheer and slap him on the back. Meanwhile, the viewer hears an announcer's voice:

In 1981 Barney Frank's colleagues named him rookie of the year in Congress. They were impressed with how Barney chopped millions of dollars in wasteful farm subsidies, how he helped stop the Republicans from cutting Social Security, how he opposed the Reagan tax program because it favored the rich over average people, and how he even stood up to a Democratic tax plan that favored big oil.[6]

Fig. 7-2. Gary Yanker, *Prop Art* (New York: Darien House, 1972), p. 20.

Figures 7-2 and 7-3 depict both stereotypes. The appeal of the Australian Labor Party is obvious. The other message was released by United States Senator Robert Kerr when he sought the presidential nomination. It was a full-page reprint of the front page of his hometown paper, emphasizing that he is powerful, which, in his opinion, is what the presidency called for.

The Strategy of Creating and Selling an Image

To carry an image of power, politicians must have enormous egos. The media delight in putting a pin in the candidate who has or is trying gain a god-like image. This gives those who create and sell public images yet another problem—one that plagued Tom Dewey. Dewey began his political career as a crusading district attorney, which carried him to the governorship of the State of New York. Then twice he was his party's nominee for president.

Dewey was extremely self-conscious about his height (5'8"), which he felt detracted from his "image" as a forceful Governor of the nation's largest state and as the potential president of the United States. He insisted on sitting on a telephone book when *Life* Magazine photographed him in the New York Governor's office so that he would not be dwarfed by the huge Governor's chair. When this tidbit found its way to the press, delighted Democratic opponents seized on it to portray him as a man with a synthetic personality.[7]

On occasion, incumbent candidates use strategic techniques to convert an unfavorable image to one that, though unpopular, still exudes power and competence. For example, in the 1978 race for Governor of New York, one of the nation's best political media men, David Garth, manipulated Governor Hugh Carey's much-publicized indifference to public appearances and ribbon-cutting ceremonies and even publicized Carey's propensity to rubbing the press and

Fig. 7-3. Ad insert, Oklahoma Robert S. Kerr for President
Club, *Ada Evening News*, Ada, Oklahoma, 1956.

legislators the wrong way. He sold Carey to the voters as a great, but strong-willed, administrator whom nobody (but the voters) liked.[8]

The Challenger's Strategy

When running behind, challengers can't be choosy and must seize issues that will turn the voter against the status quo. Figure 7-4 depicts three TV commercials sponsored by parties who were out of power. In 1980 the Republican National Committee sponsored a television and radio commercial where audiences heard the barking drawl of "Mad as Hell" Eddie Chiles, Chairman of the Western Com-

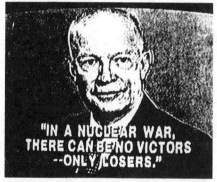

Fig. 7-4. Richard L. Gordon, "Democrats Test Ads in D.C.," *Advertising Age,* March 12, 1984; "Congress: GOP Fall Offensive," *Newsweek*, April 21, 1980.

pany, a Fort Worth oil supply firm. "What are you mad about today, Eddie Chiles?" asked an announcer, and Chiles, a Connolly-turned-Reagan Republican, unleashed an attack on every elected official to his political left. Then, with a background of patriotic fife-and-drum music, Chiles declared, "I'd trade the whole bunch of liberals in Congress for some straight shooters who haven't lost all their marbles."

In 1984, the Democratic National Committee attacked President Reagan for his policy of proliferating nuclear weapons by using a commercial featuring President Eisenhower stating, "In a nuclear war, there can be no victors—only losers." The Democratic National Committee also sponsored a television commercial that attacked President Reagan for his insensitivity to women's issues.

When creating their strategy, wise challengers don't focus on their opponent's power, importance, or seniority. The clever challenger tries to use their own power and influence against an incumbent. This is what opponents did against one-time Speaker of the House "Uncle Joe" Cannon, one of the most powerful men in U.S. history. His critics criticized him for his staunch and unflinching faith in the status quo, with wisecracks such as, "If Cannon had attended the caucus on creation, he would have been loyal to chaos."[9]

Another way to turn power and influence against an incumbent is to indicate that it smacks of dictatorship. During President Nixon's first term of office, detractors accused him of instituting an "imperial Presidency." This accusation is what U.S. Senator McGovern used when he ran against President Nixon in 1972. McGovern's television ads tried unsuccessfully to intimate that if Nixon were reelected freedom would be destroyed.

Most challengers feel that strategically they must criticize their opponent but don't want to get in the mud themselves, so they let someone else speak for them. The McGovern for President Committee did this with a television commercial: The screen was filled with the word "NIXON" in orange against a black background. Throughout the commercial, the letters changed in color from orange, to blue, to green, to yellow, to red. Meanwhile, the announcer said, " 'People have deep feelings about President Nixon.' " The camera switched to a woman who said, " 'He has put a ceiling on wages and has done nothing about controlling prices.' " Then a man said, " 'The one thing I knew during his last four years was that he knew that in some way he would have to please me come this election. And what frightens me is that if he gets in again he doesn't have to worry about pleasing me any more.' " A second woman cut in with, " 'He was caught in the act of spying and stealing. They used to go to jail for these things. He is the president and should set an example.' " Then a third woman spoke: " 'There always seems to be some big deal going on with the Nixon people, some wheat deal or something.' " The camera switched to a fourth woman. She said, " 'When I think of the White House, I think of it as a syndicate, a crime outfit, as opposed to, you know, a government.' " Then the camera picked up a fifth woman, " 'All I know is that the prices keep going up and he is president.' " A second man gave his opinion: " 'I think he's smart. I think he's sly. He wants to be the president of the United States so badly he will do *anything*." The TV screen then showed "McGovern" in white letters on a black background. The announcer said, " 'That's exactly why this is brought to you by the McGovern for President Committee.' "[10]

Avoiding Specifics

On occasion, a candidate, particularly a challenger, must strategically offer detailed criticism while avoiding difficult controversial solutions. One strategy is to resort to the rhetorical question. For example, in a debate with President Jimmy Carter, challenger Ronald Reagan used a rhetorical question to negatively focus on Carter's record:

> Next Tuesday, all of you will go to the polls, and stand there in the polling place and make a decision. I think when you make that decision it might be well if you ask yourself, are you better off than you were four years ago? Is it easier for you to go and buy things in the stores than it was four years ago? Is there more or less

unemployment in the country than there was four years ago? Is America as respected throughout the world as it was? Do you feel that our security is as safe, that we're as strong as we were four years ago?[11]

Candidates for less prestigious offices have used the same strategy. Figure 7-5 shows an ad used by Democratic candidate Al Brisbois in his unsuccessful campaign to unseat Tom Swayze, who at the time was at the pinnacle of his power as speaker of Washington state's legislative House of Representatives.

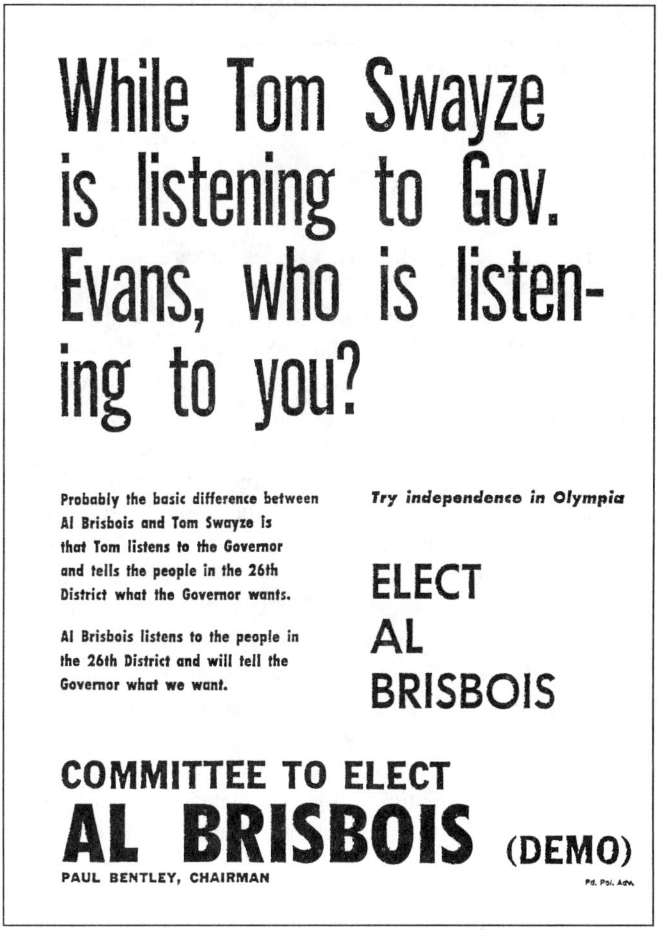

While Tom Swayze is listening to Gov. Evans, who is listening to you?

Probably the basic difference between Al Brisbois and Tom Swayze is that Tom listens to the Governor and tells the people in the 26th District what the Governor wants.

Al Brisbois listens to the people in the 26th District and will tell the Governor what we want.

Try independence in Olympia

ELECT AL BRISBOIS

COMMITTEE TO ELECT
AL BRISBOIS (DEMO)
PAUL BENTLEY, CHAIRMAN

Pd. Pol. Adv.

Fig. 7-5. Newspaper Ad, *Tacoma News Tribune*, Tacoma, Washington, November 2, 1970.

Chapter 55

Trends, Time, and Momentum

> The strategist doesn't just kill time . . . he works it to death.
> —Anonymous
>
> Politics is just like show business. You need a big opening. Then you coast for awhile. Then you need a big finish.[1]
> —Ronald Reagan, 1960

Momentum

Typically, as campaigns start there is a large percentage of undecideds who lean in one direction or the other.[2] Since the voters are inclined to switch to a candidate because they believe they are moving toward majority consensus, one strategy is to give the voter a feeling that the candidate is forging ahead.

This strategy was used in a television commercial during the 1980 New Hampshire presidential primary: A plane taxis toward the camera at night in driving rain. Presidential candidate George Bush walks through the rain with Hugh Gregg, the manager of his New Hampshire organization. There is loud chanting off-camera, "We want Bush," and Bush is shown in the midst of an adoring crowd. An announcer, speaking over the crowd, says: " 'Not just here, but in every state that he's been, the spirit of the Republican party has soared to meet the real opportunity of the 1980s. What has won out is very simple" great personal energy, experience, and knowledge at the highest levels. Quality. Ladies and gentlemen, this is George Bush.' " The camera shifts to Bush, who speaks breathlessly, " 'Thank you. Thank you. I bring you word from across America. We're going all the way!' " White letters then flash against a blue background: " 'George Bush for President.' " And the announcer says, " 'George Bush. A President we won't have to train.' "[3]

This type of momentum won't work for candidates seeking lesser offices who are not blessed with media attention. Most candidates, then, must depend upon the circumstances of their campaign to design their own strategy for building momentum.

All-Out Scramble Strategy

Typically, the all-out scramble strategy is to "run full speed ahead and hellbent for election." This is what John F. Kennedy did when he ran for President in 1960; he made a maximum effort from the beginning.

Republican Norbert Tiemann also used the all-out scramble when he ran against Val Peterson for Governor of Nebraska. Tiemann made six hundred appearances and traveled over 65,000 miles, to edge out the favored Peterson by 15,000 votes. However, there is a downside to this kind of campaign effort. His campaign manager, David Pierson, commented, "When election day came, we figured he was just about fourteen hours away from total collapse."[4]

Peaking Strategy

Some very savvy political personalities have avoided the all-out scramble strategy. President Franklin Roosevelt for one constantly reminded his intimates that the problem with this strategy is that, "It is difficult to maintain the highest note of the scale."[5] Instead, Roosevelt used peaking strategy. As in football, where there is the fourth-down punt, or in baseball, where there are two men on bases, two "outs," and a batter is walked to fill the bases, so in a political campaign there is what is strategically known as "peaking." Its purpose is to create a "snowball effect" near the end of a campaign so that support seems to rise almost uncontrollably. In its classic application, this strategy brings the campaign to a crescendo on election day.

The term "peaking" was probably first used by those studying the popularity charts submitted by pollsters, which displayed a line showing the rise and fall in a candidate's popularity until it formed a peak. Vice President Richard Nixon popularized the term during the 1960 Nixon-Kennedy campaign, when his strategy called for a steady rise in activity and intensity, peaking once about three weeks before election day and then again just as voters went to the polls.[6]

To peak in his New York campaign for Governor, Nelson Rockefeller ran 74 television commercials during the week of October 18, 1968. These commercials were seen an average of 9.8 times by 91 percent of all homes with television in New York City.[7]

Other candidates create the effect of peaking by magnifying favorable endorsements, the results of an opinion poll, or other dramatic events just before the election. In 1952, for example, the United States was engaged in the Korean War during a presidential campaign. Both candidates for President recognized the mounting war casualties and its economic burden and that the public desired peace, but they were unwilling to encourage an American default, which might jeopardize the nation's allies. Early on, General Eisenhower had an almost insurmountable lead. When the public opinion polls showed Eisenhower's lead slipping away the hero of Normandy electrified the voting public by saying, "If elected, I will go to Korea." While Eisenhower was careful not to promise anything concrete, it was enough to persuade the voters that this respected military leader could somehow achieve peace. It was not until after President

Eisenhower, made his trip to Korea that the public realized this was far from the diplomatic coup they had expected.[8]

Snowball Strategy

Some strategists try to artificially create the momentum necessary for either the scramble or peaking strategies in a major campaign. For example, a major candidate can schedule events in halls so small that they can't handle the expected crowd, or the candidate can arrange events where a large number of voters have already congregated.

John F. Kennedy created the snowball effect in another way. After a day of strenuous campaigning, his schedulers arranged for an airport car caravan that would hit downtown at noon when office workers were on their lunch break.[9]

The snowball strategy took an unusual twist in the 1970 race for Governor of Virginia in a contest between Republican Linwood Holton and Democrat Bill Battle. At the time, Virginia was considered to be a Democratic state. Battle was a former ambassador to Australia who had an old Virginia family name. To overcome this edge, Republican Holton's public relations people focused on mock elections for governor held by high school students. The Young Republicans lined up the state's high school leaders and with their help managed to win a mock election every day during the final three weeks of the campaign. Of the twenty-two mock elections publicized by a friendly press, Holton won twenty. His campaign gathered momentum, and Linwood Holton became one of the few Republicans ever to govern that state.[10]

Using Money to Create Momentum

When the strategy calls for massive last-minute campaign advertising, there can be no blitz unless there's money in the treasury, so campaign spending must be paced to leave enough money for last-minute advertising volume. For example, the candidate might expend half of the available campaign funds during the first three quarters of the time available, leaving the second half for the last one quarter.

In 1974, U.S. Senator Robert Dole of Kansas was opposed by Congressman Rob Roy. Early polls showed Dole ahead by more than twenty points. Then Roy launched a $100,000 television cam-

Fig. 7-6. James Ertel, *How to Run for Office* (New York: Sterling Publishing, 1960), p. 66.

paign featuring a bitter, bruising attack on the incumbent. At first Dole began losing his advantage; by mid-October all published polls showed him trailing. But when Roy had exhausted his resources and the charges against Dole were going stale, the incumbent threw everything he had into a last-minute counter-strategy. He brought in big outside names and dramatically increased his television coverage. Roy, unable to match this effort, was forced to watch helplessly as his campaign, which had already peaked, trailed off. Dole drew even in the polls and went on to win.[11]

Strategy and Trends

If there is a prevailing political trend, the candidate running with it tries to ride its crest like a ship under full sail running with the wind. When pursuing this strategy, a candidate or party locates a trend and tries to simplify what is bothering the voters. If it can be embodied in a headline, the candidate repeats it until it pierces the voter's stream of consciousness. Most incumbents do not even mention a challenger. Instead, they ride the tide and take credit when things are going well. For example, a commercial for incumbent President Ronald Reagan in his 1984 re-election campaign features footage of happy Americans in all walks of life performing daily tasks. As the pictures flash on and off the screen, an announcer says, "It's morning again in America. Today, more men and women will go to work than ever before in our country's history. With interest rates at about half the record highs of 1980, nearly 2,000 families today will buy new homes . . . more than at any time in the past four years. Under the leadership of President Reagan, our country is prouder and stronger and better. Why would we ever want to return to where we were less than four short years ago?"[12]

Running with the political wind is often nothing more than keeping a noncontroversial profile. Under these circumstances, classic strategy is to persuade voters to choose an alternative, unknown candidate, by painting the opposition as a political evil. In 1964, a popular Baltimore county executive, Ted (Spiro) Agnew, used this strategy when he was recruited by the Maryland Republican organization and ran for governor unopposed in the Republican primary.

Looking at the opposition primary, Agnew's strategists assessed the three candidates for the Democratic nomination and shrewdly determined that the Democratic nominee would be either too liberal, too racist, or too much of a machine candidate for universal appeal. Agnew's advertising consultant, Robert Goodman, explained that as the campaign started, there was a bitter Democratic gubernatorial primary. Since they did not want to be committed on any issues that might prevent Agnew from later altering his position, they decided to sell "pure personality."

Agnew's campaign committee flooded the state with "Ted Agnew is your kind of man for Governor" billboards and bumper stickers. Agnew's big money was spent on radio and TV advertising. His commercials featured a swing orchestra playing what became known as "The Song."

My kind of man, Ted Agnew is my kind of man,
Ted Agnew is a great new talent for Governor, And what's more,
He's your kind of man, Ted Agnew is taking your stand,
Ted Agnew is a bright light shining, Ted Agnew is that new day dawning,
Ted Agnew is the time to move to Maryland with our kind of man."[13]

Mr. Goodman summarized the advantages of selling pure personality by saying, "It encouraged a coalition with people who found it hard to support the Democratic nominee whoever he might be. And it suggested Agnew was their type of man."

Riding a political trend is not easy. This is in part because often there is more than one political wind blowing in different directions at the same time. When political winds collide, they frequently create a cross-current, making it almost impossible to see a clear prevailing trend.

Such a cross-current occurred when Franklin Delano Roosevelt sought to break a "no third term presidential tradition" and be the first president to serve three terms. This tradition convinced a number who had voted Democratic to support a displaced Democrat-turned-Republican, Wendell Wilkie. In that election, many of Roosevelt's former supporters voted for Wilkie, including former New York Democratic Governor Al Smith; Roosevelt's one-time close friend and advisor, Raymond Morley; former Secretary of War in the Roosevelt cabinet, Hugh Johnson; and John L. Lewis, long-time president of the United Mine Workers and founder of the CIO.

Yet the threat of World War II hung over the country, which permitted Roosevelt to take advantage of another cross current—one favoring a strong hand in time of crisis. In the final analysis, the voting public chose Roosevelt's experience.[14]

Running Against a Trend

Candidates running against a trend need to get out of its way. The usual strategy in this case is to play down party affiliation, or any other factor that seems to be irritating voters, and attract attention to themselves as individuals.

In the 1958 New York gubernatorial election, Governor Averill Harriman recognized a strong national trend running against the Republicans, so he tried to tie his state campaign to national issues. Harriman's Republican opponent, Nelson Rockefeller, saw the same thing. Rockefeller played down his party affiliation, absenting himself from the welcoming party when the Republican President of the United States visited New York, and concentrated his energy on a vigorous street-side campaign. This gave Rockefeller an opportunity to contrast his warm personality with the austere personality of incumbent Governor Harriman.[15]

Making Strategic Use of Time

It was a Sunday when U.S. Senator John F. Kennedy made a campaign stop in the Green Bay Packers' hometown, Green Bay, Wisconsin, and the Packers football team was playing a home game. Mounting the platform, Kennedy brought down the house when he said, "Ladies and gentlemen, I intend to cut it short and be out of here in plenty of time to permit those of you who are going to see the Green Bay Packers to leave. I don't mind running against Mr. Nixon, but I have good sense enough not to run against the Green Bay Packers."[16]

A political campaign is a huge ball of chores with many layers. Timing plays a sophisticated and even decisive role in determining when they are peeled off, one layer at a time. Time can be a problem for politicians who procrastinate. For instance, in a race for a minor office, the most effective strategy may be for the candidate to go door-to-door, but since they can only cover a few voters an evening, the candidate must start anywhere from three weeks to six months before election day.

While on the stump during a political campaign, most organizations allow each speaker three to five minutes to present their platform, and insist that time limits be honored when the candidates make their campaign speeches.[17] Thus, it is imperative that candidates not only know what they are going to say, but keep it within the allotted time limits.

Timing and Identification Strategy

Time has another facet. Most candidates for major or minor offices have to overcome identification problems, at least as the campaign opens and then as the campaign progresses. An example of how identification strategy shifts throughout a campaign can be seen in the efforts of Joseph Alioto, an unknown running for Mayor of San Francisco. Alioto hired communication specialist Tony Schwartz to write his radio and television commercials. Schwartz first turned out a series of low-key radio and television spots that emphasized Alioto's personal feelings about a wide range of social problems. As election day approached, Alioto emphasized what Schwartz considered to be the strong points, which contrasted with the unrealistic positions taken by other front-runners. Finally, a principal challenger, who held another political office, emerged from the pack. Then Schwartz had Alioto attack this opponent's record.[18]

When the campaign is coming down the home stretch, the candidate can't afford to listen to the activists who have followed the campaign. Usually they are tired of the same television commercial, billboard, or newspaper ad, and they argue that everyone they know has already decided who they're going to vote for. But the candidate should remember that it is necessary to bore those who are already going to vote to reach low-interest voters. These low-interest voters, strategist Edward Schwartzman says, "Are the 20 to 25 percent of the registered voters who do not make up their minds until late in the campaign and who frequently cast the 'swing' or determining votes in the election."[19]

Late in the campaign, candidates often find they are being drowned out by the heavyweights who use television to land their most telling blows. A change of pace may be necessary to pierce the undecideds' stream of consciousness. Even though television is considered the most effective medium in most statewide races, late in Michigan Governor Milikin's 1970 campaign, public-opinion pollsters found that his television advertising no longer seemed to be impressing the voter. He canceled most of his television commercials and in their place ordered a newspaper supplement. In all, Governor Millikin distributed three million supplements to the Sunday newspaper on the second to last and the last Sundays preceding the election.[20]

When the campaign has been heated and bitter, a candidate's image may need rehabilitation. Then a candidate for major office who commands attention might change the pace by using the hearth, the family, and the dog as appropriate props to close the campaign. In 1980 both Democratic and Republican presidential campaigns retreated to safe programming on election eve. Carter used a twenty-minute appeal moderated by actor Henry Fonda. Reagan bought half an hour on all three networks to talk of his vision for America, saying,

> "Last year I lost a friend who was more than a symbol of the Hollywood dream industry. To millions he was a symbol of our country itself. Duke [John] Wayne did not believe our country was ready for the dustbin of history. Just before his death he said in his own blunt way, 'Just give the American people a good cause, and there's nothing they can't lick.' "[21]

The Lesser Candidate and Identity Strategy

When candidates running for lesser office are being drowned out during the final days of a campaign, they can make one of two choices. They can put their best foot forward a few days earlier when there is less competition for media attention, or they can hold a big attention-getter just before the election. This can take the form of creative advertising that depends on more than a choice of design, color, and materials. For example, special door-hanger cards can be designed for doorknobs with a packet of instant coffee stapled to each card. These cards can be distributed to each potential voter the night before the election, with copy that says, "Good morning. It's Election Day and time to go to the polls and vote. But before you give your support to _____, have a cup of coffee on her. Remember she'll represent us well in the legislature."[22]

Chapter 56

Issues

> Papers today say "What would Lincoln do today? . . . . Being a
> Republican he would vote the Democratic ticket. Being in sympathy for
> the underdog he would be classed a Radical Progressive. Having a sense
> of humor he would be called an eccentric.
> —Will Rogers[1]

The Political Conception

It is common for politicians to mistakenly believe that elections are won or lost on the basis of issues. It is also common for the public to believe that candidates and their advisors use issues to manipulate voters. These conceptions are more or less true.

Candidates for public office need not always be prepared with a position. Not all campaigns rise and fall on volatile issues. For some offices the issue is constant, for example, efficiency in the administration of government functions. Under these circumstances, the candidate may have to show more than a desire to see that everyone pays their fair share of the costs. The public may insist on a detailed plan to ensure that administrative overhead is reduced in a particular function of government. Here, the candidate must be armed with research if he or she is to justify a stand, but this is not a controversial issue.

In any campaign, if the candidate is not prepared with sufficient research to give intelligent answers, that in itself will become an issue. There should be sufficient research so that a candidate doesn't appear to be ignorant of the cutting issues that vary from campaign to campaign. On occasion environmental issues will be hot and candidates will be trampling over each other to show their support. On another occasion the issue might be a religious versus social issue—for example, providing condoms to public high school students to curb the spread of AIDS or making abortion illegal, except in the case of rape, incest, or when the woman's life is in danger.

In some constituencies, strengthening affirmative action for women and minorities is an issue. On other occasions, the issue might involve a clash between church and state—for example, giving families tax credits for each child attending private or parochial schools, or banning doctors at federally funded clinics from providing information on abortion to their patients. Again, research is the key to having an answer for the media no matter what the prevalent issue is.

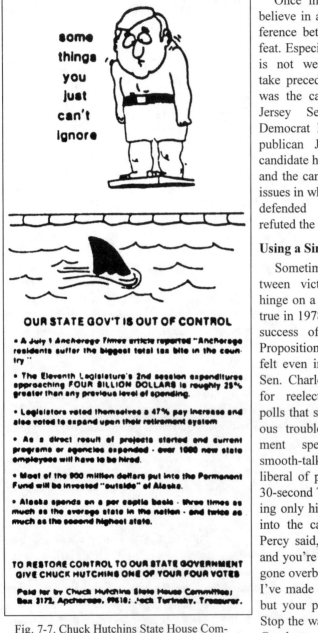

some things you just can't ignore

OUR STATE GOV'T IS OUT OF CONTROL

• A July 1 *Anchorage Times* article reported "Anchorage residents suffer the biggest total tax bite in the country."

• The Eleventh Legislature's 2nd session expenditures approaching FOUR BILLION DOLLARS is roughly 25% greater than any previous level of spending.

• Legislators voted themselves a 47% pay increase and also voted to expand upon their retirement system

• As a direct result of projects started and current programs or agencies expanded · over 1000 new state employees will have to be hired.

• Most of the 900 million dollars put into the Permanent Fund will be invested "outside" of Alaska.

• Alaska spends on a per capita basis · three times as much as the average state in the nation · and twice as much as the second highest state.

TO RESTORE CONTROL TO OUR STATE GOVERNMENT GIVE CHUCK HUTCHINS ONE OF YOUR FOUR VOTES

Paid for by Chuck Hutchins State House Committee; Box 3172, Anchorage, 99510; Jack Turinsky, Treasurer.

Fig. 7-7. Chuck Hutchins State House Committee, ad placed in Anchorage Times, November 3, 1980.

Once in a while voters who believe in an issue make the difference between victory and defeat. Especially when a candidate is not well-known, issues can take precedence over images, as was the case in the 1978 New Jersey Senate race between Democrat Bill Bradley and Republican Jeffrey Bell. Neither candidate had held political office and the campaign became one of issues in which each advocated or defended his party line and refuted the other's.[2]

Using a Single Strategic Issue

Sometimes the difference between victory and defeat can hinge on a single issue. This was true in 1978, when, following the success of California's tax-cut Proposition 13, the hysteria was felt even in Illinois, where U.S. Sen. Charles Percy was running for reelection. Responding to polls that showed he was in serious trouble concerning government spending, this urban, smooth-talking, free-spending liberal of past campaigns used a 30-second TV commercial featuring only himself. Staring straight into the camera, close to tears, Percy said, "I got your message and you're right. Washington has gone overboard, and I'm sure that I've made my share of mistakes, but your priorities are mine too. Stop the waste. Cut the spending. Cut the tax."[3]

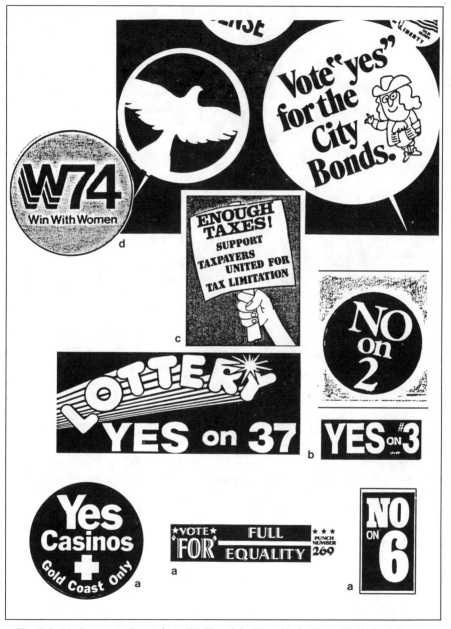

Fig. 7-8. (a) *Campaign Specialists '76* (Ferndale, New York: Votes Unlimited Corporation, (b) *Time,* November 19, 1984, (c) "Wild Cards on the Ballots," *Time,* October 30, 1978, (d) "The Year of the Woman," *Newsweek,* November 4, 1984.

Her name is Nancy.
She's nine years old. In four years
she will be a drug addict.

Fig. 7-9. "23 Winning Ideas for Political
Advertisers" (New York: Bureau of
Advertising, 485 Lexington Avenue), n.d., p. 8.

Percy then added that if he were not sent back to Washington there was no way he could effectively deliver the message to his colleagues, and apparently it worked. Percy was reelected—just barely—to the U.S. Senate.

But victory hinging on a single issue is rare. In the real world, victory depends upon the voters' total impression. Issues—or any one issue—are but one of several forces that help shape that impression.

As Canadian Liberal party pollster Angus Reid once noted, "It is rare that we have elections fought on the pros and cons of an issue."[4] This is simply because in normal circumstances, it is hard to find an issue upon which candidates disagree that so envelopes the voter that it alone influences his or her vote. See Figure 7-10 for an illustration of the several issues that affected U.S. Sen. Warren Magnuson's reelection campaign in 1968.

The gap in voter interest in issues was illustrated during President Franklin Roosevelt's administration when Cordell Hull was the Secretary of State. Hull liked to sound out public sentiment before making important decisions. On one occasion he wrote to the editor of a weekly newspaper in Arkansas asking how the people in that part of the country would react if the State Department granted recognition to a controversial country in the Near East. In a few days the answer came back. "Cordell," it said, "they don't give a damn."[5]

It is a rare campaign where victory depends on solving (or failure to solve) a particular problem, as shown by a poll taken when Reagan was running for the presidency in 1980. The reigning issues and the percentage of those who said the candidate's position even affected their vote were: national defense 27%, income tax policy 10%, reduce government spending 25%, women's rights 7%, draft registration 11%, ownership of Panama Canal 1%, abortion 11%, other 8%.[6]

Fig. 7-10. Newspaper ad, Committee for Maggie, Senator Scoop Jackson, Chairman, *Seattle Times*, September 3, 1968.

Using Strategic Issues To Mold the Candidate's Image

To illustrate how issues help create a candidate's total image, look at one-time New York Governor Nelson Rockefeller. As he concluded his first term, he took an extensive poll. When the results were in, he had to face the fact that he was unpopular. This called for unusual market strategy. When Rockefeller's strategists planned his reelection campaign, they decided first to sell the record of the Rockefeller administration. To do this, they created television and radio commercials that played down Rockefeller as an individual. However, these strategists recognized that on election day the voters would vote not just for a program, but for a man, so when the advertising campaign had publicized Rockefeller's record and the polls showed that his image had begun to improve, they featured the Governor himself.[7]

Further perspective is provided by taking a look at the Canadian National election of 1977. A doctrinaire Progressive Conservative party led by Charles Joseph (Joe) Clark didn't have the clear majority necessary to rule, so they had to resort to a coalition with a minor party. Believing they had a mandate to change the government philosophy, they pressed on, attempting to enact a whole host of legislative proposals.

After less than a year in power, the coalition broke. Then in 1978 Clark and his Canadian Progressive Conservatives party used a general election to take his image to the people. Although he wanted to highlight his philosophy, those planning Prime Minister Clark's campaign recognized that the issues were so intricate that they could not hold the voters' interest if the policies were debated on their individual merits, so Clark attempted to sell the simple theme, "Real change deserves a fair chance" (Figure 7-11).

Major issues may or may not be the key to winning any particular election, but it is interesting to note though how important it is for candidates to keep track of issues. In the 1976 presidential campaign, both Ford and Carter carried briefing books that ran some fifty pages summarizing their positions on almost every conceivable campaign issue.[8]

Exploiting an Issue

Occasionally a candidate personalizes an issue that for a time becomes a part of his political personality. This strategy was used vigorously by the late U.S. Senator Joe McCarthy of Wisconsin.

Judged by today's standards, McCarthy was a radical when he conducted his crusade against a real or imagined Communist threat. But this threat flourished during the Cold War following World War II and his opinions were in accord with what was a majority climate. Roy Cohen, who served as McCarthy's principal aide and confidant during his heyday, painted a vivid picture of how his boss

Take a look at answers for the 80's

If you believe curbing inflation begins with sound economic management

If you believe Canada should pull its weight in the world

If you believe small businesses, farmers, and fishermen deserve a break

If you believe owning a home is a right of the average Canadian

If you believe Canada must rely on its own energy resources

If you believe you have a right to know what you're voting for

Real change deserves a fair chance
Monday, vote Progressive Conservative. P❋C

Fig. 7-11. Newspaper ad, Progressive Conservative Party of Canada, *Vancouver Province*, February 15, 1978.

decided upon an anti-Communist strategy. In his book, *McCarthy*, Cohen wrote:

Joe McCarthy bought anti-Communism and made his opposition to Communism the centerpiece of his political career in much the same way that the other people purchased an automobile. The salesman showed him the model; he looked at it with interest. He examined it more closely. He kicked the tires, sat at the wheel, swiveled in the seat, asked questions, and bought it. It was just as cold as that.[9]

McCarthy became the personification of anti-Communism.

Most Candidates Try to Exploit Safe Issues

So far, we have looked at extremes. More often than not, though, a candidate tries to ride what is popular, hoping to avoid controversy. For example, in his 1966 reelection campaign of New York, Governor Nelson Rockefeller let his advertising people use a TV commercial that featured two fish puppets, one of which wore a press hat and microphone to resemble a reporter engaged in a conversation with the other, as follows:

Reporter: You, sir.
Fish: Uh huh.
Reporter: Pure waters?
Fish: Oh, oh yeah.
Reporter: This program, sir, is wiping out water pollution in New York within six years.
Fish: Well, it was pretty smelly down here.
Reporter: By the end of summer, the Governor will have called in every major polluter for a hearing.[10]

The background announcer spoke of a clean environment in broad terms. Neither Rockefeller—nor others who have used the same theme—told the voter how much a clean, safe environment might cost in taxes or how many jobs may be lost if a polluting industry was shut down.

On occasion, a candidate does not have to search for a popular issue. An opponent or someone else may go too far when making an attack and create the issue. This happened in the early 1970s during the public confrontation between the political and military establishment and opponents to the Vietnam War. Military recruiting stations were the targets of many peaceful protests. But, on one occasion, a bomb was exploded at a recruiting station. Although no one was hurt, it triggered violent public reaction. Washington State Senator John G. McCutcheon, who at one time had been a U.S. Attorney, made headlines when he was the first to condemn the bombing. His statements proved so popular that they were made part of a brochure that helped him through a tough reelection campaign (Figure 7-12).

When Candidates Try To Ride the Same Issue

When there is a really popular issue, the politician's best strategy is to be first to lead the parade. Ries, Cappiello, and Caldwell, authors of *The Positioning Era*,[11] illustrate the importance of this strategy by asking: "Who was the first

Fig. 7-12. Brochure, Re-Elect State Senator John T. McCutcheon, State of Washington, 1970.

Fig. 7-13. Oliphant © Universal Press Syndicate. Reprinted with permission. All rights reserved."

person to fly solo across the North Atlantic?" Then they ask: "Who was the second person to fly solo across the North Atlantic? Not so easy to answer, is it?"

It is reasonable to conclude that the candidate who first embraces a popular issue has the best chance of making it part of his or her image. Like Hertz in rental cars, Coke in cola, and Sanka in decaffeinated coffee, the first candidate to occupy a position in the voter's mind is hard to dislodge. However, it is rare that the candidate is blessed with a political exclusive. Being realistic, a candidate with a popular issue is like a dog with a bone. He or she will find that they must fight to protect it against others, especially his or her opponent, because opponents will not only recognize the issue, but promote their own solutions.

After all, "IBM didn't invent the computer, Sperry Rand did. But IBM was the first to build the computer position in the prospect's mind." The public has a tendency to associate the program with the better-known candidate, especially if there is an incumbent. Nowhere can this be better illustrated than in 1978 when California passed Proposition 13, limiting property taxes. After public opinion polls showed the proposition's impending landslide victory, everyone from Governor Brown (who had till then opposed it) to Congress, and even the president, rode the revolt (see Figure 7-13).

Chapter 57

Voter Loyalty Versus Ticket-Splitter Strategy

> I always voted my party's call and I never thought of thinking for myself at all.
> —HMS Pinafore, Gilbert and Sullivan
>
> And then there is the Ticket Splitter: The unstable and unattached with their heads buried in the sand, which makes them a tempting target.
> —Anonymous

In the United States, millions of voters are ticket splitters, but they split their tickets for a reason. Understanding the ticket splitter depends on understanding as a fact of life that the voter has political loyalty, so I will review the basics of political loyalty and ideology, then discuss why millions of voters find it easy to deviate from old political loyalties.

In 1980 and 1984, only 52.2 percent of the total U.S. voting-age population—registered and unregistered—voted for president, and less than 48 percent voted for Congress.[1] There is always an opportunity for victory if a political party can get more voters to the polls on election day. Political parties, then, find that it is good strategy to allocate their resources toward getting out the vote and place a priority on those who will support the party when they go to the polls.[2]

Dr. Ernest Dichter, a leading psychologist and researcher in the field of consumer relations, explains why. "Suppose you want to sell an over-the-counter drug. You'd be much better off to target the hypochondriacs and sell to them rather than to advertise all over the lot. And if you want to sell an electric carving knife, you have a much better chance of selling it to somebody who already has five gadgets in his house. He'll buy gadgets 6, 7, and 8."[3]

Campaign strategists also know that most of the American electorate are economic and hereditary voters. That is, they are born into their parents' party or they follow their economic interests when making their choice, and then continue throughout their lives to favor that party in most elections. Election records show that in some precincts party loyalties are so strong that being a candidate of a particular party outweighs almost any obstacle the candidate might face. For example, the Massachusetts precincts that most strongly supported the liberal Democrat U.S. Senator Ted Kennedy were the same ones that sent conservative Democrat Louise Day Hicks to Congress. In 1970, they were the precincts in which George Wallace had his best Massachusetts Democratic primary showing.[4]

Statistics also show that in precincts strongly favoring a particular party, if candidates can drag nonvoters to the polls, they will also vote for the party's choice in the same proportion. Party strategists, then, try to pile up majorities in these areas, since the size of the party majority affects not only local candidates but the ability of the party to elect officials at a state or federal level. To pile up majorities, strategists follow a get-out-the-vote strategy in which the candidate and his or her campaign organization works to be sure voters in friendly precincts are registered and go to the polls.[5] Of course, this assumes calm political seas when voters follow their normal political instincts. Economic conditions, a hostile press, a dynamic opposition leader, or the pull of compelling issues can produce unexpected results.

Unexpected results can happen even when machine control exists. When Tammany had absolute control of New York City, boss William March Tweed told a New York paper, "As long as I count the votes, what are you going to do about it?" Later, though Tweed had an invincible machine and still counted the votes, public outcry following newspaper attacks reduced his victory margin and reduced his party's ability to overcome opposition margins elsewhere. Tweed-supported candidates for state and national office were also defeated.[6]

Keep in mind that the opposition will find a wide variety of ways to use statistics concerning party loyalty. After Vice President George Bush tried and failed to become the first Texas Republican in the United States Senate, the party chairman, Peter O'Donnell, had the task of electing John Tower. Describing how the Republicans used precinct information to prioritize, he said, "We took the George Bush for U.S. Senate race of 1964, calculated the percent of the Republican vote for each precinct, arranged the precincts in order of absolute Republican strength." Then he explained that they targeted "the places where Bush received forty percent or more of the vote because they promised the greatest productivity per hour spent."[7]

Getting out the vote has another twist. When one realistically scans the political terrain, Democrats have the greater potential for gaining votes when registering and getting out the vote, simply because those with the higher incomes generally vote Republican, potentially out-voting the low-income Democratic voter. Only 58 percent of the registered unemployed vote even at the best turnout, while 71 percent of those registered and employed cast their ballots.[8] This is why master strategist Matt Reese recommends that Democratic doorbellers ignore areas clearly favoring the opposition on the theory that it will stir their interest and work the loyal (Democratic) areas to death.[9]

Party Loyalty Versus the Political Snob

While there are nonpartisan and bipartisan registration and get-out-the-vote drives and, in isolated instances, organizations such as labor unions make it a point to register their members, their effectiveness is limited to a single campaign. Effective year-in, year-out effort depends on an effective party organization.

If the party is to register voters, get them to the polls, and carry out other chores necessary to put on a political campaign, there must be workers loyal to the party organization. However, this type of activity does not appeal to political snobs, reformers, intellectuals, and members of the press who label the party organization a machine. All too often these individuals refer to party workers as political hacks.

The party may be a machine in the eyes of its critics. However, thousands of people who donate their labor think proudly of themselves as loyal members of a political party. Naturally, they want to be sure that, if elected, the official will not consider them political lepers. This constitutes a problem for the candidate who wants to present a nonpolitical image. When a candidate does not want to be tarnished by associating with a political machine and declares him- or herself to be independent, they insure the resentment of party leaders and volunteer workers who are loyal to the party organization.

This happened in 1924, when New York City's Tammany machine was an issue. The Democratic National Convention deadlocked for days, then nominated a dull, but respected, Wall Street lawyer, John W. Davis. This man was more at home in the boardroom or at the opera than with political workers. He took the stance that he was above politics. Still, being the Democratic nominee for president, he had to come to New York City's Tammany headquarters during the campaign. When Davis arrived, he said nothing as he passed down the line shaking hands. When Tammany chief Tom Spellacy, told him, "These men are here to help elect you," Davis replied, "Strength to their arms." He seemed to be at a loss for words. After a minute he added, "We want every man in the boat and every man with an oar." A few minutes later, Spellacy interrupted another long period of silence with what seemed to Davis to be an astounding suggestion. He said, "Tell them you are an organization man." A little befuddled, the candidate replied, "Oh, yes, I am an organization man." Then, as far as Davis was concerned, the visit was over, and he turned to speak to a correspondent of the Boston *Globe*.[10] Disdainful as Davis may have been at the time, New York City turned out to be one of the few bright spots in his otherwise disastrous defeat.

Basic Party Strategy and Ideology

Prior to 1932, both the Democratic and Republican parties were split internally. The Republicans had their conservative "stand-patters," epitomized by U.S. Senator Mark Hanna of Ohio and Roscoe Conklin of New York. And so did the Democrats, as evidenced by New York Governor and later President Grover Cleveland, who was strongly connected with the Wall Street bankers led by William C. Whitney. At the same time, both parties had radical wings. William

Jennings Bryan from Nebraska and "Pitchfork" Ben Tillman of South Carolina were radical Democrats. Moving into the 20th century, the Republican party had its radicals, the "progressives," epitomized by "Fighting" Bob Lafollette, Governor and later U.S. Senator from Wisconsin, and Hiram Johnson, who held the same offices in California. The Democratic liberals were epitomized by New Jersey Governor, and later President, Woodrow Wilson.[11]

Where ideology touches off an interparty fight, voters with strong feelings do cross party lines. When they do, they usually vote for the candidate with the philosophy closest to their own. Nowhere is this better illustrated than when maverick Democrat, Ohio's Governor, Frank Lausche, was running for reelection in 1944. At the time he carefully projected a conservative image, which contrasted with the liberal one carried by his party. During that campaign, he completely ignored the Democratic regulars and openly courted the Republican ticket splitter and the conservative press. In his campaign speeches he encouraged the voters regardless of party to look for his name and vote. In that election, he won the governorship by 112,000 in a state that voted largely anti-Democratic.[12]

When issues are powerful enough to polarize the voters, they are powerful enough to encourage interparty ideological splits. This was the case when the first Republican president, Abraham Lincoln, was elected. In that campaign, the dominant Democratic party was split four ways. Two generations later, the shoe was on the other foot. When Democrat Woodrow Wilson became president, former Republican President Teddy Roosevelt ran as third party nominee of the Progressive party on the Bull Moose ticket against a regular Republican President William Howard Taft.[13]

Given these ideological differences, a third party would seem logical, yet self-appointed, maverick political generals have historically been wrong when estimating the number of voters who will follow when they leave one of the dominant parties to form a third. When a strong third party emerges, the dominant party strategist must treat the third-party voter like a loose football because they split the vote in many different directions for many different reasons.

One of the more interesting demonstrations of ticket-splitting took place in 1965. Right-wing editor of the *National Review* William Buckley ran for Mayor of New York City on the conservative ticket against liberal Republican John Lindsay and regular Democrat Abraham Beame. In that race Buckley didn't expect to win. In fact, when asked what he would do if he were to receive a majority, he said, "Demand a recount."[14] Still, taking portions of his support from both candidates, Buckley polled a sizable vote. Public opinion polls conducted during and after the election showed, as expected, that he took some of the conservative Republican votes who might have supported Lindsay. But the polls also showed that, being an Irish Catholic, he hurt Abraham Beame's candidacy by luring off Irish Catholic voters who had been traditionally counted in the

Democratic column. More strategically important to the outcome was conservative Buckley's attacks on Republican Lindsay's liberal views, which persuaded thousands of liberal Democrats to desert Beame and vote for Lindsay.

Manipulating Basic Ideological Loyalty

When there is a two-party fight, an open primary, and a serious ideological split in the opposition party, a moderate or centrist, when running against a strident conservative or liberal, often finds support from a sizable liberal or conservative block of votes from the opposition.

This sets the stage for another classic political strategy designed to hold the party vote while directing an appeal to independents and a substantial number of the opposition. These voters are tempting targets. Why? Assume a 7-percent switch from one candidate to another. In a head-to-head contest, not only is there a 7-percent gain, but there is a 7-percent loss by the opposition. This represents a 14-percent shift.

A united party organization is essential if the candidate is to successfully carry out such a strategy. This was the case in 1972, when President Nixon was elected by a landslide while pursuing this centrist strategy. He succeeded in getting 94 percent of the Republican vote, 66 percent of the independent vote, and an astonishing 42 percent of the Democratic vote.[15]

But this doesn't always happen. Indeed, centrist strategy may backfire if the party regulars see the candidate as a traitor. The maverick who deserts party philosophy then becomes a target of the regular party faithful. This counter strategy worked in the 1978 New Jersey primary, when a small group of conservatives engineered the defeat of Clifford Case, the leader of the liberal faction of the Republican party in the U.S. Senate. The defeat was unexpected because Case had represented New Jersey as either Congressman or United States Senator for 34 years. The official Republican party had presumably closed ranks behind him. He had wide newspaper commendation and the endorsement of every Republican legislator and county chairman in the state. Early polls showed him leading his primary opponent three to one. Still, he lost in the primary to a 34-year-old conservative, Jeffrey Bell, who had been a staff man for Ronald Reagan during Reagan's unsuccessful 1976 presidential primary campaign only two years before.

When Bell surveyed his prospects, he noted that, in spite of his endorsements, Case had many enemies within the party, as shown by the fact that in 1972 Case's virtually unknown primary opponent got 30 percent of the primary vote. Bell's strategy called for a right-wing political stance and to tying down the conservatives. Using campaign money, nearly all of which was raised by direct mail from anti-Case out-of-state conservatives, Bell spent $400,000 for radio, television, and newspaper advertising to gain name recognition, while Case spent $100,000. But that was not the key.

In New Jersey, voters register by party and nominate in a party primary. Bell's strategy was to overwhelm Case by getting the conservatives out to vote in a light-voter-turnout primary.[16] To do this, his organization spent $100,000 going to the courthouses throughout the state and painstakingly copying the names of all registered Republicans. Later, his crews conducted a telephone canvass of the registered Republicans and identified the anti-Case voters. Then, Bell's organization moved heaven and earth to get those who harbored anti-Case feelings to the polls on primary election day. This strategy succeeded in defeating an over-confident Senator Case by approximately 4,000 votes. However, Bell's primary success turned to ashes in the finals when thousands who had supported Case turned to the Democrat Bill Bradley.

Picking up the Pieces

Interparty wrangling always costs votes, and on occasion such wrangling causes the candidate to commit political suicide. Then a candidate will benefit by the deflection of party voters who have become infected by the bitterness of the primary and who refuse to support their party's nominee. Some voters will even switch to the nominee of the other party as the lesser of two evils. To encourage this support, the opposition candidate avoids a positive stance and takes the strategic position of the French Premier George Clemenceau, when replying to a reporter who commented, "But Premier, you have so many enemies." The wily Clemenceau thoughtfully replied, "Yes, but I also have as friends the enemies of my enemies."[17]

This is what happened in the presidential campaign of 1886 when the eastern part of the nation perceived the great orator of that day, William Jennings Bryan, as a radical who divided the nation by advocating the "free coinage of silver." The establishment candidate, U.S. Senator William McKinley, sat like a potentate on his "front porch" in Ohio receiving visiting political figures from all parts of the United States. When asked about free silver, he claimed that he supported both "sound money, gold and free silver." Then he diverted their attention to a protective tariff.[18]

Such a vacillating message won't fly in this day of modern communication. In almost every election there is a contest where this fantasy explodes like an atom bomb. For instance, when U.S. Senator Goldwater was nominated against President Lyndon Johnson in 1964, he decided to make headlines and political history by standing up to the powerful entrenched interests of that day. Goldwater went into the Tennessee Valley with a chip on his shoulder and condemned the Tennessee Valley Administration. And he went to the cornbelt to lambaste farm subsidies, to California to discuss the Arizona water problem, and to West Virginia to criticize LBJ's "war on poverty."

Given enough time and a favorable press, the strategy might have worked, but it didn't in 1968. Like other prominent anti-establishment men and women, Goldwater found in that campaign that the news media portrayed his otherwise courageous and sincere acts as the antics of a right-wing radical.[19]

Goldwater's experience was repeated in 1972 by by Democratic nominee George McGovern, who preached a mildly radical message. His opponent, President Nixon, didn't debate. Nixon avoided controversial issues and won by exuding the image of sanity and confidence. He depended on a massive number of TV spots that closed with "Richard Nixon is a man with compassion, courage and conscience . . . that's why we need President Nixon now more than ever."[20]

Ticket Splitting: The Strategy of the Independent Banner

When a candidate offers himself or herself as an alternative to an opponent with a split party, they are attempting to exploit the enmity in a way that creates a behavioral shift without the accompanying backlash. When they organize support for their candidacy under an independent banner, they enable those who want to vote for the opposition to do so without sacrificing their cherished party status.

Following the classic formula, ticket splitters begin by meeting secretly with the opposition leaders, who are dissatisfied with their party's choice. They encourage these leaders to form independent committees headed by prominent members of the opposing political faith. In 1972 President Nixon's campaign used John Connolly, former Democratic Governor of Texas.

The supporting committee should have as many prominent people from the opposition party as possible. In 1964 when the Republicans from the "Eastern Establishment" were dissatisfied with Goldwater, they supported a National Independent Committee for Johnson and Humphrey. Its membership sounded like a blue book of American industry and finance. The roster included:

. . . Eisenhower's second Secretary of the Treasury, Robert B. Anderson; Mercy & Company's John T. Connor; American Electric Power's Donald C. Cook; Wall Street's John L. Loeb; two Boston Cabots; Detroit's Henry Ford II; Morgan Guaranty Trust Company's Thomas S. Lamont; the most frequently elected corporate director of them all, Sidney J. Weinberg; Eisenhower Cabineteer Maxwell M. Rabb; war hero James M. Gavin; publisher Cass Canfield; Xerox's magician, Sol M. Linowitz; Phillips Petroleum's K. S. Adams; and many more.[21]

Appealing to the Growing Body of Independents

There is no question that changes in lifestyle—and the pursuit of the good life—have contributed to party decline. In times past, the economics of poverty,

Fig. 7-14. Newspaper ad, Washington State Democrats
for Nixon, *Seattle Times*, November 2, 1972.

the presence of minorities, and the union vote caused Democrats to dominate big-city politics. Middle to upper income voters, believing they had to protect their interests, reacted; these white farmers and business and professional people, with Republican leanings, dominated the suburbs, towns, and farms.

Appealing to the Growing Body of Independents

There is no question that changes in lifestyle—and the pursuit of the good life—have contributed to party decline. In times past, the economics of poverty, the presence of minorities, and the union vote caused Democrats to dominate big-city politics. Middle to upper income voters, believing they had to protect their interests, reacted; these white farmers and business and professional people, with Republican leanings, dominated the suburbs, towns, and farms.

Then, during the 1950s, '60s, and '70s, middle class white voters began to move to the suburbs. This diluted the traditional coalition. By 1970, the United States census showed that roughly 25 to 30 percent of the vote came from the cities, and 35 to 40 percent came from the suburbs, with the balance being distributed between the small towns and farm areas.[22]

As the city dwellers moved, the suburbs were no longer the exclusive preserve of the traditionally affluent, white, Protestant Republicans. Instead, suburbs became a mix. Much of the new influx was labor union members and government employees, some with racial, ethnic, or religious ties who traditionally voted Democratic. From this it might be assumed that the voting patterns of the suburbs would be Democratic, but this didn't happen. These new residents were no longer strategically committed to the Democratic party, but they could not be counted on to vote Republican either. They became ticket splitters.

Before discussing these ticket splitters, it needs to be made clear that there are real independents, or as S. E. Asch describes them, "hold-outs"—voters who are likely to maintain their own independence in the face of contrary opinion.[23] But they are not typical. Deep down most of those who claim they are independents still have partisan leanings.

During the mid-twentieth century, these independent ticket splitters have slowly increased. In 1932, they were 3.19 percent of the voting population. By 1964, they were up to 7.2 percent. In recent years, their numbers have grown to 31 percent.[24]

How and Why Voters Split Their Tickets

How voters split their tickets depends upon economics, religion, labor union ties, etc. How does the candidate classify this vote? According to the strategists' calculations, these voters should be divided into "Republican swing voters" and "Democrat swing voters" because researchers' analyses have shown that these voters will vote the straight party line with only one or two exceptions. They cross over when they come to the weakest or most controversial of the party's candidates. So in general, they have partisan leanings. Usually, they are slightly younger, somewhat more educated, somewhat more white-collar than the rest of the electorate and consider it fashionable not to be tied to a particular party.

The increase in ticket splitting has had its effect on one-party states. In the four elections prior to the 1976 presidential contest, every state except Massachusetts, Arizona, and the District of Columbia had elected both Republicans and Democrats to statewide office. These voters don't split their tickets for the same reasons. Once in a while political differences are so drastic that people of the same party do split. For example, when Republican ex-Klan leader David Duke was running for governor of Louisiana, he proved to be an embarrassment to the national Republican administration. In that campaign, George Bush, the Republican President of the United States, said that if he were a resident of Louisiana he would vote for Duke's Democratic opponent, ex-governor Edwin Edwards. He described Duke as an insecure charlatan with an ugly record of racism and bigotry.[25]

Here are a few of the conflicting reasons voters give when asked why they split their tickets. In most cases, voters cross party lines because they see no need to change an incumbent who represents the brand they are now using, or because their party's candidate does not support a cause that has caught their fancy. Some ticket splitters rebel against extremes, while others become ticket splitters because they have been programmed by the public media to object to the nominee of their own party. In recent political history, zealots expounding both liberal and conservative philosophies have captured control of their party's convention, and nominated their candidates for president of the United States. Both candidates, one a conservative and the other a liberal, were reasonable individuals. But their strategy gave them, at least temporarily, a radical image.

During the 1964 campaign, the political evangelists of the far right wanted a "choice not an echo." They transferred their radical conservative image to Barry Goldwater. The media portrayed Goldwater as a radical who wanted to junk Social Security, sell TVA, and put nuclear weapons in the control of the field commanders.[26] As a result, millions of Republicans became ticket splitters and voted against Goldwater. He was able to garner only 52 electoral votes, while his successful opponent, President Lyndon Johnson, received 486.

In 1972, another political persuasion interpreted the anti-Goldwater vote as a reaction against his right-wing philosophy, rather than a radical image. The Republicans "moved heaven" and "raised hell" to nominate Senator George McGovern. When the left-leaning liberals transferred their radical image to McGovern, he met the same fate that Goldwater had eight years before.

Locating Ticket Splitters

Both the ideological right and left believe that ticket splitters constitute a decisive block. Conventional liberals perceive the ticket splitter as a liberal leaning centrist. Conventional conservatives perceive the ticket splitter as a conservative-leaning centrist, and each side passionately believes that ticket splitters are ripe for conversion to their strident point of view.

How does the strategist locate the ticket splitter? Campaign volunteers can canvass voters and ask revealing questions. They can also conduct scientific polls or market surveys to identify precincts where ticket splitters are likely to live, or the campaign organization can study historically persuadable precincts.

When using historical data, the strategist starts with the highest partisan vote getter (say Governor) and subtracts the votes of the lowest partisan on the same ticket (say an unsuccessful candidate for state treasurer). The strategist calls this difference the persuadable vote. For example, assume the unsuccessful Democratic candidate for state treasurer received 700,000 votes. This is the party vote base. Then assume a successful Democratic candidate for governor received 1 million votes. The difference represents ticket splitters or the persuadable vote.

Before taking the difference at face value, there must be adjustments for such things as voter falloff. For example, normally there are more votes cast for governor than for state treasurer. Then the strategist must make assumptions. For example, the candidate for governor might benefit from a strong hometown vote, or the candidate for governor might suffer because he or she did not come from the center of a state's population, etc. When adjustments are completed, the strategist has a formula that can be used to locate the ticket splitters, who account for a substantial part of the 300,000 difference.

A candidate with the resources can use modern polling to construct a market sample that identifies the ticket-splitters and, more important, the image or issues that motivate them. Then, using these polls, a sample can be constructed that gives the strategist a profile of the voter that may be persuaded to split his or her ticket. This is what the one-time knight of industry, Republican George Romney, did when he wanted to be Governor of the State of Michigan. Fresh from marketing automobiles, Romney used marketing surveys to determine the type of individuals (and precincts) that were likely to deviate from their normal Democratic patterns. In his case, the voters turned out to be Democratic-leaning white-collar or highly skilled industrial workers who earned a higher than average wage. They were slightly more Catholic than Protestant and generally located in the suburbs.

With survey information in hand, Romney tailored his public image to fit the ticket splitters' expectations. Then he used the media, political foot troops, direct mail, and banks of professional telephone operators to carefully target the ticket splitters.[27] Of course this strategy received publicity, and it had critics—so much so that in 1965, the Washington DC press corps used this parody in its annual gridiron dinner, where they verbally roast the leading political figures of the day:

The Lord above said "Romney, choose a party"
But didn't say for which team I should bat
And so I choose the grand old party but
    with a little bit of luck
They'll mistake me for a Democrat.[28]

But no one can quarrel with the fact that Romney's strategy worked. As a Republican from a Democratic state, Romney managed to survive the Goldwater landslide, retire undefeated, and leave behind a perfected strategy that kept the Republicans in control of the Michigan governorship for the balance of a generation.

Chapter 58

The Complex World of Economic Interests

> Politics is the science of how who gets what, when and why.
> —Sydney Hillman, one-time president of the Amalgamated
> Clothing Workers of America and chairman of C.O.P.E.[1]
>
> We came to a decision some time ago that the only way we could
> change the political fortunes of the petroleum industry was to change
> Congress.
> —Harold Scroggins, industrial lobbyist[2]
>
> Important as geography is, terrain cannot be measured in geographic
> terms alone. He who always plows a straight furrow is in a rut.
> —Howard Kandel[3]

Economics and Its Impact on Political Strategy

Voters are not one big economic blob. They are human beings with opinions motivated by loyalty, interests, predispositions, and conflicting self interests. They are men or women, registered or unregistered to vote, married or single. Most have a family. All are at least 18 years old and they are young, middle-aged, or old, though most are between 35 and 65.[4]

Most voters are loyal to a race, ethnic origin, geographic area, or religion. Most are middle class, but a few are rich and others are poor. Usually their income is derived from an occupation. All voters pay taxes, but at different rates. Often they have equity in a home, a car, or furniture and buy insurance. Many own stocks, bonds, or rental property. Most have a hobby, and millions belong to one or more of a great variety of different social, union, business, or fraternal organizations. Some drink liquor, beer, or wine. Millions smoke cigarettes, cigars, or a pipe, but most abstain.

Voters have a wide variety of different social and economic views. Some enjoy gambling while others feel it is evil. Millions are partisans who are pro- or anti-abortion. They favor or oppose unions and have differing views on nuclear arms and how we deal with foreign nations. And these are only a few of the things that categorize voters. Any one or a combination of these factors can determine or at least influence the voter's choice at the polls. And these different tastes and inclinations have been manipulated by politicians since the origin of our democracy.

The political loyalties of most voters are mixed—they ususally have one or more psychological pulls. When these pulls conflict, normally the voter has trouble sorting them out. Take labor unions, for example. Some of their members have other loyalties they consider more important than their union affiliation. Or an endorsement by a union may not deliver the union vote because the voters have little interest in who occupies a minor public office. Many young people are not registered, and there are millions who belong to a politically oriented church who do not follow its leadership.

Politicians profess to believe that every voter has an interest in those who govern. While this may not be entirely true, no doubt the political trick is to find the issue or issues that will attract the attention of these special interests. The Democratic National Committee, recognizing this fact, advises its candidates: "Remember, your campaign can't do everything everywhere. And it shouldn't. At least you can apply your resources where they'll do the most good. Play the percentages. Target your campaign."[5]

The best way to target your campaign is to categorize the voting population by what they have in common—area, economic status, race, age, sex, religion, political views on specific issues, etc.—all differences that separate people into what are loosely termed blocks. Candidates then use an endorsement, an economic issue, an occupation, social ties, etc., to identify with the voter.

When calculating the vote to be gained, the candidate should not believe everything any one interest or organization promises; more often than not their political judgment is slanted. One of President John Kennedy's favorite stories illustrates just how slanted this judgment can be.

Shortly after the turn of the century, a group of newspaper publishers zealously pursuing their own economic interests allegedly came to the powerful Speaker of the United States House of Representatives, "Uncle" Joe Cannon. They promised to elect Cannon president of the United States if he would agree to change his position to support the House's lower tariff on newsprint from Canada.

"Two thousand years ago," Uncle Joe supposed thundered, "Christ was taken up on a high mountain by the devil, who showed him the whole country below them, and promised him all of it if he would adore him." Then Uncle Joe removed the cigar stump from between his teeth and with a touch of belligerence looked up at the publishers and said, "Now it so happened that the devil, who was offering all that property, didn't own an inch of it, and neither do you."[6]

The political strategist must remember that no one political force delivers 100 percent of its members or its class. Let's consider a farmer, a professional person, or a union member. They differ in interests, race, ethnic origins, religion, left or right wing political philosophy, etc. When they vote, any one or a combination of motivations might outweigh the interests of where they live or their occupation. In the next few pages, we will examine different ways candidates have successfully targeted particular interests.

Women

In his 1970 campaign, Governor Rockefeller of New York State used a multi-issue approach. He used scores, perhaps hundreds, of pamphlets, all designed to tell different citizens where Rockefeller stood on their issues. These publications included something designed especially for women called a "Rockefeller Mini Kit." It included a litter bag imprinted with the words, "Let's Work Together for a Cleaner New York—Nelson A. Rockefeller," a pamphlet entitled, "How to Start A Women's Write-in for Rockefeller," and a pamphlet entitled, "Some Facts for Women from Governor Rockefeller's Record," which explained why Governor Rockefeller appointed over one thousand women to positions of high public trust, etc.[7]

Fig. 7-15. James M. Perry, "The Rockefeller Campaign is the Biggest, Maybe the Best," *The National Observer*, October 26, 1970, p. 19.

Veterans

Most of the political heat is generated by nonpartisan groups that have financial, emotional, or geographic interests. Let's look at veterans' organizations. These organizations see legislation through the eyes of their members, veterans proudly fought for their country and believe they are entitled to public benefits. Understandably, their loyal membership constitutes a responsive target for those who propose "veteran legislation." See Figure 7-16 for an example of a direct mail piece directed to veterans and their families.

War veterans' organizations also have other interests. Most passionately believe that the United States must be prepared to meet and dispose of any potential foreign enemies. In their mind, military preparedness is the only way, so their members usually respond to radio and television commercials—like one used by Reagan that begins by showing a Soviet military parade followed by quick glimpses of tanks, a red flag, Brezhnev, and missile carriers. The announcer says, " 'Ronald Reagan spoke out on the danger of the Soviet arms buildup long before it was fashionable. He's always advocated a strong national defense and a position of leadership for America. He has a comprehensive program to rebuild our military power.' " The TV picture then shows Ronald Reagan, wearing a blue suit, red tie, and white shirt, against a black background, saying: " 'We've learned by now that it isn't weakness that keeps the peace, it's strength. Our foreign policy has been based on the fear of not being liked. Well, it's nice to be liked, but it's more important to be respected.' " The final frame shows white letters on a bright blue background: REAGAN[8]

Geography, the "Home Town" Phenomenon

In politics as in sports, voters have a tendency to favor candidates with whom they have a geographic affiliation. Note these words spoken by one of the most successful of the nation's political practitioners, Richard Nixon:

"It's good to be back home in Indiana." (October 26, 1970)
"I also own property in Florida." (October 27, 1970)
"I was born in the little town of Loma Linda (California)." (April 14, 1969)
"Thanks for this wonderful welcome to my home county, Orange County." (July 15, 1969)
"I speak to you as a former Virginian" (October 28, 1970)
"What a proud moment it is for me to be addressing the nation . . . from my home state of California." (October 31, 1970)[9]

The Rural Strategy

Geographic or social ties have a strong political pull. But they are even stronger when geography is combined with the constituent's economic interests. To prove that this strategy is not new, let's examine the exploits of Teddy Roosevelt, who led a cavalry unit in the Spanish-American War and later served as governor of the nation's most populated state, New York. Here he enhanced his image by fighting entrenched political machines and was then chosen by the political bosses of his party to be vice president, not because they wanted him as a

Fig. 7-16. Mailer, Committee to Re-Elect Senator Greive, Seattle, Nov. 1970.

leader, but because his colorful personality balanced the bland man who was their presidential standard bearer.

Upon the assassination of President McKinley, this vice president, Teddy Roosevelt, succeeded to the presidency. After serving the balance of McKinley's term and prior to the Republican convention where he sought his party's nomination for a full term, Roosevelt invited Republican delegates to come by rail and visit him at his estate in Oyster Bay, New York, which was in part a farm.

When the Kansas delegation came to visit, they were met by the president without coat or collar. After expressing his "delight" at seeing them, the president explained that he was dressed in this way because, like the delegates, he was a farmer, and it was the season for putting in the hay. To solidify this image, he invited them to come down to the barn and talk things over while he performed his chores. When the party arrived at the barn, there was no hay. "James," the president shouted to a man in the loft, "Where's that hay?" "I'm sorry, sir, I was going to throw it into the loft," James said, poking his head out from the loft, "but I just ain't had time to throw it back since you forked it up for yesterday's delegation."[10]

Teddy Roosevelt is not the only candidate who publicized his rural ties. Adlai Stevenson, Sr., who made his mark as governor of an industrial state, Illinois, and was supported by big labor and nearly all of the nation's big city political organizations, used the fact that he was a gentleman farmer when he was a candidate for president.

Another way to appeal to rural voters is to exploit the latent anti-big city, anti-big government, feeling that is prevalent in parts of the western United States. They do not mention agro-business ranchers, miners, and oil interests, but appeal to voters who live in parts of the United States in which life is as it appears in Westerns, and where its citizens want to keep it that way.

Here is an example of a TV commercial that appeals to the rural voter, one of political consultant Robert Goodman's success stories: The camera focuses on three cowboys saddling up. Reminiscent of Paul Revere's ride or the Pony Express, one is holding up a proclamation. They mount and ride off through a stream, galloping over the crest of a hill with a dog running behind. Meanwhile, there is Western background music and an announcer who says, " 'The Wallop Senate drive begins here.' " Then the camera switches back to the three riders. The one with the proclamation chants in a deep bass voice: " 'Come join the Wallop Senate Drive! The Wallop Senate Drive! It's alert and it's alive and it's Wyoming to the spurs, The Wallop Senate Drive!' " Then the riders fade.

Another rider, Malcolm Wallop, comes into view. He wears a blue business suit and a white cowboy hat. "The camera is near ground level, making Wallop and his horse look huge." The camera shows "scores of men on horseback following Wallop." Then the camera shows them parading through a town where

for President ADLAI E. STEVENSON

the man America needs

Fig. 7-17. Pamphlet, Volunteers for Stevenson, Chicago, Illinois, 1952.

a crowd, "with American flags and Wallop pennants, waves and cheers." Then the announcer says, " 'Go forth for Wyoming, Malcolm Wallop. Tell them in the United States Senate that the people of Wyoming are proud of their land and life, and that a Wyoming Senator will fight every intrusion upon it. That you, Malcolm Wallop, will serve the nation best by serving Wyoming first—the very special needs of this great state. And by so doing share its blessing with America.' " Then

Fig. 7-18. From "No; Seriously; I Want You to Look at the Camera and Say, 'Ride with Me, Wyoming!' " *Washington Monthly*, July-August 1980. Used by permission.

back to the jingle words: "Come join the Wallop Senate Drive!" Screen fades in around Wallop's face. The announcer's voice says: " 'Malcolm Wallop for United States Senate. Ride with us, Wyoming!' "[11]

Wallop's strategy also had political teeth. It ridiculed Congress and incumbent U.S. Senator Gale McGee in particular, claiming they were responsible for over-regulating every part of life, as exemplified in another commercial, which featured a cowboy riding his horse across the prairie. The camera focused on his bedroll and, of all things, a portable toilet strapped on a donkey's back. An announcer says, " 'Now they say if you don't take the portable facility along with you on a roundup, you can't go!' "[12]

The Labor Strategy

The Yale Communications Research Program studying elections found voters follow institutional recommendations when they consider then credible, trust-worthy, or close to their interests.[13] So it comes as no surprise that the most prized political endorsements come from prestigious organizations with large memberships.

Nationally, organized labor holds a strategic position. It plays some role in most campaigns for state and local offices. Labor's power lies in its ability to turn out its members, who theoretically support and endorse candidates. Labor political involvement dates back some years, and became a strident national force when the heir to the Mennen Fortune, a young Soapy Williams, began his campaign to become Michigan's governor. At that time, it was assumed by most of the political pundits that he had little or no chance of beating the entrenched Republican machine of that day. That was until the United Automobile Workers, fresh from organizing the Detroit plants, started flexing their political muscle. With their help and resources, this young political unknown became governor.[14]

Since that time, organized labor has become the most powerful of the special interests. As a whole, labor is still faithful to the Democrats. Union members have traditionally made up a third of the Democratic vote. Labor's endorsement is especially important in the primary when Democratic nominees are chosen.

Fig. 7-19. Brochure, Democratic National Committee, Washington, DC, 1944.

Strategy and the Professional

The political leanings of professionals are less easily classified. Former Congressman Bradford Morse of Massachusetts used to say, "In the course of the month, every male gets a haircut. There were 137 barbers in my district, and I got to know every one of them on a first name basis. These fellows were campaigning for me every day, not realizing they were doing so. They simply commented to their customers that I had been in the shop."[15]

How professionals operate depends on their special interests. For example, when glib politicians say they support education while they advocate cutting "frills," they may be losing the teachers. What the candidates and the press term frills may be in the eyes of the teacher essential to a good education.

Educators do not depend upon their vote alone when flexing their strategic muscle. They rely on natural allies—janitors, custodians, school bus drivers, clerical personnel, PTAs, parents' clubs, and finally the alumni. Most teachers are registered voters and the National Educational Association, the strongest of several highly organized education groups, claims that teacher turnout at the polls habitually runs more than 90 percent. Like organized labor, they endorse, contribute to, and carry out all manner of campaign chores. In the 1976 presidential election, the teachers' national organization mailed a postcard to each teacher urging that they support Jimmy Carter because, "after eight years of vetoes and cutback, we need a friend in the White House."[16]

Most other professions are not that well organized. Typically, they content themselves with newsletters that inform their members of an incumbent's record or a candidate's position on issues in which they have an interest. A few organizations use paid advertising to criticize candidates they consider unfriendly. This happened in the 1980 congressional campaign, when the National Association of Realtors touched off a row with the congressmen to whom they gave low marks. One of these congressmen, Wisconsin Representative David Obey, objected because the realtors used misleading television ads to charge that his vote against legislation they favored "would mean 3.6 percent higher inflation, fewer jobs, less family income."[17]

These examples only scratch the surface. There are as many strategies for influencing as there are professions. For example, the college community attaches significance to the fact that a candidate has a college background. And it helps to be a professor or an alum, or at least have educational qualifications, as shown in an ad (Figure 7-20) designed to target those who teach and work in a university area.

Business Strategy

Unlike mass membership organizations, individual business doesn't have thousands of members they can persuade to go to the polls. When it comes to specific objectives, businesses do not always agree among themselves. Still, business and politics have mixed since the early foundations of our country.

Fig. 7-20. Newspaper ad, Committee to Elect Booth Gardner, *Tacoma News Tribune*, October 20, 1978.

Business power lies in the ability to make political contributions to influence public media, and to mobilize the community where local jobs are at stake.

For example, United States Senator Ernest McFarland of Arizona lost Cochise County, Arizona, by 185 votes in 1952 and by 2,537 votes in 1958. The reason for the difference can be explained. During the second campaign, when McFarland came to Cochise County he was greeted by a sullen group of copper miners. They were responding to an ad run by their employer in the local newspaper that said, "When McFarland was in the Senate, he voted against a four cent peril point protective tariff for copper. If that tariff were in force today, you would probably be on the job instead of being out of work. When the former Senator asks you to vote for him today, why don't you ask him why he didn't vote to protect your job when he had the chance?"[18]

Usually the strategy is not this specific, yet when employing this strategy, the business interests do not mention profits or even jobs. Rather, business leaders influence the local media, because they are respected community leaders. They concentrate on themes that characterize the office holder or candidate as a friend or an enemy of good government.

The Strategic Negatives of an Endorsement

Of course there are campaigns where the endorsements of some respected professionals may not be welcome. Typically, real estate brokers, land developers, bankers, personal injury lawyers, or tavern operators, can help as individuals, but as a group, their endorsement might hurt a candidate's campaign because the opposition can argue that once elected, the candidate is obligated to react favorably to their "selfish" special interests.

As a case in point, let's look at a profession whose individuals are universally admired and respected: the American doctor. The average voter will be impressed if his or her doctor is backing a candidate. However, when speaking on health care and economics, no one, except possibly doctors, would want public economic decisions made by the American Medical Association.

When it comes to specific objectives, voters frequently view profits to be at odds with public interests. With this in mind, businesses use a whole host of nonpartisan fronts. This is what the California stock and bond people did when they found their sales suffering in the summer months because of the time difference between Wall Street in New York City, which was on daylight time while California was on standard time. After they tried their own daylight saving initiative with the voters and failed, they changed strategy and persuaded the California State Junior Chamber of Commerce to become the official sponsor of a second daylight-saving initiative. In that campaign, daylight savings time was sold to California voters as necessary to give children and adults an extra hour of daylight in which to play.[19]

In addition to the traditional issues, there are other less apparent, but nevertheless potent, special interest groups. For instance, throughout virtually every constituency we find homeowner voters who have paid a premium for a home because it has a view. Anyone with an investment in a view cannot help but fear anything that might interfere with it. These property owners will certainly read a letter that begins something like this:

"Dear _____: Knowing your interest in our continuing battle to prevent the construction of high rise buildings that block homeowners' view of our waterfront, I think a progress report is in order."

This introduction is typical of a strategy used by candidates to approach voters who have narrow interests. However, candidates should not expect those with special interests or concerns to knock at their door. Usually he or she must work at rooting out and categorizing these special interests.

Chapter 59

The Politics of Diversity (Age, Gender, Race, Ethnics, Religion, Etc.)

> In our age there is no such thing as "keeping out of politics"; all issues are political issues.
> —George Orwell[1]

Strategy and Age

Strategically, the most profitable target is the voter who has reached middle age. Sixty-nine percent of the registered voters 45 to 50 years of age report they voted. But the highest percentage goes to those voters from 50 to 70, where 79 percent voted.[2]

And why not? These voters are worried about inflation and taxes that erode their investments, their pensions, and the election of those who threaten to cut their Social Security check or Medicare benefits. Elderly voters are also strategically important because they have children who vote and, if they are so inclined, they have time for campaign chores. In recent years, as proven by President Reagan and the resurgence of one-time U.S. Senator, still Congressman, Claude Pepper, there is growing evidence that the older voters have empathy for their own.

When elderly candidates run for office, they present their younger opponents with a strategic dilemma, such as that faced by one-time U.S. Senator John Tunney of California when his challenger was 73-year-old retired right-wing college president S. I. Hayakawa. Tunney, who was many years Hayakawa's junior, feared any mention of Hayakawa's age might alienate the millions of elderly whom Tunney had been courting. So Tunney contented himself with a sly reference to his opponent's age with the slogan, "It's not his age to which I object, but the age of his ideas."[3]

The young voter presents an even more complex strategic problem. Historically, they have a poor voting record. In 1982 only 49 percent of the nation's eligible voted. Still, the general statistics looked good compared to the 25 percent of the eligible 18- to 24-year-olds who participated.[4] An explanation is that the young live in a different political world than their elders. They are influenced by the disc jockeys in their radio stations, by ads in the publications they read, and by direct mail that has little appeal to their elders.

The youth vote presents the candidate with mass contradictions. For example young voters are concerned with controversial issues that touch their lifestyle, such as compulsory draft registration, legalizing of marijuana, reduction of the drinking age, the refusal of straight-laced landlords to rent to young adults who are not married, etc. Yet, for all their controversial views and talk of youth rebellion, the majority of those who do vote stay with the views and candidates favored by their parents. Even more significant, talk of revolt has a tendency to run its course, and rebellion dies as they grow older.

College students are an example. They often break, at least temporarily, with the political views of their parents. If the candidate is seriously pursuing the college student vote, he or she should target "from within." Candidates using this approach recruit students and professors and have them communicate with their peers through the college newspaper, radio, and in some cases through television.[5]

Appealing to the Woman Voter

Voter attitudes have changed dramatically since 1928, when the Democrats nominated for President a "wet" Al Smith who favored changing the laws that prohibited the sale of alcohol. The secretary of the Democratic party, Clement L. Shaver, an ardent prohibitionist, created a sensation by publicly endorsing Hoover. When the reporters asked Shaver about the endorsement, his only reply was, "Are you married?"[6]

Fig. 7-21. Dik Browne, "Hagar the Horrible," *Chicago Tribune*, May 29, 1985.

There are many cross currents when seeking the women's vote. Women actually represent a majority of all voters, but they usually do not vote as a block. And it is not clear how ready married woman voters are to vote differently than their husbands. Political analysts note that women candidates often get a "special interest" label. This perception grew in 1984 when feminists, working through the

Fig. 7-22. *Tacoma News Tribune*, September 17, 1992. Used by permission.

National Organization for Women, openly pressured Walter Mondale to nominate Congresswoman Geraldine Ferraro. While CBS exit polls showed that some women did come to the polls because the Democrats nominated Geraldine Ferraro for Vice President, far more women voted for Reagan than for the Mondale-Ferraro ticket. It was argued that Ferraro's presence on the ticket did not affect the male voter, but in the final analysis it did.[7]

Without pursuing the "women candidates strategies" in depth, we can say that traditional strategy favors an appeal that envisions women as guardians of public morals. Florida singer Anita Bryant was among those who have successfully played this traditional role. She reacted when a 1975 Dade Metropolitan County Commission ordinance mandated the hiring of "otherwise qualified homosexuals" as teachers in private and parochial schools. After recruiting religious and establishment-oriented forces, she led a fight that repealed this ordinance, which she believed would "encourage converts among the young to a glamorized, deviate life style."[8]

Public attitude toward women candidates, though, is undergoing change. Advocates cite the political career of Sally Sanford as an example. She was married six times. Earlier in life she was a bootlegger, speakeasy proprietor, and the madam of San Francisco's most famous brothel. Later, she was a restaurant owner and a city councilman, and then Mayor of Sausolito, California. During her political career she received the distinguished citizen's award from the City of San Francisco and the Paul Harris Fellowship award from Rotary International.[9]

Although both the traditional and feminist views have been used to distinguish female candidates in the past, women candidates—like Minnesota Lieutenant Governor Marlene Johnson, a Democrat and former board member of the feminist National Women's Political Caucus—are concerned that so-called women's issues may be hampering their appeal. Johnson, like other female politicians, backed away from the feminist label and reached for a more "mainstream" image.[10]

Republican pollster Richard Wirthlin found that women's groups "alienated" many voters by "trying to speak as if women's issues were simply ERA and choice on abortion." In contrast, the Republicans avoid the feminist agenda and take a broader approach. They go after their votes with specific ads on inflation, nuclear war, and other issues keyed to their concerns and lifestyles.

This is consistent with how women are focusing on a new image in other pursuits. "We must broaden our scope on economic issues. We don't have any choice," says Cleta Deatherage, a former Oklahoma state legislator, who is general counsel of Citizens National Bank & Trust Co., Oklahoma City.[11] Missouri state legislator Karen McCarthy, who is pursuing a business career in Kansas City to complement her political career, says, "Advisers say to be sure to distance myself from this 'woman's thing' and get into a business persona."[12]

Many feminists welcome the effort to broaden their base and choose their battles more carefully. Cleta Deatherage insists, though, that because of real sex discrimination, it is important that women politicians work together. If possible, they should avoid conflicts among themselves when pursuing their political goals. Otherwise, they will meet the fate shared by seven National Women's Political Caucus members who ran against each other for one Wisconsin legislative seat— and lost to a man.[13]

Sex and philosophy aside, women political activists can point to exit polls showing that the woman's vote was crucial in electing Democratic Senators Paul Simon of Illinois and Tom Harkin of Iowa as well as candidates in other races. Kathy Wilson, President of the National Women's Political Caucus, says her organization is sharpening its long-range focus, concentrating on targeted areas and "attempting to create a climate in certain districts that makes a woman the logical successor."

There is no question that the number of women office holders is increasing. Geraldine Ferraro, who "blazed the trail, showed that women can stand up to the pressure,"[14] is no longer alone. Republican Sandra Day O'Connor is on the Supreme Court. Women now occupy approximately 18.2 percent of the seats in

U.S. legislatures, approximately 60 percent of which are Democrats. In 1991, 31 women sat in Congress. Of the 29 House members, 20 were Democrats, 9 Republicans. Just two women were in the Senate, a Democrat and a Republican.[15] The States of Washington, Connecticut, Kentucky, and New Hampshire have elected Democratic women governors. And a number of cities have chosen women mayors, as illustrated by the 1983 graph from *USA Today* shown in Figure 7-23.

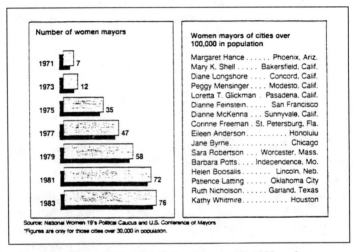

Fig. 7-23. Karen Loeb, *USA Today*, January 27, 1983, p. 2.
Copyright 1983, USA Today. Reprinted with permission.

Race, Ethnicity, and Political Strategy

There is evidence that voters with a clearly defined ethnic heritage favor one of their own. As already pointed out, in recent years the Jewish voter and the black voter have consistently supported Democrats. Yet a New Yorker of Jewish heritage, one-time Republican United States Senator Jacob Javits, did well with the normally Democratic, Jewish population. And the four city wards in Boston where most blacks live supported Edward William Brook, a black Republican, for the office of State Attorney General and for United States Senator.[16]

Aided by empathy for each other, blacks and other minorities have registered and turned out in large numbers to elect black mayors in Atlanta, Los Angeles, Chicago, Washington, DC, Cleveland, Philadelphia, and Gary, Indiana. Eighty percent of the blacks who voted supported a black candidate, Jessie Jackson, in the 1984 Presidential primaries. And in Denver, which has a predominantly white population, the 1991 race for mayor was particularly noteworthy in that both of the finalists were black men, Denver City Auditor Wellington Webb and District Attorney Norm Early.[17]

In spite of this success, the fact remains that during the last 50 years of U.S. politics, black voters have traditionally had a poorer turnout record than white voters. Yet that historical precedent was overturned during the 1991 race for governor in the state of Louisiana. That election featured one-time imperial wizard of the anti-black Ku Klux Klan running against one-time governor Edwin Edwards, who was a champion of minority rights. Given this choice, the black turnout was an unbelievable 80 percent and exceeded the white vote in that election.[18]

Where they perceive it is in their interest, ethnics also vote as a block. For example, in 1916 when President Woodrow Wilson was campaigning for re-election to the presidency and emphasizing that "he kept us out of war," the German sections of New York and Chicago, who had no desire to see themselves engaged in a battle against their ancestral homeland, strongly supported his candidacy. But after Wilson led the nation into the first World War against Germany, a study of the same wards following the Armistice showed the voters of German extraction had switched. They opposed Wilson's peace plans, including the League of Nations, and supported Harding's "return to normalcy" and "isolation from foreign affairs."[19]

Looking at the "let's vote for one of our own strategy," candidates with knowledge and ingenuity have found it strategically profitable to emphasize what they have in common with the voter. William Randolph Hearst, remembered because of his publishing empire, was also a U.S. Congressman and a candidate for Mayor of New York City. His opponent, George B. McClellan, had an unusual weapon: He was fluent in German, Italian, and French. When McClellan took the stump in ethnic neighborhoods, he had a supporter strategically planted in the audience, who invariably asked him to address the crowd in their own language. After some urging from the crowd, he would do so. No question, this gimmick was a contributing factor in his win: His vote margin was approximately one-half of one percent of the votes cast.[20]

Even where foreign languages are no longer used, ethnic heritage still influences both voters and politicians. So candidates look for ethnic ties they can profitably exploit. When a Boston blueblood, the late U.S. Senator, Everett Saltenstill, faced an Irish Catholic electorate in the State of Massachusetts, he dug up some ancient Irish ancestors that entitled him to be a member in good standing of the Charitable Irish Society—a membership he publicized when he ran for Lieutenant Governor, Governor, and U.S. Senator.[21]

President Richard Nixon appealed to ethnics when he exploited not only his own heritage, but that of his wife, Pat's, when he said:

> "Mrs. Nixon's father was Irish, and on my side, my mother was Irish. So between us, you have one." (March 17, 1969)

"... my wife, whose mother was born in Germany, and our two daughters are therefore one-fourth German." (August 7, 1969)

"At the Parliament in Bonn, she (Mrs. Nixon), could say; "This is not my fatherland, but it is my mother's land." (August 7, 1969)[22]

Where no such obvious bond exists, the sophisticated strategist might organize a committee composed of group members to support his or her candidacy. Thus, there might be "Italians for Commissioner Tracy Owens," "Asians for Senator Gordon Herr," "Irish for Representative Frank Connor," a "Mexican American Committee for Senator Papajonni," or "Black Voters in Support of Mayor Dave Mooney."

Beyond these examples, race and ethnic strategy can be a can of worms. Up until the latter part of this century, bigoted white Southern politicians used the, "We have got to keep them (the blacks) in their place" strategy. In 1952, Frank Graham, former president of the state university and a racial moderate, led his opponent in the North Carolina senatorial primary by 53,383 votes. His runoff opponent in the Democratic primary was a former president of the American Bar Association, Willis Smith. Smith used stump radio and newspaper ads to tell the voters, "If you want your wife and daughter eating at the same table with Negroes, vote for Graham." Both the blacks and bigoted white voters got the message. Blacks supported Graham as a block, but their voting numbers were small. Smith rallied the bigoted white vote and defeated Graham by 20,000 votes.[23]

As racial minorities have come of age politically, bigotry is less and less open. White candidates no longer find it fashionable to openly exploit races, so they have substituted other racial strategies. Starting in the last part of the 19th century and the early part of this one, in the small towns of the East and in most cities of the north, Midwest, and far West, was the era of the "WASP" (white Anglo-Saxon Protestant) political strategy. North of the Mason Dixon Line, this strategy was to approach the electorate as though they were sterile robots. Major politicians and the press of that day labeled an appeal to a racial or ethnic minority as "un-American."

The WASP strategy sounded good on paper, but as a practical matter, it lessened the political influence of the minorities, who were drowned out by the greater numbers and the affluence of the white population. As time went on, the minority populace became more sophisticated. Working through their leaders, these voting blocks entered into informal alliances with politicians who supported what they considered to be their legitimate political objectives.

Today's racial strategy is determined more by conditions in the district, county, or state in which the candidates are running. For example, "The Statue of Liberty might have been the right choice for Ukrainians or Italians," says Robert Estrada, a Texas attorney who led the Reagan-Bush Hispanic campaign. "But for most Hispanics, the port of entry into the country was the Rio Grande."[24]

One thing is clear: Today most black and other racial minorities are Democrats. This was not always true in New York City in the decades after the Civil War. For example, the black population did not respond to every Democratic promise of social legislation. Manhattan blacks, as many blacks elsewhere, remained faithful to Lincoln's party, who freed the slaves. That was until the dawn of Franklin D. Roosevelt's New Deal, when, with other racial minorities, at least 80 percent of the black vote supported the Democrats. In recent years the Democrats have combined the blacks with another powerful minority, the Hispanics.

Today, it doesn't pay a candidate to have two racial strategies. And what is more important, good conscience as well as good politics requires that the candidate consider how any racial or ethnic commitment will affect the other formal or informal coalition partners. An example of a strategy gone awry started in the all-black Ward No. 17 in Baltimore, Maryland. During the presidential election, this ward gave Democrat Lyndon B. Johnson virtually all of its vote and was considered to be a Democratic stronghold.

Two years later, George P. Mahoney won the Democratic nomination for Governor. During the final election he took the central city for granted and strategically tried to add the vote of the all-white suburbs, whom he perceived as being violently opposed to a ballot issue that would void restrictive real estate contracts preventing blacks from moving into their neighborhoods. In an effort to appeal to the suburbs, Maboney coyly used the political slogan, "Your home is your Castle . . . Protect it."

On election night 1964, black leaders and organizations retaliated. At first the CBS computer systematically rejected reports that the black ward, who had given 95 percent of their vote to Democratic President Lyndon B. Johnson two years earlier, could be giving 93 percent of their vote to Mahoney's Republican opponent. But eventually the returns showed CBS's projections were mistaken. When the votes were counted, Maryland's next Governor was a Republican, Spiro Agnew, who later became Vice President of the United States.

Race continues to play a very real part in the electoral process. For example, second- and third-generation Irish, Italian, and Polish voters who live north of the Mason-Dixon Line have moved to the suburbs. They don't react to old-fashioned bigotry, but they do buy a strategy that criticizes programs designed to aid inner cities. They insist that the suburbs should not pay to rehabilitate this area where blacks, Hispanics, and other minorities still make their home, even if it is necessary to alleviate conditions from which they escaped by moving.

In states where there is major Hispanic impact, such as Texas, California, Florida, and New Mexico, demographers say Hispanics constitute the fastest-growing segment of the population. The percentage of Hispanics who register to vote has already doubled in the past decade and is growing, thanks to aggressive registration efforts, and they will play a big role in national political races in the years ahead.

For years, Democrats relied on old-fashioned stump politicking to turn out the Hispanic vote. They courted Hispanics with chili cook-offs and barbecues. But with some 16 million Hispanics now living in the U.S., that's changing. "Today, the Democratic party can't expect to hold tamale parties and count on Hispanics voting Democrat," says Richard Hamnen, president of Bravo Communications Inc., an Austin, Texas-based media consulting firm whose advertisements contributed to the massive Hispanic turnout that put Mark White, a Democrat, in the governor's office in 1982.

While it is too early to draw any firm conclusions, Republicans have attempted to draw a portion of the Hispanic vote, which up until now has been Democratic, by using ads that emphasize traditional Hispanic values such as patriotism, hard work, and family. In one advertisement, a Hispanic woman said President Reagan had made her proud of a country that was once again "fuerte," or strong. Another commercial featured a young Hispanic soldier who said President Reagan's defense policies allowed him to wear his uniform with pride. A small-business man starred in another commercial, beaming with pride because sales had improved.[25]

Appealing to Those With a Religious Conviction

Separation of church and state sounds good in theory, but as a practical matter, religious muscle has always played a part in political life. Back when congressional candidate Abraham Lincoln was opposed by the circuit-riding, fire-and-brimstone religious spellbinder, the Reverend Peter Cartwright, he decided to attend one of Cartwright's services. During the ceremony Cartwright shouted, "All those desiring to lead a new life, give their hearts to God, and go to heaven stand." Most stood. Then he went on, "All who do not wish to go to hell stand." Everyone except Abraham Lincoln rose. While everyone in the meeting hall was looking at Abe, Cartwright shouted, "I observe that many people responded to the first invitation to give their hearts to God and go to heaven; and I further observe that all of you, save one, has indicated they do not desire to go to hell. May I inquire, Mr. Lincoln, where are you going?" Lincoln rose and, after a long pause said, "I came here as a respectful listener. I did not know I was going to be singled out. Now, brother Cartwright asked me directly where am I going. I desire to reply with equal directness. I am going to Congress."[26]

Today we find mainline religious leaders are turned off by the way politically motivated religious firebrands of the past exploited doctrines. For example, when the Democrats nominated a Catholic, Al Smith, for President, he was attacked by a leading religious fanatic of that day, Billy Sunday, who purported to be speaking as an ambassador of God out to defy the forces of hell. He described Smith's male

Fig. 7-24. Interlandi, *Los Angeles Times*, October 5, 1980. Copyright, 1980, Los
Angeles Times. Reprinted by permission.

supporters as whiskey politicians, bootleggers, crooks, and pimps and his New
York female supporters as street-walkers. A respected "mainline" national
religious publication of that day said, "(New York) Governor Smith has a
constitutional right to run for president . . . and we have a constitutional right to
vote against him, because he is a Catholic."[27]

Currently, most traditional mainline religious leaders shy away from active
participation in political campaigns and limit their political pronouncements to
occasional outbursts against what they consider sin, because they argue that
religious involvement violates the doctrine of separation of church and state.

In the USA, traditional religious doctrines have slowly eroded as a political
barrier—so much so that those who made Smith's religion an issue would have
been shocked that by 1984 two Bible-Belt Southern Baptist bastions (Oklahoma
and Alabama) elected Roman Catholic Republican Senators, just as they would be
shocked that the nation's most Roman Catholic state (Rhode Island) elected two
WASP Senators, both of whom (under some conditions) advocated federally-
funded abortions.[28]

This trend has been met by a political cross-current, one that has little to do
with religious doctrines. For generations, religious leaders have recognized the

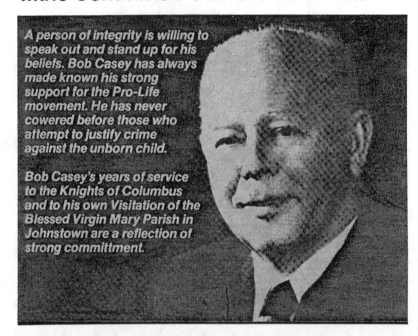

Bob Casey
...the Committed Catholic candidate

A person of integrity is willing to speak out and stand up for his beliefs. Bob Casey has always made known his strong support for the Pro-Life movement. He has never cowered before those who attempt to justify crime against the unborn child.

Bob Casey's years of service to the Knights of Columbus and to his own Visitation of the Blessed Virgin Mary Parish in Johnstown are a reflection of strong committment.

- **Choose the candidate with a reverence for life.**
- **Choose the candidate with the courage of his convictions.**
- **Keep the State Treasurer with a record of performance.**

VOTE FOR STATE TREASURER BOB CASEY

Paid for by the Committee to Elect Bob Casey
John Durbin, Treasurer

Fig. 7-25. Newspaper ad, Committee to Elect Bob Casey, Scranton Catholic Light, Scranton, Pennsylvania, April 20, 1980.

church has a obligation, or at least a role, in forming social, humanitarian, and economic attitudes, so they justify political involvement where it avoids doctrines and concentrates on public morals.

During his 1988 presidential campaign, former televangelist Pat Robertson found it necessary to run a 30-minute campaign commercial in which he discussed media prejudices against a Southern Baptist and clergyman. In the commercial Robertson argued that neither of these facts should be a liability; his religious affiliation should not turn off voters and certainly should not disqualify him.[29]

Yet for generations candidates have strategically used the moral precepts preached by organized religion, which is what Orval Faubus did a generation ago when he toured the Bible Belt promising that if he was elected Governor he would move against sinfulness, gambling, and prostitution by closing "the flesh pots of Hot Springs, Arkansas." After Faubus was elected, he ignored what he had called a "flagrant violation of the law by this sinful community." When he ran for re-election, his opponents raised this as an issue and faubus replied, "If there were violations going on, Hot Springs has plenty of judges, police, officials, and other means of enforcement. If I did something about it, they'd call me a dictator."[30]

Organized religion has found other ways to use its political clout in support of the concept of morality. For example, the Catholic Church does not endorse candidates, but it has resorted to political means when Catholic schools were threatened. Their teachings have also provided a favorable environment for anti-abortion activists.[31] In Utah and Idaho for almost a century the Church of the Latter Saints (the Mormons) has supported and opposed legislation and are active against the enactment of the national Equal Rights Amendment. In the 1960s, a black Baptist minister, the late Martin Luther King, Jr., formed the Christian Leadership Conference, which used churches to help recruit, rally supporters, raise money, and aid the forces that opposed racial discrimination.

Another example of church involvement with political issues came in 1979 when the Reverend Jerry Falwell, already familiar to millions of Americans through his program, "The Old Time Gospel Hour," actively objected to the proliferation of abortion, homosexuality, and pornography, and opposed the U.S. Supreme court's ruling to reject the right to prayer in the public schools. Falwell organized a "Moral Majority" network that at one time boasted four million lay members led by 72,000 ministers in all fifty states and who he claimed registered three million new voters and raised $5 million dollars. This was strategically spent in key races to elect sympathetic candidates.[32] In 1980 the Internal Revenue Service formally recognized the existence of the resurgence of this religious political involvement when it ruled that the United Church of Christ could interpret, publish, and circulate congressional voting records without jeopardizing its tax-exempt religious status.[33]

Some segments of the religious community argue that the need for racial equality alone justifies the bending of the so-called doctrine of separation of church and state. Black minister Reverend Jesse Jackson made extensive use of black churches in his race for the Democratic presidential nomination. In the

Pennsylvania primary, for example, Jackson's state campaign chairman was a Philadelphia minister, as were his state youth coordinator and office manager. The black churches and black ministers urged their parishioners to vote for Jackson. One of them, the Reverend James Hall of Philadelphia, said that Jackson "is giving us a vehicle to implement what we have been preaching." And Jackson himself told ABC News Nightline, "What labor was supposed to be to Mondale . . . what big business is to Reagan, the black church has been to this campaign."[34]

Informal Influences and Voter Loyalty

Just as voters are influenced by geography, race, or ethnic origins, voters have an emotional allegiance to candidates who are members of their business, profession, hometown, or church. This sense of loyalty is not limited to those with formal affiliations. In general, however, it pays those who want to pursue public office to follow the advice of Los Angeles political consultant, Hal Avery—a man who has made a career out of appealing to the electorate who have no fixed political views. When advising his candidates, Avery says they should earn their leadership spurs working in a church or a fraternal, political, or Chamber of Commerce organization. Belonging to such a group not only gives the candidate exposure, but conveys to the fellow church, club, or fraternal members an image of being "one of their own."[35]

Candidates, like sports teams, have always been conscious of local loyalties. Probably the most striking example of a politician who capitalized on such connections was a United States Senator from Pennsylvania, James J. Davis. In the 1920s and 1930s Puddler Jim (as he was known) ran the Moose lodge in his home state, but he was also active in the Masons, Mystic Shrine, Grotto, Fellows of the Knights of Pythias, Elks, Foresters, Protected Home Circle, Knights of the Golden Eagle, Woodman of the World, and Maccabees.[36]

Candidates with local affiliations like these have extorted local voters to support "a home town candidate," but candidates without "home town" roots have had to evolve strategies to overcome this barrier. For example, after President John Kennedy was assassinated, his brother Robert, who had been Attorney General, decided to run for the U.S. Senate, not from his home state of Massachusetts, but from New York. To overcome the carpetbagger image, Bobby Kennedy set out to ride the coattails of past New York statesmen. During some of his TV commercials he looked straight into the camera and said:

> I want to be a United States Senator like Senator Wagner (of New York) was a United States Senator, and like Herbert Lehman (of New York) was a United States Senator. Where would they have been when the education bill came up in 1961? Senator Lehman would have been on the floor of the United States Senate leading the

fight for federal aid to education. Where was my opponent, Senator Keating? Senator Keating voted against the education bill in 1961.

Scotty Reston said that the education bill in 1961 was a test of our national purpose. Senator Keating voted against that bill. Where would Herbert Lehman have been? Where would Robert Wagner have been? They would have been in the forefront. They would have been leading the fight. That's what kind of a Senator the State of New York deserves.

Then the announcer's voice said: "Let's put Robert Kennedy to work for New York."[37]

Weighing Loyalties Against Each Other

Generally, there is an informal ranking of a candidate's attributes and the loyalties they engender. For example, a common economic interest—or in the case of the voter who is a member of a minority, a common race—has the strongest psychological bond. After that, it is the voters' religion and this religion's ability to engender voter loyalty. Generally, a common religious bond is stronger than a fraternal affiliation and geographic affiliation. For this reason candidates have always found a way to capitalize on their religious leanings.

When "Kingfish" Huey Long stumped rural south Louisiana in the early 1930s, a local leader in Southern Louisiana told Huey: "You're from the Bible Belt (The Protestant North). But remember, now you're in Cajun country where we got mostly Catholics." Throughout that day, as he spoke in every small town, Huey would begin with this story: "When I was a boy, I would get up at six o'clock in the morning on Sunday, and I would hitch our old horse up to the buggy and I would take my Catholic grandparents to mass. I would bring them home, and at ten o'clock I would hitch the old horse up again, and would take my Baptist grandparents to church."

On the way back to Baton Rouge that night the local leader complimented Huey, saying: "Why, Huey, you've been holding out on us. I didn't know you have any Catholic grandparents." "Don't be a damn fool," replied Huey. "We didn't even have a horse."[38]

Chapter 60

The Coattail Mystique

> There is a new fashion sweeping the country: skirts are shorter, pants are tighter, and the L.B.J. coattails are going out of style.
> —Richard Nixon[1]
>
> In most campaigns it is someone's recommendation that accounts for most of the vote changes that occur during an election campaign.
> —Professor Joseph T. Klapper[2]

The Mystique of Political Association

Well-known political names do influence millions of voters. They are especially helpful to candidates when a popular political figure—say a president, prime minister, or governor—is leading their party's ticket. Replying to Alfred Iverson of Georgia, Congressman Abraham Lincoln described this phenomenon as riding the coattails. He spoke to the United States House on July 27, 1848, saying:

> Mr. Speaker, old horses and military coattails, or tails of any sort, are not just figures of speech. . . . The gentleman from Georgia . . . says we have deserted all our principles, and taken shelter under General Taylor's military coattail. . . . Has he no acquaintance with the ample military coattail of General Jackson? Does he not know that his own party has run the last five Presidential races under that coattail, and that they are now running the sixth under the same cover. . . ?

The military connotation soon fell by the wayside and coattails came to mean the ability of a leader to transfer support at an election.[3] What Lincoln was describing was the mystique of voter association. Occasionally, this is seen when candidates wrap themselves in the images of past heroes.

What Lincoln so wisely observed has continued to be true down through the years. As shown in a graph (Figure 7-26) taken from *USA Today* following the 1984 Reagan landslide, the presidential coattail effect continues to influence elections for congressional offices. But the coattail effect has ramifications beyond the direct effect on congressional elections. The endorsement of and even the association with powerful, important, and instantly recognized personalities can and often does add stature to a candidacy.

Candidates who benefit from this mystique find prestige because they associate with world, regional, or state leaders, as seen in the Averill Harriman brochure when he aspired to the presidency (Figure 7-27). This piece emphasized his association with President Roosevelt, Winston Churchill, and even Stalin.

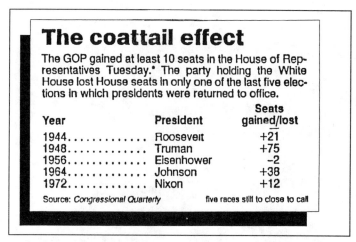

The coattail effect

The GOP gained at least 10 seats in the House of Representatives Tuesday.* The party holding the White House lost House seats in only one of the last five elections in which presidents were returned to office.

Year	President	Seats gained/lost
1944	Roosevelt	+21
1948	Truman	+75
1956	Eisenhower	-2
1964	Johnson	+38
1972	Nixon	+12

Source: *Congressional Quarterly*   five races still to close to call

Fig. 7-26. "The Coattail Effect," *USA Today*, November 8, 1984. Copyright 1984, USA Today. Reprinted with permission.

When Hugh Scott was the minority leader of the United States Senate, he also demonstrated that the coattail mystique works. When he ran for re-election in 1970, his television commercials showed a young boy walking up the steep steps of the capitol building, past the guards, and knocking on a huge wooden door. The door opened and the boy was greeted by U.S. Senator Hugh Scott, who informed the boy that this used to be Thomas Jefferson's office. Scott said that Jefferson had the right idea about government, which was "trust in people." The television commercial continued with Senator Scott telling the boy:

. . . there are a lot of things right about America, but there are some things wrong. And my job is to find out what's wrong and make it right. By the time you start college, Billy, things are going to be a lot better in America.

That's a promise. I've worked with six different presidents: Franklin Roosevelt, Harry Truman, Dwight Eisenhower, John Kennedy, Lyndon Johnson, and Richard Nixon. All great men, and I got things done with all of them. Now, let's go over to the Senate restaurant and I'll buy you a Coke."

As they walked off, the announcer's voice could be heard saying, "Day in, day out, using energy and persuasion, one man fights for our state as he works for our nation. The most powerful Senator we ever had: Scott of Pennsylvania."[4]

In the closing days of the 1965 campaign for the New York's U.S. Senator, polls showed that Robert Kennedy and the incumbent were running close. Then Fred Papert and George Lois came up with a 20-second television spot that tilted a large undecided vote into Kennedy's column. The commercial very briefly compared both the Democratic and Republican nominees. It recognized that

Fig. 7-27. Brochure, National Committee for Harriman for President, New York.

Fig. 7-28. George Lois and Bill Pitts, *The Art of Advertising*
(New York: Harry N. Abrams, Inc., 1977), pp. 103, 110, 111.

Bobby was heir to the legend of his assassinated brother, President John F. Kennedy. Then the commercial ended with the question shown in Figure 7-29.[5]

Under some circumstances, the mystique of voter association has carried even beyond the rational. For example, sometimes candidates benefit by confusion with politicians who have the same last name. In 1946, a veteran political figure, Homer Holt, became Governor of West Virginia, and no-relation newcomer Rush Holt was elected the youngest member of the United States Senate in history. In the years from 1952 to 1963, the same situation arose in the State of Washington when it was represented by two Magnusons. One, Warren, was a popular United States Senator, and the other, no relation, Don Magnuson, was elected Congressman at large.[6]

Individual Endorsement Strategy

Individual endorsements are not an exclusively political phenomenon. On the contrary. Endorsements have been used over and over again in commercial

Fig. 7-29. George Lois and Bill Pitts, *The Art of Advertising*
(New York: Harry N. Abrams, 1977), pp. 105-106.

advertising. In 1893, Lillie Langtry posed in a wooden bath tub for Pears soap.[7]
In the early 1930s, advertising pioneers like Albert Lasker used ads to create a
sophisticated female smoker image with slogans like, "Luckies are kind to your
throat," and "I protect my precious voice with Lucky Strikes." He got testimonials
from people supporting these claims. When President Coolidge retired from the
White House, Lasker sent Mrs. Grace Coolidge, who didn't smoke, a $50,000
check with a note telling her that the money was hers if she would sign a Lucky
Strike testimonial. Although the retiring First Lady rejected his offer, other
prominent women did not. For example, Lasker got Luckies endorsements from
the entire female roster of the Metropolitan Opera.[8] As we can see in Figure 7-30,
Ronald Reagan was one of the movie stars recruited to advertise Chesterfield
Cigarettes.

At election time, friendly politicians traditionally say complimentary things
about their party's candidates which are used in mass media advertising, or on the
literature they distribute door to door. An example is the brochure used by a one-
time congressional staffer in his first candidacy for Congress (Figure 7-31). The

Fig. 7-30. Advertisement, The Liggett Group, Inc., Raleigh, North Carolina.

brochure features endorsements from both of the state's U.S. Senators and the incumbent congressman, who had chosen not to run.

Frequently, because of the perception that endorsements, particularly group endorsements, put the candidate in someone's political pocket, strategists limit

★★★

People are talking about
NORM DICKS

Maggie says:
"Norm Dicks has spent the past seven and one-half years serving the people of Washington State, and serving them extraordinarily well, with integrity, intelligence, and his own special brand of enthusiasm."
—Senator Warren G. Magnuson

Scoop says:
"In recent years, I have worked almost daily with Norm Dicks. I have seen the high quality of his performance, and the great depth of his understanding, on literally dozens of problems affecting Washington State and the Sixth District. He is tough, smart, honest and concerned—and he would be a first-rate representative in Congress."
—Senator Henry M. Jackson

Norm Dicks for Congress Committee
210 Broadway, Tacoma, Wa
Booth Gardner, Chairman
Tacoma – 383-3976
Bremerton – 479-3932

★★★★★★★★★★★★★★★★★★★★★★★★★★★★

4. Bremerton needed help to fight crime. We had to get an additional squadron of armed forces police for PSNS. Maggie assigned Norm Dicks to the job, and he got it done.
—Mayor Glenn Jarstad, Bremerton

5. When the bureaucrats in Washington kept stalling our Trident impact funds, our school funds, and even an essential sewer project, Senator Magnuson and Senator Jackson told Norm Dicks to cut through the red tape. And that's just what Norm did, with great results for the whole county.
—Kitsap County Commissioners Gene Lobe, Bill Mahan, and Frank Randall

3. The dynamic Dicks, should he be elected, would be one of the most impressive freshman Congressmen in years from any state.
—Editorial in Argus, Pacific Northwest's independent magazine of news, comment, and opinion

6. Congressman Floyd Hicks said he thinks Dicks would be an effective replacement because, as Magnuson's top aide, he has made valuable contacts that would give him an advantage as a freshman Congressman.
—A. Robert Smith, reporting from Washington, D.C. in the Tacoma News Tribune

Part of the best team any state has ever had on Capitol Hill: Senator Jackson, Norm Dicks and Floyd Hicks.

About Norm Dicks, Democrat for Congress:

Norm Dicks was born and raised in the Sixth District. He was a star athlete and scholar at West Bremerton High School and the University of Washington, where he played in the Rose Bowl and won All-Coast academic honors. After working in private industry, he graduated from the UW Law School in 1968, and went to work for Senator Magnuson. As Magnuson's top assistant, Norm was responsible for both national legislation and laws and appropriations dealing directly with the State of Washington and the Sixth District. In April 1976, Norm left Senator Magnuson's staff to run for Congress.

Fig. 7-31. Brochure, Norm Dicks for Congress Committee, 1976.

endorsements to situations where the candidate is under attack—when they call on prominent people as character references—or in situations where a candidate is in danger of being overwhelmed by a better-known opponent.

For example, in November 1977 there was a political contest between the sons of two of New York's most powerful men. One was Robert Wagner, Jr., son of New York Mayor Robert Wagner and grandson of the U.S. Senator by the same name. The other was Andrew Stein, son of millionaire Jerry Finkelstein. Both candidates had previously held office (Wagner as Councilman and Stein as Assemblyman). To overcome Wagner's family name familiarity, Stein used endorsements from such national figures as Hubert Humphrey, Edmund Muskie, and Edward Kennedy to tip the balance in his favor.[9]

Another flip side is that an endorsement by a prominent individual often carries with it opposition from the endorser's enemies. A candidate conscious of this criticism can bypass endorsements from politicians and use endorsements from local prominent individuals.

Getting and Using the Endorsement

The Democratic National Committee suggests that candidates make a demographic analysis of key subgroups long before filing. Then the candidates systematically call on their leaders, many of whom would be insulted if the candidate didn't inquire as to their political objectives and ask for support. Here the candidate's knowledge of the organization's objectives and reactions to those goals become important. In fact, the type of reception a candidate receives depends on whether the candidate knows and agrees or disagrees with the organization's political objectives.

If the organization has loyal supporters and if what their leaders want is within reasonable limits, the candidate can expect that many others are making the same pilgrimage. As often happens, all or most of the candidates agree to support the leaders' objectives, so the leaders must select from among the ambitious politicians those they will recommend to their followers.

Other things being equal, the candidate's personal contacts, style, personality, and chances of winning become important. I. Lynn Mueller, of Robert Lynn Associates, Ltd., tells of a relatively unknown candidate for Governor who followed each early contact by sending a personal note by mail. Mueller says that although this candidate was in reality only known to the leaders themselves, within a period of two or three months he was being heralded as a bright new star and a real comer.[10]

A Strategy for Creating an Endorsing Committee

There is no formula for acquiring a group's political endorsement. Usually, the candidate targets by mail or by placing ads in the group's bulletins or newspapers.

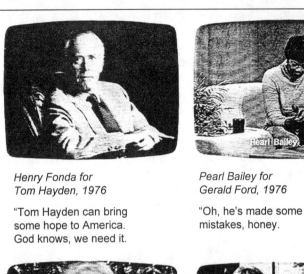

Henry Fonda for
Tom Hayden, 1976

"Tom Hayden can bring
some hope to America.
God knows, we need it.

Pearl Bailey for
Gerald Ford, 1976

"Oh, he's made some
mistakes, honey.

Carroll O'Connor for
Edward Kennedy, 1980

"I'm afraid Jimmy's
depression is going to be
worse than Herbert's"

Mary Tyler Moore for
Jimmy Carter, 1980

"Men and women truly con-
cerned about women's freedom
are going to vote for Jimmy
Carter"

Fig. 7-32. Used by permission of L. Patrick Devlin, Curator, Television
Political Advertising Collection, University of Rhode Island.

But one of the best strategies was used by Governor, later U.S. Senator, John
Chaffee of Rhode Island.

First, Chaffee asked a few friends in a number of different businesses and
professions to form internal committees. If they were from medicine, they might
use a letterhead, "Doctors for Chaffee, Thomas A. Perry, M.D., Chairman," with a
few prominent physicians listed down its left side. The letter went to other doctors

in the state and read in part: "As was done in connection with the last campaign for Governor, an organization is being formed to make known the endorsement of Governor Chaffee by Rhode Island doctors." This was followed by an explanation of the kind of job the Governor had done with emphasis on his interest in medicine, etc.

Then the letter concluded: "May we include your name on the list of 'Doctors for Chaffee'? Please mail the enclosed card without delay." The card said: "Please enroll me in 'Doctors for Chaffee.' In any public list of Governor Chaffee's supporters, you may include my name." As soon as they received about a hundred replies, they ran off more stationery with the new names, which they used to send a follow-up letter saying, "We haven't heard from you. How about joining?" When these new names came back, a release was given to the newspapers saying that 237 doctors had joined in endorsing Chaffee. Then another letter followed to the others in that profession, saying, "While each of us may not always agree with Governor Chaffee's position on every single proposed measure affecting us as doctors, we believe he is worthy of our support." The letter was then signed by the Chairman, followed by a greatly enlarged list of doctors.

This technique was repeated with other groups such as lawyers, teachers, nurses, attorneys, engineers, architects, cleaners, insurance salesmen, building contractors, etc. Evaluating the technique, Chaffee commented, "There is no question but that such endorsement letters can spell the difference between victory and defeat . . . in my first election we used a lot of groups; 320,000 people voted, and I only won by 398 votes."[11]

Candidates can target particular constituencies without having a mailing list or an inside contact. In some instances he or she can use a listing by business or occupation in the yellow pages of the telephone directory to make their own prospect lists of businesses or professions.

Endorsement Strategy Pitfalls

No names should be used as an endorsement until the campaign organization has a signed authorization. This is true even when the endorser is predisposed to cooperate. Simply telephoning and asking permission to use names can result in problems. A phone call gives the candidate little protection when the endorser changes his mind, and this problem becomes more difficult when a candidate isn't attempting to use an endorsement, only publicizing legitimate praise that he or she has received from individuals or organizations.

In 1965 Washington State's very popular Lieutenant Governor John Cherberg was running for Mayor of Seattle. He published excerpts from letters he had received from a variety of groups and individuals praising him for work he had done on their behalf. The weekend before the election, some of those who had made favorable remarks in the past held a press conference, endorsed Cherberg's opponent, and signed a devastating ad, with the headline, "You can't use us, John." It was significant that the wafflers did not say that they had been quoted incorrectly in Cherberg's brochure. Still, their comments left the impression that the material in Cherberg's brochure and advertising were not true, and he was defeated.

If the candidate wants to use a favorable statement, and, fearing change of heart, is afraid to ask for permission, he or she should use a headline such as, "The true worth of a candidate is not judged by a political endorsement made at election time. A far better criteria is the unsolicited comments made by those who appraise his or her work during years of service." Then as a part of the copy note the date and place the laudatory comments were made.

How should the candidate react when those who have actually made positive statements hold a press conference saying that they do not endorse the candidacy? There should be no attempt to explain; that might signal a retreat. Instead, give a statement such as this to the reporters: "The question is, did I deserve the praise at the time the comments were made? I rest my case on what was said when the statement was made, not on the basis of the waffler's decision to support someone else in an election."

Any attempt to use the back door to a prominent individual's personal following without permission can be a political disaster, as congressional contender, John Nance Garner (no relation to the former vice president) learned in the 1978 campaign. Analyzing the conservative trend sweeping the nation, Garner used a commercial featuring an impersonator whose voice closely resembled that of national newscaster, Paul Harvey. In typical Harvey style, the sixty-second radio spot took the government workers in Washington, DC, to task for using electric erasers, claiming, "this plug-in costs the government $16," and it ended with a Paul Harvey-like sign off, "Good Luck."

Given Garner's political stance, this commercial seemed both appropriate and effective, but Garner didn't count on the reaction of the real Paul Harvey. In one of his daily radio broadcasts Harvey's faithful followers heard the following comment: "Paul Harvey does not endorse any political candidate for office. Now and then some candidate uses the canned voice of a professional impersonator who implies otherwise. The most recent attempt I understand is in Seattle. But again, the real Paul Harvey does not endorse any partisan politician and certainly would never endorse one who tries to deceive voters."[12]

Politics is a profession in which relationships change overnight, so the candidate should always be on the lookout for situations that will be helpful. An endorsement given on a different occasion by an opponent can be gold. In the 1984 presidential primary, when U.S. Senator Gary Hart and former Vice President Fritz Mondale were opposing each other for the Democratic nomination, a Hart TV commercial quoted what Mondale had said of him on an earlier occasion, when he described Hart as "one of the most compassionate public servants I have ever known in my life. He is brilliant." Then Hart's TV commercial announcer continued: "Now that he's an opponent, Mr. Mondale is attacking Mr. Hart bitterly, recklessly. . . . Oh, how Mondale wishes we'd forget that he once said, 'If we lost Gary Hart, it could change the course of this entire nation.' "[13]

Fig. 7-33. "23 Winning Ideas for Political Advertisers" (New York: Bureau of Advertising, n.d.), pp. 11, 13.

Chapter 61

Opportunism, Deception, Commitment, and Morality

A politician these days has to sit on a fence and still keep both ears to the ground.
   —Allan Lamport, Former Mayor of Toronto[1]

This man has no principles, public or private. As a politician his sole spring of action is an inordinate ambition.
   —Alexander Hamilton, speaking of Aaron Burr[2]

Those who treat politics and morality apart will never understand one or the other.
   —John Morley[3]

The Truth Versus. . . .

Candidates have moral requirements, the most important of which is the obligation to tell the truth. While outright lying is rare, though, there are some successful politicians who have used "white lies" to win a political campaign. One of those was Joe McCarthy, who served as United States Senator from Wisconsin. During his career, McCarthy caught the political wind not only once, but several times.

McCarthy ran first as a Democrat for a local political office and was defeated. Three years later, after sizing up the prevailing winds, he ran as a Republican and was elected a circuit judgeship. In that office he was noted for granting quickie divorces and for making decisions that were overturned by the state supreme court. Then came the war years. McCarthy took a leave of absence from his official duties and enlisted in the Marine Corps.

When World War II was over, terming himself "Tail Gunner Joe," McCarthy filed for United States Senator. Actually the records show that while in the service McCarthy was "an intelligence officer and that he was never a tail gunner, and he saw no combat duty." But this was never publicized—until after he rode the lie to victory and was a U.S. Senator.[4]

The Most Common of Moral Lapses—Contradictory Statements

The candidate is making contradictory statements when he or she tells one side what they want to hear, and takes a different position with those who feel strongly in the other direction.

Direct mail specialist Lynn Mueller tells how he marketed a Republican candidate. After noting whether the precincts had been carried by a liberal or conservative during the last Democratic primary, Mueller designated each precinct as either liberal or conservative. Mueller billed his candidate as a "problem solver," who adopted either a liberal or a conservative approach. Then he drafted two letters for circulation. One led the recipients to believe the candidate was a liberal. The other letter led voters to believe the candidate favored a conservative position. Then, depending upon the majority persuasion, Mueller mailed either a liberal or a conservative message to the registered Democratic voters in that precinct.[5]

While these deceptions are questionable, it is not fair to condemn every candidate who openly seeks an innovative way to ride the political fence. For example, in the 1924 Presidential election, the unsuccessful Democratic nominee was Wall Street lawyer, John W. Davis. Although Davis was personally dry (a nondrinker), he knew he was far behind, so, hoping to get the big city wet vote, Davis gambled on a wet position. At the same time, he tried not to offend the historically bone-dry Democrats of the rural South. When he made his campaign swing, Davis tried to ride both horses. He proclaimed that he believed in "personal liberty," which he defined as the local option to have beer and wine, and left each jurisdiction free to decide the issue for itself. But his strategy didn't work. The drys publicly and loudly complained that Davis's pious expressions were in reality wet code words.[6]

When the Candidate Has an Obligation to Tell the Whole Truth

The candidate has a special obligation to tell the whole truth to those who vote with their heart, particularly single-issue voters. To single-issue organizations, such as those who take a pro or anti stand on abortion, ERA, gun or rent control, or control of pornography, the candidate has a moral obligation to know what the organization wants and to not promise to support their objectives unless he or she will honestly support their position after the election.

Of course, there are often two sides to an alleged commitment. The candidate may not give a single-issue group an iron-clad promise. A candidate can agree in part with a controversial position and even reject any formal endorsement by a leader or organization and still accept the endorsement of an independent committee of individuals who are from the group.

This does not imply that a candidate is not free to strategically avoid an issue, especially if, in their opinion, there is no right or wrong position. For example, if a town is embroiled in where a public facility should be built and the two sites under consideration are equally acceptable, the candidate can say she has not yet made up her mind or that she or he needs more facts before answering. Under other circumstances, a candidate has a moral right to strategically avoid confrontation on issues, and to go on addressing other issues which the voters are interested in.

Under most circumstances, a wise opportunist tries to acquire support by a mild commitment—one that is not so inflammatory that it will turn off other support. The front runner, usually the incumbent, settles for a promise to "consider reforms," "to examine the issue," or "not to make a decision without hearing from the barnburner." The 1924 presidential campaign provides an illustration. When the nation was debating the fate of the eighteenth amendment, which had prohibited the sale of liquor in the United States, the vote was violently split. The Republicans ignored the issue, preferring to stay "cool, though dry, with Coolidge." The third party, the Progressives—led by Wisconsin's fighting Bob LaFollette—like the Republicans, were dry, but focused their campaign on social reform.[7]

Softening a Hostile Confrontation

Sometimes the candidate must take a stand that runs counter to what a group perceives as their interests. But William Albin had the key to softening a hostile confrontation; he said that, "Opinions have this in common with entrenchments that they offer an obstinate resistance to a frontal attack, but not to a turning movement."[8] Applying this psychology, the best way to handle those who disagree with the candidate is to point to something else about the candidate that they do agree with and, in the process, pick up the votes of those who agree with the candidate for some other reason.

If the candidate disagrees with a part of his or her constituency on a popular issue and must face a hostile audience, the candidate should heed the advice of Gordon Alport and Leo J. Postman, writing in the Transactions of the New York Academy of Science: "Change the message to fit existing concepts and attitudes."[9]

For example, in the 1960 congressional election, Congressman Bradford Morse, a Massachusetts Republican, had to face a Polish Catholic constituency who wanted Federal support for the students who attended church schools. He had to ask them to support him against the opposition Democrat, who was advocating this Federal assistance while his party, the Republicans, were not. Congressman Morse searched for an explanation that permitted him to appeal to these constituents without deserting his party's position. He enhanced his political image by reminding his constituents, who had relatives in Poland, "You know what happened to the church school system . . . where the state intruded into religious affairs." Then he explained that he opposed the aid because it presented a danger of Federal control over church and school, as had already occurred in Poland.[10]

The Classic Confrontation

If a candidate must take a stand that runs counter to what the constituency or a group perceives to be their interests but the candidate is not totally opposed to their views, he or she could follow strategy suggested by Margaret Heckler, a member of President Reagan's Cabinet, and later Ambassador to Ireland. During the 20 years she served in Congress, she tried to appeal to those with whom she had some disagreement by promising that they could talk to her on any important issue whenever they wished. As Heckler once explained when she was still Congresswoman, there is always a percentage of the constituency that will find such an image frank and refreshing, and some otherwise hostile voters will be persuaded to deviate from the traditional view and give the honest candidate the vote.[11]

Now we move to another facet. Assume the candidate is not deeply committed. Political opportunities are a mixed bag, and it is up to the candidate to balance the tradeoffs. A candidate should calculate the risk before taking a stand just to please a barn-burner group. Some voting blocks are so controversial that open support of their cause will be a political disaster because their issue lays the candidate open to the charge that he has sold out, or support might cause a backlash from another group, class, or organization that holds a different economic, philosophical, or religious view. However, the candidate with the uphill climb must still attract new support. This often means taking risks.

In 1938, Frank R. Kent described the political encounter with antivivisectionists who opposed the use of animals for medical research, because they considered it to be working against the interests of humanity. At one of the five or six places at which a candidate for Mayor of Baltimore spoke one evening, there was an audience composed exclusively of antivisectionists. As he entered the hall, his local leader whispered, "These people don't give a damn about the tax rate or the schools or the health department, or any other issue of the campaign. All they care about is this antivivisection stuff. If you are with them on that, they will be with you. And if you are against them, they will be against you to the man; and they are worth about 1,500 votes." Up until that moment, the candidate had scorned these people as kooks. After considering the votes, however, the candidate gave lip service to their cause.[12]

Deception

Telling both sides what they want to hear and riding the fence are not the only ways deception can be used in a campaign. The unscrupulous will go overboard when describing the opposition. A classic example occurred during a 1950 Florida campaign for U.S. Senator—one that was so close it was widely assumed that Republicans won the day by switching their registration to vote for George Smathers in the Democratic primary.

One of many reasons for the switch was a letter sent by the president of the Florida Young Republicans Club to all members, urging them to "forget party ambitions just this once to support (Democrat) George Smathers," because a vote for the then U.S. Senator Claude Pepper was a vote "to support Stalin and the Communists."[13] Candidates, even those that are demagogues, usually stop short of such vicious rhetoric.

Resourceful candidates find many ways to stretch the truth. When one-time Republican Mayor of New York City Fiorello LaGuardia, the son of an Italian father and a Jewish mother, sought a congressional seat in a district that included a large Jewish vote, some say he accused his opponent of starting a rumor that he was anti-semitic so he could stage a publicity stunt. He challenged his opponent to a debate and stipulated that it must be in Yiddish, which only LaGuardia, who had for some years worked as an interpreter on Ellis Island, could do.[14]

Deception is more than a moral problem. The candidate trying to get away with it is probably courting political disaster when the deception is exposed. Under these circumstances, the moral question is, how does the deception affect the voters and if they knew they were being deceived, would the voter still vote for that candidate?

Opportunism

Call it opportunism or not, on occasion some prominent politicians have been willing to ignore pitfalls and moral scruples in an effort to tie up a crucial voting block. In 1944, a young Thomas Dewey was running for President against Franklin Roosevelt. At the time, Roosevelt, the internationalist, had incurred the wrath of the U.S. Communists because he had condemned the Russians for temporarily cooperating with the Nazis in carving up Poland. For a brief historical moment, the Republican party tried to tie up the vote of their bitter arch enemies, the Communists by advertising Tom Dewey's opposition to Roosevelt's so-called imperialist internationalist in the official Communist newspaper in the U.S., the *Daily Worker*.[15]

Putting opportunism in perspective, no one can rightfully criticize a candidate for watching and taking advantage of an opportunity. Certainly, sincere committed candidates are entitled to dream of opportunities that permit them to pursue a cause that will galvanize the majority and catapult them into public office.

To illustrate further, let's go back to when women were first given the right to vote in the United States, when the majority of voters no longer condoned such things as a public hanging or the old-fashioned barroom where liquor, prostitution, and gambling had flourished. Even after women got the right to vote, Seattle, like other seaport cities in that male-dominated era, was running "wide open" until the late twenties when the wife of a university professor, Bertha Landis—dubbed "Big Bertha" by her critics—won a place on the city council. Although Landis continued talking against "illegal girls, gambling and bootlegging," she was ignored by the male city fathers. Then, His Honor, the

Mayor, "Doc" Brown, and several members of the city council, left the city for a convention of city officials in Atlantic City. By a process of elimination Landis became acting Mayor.

Seeing her chance, the acting mayor summoned the chief of police to her office and demanded that he fire officers she claimed were winking at the law. The chief stood his ground and refused to follow her orders. Bertha fired him on the spot. Then she appointed herself chief. Thereafter, she made headlines across the nation as she led police raids that "closed the city." And the city stayed closed until the Mayor could hurry back via railroad from the East Coast and rescind her actions. Later, strategically using the "open versus closed city" as an issue, Landis filed for mayor in the next election. She defeated the incumbent and became the first woman mayor of a major city in the United States.[16]

Opportunists are not to be condemned because they try to please a crowd, but they are subject to criticism when they have no philosophical roots or if they push under what they believe to stay on top of a popular trend. One unsuccessful Southern candidate for governor made this statement:

> The difference between me and the others is I refuse to use the race issue. I can read the Constitution. There ain't no use in goin' out and lyin' to people. I coulda hung a nigger in every stump, but I just didn't go for that kinda politics. It don't get you nothin' in the long run. Folks give me hell about bein' a nigger-lover. Hell, I don't know nothin' about that. They was just against me 'cause I wouldn't hang niggers. There ain't no use in runnin', that's all. It's the old Southern custom. I guess I just wasn't aggressive enough to suit 'em.

You may not believe this, but these were the words of George Corley Wallace—the same Wallace who later won the governorship by vowing that he would stand in the door of any Alabama school to prevent integration and who concluded his inaugural speech by saying, "In the name of the greatest people that ever trod this earth, I draw the line in the dust and toss the gauntlet before the feet of tyranny. And I say segregation now! Segregation tomorrow! Segregation forever!"[17]

And it was this same Wallace who also, after years out of office, courted the black vote and was again elected Governor in 1983. He then invited the press to publish the fact that he was entertaining Chicago-based Reverend Jesse Jackson, a black candidate for President of the United States, in his office and was instrumental in getting Jackson the chance to address a joint session of the Alabama legislature.

Part 8

Reporting, Regulation, and Taxation

of Campaign Funds

Chapter 62

Public Disclosure

> The system is a witch's brew unless the candidate hires lawyers and
> accountants to keep things straight.
> —Ross Cunningham, veteran political editor[1]

Brief History of U.S. Campaign Finance Reform

The need for campaign finance reform was recognized as early as 1907 when
President Theodore Roosevelt recommended public financing of federal elections
and a ban on private contributions. Congress didn't adopt Roosevelt's
suggestions, but in 1910 it enacted laws prohibiting corporate contributions and
limiting the amount of money a candidate could spend.

At that time, most state legislatures also enacted laws to control campaign
spending. Typical of these was a 1915 Kansas law limiting contributions to $500
for state senators and representatives (who, at the time, earned less than $1,000
per year).[2] Although there was some public outcry and the Kansas legislation was
considered a significant reform, the real push came from the sitting politicians,
especially U.S. Senators, who until that time had been chosen by the state
legislatures and feared rich candidates might contest their seats.

Eventually, the new laws restricting campaign spending were tested. The
guinea pig was Truman H. Newsberry of Michigan. After he received a majority
of the votes in his state for U.S. Senator, he was tried in 1918 by the sitting United
States Senators for spending $195,000 and found guilty of violating the law. He
was deprived of his office in spite of his defense that he had to spend to compete
with his opponent, Henry Ford, whose name was a household word. Later, the
Senate's decision in Newsberry's case was held unconstitutional by the Supreme
Court, but when the Senate seated Newsberry, he resigned. Having made his
point, Newsberry said that "further service would be futile."[3]

Following the U.S. Supreme Court's decision, Congress drew together the
surviving provisions of the federal election law and enacted the Federal Corrupt
Practices Act of 1925. In this act, Congress attempted to set upper spending limits
and prohibit contributions in excess of $5,000 to any candidate for federal office.
The following year, when the U.S. Senate found that William S. Vare spent
$786,000 in Pennsylvania, and Frank L. Smith spent $458,000 in Illinois, both
Vare and Smith were denied their U.S. Senate seats.[4]

While there was widespread public support for the Senate's action, the fact remained that it was the members of the Senate—the most exclusive club in the world—and not the voters who were responsible for Vare and Smith's rejections.

During the 1930s and 1940s, the campaign spending laws came under attack. Critics representing all different shades of opinion claimed that what was thought earlier to be reform handicapped those who wanted to change the status quo. When public support waned, these laws were more or less ignored.

Modern Disclosure Legislation

The power of money to control elections was not uniquely an American concern. The British also tried to curb campaign spending with the Representation of the People Act, which restricted preelection spending to slightly over $2,000 to each Parliamentary candidate and contained an unwritten understanding that political parties could use election posters, but they would not use newspaper, radio, or TV advertising.

In February 1974, Britain's tiny Liberal party, headed by Jeremy Thorpe, ignored this understanding. Thorpe's party spent $60,000 on newspaper advertising that carried the slogan: "*You* can change the face of Britain. Take power. Vote Liberal." Although the ads did not result in Thorpe's party being elected, they broke the barrier. In the elections that followed, all political parties used newspaper and TV advertising.[5]

Meanwhile, campaign spending had gotten out of hand in the United States with powerful special interests recklessly spending huge sums to influence elections. But a new wave of spending reform created federal, state, and local legislation requiring candidates, their political committees, and other politically active interests to make periodic public disclosure of campaign contributions and expenditures. The 1971 federal act, for example, made significant reforms. It eliminated the overall ceiling on campaign contributions and limited the amount of expenditures that candidates for president, vice president, or U.S. senator or representative could make from their personal funds or from the funds of their immediate families.[6] The Act also experimented with a limit on the amount that could be spent in a presidential campaign and allowed taxpayers to direct a dollar of their federal income tax payments toward financing it.

To pass this legislation, Congress had to negotiate with President Nixon, who refused to sign unless Congress agreed to delay public funding until the 1976 presidential election, so it did not affect his 1972 campaign. Ironically, the rampant campaign abuses of that election drove Mr. Nixon from office. Disclosures at the Watergate hearings following the election revealed that during the campaign Nixon's lieutenants solicited and spent an unprecedented amount in campaign contributions, some of which were illegally collected from corporations.

Fig. 8-1. "Newspaper ad, the Liberal party in Britain," *Advertising Age*, February 25, 1974.

A study by Representative Les Aspin of Wisconsin showed the Committee to Re-elect President Nixon indirectly received substantial sums from the one hundred largest defense contractors. These contributions came through their 413 directors, senior officials, and stockholders. Oil companies were responsible for almost $5 million in contributions. Disclosures forced by a Common Cause lawsuit showed $1,176,500 came from interests associated with Gulf Oil, while ten other companies gave more than $100,000 each.[7]

The 1972 orgy of big giving renewed interest in contribution limits. By August 1974, the number of states imposing ceilings on campaign gifts rose from seven to seventeen. Most states held donations to gubernatorial campaigns under $5,000, but others enacted tighter restrictions. New Jersey, for example, set the limit at $600, which was matchable under that state's public financing plan.

In 1974, Congress also reinstated contribution limits applicable to federal candidates and created a Federal Election Commission, which became a model for other jurisdictions. Amendments to the Federal Election Act imposed limits on both expenditures and contributions. They imposed a limit of

Fig. 8-2. Gary Yanker, *Prop Art* (New York: Darien House, Inc., 1972), p. 88.

$1,000 for each election on an individual's annual contribution to a candidate for federal office, which, except for presidential campaigns, is defined as primaries, runoffs, and general elections. A limit of $5,000 was imposed on contributions made by any political committee or candidate. In any election, the total aggregate individual political contributions to candidates for federal offices was limited to $25,000 annually. The act banned contributions by foreign nationals who were not United States residents, and specified that checks rather than cash were to be used if the contributions exceed $100.[8]

State Laws

Most public disclosure legislation requires a statement be filed with the disclosure commission and an official bank account be established before soliciting campaign expense money. A treasurer must be appointed who receives contributions and is responsible for recordkeeping and making expenditures. The candidates are deemed to have knowledge of the contributions and expenditures made on their behalf.[9] All expenditures, other than those from petty cash, must be made by check drawn on the campaign's official account.[10]

Federal law specifically prohibits national banks and federally chartered savings and loan associations from making contributions or expenditures in connection with any election. Also, federal candidates are subject to some state laws. For example, most congressional candidates must file a copy of every report and statement with the state in which the candidate seeks federal office. States also control the primary election date and who is eligible to vote and, in some cases, require that all candidates make a personal financial disclosure.

Candidates for federal office do not have to comply with laws in some states that require information on campaign advertising not required by the Federal Election Act.[11] Also the federal act superseded a Houston ordinance that required federal election-related campaign materials to include an anti-litter warning.[12] Corporation-sponsored federal political action committees do not have to comply with state laws prohibiting payroll deduction when they collect contributions for use in federal campaigns.[13] And federal candidates who are state officials do not have to comply with state laws that ban lobbyists' money when raising funds for their federal election campaigns.[14] However, federal candidates do have to comply with state laws requiring their party affiliation and laws that require their campaign pieces to carry the names and addresses of campaign secretaries or chairmen responsible for their advertising.

These state campaign laws taken as a whole are a hodgepodge of at least fifty different state variations, and include countless local statutes adopted by cities, counties, and other governmental entities. Problems come when candidates apply whichever law, federal or state, will work to their best advantage. Veteran politician Ken Birkhead, a one-time member of U.S. Senator Thomas J. McIntyre's staff, claims he saw a candidate in the senate (not his boss) shake hands with a contributor and come away with a $1,000 bill stuck to his palm.[15] The fact that the contribution was in cash does not mean the money was tainted. Unlimited cash contributions are permitted by most state laws. However, Birkhead's concern was that the candidate he saw was running for a federal office where cash gifts of over $100 must be immediately returned to the donor.[16]

Local regulations have little uniformity. For instance, when filing under some laws, the candidates notify the election commission and do nothing more until they file a final report of contributions and expenditures. Other laws require only two or three reports, while some demand a running weekly account of contributions and expenditures. Some local laws do not require reports below a threshold of $500 or $1,000, while others require a complete accounting, even to the petty cash used to pay for ongoing small expenses.

Local and state laws differ in how they track lobbyists' contributions. Some jurisdictions require that all lobbyists report the source of their gifts so there is a paper trail for tracking how much money the lobbyists' employers have contributed. Then the voter can decide the effect this money has on public officials who make decisions involving their interests.

A few jurisdictions require that candidates identify and declare their source(s) of personal income. Even when candidates disclose personal income, state laws have conflicting philosophies. For example, some states require an itemization of all sources of income, as well as major creditors, and any business in which they have invested along with its major customers or clients, while other state laws only require the public official and/or candidate to list income by category, meaning candidates do not have to disclose the names of or their dealings with individuals. Thus, a lawyer legislator can protect an attorney-client relationship. In some jurisdictions, specific information as to the source of a candidate's regular income is confidential, and only comes to light if a complaint is filed that puts his ethics in question.

Sometimes a local disclosure statute is easily circumvented—for example, when political committees need only to use their "best efforts" to obtain required information. For example, during a 1975 campaign for Los Angeles City Council, William Dauer, a Chamber of Commerce executive, and Sam Stewart, a Bank of America president, organized a political lunch. They invited forty California businessmen, who listened to candidates and asked questions. During the course of the meal, Dauer and Stewart took up an anonymous collection. The $17,000 they picked up was given to J. Hershey Kopp. He dispensed the money to local candidates through five committees with names such as "The Downtown Luncheon Committee." When the press inquired about the source of the money, Kopp said simply, he "couldn't remember" who was there.[17]

Speaking broadly, the laws and regulations concerning public disclosure not only vary but are also constantly changing. New procedures are constantly being suggested and instigated. A few states are considering limits on campaign contributions from political action committees (PACs). Most jurisdictions are considering legislation to limit campaign expenditures and provide public financing. In still others, there are proposals to allow voters to recall a legislator who violates public-disclosure laws. Because of these constant changes and differences in enforcement, candidates bound by a disclosure law must carefully review applicable local, state, or federal statutes.

To get a bird's-eye view of public disclosure, it's important to look at federal rather than state or local legislation. Those candidates who have a specific problem should get advice from the Internal Revenue Service or from federal or local election commissions. Most, if not all, issue advisory opinions such as the 163 advisory opinions issued in 1975, the first opinions given by the State of Kansas Ethics Commission.[18]

E. Chart on Who May Be Solicited

Who May Be Solicited	By Corporation	By Labor Organization	By Incorporated Membership Organization[1]	By Incorporated Trade Association
• Anytime	• Executive and administrative personnel and families • Stockholders and families	• Members and families	• Noncorporate members[2] • Executive and administrative personnel and families	• Noncorporate members • Executive and administrative personnel and families • With prior approval, corporate members' executive and administrative personnel, stockholders and the families of both
• Twice Yearly[3]	• Nonexecutive and nonadministrative personnel and families	• Nonmember employees and families • In corporations that employ members of the labor organization, corporate nonmember employees, stockholders and the families of both		• Nonexecutive and nonadministrative personnel and families

[1]These rules apply, as appropriate, to corporations without capital stock and incorporated cooperatives.
[2]If a membership organization has stockholders as well as members, it may also solicit its stockholders and their families.
[3]Individuals who may be soliticed at any time may also be included in a twice-yearly solitication.

Fig. 8-3. From Appendix E, Campaign Guide for Congressional Candidates and Committees (Washington, DC: Federal Election Commission, 1982), p. 56.

U.S. Federal Legislation

Federal legislation provides that the laws be triggered when the aspirant becomes a candidate, which encompasses "those formally qualified for the ballot, incumbents seeking reelection and individuals who have received contributions or made expenditures to test the political waters."

The federal act is also triggered when a club, association, or other group of persons becomes a political committee. This happens when they receive money to make political contributions or expenditures exceeding $1,000 in a calendar year, and they use it to support one or more federal candidates. The act can also be enforced once an entity establishes a separate, segregated fund, independent of a candidate, with money collected from individuals who are affiliated with a

5

E. Chart on Contribution Limits

Contributions from	To Candidate or His/Her Authorized Committee	To National Party Committee[1] Per Calendar Year[2]	To Any Other Committee Per Calendar Year	Total Contributions Per Calendar Year
Individual	$1,000 per election[3]	$20,000	$5,000	$25,000
Multicandidate committee[4]	$5,000 per election[3]	$15,000	$5,000	No limit
Party committee	$1,000 or $5,000[5] per election[5]	No limit	$5,000	No limit
Republican or Democratic Senatorial campaign committee,[6] or the National Party Committee, or a combination of both	$17,500 to Senate candidate per calendar year in which candidate seeks election	Not applicable	Not applicable	Not applicable
Any other committee or group[7]	$1,000 per election[3]	$20,000	$5,000	No limit

[1]For purposes of this limit, each of the following is considered a national party committee: a party's national committee, the Senate campaign committees and the National Congressional committees, provided they are not authorized by any candidate.

[2]Calendar year extends from January 1 through December 31. Individual contributions made or earmarked to influence a specific election of a clearly identified candidate are counted as if made during the year in which the election is held.

[3]Each of the following elections is considered a separate election: primary election, general election, run-off election, special election, and party caucus or convention which has authority to select the nominee.

[4]A multicandidate committee is any committee with more than 50 contributors which has been registered for at least 6 months and, with the exception of state party committees, has made contributions to 5 or more Federal candidates. A candidate committee should check with the FEC to determine whether a contributing committee has qualified as a multicandidate committee.

[5]Limit depends on whether or not party committee is a multicandidate committee.

[6]Republican and Democratic Senatorial campaign committees are subject to all other limits applicable to a multicandidate committee.

[7]Group includes an organization, partnership or group of persons.

Fig. 8-4. From Appendix B, Campaign Guide for Congressional Candidates and Committees (Washington, DC: Federal Election Commission, 1982), p. 46.

corporation or union. These membership organizations or political committees are considered PACs. A political party organization that makes contributions or expenditures in a federal campaign in excess of $1,000 per year, or that receives contributions exceeding $5,000 a year or spends more than $5,000 a year in activities related to federal elections, qualifies as a political committee.

Political committees must register and file periodic disclosure reports with the Clerk of the United States House and the Secretary of the United States Senate. When a candidate or an organization registers and reports, all records are made available to the public by the office of public records, where they can be copied. The limitations imposed by federal law are found in Appendix B of the Campaign Guide for Congressional Candidates and Committees (shown in Figure 8-4).

When candidates for a federal office file periodic reports with the Federal Election Commission, the sponsor need not be identified on small items, such as campaign pins or buttons. But if advertising is authorized by the candidates their campaign must state that it has been authorized and identify the person who has paid for it—for example, "Paid for and authorized by the candidate." If a piece of advertising is not authorized by the candidate or those responsible for the campaign, the communication must identify the person who paid for it and state that it has not been authorized. For example, "Not authorized by any candidate. Paid for by Freeze '89."

The federal act also requires routine listing of all expenditures of more than $1,000 made between 2 and 20 days before an election. Last-minute expenditures must be filed with the Secretary of the Senate or the Clerk of the House within 24 hours and disclosed a second time in the next scheduled report.[19] No post-primary reports are required under federal law, but a post-general-election report has to be filed within 30 days after the general election.[20]

Corporations and Labor

Federal law restricts contributions to federal candidates from national banks and unions as well as from firms doing business with the federal government, and 31 states prohibit contributions from corporations. What's more, these restrictions are strictly enforced. For example, the federal and most state election commissions have taken the position that, when a campaign committee sells photographs of the candidate—or books, watches, or medallions bearing his or her likeness—the candidate committees are raising funds. The amount remaining after deducting the cost of the item to the candidate is considered a contribution.[21] However, they look at it differently when a private corporation retails the campaign article and gives a portion of the profit to the candidate's campaign. The Federal Election Commission once held that an Indianapolis corporation could not underwrite the production and marketing expenses of a "Congressman Dick Lugar T-Shirt" and then transmit a $1.00 certificate to his campaign for every shirt sold.

The Federal Election Commission also ruled that the sale of poll results by the Philadelphia-based Wendell Young for Congress Committee to a local of the United Food and Commercial Workers Union would be a prohibited union contribution, because the candidate would get the poll results while recouping the $9,400 fee it had paid for the polling.

However, both labor and corporations are entitled to make internal communication without reporting. This permitted the Sun Company to circulate written materials prepared by the corporation to its executives and stockholders and their families and it probably helped reelect Congressman Allen E. Ertel of Pennsylvania.

A corporation or labor organization that customarily makes its meeting rooms available to civic and community groups may also offer them to political committees. However, the offer must not be partisan and must be on the same terms as those given to others.[22]

Both labor and the corporation can participate in nonpartisan communications, such as distribution of official registration and voting information produced by election officials. They can also participate in a nonpartisan effort to encourage voters to get to the polls or use their funds to support such things as nonpartisan candidate debates.[23]

Even when federal or state laws ban corporate contributions, that does not prohibit corporate contributions to corporate employees. The commission held an executive of the Brunswick Corporation violated the law when he used television to praise Oklahoma Congressman Jim Jones, in an ad paid for by Congressman Jones' reelection committee, because the endorsement was the work of a volunteer, even though the employee was identified as a company official.[24]

A candidate or a campaign committee may accept, without reporting, free legal or accounting advice to help comply with the reporting statutes. Thus, corporations and labor organizations may pay for legal and accounting service rendered by their employees to federal candidate committees if the costs incurred are reported, and the services are rendered solely to ensure compliance with the Act.[25]

Political Action Committees (PACs)

Corporations, federal chartered banks, and unions cannot contribute to a candidate for federal office, but officers, stockholders, and their immediate families can establish a separate, segregated account called a political action committee (PAC). PACs must be independent of the corporation, bank, or labor union, and must comply with reporting requirements.[26] Figure 8-5 shows the steady growth of PACs since 1975.

There are limitations on who can be solicited. For example, the union can only solicit its members while corporate PACs can only solicit stockholders, executives, and administrative personnel and their families. Other limitations on who can be solicited are set out in the *Campaign Guide for Corporations and Labor Organizations*, published by the Federal Election Commission.

When enforcing these provisions, the Federal Election Commission restricts solicitation of company employees and stockholders who do not work directly for companies that it controls. For example, American Health Capital, a New York corporation, was not permitted to solicit contributions to its PAC from the executive and administrative employees of a joint venture partnership, even though its wholly-owned subsidiary owned 40 percent. And American Health Capital could not solicit from the employees and stockholders of a Delaware

STATISTICS

1983 PAC GROWTH

Although growing at a slower rate than in past years, the number of PACs registered with the FEC continued to increase during 1983. By January 1, 1984, there were 3,525 PACs, an increase of 4.5 percent over the 3,371 PACs registered on January 1, 1983. (The term PAC or political action committee refers to any political committee not authorized by a federal candidate or established by a political party.)

Figures releasted by the FEC in mid-January show that yearly increases in the number of PACs from January 1, 1975, through January 1, 1984, have averaged 22.3 percent. The largest increase in PAC growth occurred between January 1, 1975, and January 1, 1977. During this two-year period, PAC numbers grew by 88.5 percent (from 608 PACs in January 1975 to 1,146 PACs in January 1977).

The graph below plots the growth of PACs between 1975 and 1984. Figures show that 608 PACs existed at the beginning of 1975. By the end of 1976, that number had risen to 1,146 and by January 1984 had reached 3,525. The graph does not reflect the financial activity of PACs.

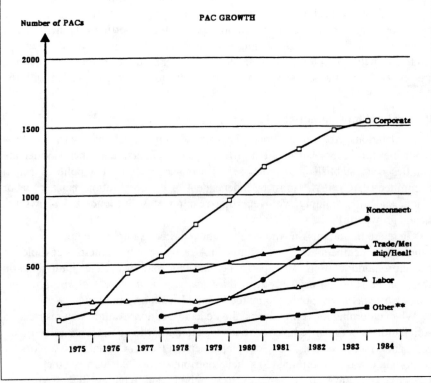

Fig. 8-5. Federal Election Commission Record, March 1984.

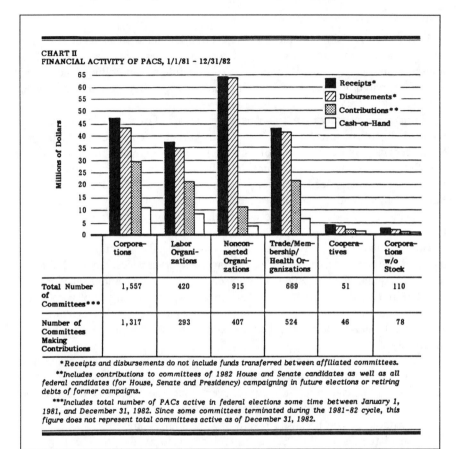

Fig. 8-6. Federal Election Commission Record, March 1984.

corporation in which a subsidiary controlled 100 percent because both were controlled by an independent board, who in theory made corporate decisions.[27] Figure 8-6 shows the financial activity of various PACs over a 2-year period.

Contributions from Foreign Nationals

Because U.S.-based foreign nationals are not permanent residents, they are prohibited from making political contributions. In one case, however, the Federal Election Commission held that the Budd Company in Pennsylvania retained its autonomous corporate identity, permitting employees to continue their PAC even after the company became a wholly-owned subsidiary of a West German corporation.

In-Kind Contributions

Under the provisions of all disclosure laws, candidates can receive gifts of signs, supplies, mailing lists, etc., as well as professional services such as transportation, preparation of advertising copy, printing, and polling. The same is true of campaign headquarter space, furniture, rent, etc. But the fair market value of these in-kind services must be reported.

Normal volunteer living or travel expenses on behalf of a candidate need not be reported in most jurisdictions because it is not deemed a contribution.[28] Supporters can volunteer the use of their homes or a community room in a club or church for occasional limited campaign activity without reporting. Under federal law, these supporters need not report a luncheon to hear a candidate, as long as the food, beverages, and invitations used remain under $2,000.[29]   Also a vendor can sell food and beverages at cost to a campaign without making a contribution as long as the lost profit does not exceed $1,000 per candidate.[30]

Beyond this, most jurisdictions insist that in-kind contributions, especially those of corporations, bank, or union facilities or services, be paid for and reported. Again, federal law makes exception and contributions need not be reported in the case of minor office equipment and occasional use of corporation or union equipment, such as phones or copying equipment. If "incidental use" is exceeded, the organization must be reimbursed within a reasonable time for using the facility.

Federal law requires reimbursement when a candidate uses a corporate plane for a campaign activity. This rule was applied to a candidate for United States Senator from Pennsylvania, Ed Howard, even though he was the sole stockholder of the corporation that owned the aircraft. However, the rate applicable was for an aircraft without a pilot, because Howard flew the aircraft himself.[31]

When distinguishing between contributions made by the PAC and by their sponsoring organization, the Federal Election Commission is very technical. For example, in 1984 the Sierra Club, a tax-exempt nonprofit corporation that advocates environmental issues, sponsored a PAC. The Federal Election Commission held that the PAC could not use 20 Sierra Club employees who used Sierra Club facilities to provide candidates with campaign services.

In the case of the American Medical Association Political Action Committee's PAC, since their plan involved reimbursement by the PAC after the services were performed, the commission held that it could make in-kind type contributions to U.S. House and Senate candidates if it did not use the AMA's office facilities and if the PAC paid the sponsoring organization in advance for the consulting services of AMA employees.[32]

Chapter 63

News, Publicity, and Public Disclosure

Disclosure and News Coverage

Campaign support also comes in the form of news stories, commentaries, and editorials. Left-wing Congressman Hugh Delacy told his audience in 1946, "We need your money to compete with Homer Jones [the opposition candidate], who has three pieces of literature [the three daily newspapers] going in every home in the district every day." He was alluding to his opponent's support by the Seattle dailies. Although this can be true in any political race, federal law avoids tampering with freedom of the press, which would go against the First Amendment to the Federal Constitution.

Where the newspaper, magazine, or television station is owned or controlled by the candidate or his or her political committee or party, Congress places such coverage inside the federal election law. When William L. Armstrong, principle stockholder and director of the publishing company that owned the Colorado Springs *Sun* newspaper and radio station KOSI AM/FM, filed for a seat in Congress, the Federal Election Commission ruled that his properties were required to report unless they gave equal coverage to all opposing candidates, and that if they favored Armstrong's candidacy, the commentaries and editorials favorable to the candidate or unfavorable to his opponent were to be considered in-kind contributions. The commission further ruled that such in-kind contributions would be illegal under federal law. Armstrong was prohibited form accepting corporate contributions because the media properties were incorporated.[1]

Federal law, as interpreted by the Federal Election Commission, places other restrictions on media aid to a candidate. The commission held that giving Congressman Harold S. Sawyer of Michigan free NBC videotapes of his television appearance on the news so he could use them in connection with his re-election campaign would constitute a prohibited corporate contribution because NBC did not have an established policy of providing free videotape segments to any individual who appeared in a newscast. The commission continued that Congressman Sawyer could use the videotape if he paid "the amount which NBC regularly charges to any person who requests a copy of the videotape segment."[2]

Political Parties

If a political party organization contributes or makes expenditures of over $1,000 per year, or if it spends over $5,000 per year on non-exempt federal election activities, it must file periodic financial reports.

When a state or national party gives directly to a federal candidate, this counts as a contribution and is subject to monetary limits. But a party can ask its own "independent expenditures" on behalf of the party's nominees, which are not considered contributions, even though these expenditures may be coordinated with their candidates for the U.S. House and Senate.[3]

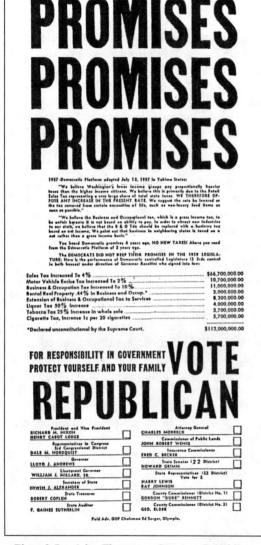

Fig. 8-7. Ad, Thurston County Republican Central Committee, Washington State, *The Daily Olympian*, November 1, 1958.

In addition, a local party organization may pay for basic campaign materials such as pins, bumper stickers, handbills, or brochures, to be distributed to volunteers on behalf of the party's nominees. These are not considered contributions or expenditures if: (a) they contain no general public political advertising, (b) the distribution is person-to-person or by direct mail, (c) payment is not made from funds contributed specifically for a particular candidate, (d) the payments are not made from funds donated by the national party specifically for this purpose, and (e) the national committee has not given these materials to the local organization for distribution.[4]

Federal regulations also permit a local party organization to prepare for distribution by campaign workers or direct mail a slate card or sample ballot which includes federal candidates, such as the one shown in Figure 8-7. The card or ballot must include three or more candidates and must identify the office sought and their party. It must not include any biographical information or political views.[5]

A voter registration or get-out-the-vote drive can be conducted by a local party organization on behalf of its party in the general election without its costs being considered contributions or expenditures. Expenses for phone banks operated by volunteer workers are also exempted, provided any reference to a candidate for the U.S. House or Senate is incidental. Otherwise, the cost is attributable to the federal candidate and is considered a contribution, which counts against the party's maximum.[6]

A local party organization engaged in both federal and non-federal election activities must be organized so that if union or corporate contributions are not permitted under state law, they are not used to finance federal election activities. For example, the Republican Executive Committee of Jefferson County, Kentucky, was a registered federal political committee that could not accept corporate advertising in its political magazine, *Today's Republican*, unless they could show that the publication contained no specific or general reference to federal candidates or that the payment for corporate advertisement was not used to defray publication costs, but spent exclusively for non-federal purposes.[7]

Chapter 64

Impact of the U.S. Supreme Court on Disclosure Legislation

The Courts and Public Disclosure

Under the 1971 Federal Election Act and its 1974 Amendments, there were limits on what individuals and groups could contribute to candidates for federal office, what committees could contribute, what individuals and groups could contribute to independent committees, and what individuals could contribute to their own campaigns. Then just as the presidential primary season was getting under way, on January 30, 1976, the U.S. Supreme Court decided to challenge the Federal Election Act.

The suit was brought by independent U.S. Senator James Buckley and former U.S. Senator Eugene McCarthy. The decision, *Buckley v. Valeo*, was a mixed bag. The Court upheld the law—the $1,000 limit on individual contributions and the $5,000 limit on a PAC contribution to a single candidate—and the court favored the public financing of presidential campaigns. At the same time it threw out: (a) limitations on independent expenditures in support of federal campaigns, (b) the method of appointing the Federal Election Commission (this was soon remedied by legislation), and (c) the limitations on the amount a candidate for federal office could spend on his or her campaign.[1]

Following the holding in *Buckley v. Valeo*, there was no financial limit on what candidates could spend or how much they could spend of their own money. The Federal Election Commission has since held that for campaign purposes both husband and wife have equal access to community property and permit a husband or wife who has separate property to make unlimited loans to the other for campaign purposes.

However, when William E. Shluter of New Jersey ran for Congress, he tried to stretch the "spouse rule" to include other family members, arguing that he should be able to accept money from family members to defray living expenses because his personal funds were depleted and he could not replenish them because of the time he had to spend campaigning. The Federal Election Commission refused to stretch the rule. They held that family contributions may not exceed $1,000 per donor per election.[2]

The decision in *Buckley v. Valeo* highlights the differences in how the U.S. Supreme Court and politicians view campaign legislation. Most political observers justify limits on campaign expenditure. They argue that in this world of television, radio, and high-speed presses that a political campaign is an emotional short-run experience similar to advertising where it is possible to dominate the consumer's mind. Further, they argue that in the short run it may be impossible to dislodge an impression once it is implanted.

When the case was heard, it was argued that where candidates use expensive multi-media political campaigns and the rich are permitted unlimited use of money to campaign, it gives an advantage to men like Democrat Jay Rockefeller, who followed his Republican uncles—Nelson of New York and Winthrop of Arkansas—into politics to become both Governor and U.S. Senator from West Virginia. In his 1984 re-election campaign, Jay spent roughly $12 million dollars to achieve election to the U.S. Senate, mostly from his own pocket. This $12 million, when divided by the votes he received, equals $31 per final election vote.[3]

The United States Supreme Court didn't seem impressed with the argument. They held that if an officeholder or potential officeholder receives campaign money, it could influence his or her subjective judgment and that Congress has a right to insist that the source be exposed and to impose limitations on how much any one person or source could contribute. And it was within Congress's rights to place limits on sources from whom money could be received. Where there was no potential officeholder to influence, the Court reasoned there were no subjective components and, thus, no corruption.[4]

In 1978, another case carried this rationale further. The sole question decided was whether the corporation had a First Amendment right to use its money to oppose an initiative submitted to voters. The court upheld the right of a corporation to spend general corporate funds to oppose a referendum that was in conflict with the corporation's interests.[5] This interpretation benefited organizations such as the National Association of Women (NOW) in their effort to get the proposed Equal Rights Amendment ratified, because they did not have to identify and disclose their contributors.

Later, the Federal Election Commission applied this reasoning to the National Right to Life Committee, holding that the committee did not have to report costs it incurred when distributing congressional voting records on abortion-related legislation even though the vote was characterized as either "pro-life" or "pro-abortion." This is because the voting records did not urge the reader to support a Senator or Representative based on his or her vote on any issue.[6]

Wild-card Political Organizations

The Supreme Court decision in *Buckley v. Valeo* had another effect. It struck down any limit on what an independent PAC could spend, provided it was not the alter ego of a candidate, corporation, or union, and that an independent PAC's advertising did not count as either a contribution to or expenditure by the candidate's campaign.[7]

Fig. 8-8. "The Conservative Political Action Committee," *The Dallas Morning News*, October 30, 1981.

This opened a Pandora's box that let loose a cyclone of political smear advertising. To illustrate, see the ad for the National Conservative Political Action Committee (Figure 8-8). In small print it carries a notation that it is not authorized by any candidate or committee of the candidate. Since this type of activity was not favored by those who drafted the federal legislation, the Federal Election Commission is very strict when regulating so-called independent expenditures. If these expenditures are made in cooperation or consultation with or at the suggestion of a candidate, they're considered in-kind.

To draw a distinction, if an independent individual or PAC purchases a newspaper advertisement supporting Jane Candidate without ever contacting the candidate or any of his campaign staff, it is considered an independent expenditure. However, if Jane Candidate or her campaign staff are asked and give any advice, this makes the expenditure an in-kind contribution, which when combined with all others, is limited to $1,000 per candidate per election.

For this reason, the Federal Election Commission held that the anti-nuclear organization, Freeze Voter '84, did not act independently when it placed advertising in support of candidates in the general election. Their contributions were in-kind because the organization had already donated paid staff in its primary campaign. This had compromised its independence which, together with any previous contribution, was limited to $1,000 for each election, instead of being unlimited independent expenditures.[8]

The federal law provides further that when a contribution is made to a political committee that makes independent expenditures exclusively in support of, or in opposition to, a single federal candidate, it is subject to the statutory limit. For example, if a donor contributes $1,000 to an independent committee established exclusively on behalf of John Candidate, that donor may not give John Candidate more because then the donor would exceed the $1,000 limit.[9]

Independent PACs must file a report at the end of any reporting period with the Federal Election Commission, in which they itemize each expenditure exceeding $200. In addition, the total of all independent expenditures of $200 or less must be reported.[10] The report must include the name, mailing address, occupation, and name of employer of each person who contributes more than $200, and the committee must certify that the expenditure meets the federal standard of independence.

Enforcement

Violations of the Federal Election Act range from making contributions in somebody else's name to filing records that fail to identify certain contributions. Complaints alleging a violation of the act may be initiated by an individual or group, who must file a formal, notarized complaint, or complaints may be based on information obtained during the course of Federal Election Commission supervisory responsibilities. Fortunately, the commissions and legislative bodies administrating these laws usually favor informal efforts to correct or prevent

566   THE BLOOD, SWEAT, AND TEARS OF POLITICAL VICTORY

violations. All information regarding an enforcement case is strictly confidential until the case is closed.

Where the law is subject to more than one interpretation, most laws permit a candidate to seek an advisory opinion. No person will be subject to any sanctions if he or she acts in accordance with their opinion, and the opinion may also be relied on by anyone else. Furthermore, there are situations in which a candidate may not be required or even responsible for reporting. This is because often money can be used to influence in ways that do not fit orthodox molds. For example, in 1952, prior to this legislation, Joe Kennedy, the father and patriarch of the Kennedy clan, which included President John and United States Senators Bobby and Ted, lent the publisher of the financially pressed *Boston Post* $500,000. Shortly afterwards, the *Post* switched from supporting United States Senator John Cabot Lodge to supporting John Kennedy, who was a candidate for Lodge's seat.[11]

In spite of the fact that enforcement is lenient where the violator is ignorant or the law is subject to more than one interpretation, candidates and/or contributors do break the law. Penalties include public reprimand and payment of a civil penalty. In flagrant cases, the Federal Election Commission may file civil suit against the respondent in federal district court. If the matter involves knowing and willful violation, the commission can refer the case to the United States Justice Department.

This was the case in 1974, when Watergate Special Prosecutor Leon Jaworski prosecuted George M. Steinbrenner, III, Chairman of American Ship Building and a general partner in the New York Yankees. Steinbrenner's corporations allegedly contributed money to the campaign of former President Nixon and members of Congress, but Steinbrenner denied intending to violate the law. Nevertheless, he pleaded guilty to two felonies—conspiring to violate the campaign contributions law and aiding and abetting obstruction of an investigation—and was fined $15,000.[12]

Chapter 65

The Internal Revenue Service

> If Patrick Henry thought taxation without representation was
> bad, he should see it with representation.
> —Handy News[1]

Political Contributions and the Gift Tax

Most United States political organizations, including candidate committees, have a tax exempt income that consists in part of contributions, membership dues, and assessments. This was not always so. Originally, the Internal Revenue Service took the position that political contributions were subject to the gift tax.[2] The IRS position was confirmed by the United States Supreme Court. Then in 1975 Congress amended the Internal Revenue code to provide that a transfer of money or other property to a political organization and used by the organization to influence political opinion would not be subject to gift tax.

For example, today contributions in the form of ticket purchases to political functions are not taxable as long as the candidate's political campaign is not primarily motivated by a desire to confer entertainment on the contributor.[3] However, political organizations are taxed on interest, dividends from investments, income from commercial activities, and gains from sales of appreciated property. So a political organization that wants to protect its tax-exempt status must keep detailed substantiating records.[4]

Political Expenses as a Business Deduction

Candidate expenses, which include campaign travel, advertising, and assessments imposed by the political party, are not deductible as business expenses.[5] After a candidate is successful in winning or retaining office, there will probably be deductible expenses incurred in carrying out his or her duties.[6] However, a legislator's expenses in attending his party's political convention are not deductible as business expenses as they have no direct relation to legislative business.[7]

Contributions to Finance Tax Credit

A congressional candidate's expenditures for return trips home during the campaign, expenses incurred in raising political contributions, and polling and research expenses all qualify for tax credits.

Federal law does permit political contributors to take an income tax deduction of $50 ($100 for married couples). A tax credit for political contributions is

Fig. 8-9. Pledge card, Washington State Democrats, 1976.

allowed only if it is reported to the IRS. Even then the taxpayer must be prepared to account. [8] If asked, the taxpayer/donor is subject to other limitations and must produce a written receipt. A canceled check generally meets this requirement. Contributions of services or property do not qualify for tax deductions. A tax credit is allowable only if the contribution is made in money. [9]

Political contributions are eligible for tax credit only if they are used for expenditures incurred in the political campaign. For example, potential candidates may seek early contributions to finance opinion polls and surveys, but if the candidate does not file, the deduction or credit will not be allowed. [10] The same rule applies to situations in which candidates publicly announce their candidacy and solicit contributions, but for some reason are ineligible. The tax credit is not allowed by the Internal Revenue Service. If the contributor has taken a deduction, an amended return is required.

Tax Consequences

The Internal Revenue Code exempts nonprofit business leagues, chambers of commerce, boards of trade, and similar organizations from tax, but makes an exception with respect to unrelated business income. Neither the statute nor the regulations prohibit such groups from making political contributions.[11]

The same is true of labor unions. While their unrelated business income is subject to federal tax, most of their dues income is exempt. Again, the revenue code does not specifically prohibit political contributions by either corporations or tax-exempt labor associations, but the Federal Corrupt Practices Act does, and, in some jurisdictions, states prohibit such contributions.[12] As discussed in Part 2, to get around this, unions and corporations have established separate political funds (PACs) to dispense voluntary political contributions.[13]

In the past it was possible for political parties, clubs, and occasionally candidates to circumvent both the IRS code and the prohibitions against union and corporate contributions by simply publishing programs or books in which they sold advertising. The purchasers of the ad treated the expenditure as advertising, not a contribution. This permitted the special interests who bought advertising to avoid income tax liability by writing off the ad as a business expense.

When the Democrats published their convention book as a memorial to President Kennedy in 1964, the ads were $5,000 a page. This advertising was sold to corporations doing business with the federal government, and many of these were subject to federal regulations that prohibited them from contributing. Congress has since amended the law to make it illegal to write off this advertising as a business expense.

However, the IRS still permits a corporation to deduct its expenditures for advertising of a general commercial nature, if the advertising is designed to encourage the public to register, vote, and financially support the candidates of their choice. But the advertising must be in commercial media that are politically impartial and must qualify as "good will" advertising.[14] For instance, in 1976, television ads were jointly sponsored by the National Advertising Council and The National Association of Secretaries of State, showing a non-voter whose candidate had lost because he did not vote. This ad was aimed at some 70,000 eligible Americans who did not vote.

The IRS also permits a business taxpayer to deduct expenditures made to encourage its employees to register and vote. The employer can deduct the costs incurred in sponsoring a political debate, where all candidates for that office are given an equal opportunity to present their views; and employers can deduct payroll expenditures made to employees to cover the time they took off to vote. These deductions are justified by claiming that sponsorship improves employee morale.

Fig. 8-10. Democratic convention book, *Toward an Age of Greatness* (Washington, DC: Democratic National Committee, 1964), cover and p. 10.

Restrictions and Penalties Imposed on Other Corporate Political Activities

Specific increases in corporate salaries or bonuses paid with the understanding that the employee will contribute the funds to a political candidate are not tax deductible. Similarly, a corporation may not deduct contributions made by paying counsel fees for professional services not rendered, or by paying for merchandise not received. Indeed, such expenditures give rise to civil and criminal penalties.[15] However, that does not mean that under unusual circumstances there are not exceptions. For example, the IRS permitted an unincorporated consultant to write off as a tax loss costs and expenses incurred, but only after the vendor had tried standard techniques, including litigation, to recover what was owed.

Fig. 8-11. Warren G. Magnuson campaign button.

Beyond these typical expenditures, there are risky devices some candidates use to avoid or lessen income tax liability, but they should not be used without legal and accounting advice. Without attempting to justify these fundraising tax writeoffs, candidates should be aware that there are donations and sales of a wide range of items such as animals, race horses, and even antique cars. The manipulation starts when these items are donated to a campaign, continues when they are resold at a profit by the campaign organization, and ends when the proceeds are used to finance the campaign effort.[16]

To illustrate, a young man from a wealthy family was running for mayor. His campaign was blessed by the donation of a house and lot by his uncle, who had held it as a rental unit for many years. The uncle used a depreciated value for the house and paid no income tax on the transfer of the property, because it did not result in an income gain.[17] The campaign committee promptly sold the house and lot to the candidate's stepfather, realizing a handsome profit. The campaign committee paid income tax on the profit, because the property was not a contribution.

Under these circumstances, the political organization may elect to compute its tax at a 30 percent tax rate if it qualifies as capital gains income. As we can see from Table 8-1,[18] it can calculate the tax at the standard rate. Whatever income tax they paid was far less than the rich uncle would have had to pay if he had taken the money out of his current income.

Range	Rate
0-$25,000	15%
$25,000-50,000	$3,750 + 18%
50,000-75,000	8,250 + 30%
75,000-100,000	15,750 + 40%
100,000 +	25,750 + 46%

Table 8-1

Now let's look at the tax position of the wealthy stepfather, who paid an inflated price for the house and lot when he purchased it. He didn't pay any income tax on the transaction because he had held the house for more than two years, and he sustained a tax loss when he sold it at its appraised value.

Internal Revenue Enforcement

If a political candidate diverts campaign contributions to his or her own personal use, the amounts diverted constitute taxable income. Failure to report diverted contributions and pay tax on them may subject the candidate to the penalty for civil tax fraud or to criminal prosecution for income tax evasion. The IRS knows that raising campaign money and financing a campaign is a volatile, short-run, emotional experience. It has established a political campaign contribution compliance section to ferret out the activities relating to political slush funds.[19]

When the Internal Revenue Service finds the contributor who has cheated on taxes, he or she can expect the same fate suffered by a man who was a dominant figure on the California political scene from 1932 to 1949. This California lobbyist used money, conviviality, and favors to virtually control legislators and whole legislative committees. He worked from the fourth floor suite in the Senate Hotel across from the State Capitol, relaying his orders through legislative assistants. After the press dubbed Artie Samish "King of the Legislature" because he seemed untouchable, he ran into trouble with the IRS and was tried and convicted by the federal government for income tax evasion.[20]

"Well, thank goodness we're only *morally* bankrupt."

Fig. 8-12. C'Barsotti's People, *USA Today*, March 1, 1985. Copyright 1985, USA Today. Reprinted with permission.

Loans and Contributions

Years ago, taxes on campaign contributions were treated differently than loans. If the candidate or campaign committee could not pay, the donor could write the loan portion off as a bad debt. In some instances contributors attempted to get this write-off even when there was no prior agreement that the money given was a loan. But getting this write-off often depended upon the candidate. In 1973, for example, one-time Georgia Governor Lester Maddox was unable to pay the banks. They pressed him for payment after he was defeated in his comeback effort. Some co-signers, such as Georgia State Senator, Gene Holly, paid off, saying, "It was sort of like a horse race, but in a horse race you get to win, place, or show. . . . I only bet to win, and I lost." Others wanted to write the loans off as bad debts, but they were stymied because they had to prove Maddox was insolvent, and he refused to declare bankruptcy.[21]

When it became fashionable for big contributors to give money as loans rather than contributions, Congress and most states plugged what had become a loophole. To most, disclosure laws have provisions that govern loans, promissory notes, or security instruments used by or for the benefit of the candidate. These require a filing with the appropriate disclosure commission, which must show "the names and addresses of the lender and each person liable directly, indirectly, or contingently, and the date and amount of each loan, promissory note, or security instrument." The loan is considered to be a contribution until it is paid back.[22]

Surpluses, Debts, and Debt Settlement

Once an aspirant declares his candidacy and accepts contributions, most laws keep the campaign funds alive indefinitely. If contributions exceed the amount needed to defray campaign expenditures, they may be used for a future election or diverted to an ally's campaign.[23]

The IRS and the Federal Election Commission also permit candidates with surplus campaign funds and who already hold or are elected to other offices to transfer those funds to a new office account. The funds are then used to defray expenses which in the officeholder's judgment are expected when carrying out his or her duties, but for which no provision was made for reimbursement by the political entity. This could include trips to a party convention, flowers in the event of a death of an associate, or the expenses of hosting a dinner party in which political rather than strictly governmental matters are discussed. They can also be used to defray the officeholder's contributions to the state or local party, to another candidate or political committee, or to repay loans made to the candidate.

If surplus campaign funds are transferred to the officeholder's account, they can be included as gross income for the year the funds are transferred, but the amounts disbursed from the office account as ordinary and necessary expenses can be offset by deducting the expenses under the Federal tax code. And, of course, they can be used to cover the expense of future elections.

Gifts made to support a candidate in a non-election year are counted as gifts in the year of the election. For example, in 1978, campaign committee reports for U.S. Senator John Melcher of Montana indicated that the committee had sufficient funds on hand to satisfy all outstanding debts from the 1976 campaign and that Melcher was still receiving and expending funds. Melcher asked the Federal

Election Commission for advice and they told the senator that the contributions received would count against the 1982 primary election contribution limits.

Surplus campaign funds can also be given to charity. The Federal Election Commission ruled that Senator James B. Pearson of Kansas could transfer $100,000 in excess campaign funds for the purpose of establishing a fellowship program at the University of Kansas.[24]

Where an election debt exists, most election commissions have taken the position that the candidate's status continues until all debts and obligations arising in connection with that election are paid. When raising money to liquidate these debts, most states follow the Federal Election Commission. It requires that all solicitations for contributions being used to extinguish past debts include a clear notice of that purpose, and persons who contribute in excess of $100 to this cause must expressly restrict their use to past debts in writing.

Under unusual circumstances it is possible to settle with campaign creditors for less than the amount owed. But under federal law the debtor (committee) must file a debt settlement statement, which must detail: (a) the steps taken to pay the debt, as well as the efforts made by the creditor to obtain payment, and (b) the terms of and an indication that the creditor is in agreement with the settlement. This is subject to Federal Election Commission review. If it approves the debt settlement, the committee may stop reporting the debt once the final payment is made to the creditors.[25]

Under most state laws, when a public official is defeated or retires, his friends and supporters can organize a fundraiser for the individual without being required to register and report as a political committee. This was the case with Republican minority leader John Rhodes of Arizona when, upon his retirement, a commemorative dinner was held. The donors were informed that this was a private fundraiser to honor a former public servant for his years of service and the proceeds netted after expenses were to go to him personally.[26] The dinner was a true testimonial because it was nonpartisan, did not advocate the election or defeat of any candidate, and was not held for the purpose of influencing Mr. Rhodes' nomination or election.[27]

Although local jurisdictions differ, most follow the Federal Election Law and ban diversion of donated funds to personal use. The Federal Election Commission, for example, applies this rule to political donations that are co-mingled with the candidate's personal funds, rendering identification impractical. In fact, funds are considered to have been diverted unless it can be shown that contributors' funds were used for campaign purposes, repaid to contributors, or otherwise disposed of as permitted by law.

Part 9

Conclusion

Chapter 66

To Run or Not to Run? Making the Decision

> The Christopher Columbus expedition, in which he "discovered"
> America, has all the elements of a modern political campaign: When he
> started he didn't know where he was going. When he got there, he didn't
> know where he was. When he got back, he didn't know where he had
> been. And he did the whole thing on borrowed money.[1]
>
> Don't be afraid to raise dumb questions; they're easier to handle than
> dumb mistakes.[2]

Before making the commitment to run for office, every potential candidate needs to consider a number of factors carefully. This chapter provides a review of these factors and the questions a candidate and his or her campaign advisors might ask themselves.

The Product: Understanding What's Being "Sold"

Every potential candidate needs to understand exactly what a successful political campaign entails. A campaign is not an attempt to push issues (although it may do so), or to inflate the candidate's ego (although it usually does that as well), or to attack an opponent's record, or to raise money. No, much as Americans glorify the democratic process and take pride in its workings, the naked truth is that a campaign is nothing more than a sales effort to create and intensively merchandise an image of a candidate whose character and personal convictions are usually virtually unknown by the vast majority of the electorate.

Occasionally the candidate gets elected simply because the voters admire him or her as an individual, or because the candidate has been chosen by a particular political party, or because he or she is the champion of a particular issue. But for most political aspirants, this is not the real world. The candidate's image is all important and this image is bound to the candidate's qualifications. So it is important that a candidate learn and/or review the duties and responsibilities that he or she would have if elected to the office. This information can be gained by attending classes at an educational institution, through on-the-job training, or as a result of intensive personal study, including library research and contact with current officeholders.

Having accepted the somewhat harsh reality of what campaigning is, the potential candidate must ask, "What exactly is the image I am attempting to sell the voter?" Along with this question a candidate should also ask: "Do I *already* have an image among the public and/or the media?" If so, how does this image

Fig. 9-1. Editorial cartoon, "Weevil for President," *Seattle Post-Intelligencer*, February 3, 1992, p. A9. Reprinted courtesy of the *Seattle Post-Intelligencer*.

correspond to: (1) the likely issues of the election (relative to the office in contention), (2) the makeup of the constituency, (3) the opponent's image, and (4) the prevalent stance of the media?

If the candidate lacks a clearly defined image, a thorough assessment of the issues, the constituency, the opponent(s), and the media will provide a good idea of the kind of image that must be created or at least what aspects of an image should be emphasized. This assessment and the subsequent creation of an appropriate political image can be complex.

Basically, the candidate's image consists of a mix of name familiarity, character, personality, charm, age, party, and issues. The vast majority of candidates, though, find it both sufficient *and necessary* to emphasize only one or two of these aspects. This is because it is important not to project an overly complex image; the more facets of an image a candidate tries to sell, the less emphasis can be devoted to each facet-and this dilutes the candidate's political image.

George Washington sold his image as a hero of the Revolutionary War. Similiarly, General Dwight Eisenhower was elected because the media created a "hero of Normandy" image for him. Political images can be created and sold like other commercial products and the best images are timely, powerful, and relatively simple.

The potential candidate must carefully evaluate the effort and cost required to create a winning image or to successfully market an existing image. He or she may want to change some elements of an existing image, but this can be both difficult and expensive, and the candidate's opposition will often do everything to make it even more so.

For example, if the candidate has a drinking problem, has he or she reformed? If so, are they an active member of Alcoholics Anonymous? When the one-time wizard of the local Ku Klux Klan, David Duke, ran for governor of Louisiana, he freely admitted his past affiliation with the Klan, but argued that he had since become a born-again Christian and that his past affiliations were no longer an influence in his life.

Perhaps an issue can be created that will enhance the candidate's image while diminishing the opponent's. Or maybe a critical segment of the electorate can be identified that will enable the candidate to identify which aspects of his or her image to emphasize. Or perhaps the media can be used to inadvertently enhance the candidate's image. *But Beware!* It's important to remember that the media's sword has two edges. Perhaps aspects of the opponent's image can be identified that are both crucial to his/her prospects for winning and vulnerable to attack.

Again, it is necessary to explore these possibilities in order to get a feel for the scope and intensity of the effort that will be needed to be competitive. The potential candidate must then assess what resources can be brought to bear-budget, volunteer labor, personal contacts, etc.-and realistically evaluate the chances of winning before making a commitment to run.

Major campaigns hire professional image builders because of their experience and ability to draw from public opinion sampling. Those running for high office spend huge sums on such consultants. For example, in the 1988 presidential primary, Michael Dukakis spent $5,668,747, while George Bush spent $5,171,695 for media advice and TV production alone. If all of the leading candidates are included-Michael Dukakis, Pat Robertson, George Bush, Robert Dole, Albert Gore, Jr., and Richard Gephardt-the total spent in that presidential primary was $26,295,590.[3]

Once a candidate's personal image is created it can be difficult to maintain. This is illustrated by an incident from a campaign in which the candidate miscalculated the power of his own image. At the time of this incident, "Teddy" Roosevelt had already served two terms as president of the United States, but still had a huge following. After four years of retirement, Roosevelt sought a third term, not as the nominee of the Republican party, but as a nominee of the maverick Progressive party known as the "Bull Moose ticket."

On October 14, 1912, while Roosevelt was speaking in Milwaukee, a would-be assassin fired a shot at his heart. The bullet penetrated Teddy's coat, vest, and glasses case, but was deflected by a 100-page speech written on heavy paper folded over in his pocket. The bullet lodged painfully against his fifth rib. After a brief medical examination, Roosevelt's doctor told him that he had suffered a serious, but not immediately life-threatening wound. Roosevelt exclaimed, "This is my big chance; I am going to make that speech if I die doing it."

Roosevelt went back and faced the crowd that was still in place waiting to see whether he was dead or alive. He pulled the speech from his coat pocket with bullet holes in plain view to all, unbuttoned his vest to reveal his blood-stained shirt, and delivered his speech to an ecstatic crowd and very excited press.[4]

Teddy Roosevelt thought this display of courage under fire would turn his faltering campaign around, but it didn't. The Republican vote split. Though Roosevelt received 27.4 percent of the popular vote in the three-way election, exceeding that for incumbent President Taft, Taft kept the support of the regular Republican machinery.[5]

No single display of courage could propel Roosevelt to victory for several reasons. First, the attempted assassination was the act of an insane man; Roosevelt couldn't blame any opposing group or candidate. True, Roosevelt showed great courage under fire, but he had already earned this image as a colonel in the U.S. Cavalry, leading the Rough Riders during the Spanish American War. As President, Roosevelt had sent the U.S. fleet around the world, enunciating the famous doctrine, "Walk softly but carry a big stick." Even after Roosevelt left the presidency, he was known for the courage he displayed on big-game hunts in Africa. And in this campaign, he had shown courage when he broke with the Republican party and ran as an independent.

Secondly, no single display of courage was enough to overcome the way old-line Republican view of Roosevelt as a man who had deserted their conservative philosophy and was proposing "radical socialist" reforms with which they violently disagreed. Roosevelt was also competing with a third candidate, Woodrow Wilson, who preached a liberal political philosophy similar to Roosevelt's, but with the unified support of the Democratic party.

Finally, there was no radio or television, so Roosevelt's act of courage had to be presented to the voter through the eyes of a conservative press.

The Battleground: Assessing the Office and Crucial Issues

Most successful political campaigns are built around both an image and an issue. The issue can be either negative or positive and probably won't be what the candidate himself or herself wants to promote. Rather, the issue often depends on who the candidate is attempting to appeal to and this often has to do with the makeup of the candidate's constituency.

Issues differ from office to office and from campaign to campaign. For example, saving taxpayers' money may dominate. In this case, the voter's choice might depend on the candidate's desire to see that everyone pays their own way. Or the voter may insist on more efficient government services. Under other circumstances, the voter may favor the candidate that supports additional taxes if extra taxes ensure governmental solvency or the delivery of additional services.

A candidate for Congress might advocate legislation requiring able-bodied people on welfare to work for their government checks, or advocate offering college loans in return for military or nonmilitary service, or enforcing tougher laws restricting immigration into the United States. In a state legislative race, the issue could be mandatory death penalty for people convicted of murder, or environmental legislation may be the cutting issue. In a quest for either state or federal office, there are always universal issues such as separation of church and state, for example, a constitutional amendment to permit prayer in schools.[6]

Even if an otherwise qualified candidate is not ready to take a position, he or she must still understand the issues in his or her particular race and do sufficient research to permit intelligent discussion. Knowledge gained from issues research can be enhanced by key information about the constituency. For example, does it have a great number of older retired people, or young university students and faculty, or does it consist primarily of young parents? Census information can help decide the economic status of this constituency and whether they are members of a particular racial or ethnic minority.

With this information, other questions may arise: Is this an affluent suburban or high-rise area or is there a major university? If so, does the majority in this area traditionally support only candidates of a certain academic or economic status? Also, if additional issues arise as the campaign progresses, candidates must make a serious effort to learn what they are and determine a position so they are ready when they speak, debate, or are interviewed.

A Closer Look at the Constituency

A constant, recurring theme in any political race is that success, with or without party support, often depends upon the constituency. Evidence of this support is found in statistical information gathered by state, federal, or local census-information keepers, which can help the candidate decide if race, gender, income, ageism, or youth is a factor in the candidate's constituency.

I suggest that any woman running for office-or even thinking about it-consult books written in the past few years directed at the special problems women encounter when entering the political arena. It's unfortunate that, although great progress has been made, the American voter has still not reached the point where they treat women candidates with an even hand.

Fig. 9-2. Covers of books aimed at women campaigning for political office: Jewel Lansing, *Campaigning for Office: A Woman Runs* and *101 Campaign Tips for Women Candidates and Their Staffs* (Saratoga, CA: R&E Publ., 1991); The Women's Political Action Group. *The Women's 1992 Voting Guide*. Used by permission.

If the campaign is state-wide, the candidate should get a feel for what parts of the constituency can be appealed to, as well as for what difficulties may be experienced when attempting to convince voters of diverse backgrounds to vote for him or her.

To a lesser extent in district, city, or county races the candidate should schedule personal appearances so he or she can reach all geographic pockets of the population. A computer can be used to digest statistical information and information gathered from local census and election bureaus. Such information not only helps the candidate emphasize the right issues, but can also be a key to determining the best places for the candidate's personal appearances.

The candidate or the campaign advisors can do more than check official records. They can talk to other political candidates or party officials who have campaigned in that or similar constituencies. These more experienced people may be aware of other considerations. If the candidate is a minority, his or her inner circle will want to know if the constituency has ever elected a minority candidate and, if so, how often. If the candidate is a homosexual, he or she should consider the impact if this factor is publicized. While today the candidate's sexual preference may still be a handicap with some voters, that's not always the case. In one liberal New York City council race in a district where up to 25 percent of the voters were gay, it was revealed that the two finalists were Tom Duane, an admitted gay, and Liz Abzug, a lesbian.[7]

Constraints: Assessing Partisan Political Organizations and Other Special Interests

Candidates must recognize that special interest organizations within their constituency will dominate most partisan and nonpartisan contests. If the political office is one that is traditionally won by a partisan Democrat or Republican, the question arises, is there an effective organized political party in that constituency? If so, does the aspirant share the majority philosophy? Assuming the answer to both questions is yes, the candidate should find out who the organizational dynamos are, and then try to win their support.

In addition, in most major campaigns, a good plan involves examining the likely actions of more than the political party component. The candidate should not decide too soon to condemn specific or even general special interests. The aspirant must consider the voters who owe their allegiance to or are influenced by special interests, including labor unions, political business groups, teachers, associations of retired people, or veterans organizations. These are only a few of a host of organizations that engage passively or actively in the political process.

The Competition: Assessing The Opponent

Candidates should realize that incumbents have a built-in advantage because normally the electorate is satisfied with their brand. Candidates should also recognize that it is very difficult to run against nominees of the dominant political party or opponents with vastly superior campaign funds.

However, incumbents do lose-usually because they have permitted their campaign apparatus to fall into disrepair. Sometimes they fail to fully realize that volunteers are temporary, and they are unable to recruit them again when they seek another term of office. For example, General Dwight Eisenhower attracted thousands of volunteers with no political experience when he first filed. However, with time and exposure, the General's war hero image blended into the political landscape, and the volunteers pursued new and different goals. Though Eisenhower didn't lose the race for a second term, his popular vote percentage dropped significantly. He wondered aloud to his aide, Sherman Adams, "What happened to all those people with stars in their eyes who sailed balloons and rang doorbells for us in 1952?"[8]

Once the candidate has decided on the image he or she wants to project and has conducted some research regarding the constituency and pertinent issues, a good look should be taken at the opponent's image. So before the candidate and his or her inner circle make any important campaign decisions, they should conduct opponent research and ask a few questions.

Does the opponent have a more attractive image than the candidate? What is the opponent's public record? Is the opponent personally unpopular or associated with an unpopular political issue that divides the constituency? If the opponent is an incumbent, will the aspirant's candidacy fail because the voters in this constituency have a tendency to stick with the brand they are using? Is the incumbent's health such that he or she is unable to campaign?

Once these questions have been answered the candidate or campaign staff advisors should explore what tactics the opposition is likely to use against them. If these tactics can be identified, they should then be carefully considered, and the candidate's plan should include necessary countermeasures. At times the candidate may want to launch an attack on the opposition, but he or she should be aware that the public tends to dislike candidates who throw mud and that the attacker runs a serious risk of counterattack.

The lethal effect of the counterattack was demonstrated in Chicago in the March 1992 primaries. In that race, redistricting threw two incumbent congressmen against each other. Marty Rosso, in a flyer attacking his former colleague, Congressman William Lipinski, said, "Marty Rosso writes the laws and Bill Lipinski breaks them." The text went on to accuse Lipinski of hustling public employees and enriching himself at public expense. Lipinski replied with a radio commercial that recited a long list of corporate campaign contributions made to Congressman Russo, and then told the voters bluntly, "He's for sale. Are you?" Rosso lost.[9]

When looking for the opponent's weak points, the strategist should look at any other election campaigns in which the opponent participated and research both favorable and unfavorable publicity the opponent received that is likely to impact the election. If research shows that the opponent has enemies, they should be contacted and even cultivated if there is a possibility of the candidate gaining their support. Research will also reveal the opponent's political allies, campaign financing, and any potential political skeletons.

But is a political attack worth diverting the campaign staff from the positive aspects of the campaign? While there are exceptions, in general attackers should avoid anything they think may boomerang. This usually means sticking to simple propositions and repeating information that has already been published in the media.

A Loose Cannon: Assessing the Media

The candidate's public image is created in a number of different ways, but generally depends upon how the media perceives his or her candidacy. If the aspirant has a good public image, it should be promoted in every way possible.

But what if the media has saddled an aspirant with an unflattering public image? In rare cases a candidate can turn this situation around, but only after some painful and/or embarrassing self-analysis. This self examination should include everything about the candidate's present and past public record, along with sex, race, religion, place of residence, union orientation, etc.

It may be that the candidate's religious, economic, or social beliefs conflict with those of the majority. Or it may be that the candidate has a preexisting stain on his or her political record. For example, there may have been a minor scandal or it could be that he or she was convicted of a minor crime, which won't appeal to the voters.

The aspirant should realistically examine the media's interest in the campaign. Will they cover it? If so, how are they likely to do it? How can they be interested, influenced, or in some cases persuaded? And how can their influence be overcome if for one reason or another they desire the candidate's defeat?

If the campaign planners find the media lukewarm or hostile, in most cases it is important to restrain the candidate and even his or her supporters from trying to lash out. As Mark Twain, who was a newspaperman, once said, "I dislike [such] arguments. . . . They are always vulgar and often convincing."[10]

Aside from debating with the media or using influence to neutralize the media's negative effects, the candidate can attempt to distract the voter from any media charges. Positive aspects of the campaign can be emphasized to balance unfavorable criticism. Unfortunately, there is no one "positive aspect" that will distract the voter in every case, except maybe a candidate's personal interest in the constituents and their problems.

Most successful candidates have merchandised this personal interest in their constituency, and on rare occasions this interest can even be used to overcome media hostility. Nowhere is this better demonstrated than in the political career of William Langer, a three-term governor of North Dakota, who, while in office, was indicted and convicted of a technical charge relating to the collection of funds, a federal felony.

Langer's public image was greatly damaged when the federal judge who presided over his initial conviction congratulated the jury on their decision. Langer's conviction was applauded by the press and welcomed by many of his former associates, who were delighted to be rid of him. When Langer was sentenced, eighteen months after he was recalled as Governor, his conviction was reversed by the appellate court. He was tried again, but there was a hung jury. A third trial ended in acquittal, but still Langer's image was not redeemed in the eyes of the media.

Even after unmerciful press attacks, though, Langer bounced back politically and was elected to the U.S. Senate where he had the distinction of being the only sitting member in its history to have been previously convicted in federal court of a felony.[11]

In spite of his success at the polls, "Wild Bill" Langer, as he became known, never won over the news media. While in the U.S. Senate, the media scoffed at Langer because he was the body's leading introducer of private bills to aid individuals. They ridiculed him when he asked the vicar of Old North Church in Boston to place a lantern in the belfry to give the United States a Paul Revere-style warning when Winston Churchill was coming to the United States. The media pronounced Langer politically dead after a poll of national press correspondents labeled him "the nation's worst U.S. Senator."

While on the stump in the 1952 primary, "Wild Bill" returned some of the media fire by always introducing reporter Alden MacLachlan of Bismark, representing Associated Press, as "the reporter from the *Fargo Forum . . .* who follows me around to write lies about me." Langer would then say to MacLachlan, "Stand up and let's see what your kind of man looks like."[12]

But what did "Wild Bill" represent to his constituency? He was a controversial populist-a leader of the maverick Republican organization called the Non-Partisan League. His constituents remained on his side because they expected the press to say rotten things. After all, Langer had attacked almost every special interest and fought with virtually every politician and every newspaper in his state.

But more important, Langer was a governor and United States senator who never lost the common touch. Even today, years after Langer's death, he is remembered in his native North Dakota, not for the label the press put on him, but for his smile, his handshake, and the compliments he gave women on their children and men on their crops. One of Langer's key lines was, "If you have a problem, write to me." And he is remembered by the thousands to whom he sent letters signed "Bill" that marked almost every North Dakota birth, death, marriage, graduation, and golden wedding anniversary.[13]

Building an Organization

Realistic candidates set goals knowing that in the real world many goals will not be identified until after the campaign is in full swing. Then they examine the contingencies, think through their options, and draw conclusions. As Henry Ford II stated when speaking of the auto industry: "Nobody can really guarantee the future. The best we can do is size up the chances, calculate the risks involved, estimate our ability to deal with them, and then make our plans with confidence."[14]

Concerning campaign funds, the candidate should discuss with his or her advisors what it is going to take financially to run for political office. How much money will the opponent raise and will the campaign be able to match or exceed the opposition's financing? Are there friends and others with like interests or views willing to contribute? How can the candidate bargain with special interests? Do these special interests insist on an incumbent or sure winners? Must the candidate be a shoo-in before getting their contributions? If all else fails, does the candidate have access to the funds necessary to run a traditional campaign? If not, does strategy exist to enable the candidate to overcome an opponent with superior financing?

An underfunded contender might consider doing what William Webb did. Weeks before the primary, this Denver city auditor and candidate for mayor ran out of campaign money. Webb's lack of funds left him with two options: He could quit, which he declined to do, or he could adopt an alternative low-budget plan, which he did. Taking advantage of his low budget, Webb condemned big-money politicians and worked the city streets. By spending one night each with forty Denver families, he garnered considerable publicity. This low-budget campaign led him to political victory over his better-financed opponent, and he became Denver's first black mayor.[15]

It is important that the candidate get an early start recruiting both paid personnel and the needed volunteers. As volunteers join the team, campaign insiders should be able to match them with a list of specific tasks-telephoning, raising money, putting up signs, ringing doorbells, etc.

Also, a number of federal, state, and local regulations govern the conduct of the campaign, most dealing with the collection and spending of campaign money. The campaign must appoint a competent, willing person to read and digest these regulations, and then inform those who are running the campaign. This is necessary because: (1) there are serious penalties if these regulations are not complied with and (2) because these regulations usually require a special fund and the designation of a person with whom the campaign funds are deposited who accounts to the government for the disbursements.

Campaign Advertising

Part 4 of this book is devoted to a detailed discussion of campaign advertising. But, in summary, there is a need for expert advice. Without it the candidate will get lost in media details and methods. In general, most of the money spent during the political campaign will be for advertising. Advertising decisions are complex and involve not only demographics but a series of choices such as: Does the candidate want yard signs? Will direct mail be used? Should there be newspaper, radio, or television ads? Then there are decisions to make concerning advertising-creativity, technique, text color, strategy, etc. The candidate and/or campaign advisors need to decide whether the campaign can afford professional help in designing, creating, and distributing their message.

For advertising purposes, research and statistics show where the voters live as well as the usual voter turnout, which varies from election to election. For example, there is a substantial difference between those who vote during presidential campaign years and the number and profiles of those who turn out when only local candidates are on the ballot. After carefully researching the residents, the turnout, and other statistical data, planners need to decide how often specific voters go to the polls. The candidate and his or her advisors should discuss tailoring a message and then using direct mail, telephone, or door-to-door solicitation to target those likely to vote in that election.

Placing Limitations on Planning

The realistic candidate must place planning limitations. Why? Because planners can become so fascinated with the details and controversies of planning that winning the election becomes secondary. There are literally hundreds of thousands of people who imagine themselves as political strategists. For them the goal is the act of giving advice, thus boosting their own egos. At best overplanning wastes time; at worst it can seriously snarl the campaign. As the campaign progresses the candidate must always be on guard to prevent overplanning.

After the candidate and his or her spouse-or a close circle of friends-have honestly and pragmatically discussed relevant questions, the campaign tasks should be categorized and priorities established. A calendar should be looked at and a timetable laid out for completion of campaign tasks. The plan should allow extra time and address what to do when some essential task is late or not performed.

After each portion of the analysis is completed, the candidate should organize the notes and type a written outline so the many facets can be critically examined.

Note that campaigns are often volatile. Political loyalties shift. Copies of campaign plans can be secretly circulated, so a written report may not be an appropriate place to detail the candidate's weaknesses.

Once a plan is adopted, the candidate, staff, and advisors must get out and carry the plan through. This is when the most important element of a campaign becomes energy and hard work. See the Campaign Preliminaries nutshell for a summary of the steps to building a plan.

Puncturing the Hard Work Myth

It is a myth that hard work and personal contact are the only things necessary to achieve political victory. Candidates nominated by their party often conduct vigorous and extensive campaigns but are still defeated by those who appear not to work at all-the so-called "front porch" candidates.

★ ★ ★ ★ ★ ★ ★ ★ ★ ★ ★ ★ ★

Campaign Preliminaries

	Target Date	Date Compl.
Study then determine requirements of the office:	_____	_____
Can candidate run an effective campaign?		
Will his/her health allow running?		
Are there handicaps?		
Will personal life or business interfere?		
Any problems in his/her past?		
Will the candidate's family be supportive?		
How recognizable is the candidate's name?		
How much support does he or she already have?		
List potential sources of financial support.	_____	_____
Estimate, then calculate campaign costs.	_____	_____
Identify issues and discuss candidate's positions.	_____	_____
Draft a general campaign strategy and run it past friends and supporters. (Be prepared to withdraw if candidate has no chance of making a decent showing.)	_____	_____
Compose a personal fact sheet: (a) qualifications (b) positions on issues.	_____	_____
Draft a preliminary schedule.	_____	_____
Form an organizing committee.	_____	_____

★ ★ ★ ★ ★   **In A Nutshell**   ★ ★ ★ ★ ★

For example, twice the voters of the United States were treated to a campaign featuring the golden orator, William Jennings Bryan. In both campaigns Bryan vigorously toured the country in his quest for the presidency. But in 1896 he was defeated by U.S. Senator William McKinley, who, long before television, was able to conduct a successful campaign from his front porch.

In 1916, one-time New York Governor Charles Evans Hughes, later appointed to the U.S. Supreme Court, sought the presidency. He made a long transcontinental trip but was beaten by President Woodrow Wilson, who conducted a front porch campaign from his home in New Jersey.

In 1920 Warren Harding was elected from his front porch, while the Democratic candidate, Ohio's Governor Cox, was defeated in spite of an extensive and unsuccessful transcontinental tour.[16]

Despite evidence to the contrary, many candidates still believe they can win by outworking the incumbent. Unfortunately, the prospects of victory are controlled by many elements in a political environment as well as the candidate's personal life. This leads to one last important consideration, whether the candidate's spouse and family are willing to make sacrifices for the sake of the campaign. Most spouses hate life on the campaign trail. If this is the case, the campaign may exact a price from the aspirant's family life.

On the other hand, the candidate may have a spouse who shares their enthusiasm. This was the case of a politician, John O. Brown, who amassed millions franchising Kentucky Fried Chicken restaurants. After he married former Miss America Phyliss George, she encouraged him to run for Governor of the State of Kentucky. After his election, she basked in his victory, commenting in a television interview that, "Most of John's celebrity status came when he married me. . . . I have to help him and teach him how to deal with it."[17]

Risks

Obviously, even skilled and industrious campaigners can and do lose. This is because the outcome of a campaign is not controlled by elements that can be counted upon to work the same way each time. Because of this, political pundits are often wrong when they say a defeated candidate's political career is over. For example, they were wrong in the case of the most illustrious of our presidents, Abraham Lincoln. Lincoln lost his job in 1832 and later that year ran for the Illinois legislature and was badly defeated. He ran for Speaker of the Illinois House of Representatives in 1839 and lost. Lincoln was overwhelmingly defeated in a bid for nomination for Congress in 1843, rejected for appointment to the United States Land Office in 1849, and defeated when he sought the nomination for Vice President in 1856. But eventually, Honest Abe's luck changed. He became president and saved the Union.

And Lincoln is not alone. If the political pundits had been right when Franklin Roosevelt, Harry Truman, Lyndon Johnson, Richard Nixon, George Bush, and Ronald Reagan lost, these men would not have become presidents. So even the best-run campaign cannot insure victory and the prognosticators cannot guarantee accuracy.

Being a Good Sport

A loser is still expected to be a good sport. A smart winner leaves past bitterness and vindictiveness behind. An incident illustrating the importance of this took place in 1950 when a respected professional political campaign manager, Stephen Shadegg, was actively working for Carl Hayden, who eventually served as United States Senator from Arizona for 40 years. In that campaign, Hayden was challenged by a vigorous, well-financed opponent put into the race by two special interest groups. When Hayden won despite this opponent, Shadegg said, "The world was ours. The voters had just said so."

Later that week, Shadegg met with the Senator to have a victory drink at a swank rendezvous located on top of the Hotel Westward Ho in Phoenix. When they discussed public reaction to their victory, Shadegg, in a happy frame of mind, casually asked the Senator what he did the day after the primary. Hayden replied that he paid his respects to the men who had sponsored his opponent. Reacting to Shadegg's astonishment, the Senator grinned and said, "Let me tell you something, Steve. Never give your enemies any more reason than they already have to go on hating you."[18]

For a practical overview of campaign detail, please refer to the following nutshell.

Conclusion

Why men and women choose to compete for office in such a confusing and unpredictable environment can't fully be explained, but one thing is certain-the majority who run for political office find it consuming, fascinating, and exhiliarating. Hundreds of thousands of candidates are willing to take the risks and suffer the heartaches.

Some thirty years ago a novelist named Edwin O'Conner wrote a book entitled *The Last Hurrah* in which a slightly corrupt, political charmer who loved the rough-and-tumble political life ran for Mayor of Boston just one more time to prove to himself that he was not finished. As the book concluded, he was on his deathbed. Among those gathered around was a clergyman who had been a long-time enemy, but who had decided it was time to forgive and to be generous to his old foe. When everyone thought the old politician was dead, the clergyman tried to deliver a sermon to the others at the bedside, saying, "Well, no matter what some may have thought in the past, it is different now. And I think I can say this, that knowing what he knows now, if he had it to do all over again, there is not the slightest doubt but that he would do it all very, very differently." Hearing these words, the dying politician stirred and raised himself slightly. Those gathered at this bedside saw his eyes open for the last time. In them was a challenging, mocking gleam, and they heard him say in a hoarse whisper, "The hell I would."[19]

A Practical Overview of the Campaign

Before Candidate Decides to File

Confer with family and friends, estimating support and experience, as well as requirements of campaigning and then serving in office.

Assess opposition; discuss their strengths and weaknesses.

After Candidate Decides

Form campaign committee.

Set up files, recordkeeping procedures.

Make preliminary drafts of (a) theme, (b) campaign plan, (c) budget. (Don't be concerned if you can't fill in the details.)

Strategy

Structure the temporary campaign committee.

Outline a broad preliminary campaign strategy (add details later).

Money

Estimate costs (add details later).

Solicit friends and associates for early money to hold announcement event(s).

Print pledge cards and candidate fact sheet for early fundraising.

Set up a campaign bank account.

Register the campaign committee with the public disclosure agency. Learn where reports will be sent.

Nuts and Bolts

Assemble materials (e.g., photos (some showing prospective candidate in action) and copies of pertinent records).

Where available, order (a) precinct maps & walking lists, and (b) mailing labels from the election department.

Where required, get sign permits.

File public disclosure reports.

File a statement of qualifications for the voter's pamphlet.

Get endorsements.

Campaign Calendar / Filing Deadlines

File nomination papers where required, signed by any needed sponsors.

Kickoff publicity event (preferably a Saturday or Sunday)

Collect endorsements to use in ads (schedule cutoff dates)

Collect "Dear Friends" return cards.

Start coffee hours.

Choose dates to start: (a) phone bank, (b) "foot soldiers" in precincts, including shopping centers.

Start fundraising events.

Send "Dear Friends" fundraising letters with contribution-return envelopes. Follow up with phone calls.

★ ★ ★ ★ ★ **In A Nutshell** ★ ★ ★ ★ ★

★ ★ ★ ★ ★ ★ ★ ★ ★ ★ ★ ★ ★ ★

A Practical Overview of the Campaign (cont.)

Campaign Calendar / Filing Deadlines (cont.)

Hold attention-getting and newsmaking events (e.g., auto caravan, door-to-door canvass & pamphlet blitz).

Advertising

Schedule TV and radio ads. Time must be purchased early, requiring early money, decisions on types, issues to be covered, etc.)

Send a major direct-mail campaign piece to all area voters.

Post and/or distribute yard signs & bumper strips. Start posting first batch of signs to stimulate campaign momentum. Check to see signs in place.

Create a phone bank for various campaign functions—e.g., to gather names of supporters, to get votes, as polling device to see how candidate is faring.

Evaluate effectiveness of advertising as well as issues and personalities impacting the campaign. Issue news releases (or if candidate packs

enough clout, hold news conferences).

Recheck radio and TV spots; change if necessary & add endorsements where appropriate.

Send mailing(s).

Post second wave of signs.

Schedule newspaper ads. Timing and content depend on advertising strategy and whether paper is daily or weekly. News and ads usually go together in weekly papers (cover issues).

Send in final newspaper ads (with names of endorsers where appropriate).

Election Day and Just Prior

Order supplies for victory party (refreshments, serving utensils, balloons, video and audio & video tapes, novelties).

Place final ads.

Run get-out-the-vote phone bank starting four hours before polls close.

Station supporters with placards along main commuter roads.

Hold the victory party!!!

★ ★ ★ ★ ★ **In A Nutshell** ★ ★ ★ ★ ★

$ $ $ $ WARNING $ $ $ $

Today, campaign costs and contributions have soared beyond the wildest predictions. Though dollar amounts quoted throughout this book are historically correct and valuable as general percentage guidelines, dollar amounts more than two to four years old should not be depended upon for structuring campaign budgets.

Chapter Notes

Chapter Notes

Part 1—Merchandising the Common Touch

Preface

1   Readers Ask, *Campaign Insight*, Wichita, Kansas, September, 1971.

Chapter 1—Introduction to Reality

1.   "Quotable Quotes," *Readers Digest*, February 1980, p. 80.
2.   Bill Adler, *The Washington Wits* (New York: The Macmillan Company, 1967), p. 71.
3.   Robert E. Began, *Persuasion in Advocacy* (Washington, DC: Association of Trial Lawyers, 1976).
4.   Richard Reeves, *A Ford, Not a Lincoln* (New York: Harcourt, Brace Jovanovich, 1974), p. 15.

Chapter 2—The Perils of the Top Brass

1.   Edward F. Murphy, 2,750 *One-Line Quotations For Speakers, Writers and Raconteurs* (New York: Crown Publishers, 1981), p. 20.
2.   Ibid.
3.   Peter ODonnell, Planning the Campaign, *Ways to Win* (Washington, DC: Republican National Committee, 1968), p. 17.
4.   Jacques Weher, Daily Spells Out Reagans Fight Plan, *Advertising Age* [Chicago, IL], July 21, 1981, pp. 1 & 89.
5.   Rubin, Making The Campaign Succeed, p. 156.
6.   Robert Bonitati, Managing to Manage Volunteers, *Ways to Win* (Washington, DC: Republican National Committee, 1968), p. 132.
7.   Stephen Shadegg, *The New How to Win an Election* (New York: Taplinger, 1972), p. 154.
8.   Robert L. Goodman, "Getting Across With Advertising," *Ways to Win* (Washington, DC: Republican National Committee, 1968), p. 60.
9.   Richard L. Williams, The Advance Men, *Life*, October, 1952, p. 135.
10.   Shadegg, *How to Win an Election*, p. 154.
11.   Herbert M. Baus and William B. Ross, *Politics Battle Plan* (New York: MacMillan, 1968), p. 206. Reprinted with the permission of Simon & Schuster, Inc., from *Politics Battle Plan* by Herbert M. Baus and William B. Ross. Copyright © by Herbert M. Baus and William B. Ross.
12.   Joseph F. Sullivan, *The New York Times*, November 20, 1977, p. 1-A.
13.   Sidney Yudain, "The Way It Was," *Roll Call* [Capitol Hill newspaper, Washington, DC], July 14, 1977, p. 8.

Chapter 3—Smilin', Recognizin', and Charmin'

1.   "Quotable Quotes," *Readers Digest*, November 1976.

2   Stephen J. Skubek and Hal E. Short, *Republican Humor* (Washington, DC: Acropolis Books, 1976), p. 151.

3.   Speech Accepting the Democratic Nomination for President, 1976.

4.   Cited in William Safire, *Safire's Political Dictionary* (New York: Ballantine Books, 1978), p. 44.

5.   James Ertel, *How to Run for Office* (New York: Sterling Publishing Co., 1960), p. 120.

6.   Ibid., p. 133.

7.   Quoted in Nancy McPhee, *The Book of Insults, Ancient & Modern* (New York: St. Martins, 1978), p. 124.

8.   Margaret Truman, *Harry S. Truman* (New York: Pocket Books, 1972), pp. 25-26.

9.   Marshall Frady, *Wallace* (New York: World Publishing Company, 1970), p. 100.

10.   Congresswoman Margaret Heckler, "Through Leaders and Special Interest Groups," *Ways to Win* (Washington, DC, Republican National Committee, 1968), p. 109.

11.   David Fink, "Politicians Like To Be Liked," *USA Today*, October 31, 1984. Copyright 1984 USA Today. Reprinted with permission.

12.   Brooks Jackson, "A Senators Advice: Dont Give Consent To Re-election Debate," *The Wall Street Journal*, May 2, 1985. Reprinted by permission of *The Wall Street Journal*, © Dow Jones & Company, Inc.   All rights reserved worldwide.

13.   Ibid.

14.   Ertel, *How to Run for Office*, p. 54.

15.   Carl P. Rubin, "Do It Yourself Campaigning," *Ways to Win* (Washington, DC: Republican National Committee, 1968), p. 157.

16.   Fink, Politicians Like To Be Liked

17.   Jackson, "A Senators Advice." Reprinted by permission of *The Wall Street Journal*, © Dow Jones & Company, Inc.   All rights reserved worldwide.

18.   Ibid.

Chapter 4—Merchandising the Common Touch—Machine Style

1.   Abraham Lincoln, in Illinois State Register, February 21, 1840.

2.   Dale Carnegie, *How to Win Friends and Influence People* (New York: Pocket Books, 1975), p. 30.

3.   Michael Barone, "Nonlessons of the Campaign," *New York Times Magazine*, November 28, 1976, p. 37.

4.   Henry Luther Stoddard, *Presidential Sweepstakes* (New York: G. P. Putnam's Sons, 1948), pp. 39-40, 202-203.

5.   Richard Hofstadter, *The American Political Tradition & The Men Who Made it* (New York: Vantage Books, 1973), p. 63.

6.   Len O'Conner, *Mayor Daley and His City* (New York: Avon Books, 1975, pp. 114, 115, 157, 179, 212.

7.   John Gunther, *Inside the USA* (New York: Harper & Harper, 1947), p. 345.

8.   Alfred Steinberg, *The Bosses* (New York: The New American Library, 1974), pp. 39-42.

9.   Steinberg, *The Bosses*, p. 41.

10. Barone, "Nonlessons of the Campaign," p. 37.

11. Morris Markey, *Ward Heelers*, September 1947, Vol. 1, No. 7.

12. Ertel, *How to Run for Office*, p. 40.

13. Robert Sherrill, *Gothic Politics in the Deep South: Stars of the New Confederacy* (New York: Ballantine Books, 1969), p. 123.

14. Frank R. Kent, *The Great Game of Politics* (Garden City, New York: Doubleday and Co., 1935), pp. 42-44.

15. William Devlin, *Ways to Win* (Washington, DC: Republican National Committee, 1968), p. 124.

16. George S. Blair, *Government at the Grass Roots* (Pacific Palisades, CA: Palisades Publishers, 1977), p. 78.

17. Steinberg, *The Bosses*, pp. 39-42.

18. Ralph Coghlan, *St. Louis Post-Dispatch* (cited in *Inside U.S.A.*, by John Gunther (New York: Harper & Harper, 1947)), p. 592.

Chapter 5—Changing the Guard: Goodbye Machine, Hello Volunteer

1. William Riordon, *Plunkett of Tammany Hall* (New York: E. P. Dutton & Co., 1963), p. 11.

2. Lynn Mueller, "Political Direct Mail Can Be Useful Candidate Tool," *Direct Marketing*, 1971, p. 30.

3. Dick Simpson, *Winning Elections* (Chicago: Swallow Press, 1972), p. 47.

4. Ibid, p. 30.

5. "Young Democrats and Republicans Give Tips For Turning Out the Youth Vote," *Campaign Insight*, July 1970.

6. Robert Bonitati, "Managing To Manage Volunteers," p. 130.

7. Ertel, *How To Run For Office*, pp. 114-115.

8. Nancy Pederson, "Sign at Retirement Village, Palm Springs," *Reader's Digest*, August 1977.

9. Baus and Ross, *Politics Battle Plan*, p. 210.

10. Bonitati, "Managing to Manage Volunteers," p. 132.

11. James A. Farley, *Behind The Ballots: The Personal History of a Politician* (New York: Harcourt, Brace, 1938), p. 193.

12. Goodman, "Getting Across with Advertising," p. 61.

13. *USA Today*, November 5, 1984, p. 3.

14. William E. Mosher, "Party and Government Control at the Grass Roots," *National Municipal Review*, 24, 1935, pp. 15-18.

15. *The Wall Street Journal*, November 2, 1984, p. 23.

Chapter 6—Doorbelling

1. Jack Alexander, "The Senate's Remarkable Upstart," *The Saturday Evening Post*, August 9, 1947, p. 52.

2. Carnegie, *How To Win Friends and Influence People*, p. 110.

3. James M. Perry, *The New Politics* (New York: Clarkson N. Potter, 1968), p. 100.

4. Edward Schwartzman, *Campaign Craftsmanship* (New York: Universe Books, 1973), p. 212.

5. Dennis Farney, "A Modern Machine: How Savvy Matt Reese, a Political Consultant, Gets Out the Winning Vote," *The Wall Street Journal*, March 23, 1972, p. 22.

6. Julia Brodigan, "Volunteers Help Republican Win Major Office," *Campaign Insight* [Wichita, Kansas], August 5, 1975.

7. *Let's Talk About Running for Office* (New York: National Association of Manufacturers, 1968), p. 33.

8. Ibid.

9. Ibid, p. 82.

Chapter 7—Person to Person: The Power of the Telephone

1. Paul Dickson, *The Official Explanations* (New York: Dell Publishing, 1981), p. 205.

2. John Robert Colombo, *Colombo's Hollywood* (Toronto: W. Collins and Sons, 1979), p. 160.

3. Herbert V. Prochnow and Herbert V. Prochnow, Jr., *A Treasury of Humorous Quotations* (New York: Harper and Row, 1969), p. 326.

4. Gunther, *Inside the USA*, p. 23.

5. Farney, "A Modern Machine," p. 22.

6. "Got Your Message," *Time*, November 20, 1978, p. 16.

7. James M. Perry, "How Innocent Voters Are Now Being Wooed By Computers," *National Observer*, September 1967, p. 18.

8. Shadegg, *How to Win an Election*, p. 133.

9. Perry, "How Innocent Voters Are Now Being Wooed By Computers," p. 18.

10. Schwartzman, *Campaign Craftsmanship*, p. 211.

11. Robert V. Doyle, "Ma Bell: A Great Campaign Auxiliary," *Campaign Insight*, November 1973.

12. "Got Your Message," *Time*, November 20, 1978.

13. Murray Roman, "Call for Professional Telephone Politicking," *Advertising Age*, January 21, 1980, p. 12.

14. Shadegg, *The New How to Win an Election*, p. 126.

15. Ed Heavey, Candidate For Attorney General, *Washington State Campaign Handbook*, 1972, p. 2.

16. Farney, "A Modern Machine, p. 22.

17. Edmund Fuller, *2500 Anecdotes For All Occasions* (New York: Dolphin Books, 1961), p. 39.

18. Schwartzman, *Campaign Craftsmanship*, p. 123.

19. National Association of Manufacturers, *Campaign Manual* (New York, 1968), pp. 80-81.

Part 2—The Money Ritual

Chapter 8—Drawing the Budget

1. John Bartlett, *Bartlett's Quotations* (New York: Doubleday, 1942), p. 128.

2. "Where the Money Goes," *Campaign Insight*, June 1971.

3.   *The Royer Report, Charles Royer for Mayor Campaign*, Seattle, Washington, June 1977.

4.   Nick Thommesch, *Seattle Times*, November 1980.

5.   Democratic Hopefuls in Mayoral Race Looking to Late Effort and T.V., *New York Times*, September 4, 1977.

6.   Michael S. Berman, Speaker, National Conference on Political Fund Raising, University of Chicago, Dec. 15-16, 1976.

7.   Leon H. Harris, *The Fine Art of Political Wit* (New York: E. P. Dutton Co., 1958), p. 258.

8.   James C. Hume, *Podium Humor* (New York: Harper & Row, 1975), p. 236.

9.   Berman, Speaker, National Conference on Political Fund Raising.

10.   Baus and Ross, *Politics Battle Plan*, pp. 324-326. Reprinted with the permission of Simon & Schuster, Inc., from *Politics Battle Plan* by Herbert M. Baus and William B. Ross. Copyright © by Herbert M. Baus and William B. Ross.

Chapter 9—Facing the Gamble

1.   Columbo, *Columbo's Hollywood*, p. 119.

2.   Ibid.

3.   Ibid. p. 189.

4.   Dr. Hunter S. Thompson, *Fear And Loathing on the Campaigning Trail '72* (New York: Popular Library, 1973), p. 267.

5.   Paul Steiner, ed., *Stevens on Wit & Wisdom* (New York: Pyramid Books, 1965), p. 24.

6.   George Bush, "Responsibilities of a Candidate," *Ways To Win* (Washington, DC: Republican National Committee, 1968), p. 31.

7.   Ken Johnson, *The Political Campaign* (pamphlet).   Washington State Democratic Central Committee, 1969), pp. 15-16.

8.   Brooks Jackson, "Direct Mail Pays Off," *The Wall Street Journal*, April 3, 1984.

9.   Gerald J. McCullough, "Pennsylvania: The Failure of Campaign Reform," in Herbert E. Alexander, ed., *Campaign Money: Reform and Reality in the States* (New York: The Free Press, 1976), pp. 248-249.

10.   George Thayer, *Who Shakes The Money Tree?* (New York: Simon & Schuster, 1973), p. 145.

11.   Prochnow and Prochnow, Jr., *A Treasury of Humorous Quotations*, p. 51.

12.   Thayer, *Who Shakes the Money Tree?*, pp. 75-76.

13.   Arnold Steinberg, *Political Campaign Management* (Lexington, MA: Lexington Books, 1976), p. 140.

Chapter 10—Yes, Virginia, There Is a Santa Claus

1.   "Yes, Virginia There is a Santa Claus," *New York Sun*, September 21, 1897.

2.   Jolene Unsoeld, *Common Cause Survey For Washington State* (Olympia, WA: Common Cause, 1974).

3.   Frank Lyman, "Democratic Race Mounts Final Drive With Heavy Campaign Spending," *New York Times*, September 4, 1977.

4.   Thayer, *Who Shakes The Money Tree?*, pp. 15-16.

5. Lyman, Democratic Race Mounts Final Drive.

6. Quoted in Safire, *Safire's Political Dictionary*, p. 220.

7. Herbert E. Alexander, *Money in Politics* (Washington DC: Public Affairs Press, 1972), p. 140.

8. Baus and Ross, *Politics Battle Plan*, p. 79.

9. Thayer, *Who Shakes The Money Tree?*, pp. 126-145.

10. Thayer, *Who Shakes The Money Tree?*, pp. 126-145.

11. 1968 Election Handbook, *New York Times*, p. 153.

12. Ibid.

13. Susan Littwin, "How The West's Best Fund Raiser Gets His Hand In Your Pocket," *New West*, December 6, 1976, p. 13.

Chapter 11—Yes, Virginia, Sometimes Santa Claus Is More Interested in a Cause, a Job, or the Triumph of a Party Than in Christmas

1. Fuller Warren, *How To Win in Politics* (Tallahassee, Florida: Peninsular Publishing Company, 1949), p. 52.

2. Baus and Ross, *Politics Battle Plan*, p. 86. Reprinted with the permission of Simon & Schuster, Inc., from *Politics Battle Plan* by Herbert M. Baus and William B. Ross. Copyright © by Herbert M. Baus and William B. Ross.

3. Ralph Friedman, "Nuclear Issues in Oregon," *Advertising Age*, October 11, 1976.

4. Thayer, *Who Shakes The Money Tree?*, p. 176.

5. Robert Richards, *San Diego Union*, July 20, 1960.

6. Howell Raines, "Georgia: The Politics of Campaign Reform," in Alexander, *Campaign Money*, p. 213.

7. Ibid.

8. Joel Connelly, "Big Bucks Add Up in the Second District," *Seattle Post-Intelligencer*, August 28, 1978.

9. Thayer, *Who Shakes The Money Tree?*, p. 128.

10. *Seattle Times*, United Press International Dispatch, July 23, 1976.

11. James M. Perry, "Liberals Find A Use For the Reagan Crowd—As a Rallying Cry," *The Wall Street Journal*, March 30, 1981.

12. Riordon, *Plunkett of Tammany Hall*, p. 73.

13. Title 8, U.S.C., Section 61(a).

14. David W. Adamany and George L. Agree, *Political Money* (Baltimore: Johns Hopkins University Press, 1975), p. 41.

15. Jerome Kelly, "California: A New Law," in Alexander, *Campaign Money: Reform and Reality in the States*, (New York: The Free Press, 1976), p. 19.

16. Title 18, U.S.C., Section 61 (a).

17. Kelly, "California," in Alexander, *Campaign Money*, p. 19.

18. Brian T. Usher, "Ohio: A Tale of Two Parties," in Alexander, *Campaign Money*, pp. 260-261.

19. "Biggest Spellman Donor," *Seattle Times*, March 4, 1981.

20. Riordon, *Plunkett of Tammany Hall*, p. 74.

21. II Code of Federal Regulations, 104.3(b) 3 VIII and 110.7 (e).

22. II Code of Federal Regulations, 100.7 b (4)-(5)-(6)-(7)-(8).

23. II Code of Federal Regulations, 100.7 b (4)-(5)-(6)-(7)-(8).

24. Pamphlet, Minnesota Democratic Farmer Labor Party, State Central Committee Sustaining Membership Program, 1974.

25. "How California State Senator Overcame Special Interest," *Campaign Insight*, May 1, 1974, p. 3.

Chapter 12—PACs and How They Get What They Want for Christmas

1. Riordon, *Plunkett Of Tammany Hall*, p. 73.

2. Michael Jackman, *Crown Book of Political Quotations* (New York: Crown Publishers, 1982), p. 217.

3. Adler, *The Washington Wits*, p. 98.

4. Adamany and Agree, *Political Money*, p. 39 (2), p. 40.

5. Robert Healy, "Massachussetts, Corruption and Cleanup," *Campaign Insight, Reform and Reality in the United States* (New York: The Free Press, 1976), p. 158.

6. "Mormons Rushed Money To ERA Foes," *Idaho Statesman*, April 21, 1980.

7. Bobby Baker and Larry L. King, *Wheeling And Dealing* (New York: W. W. Norton and Co., 1978), p. 86.

8. Usher, "Ohio," in Alexander, *Campaign Money*, p. 266.

9. Jon Ford, "Texas: Big Money," in Alexander, *Campaign Money*, p. 99.

10. Sig Mickelson, *The Electric Mirror* (New York: Dodd, Mead & Company, 1972), p. 243.

11. Ibid., p. 242.

12. II Code of Federal Regulations, S114.(1),(5).

13. II Code of Federal Regulations, S114.5.

14. "Doctors Top Givers In U.S. Politics," *Seattle Times*, January 25, 1979.

15. II Code of Federal Regulations, S1325.1.

16. II Code of Federal Regulations, S114.5 (3)(3).

17. Thayer, *Who Shakes The Money Tree?*, p. 151.

18. Peter Rinearson, "Legislative Races Are More Costly," *Seattle Times*, August 4, 1979.

19. Adamany and Agree, *Political Money*, p. 40.

20. Brooks Jackson, *The Wall Street Journal*, April 1, 1985, p. 44. Reprinted by permission of *The Wall Street Journal*, © Dow Jones & Company, Inc. All rights reserved worldwide.

21. Ibid.

22. 26 U.S.C. 271.

23. Brooks Jackson, *The Wall Street Journal*, p. 44. Reprinted by permission of *The Wall Street Journal*, © Dow Jones & Company, Inc. All rights reserved worldwide.

24. Raines, "Georgia," in Alexander, *Campaign Money*, pp. 201, 202, 203, 207.

25. Jackson, *The Wall Street Journal*, p. 44.

26. Anonymous, *Washington Merry-Go-Round* (New York: Horace Liveright Inc., 1931), p. 163.

27. II Code of Federal Regulations 114.3 (c) (i) (ii).

28. Bill and Nancy Boyarsky, *Backroom Politics* (Los Angeles, CA: J. P. Tarcher, , 1974), p. 107.

29. II Code of Federal Regulations, S114.5(3) (3).

30. David Ignatium, "Despite Liberal Laws, Most Companies Shun Partisan Politicking," *The Wall Street Journal*, October 27, 1976.

31. II Code of Federal Regulations, 114.3(c) (i) (ii).

32. II Code of Federal Regulations, 114.3(a) (vi) and (vii).

33. Robert W. Merry, *The Wall Street Journal*, February 10, 1984.

34. Adamany and Agree, *Political Money*, p. 38.

Chapter 13—Like Christmas Spirit the Gifts Improve with Prospects of Victory

1. Thayer, *Who Shakes The Money Tree?*, p. 34.

2. Ibid., p. 94.

3. Jackson, *The Wall Street Journal*, February 5, 1984. Reprinted by permission of *The Wall Street Journal*, © Dow Jones & Company, Inc. All rights reserved worldwide.

4. Al Polczinski, "Kansas: Reform and Reaction," in Alexander, *Campaign Money*, pp. 173-174.

5. Michael Wheeler, *Lies, Damn Lies and Statistics* (New York: Liveright, 1976), p. 114.

6. Ibid., pp. 114-115.

7. Jerry Landaver, *The Wall Street Journal*, October 13, 1980.

Chapter 14—The Ethics, The Wise Men Who Came Bearing Gifts

1. Columbo, *Columbo's Hollywood*, p. 105.

2. Thayer, *Who Shakes the Money Tree?*, p. 208.

3. Leonard Louis Levinson, *Webster's Unafraid Dictionary* (New York: Collier Books, 1978), p. 192.

4. Robert Ripley, *Ripley's Believe It Or Not* (New York, June 1948), p. 78.

5. Mark Green and Michael Calabrese, *Who Runs Congress?* (New York: Bantam Books, 1979), pp. 3-4.

6. Thayer, *Who Shakes the Money Tree?*, p. 150.

7. Gunther, *Inside the USA,* p. 426.

8. Richard Larsen, *Seattle Times*, November 6, 1970.

9. Hank Fischer, "Sustaining Members Drive Pamphlet," Minnesota Farmer Labor Party, 1975.

10. Alexander, *Money in Politics*, p. 121.

11. McCullough, "Pennsylvania," in Alexander, *Campaign Money*, pp. 237-238.

12. Ross Cunningham, *Seattle Times*, September 20, 1975.

13. Boyarsky, *Backroom Politics*, p. 104.

14. Ross Cunningham, *Seattle Times*, September 20, 1976.

15. Anonymous, *Washington Merry-Go-Round*, p. 101.

16. Peter Rinearson, *Seattle Times*, February 8, 1981.

17. Ross Cunningham, *Seattle Times*, September 20, 1975.

18. Thayer, *Who Shakes the Money Tree?*, p. 50.

19. Ford, "Texas," in Alexander, *Campaign Money*, pp. 248-249.

20. Ibid.

21. *Greive v. Evans* Campaign Committee, Washington State Superior Court for Thurston County, Case No. 43523.

22. Senator Thomas J. Dodd, "Government and Graft: There Is No Code of Ethics," *Morals* (Cowles Education Corporation, 1968), p. 20.

23. Theodore H. White, *The Making of a President 1960* (New York: Pocket Books, 1964), p. 131.

24. William Mansfield, "Florida: The Power of Incumbency," in Alexander, *Campaign Money*, p. 50.

25. Kelly, "California," in Alexander, *Campaign Money*, pp. 19-20.

26. Ibid.

27. Ibid., pp. 20-21.

28. Tim Carrington, *The Wall Street Journal*, February 7, 1984.

29. Alexander, *Money in Politics*, p. 165.

30. Adamany and Agree, *Political Money*, p. 41.

31. Note that the contribution was in 1978 dollars. Green and Calabrese, *Who Runs Congress*, pp. 6-7.

32. "Teachers Tie Election Case to Single Issue," *The Wall Street Journal*, October 3, 1980.

33. Mansfield, "Florida," in Alexander, *Campaign Money*, p. 58.

34. McCullough, "Pennsylvania," in Alexander, *Campaign Money*, p. 235.

35. Peter Rinearsen, *Seattle Times*, February 8, 1981.

36. Howell Raines, "Georgia," in Alexander, *Campaign Money*, p. 217.

37. "Foley Backers," *Spokane Daily Chronicle*, August, 1978.

38. Adamany and Agree, *Political Money*, pp. 39-40.

39. "Doctors Top Givers in U.S. Politics," *Seattle Times*, January 25, 1979.

40. Ibid.

41. Raines, "Georgia," in Alexander, *Campaign Money*, p. 217.

42. Joel Connelly, *Seattle Post-Intelligencer*, August 23, 1978.

43. "Six Methods Of Raising the Political Buck," *Campaign Insight*, April 1973, p. 6.

44. Kelly, "California," in Alexander, *Campaign Money*, p. 20.

45. George Thayer, *Who Shakes The Money Tree?* (New York: Simon & Schuster, 1973), p. 151.

46. Ibid.

Chapter 15—Selection, Direct Solicitation, and Seduction

1. Floyd Martin Clay, *From Huey Long to Hadacol* (Gretna, Louisiana: Pelican Publishing Company, 1973), p. 59.

2. Leonard Louis Stevenson, *Webster's Unafraid Dictionary* (New York: Collier Books, 1978), p. 211.

3. Hank Parkinson, *Winning Your Campaign* (Englewood Cliffs, New Jersey: Prentice-Hall Inc., 1970), p. 43.

4. Hank Parkinson, *Winning Your Campaign* (Englewood Cliffs, New Jersey: Prentice-Hall, 1970), p. 49.

5. Tom Coffman, *Campaign Insight*, April 15, 1974.

6. Edward J. Flynn, *You're the Boss* (New York: Viking Press, 1947), p. 106.

7. Kelly, "California," in Alexander, *Campaign Money*, p. 19.

8. Doug Underwood, *Seattle Times*, April 8, 1984.

9. Tom Coffman, *Campaign Insight*, April 15, 1974.

10. McCullough, "Pennsylvania," in Alexander, *Campaign Money*, p. 245.

11. Susan Littwin, "How The West's Best Fund Raiser Gets His Hand In Your Pocket," *New West*, December 6, 1976, p. 13.

12. Mary Ellen Leary, *Phantom Politics: Campaigning In California* (Washington, D.C.: Public Affairs Press, 1977), p. 77.

13. Susan Littwin, "How The West's Best Fund Raiser Gets His Hand In Your Pocket," p. 13.

14. Thayer, *Who Shakes The Money Tree?*, p. 145.

15. Susan Littwin, "How The West's Best Fund Raiser Gets His Hand In Your Pocket," p. 13.

16. Alexander, *Money in Politics*, p. 81.

17. Michael S. Berman, Speaker, National Conference on Political Fund Raising, University of Chicago, Dec. 15-16, 1976.

18. Speaker, National Conference on Political Fund Raising, University of Chicago Center, Dec. 15-16, 1976.

19. Alexander, *Money in Politics*, p. 64.

20. Brochure, Parker for Congress Campaign, Tacoma, Washington, 1974.

21. Alexander, *Money in Politics*, p. 163.

22. Baus and Ross, *Politics Battle Plan*, p. 137.

23. II Code of Federal Regulation, SIIO.4 (a)(1) and (3)(ii).

24. Thayer, *Who Shakes the Money Tree?*, p. 143.

Chapter 16—Salesmanship . . . Via Direct Mail

1. Evan Esar, *20,000 Quips and Quotes* (Garden City, New York: Doubleday and Company, Inc., 1968), p. 479.

2. Carl Bender, Speaker, National Conference on Political Fund Raising, University of Chicago, December 15-16, 1976.

3. Richard Larsen, *Seattle Times*, November 1, 1970.

4. Betty Kroll, Stern's Law . . . There's No Such Thing as a Political Liability, *Campaign Insight*, October, 1972.

5. Baus and Ross, *Politics Battle Plan*, pp. 74-75.

6. David Burnham, "Mondale Forces Engage in Computer Dating," New York Times Service, *Seattle Post-Intelligencer*, February 2, 1984.

7. Tom Collins, Speaker, National Conference on Political Fund Raising, University of Chicago, Dec. 15-16, 1976.

8. Robert Timberg, "N.C.P.A.C. Means Business for Friends on the Right," *Baltimore Sun*, July 1, 1982.

9. James Ridgeway, *Seattle Post-Intelligencer*, June 20, 1982, pp. 15-16.

10. Bob Donath, "Viguerie Has Long Range Goal for Conservatives," *Advertising Age*, September 20, 1976.

11. Ibid.

12. Perry, "Liberals Find a Use for the Reagan Crowd."

13. Carl Bender, Speaker, National Conference of Political Fund Raising, University of Chicago, December 15-16, 1976.

14. Thomas Collins, Speaker, National Conference on Political Fund Raising, University of Chicago, December 15-16, 1976.

15. William Endicott, "Florida: The Power of Incumbency," in Alexander, *Campaign Money*, p. 134.

16. Thomas Collins, *Direct Marketing*, November, 1973, p. 27

17. Littwin, "How The West's Best Fund Raiser Gets His Hand In Your Pocket," p. 32.

18. Thomas Collins, Speaker, National Conference on Political Fund Raising, University of Chicago, December 15-16, 1976.

19. Baus and Ross, *Politics Battle Plan*, pp. 74-75.

20. Alexander, *Money In Politics*, p. 142.

21. Carl Bender, Speaker, National Conference on Political Fund Raising, University of Chicago, December 15-16, 1976.

22. Thomas L. Collins, The Political Battle in the Mail, *Direct Marketing*, November, 1973, p. 28.

Chapter 17—Cash, Calories, and a Slice of Heaven

1. Quoted in Safire, *Safire's Political Dictionary*, p. 620.

2. *The Official Ronald Wilson Reagan Quote Book* (St. Louis, Minnesota: Chain-Pinkham Books, 1980), p. 19.

3. Flyer, "Campaign Money," Democratic National Committee, Washington, DC, February 1958.

4. Alexander, *Money in Politics*, p. 131.

5. Michael S. Breman, Speaker, National Conference on Political Fund Raising, University of Chicago, Dec. 15-16, 1976.

6. National Association of Manufacturers, *Let's Talk About Running for Office*, p. 60.

7. Shirley Polikoff, Speaker, National Conference on Political Fund Raising, University of Chicago, Dec. 15-16, 1976.

8. Ibid.

9. Richard W. Larsen, "What It Takes to Get Elected to Congress," *Seattle Times*, November 1, 1970.

10. Safire, *Safire's Political Dictionary*, p. 620.

11. *The Seattle Sun*, October 22, 1980, p. 6.

12. Littwin, "How the West's Best Fund Raiser Gets His Hand in Your Pocket," p. 13.

Chapter 18—Adding a Touch of Imagination and. . . .

1. Baxter Lane, *Scrapbook of Famous Quips and Quotes* (Amarillo, Texas: Baxter Lane Co., 1974), p. 43.
2. Gregory Jaynes, "Letting The Good Times Roll," *Time*, February 6, 1984.
3. "Tea Dances, Toe Dances, Judo Chops and All that Jazz, Fundraisers," *The Royer Report*.
4. Anonymous from the floor, National Conference on Political Fund Raising, University of Chicago, Dec. 15-16, 1976.
5. Richard Smith & Edward Dector, *Oops!* (New York: Rutledge Press, 1981), p. 38.
6. *The Royer Report*.
7. Richard Larsen, *Seattle Times*, November 1, 1970.
8. Anonymous from the floor, National Conference on Political Fund Raising, University of Chicago, Dec. 15-16, 1976.
9. George Thayer, *Campaign Insight*, February 1970.
10. Thayer, *Who Shakes The Money Tree?*, p. 84.
11. Governor Paul Laxalt, *Campaign Insight*, October 1972.
12. Dick West, "A Little Of Nothing," *Roll Call* [Capitol Hill newspaper, Washington, DC], May 25, 1978.
13. Bill Young, administrative staff aide to Speaker Crimm, May 27, 1981.
14. *The Royer Report*
15. Democratic Farm Labor Party, *1976 D.F.L. Legislative Handbook*, Minnesota, 1976, p. 9.
16. Norman Ackley For State Representative Bash, Seattle, Washington, 1964.
17. Thayer, *Who Shakes The Money Tree*, pp. 68-69.
18. Thayer, *Who Shakes The Money Tree*, p. 84.

Chapter 19—After the Votes are Counted: Winners, Losers

1. Adamany and Agree, *Political Money*, p. 41.
2. Anonymous suggestion from the floor, National Conference on Political Fund Raising, University of Chicago, Dec. 15-16, 1976.
3. Richard W. Larsen, "Friends Roast Durkan," *Seattle Times*, May 3, 1977.
4. Jill Buckley, Speaker, National Conference on Political Fund Raising, University of Chicago, Dec. 15-16, 1976.
5. Murphy, *2,750 One-Line Quotations*, p. 97.
6. Lewis C. Henry, *Best Quotations for All Occasions* (Greenwich, Connecticut: Premier Books, Inc., 1955).
7. Douglas Caddy, *The Hundred Million Payoff* (Washington, DC: Public Policy Press, 1974), p. 53.
8. N. H. Magel and S. K. Magel, *The Complete Letter Writer* (New York: Pocket Books, 1973), pp. 47-53.

Part 3—Polling

Chapter 20—The Political Poll

1.   Jackman, *Crown's Book Of Political Quotations*, p. 66.
2.   From "Quote Lines," *USA Today*, January 31, 1984.
3.   Arthur Tobier, *How McGovern Won The Presidency* (New York: Ballantine Books), 1972, p. 71.
4.   David Halberstam, "How Television Failed the American Voter," *Seattle Post-Intelligencer*, January 11, 1981.
5.   Mike Royko, Exit Lying, *Seattle Times*, March 16, 1984.
6.   Jack J. Honomichl, "Research Acts as Reagans Eyes," *Advertising Age*, November 5, 1984.
7.   Ibid.
8.   Allen Otter, Computing Democratic Winner in 72, *The Wall Street Journal*, December 11, 1970.
9.   Shadegg, *How to Win an Election*, p. 134.
10.   Herbert Block, *H. R. Block Special Report* (New York: W. W. Norton, 1974), p. 64.
11.   Wheeler, *Lies, Damn Lies and Statistics*, p. 250.
12.   John Glee and Ralph F. Shawain, "California Votes on Utopia" (*Saturday Evening Post*, 1938), p. 8.
13.   "Dukakis Poll," *Boston Globe*, October 21, 1982.
14.   Ibid.
15.   Dan Nimmo, *The Political Persuaders* (Englewood Cliffs, NJ: Prentice Hall, 1970), p. 93.
16.   In-House Polling, *Target 76* (Washington, DC: Democratic National Committee, 1976), p. 70.
17.   Wheeler, *Lies, Damn Lies and Statistics*, p. 70.
18.   Dr. George Gallup, *The Pulse of Democracy* (New York: Simon and Schuster, 1940), p. 68.
19.   Schwartzman, *Campaign Craftsmanship*, p. 107.
20.   Wheeler, *Lies, Damn Lies and Statistics*, p. 107.
21.   Ibid., p. 81.
22.   *Statistical Abstract of the United States, 1981* (United States Bureau of the Census), p. 25.
23.   Ernest Dichter, "Motive Interpreter," *Journal of Advertising Research*, June 1977.
24.   Walter DeVries and Lanee Terrance, *The Ticket Splitter: A New Face in American Politics* (Grand Rapids, MI: Eerdmans Publishing, 1972), p. 110.
25.   Steinberg, *Political Campaign Management*, p. 242.
26.   "In-House Polling," *Target 76* (Washington, DC: Democratic National Committee), p. 18.
27.   Schwartzman, *Campaign Craftsmanship*, p. 188.
28.   "In-House Polling," *Target 76*, p. 5.

29. James Brown and Philip Seib, *The Art of Politics: Electoral Strategies and Campaign Management* (Alfred, 1976), p. 201.

30. Richard M. Scammon and Ben Whittenberg, *The Real Majority* (New York: Coward McCann, 1970), p. 34.

31. "In-House Polling," *Target 76*, p. 8.

32. Wheeler, *Lies, Damn Lies and Statistics*, p. 80.

Chapter 21—Measuring Name Familiarity and Performance

1. Evan Esar, *20,000 Quips & Quotes* (New York: Doubleday, 1968), p. 563.

2. Shadegg, *How to Win an Election*, p. 143.

3. *Target 76* (Washington, DC: Democratic National Committee, 1976).

4. Steinberg, *Political Campaign Management*, p. 188.

5. Arthur Dudden, *Pardon Us, Mr. President* (New York: Barnes, 1975), p. 240.

6. Jackson, "A Senator's Advice," May 2, 1985. Reprinted by permission of *The Wall Street Journal*, © Dow Jones & Company, Inc. All rights reserved worldwide.

7. Steinberg, *Political Campaign Management*.

8. Wheeler, *Lies, Damn Lies and Statistics*, p. 185.

9. Murray B. Levin, *The Complete Politician* (Boston: Beacon Press, 1961), p. 202.

10. Richard H. Schweitzer, *The 1968 Election in the State of Washington* (Republican State Central Committee, November 1980).

11. "Campaign Consultant Program," *Target '76* (Washington, DC: Democratic National Committee), p. 5.

12. Nimmo, *The Political Persuaders*, pp. 93-94.

13. Marvin R. Weisbord, *Campaigning For President* (Washington Square Press, 1966), p. 221.

Chapter 22—In-Depth Polling

1. Quoted in "Quotelines," *USA Today*, January 31, 1984.

2. Lickty & Wagner, "Cartoon Quips," *Reader's Digest*, November 1980, p. 71.

3. Lorene Hanley Duquin, "The Pluses and Minuses of Do-It-Yourself Polling," *Campaigns & Elections*, 1984), p. 35.

4. Christopher Hitchens, "Voting in the Passive Voice: What Polling Has Done to American Democracy," *Harper's*, April 1992, p. 47.

5. *Congressional Quarterly Guide to U.S. Elections* (Washington, DC, 1975), p. 506.

6. Ibid.

7. Nimmo, *The Political Persuaders*, p. 92.

8. Steinberg, *Political Campaign Management*, p. 187.

Chapter 23—The Pitfalls of Evaluation

1. "Quotable Quotes," *Reader's Digest*, May 1977, p. 177.

2. Elizabeth Hartmann, "Public Reaction to Public Opinion," *Public Opinion Quarterly*, 1968, p. 295.

3. Jack J. Honomichl, "The Political Pollsters Reach Superstar Status," *Advertising Age*, February 28, 1983.

4. *The Everett Herald*, November 4, 1981.
5. Louis Harris, "Election Will Be Close," *USA Today*, January 31, 1984.
6. Kevin Phillips, *Spectrum*, February 7, 1983.
7. Steinberg, *Political Campaign Management*, p. 188.
8. Wheeler, *Lies, Damn Lies and Statistics*, p. 279.
9. Ibid., p. 276.
10. Nimmo, *The Political Persuaders*, p. 100.

Chapter 24—Balancing Image and Issues

1. "Quotable Quotes," *Readers Digest*, May 1977, p. 177.
2. "In-house Polling," *Target '76*, p. 18.
3. Duquin, "Do-it-yourself Polling," p. 20.

Chapter 25—Is Polling Really Worth the Cost?

1. Schwartzman, *Campaign Craftsmanship*, p. 92.
2. Charles W. Boll and Albert H. Cantril, *Polls* (Cabin John, MD: Seven Locks Press, 1972), pp. 127-128.
3. Ted Worner, "If You Think You Were Surprised," *Roll Call* [Newspaper of Capitol Hill, Washington, DC], November 23, 1978.

Chapter 26—Reaction to Polls

1. From "Quote Lines," *USA Today*, January 31, 1984.
2. M. Truman, *Harry S. Truman*, pp. 60.
3. Duquin, "Do-It-Yourself Polling," p. 21
4. Tobier, *How McGovern Won the Presidency*, p. 71.
5. Honomichl, "The Political Pollsters Reach Superstar Status."
6. James M. Perry, *The New Politics* (New York: Clarkston N. Potter, 1968), p. 79.
7. Ibid.
8. Allan Brownfield, "American Politics," *Roll Call* [Capitol Hill newspaper, Washington, DC], October 1976.
9. Dudden, *Pardon Us, Mr. President*, p. 166.
10. Beth Bogart, "Polls Shape Politicians and Campaigns," *Advertising Age*, February 28, 1985.
11. W. A. Swanberg, *Citizen Hearst* (New York: Charles Scribner and Sons, 1971), p. 29.
12. Ad pamphlet produced by the Radio Advertising Bureau, New York, 1969, p. 2.

Part 4—Advertising

Chapter 27—Political Advertising Techniques

1. Budden, *Pardon Us, Mr. President!*, p. 150.
2. Joe McGinnis, *The Selling of the President* (New York: Pocket Books, 1975), p. 21.
3. Joseph A. St. Amant, United Press International. "Speeches High Road to Hill," *Baltimore Sun*, May 10, 1962.

4.   J. V. Stewart, *Repetitive Advertising in Newspapers* (Hinsdale, IL: Dryden Press, 1973), p. 182.

5.   Dichter, "Motive Interpreter," *Journal of Advertising Research*, p. 3.

6.   Safire, *Safire's Political Dictionary*, p. 802.

7.   Nimmo, *Political Persuaders*, p. 162.

8.   Don Grant, "Bob Dole a Big Ad User in 13 Election Victories," *Advertising Age*, October 11, 1976, p. 69.

9.   Edwin Diamond and Stephen Bates, *The Spot: The Rise of Political Advertising on Television* (Cambridge, MA: MIT Press, 1984), p. 245.

10. Bill Abrams, "More Ads Are Squeezed into Less," *The Wall Street Journal*, October 27, 1983.

11. Erick Fettman, "Pink Panther Trounce," *New York Post*, November 15, 1978.

12. Diamond and Bates, *The Spot,* pp. 277-278.

Chapter 28—What Distinguishes the Image of Mickey Mouse From Other Mice?

1.   Jackman, *Crown's Book of Political Quotations*, p. 66.

2.   Warren, *How To Win in Politics*, p. 120.

3.   Ruth and Norman Lloyd, *The American Heritage Song Book* (New York: American Heritage Publishers, 1968), p. 112.

4.   Tony Schwartz, *The Responsive Chord* (New York: Anchor Books, Doubleday, 1974), p. 76.

5.   Joseph T. Klapper, *The Effects of Mass Communication* (Glencoe, IL: The Free Press, 1960), p. 111.

6.   David Halberstam, "President Video," *Esquire*, June 1975, p. 94.

7.   Klapper, *The Effects of Mass Communication*, p. 111.

8.   Myles Martel, "Political Campaign Debates," *The Journal of Political Action, Campaigns & Elections*, Winter 1984, p. 15.

9.   "How Television Failed the American Voter," *Seattle Post-Intelligencer*, January 11, 1981.

10. "Incredible Honest Ads Won For Lindsay," *Advertising Age*, November 10, 1969.

11. Ibid.

12. Conversation with Deak Davis, January 1950. Davis was a long-time lobbyist and philosopher who followed the Washington State legislative process.

13. Toni Delacorte, Judy Kimsey, and Susan Halas, *How To Get Free Press* (New York: Avon Books, 1981), p. 155.

14. Shadegg, *How to Win an Election*, p. 46.

15. "The Media Mesmerists," *Time*, October 20, 1978.

16. George Lois & Bill Pitts, *The Art of Advertising* (New York: Harry N. Abrams, 1977), pp. 104-107.

17. Elliot Roosevelt and James Brough, *The Untold Story: The Roosevelts at Hyde Park* (New York: Dell Publishing, 1973), pp. 53-56.

18. Ibid.

19. Jennifer Pendleton, "Vote Trail Ends with Harsh Talk," *Advertising Age*, June 4, 1984.

20. Diamond and Bates, *The Spot*, p. 326.

21. Norman Mailer, *Running Against the Machine* (New York: Doubleday, 1969), p. 294.

Chapter 29—Image Weak, Dull, or Unpopular? Change It or Use Someone Else's

1. Esar, *20,000 Quips & Quotes*, p. 563.

2. Harris, *The Fine Art of Political Wit*, p. 242.

3. John Gunther, *Taken at the Flood* (New York: Harper and Brothers, 1960), p. 76.

4. Jane Mayer, *The Wall Street Journal*, May 8, 1984.

5. Walter Weintz, "Republicans Find Lists," *Direct Marketing*, November 1972, p. 40.

6. James Michael Curley, *Boston Herald*, December 8, 1944.

7. Edward Heavey for Attorney General, Washington State Campaign Handbook, 1971.

8. Grant, "Bob Dole a Big Ad User," p. 69.

9. Diamond and Bates, *The Spot*, p. 314.

10. James W. Perry, "The Rockefeller Campaign Is the Biggest, Maybe the Best," *National Observer*, October 26, 1970.

11. Diamond and Bates, *The Spot*, pp. 328-329.

12. David Zimmerman, *USA Today*, December 21, 1983.

13. David M. Alpert, "Gamesmanship," *Newsweek*, November 20, 1978.

14. "Incredible Honest Ads Won for Lindsay," *Advertising Age*, November 5, 1969.

15. AP Dispatch, *Seattle Times*, October 18, 1979.

16. Goodman, "Getting Across with Advertising," p. 66.

Chapter 30—Comprehension, Targeting, Repetition, and Momentum

1. Quoted in McPhee, *The Book of Insults*, p. 69.

2. Prochnow and Prochnow, Jr., *A Treasury of Humorous Quotations*, p. 301.

3. Richard L. Gordon, "Political Shift," *Advertising Age*, September 1, 1980.

4. David Ogilvie, *Advertising Age*, August 1, 1983.

5. Jack Trout and Al Riess, *Advertising Age*, April 24, 1972.

6. Hank Parkinson, *Campaign Insight*, April, 1970, p. 4.

7. Stanley Kelley, Jr., *Professional Public Relations and Political Power* (Baltimore, Maryland: Johns Hopkins Press, 1966), p. 128.

8. Nick Thimmesch, "Obscene Vote Buying In West Virginia," *Seattle Times*, November 11, 1980.

9. Diamond and Bates, *The Spot*, 249-252.

10. J. V. Stewart, *Repetitive Advertising in Newspapers* (Hinsdale, IL: Dryden Press, 1973), p. 182.

11. Ernest Gruening, *Money Battles* (New York: Liveright, 1973), p. 511.

12. Schwartz, *The Responsive Chord*, p. 83.

13. Stewart Emmrich, "Candidates' T.V. Spots Start to Fill the Air," *Advertising Age*, January 24, 1984.

Chapter 31—Brochures, Pamphlets, or Tabloids

1. Malcolm S. Forbes, *Readers Digest*, May 1977, p. 77.
2. Frank Rowsome, Jr., *The Verse by the Side of the Road*, (Brattleboro, VT: Stephen Green Press, 1965), p. 68.
3. Leary, *Phantom Politics*.
4. Paul F. Healy, Nobody Loves Clarence, *Saturday Evening Post*, March 25, 1950, p. 38.
5. Bob Strong, "Graphics That Grab You," *Campaign Insight*, November 1974, p. 8.
6. Delacorte, Kimsey, and Halas, *How to Get Free Press*, p. 165.
7. William L. Roper, *Winning Politics* (Radnor, PA: Chilton Book Company, 1978), p. 122.
8. Bob Stone, "If You Can't Test Your Market, Follow These Principles," *Advertising Age*, August 3, 1970, pp. 41-42.
9. Delacorte, Kimsey, and Halas, *How to Get Free Press*, pp. 116-167.
10. Nimmo, *The Political Persuaders*, p. 126.
11. Cited in Matthew Josephson, *The Politicos, 1865-1896* (New York: Harcourt, Brace and World, 1938/1966), pp. 646-647.
12. Bob Donath, "Ford Agency Planning To Finish Strong With Ads," *Advertising Age*, November 18, 1976, p. 1.

Chapter 32—Persuasion Via the Printed Word

1. Prochnow and Prochnow, Jr., *A Treasury of Humorous Quotations*, p. 7.
2. *Winning Ideas For Political Advertisers* (New York: Bureau of Advertising, n.d.), pp. 1, 7.
3. Bernice Kanner, "TV vs. Print Study Finds Readers More Attentive," *Advertising Age*, August 7, 1978.
4. William Taylor, *Campaign Insight*, June 1963.
5. *Winning Ideas for Political Advertisers*, pp. 1, 7.
6. Ibid., p. 15.
7. David Ogilvy, *Confessions of an Advertising Man* (New York: Atheneum Publishers, 1963), p. 105.
8. John Caples, *Advertising Age*, April 10, 1978, p. 19.
9. John Sackheim, *My First 60 Years in Advertising* (Blue Ridge, PA: Tab Books, 1975), p. 180.
10. David Ogilvy, "Ogilvy on Advertising," *Advertising Age*, August 1, 1983.

Chapter 33—Politics Versus the Business of Broadcasting

1. Harry V. Wade, *A Treasury of Humorous Quotations* (New York: Harper and Row, 1969), p. 281.
2. Leary, *Phantom Politics*, p. 48.
3. Mickelson, *The Electric Mirror*, p. 93.

4.   Sherrill, *Gothic Politics*, p. 85.

5.   Burt Schorr, "The Rush For Political TV Time," *The Wall Street Journal*, May 26, 1976.

6.   Susan Spillman, "Radio Stations Cool to Politics," *Advertising Age*, February 20, 1984.

7.   Ibid.

8.   *Red Lion Broadcasting Co. v. Federal Communications Commission*, 395, U.S. 367, 1967.

9.   Schwartz, *The Responsive Chord*, p. 9.

10.   Delacorte, Kimsey, and Halas, *How To Get Free Press*, p. 163.

11.   "Time is Ripe for Radio Ad Growth," *Advertising Age*, May 29, 1978.

12.   Spillman, "Radio Stations Cool to Politics."

13.   Bernard Weintaub, "Radio Ads Have Become Big Ammunition," *New York Times*, Feb. 8, 1980.

14.   Radio Commercial, Re-elect Jackson U.S. Senator, KBAM Radio, September 30, 1982.

15.   Radio Advertising Bureau Inc., New York, 1969, p. 3.

16.   Schwartz, *The Responsive Chord*, pp. 90-91.

17.   Diamond and Bates, *The Spot*, p. 242.

18.   Malcolm D. MacDougall, *We Almost Made It* (New York: Crown, 1977, p. 21.

19.   Alfred L. Malabre, Jr., "Sick of the T.V. Ads for Politicians, You Reach for the Radio, You Get a Nasty Shock," *The Wall Street Journal*, May 15, 1972.

20.   Spillman, "Radio Stations Cool To Politics."

21.   Malabre, "Sick of the T.V. Ads.

22.   Sidney Yudain, *Roll Call*, Washington, DC, September 23, 1976, p. 21.

23.   Spillman, "Radio Stations Cool To Politics."

Chapter 34—Television

1.   Thomas E. Patterson and Robert D. McClure, *The Unseeing Eye: The Myth of Television Power in National Politics* (New York: G. P. Putnams Sons, 1976), p. 59.

2.   Donna Woolfork Cross, *Media Spark* (New York: McCann, 1983), p. 167.

3.   David Halberstam, "How Television Failed the American Voter," *Seattle Post-Intelligencer*, January 11, 1981.

4.   Ibid.

5.   Mickelson, *The Electric Mirror*, p. 104.

6.   Schwartzman, *Campaign Craftsmanship*, p. 164.

7.   Stewart Emmrich, "Newspapers Actively Seeking Politicians Vote—For Ad Buys," *Advertising Age*, December 12, 1983.

8.   Leary, *Phantom Politics*, p. 77.

9.   Diamond and Bates, *The Spot*, p. 308.

10.   "Brown Brings Show Biz to Wisconsin," *Advertising Age*, March 31, 1980.

11.   Jennifer Pendleton, "Vote Trail Ends With Harsh Talk," *Advertising Age*, June 4, 1984, p. 67.

12.   Joel Connelly, *Seattle Post Intelligencer*, October 24, 1984, p. 10A.

13. Fred L. Zimmerman, Message for the Media, *The Wall Street Journal*, May 10, 1972.

14. Robert Sam Anson, "The World According To Garth," *New Times*, October 30, 1978, p. 25.

15. Steinberg, *Political Campaign Management*, p. 11.

16. Zimmerman, "A Message For The Media," p. 33.

17. Leary, *Phantom Politics*, p. 88.

18. Bernard Weinroup, "Presidential Candidates Ponder," *Seattle Post Intelligencer*, February 17, 1980.

Chapter 35—Shake Hands With Every Voter Through the Mail Box

1. Shubek and Short, *Republican Humor*, p. 139.

2. Esar, *20,000 Quips & Quotes*, p. 497.

3. "Tinkham, the Mighty Hunter," *Time Magazine*, December 16, 1940, pp. 72-73.

4. *The Encyclopedia Americana*, 1960 ed. (Washington DC: Americana Corporation, 1960), p. 139.

5. Schwartzman, *Campaign Craftsmanship*, p. 208.

Chapter 36—The Magic of Personalization

1. James A. Farley, *Behind the Ballots: The Personal History of a Politician* (New York: Harcourt, Brace, 1938), pp. 192-193.

2. *Let's Talk About Running for Office*, p. 17.

3. *Campaign Insight*, 3(9), December 19, 1972.

4. Farley, *Behind the Ballots*, p. 193.

5. Sherrill, *Gothic Politics*, p. 123.

6. Robert Beuhler, "Reaching Voters By Mail," *Ways To Win* (Washington, DC: Republican National Committee, 1968), p. 79.

7. James M. Perry, "Almost Perfect Campaign," *The National Observer*, January 9, 1967.

8. Steinberg, *Political Campaign Management*, p. 179.

9. James M. Perry, "Wooing the Voters With a Computer," *The National Observer*, January 11, 1967.

10. Warren, *How to Win in Politics*, p. 128.

11. Martin Schram, *Running for President: A Journal of the Carter Campaign* (New York: Pocket Books, 1977), p. 28.

12. Perry, "The Rockefeller Campaign Is the Biggest, Maybe the Best."

13. Klapper, *The Effects of Mass Communication*, p. 80.

14. Carnegie, *How To Win Friends and Influence People*, p. 150.

15. J. K. Westerfield, *Readers Scope*, September 1947, p. 37.

16. Congressman George Bush, *Ways To Win* (Washington, DC: Republican National Committee, 1968), p. 30.

17. Perry, "The Rockefeller Campaign Is the Biggest, Maybe the Best."

18. Bill Adler, *The Reagan Wit* (Aurora, IL: Caroline House Publishers, 1981), p. 37.

19. Robert Buehler, "Reaching Voters By Mail," *Ways to Win* (Washington, DC: Republican National Committee, 1968), p. 79.

20. Stone, "If You Can't Test the Market," pp. 41-42.

21. *Let's Talk About Running For Office*, p. 17.

Chapter 37—Billboards

1. Lewis and Faye Copeland, *10,000 Jokes, Toasts, and Stories* (New York: Doubleday, 1965), p. 792.

2. Cited in Josephson, *The Politicos*, p. 647.

3. "The Low Priced Spread," *Forbes*, January 15, 1977, p. 64.

4. *The First Medium* (New York: Institute of Outdoor Advertising, 1974), p. 17.

5. *Advertising Age*, September 20, 1976.

6. "The Low Priced Spread," p. 64.

7. *The First Medium*, p. 17.

8. Ibid, p. 26.

9. James MacGregor Burns, *John Kennedy: A Political Profile* (New York: Avon Books, 1960), p. 115.

10. *The First Medium*, p. 20.

11. Ibid.

12. Ogilvy, "Ogilvy on Advertising," p. 14.

13. Clark Kissinger, *Members of Students for a Democratic Society vs. New York City Transit Authority*, 274 F. Supp. 438.

14. Ogilvy, "Ogilvy on Advertising," p. 49.

15. Goodman, "Getting Across With Advertising," p. 67.

Chapter 38—Yard and Roadside Campaign Signs

1. Rowsome, *The Verse by the Side of the Road*, p. 68.

2. Schwartz, *The Responsive Chord*, p. 82.

3. "Todd Appears To Be the Winner in Tukwila," *Seattle Times*, November 16, 1979, p. B-6.

4. Gary Yanker, *Prop Art* (New York: Darien House, Inc., 1972), p. 88.

Chapter 39—Designing, Assembling, and Posting Signs

1. Rowsome, *The Verse by the Side of the Road*, p. 68.

2. Myles Martel, "Political Campaign Debates," *The Journal of Political Action, Campaigns & Elections*, Winter 1984, p. 33.

Chapter 40—Automobile Signage

1. Shadegg, *How to Win an Election*, p. 69.

2. Ibid.

3. *Let's Talk About Campaigning* (New York: National Association of Manufacturers, 1968), p. 68.

4. Frady, *Wallace*, p. 123.

Chapter 41—The Idea File

1. Schwartzman, *Campaign Craftsmanship*, p. 160.
2. Jeff Wainscott, "Don't Neglect Opponent Research," *Campaign Insight*, October 7, 1972, p. 4.
3. Lois and Pitts, *The Art of Advertising*, pp. 104-107.
4. Steinberg, *The Bosses*, p. 78.
5. Shadegg, *How To Win an Election*, pp. 32-33.
6. Schwartzman, *Campaign Craftsmanship*, p. 72.
7. *Election Handbook on Radio Advertising* (New York: Radio Advertising Bureau, 1969), p. 10.
8. Delacorte, Kimsey, and Halas, *How to Get Free Press*, p. 161.
9. Schwartzman, *Campaign Craftsmanship*, p. 197.
10. "Gimmick Sales Off," *Campaign Insight*, October, 1972, p. 3.

Part 5—Anatomy of a Smear

Chapter 42—Fairness: Motivation and the Political Predator

1. Prochnow and Prochnow, Jr., *A Treasury of Humorous Quotations*, p. 21.
2. Gunther, *Inside the USA*, p. 34.
3. P-I News Services, *Seattle Post-Intelligencer*, September 15, 1984.
4. Martel, "Political Campaign Debates," p. 16.
5. Sherrill, *Gothic Politics*, p. 161.
6. Wainscott, "Don't Neglect Candidate Research," p. 1.
7. John Deardorff, "Researching Issues and the Opposition," *Ways to Win* (Washington DC: Republican National Committee, 1968), p. 92.
8. D. Duane Cummins, *Consensus and Turmoil: The 1950's and 1960's* (Mission Hills, CA: Benziger Publishing, 1972), p. 11.
9. "O'Connor: Machismo in Reverse," *Newsweek*, November 4, 1974, p. 27.
10. Baus and Ross, *Politics Battle Plan*, p. 152. Reprinted with the permission of Simon & Schuster, Inc., from *Politics Battle Plan* by Herbert M. Baus and William B. Ross. Copyright © by Herbert M. Baus and William B. Ross.
11. *New York Times v. Sullivan*, 84 S. Ct. 710, 1964; *Garrison v. Louisiana*, 379 U.S. 64, 1964.
12. William E. Miles, "Crazy Campaign Capers," *American Legion Magazine*, April 1980, pp. 14-15.
13. Maurine Christopher, *Advertising Age*, Chicago, Illinois, January 9, 1984.

Chapter 43—Packaging the Smear

1. Harris, *The Fine Art of Political Wit*, p. 130.
2. *Campaign Insight*, May 1, 1975, p. 6.
3. Mansfield, "Florida," in Alexander, *Campaign Money*, p. 50.
4. "The House: A Silver Lining for the Democrats," *Time*, November 19, 1984, p. 89.
5. Ertel, *How to Run for Office*, p. 10.

6.   Swanberg, *Citizen Hearst*, p. 229.
7.   David Burner, *Politics of Provincialism: The Democratic Party in Transition, 1918-32* (New York: W. W. Norton, 1975), p. 185.
8.   Ibid, pp. 183-184.
9.   Deardorff, "Researching Issues and the Opposition," p. 92.
10.   Jennifer Pendleton, "Vote Trail Ends with Harsh Talk," p. 67.
11.   George E. Mowry, *The California Progressives* (New York: New York Times Book Company, 1957), pp. 126-129.
12.   Truman, *Harry S. Truman*, pp. 13-15.
13.   Cited in Josephson, *The Politicos*, pp. 210-214, 373.

Chapter 44—Innuendo and Affirmative Ridicule

1.   Jackman, *Crown's Book of Political Quotations*, p. 192.
2.   Edwin P. Hoyt, *The Nixons, an American Family* (New York: Random House, 1972), pp. 261-262.
3.   "They Laughed When I Ran For Office—And I Am Glad," *Campaign Insight*, January 10, 1971.
4.   Diamond and Bates, *The Spot*, p. 177.
5.   "Taking Those Spot Shots," *Time*, September 29, 1980, p. 19.

Chapter 45—Opposition Research

1.   William H. Roylance, *Complete Book of Insults, Boasts and Riddles* (New York: Parker Publishing, 1972), p. 65.
2.   Richard Hofstader, *The American Political Tradition and the Men Who Made It* (New York: Vantage Books, 1974), pp. 148-149.
3.   Warren, *How to Win in Politics*, p. 24.
4.   Martel, "Political Campaign Debates," p. 22.
5.   Deardorff, "Researching Issues and the Opposition," p. 92.
6.   Shadegg, *How to Win an Election*, p. 76.
7.   Deardorff, "Researching Issues and the Opposition," p. 89.
8.   "The House: A Silver Lining for the Democrats—Sort Of," *Time*, November 19, 1984, p. 91.
9.   Deardorff, "Researching Issues and the Opposition," p. 89.
10.   Baus and Ross, *Politics Battle Plan*, p. 134.
11.   Ibid.
12.   Green and Calabrese, *Who Runs Congress?*, p. 176.
13.   Shadegg, *How To Win an Election*, p. 83.
14.   Wainscott, "Don't Neglect Opponent Research," p. 1.
15.   Nick Thimmesch, "Obscene Vote-Buying in West Virginia," *Seattle Times*, November 11, 1980.
16.   Charles Roberts, "This Way Out," *Reader's Digest*, May 1975, p. 82.
17.   Healy, "Nobody Loves Clarence," pp. 38-76.
18.   Shadegg, *How to Win an Election*, pp. 91-97.

Chapter 46—Backlash

1. Colombo, *Colombo's Hollywood*, p. 24.
2. Bernard Weinroup, "Presidential Candidates Wonder Where to Place Their TV Spots," *Seattle Post-Intelligencer*, February 17, 1980, p. 3.
3. Diamond and Bates, *The Spot*, pp. 332-333.
4. Miles, "Crazy Campaign Capers."
5. Cited in Josephson, *The Politicos*, pp. 207, 208, 365, 367, 368.
6. Murray B. Levin, *Kennedy Campaigning* (Boston, MA: Beacon Press, 1966), pp. 210-211.
7. Max McCarthy, *Elections for Sale* (Boston, MA: Houghton Mifflin, 1972), pp. 57-58.
8. Oklahoma Showdown, *The Wall Street Journal*, October 23, 1984.
9. Cummins, *Consensus and Turmoil*, p. 131.
10. *American Heritage Dictionary of the English Language* (New York: American Heritage Publishing, 1971), p. 809.
11. Cummins, *Consensus and Turmoil*, p. 131.

Chapter 47—Looking Piously Toward Heaven While Raising Hell

1. Quoted in McPhee, *The Book of Insults*, p. 131.
2. "Mud Flies in Carolina Senate Race," *Advertising Age*, May 16, 1977.
3. Maurice Carroll, "Koch Out in Street for Final Weekend," *New York Times*, November 6, 1977.
4. Information obtained by telephone from the Washington office of United States Senator Wendell Ford, Democrat, Kentucky, May 18, 1982.
5. Information gathered in Florida during the Peppers/Smathers campaign by Rubin Kline, *Miami Life* publisher.
6. Patterson and McClure, *The Unseeing Eye*, p. 119.
7. Nora Sayre, "Hollywood," *Seattle Times*, March 28, 1982.
8. John Wilson, "Heavy Gambling by O'Connell Widely Known," *Seattle Times*, October 14, 1968, p. 1.
9. John Wilson, "Gorton Suspends Top Aide Over Unauthorized Probe of Rosellini's Despicable Act of Political Espionage," *Seattle Times*, October 29, 1972.
10. John Wilson, "Dysert Tells His Version of Rosellini Past," *Seattle Times*, Oct. 20, 1972.
11. Burner, *The Politics of Provincialism*, p. 202.
12. Steinberg, *The Bosses*, p. 78.
13. Swanberg, *Citizen Hearst*, pp. 28, 81, 287.

Chapter 48—Reducing the Target or . . . the Fine Art of Being a Cautious Jellyfish

1. Esar, *20,000 Quips and Quotes*, p. 735.
2. Bert Randolph Sugar, *The Book of Sports Quotes* (New York: Quick Fox, 1979), p. 2.
3. Robert Orben, "Orben's Current Comedy," *Readers Digest*, February 1975, p. 71.

4.   Quoted in McPhee, *The Book of Insults*, p. 121.

6.   Bill Nichols, "The Choice: Rapscallion or Racist," *USA Today*, November 15-17, 1991, p. 2. Copyright 1991, USA Today. Reprinted with permission.

7.   James C. Hume, "Never Underestimate the Power of the Ploy," *Readers Digest*, July 1978, p. 34.

8.   "United States Senator John Chaffee," *Ways to Win* (Washington DC, Republican National Committee, 1968), p. 112.

9   "Larkin's Ads Called Deceptive by Rice," *Seattle Times*, October 25, 1978.

10.   Weisbord, *Campaigning for President*, p. 112.

11.   Cited in Matthew Josephson, *The President Makers: The Culture of Politics and Leadership in an Age of Enlightenment, 1896-1919* (New York: Frederick Ungar Publishing Co., 1940/1964), pp. 166-167.

12.   Safire, *Safire's Political Dictionary*, p. 124.

13.   Weisbord, *Campaigning for President*, p. 227.

14.   "Reagan Winner of Doublespeak Award," *Seattle Times*, November 22, 1980.

15.   Stephen Hill and Milton Kaplan, *The Ungentlemanly Art* (New York: MacMillan Company, 1968), p. 126. Reprinted with the permission of Simon & Schuster, Inc., from *The Ungentlemanly Art: A History of American Political Cartoons* by Stephen Hess and Milton Kaplan. Copyright © by Stephen Hess and Milton Kaplan.

16.   Clarence L. Townes, "The Minority Voter," *Ways To Win* (Washington, DC: Republican National Committee, 1968), p. 116.

17.   Bill Adler, "They Get Along Like Two Peeves in a Pod," *Readers Digest*, August 1976, p. 89.

18.   Kevin Cash, *Who the Hell Is William Loeb?* (Manchester, NH: Amoskeag Press, 1976), Appendix A.

Chapter 49—Change-of-Pace Ridicule

1.   Quoted in McPhee, *The Book of Insults*, p. 128.

2.   Harris, *The Fine Art of Political Wit*, pp. 146-149.

3.   Martel, "Political Campaign Debates, p. 26.

4.   Robert Sam Anson, "The World According to Garth," *New Times*, October 30, 1978, p. 25.

5.   Healy, "Nobody Loves Clarence," p. 76.

6.   Warren, *How to Win in Politics*, pp. 62-66.

7.   Grant, "Bob Dole a Big Ad User in 13 Election Victories," p. 68.

8.   Quoted in McPhee, *The Book of Insults*, p. 124.

9.   Ibid.

10.   Warren, *How to Win in Politics*, p. 173.

11.   Baus and Ross, *Politics Battle Plan*, p. 261. Reprinted with the permission of Simon & Schuster, Inc., from *Politics Battle Plan* by Herbert M. Baus and William B. Ross. Copyright © by Herbert M. Baus and William B. Ross.

12.   Josh Lee, *How to Hold an Audience Without a Rope* (Chicago & New York: Davis Publishing Co., 1947), pp. 137-138.

13.   Charles Edmundson, "How Kefauver Beat Crump," *Harper's Magazine*, January 1949, p. 83.

14. Charles A. Johnson, *Denver's Mayor Speer* (Denver: Big Horn Books, Green Mountain Press, 1969), p. 145.

15. Quoted in McPhee, *The Book of Insults*, p. 121.

16. Cited in Josephson, *The Politicos*, p. 247.

17. Diamond and Bates, *The Spot*, p. 370.

18. David Sherebman, "Reaganomics in Connecticut: Race for Congress Is Replay," *The Wall Street Journal*, October 25, 1984, p. 64.

Part 6—News as a Political Tool

Chapter 50—The Media

1. Harold Lamb, *Omar Khayyam* (New York: Doubleday, 1978), p. 109.

2. Mickelson, *The Electric Mirror*, p. 112.

3. Austin Ranney, "The Real Election Will Be on Television," *USA Today*, January 31, 1984.

4. Chief Justice Earl Warren, *Memoirs Of Earl Warren* (Garden City, NY: Doubleday, 1977), p. 161.

5. Thomas Houser, *Selling The Candidate: Ways To Win* (Washington, DC: Republican National Committee, 1967), p. 135.

6. Leary, *Phantom Politics*, pp. 54-58.

7. Ibid.

8. Ibid.

9. "Taking Those Spot Shots," *Time*, September 2, 1980.

10. Ibid.

11. Leary, *Phantom Politics*, pp. 58-59.

12. Ibid.

13. Ibid.

14. Wheeler, *Lies, Damn Lies and Statistics*, p. 202.

15. Leary, *Phantom Politics*, p. 51.

16. Ibid.

17. Ibid.

18. "Taking Those Spot Shots," *Time*, September 2, 1980.

19. Leary, *Phantom Politics*, p. 54.

20. Ibid.

21. Ibid.

22. Alfred L. Malabre, Jr., "Sick of the T.V. Ads for Politicians, You Reach For the Radio," *The Wall Street Journal*, May 15, 1972.

23. Schorr, "The Rush for Political TV Time."

Chapter 51—Publicity Mechanics

1. Colombo, *Colombo's Hollywood*, p. 112.

2. Delacorte, Kimsey, and Halas, *How To Get a Free Press*, p. 156.

3. Ibid, p. 153.

4. Allan P. Sindler, *Huey Long's Louisiana State Politics, 1920-1952.* (Baltimore, Maryland: Johns Hopkins Paperback, 1971), p. 143.

5. Jeff Greenfields, *Playing to Win: An Insider's Guide to Politics* (New York: Simon & Schuster, 1980), pp. 139-140.

6. Leary, *Phantom Politics*, p. 53.

7. Richard T. Fleming, *Ways To Win* (Washington, DC: Republican National Committee, 1968), p. 102.

8. Stanley E. Cohen, *Advertising Age*, June 27, 1983, p. 24.

9. Albert R. Hunt, *The Wall Street Journal*, May 20, 1977.

10. Leary, *Phantom Politics*, p. 53.

11. Susan Parker, John Lindsay, and Henry W. Hubbard, "Fresh Faces of '78," *Newsweek*, March 20, 1978.

12. Leary, *Phantom Politics*, pp. 17-18.

13. Ibid.

14. Iginas Giyserm, *Ways To Win* (Washington, DC: Republican National Committee, 1977), p. 17.

15. Delacorte, Kimsey, and Halas, *How To Get Free Press*, pp. 159-160.

16. Leary, *Phantom Politics*, p. 53.

17. Wheeler, *Lies, Damn Lies and Statistics*, p. 208.

18. "Carter Still Plans to Make Seattle Tonight," *Seattle Times*, November 3, 1980.

19. Wheeler, *Lies, Damn Lies and Statistics*, p. 208.

20. Jackson, A Senator's Advice.

21. Wheeler, *Lies, Damn Lies and Statistics*, p. 202.

22. Reeves, *A Ford, Not a Lincoln*, p. 20.

23. Charlotte Perry, *Los Angeles Times*, April 2, 1980.

24. David Halberstam, "How Television Failed the American Voter."

25. Leary, *Phantom Politics*, p. 62.

26. Sherrill, *Gothic Politics*, pp. 156-157.

27. Schwartz, *The Responsive Chord*, p. 98.

28. Delacorte, Kimsey and Halas, *How to Get Free Press*, pp. 161-162.

29. Warren, *How to Win in Politics*, pp. 54-55.

30. Herb Robinson, "Monthly Awards to Honor the Best of Reader Mail," *Seattle Times*, January 13, 1985.

31. Harvey Yorke and Liz Doherty, *The Candidate's Handbook For Winning Local Elections* (Novato, CA: Harvey Yorke, 1982), p. 54.

32. Herb Robinson, *Seattle Times*, January 13, 1985.

33. Paul M. DeGroot, *Seattle Times*, October 21, 1979.

Chapter 52—Organizing Public Relations

1. Jane Mayer, "Hart's Press Chief Focuses on Strategy and Issues," *The Wall Street Journal*, April 10, 1984.

2. Robert Zimmerman, *Ways To Win* (Washington, DC: Republican National Committee, 1968), p. 70.

3. Hank Parkinson, *Campaign Insight*, June 1976.

4. Ibid.

5. Ibid.

6. Leary, *Phantom Politics*, p. 27.

7. Clarence L. Townes, *Ways To Win* (Washington, DC: Republican National Committee, 1968), p. 12.

8. Mel Grayson, *Advertising Age*, March 19, 1973

9. Hank Parkinson, *Campaign Insight*, June 1970.

10. Clarence L. Townes, Jr., *Ways To Win* (Washington, DC: Republican National Committee, 1968), p. 122.

11. "Stein Questions Wagner's Links," *New York Times*, November 6, 1977.

12. Henry Bellmon, *Ways To Win* (Washington, DC: Republican National Committee, 1968), p. 97.

13. Lynn Nofziger, *Ways To Win* (Washington, DC: Republican National Committee, 1968), p. 164.

14. Casey Corr, "College Professors Given Hints on Handling Press," *Seattle Post-Intelligencer*, March 3, 1984.

15. Carol H. Falk, "GOP's Own TV Tutor Teaches Candidates," *The Wall Street Journal*, October 20, 1970.

16. Ibid.

17. Patterson and McClure, *The Unseeing Eye*, p. 98.

18. Falk, "GOP's Own TV Tutor Teaches Candidates."

19. Falk, "GOP's Own TV Tutor Teaches Candidates."

20. Burns, *John Kennedy: A Political Profile*, p. 217.

21. Allan P. Sindler, *Huey Long's Louisiana State Politics, 1920-1952* (Baltimore, MD: Johns Hopkins, 1971), p. 143.

22. Burns, *John Kennedy: A Political Profile*, p. 218.

23. Lynn Nofziger, *Ways To Win* (Washington, DC: Republican National Committee, 1968), p. 164.

24. Jane Mayer, "Hart's Press Chief Focuses on Strategy," *The Wall Street Journal*, April 10, 1984.

Chapter 53—The Perils of Provocation

1. Prochnow and Prochnow, Jr., *The Public Speakers' Treasure Chest*, p. 199.

2. Colombo, *Colombo's Hollywood*, p. 82.

3. Leary, *Phantom Politics*, pp. 47-48.

4. "Mayor's Non-Campaign Campaign," *The New York Times*, November 6, 1977.

5. "Bomb Scare," *Seattle Times*, August 14, 1984.

6. Margaret M. Heckler, "Through Leaders and Special Interest Groups," p. 105.

7. Warren, *Memoirs of Earl Warren*, pp. 164-165.

8. James Thomas Flexner, *Washington, the Indispensable Man* (Boston: Little, Brown, 1974).

9. Joseph H. Cooper, *The Wall Street Journal*, February 21, 1984.

10. Baus and Ross, *Politics Battle Plan*, p. 311. Reprinted with the permission of Simon & Schuster, Inc., from *Politics Battle Plan* by Herbert M. Baus and William B. Ross. Copyright © by Herbert M. Baus and William B. Ross.

11. Baus and Ross, *Politics Battle Plan*, pp. 314-315.

12. Swanberg, *Citizen Hearst*, p. 298.

13. Baus and Ross, *Politics Battle Plan*, p. 311. Reprinted with the permission of Simon & Schuster, Inc., from *Politics Battle Plan* by Herbert M. Baus and William B. Ross. Copyright © by Herbert M. Baus and William B. Ross.

14. Jeff Greenfield, *Playing To Win* (New York: Simon & Schuster, 1980), p. 134.

15. Roper, *Winning Politics*, p. 108.

16. Jane Mayer, *The Wall Street Journal*, April 10, 1984.

17. Kevin Cash, *Who the Hell Is William Loeb?* (Manchester, NH: Amoskeag Press, 1975), Epilogue, Appendix A, pp. 16, 17, 18, xix, xx, xxi.

18. Richard Smith and Edward Decter, *Oops!* (New York: Rutledge Press, 1981).

19. Jeff Greenfield, *Playing to Win* (New York: Simon & Schuster, 1980), p. 151.

Part 7—Political Strategy

Chapter 54—Examples of Strategic Technique

1. Steinberg, *Political Campaign Management*, p. 64.

2. Shadegg, *How to Win an Election*, p.43.

3. Donald Delano Wright, "President Taft Was Gored By The Bull Moose," *Seattle Times*, September 9, 1984.

4. Winthrop Griffith, *Humphrey: A Candid Biography* (New York: William Morrow & Co., 1965), p. 115.

5. Martel, "Political Campaign Debates," p. 16.

6. Griffith, *Humphrey, A Candid Biography*, p. 115.

7. Gunther, *Inside the USA*, p. 427.

8. The Media Mesmerists, *Time Magazine*, October 20, 1978.

9. Cited in Safire, *Safire's Political Dictionary*, p. 429.

10. Diamond and Bates, *The Spot*, pp. 212-213.

11. Martel, "Political Campaign Debates," p. 25.

Chapter 55—Trends, Time, and Momentum

1. Adler, *The Reagan Wit*, p. 32.

2. Ertel, *How to Run for Office*, p. 66.

3. Diamond and Bates, *The Spot*, pp. 267-268.

4. Cited in Safire, *Safire's Political Dictionary*, p. 525.

5. Ibid.

6. Ibid.

7. James Perry, *The National Observer*, January 9, 1967.

8. Baus and Ross, *Politics Battle Plan*, pp. 118-135. Reprinted with the permission of Simon & Schuster, Inc., from *Politics Battle Plan* by Herbert M. Baus and William B. Ross. Copyright © by Herbert M. Baus and William B. Ross.

9. Burns, *John Kennedy: A Political Profile*, p. 217.

10. John A. Burgess, "Debunking the Expert," *The Association of Trial Lawyers of America*, 1976.

11. Grant, "Bob Dole a Big Ad User in 13 Election Victories," p. 69.

12. Pat Sloan and David Snyder, "Reagan Team Opening Blitz Hails America," *Advertising Age*, May 21, 1984.

13. Goodman, Getting Across With Advertising, p. 61.
14. John Gunther, *Roosevelt in Retrospect* (New York: Pyramid Books, 1961), p. 323.
15. Ertel, *How to Run for Office*, pp. 66-67.
16. Wheeler, *Lies, Damn Lies and Statistics*, p. 277.
17. Delacorte, Kimsey, and Halas, *How to Get Free Press*, p. 150.
18. Grant, "Bob Dole a Big Ad User in 13 Election Victories," p. 68.
19. Schwartzman, *Campaign Craftsmanship*, p. 208.
20. "Ticket Splitters: A New Face in American Politics, 1970," *Campaign Insight*, 1974, p. 8.
21. Diamond and Bates, *The Spot*, p. 289.
22. "Gimmicks That Work," *Campaign Insight*, November 1972, p. 6.

Chapter 56—Issues

1. Dudden, *Pardon Us, Mr. President*, p. 405.
2. Martel, "Political Campaign Debates," p. 18.
3. "Got Your Message," *Time*, November 20, 1978, p. 16.
4. John Hay, "The Battle of the Image Men," *Maclean's*, August 6, 1984.
5. Ertel, *How to Run for Office*, p. 96.
6. Jack J. Honomichl, "The Marketing of A Candidate," *Advertising Age*, December 15, 1980, p. 66.
7. James Perry, *The National Observer*, January 9, 1967.
8. Bob Donath, "From Plains to President," *Advertising Age*, November 8, 1976.
9. Roy Cohen, *McCarthy* (New York: The New American Library, 1968), p. 8.
10. Baus and Ross, *Politics Battle Plan*, p. 332. Reprinted with the permission of Simon & Schuster, Inc., from *Politics Battle Plan* by Herbert M. Baus and William B. Ross. Copyright © by Herbert M. Baus and William B. Ross.
11. Jack Trout and Al Ries, *The Positioning Era* [a slide presentation] (New York: Ries-Cappiello Caldwell, 1972), slides 19, 20, 21, & 22.

Chapter 57—Voter Loyalty Versus Ticket-Splitter Strategy

1. *Abstract of the United States, 1981* (U.S. Bureau of Census, Current Population Reports), p. 25.
2. George J. Church, *Time*, November, 19, 1984.
3. "Ernest Dichter, Motive Interpreter," *Journal of Advertising Research*, June, 1977, p. 6.
4. Richard Scammon, *Newsweek*, October, 25, 1971, p. 41.
5. Ertel, *How to Run for Office*, p. 60.
6. Morton Keller, *The Art and Politics of Thomas Nast* (London: Oxford University Press, 1968), p. 127.
7. O'Donnell, *Ways To Win*, p. 21.
8. "Excerpts from U.S. Census Bureau 1970 Census," *Area Mechanics*, February 8, 1971.
9. Farney, "A Modern Machine," p. 22.
10. Burner, *The Politics Of Provincialism*, p. 134.

11. Mowry, *The California Progressives*, pp. 102-104.
12. Gunther, *Inside the USA*, p. 420.
13. *Information Please Almanac Atlas and Yearbook*, 29th ed., 1975, p. 53.
14. Safire, *Safire's Political Dictionary*, p. 678.
15. Richard Scammon and Ben J. Whittenberg, *The Real Majority* (New York: Coward-McCann, 1970), p. 21.
16. "The Bell Tolls For Case," *Time*, June 19, 1978.
17. Mowry, *The California Progressives,* pp. 102-104.
18. Cited in Josephson, *The Politicos*, p. 654.
19. Baus and Ross, *Politics Battle Plan*, p. 195. Reprinted with the permission of Simon & Schuster, Inc., from *Politics Battle Plan* by Herbert M. Baus and William B. Ross. Copyright © by Herbert M. Baus and William B. Ross.
20. Patterson and McClure, *The Unseeing Eye*, p. 97.
21. Baus and Ross, *Politics Battle Plan*, p. 234.
22. Steinberg, *Political Campaign Management*, p. 36.
23. S. E. Asch, *Social Psychology* (New York: Prentice Hall, 1952), p. 127.
24. *U.S. News and World Report*, September 18, 1978, p. 41.
25. "Wake Up Call," *Time*, November 18, 1991, p. 23.
26. Stoddard, *Presidential Sweepstakes*, pp. 75-76, 151.
27. Devries and Terrance, Jr., *The Ticket Splitters*, pp. 74-101.
28. Adler, *The Washington Wits*, p. 219.

Chapter 58—The Complex World of Economic Interests

1. Jackman, *Crown Books Political Quotations*, p. 1.
2. Ibid, p. 171.
3. Howard Kandal, *The Power of Positive Pessimism* (Los Angeles: Price Stern Slone, 1976), p. 16.
4. Peter Frances, *Advertising Age*, September 20, 1984.
5. Patricia Krause, *Target '76* (Washington, DC: Democratic National Committee Consultation Program, 1976), p. 12.
6. Burns, *John Kennedy: A Political Profile*, p. 127.
7. Perry, "The Rockefeller Campaign is the Biggest, Maybe the Best," p. 19.
8. Diamond and Bates, *The Spot*, p. 271.
9. Amram M. Ducovny, *I Want To Make One Thing Perfectly Clear* (New York: Ballantine Books, 1971), p. 18.
10. James C. Hume, *Speaker's Treasury of Anecdotes About the Famous* (New York: Harper and Row, 1978), p 47-48.
11. "No; Seriously; I Want You to Look at the Camera and Say, 'Ride with Me, Wyoming!' " *Washington Monthly*, July-August 1980.
12. Diamond and Bates, *The Spot*, pp. 298-299.
13. Klapper, *The Effects of Mass Communication*, p. 101.
14. Richard Thruelsen, "When Michigan Woke Up, He Was Governor," *Saturday Evening Post*, February 12, 1948, p. 26.
15. Bradford Morse, "Winning in a Democrat District," *Ways To Win* (Washington, DC: Republican National Committee, 1968), p. 146.

16. Arlene J. Large, "A Different View of Voter Apathy," *The Wall Street Journal*, November 2, 1972, p. 14.

17. Ibid.

18. Shadegg, *How to Win an Election*, page 91.

19. Baus and Ross, *Politics Battle Plan*, p. 217.

Chapter 59—The Politics of Diversity (Age, Gender, Race, Ethnics, Religion, Etc.)

1. Jackman, *Crown's Book of Political Quotations*, p. 1.

2. "Excerpts from U.S. 1970 Census Bureau: Those Who Gripe the Most Usually Vote the Least," *Aero Mechanics*, February 8, 1971,

3. *The Wall Street Journal*, December 4, 1976.

4. Ellen Hume, "Big Man On Campus: Hart Revives Student Activism," *The Wall Street Journal*, March 12, 1984.

5. "Voter Turnout by Age Groups," *Campaign Insight*, August 1, 1975.

6. Burner, *The Politics of Provincialism*, p. 134.

7. Ellen Hume, "Some Women Politicians are Backing Away from Feminist Label to Expand Base of Support, Politics and Policy," *The Wall Street Journal*, April 3, 1985, p. 60.

8. "Anita and the Gays," *Newsweek*, March 13, 1975, p. 14.

9. Dave Martin, "Ex Madam Now Mayor Expects to be President in Next Life," *Los Angeles Times*, November 16, 1977.

10. Hume, "Some Women Politicians are Backing Away,", p. 60.

11. Ibid.

12. Ibid.

13. Ibid.

14. Ibid.

15. Mimi Hall, "Women Hope to Have Political Impact," *USA Today*, July 12, 1991, p. 8A.

16. Kevin B. Phillips, *The Emerging Republican Majority* (Garden City, New York: Doubleday Anchor Books, 1970), p. 105.

17. Bill Nichols, "Denver's New Mayor Puts Best Foot Forward—Because He Had To." *USA Today*, June 20, 1991, p. F1.

18. Bill Nichols, "Fence Sitters Are Quarry in Louisiana Gov's Brawl," *USA Today*, November 4, 1991.

19. Burner, *The Politics of Provincialism*, p. 233.

20. Swanberg, *Citizen Hearst*, p. 278.

21. Gunther, *Inside the USA*, p. 116.

22. Ducovny, *I Want To Make One Thing Perfectly Clear*, p. 18.

23. Sherrill, *Gothic Politics*, p. 163.

24. Matt Moffett, "Media Consultant Sosa Tailors the Pitch of GOP Candidates to Gain Hispanics," *The Wall Street Journal*, June 24, 1985.

25. Ibid.

26. Keith W. Jennson, *Humorous Mr. Lincoln* (New York: Bonanza Books, 1969), p. 40.

27. Burner, *The Politics of Provincialism*, p. 202.

28. Alan Baron, *The Baron Report*, Washington, DC, February 24, 1984.

29. Bill Nichols, "Electionline," *USA Today*, July 9, 1988.

30. Sherrill, *Gothic Politics*, pp. 92-93.

31. "Robert Shun, Party Lines: The New Realism News," *Time*, October 30, 1978, p. 6.

32. George J. Church, "Politics From The Pulpit," *Time*, October 13, 1980.

33. UPI Dispatch, "IRS Let's Church Publish Congress Voting Records," *San Diego Union*, October 9, 1980, AP2.

34. Michael Days, "Jackson Mobilizes Churchgoers," *The Wall Street Journal*, April 10, 1984.

35. Hal Avery, "Running for Office? Start Now," *Roll Call* [Capitol Hill newspaper, Washington, DC], January 21, 1971, p. 8.

36. Gunther, *Inside the USA*, p. 480.

37. Lois and Pitts, *The Art of Advertising*, pp. 104-106.

38. Floyd M. Clay, "Twelve Years," *Time*, January 29, 1940, p. 23.

Chapter 60—The Coattail Mystique

1.   Cited in Safire, *Safire's Political Dictionary*, p. 125.

2.   Klapper, *The Effects of Mass Communication*, pp. 99-103.

3.   Cited in Safire, *Safire's Political Dictionary*, p. 125.

4.   Lois and Pitts, *The Art of Advertising*, pp. 104-107.

5.   Lois and Pitts, *The Art of Advertising*, pp. 104-107.

6.   John Bosworth, *Ways To Win In Politics* (Jackson, MS: Confederate Book House, 1969), p. 95.

7.   David Zimmerman, *USA Today*, December 21, 1983.

8.   Klapper, *The Effects of Mass Communication*, pp. 99-103.

9.   Harry Stein, "What Makes Andy and Bobby Run?" *New York Times*, November 6, 1977, p. 47.

10. I. Lynn Mueller, "Political Direct Mail Can Be Useful Candidate Tools," *Direct Marketing*, February, 1971, pp. 31, 32.

11. Senator John Chaffee, *Ways To Win* (Washington, DC: Republican National Committee, 1968), pp. 112-114.

12. S. L. Sanger, "Hello, America, Harvey Doesn't Back Garner," *Seattle Post-Intelligencer*, September 28, 1978.

13. Pendleton, "Vote Trail Ends With Harsh Talk," p. 67.

Chapter 61—Opportunism, Deception, Commitment, and Morality

1.   John Robert Colombo, *Colombo's Concise Canadian Quotations* (Edmonton, Alberta: Hutig Publishers, 1976), p. 175.

2.   Quoted in McPhee, *Book of Insults*, p. 118.

3.   John Morley, *Braude's Handbook for Toastmasters* (Englewood Cliffs, NJ: Prentice Hall, 1957), p. 271.

4.   Cummins, *Consensus and Turmoil*, p. 105.

5.   Lynn Mueller, "Political Direct Mail Can Be Useful Tool!," *Direct Marketing*, Garden City, NY, 1971).

6.   Burner, *The Politics Of Provincialism*, p. 128.

7.   Ibid.

8.   William Albin, *Public Opinion* (New York: McGraw Hill, 1939), p. 217.

9.   Gordon Alport and Leo J. Postman, *Transactions of the New York Academy of Sciences*, vol. 8, series II, pp. 61-81.

10.   Bradford Morse, *Ways to Win* (Washington, DC: Republican National Committee, 1968), p. 147.

11.   Margaret M. Heckler, Through Leaders and Special Interest Groups, p. 109.

12.   Kent, *The Great Game of Politics*, p. 198.

13.   Sherrill, *Gothic Politics*, pp. 162-163.

14.   Louis Nizer, *Thinking on Your Feet* (New York: Pyramid Books, 1963), p. 139.

15.   Gunther, *Roosevelt in Retrospect*, p. 323.

16.   Marci   Whitney,   "Notable   Women,"   *Tacoma   News   Tribune*   [Tacoma, Washington], 1977, pp. 38-39.

17.   Edwin Guthman [editor of *Philadelphia Inquirer*], "Segregation Now," *Seattle Times*, June 1, 1983.

Part 8—Reporting, Regulation, and Taxation of Campaign Funds

Chapter 62—Public Disclosure

1.   Ross Cunningham, "Why Incumbent Candidates Keep Getting   Re-elected," *Seattle Times*, September 20, 1976.

2.   Polczinski, "Kansas," in Alexander, *Campaign Money*, p. 162.

3.   *Newsberry v. the United States*, 256 U.S. 232 (1921).

4.   James C. Kerby, Jr., "Congress and the Public Trust," *Report of the Association of the Bar of the City of New York*, 1970, p. 120. The Supreme Court upheld the constitutionality of this act in *Burroughs v. United States*, 290 US 534 (1934).

5.   Michael Kallenbach, "Britain's Liberal party," *Advertising Age*, January 25, 1974.

6.   18 USC 610-611 (see 1.93-1.130).

7.   Adamany and Agree, *Political Money*, pp. 36-48; Burt Neuborne and Arthur Eisenberg, *The Rights of Candidates and Voters* (New York: Avon Books, 1976), p. 124; Thayer, *Who Shakes The Money Tree?*, p. 131.

8.   David W. Adams and George E. Agree, *Political Money* (Baltimore: John Hopkins University Press, 1976), p. 48.

9.   11 CF Section 100.2(b), 40 Fed Reg 44698.

10.   Alexander, *Money in Politics*, p. 189.

11.   2 U.S.C. 441d and 11 CFR 110.11(a).

12.   AO 1982-2; AO 1982-29.

13.   Ibid.

14.   AO 1978-66.

15. 11 Code of Federal Regulation, S102.9(a)(1).

16. 11 Code of Federal Regulation, S110.4(c)(2).

17. Susan Littwin, "How The West's Best Fund Raiser Gets His Hand In Your Pocket," *New West*, December 6, 1976, p. 32.

18. Polczinski, "Kansas," in Alexander, *Campaign Money*, p. 184.

19. Code of Federal Regulations 104.5F.

20. Code of Federal Regulations, 104.5(a).

21. Curtis C. Sprout, "Federal Law Regulating Campaign Activity," *The Law of Politics on Federal & California Fair Political Practices and Election Laws*, Berkeley, CA, 1977, p. 13.

22. Code of Federal Regulations, 114.12(b).

23. Code of Federal Regulations, 114.4.

24. *Federal Election Commission* AD 1984-43, November 1984, p. 4.

25. 11 CFR 104.3(h), 11 CFR 100.7(b)(14).

26. 18 USC Sections 610-611 (see Sections 1.100-1.102 & 1.123-1.125).

27. *Federal Election Commission*, AO 1984-36, September, 1984, pp. 6 & 7.

28. 11 Code of Federal Regulations, S114.12(c)(1).

29. 11 Code of Federal Regulations, S100.4(b)(2).

30. 11 Code of Federal Regulations, S100.4(b)(5); 11 Code of Federal Regulations, S100.4(s)(i)(iii)(A).

31. *Federal Election Commission Record*, AO 1979-52, December, 1979, p. 4.

32. *Federal Election Commission Record*, AO 1984-24, September 1984, p. 7; AO 1984-37, September 1984.

Chapter 63—News, Publicity, and Public Disclosure

1. *Federal Election Commission Record*, AOR 1976-29, November 1977, p. 3.

2. *Federal Election Commission Record*, AO 1978-60, October 1978.

3. 11 CFR 110.7(b)(4).

4. 11 CFR 100.7(b)(15) and 100.8(b)(16).

5. 11 CFR 100.7(b)(9) and 100.8(b)(10).

6. 11 CFR 100.7(b)(17), 100.8(b)(18), and 106.1(c)(3).

7. *Federal Election Commission Record*, AOR 1976-65, January 1977.

Chapter 64—Impact of the U.S. Supreme Court on Disclosure Legislation

1. *Buckley v. Valeo*, 424 U.S. 1. 96 Sup. Ct. 612, 1976.

2. *Federal Election Commission Record*, C.R.F. Code 110.10B, Section 44, AOR 1976-84, 1977, p. 4.

3. Thimmesch, "Obscene Vote-Buying in West Virginia."

4. *Buckley v. Valeo*, 424 U.S. 1. 96 Sup. Ct. 612, 1976.

5. *First National Bank v. Bellotti*, 435 U.S. 763, 1978.

6. *Federal Election Commission Record*, AD 1984-22, August, 1984, p. 4.

7. *Buckley v. Valeo*, 424 U.S. 1. 96 Sup. Ct. 612, 1976.

8. 11 CFR 104.3(b)(3)(vii)(B) and 109.2(a)(1).

9. 11 CFR 110.4(b).

10. 11 CFR 10 2.9(a)(3).

11. Richard J. Whalen, *The Founding Fathers* (New York: New American Library, 1964).

12. Dick Schaap, *Steinbrenner* (New York: G. Putnam, 1982), p. 138.

Chapter 65—The Internal Revenue Service

1. Ralph L. Woods, *The Modern Handbook of Humor* (New York: McGraw Hill, 1976, p. 112.

2. IRS TI 1125, December 17, 1971.

3. IRS TIR No. 1145, February 23, 1972.

4. IRS Sec. 527(c)(1), 13.33-13.34.

5. *McDonald v. Commissioner of Internal Revenue*, 1944 323 US 57.

6. AC Code 374.

7. Rev RU1 76-64, 1976 *Int Rev Bull* No. 9 or 8.

8. Stuart J. Offer, article in *The Law of Politics on Federal & California Fair Political Practices & Election Laws* (Berkeley, CA), 1977, p. 650.

9. IRC Sections 41(c)(1), 501(c)(5).

10. Reg Section 1.41-2(d)(4)(ii), 37 Fed Reg 19143 (1972).

11. Stuart J. Offer, article in *The Law of Politics on Federal & California Fair Political Practices & Election Laws* (Berkeley, CA), 1977, p. 648-649.

12. The Federal Corrupt Practices Act (18 USC Section 610).

13. *Pipefitters Local 562 v. United States* (1972) 407 US 385, Sections 1.89-1.91.

14. *Rev Rul* 62-156, 1962-2 *Cum Bull* 47.

15. "How 3M Got Tangled Up in Politics," *New York Times*, March 9, 1975.

16. 26 U.S.C. 271.

17. IRC Section 120(d), INC Section 57(a)(9).

18. Form 1120-POL.

19. Stuart J. Offer, article in *The Law of Politics on Federal & California Fair Political Practices & Election Laws* (Berkeley, CA), 1977, p. 660.

20. Boyarsky, *Backroom Politics*, p. 117.

21. Raines, "Georgia," in Alexander, *Campaign Money*, p. 219.

22. Washington State RCW 42.17.090, CFR Section 114.10.

23. 11 CFR Section 113.2 and 41 IRC Section 527(b).

24. Opinion of the Federal Election Commission, AO 1978-87, January 1979, p. 2.

25. *Campaign Guide for Congressional Candidates and Committees*, Federal Election Commission, 1982, p. 17.

26. Dean Katz, "Funds for Magnuson or Campaign Debt?" *Seattle Times*, March 29, 1981.

27. Opinion, Federal Election Commission, May 1978, p. 4.

Part 9—Making the Decision

Chapter 66—To Run or Not to Run? Making the Decision

1. Sam Levenson, *You Can Say That Again, Sam* (New York: Pocket Books, 1975), p. 99.

2. Esar, *20,000 Quips & Quotes*, p. 563.

3.   "Costly Advice: Even Losers Win Big When Their Business Is Counseling Candidates," *Wall Street Journal*, June 7, 1988.

4.   Richard Shenkman and Kurt Reiger, *One Night Stands with American History* (New York: William Morrow, 1980), p. 83.

5.   "USA Snap Shots: A Look at Statistics That Shape the Nation." *USA Today*, May 20, 1992.

6.   "Traditional Values Play Well on Campaign," *USA Today*, January 16, 1992, p. 5A.

7.   "Gay Candidates in Close Race for NYC Council," *USA Today*, September 11, 1991, p. 2.

8.   Cited in Safire, *Safire's Political Dictionary*, pp. 767-768.

9.   David Rogers, "Windy City Democrats, Victims of Redistricting Swap Bitter Blasts as Political Traditions Clash," *The Wall Street Journal*, Thursday, March 12, 1992, Politics and Policy section, p. 14.

10.   Quoted in McPhee, *The Book of Insults*, p. 71.

11.   Gunther, *Inside the USA*, p. 230.

12.   "Wild Bill and Good Will," *Time*, July 7, 1952.

13.   Ibid.

14.   Prochnow and Prochnow, Jr., *The Toastmaster's Treasure Chest*, p. 366.

15.   Bill Nichols, "Politics '91:   Denver's New Mayor Put Best Foot Forward— Because He Had To," *USA Today*, June 20, 1991.

16.   Cited in Josephson, *The President Makers*.

17.   *The Globe* (Palm Beach, Florida), July 19, 1983, p. 21.

18.   Stephen C. Shadegg, *The New How to Win an Election* (New York: Taplinger Publishing, 1972), pp. 35-36.

19.   Edwin O'Conner, *The Last Hurrah* (Boston, Toronto: Little, Brown and Company, 1956), p. 401.

Additional Reading

Allen, Cathy. *Political Campaigning: A New Decade*. Washington, DC: The National Women's Political Caucus, 1990.

Atkins, Chester G., with Barry Hock & Bob Martin. *Getting Elected: A Guide to Winning State and Local Office*. Boston: Houghton Mifflin, 1973.

Beaudry, Ann, & Bob Schaeffer. *Winning Local and State Elections: The Guide to Organizing Your Campaign*. New York: The Free Press, a Division of Macmillan, Inc.; London: Collier Macmillan Publishers, 1986.

Ertel, James. *How to Run for Office*. New York: Sterling Publishing Co., Inc., 1960.

Gardner, Gerald. *The Mocking of the President: A History of Campaign Humor from Ike to Ronnie*. Detroit: Wayne State University Press, 1988.

Guber, Susan. *How to Win Your First Election*. Miami, Florida: The Pickering Press, 1988.

Huseby, Sandy. *How to Win an Election: A Complete Guide to Running a Successful Campaign*. New York: St. Martin's Press, 1983.

Lansing, Jewel. *Campaigning for Office: A Woman Runs*. Saratoga, CA: R&E Publishers, 1991.

Lansing, Jewel. *101 Campaign Tips for Women Candidates and Their Staffs*. Saratoga, CA: R&E Publishers, 1991.

Palmer, H. J. *How to Run for Office*. Albuquerque: Sandia Publishing Corporation, 1989.

Polsby, Nelson W., & Aaron Wildavsky. *Presidential Elections: Contemporary Strategies of American Electoral Politics*, 8th ed. New York: The Free Press (division of Macmillan), 1991.

Reinsch, J. Leonard. *Getting Elected: From Radio and Roosevelt to Television and Reagan*. New York: Hippocrene Books, 1988.

Trafton, Barbara M. *Women Winning: How to Run for Office*. Boston, Mass.: The Harvard Common Press, 1984. [foreword by Rosalynn Carter]

Women's Political Action Group, The. *The Women's 1992 Voting Guide*.

Young, Michael L. *American Dictionary of Campaigns and Elections*. Lanham, New York & London: Hamilton Press, 1987.